EXERCISES FOR

Ellsworth/Higgins

ENGLISH
SIMPLIFIED

Twelfth Edition

Christine Rauchfuss Gray
Community College of Baltimore County

Longman

New York   San Francisco   Boston
London   Toronto   Sydney   Tokyo   Singapore   Madrid
Mexico City   Munich   Paris   Cape Town   Hong Kong   Montreal

Acquisitions Editor: Matthew Wright
Senior Supplements Editor: Donna Campion
Electronic Page Makeup: Grapevine Publishing Services, Inc.

Exercises for Ellsworth/Higgins, *English Simplified,* Twelfth Edition

Copyright © 2010 Pearson Education, Inc.

1 2 3 4 5 6 7 8 9 10–BRR–12 11 10 09

Longman
is an imprint of

www.pearsonhighered.com

ISBN 10:   0-205-63407-9
ISBN 13: 978-0-205-63407-1

CONTENTS

(ESL denotes that the exercise has an ESL component. C denotes choice-type items; W denotes items asking for original written responses.)

PREFACE

The twelfth edition of *Exercises for English Simplified*, as in the eleventh edition, provides instructors with two types of exercises for assessing and developing students' writing and researching skills. Many of these exercises, however, have been updated and modified. For instructors who want quick, easy scoring, there are nearly three thousand choice-type items (exercises including these are labeled C in the table of contents). For instructors who prefer original, open-ended responses, there are hundreds of items for which students compose their own answers—words, sentences, paragraphs, even a full essay (exercises including these are labeled W in the table of contents).

The twelfth edition has further improvements:

- More exercises on writing clearly. These exercises focus on such problems affecting clarity as misused modifiers, confusing sentence construction, unnecessary words, and the confusing use of apostrophes, commas, and hyphens.

- New exercises on the simple and perfect verb tenses

- Updated research exercises reflecting the latest MLA and APA form revisions, and including evaluation of sources

- An expanded exercise on note-taking, avoiding plagiarism, and citing

- A new exercise on online writing

- New proofreading passages with multiple errors

- A more legible Answer Key format for easier scoring

Many of the improvements mentioned come from reviewers' suggestions. I would like to thank Christine Rauchfuss Gray, Community College of Baltimore County; Joseph A. Scherer, CCAC (Community College of Allegheny County), South Campus; David Borofka, Reedley College; Virginia Jansen, University of California, Santa Cruz; Kent Harrelson, Dalton State College; and David A. Sprunger, Concordia College.

1. DIAGNOSTIC TEST: Sentences, Grammar, and Paragraphs

Part 1: Sentences

In the blank after each sentence,

Write **S** if the boldfaced expression is **one complete, correct sentence.**
Write **F** if it is a **fragment** (incorrect: less than a complete sentence).
Write **R** if it is a **run-on** (incorrect: two or more sentences written as one—also known as a **comma splice** or **fused sentence**).

Example: The climbers suffered from hypothermia. **Having neglected to bring warm clothing.**   _____F_____

1. The ambulance rushed to the emergency room. **As the accident victim in the back was cared for by a medic.**

    1._____

2. The school's computers have broken down again. **All online classes have been halted and hundreds of students are angry.**

    2._____

3. **In Venezuela, gasoline was selling for twelve cents a gallon last month, a price that will never be seen again in the United States.**

    3._____

4. The Baltimore Orioles made two trades after the season had begun. **First for a shortstop and then for a pitcher.**

    4._____

5. The Black Student Union put Marcia Simpson in charge of the Multicultural Festival. **A responsibility that appealed to her.**

    5._____

6. **The children are learning how to tumble; they really seem to enjoy their acrobatics class.**   6._____

7. In ancient times, there was certainly no microscopic knowledge of germs. **It is believed that there was little scientific understanding of infections.**

    7._____

8. **Although American society may seem uncaring.** More people are volunteering to help with the homeless.

    8._____

9. **The reason for her low math score being that she did not understand basic algebra.**   9._____

10. **The march against animal cruelty was both controversial and exciting protesters pored fake blood on anyone wearing fur.**

    10._____

11. **Because scientists have learned that one sick sheep can infect an entire flock with a serious bacterial disease.**

    11._____

12. **Albert was troubled by the weeds and trash in his neighborhood.** He began cleaning up the sidewalk in front of his house.

    12._____

13. The most significant age-related changes to the eyes seem to occur in the lens and pupil; these changes account for the majority of vision limitations people experience. **As they get older.**   13._____

14. **Learning to drive a stick shift can be tricky your timing must be right.**   14._____

15. **New Orleans, Louisiana, was devastated by Hurricane Katrina in August 2005.** The city is rebuilding very slowly.   15._____

16. **When setting the table, you should always put the fork to the left of the plate.**   16._____

Part 2: Grammar

In the blank,

Write **C** if the boldfaced expression is used **correctly**.
Write **X** if it is used **incorrectly**.

Example: There **was** dozens of doughnuts on the kitchen counter.   _____X_____

1. The promise between you and **I** will always be kept private.   1. _____

2. Jill was fired from her new job, **which** made her despondent.   2. _____

3. Each member will be responsible for **their** own transportation.   3. _____

4. There **was** at least five printers in the office.   4. _____

5. Several of **us** tourists needed directions to find the Statue of Liberty.   5. _____

6. The eyes and the eyebrows nonverbally **communicates** a wide range of expressions that are universal to all people.   6. _____

7. The graduate teaching assistant and **myself** met for a review session.   7. _____

8. Surprisingly enough, presidential candidate Joan Smith was leading **not only** in the cities **but also** in the rural areas.   8. _____

9. In each lunchbox **were** a turkey sandwich, an orange, and a bottle of water.   9. _____

10. Leave the message with **whomever** answers the phone.   10. _____

11. **Having made no other plans for the evening,** Tony was glad to accept the invitation.   11. _____

12. All members of the Hispanic Society **was** urged to join the movement to bring more Hispanic families to the neighborhood.   12. _____

13. If I **were** driving to Richmond this weekend, I would take along toys for my grandsons.   13. _____

14. I bought one of the printers that **were** on sale.   14. _____

15. You and **me** will share the last sandwich on the tray.   15. _____

16. The prosecutor demanded that the witness tell her **where on the road did the car hit the dog.**   16. _____

17. The coach, as well as the team members, **has** agreed to a radio interview.   17. _____

18. The supervisor is especially fond of arranging training programs, working on elaborate projects, and **to develop budgets.**   18. _____

19. A trompe-l'œil **is when you trick the eye by making the items in a painting appear three dimensional and real.**   19. _____

20. **Whom** do you think will be planning the faculty brunch?   20. _____

21. Neither the students nor the instructor **know** where the schedule has been posted.   21. _____

22. Are you sure that it was **her** that you saw with John yesterday?   22. _____

23. Between you and **me**, the dress she made for the prom makes her look twenty pounds heavier.   23. _____

24. If Bill **had been** in school yesterday, he would have passed today's grammar test.   24. _____

25. Maryanne tutored students after school and coached the tennis team. She enjoyed doing **it** for the students.   25. _____

26. Given the candidates in the race, it's painfully clear that **us** voters didn't have much of a choice.   26. _____

27. Customers should check the apples carefully before paying; otherwise, **you** may end up with rotten or spoiled fruit.   27. _____

28. Anyone who forgets his book will not be able to take **their** report home   28. _____

29. While carrying my books to the library, **a black cat darted across my path.**   29. _____

30. Norma **only** had one issue left to raise before she could rest her case.   30. _____

31. I had no idea that **my** giving a report would create such turmoil at the meeting.   31. _____

32. We didn't think that many of **us** teenagers would get into the aquarium.   32. _____

33. Dean Robert Patterson gave Karen and **I** permission to establish a volunteer organization to tutor students from city schools.   33. _____

34. Although she often spoke harshly to others, her voice was always **pleasant** to us.   34. _____

35. Neither the librarian nor the students in the reference room **was** aware of the situation.   35. _____

36. Professor Rogers looks very **differently** since he dyed his beard and moustache red.   36. _____

37. We know it was **she** who borrowed your iPod.   37. _____

38. The audience comprised **not only juniors but also seniors**.   38. _____

39. Dr. Smith, together with thirty of his students, **are** working in a soup kitchen today.   39. _____

40. Each of three new employees **were** given a laptop computer.   40. _____

41. The candy and popcorn we bought at the movies **was** very expensive.   41. _____

42. **Standing motionless on the windswept, dreary plain,** the rain pelted my face.   42. _____

43. Regina agreed to **immediately and without delay** notify the trustees of her decision.   43. _____

44. The dean agreed to award the scholarship to **whoever** the committee selected.   44. _____

45. **Knowing that I should study**, it seemed important to turn off the television.   45. _____

46. **Who** were you looking for in the theater?   46. _____

47. The noise and the general chaos caused by the alarm **was** disturbing to the visitor.   47. _____

48. As hard as I try, I'll never be as thin as **her**.   48. _____

49. Only one of these antique chairs **is** of real value.   49. _____

50. Only my sister and **myself** were allowed to write checks at the small grocery store.   50. _____

Part 3: Paragraphs (not included in scoring)

On the back of this page, write a **paragraph** of six to eight sentences on **one** of the topics below (you may also use scrap paper):

_____

If I had to choose my favorite uncle (or aunt)

My room (or clothes, car, etc.) as a reflection of me

If I could create a new law

Caring for the environment

The best (or worst) film I have seen in the past year

2. DIAGNOSTIC TEST: Punctuation

In the blank after each sentence,

Write **C** if the punctuation in brackets is **correct**;
Write **X** if it is **incorrect**.

(Use only one letter in each blank.)

Example: Regular exercise[,] and sound nutrition are essential for good health.   ____X____

1. The local softball league voted to join the peace march[;] this afternoon the team will wear armbands and carry flags.   1._____

2. "What shoes can I show you today[?]" the salesperson asked.   2._____

3. "Will you go to the holiday dance with me["?] Maurice asked Julie.   3._____

4. Mary told the class that the newly elected officers were Duff Goldman, president[;] Sophie Jones, vice president[;] Tom Smith, treasurer[;] and Julie Chang, secretary.   4._____

5. The class expected low grades[. T]he test having been long and difficult.   5._____

6. It[']s hard to imagine life without an MVP player, a personal computer, and a cell phone.   6._____

7. Eventually, everybody has dinner at Harpoon Hannah's[;] the best restaurant in Ocean City.   7._____

8. Recognizing that sleep is a necessity for teenagers[,] the Caldwell County Board of Education voted to begin all morning classes at 9:00.   8._____

9. Mai Ling was homesick[,], she wanted to return to Beijing to see her family.   9._____

10. That is not the Watsons' dog; at least, I don't think that it is their[']s.   10._____

11. When I work in my garden, I always think of lines from Wordworth's poem "The Daffodils": "When all at once I saw a crowd, [/] A host of golden daffodils."   11._____

12. The prosecutor asked, "Were you at the crime scene?[" "]Are you sure?"   12._____

13. "The report is ready," Preston said[,] "I'm sending it to the president today."   13._____

14. Didn't I hear you say, "I especially like blueberry cheesecake"[?]   14._____

15. Joe enrolled in a small college[;] although he had planned originally to join a traveling circus.   15._____

16. Stephen moved to Denver[,] where he hoped to open a ski shop.   16._____

17. You do want chocolate ice cream[,] don't you?   17._____

18. Fifty students responded to the poll[,] asking about opening a bank branch on campus.   18._____

19. Sarah is asking for a week[']s vacation to visit relatives in Bermuda.   19._____

20. On February 21, 2012[,] Robin and Sam are getting married.   20._____

21. The womens['] lacrosse team has reached the state finals.   21._____

22. Recently, researchers have discovered that rhesus monkeys have some hidden talents[;] such as the ability to do basic math.   22._____

23. Caroline received forty[-]three e-mail messages in one hour.   23._____

24. Virginia finished her math [,] and began reading for the literature exam.   24. _____

25. Many weeks before school was out[;] he had applied for an internship at the local newspaper.   25. _____

26. Dear Sir[;] Please accept this letter of application for the teaching position.   26. _____

27. Schweitzer summed up his ethics as "reverence for life[,]" a phrase that came to him during his early years in Africa.   27. _____

28. Our communications professor asked us whether we understood the use of extended periods of silence often found in conversations among Native Americans[?]   28. _____

29. "As for who won the election[—]well, not all the votes have been counted," she said.   29. _____

30. ["]The Necessity of Recycling["] (This is the title at the head of a student's essay for an English class.)   30. _____

31. Any music[,] that is not by Mozart[,] does not appeal to Cheryl.   31. _____

32. "Election results are coming in quickly now," the newscaster announced[;] "and we should be able to predict the winner soon."   32. _____

33. More than 42 percent of all adults eighteen and over are single[,] however, more than 90 percent of these adults will marry at least once.   33. _____

34. The children went to the zoo[;] bought ice-cream cones[;] fed peanuts to the elephants[;] and watched the seals perform their tricks while being fed.   34. _____

35. ["]Happy Birthday to You["] is the most popular song in the English language.   35. _____

36. In the 1950s, department stores provided customers with valet service, elevator operators, public telephones, and personal shoppers[;] and these stores offered countless other services, such as bakeries, post offices, free gift wrapping services, and needlework demonstrations.   36. _____

37. Watch out[,] Marjorie, for the dogs in my neighbor's yard.   37. _____

38. The rival candidates for the Senate are waging an all-out campaign[,] until the polls open tomorrow.   38. _____

39. Because Henry stayed up to study[,] he didn't make it to his early class.   39. _____

40. The weather[—]rain, rain, and more rain[—]has ruined our weekend plans for an entire month.   40. _____

41. The first modern drive-in was called[,] The Pig Stand, which was a barbecue pit along a highway between Dallas and Fort Worth.   41. _____

42. The scholarship award went to Julia Brown, the student[,] who had the highest grades.   42. _____

43. Some of the technologies developed after World War II were[:] television, synthetic fibers, and air travel.   43. _____

44. Route 66[,] which was known as The Great Diagonal Way[,] was advertised as The Main Street of America.   44. _____

45. The talk show host[,] irritated and impatient[,] cut off the caller who insisted he was calling from aboard a flying saucer.   45. _____

46. I hav[']ent decided whether to stay home this weekend to do the laundry or to go to the beach with friends.   46. _____

47. Estelle Washington[,] who is the class president[,] comes from a small town near Philadelphia   47. _____

48. Author Mike Rose writes[:] "When a local public school is lost to incompetence, indifference, or despair, it should be an occasion for mourning."   48. _____

49. A note under the door read: "Sorry you weren't in. The Johnson[']s."   49. _____

50. Most of my friends are upgrading their computer security systems[,] they want to be safe from computer viruses and identity theft.

50. _____

51. This spring we began a new family vacation tradition[:] we flew to Florida to watch the Indians' spring training.

51. _____

52. "Well[,] if you want a good haircut, you must go to Chez Frenchie," said Marlene.

52. _____

53. We are going to New York City[,] we all want to skate at Rockefeller Center and visit Tiffany's.

53. _____

54. By saving her money[,] Jill was able to travel to Rome to see Vatican City.

54. _____

55. Like rats, squirrels are rodents[,] which means they must constantly gnaw to keep their teeth short.

55. _____

56. Chipmunks, although small, play a crucial role in a forest environment[,] because they harvest and hoard tree seeds.

56. _____

57. The zoologist told the students[,] that chipmunks construct extensive burrows with several well-concealed entrances.

57. _____

58. The sleeping quarters of chipmunks are kept extremely clean as they put shells[,] and waste in special refuse tunnels.

58. _____

59. "I cannot believe that you have read my book!"[,] shouted the author to the critic.

59. _____

60. In his painting [*The Three Musicians,*] the French artist Pablo Picasso included a dog under the table.

60. _____

61. I have heard[,] that Picasso's dog makes sure that the musicians keep the music at the right tempo.

61. _____

62. According to my family's written records[,] five of my ancestors were beekeepers who lived in Prussia.

62. _____

63. My hometown is a place[,] where older men still think white shoes and belts are high fashion.

63. _____

64. She spent her summers visiting her friends in Baltimore[,] where she went to the movies every Saturday night.

64. _____

65. Having learned that he was eligible for a scholarship[,] Evan turned in his application.

65. _____

66. Watching television in the 1950s[,] was boring for children because most shows were news broadcasts and plays.

66. _____

67. In the novel ["The Scarlet Letter"], Hester Prynne is forced to wear a large red A on her dress.

67. _____

68. Many Americans remember family celebrations from their childhood[,] moreover, they are seeking ways to incorporate some of these rituals into their busy lives.

68. _____

69. The jack-o'-lantern can be traced back to the Irish legend of Stingy Jack[;] a greedy, gambling, hard-drinking old farmer.

69. _____

70. After the long, harsh winter, I needed a soak[-]in[-]the[-]sun vacation.

70. _____

71. Veterans of World War I[,] who were hit hard by the Great Depression[,] received a government bonus in the 1930s.

71. _____

72. The girls['] and boys['] locker rooms had no heat.

72. _____

73. The parking lot always is full[,] when there is a concert.

73. _____

74. Dan was proud that he received all A[']s.

74. _____

75. You can reach Charles Street by turning left[,] and driving on Pratt Street.

75. _____

3. DIAGNOSTIC TEST: Mechanics, Spelling, and Word Choice

Part 1: Capitalization

In each blank, write **C** if the boldfaced word(s) **follow** the rules of capitalization.
Write **X** if the word(s) **do not follow** the rules.

Example: The Mormons settled in what is now
    Salt Lake City.   __C__

1. The *Harbor Queen* sails from Baltimore's
Inner Harbor daily.   1.____

2. I often recall the hard work of my **College**
days.   2.____

3. He attends Annapolis **high school.**   3.____

4. He attends a **high school** in Annapolis.   4.____

5. They drove **east** from Denver.   5.____

6. We presented **mother** with a bouquet of roses. 6.____

7. The children gave their **mother** a bouquet
of roses.   7.____

8. She is in France; **He** is at home.   8.____

9. "Are you working?" **She** asked.   9.____

10. I love **Korean** food.   10.____

11. We saluted the **american** flag.   11.____

12. Last **Summer** I drove to California.   12.____

13. My birthday was **Friday**.   13.____

14. I am enrolled in courses in **philosophy**
and Japanese.   14.____

15. She went **North** for Christmas.   15.____

16. Please, **Father**, lend me your car.   16.____

17. My **Cousins** welcomed me to Tennessee.   17.____

18. "Whoever roasted **Marshmallows** in the
kitchen is in trouble!" Mother said.   18.____

19. Jane does not want to attend today's
meeting of the **Porcupine Club**.   19.____

20. George and Phillip Thompson agreed to
decorate the **Classroom** for Valentine's Day. 20.____

Part 2: Abbreviations and Numbers

Write **C** if the boldfaced abbreviation or number is used **correctly**.
Write **X** it is used **incorrectly**.

Example: They drove through **Tenn**.   __X__

1. **Seven billion** people now inhabit the world. 1.____

2. I participated in a **five-hour** workshop on
interpersonal communications.   2.____

3. The play begins at **7** p.m.   3.____

4. Aaron was born on November **11th,** 1988. 4.____

5. The rent is **$625** a month.   5.____

6. The interest comes to **8** percent.   6.____

7. **Sen.** Levy voted against the bill.   7.____

8. There are **nineteen** women in the club.   8.____

9. **2008** was another bad year for flooding.   9.____

10. I wrote a note to **Dr**. Rovira.   10.____

11. [Opening sentence of a news article]
The **NAAFF** has filed for bankruptcy.   11.____

12. She lives on Buchanan **Ave.**   12.____

13. We consulted Ricardo Guitierrez, **Ph.D.** 13.____

14. Our appointment is at **4** o'clock.   14.____

15. I slept only **3** hours last night.   15.____

Part 3: Spelling

In each sentence, one boldfaced word is **misspelled.** Write its number in the blank.

Example: (1)**Its** (2)**too** late (3)**to** go.   <u>   1   </u>

1. Jane's (1)**independent** attitude sometimes was a (2)**hindrence** to the (3)**committee**.   1._____

2. (1)**Approximatly** half of the class noticed the (2)**omission** of the last item on the (3)**questionnaire**.   2._____

3. The (1)**mischievous** child was (2)**usualy** (3)**courteous** to adults.   3._____

4. At the office Jack was described as an (1)**unusually** (2)**conscientous** and (3)**indispensable** staff member.   4._____

5. Even though Dave was (1)**competent** in his (2)**mathematics** class, he didn't have the (3)**disipline** required to complete the daily homework.   5._____

6. The sociologist's (1)**analysis** of the (2)**apparent** (3)**prejudise** that existed among the villagers was insightful.   6._____

7. She was (1)**particularly** (2)**sensable** about renewing her (3)**license**.   7._____

8. It was (1)**necesary** to curb Tad's (2)**tendency** to interrupt the staff discussion with (3)**irrelevant** comments.   8._____

9. I was not (1)**sirprised** that (2)**curiosity** prompted the toddler to smear lipstick on the (3)**mirror**.   9._____

10. Tim developed a (1)**procedure** for updating our (2)**apointtment** (3)**calendar**.   10._____

11. As a (1)**sophomore** Sue had the (2)**perseverence** and (3)**energy** needed to work three part-time jobs and to raise her three sons.   11._____

12. Her (1)**opinion**, while (2)**fascinating**, revealed an indisputable (3)**hypocricy**.   12._____

13. Every day our (1)**secretery** meets a colleague from the (2)**Psychology** Department at their favorite campus (3)**restaurant**.   13._____

14. During (1)**adolescence** we often (2)**condemm** anyone who offers (3)**guidance**.   14._____

15. Based on Bill's (1)**recommendation**, his dream vacation sounded (2)**irresistable** and guaranteed to (3)**fulfill** anyone's need to escape.   15._____

Part 4: Word Choice

To be correct, the boldfaced expression must be standard, formal English and must not be sexist or otherwise discriminatory.

Write **C** if the boldfaced word is used **correctly**.
Write **X** if it is used **incorrectly**.

Examples: The counsel's **advice** was misinterpreted.   <u> C </u>

They **could of** made the plane except for the traffic.   <u> X </u>

1. A modern house is quite different **than** a Victorian house.   1.____

2. Jane **didn't barely** have any chance.   2.____

3. The plane began its **decent** for Denver.   3.____

4. Economic problems always **impact** our enrollment.   4.____

5. Jill's book **lay** where she had left it.   5.____

6. We didn't play **good** in the last quarter.   6.____

10

7. I selected a **nice** birthday card. 7._____

8. The float **proceeded** the band in the parade. 8._____

9. No one predicted the **affects** of the flu outbreak. 9._____

10. Aunt Harriet always uses **stationery** with roses and violets on it. 10._____

11. The trains at the station were **stationary**. 11._____

12. We are going to **canvas** the school district for the scholarship fund. 12._____

13. She **referred back** to her earlier research. 13._____

14. College men and **girls** are warned not to drink and drive. 14._____

15. The **principle** spoke to the parents at the meeting. 15._____

16. I **had ought** to read the assigned novel. 16._____

17. Andy made **less** mistakes than John did. 17._____

18. The family **better** repair the leaky roof. 18._____

19. The package had **bursted** open. 19._____

20. Where is John **at**? 20._____

21. We are taught to consider the feelings of our **fellow man**. 21._____

22. **Irregardless** of the warning, I drove in the dense fog. 22._____

23. The next **thing** in my argument concerns my opponent's honesty. 23._____

24. The new carpet **complements** the dining room furniture. 24._____

25. Margie was the **best** of the two singers. 25._____

26. I **ought to of** made the flight arrangements. 26._____

27. **Numerical statistical figures** show that an asteroid might collide with Earth. 27._____

28. **Due to the fact that** it rained, the game was canceled. 28._____

29. The **reason because** we're leaving is that it's so late. 29._____

30. The new porch furniture was **green in color**. 30._____

4. SENTENCES AND GRAMMAR: Parts of a Sentence

(Study 101–103, The Sentence and Its Parts)

Part 1

In the blank, write the number of the place where the **complete subject** ends and the **complete predicate** begins.

Example: Immigrants (1) to the United States (2) have helped greatly (3) in building the country.   ____2____

1. The cute little puppies (1) have wandered (2) all over the garden and (3) into the budding violets.   1._____

2. The elderly woman (1) recently (2) gave her car to her grandson (3) in exchange for having him mow her lawn for two years.   2._____

3. The intelligent young man (1) sitting in the back row (2) will be (3) an asset to the senior class.   3._____

4. Thirteen states (1) constitute the Appalachian region (2) of the eastern United States.   4._____

5. Our ivy groundcover (1) was weakened (2) by a plant fungus (3) last year.   5._____

6. The barbecued ribs (1) on the kitchen counter (2) were getting cold (3) and stringy.   6._____

7. With his new video games (1), Archie (2) visited (3) his cousins last weekend.   7._____

8. The elderly woman (1) carefully (2) chose two collections of short stories at the book sale.   8._____

9. The man (1) working on my neighbor's house (2) is a licensed plumber (3) in New Jersey.   9._____

10. When did the committee select the candidate for comptroller?
[Rewritten in subject-predicate order:
The committee (1) did select (2) the candidate (3) for comptroller when?]   10._____

Part 2

Write **S** if the boldfaced word is a **subject** (or part of a compound subject).
Write **V** if it is a **verb**.
Write **C** if it is a **complement** (or part of a compound complement).

Examples: Caroline played a superb game.   ____S____

Caroline **played** a superb game.   ____V____

Caroline played a superb **game**.   ____C____

1. The newborn **baby** cried until midnight.   1._____

2. Penelope put the **pickles** in the pantry.   2._____

3. The **horse** in the barn eats two bales of hay each week.   3._____

4. She **put** the extra fabric into her sewing basket.   4._____

5. Tonight, we're having **supper** on the garden.   5._____

6. You should never give **chocolate** to a dog.   6._____

7. The mother **gave** her daughter a vitamin each morning.   7._____

8. Ten dogs chased the big red **ball** in the park.   8._____

9. A **firefighter** came to our house to check the smoke alarms.   9._____

10. The mother gave her daughter a **vitamin** each morning.   10._____

11. The horse in the barn eats two **bales** of hay each week.   11._____

12. Cough drops cannot **cure** a cold.   12._____

13. My neighbors **worked** together to build a new playground.   13._____

14. The **children** enjoy the swing set in the back yard.   14._____

15. Mary swept the front **porch** as she waited for her guests.   15._____

16. The tiny woman put the old **lamp** on the table near the staircase.   16._____

17. Bill **was** ecstatic about finding the book he lost last week.   17._____

18. Cute **puppies** buried big white bones in my mother's garden.   18._____

19. Jim bought a **package** of spearmint gum for Cynthia.   19._____

20. For some reason, **Betty** likes to eat lemons.   20._____

Part 3

In each sentence, fill in the blank with a word of your own that makes sense. Then, in the blank at the right, tell whether it is a **subject** (write **S**), **verb** (write **V**), or **complement** (write **C**).

Example: The builders needed a _ladder_ for the new job.   _____C_____

1. Beautiful _____ grow down the street.   1._____

2. Our family likes _____ on the back porch.   2._____

3. Cabbages, onions, and _____ grow in our garden.   3._____

4. Three students in English 101 _____ their final examination.   4._____

5. The instructor was a _____.   5._____

6. As she sat on the pony, the young girl _____.   6._____

7. The Smith family sent _____ to the newly married couple.   7._____

8. The crisp, clear _____ refreshed us.   8._____

9. Many Americans _____ concerned about their health.   9._____

10. In order to win the contest, you must have _____ and skill in pitching.   10._____

5. SENTENCES AND GRAMMAR: Parts of Speech

(Study 104–110, The Parts of Speech)

Write the **part of speech** of each boldfaced word (use the abbreviations in parentheses):

noun	adjective (**adj**)	preposition (**prep**)
pronoun (**pro**)	adverb (**adv**)	conjunction (**conj**)
verb		interjection (**inter**)

Example: Shaw wrote many **plays**.   _noun_

1. **Cover** the furniture before you paint the room.   1._____

2. The men would **not** wait for the contract.   2._____

3. Stand **by** the corner until I come by to pick you up.   3._____

4. Phillip played in the sandbox until **his** mother called him inside.   4._____

5. I think he is the man **whom** you invited yesterday.   5._____

6. **If** I don't meet you at the game, I'll see you at school.   6._____

7. John **gives** his dog too many dog biscuits.   7._____

8. The young genius **quickly** won the chess match.   8._____

9. **Oh**, I thought you brought the hot dogs!   9._____

10. Put the chips on the **side** of the plate.   10._____

11. Peas **and** carrots are good for your skin.   11._____

12. The stock market **was jarred** by the price of oil.   12._____

13. A **jar** of canned tomatoes was left on our porch by a neighbor.   13._____

14. Janice put the lamp on the new **maple** end table.   14._____

15. Betsy **vowed** to lose the weight she gained at Thankssgiving.   15._____

16. **That** chair was refinished two summers ago.   16._____

17. Do you want pickles with **that**?   17._____

18. Jumping on a **trampoline** can be fun.   18._____

19. Jumping on a trampoline can also be very **dangerous**.   19._____

20. Bill **sided** with John in the argument.   20._____

21. We were out of breath **because** we ran too fast.   21._____

22. **John** showed the guests how to line dance.   22._____

23. The Queen **of** Hearts baked some lemon tarts.   23._____

24. The timid **rabbit** hopped behind the hedge.   24._____

25. The host said that **everyone** must have champagne.   25._____

26. She ate everything **except** the bratwurst.   26._____

27. You can take your cat, **but** your dog must stay home.   27._____

28. **Well**, you can take the bus to the convention center.   28._____

29. I **myself** have never driven a sports car.   29._____

30. Bill **and** Brenda washed the dishes after lunch.   30._____

31. **When** you go to the grocery store, pick up some oranges please.   31._____

32. Jill **had** to replace the toaster because it was unsafe.   32._____

33. "**Fire** the torpedoes," said the captain.   33._____

34. I **always** walk my dog right after supper.   34._____

35. **This** is my favorite time of the year.   35._____

36. Please **let** me borrow your hammer.   36._____

37. **Your** living room is a wonderful shade of purple.   37._____

38. **Where** are you going?   38._____

39. May I go **with** you?   39._____

40. **Yesterday**, I went to the movies with Leslie and Jake.　40.＿＿＿

41. I **danced** to all of the Elvis Presley songs.　41.＿＿＿

42. The mud was caked on Terry's **boots**.　42.＿＿＿

43. **Save** the last piece of cake for your grandmother.　43.＿＿＿

44. The kitten and puppy became **best** friends.　44.＿＿＿

45. **This** house has the most interesting garden on the block.　45.＿＿＿

46. **Yesterday** was her birthday.　46.＿＿＿

47. If **Bill** goes fishing, I will have to buy the bait.　47.＿＿＿

48. **After** we bought a cat, all the mice disappeared.　48.＿＿＿

49. **After** the opera, we went to a French cafe on the river.　49.＿＿＿

50. We walked **slowly** to the final exam in math.　50.＿＿＿

6. SENTENCES AND GRAMMAR: Parts of Speech

(Study 104–110, The Parts of Speech)

Part 1

In the first blank in each sentence, write a word or word group of your own that **makes sense**.
Then in the blank at the right, tell what **part of speech** your word or word group is (use the abbreviations in parentheses):

noun	adjective (**adj**)	preposition (**prep**)
pronoun (**pro**)	adverb (**adv**)	conjunction (**conj**)
verb		interjection (**inter**)

Example: The singer wore a *gaudy* jacket.   ____adj____

(Collaborative option: Students work in pairs, alternating: one writes the word or word group, the other names the part of speech.)

1. The book you ordered should arrive _____.   1._____
2. May I _____ you on Friday?   2._____
3. This evening, we washed the _____dishes in the sink.   3._____
4. _____ seemed nervous to the teacher.   4._____
5. Is _____ your book?   5._____
6. The _____ was silky smooth.   6._____
7. My _____ vacation proved quite hazardous.   7._____
8. _____! The ball rolled into the lake.   8._____
9. Many _____ bulbs in our garden have been eaten by deer.   9._____
10. This plane goes _____ Cleveland.   10._____
11. Jane should have put the book _____ the table.   11._____
12. _____ the baby in the stroller.   12._____
13. Tom found a _____ and took it home.   13._____
14. Ms. Brooks gave her secretary a _____ desk set.   14._____
15. Martina cleaned the kitchen counter with a _____.   15._____
16. Approach that pit bull dog _____ carefully.   16._____
17. Arles is in France, _____ Aachen is in Germany.   17._____
18. Dorothy was _____ of Marcia's Jaguar.   18._____
19. _____ he won the lottery, he bought his mother a house.   19._____
20. _____ of the runners collapsed from foot injuries.   20._____
21. _____ runners collapsed from the heat.   21._____
22. Sheila was spending her money _____.   22._____
23. The bus has _____ been more popular than the subway.   23._____

24. We took a _____ to Grandmother's house in the woods.   24. _____

25. _____! That's a cool car you're driving.   25. _____

Part 2

In each blank, write the **correct** preposition: **at**, **in**, or **on**.
(In some blanks, either of two prepositions may be correct.)

Example: Francis lives <u>in</u> an apartment <u>on</u> Broadway.

    Luella Smith, a retired teacher, lived _____ a pleasant street _____ a small town _____ the Midwest. Most mornings she awoke promptly _____ six, except _____ Sundays, when she slept until eight. Then she would ride to worship _____ her 1987 Ford or _____ her old three-speed bicycle. Often she was the first one _____ her house of worship. Later she had lunch _____ her favorite restaurant, which was _____ Elm Street _____ a near-by town.

7. SENTENCES AND GRAMMAR: Uses of Nouns

(Study 112, Using Nouns)

Part 1

In the blank, tell how the boldfaced word in each sentence is **used** (use the abbreviations in parentheses):

subject (**subj**)	indirect object (**ind obj**)	appositive (**app**)
subject complement (**subj comp**)	object complement (**obj comp**)	direct address (**dir add**)
direct object (**dir obj**)	object of preposition (**obj prep**)	

Example: The passenger gave the **driver** a tip.   ___ind obj___

1. The wait **staff** gathered to hear that night's specials.   1._____
2. We went to the circus without the **children**.   2._____
3. We considered John the **leader**.   3._____
4. We considered **John** the leader.   4._____
5. The children threw the birds bread **crusts**.   5._____
6. Jackson will be the **head** of the committee   6._____
7. The tall grass grew in the back **pasture**.   7._____
8. **Martin**, you must come home immediately.   8._____
9. Ladies and gentlemen, Phyllis Betz is the **winner** of the chess match.   9._____
10. The young singer, **Jane Monroe**, appeared nervous.   10._____
11. Antilock brakes give the **driver** more control.   11._____
12. These brakes have become a **source** of controversy.   12._____
13. These brakes have become a source of **controversy**.   13._____
14. Misapplication of these brakes has caused some **accidents**.   14._____
15. Which **ice cream** is your favorite?   15._____
16. Which kitten will **you** adopt?   16._____
17. We pitied the veterans who were begging on the city's **streets**.   17._____
18. Redundancy, needless **repetition**, can put an audience to sleep.   18._____
19. Marie, give that **customer** a fresh cup of coffee.   19._____
20. **Marie**, give that customer a fresh cup of coffee.   20._____
21. The company named Jennifer the **winner** of the lottery.   21._____
22. Tiger Woods has already become a legendary **golfer**.   22._____
23. The mother baked the **children** cookies.   23._____
24. Their cheating made Fred the **loser** in the poker game.   24._____
25. Fred, a trusting **fellow**, never caught on.   25._____

In each sentence, fill in the blank with a noun of your own that **makes sense**. Then in the blank at the right, tell how that noun is **used** (use the abbreviations in parentheses):

subject (**subj**)   indirect object (**ind obj**)   appositive (**app**)
subject complement (**subj comp**)   object complement (**obj comp**)   direct address (**dir add**)
direct object (**dir obj**)   object of preposition (**obj prep**)

Example: We sang songs far into the _night_.   ___obj prep___

(Collaborative option: Students work in pairs, alternating: one writes the word, the other names its use.)

1. First prize was a brand-new _____.   1. _____

2. _____, please make more coffee.   2. _____

3. The new _____ in town should expect a warm welcome.   3. _____

4. Every autumn the region's trees, mostly _____, delight touring leaf-peepers.   4. _____

5. Brad's CD collection contains mostly songs by _____.   5. _____

6. Before the literature examination, Professor Ferrano gave the class a(n) _____.   6. _____

7. Paula's attitude made her a(n) _____ to many classmates.   7. _____

8. Warmhearted Pat gave the _____ a hug.   8. _____

8. SENTENCES AND GRAMMAR: Complements

(Study 112B, Complements)

Part 1

In the blank, tell how each boldfaced complement is **used** (use the abbreviations in parentheses). If any complement is an adjective, **circle** it.

subject complement (**subj comp**) object complement (**obj comp**)
direct object (**dir obj**) indirect object (**ind obj**)

Examples: The ambassador delivered the **ultimatum**. _____dir obj_____
The queen became (furious.) _____subj comp_____

1. The Baltimore Orioles have been my favorite **team** for years. 1._____
2. Christine gave her **dog** a good bath. 2._____
3. The city lost many **jobs** after September 11, 2001. 3._____
4. Kenneth declared English his **major**. 4._____
5. The guide gave us **directions** to the Tomb of the Unknown Soldier. 5._____
6. Friends, Romans, countrymen, lend **me** your ears. 6._____
7. The soprano completed her **practice**. 7._____
8. She sounds **happier** every day. 8._____
9. **Whom** did you meet yesterday? 9._____
10. Will the company make **Jason** another offer? 10._____
11. Parents will often promise noisy **children** anything to quiet them. 11._____
12. The group had been studying **anthropology** for three semesters. 12._____
13. Her former employer gave **her** the idea for the small business. 13._____
14. Judith Ashby named the **SPCA** her beneficiary. 14._____
15. She is an **instructor** at the local community college. 15._____
16. At the ceremony, John became the newest **member** of the Honors Society. 16._____
17. The man in the gray suit gave ten **dollars** to the beggar. 17._____
18. He considered her a **genius**. 18._____
19. Select whatever wrapping **paper** you like for the wedding gift. 19._____
20. The company made her **manager** of the branch office. 20._____
21. Wasn't the Juicy Couture model **glamorous**? 21._____
22. The besieging troops gave the surrounded city an **ultimatum** this morning. 22._____
23. Most drivers don't use turn **signals**. 23._____
24. John grew **downcast** at the news. 24._____
25. Tim grew **tomatoes** over the summer. 25._____

26. The realtor found the **Smiths** a wonderful house.   26. _____

27. Martina found the children **rude**.   27. _____

28. A few passengers were tossing **the youngsters** coins from the ship.   28. _____

29. The fur on the collar of the jacket feels very **soft**.   29. _____

30. The next available time for an appointment will be **Tuesday**.   30. _____

Part 2

In each sentence, fill in the blank with a complement of your own. Then in the blank at the right, **tell what kind** of complement it is.

subject complement (**subj comp**)   object complement (**obj comp**)
direct object (**dir obj**)   indirect object (**ind obj**)

Example: The test results were _inconclusive_.   _subj comp_

(Collaborative option: Students work in pairs, alternating: one writes the word, the other names the kind of complement.)

1. This prescription drug is _____.   1. _____

2. The television host has an anonymous _____.   2. _____

3. Santos named Ahmed his _____.   3. _____

4. Last year, my neighbors did _____ a favor.   4. _____

5. News of the Halloween party attracted _____ throughout the school.   5. _____

6. The recent letter from her mother gave _____ much relief.   6. _____

7. To keep the young boy busy, they designated him _____.   7. _____

8. She did not seem especially _____ about the award.   8. _____

9. SENTENCES AND GRAMMAR: Uses of Nouns

(Study 112, The Uses of Nouns)

First write a sentence of your own, using the boldfaced verb. Include the parts mentioned in parentheses (in the order given). Then **identify** each of those parts by writing its name under the proper word (use the abbreviations given below):

subject (**subj**)   object complement (**obj comp**)
subject complement (**subj comp**)   object of preposition (**obj prep**)
direct object (**dir obj**)   appositive (**app**)
indirect object (**ind obj**)   direct address (**dir add**)

_____

Example: designated (subject, direct object, object complement) <u>The teacher designated Paul the class librarian.</u>
                                                                        subj   dir obj   obj comp

(Collaborative option: Students work in pairs, alternating: one writes the sentence, the other identifies the uses.)

1. **destroyed** (Subject, direct object) _____

_____

2. **grew** (Subject, subject complement) _____

_____

3. **sent** (Subject, indirect object, direct object) _____

_____

4. **considered** (Subject, direct object, object complement)_____

_____

_____

5. **sat** (Subject, appositive)_____

_____

6. **get** (Direct address, understood subject, direct object) _____

_____

23

7. **has obtained** (Subject, object of preposition, direct object) _____

_____

_____

8. **may show** (Subject, indirect object, direct object) _____

_____

9. **may become** (Subject, object of preposition, subject complement) _____

_____

_____

10. **made** (Subject, direct object, object complement) _____

_____

_____

11. **might have been** (Subject, appositive, subject complement) _____

_____

_____

12. Choose your own verb. (Subject, direct object, appositive, object complement) _____

_____

_____

10. SENTENCES AND GRAMMAR: Verb Tenses and Forms

(Study 115, Principal Parts, and 116, Tenses and Forms)

Part 1

Identify the tense or other form of the boldfaced verb (use the abbreviations in parentheses):

present (**pres**)	past perfect (**past perf**)
past	future perfect (**fut perf**)
future (**fut**)	conditional (**cond**)
present perfect (**pres perf**)	perfect conditional (**perf cond**)

Example: They **spoke** too quickly for us to understand them.   ___past___

1. Her dental work **cost** $8,000.   1. _____
2. The train **will** surely **depart** on time.   2. _____
3. By next summer we **shall have lived** in this house for ten years.   3. _____
4. Lenoir, a small town in North Carolina, **has elected** a new mayor.   4. _____
5. We **arrived** at the airport at noon, just in time to catch our flight.   5. _____
6. If the study were flawed, it **would be rejected**.   6. _____
7. **Will** she **be** the new swimming champion?   7. _____
8. American flags **appeared** all over the city.   8. _____
9. At first, they **had** not **believed** the rumors.   9. _____
10. If it hadn't rained, I **would have played** tennis last night.   10. _____
11. The company **guaranteed** that the package would arrive in the morning.   11. _____
12. Marcia **will learn** to drive this summer.   12. _____
13. The children **have created** a sand castle on the beach.   13. _____
14. **Have** you an extra soft drink?   14. _____
15. By noon, Shelley **had had** eight apples.   15. _____
16. I **did have** lunch at the new diner.   16. _____
17. The family **has planned** a vacation.   17. _____
18. She **had studied** for five hours when she took the exam.   18. _____
19. Last week the flu **hit** five staff members.   19. _____
20. This Friday **would have been** my grandmother's hundredth birthday.   20. _____
21. **Would** you **give** me a ride home this afternoon?   21. _____
22. Congress **will have adjourned** by the time the law expires.   22. _____
23. Michael **has applied** for a junior year abroad.   23. _____
24. **Is** it fair for you to turn me down?   24. _____
25. The police **stormed** the criminals' hideout.   25. _____

In each blank, write the needed **ending**: **ed** (or **d**), **s** (or **es**), or **ing**. If no ending is needed, leave the blank empty.

Example: Every boy jump_____ into the pool.   Every boy jump<u>ed</u> into the pool.

Today, the old mansion stand _____ alone in the field, about one mile from the highway. No one has live____ there for years. Children have consider_____ it haunted because it seem_____ to have lights on and people inside. When I was a child, I visit_____ the house many times. I remember _____ that the boards on the porch creak _____ and the windows rattle_____. Inside, I could see that plaster had fall _____ from the walls, and some steps on the staircase were broke____. The ceiling sag____, and the carpets were roll _____ up. I wonder_____ who had live_____ there long ago. In the backyard, a black cat jump_____ out of a broke_____ window. That frighten____ me. Although I thought the house was haunt_____, flowers were bloom_____ in the garden, but weeds had nearly overtake_____ them. I look_____ in the kitchen window and saw an old gas stove that had rust_____. Water drip_____ from the faucet, and a dish of cat food had been place_____ on the floor. Maybe the cat was not starv_____ as I had thought it was. A dog howl_____, and that fill_____ me with terror. I decide_____ that it was time for me to leave.

Yesterday, my best friend from childhood and I visit_____ the house. We recall_____ the adventures we had as children when we explor____ the house. Now, it look_____ like a big empty house; we are no longer scare_____ by it. It seem_____ as if someone has been tend _____ to it because the lawn has been mow_____, and the porch has been paint_____. I saw kittens play____ in the grass. Maybe the black cat I saw years ago was their great-great-grandmother.

11. SENTENCES AND GRAMMAR: Verbs—Kind, Tense, Voice, and Mood

(Study 114, Kinds of Verbs; 115, Principal Parts; 116, Tenses, Forms; and 118, Avoiding Verb Errors)

Part 1

Write **T** if the verb is **transitive**.
Write **I** if it is **intransitive**.
Write **L** if it is **linking**.

Example: The house **looked** decrepit.   ___L___

1. John **ate** a banana sandwich while he waited for Lorenzo.   1._____
2. The young mother **appeared** worried about her baby's cough.   2._____
3. **Put** your wet shoes on the front porch.   3._____
4. Johnny **opened** his gifts at the party.   4._____
5. The island **lies** not far off the mainland.   5._____
6. The plane for Topeka **had left** by noon.   6._____
7. **Set** the vase carefully on the table.   7._____
8. Mary **remained** calm during the argument.   8._____
9. A blanket of smog **lay** over the valley.   9._____
10. The bus **departed** five minutes ago.   10._____
11. Never **interfere** in another person's quarrel.   11._____
12. The chef **brought** the roast to the couple's table.   12._____
13. My friend **grew** nervous.   13._____
14. Jill **was amazed** by the magician.   14._____
15. Women **have been** leaders in ways that are not always noticed. 15._____

Part 2

Rewrite each boldfaced verb in the tense or form given in parentheses.

Example: Now the Johnsons **live** near the county line. (present perfect)   *For the past year, the Johnsons have lived near the county line.*

1. The train **goes** past my house every evening. (past)

   _____

   _____

2. Marcia **rode** her horse to the highest summit on the ranch. (present perfect)

_____

_____

3. The Super Pie and Cake Company **appointed** Chris its sales manager. (past perfect)

_____

_____

4. The Orioles **will win** the pennant by next fall. (future perfect)

_____

_____

5. The drought in California **will continue** without relief from rain. (conditional)

_____

_____

6. The houseplants on the porch **will die** without daily watering. (perfect conditional)

_____

_____

7. The new executive board **controls** the cost of the stock shares. (present progressive)

_____

_____

8. The Zippy Skateboard Company **wants** an imaginative designer for its new line. (past emphatic)

_____

_____

9. The Piffle Company **seeks** a new sales manager. (present perfect)

_____

_____

10. The Piffle Company **seeks** a new sales manager. (present perfect progressive)

_____

_____

Part 3

First write **A** if the boldfaced verb is in the **active voice** or **P** if it is in the **passive voice.** Then **rewrite** the sentence in the opposite voice (if it was active, make it passive; if it was passive, make it active). If necessary, supply your own subject.

Examples: A car **struck** the lamppost.   _____A_____
           The lamppost was struck by a car.

           The stage door **was left** open by Larry.   _____P_____
           Larry left the stage door open.

1. One name **was** inadvertently **omitted** from the list.   1._____

2. The bride **wore** her grandmother's wedding gown.   2._____

3. The media **bashed** the incumbent's speech.   3._____

4. The meeting **was called** to order.   4._____

5. The ancient city of Pompeii **was** completely **destroyed** by a volcanic eruption.   5._____

6. San Salvador Island **was** the first island **visited** by Christopher Columbus.   6._____

7. Younger voters **have selected** a presidential candidate.   7._____

8. The prosecutor **subjected** the witness to a vigorous cross-examination.   8. _____

_____

_____

9. By dawn, the scoutmaster **will have prepared** breakfast over the campfire.   9. _____

_____

_____

10. Vernon **was stung** by bees while weeding his garden.   10. _____

_____

_____

11. The left fielder **threw out** the runner.   11. _____

_____

_____

12. Animal rights activists **have begun** a campaign against fur coats.   12. _____

_____

_____

Part 4

Write the tense of each boldfaced verb in the blank line in the right column.

_____

Example: Marcy **went** to the market this morning.   ___Past___

1. John thought that Jim **had tried out** for the lacrosse team.   1. _____

2. By midnight, we **will have driven** over 600 miles.   2. _____

3. "Don't leave your laundry in the bathroom," Maria's grandmother **told** her.   3. _____

4. We **had** just **finished** the fish when the dessert arrived.   4. _____

5. Intrigued by weather, Michelle **has become** a meteorologist.   5. _____

6. Mark **had eaten** four apples by noon.   6. _____

7. "**Will** you **make** cookies today," the little boy asked his mother.   7. _____

8. The teens **cleaned** the kitchen, much to their mother's surprise.   8. _____

9. Marcia **likes** to wear her red plaid boots in the rain.   9. _____

10. As the ship left the dock, the passengers **waved** to their friends and families.   10. _____

11. By the time Josh returned home, the puppy **had eaten** the entire cake.   11. _____

12. Children who are taught manners **will** often **become** polite adults.   12. _____

30

13. I hope that by the day's end I **will have eaten** only 1000 calories.

14. Do you like the way she **handles** her new truck?

15. The crew **put away** the boats before the athletic meeting began.

13._____

14._____

15._____

Part 5

Rewrite each sentence in the **subjunctive** mood.

Example: Today the sky is sunny.

 I wish the sky <u>were</u> sunny today.

1. Phillip is in the parade this afternoon.

 I wish Phillip _____ in the parade this afternoon.

2. I am a gardener; I plant tulips in the spring.

 If I _____ a gardener, I would plant tulips in the spring.

3. The teenagers protested; the city reopened the skateboard park.

 The teenagers protested that the skateboard park _____ reopened.

4. You should take the exam today.

 If I _____ you, I would take the exam today.

5. Justine is a good painter and has won several prizes.

 If Justine _____ a good painter, she could win several prizes.

12. SENTENCES AND GRAMMAR: Verbals

(Study 117, Distinguishing Verbals from Verbs)

Part 1

Identify each boldfaced verbal by writing

    inf for infinitive   **pres part** for present participle
    ger for gerund   **past part** for past participle

Example: The **outnumbered** soldiers surrendered.   past part

1. July is one of the worst months **to make** meringue for a pie.   1._____
2. Usually, the humidity in the air prevents the egg whites from **peaking.**   2._____
3. Cecilia has a cake recipe that says **to add** eight eggs.   3._____
4. By **adding** the eggs, she will have a very moist cake.   4._____
5. Roy believes that **added** milk makes the cake moister.   5._____
6. **Encouraged** by their initial weight loss, Cecilia and Roy no longer ate cakes.   6._____
7. **To lose** more weight, they had to both diet and exercise.   7._____
8. By **losing** weight, they felt better and looked healthier.   8._____
9. **Craving** the delicious cake, Cecilia ate two slices after Roy left for school.   9._____
10. Because Cecilia likes **being** thin, she no longer eats desserts.   10._____
11. Roy, **driven** by hunger, made a huge salad with tomatoes, cucumbers, and spinach.   11._____
12. **Seeing** the salad, Cecilia prepared one for herself.   12._____
13. **Concerned** about their weight gain, the couple now uses a new cookbook.   13._____
14. The purpose of this cookbook is **to increase** the number of fresh vegetables.   14._____
15. **Losing** weight became a priority after they visited the doctor.   15._____

Complete each sentence with a verbal or verbal phrase of your own. Then in the blank at the right, tell how it is **used** (use the abbreviations in parentheses):

subject (**subj**)	object of preposition (**obj prep**)
subject complement (**subj comp**)	adjective (**adj**)
direct object (**dir obj**)	adverb (**adv**)

Examples: <u>Faced with the evidence</u>, the suspect admitted the crime.   <u> adj </u>

The suspect was accused of <u>absconding with company funds</u>.   <u> obj prep </u>

(Collaborative option: Students work in pairs, alternating: one writes the word or phrase, the other identifies its use.)

1. _____ is no way to greet the day.   1. _____

2. Chang likes _____.   2. _____

3. The _____ crowd rose to its feet.   3. _____

4. The mechanic opened the hood of the car [why?] _____.   4. _____

5. Professor Bigley's obsession is _____

_____.   5. _____

6. I earned an *A* in her course by _____

_____.   6. _____

7. The huge motor home, _____

_____, lumbered up the mountain road.   7. _____

8. As a last resort the officials tried _____

_____.   8. _____

9. My ambition since childhood has been _____

_____.   9. _____

10. Oddly, _____

has never been one of my goals.   10. _____

13. SENTENCES AND GRAMMAR: Verbs

(Study 115, Principal Parts; 116, Tenses, Forms; and 118, Avoiding Verb Errors)

In each blank, write the **correct form** of the verb in parentheses (some answers may require more than one word).

Examples: (prefer) We have always <u>preferred</u> vanilla.
  (see) Yesterday all of us <u>saw</u> the rainbow.

1. (use) The young man had never _____ a microwave.

2. (begin) He found the instruction manual and _____ to read it.

3. (cross) They were _____ the busy street in the wrong place.

4. (blow) Trees of all sizes were _____ down in the storm.

5. (try) If I had found the courage, I would _____ _____ skydiving.

6. (drink) Drivers who had _____ alcoholic beverages were detained by the police.

7. (fly) By the time I reach Tokyo, I shall _____ _____ for thirteen hours nonstop.

8. (freeze) If they had not brought heavy clothing, they would _____ _____ on the hike.

9. (possess) The Tsar's court felt that Rasputin _____ a strange power over them.

10. (choose) The district has always _____ a Republican for Congress.

11. (bring) Sidney _____ his guitar to school last year.

12. (forbid) Yesterday, the resident assistant _____ Sidney to play it after 9 p.m.

13. (lead) Firefighters _____ the children to safety when the smoke became too dense.

14. (lay) When their chores were finished, the weary farmers _____ their pitchforks against the fence and rested.

15. (pay) The company had always _____ its employees well.

16. (ring) The pizza deliverer walked up to the door and _____ the bell.

17. (rise) We are late; the sun has _____ already.

18. (see) Then I _____ him running around the corner.

19. (shine) Before the interview, Rod _____ his old shoes.

20. (shine) Rod polished his car until it _____ brightly.

21. (break) The rebels had _____ the peace accord.

22. (shake) The medicine had to be _____ well before being used.

23. (struggle) For hours, the fox had _____ _____ [2 words—use progressive form] to escape from the trap.

24. (show) Last week, Ford _____ its new models at the automotive exhibition.

25. (mean) Daisy had not _____ to hit Mrs. Wilson.

26. (sink) In 1945, Nimitz's carrier planes _____ much of the enemy's fleet.

27. (drag) When it grew dark, the poachers _____ the dead deer to their truck.

28. (speak) If they had known who she was, they never would _____ _____ to her.

29. (swing) In his last at-bat, Pujols _____ the bat harder than ever before.

30. (throw) The pitcher had _____ a high fastball.

31. (write) A columnist had _____ that Pujols could not hit a high fastball.

32. (seek) After her divorce, Carla _____ a place of peace and quiet.

33. (admire) For years to come, people _____ _____ _____ [3 words—use progressive form] your paintings.

14. SENTENCES AND GRAMMAR: Using Verbs

(Study 115, Principal Parts, and 118, Avoiding Verb Errors)

Write **C** if the boldfaced verb is used **correctly**.
Write **X** if it is used **incorrectly**.

Examples: In chapter 1 Greg goes to war, and in chapter 10 he **died.** _____X_____
 The lake **was frozen** overnight by the sudden winter storm. _____C_____

1. The longer he stayed, the more he **payed**. 1._____
2. The pilots **have flown** this route hundreds of times. 2._____
3. The giant shark had **swam** far up the estuary. 3._____
4. The baby **has drunk** five bottles of formula. 4._____
5. My hat **was stole** when I left it at the restaurant. 5._____
6. We **have rode** the train to Chicago many times. 6._____
7. The little child **teared** open the present wrapped in bright yellow paper. 7._____
8. The student **sunk** into his chair to avoid being called on by the professor. 8._____
9. **Have** you **went** to see the new *Star Wars* episode? 9._____
10. We **should have known** that Caroline would be late for the meeting. 10._____
11. The little boy standing by the counter **seen** the man shoplift a watch. 11._____
12. I **was drawn** to the exhibit of the colorful paintings by Matisse. 12._____
13. The judge decreed that the thief **be** sent to prison for ten years. 13._____
14. The medals **shone** brightly on the general's uniform. 14._____
15. The children **swang** on the swing until their mother called them home for supper. 15._____
16. When we were small, we **wore** hats and white gloves on special occasions. 16._____
17. The author **hasn't spoken** to the news media for fifty years. 17._____
18. Jack **has wrote** his essay on the summer he hiked the Appalachian Trail. 18._____
19. I always work on the crossword puzzle while I **lie** on the couch. 19._____
20. Grandfather **is laying** down and taking a nap. 20._____
21. When Hamlet thinks he knows what Claudius has done, he **began** to plot revenge. 21._____
22. Only immigrants who could not afford first- or second-class ship fares **passed** through Ellis Island. 22._____
23. Begin by taking Route 202 to West Chester; then **take** Route 30 to Lancaster. 23._____
24. Today long-distance telephone calls cost less than they **costed** forty years ago. 24._____
25. Stella **has ran** five miles along the coastal trail every day this year. 25._____
26. Within ten minutes after someone broke into our house, the police **were notified** by us. 26._____
27. The second act complicates the conflict, but the third act **resolves** it. 27._____
28. Then I **come** up to him and said, "Let her alone!" 28._____

29. Mark **has drunk** four bottles of water since this morning.   29. _____

30. The pastor suggested that the discussion **be** postponed until the next Parish Council meeting.   30. _____

31. The cat **was** finally **rescued** hours after climbing the tree.   31. _____

32. As the curtain **rose**, Alicia is sitting alone on stage, reading a book.   32. _____

33. The scientists' report **has awoken** the nation to the dangers of eating fast food.   33. _____

15. SENTENCES AND GRAMMAR: Adjectives and Adverbs

(Study 119, Using Adjectives and Adverbs Correctly)

If the boldfaced adjective or adverb is used **correctly,** leave the blank empty.
If the boldfaced adjective or adverb is used **incorrectly,** write the correct word(s) in the blank.

Examples: Her performance was truly **impressive.**   _____
        The Yankees are playing **good** this year.   well

1. The rock star sounds **good** on her new CD.   1._____
2. Why let his innocent remarks make you feel **badly**?   2._____
3. She was the **most** talented member of the duet.   3._____
4. Her computer is in very **good** condition for such an old machine.   4._____
5. He was very **frank** in his evaluation of his own work.   5._____
6. My father spoke very **frankly** with us.   6._____
7. Her mother is the **kindest** of her two parents.   7._____
8. My stomach feels bad, and my back hurts **bad**.   8._____
9. The student looked **happy** about his grade.   9._____
10. The fire captain waited **patiently** for the fire to be extinguished.   10._____
11. I comb my hair **different** now.   11._____
12. Was the dog hurt **bad**?   12._____
13. He seemed **real** happy about making the track team.   13._____
14. The learning assistant tried **awful** hard to keep the residence hall quiet during finals week.   14._____
15. Reading Thomas Hardy's novels is a **real** pleasure.   15._____
16. The teaching assistant glanced **nervously** at the class.   16._____
17. The bus driver seemed **nervous**.   17._____
18. The campus will look **differently** when the new buildings are completed.   18._____
19. Yours is the **clearer** of the three explanations.   19._____
20. The book is in **good** condition.   20._____
21. I did **poor** in organic chemistry this term.   21._____
22. Mario looked **debonair** in his new suit.   22._____
23. Trevor felt **badly** about having to fire the veteran employee.   23._____
24. Daryl's excuse was far **more poorer** than Keith's.   24._____
25. She writes very **good**.   25._____
26. It snowed **steady** for the whole month of December in London.   26._____
27. The roses smell **sweet**.   27._____
28. He tries **hard** to please everyone.   28._____

29. John is **near** seven feet tall.   29. _____

30. He talks **considerable** about his career plans.   30. _____

31. She donated a **considerable** sum of money to the project.   31. _____

32. The **smartest** of the twins is spoiled.   32. _____

33. The **smartest** of the triplets is spoiled.   33. _____

34. The coach gazed **uneasily** at her players.   34. _____

35. He felt **uneasy** about the score.   35. _____

36. Do try to drive more **careful**.   36. _____

37. It was Bob's **most unique** idea ever.   37. _____

38. The trial was **highly** publicized.   38. _____

39. The wood carving on the left is even **more perfect** than the other one.   39. _____

40. The house looked **strangely** to us.   40. _____

41. She looked **strangely** at me, her brow furrowed.   41. _____

42. He was ill, but he is **well** now.   42. _____

43. That lobbyist is the most **influential** in Washington.   43. _____

44. The orchestra sounded **good** throughout the hall.   44. _____

45. Societal violence has **really** reached epidemic proportions in this country.   45. _____

46. He seemed very **serious** about changing jobs.   46. _____

47. Something in the refrigerator smelled **bad**.   47. _____

48. We felt **badly** about missing the tennis match.   48. _____

49. The firefighters acted **swiftly** when they received the 911 call.   49. _____

50. However, their response was not **swift** enough.   50. _____

16. SENTENCES AND GRAMMAR: Articles and Determiners

(Study 120, Using Articles and Determiners Correctly)

Part 1

In each blank, write the **correct** article: **a**, **an**, or **the**; or leave the blank empty if **no** article is needed. (In some blanks either of two answers is correct.)

Example: When the moon and a planet come close to each other in the sky, an exciting sight awaits the viewers.

_____ exciting play occurred yesterday in _____ big-league baseball game at _____ Oriole Park. _____ Oriole player dropped _____ ball in the glare of _____ sun. When _____ ball fell to _____ ground, three Oriole players ran after it; thus _____ nobody was guarding the bases for _____ Orioles. _____ crowd groaned with _____ disappointment. _____ batter from _____ other team ran around _____ bases with _____ determination. _____ Oriole player retrieved _____ ball and made _____ accurate throw that reached home plate ahead of the runner, who was called "Out!" From the crowd came _____ cheers. The Orioles won the game and celebrated with _____ champagne from _____ France. This was _____ biggest Oriole victory of the year.

Part 2

For each blank, choose from the list any correct determiner (limiting adjective), and write it in. Try not to use any word on the list more than once.

every	many	other	more	some
each	most	such	(a) little	
either	(a) few	both	much	
another	all	enough	any	

Example: They needed *another* person to help lift the car.

1. _____ country that voted for the United Nations resolution was praised.

2. _____ countries that voted against it were criticized.

3. _____ discussions took place before the vote.

4. _____ of the neutral countries tried to postpone the vote.

5. But _____ pressure was put on these countries to vote.

6. _____ effort to influence the neutral countries' vote was rebuffed.

7. Delegates from _____ countries wanted to get the voting finished.

8-9. _____ delegates had _____ patience.

10. Finally, the Secretary General declared that _____ voting would take place the next day.

17. SENTENCES AND GRAMMAR: Pronouns—Kind and Case

(Study 121, The Kinds of Pronouns, and 122, Using the Right Case)

Part 1

Classify each boldfaced pronoun (use the abbreviations in parentheses):

personal pronoun (**pers**)
interrogative pronoun (**inter**)
relative pronoun (**rel**)
demonstrative pronoun (**dem**)

indefinite pronoun (**indef**)
reflexive pronoun (**ref**)
intensive pronoun (**intens**)

Example: Who is your partner? _____inter_____

1. I made **him** an offer that he could not refuse. 1._____

2. Queen Latifah thanked **everyone** who helped her on the film. 2._____

3. **This** is the salsa recipe I told you about. 3._____

4. John **himself** built the treehouse for the children. 4._____

5. **Which** of the trains does your cousin take to New York City? 5._____

6. The man wearing the tweed blazer is the one **who** makes the decisions here. 6._____

7. I **myself** have no desire to explore the rough terrain of mountainous regions. 7._____

8. **No one** attended the meeting scheduled for late Friday afternoon. 8._____

9. Sandra carried in the books, **which** Sheila put on the shelves. 9._____

10. Set a goal **that** is realistic or you might become frustrated. 10._____

11. Be sure that you take care of **yourself** on the expedition. 11._____

12. **Neither** of the quarterbacks could attend the awards banquet last night. 12._____

13. **Whoever** did this should be removed from office. 13._____

14. Jose cut **himself** while shaving this morning. 14._____

15. These are my biology notes; **those** must be yours. 15._____

16. **Who** should be awarded the literary prize? 16._____

17. The teens **themselves** built the raft that made it through the rapids. 17._____

18. You may give this money to **whomever** you please. 18._____

Write the number of the **correct** pronoun.

Example: The message was for Desmond and (1)**I** (2)**me**.   2

1. None of (1)**we** (2)**us** plaintiffs felt that we had been adequately compensated.   1._____

2. Jennifer feeds her dog too much food. Just look at (1)**its** (2)**it's** stomach!   2._____

3. May we—John and (1)**I** (2)**me**—join you for dinner this evening?   3._____

4. Between you and (1)**I** (2)**me**, I think we need to take a study break.   4._____

5. We gave the books to (1)**whoever** (2)**whomever** wanted them.   5._____

6. Marina was elated that the song written by Jake and (1)**he** (2)**him** was dedicated to her family.   6._____

7. It must have been (1)**he** (2)**him** who wrote the article about plant safety for the company newsletter.   7._____

8. She greeted the guests (1)**who** (2)**whom** I had brought.   8._____

9. No one except (1)**she** (2)**her** could figure out Alonzo's new cell phone.   9._____

10. He is much more talented in dramatics than (1)**she** (2)**her**.   10._____

11. The secretary notified (1)**whoever** (2)**whomever** had planned to attend of the cancellation.   11._____

12. Help (1)**we** (2)**us** students to purchase a microwave for the Honors Center.   12._____

13. Does anyone know (1)**who's** (2)**whose** boots these are?   13._____

14. He (1) **himself** (2) **hisself** made all of these fishing lures out of feathers.   14._____

15. Girls like (1)**she** (2)**her** are special.   15._____

18. SENTENCES AND GRAMMAR: Pronouns—Case

(Study 122, Using the Right Case)

In the first blank, write the **number** of the **correct** pronoun.
In the second blank, write the **reason** for your choice (use the abbreviations in parentheses):

subject (**subj**)   indirect object (**ind obj**)
subjective complement (**subj comp**)   object of preposition (**obj prep**)
direct object (**dir obj**)

Example: The tickets were for Jo and (1)**I** (2)**me**.   __2__ obj prep

1. The principal gave the password to the computer to (1)**we** (2)**us** girls.   1._____ _____

2. Did you and (1)**he** (2)**him** order tickets to the Rolling Stones concert?   2._____ _____

3. All of (1)**we** (2)**us** passengers were annoyed by the crying infant in the back of the plane.   3._____ _____

4. Mr. Russell, the scoutmaster, showed (1)**they** (2)**them** how to tie a timber hitch knot.   4._____ _____

5. Julia Ward Howe, (1)**who** (2)**whom** created Mothers' Day, did so with a Mother's Day
Proclamation in 1870.   5._____ _____

6. Gail invited (1)**he** (2)**him** to the senior dance.   6._____ _____

7. Speakers like (1)**she** (2)**her** are both entertaining and informative.   7._____ _____

8. I was very much surprised when I saw (1)**he** (2)**him** at the political rally.   8._____ _____

9. Have you and (1)**he** (2)**him** completed your science project on the life cycle of the
praying mantis?   9._____ _____

10. We asked Joan and (1)**he** (2)**him** about the movie the children saw this afternoon.   10._____ _____

11. The leader of the student group asked, "(1)**Who** (2)**Whom** do you think can afford the
10 percent increase in tuition?"   11._____ _____

12. All of (1)**we** (2)**us** tourists spent the entire day at the Kit Carson Museum in Taos, New Mexico. 12._____ _____

13. It was (1)**he** (2)**him** who made all the arrangements for the dance.   13._____ _____

14. Television executives seem to think that high ratings go to (1)**whoever** (2)**whomever**
broadcasts either the sexiest or the most violent shows.   14._____ _____

15. My two friends and (1)**I** (2)**me** decided to visit Window Rock, Arizona, headquarters of the
Navajo nation.   15._____ _____

16. This argument is just between James and (1)**I** (2)**me**.   16._____ _____

17. My father always warned (1)**I** (2)**me** against drinking and driving.   17._____ _____

18. The principal said he would give the award to (1)**whoever** (2)**whomever** raised the most
money for Toys for Tots.   18._____ _____

19. If you were (1)**I** (2)**me**, would you consider flying to London with the high air fares?   19._____ _____

20. Gandhi, Mother Teresa, and Martin Luther King, Jr., are persons (1)**who** (2)**whom** I think
will be remembered as heroes of the twentieth century.   20._____ _____

21. Everyone had to clean up the campus except Marshall, Marie, and (1)**I** (2)**me**.   21._____ _____

22. The teaching assistant asked (1)**he** (2)**him** about the experiment.   22._____ _____

23. Nina was as interested as (1)**he** (2)**him** in moving to Arizona after they both retired.   23.____ _____

24. I knew of no one who has won more talent shows than (1)**she** (2)**her**.   24.____ _____

25. Rebecca gave (1)**I** (2)**me** the notes for the class I missed.   25.____ _____

26. The teachers invited (1)**we** (2)**us** parents to a meeting with the Advanced Placement coordinator.   26.____ _____

27. The dance instructor was actually fifteen years older than (1)**he** (2)**him**.   27.____ _____

28. (1)**We** (2)**Us** veterans agreed to raise money for a memorial plaque.   28.____ _____

29. Are you and (1)**she** (2)**her** planning to join the Honors Guild?   29.____ _____

30. It is (1)**I** (2)**me** who am in charge of the bake sales for the Honors Program.   30.____ _____

31. "The caller is (1)**she** (2)**her**," said Jessica as she answered the phone.   31.____ _____

32. If you were (1)**I** (2)**me**, where would you spend spring break?   32.____ _____

33. (1)**Who** (2)**Whom** do you think will be the next mayor?   33.____ _____

34. Assign the project to (1)**whoever** (2)**whomever** doesn't mind traveling.   34.____ _____

35. Caroline gave the dictionary to Marcia and (1)**he** (2)**him** so that they could complete the vocabulary exercises.   35.____ _____

36. He is the author about (1)**who** (2)**whom** we shall be writing a paper.   36.____ _____

37. Was it (1)**he** (2)**him** who won the contest?   37.____ _____

38. The only choice left was between (1)**she** (2)**her** and Matthew.   38.____ _____

39. No one actually read the book except (1)**she** (2)**her**.   39.____ _____

40. "Were you calling (1)**I** (2)**me**?" Peggy asked as she entered the room.   40.____ _____

41. Both of (1)**we** (2)**us** hated going to the math tutoring sessions.   41.____ _____

42. Imagine finally meeting (1)**he** (2)**him** after so many years of correspondence!   42.____ _____

43. The polltakers asked both (1)**she** (2)**her** and her friend some questions about the planned subway line.   43.____ _____

44. Do you suppose that (1)**he** (2)**him** will ever find time to visit us?   44.____ _____

45. José sent an invitation to (1)**I** (2)**me**.   45.____ _____

46. It was the other reviewer who disliked the movie, not (1)**I** (2)**me**.   46.____ _____

47. The dean's objection to the content of our play caused the directors and (1)**we** (2)**us** much trouble.   47.____ _____

48. The couple disagreed about (1)**who** (2)**whom** was better at rearranging the living room furniture.   48.____ _____

49. It was Thomas Jefferson, I think, (1)**who** (2)**whom** was the third President of the United States.   49.____ _____

50. The last piece of pie should go to (1)**whoever** (2)**whomever** you see first.   50.____ _____

19. SENTENCES AND GRAMMAR: Pronoun Reference

(Study 123, Avoiding Faulty Reference)

Part 1

Write **C** if the boldfaced word is used **correctly**.
Write **X** if it is used **incorrectly**.

Example: Betsy agreed with Jane that **she** was too far behind in math to catch up. _____X_____

1. Marcy campaigned for Stephanie; then she made campaign signs for Jason. None of us expected **this**. 1._____

2. Bill loves to bake cakes as a hobby, but he hasn't gained any weight. **This** surprised all of us. 2._____

3. Ms. Joseph told the students that a quiz would be given on Tuesday and the papers would be due on Wednesday. No one was expecting **that**. 3._____

4. The latest of these attacks was so vicious that the Secretary of State urged the President to respond strongly to **it**. 4._____

5. Marcia and Pearl met so she could return the purse that **she** had borrowed for the prom. 5._____

6. In Buffalo, **they** eat chicken wings served with blue cheese dressing and celery. 6._____

7. I was late filing my report, **which** greatly embarrassed me. 7._____

8. In the United States, **they** mail approximately 166 billion letters and packages each year. 8._____

9. Irene was accepted by several medical schools, but she decided to go into nursing instead. Her family was surprised by **that**. 9._____

10. The physician's speech focused on the country's inattention to the AIDS epidemic; the audience was greatly surprised by **it**. 10._____

11. The President's dog was a favorite of the media, and **he** liked all that attention. 11._____

12. They intended to climb rocky White Mountain; few hikers had ever accomplished **that** feat before. 12._____

13. Pat always wanted to be a television newscaster; thus, she majored in **it** in college. 13._____

14. The average American child watches over thirty hours of television each week, **which** is why we are no longer a nation of readers. 14._____

15. **It** was well past midnight when the phone rang. 15._____

16. The speaker kept scratching his head, a mannerism **that** proved distracting. 16._____

17. According to the Weather Channel, **it** is expected to sleet heavily in the upper Northeast this winter. 17._____

18. When Dan drives down the street in his red sports car, **they** all look on with admiration and, perhaps, just a little envy. 18._____

19. Bill told Josh that **he** could repay him next week. 19._____

20. Matthew started taking pictures in high school. **This** interest led to a brilliant career in photography. 20._____

21. **It** is best to be aware of both the caloric and fat content of food in your diet. 21._____

22. In some vacation spots, **they** add the tip to the bill and give poor service. 22._____

23. In Russo's novel *Empire Falls*, the main character seems just like **him**. 23._____

24. In some areas of California, **it** seemed as if the drought would finally end. 24._____

25. In some sections of the old history text, it seems as if **they** ignored the contributions of African Americans to the development of this country. 25._____

Part 2

Choose eight items that you marked **X** in part 1. **Rewrite** each correctly in the blanks below. Before each sentence, write its number from part 1.

Example: 26. Betsy agreed with Jane that Jane was too far behind in math to catch up.

_____

_____

_____

_____

_____

_____

_____

_____

_____

_____

_____

_____

_____

_____

_____

_____

20. SENTENCES AND GRAMMAR: Phrases

(Study 124, Phrases)

Part 1

In the first blank, write the number of the **one** set of words that is a prepositional phrase.
In the second blank, write **adj** if the phrase is used as an adjective, or **adv** if it is used as an adverb.

Example: The starting pitcher for the Giants is a left-hander.   <u> 2 </u> <u>adj</u>
           1   2   3

1. If time permits, the club members will vote today on your proposal.   1.____ ____
     1   2   3   4

2. The great white pines growing in the northern forests may soon die without more rain.   2.____ ____
      1   2   3   4

3. The lady wearing the fur stole has been dating an animal activist from Oregon.   3.____ ____
     1   2   3   4   5

4. What they saw before the door closed shocked them beyond belief.   4.____ ____
     1   2   3   4

5. The most frequently used word in the English language is the word *the*.   5.____ ____
        1   2   3

6. The need for adequate child care was not considered when the President addressed the convention. 6.____ ____
    1   2   3   4

7. The observation that men and women have different courtship rituals seems debatable
     1   2   3

   in a modern postindustrial society.   7.____ ____
     4

8. At our yard sale, I found out that people will buy almost anything if the price is right.   8.____ ____
     1   2   3

9. Until the last five minutes our team seemed to have the game won, but we lost.   9.____ ____
      1   2   3   4

10. After everyone left to attend the meeting, Nugent sneaked back for a long, quiet nap.   10.____ ____
      1   2   3   4

Some of the boldfaced expressions are verbal phrases; others are parts of verbs (followed by modifiers or complements). In the blank, **identify** each **expression** (use the abbreviations in parentheses):

verbal phrase used as adjective (**adj**)
verbal phrase used as adverb (**adv**)
verbal phrase used as noun (**noun**)
part of verb (with modifiers or complements) (**verb**)

Examples: Singing in the rain can give one a cold.   <u>noun</u>
       Gene is **singing in the rain** despite his cold.   <u>verb</u>

1. **Walking one mile each day** has helped me lose some weight.   1. _____

2. Maria is **assembling the items** to decorate a birthday cake.   2. _____

3. **To prepare the icing**, she adds vanilla flavoring to the sugar and butter,   3. _____

4. I'm trying **to resist the cake**, but its smell is tempting me.   4. _____

5. **Having run four miles**, Justin had two desserts after dinner tonight.   5. _____

6. The Clementes were **having the Robertsons to dinner that evening**.   6. _____

7. His idea of a thrill is **driving in stock-car races.**   7. _____

8. **Modeling in a local fashion show** helped Allison decide to consider modeling as a career.   8. _____

9. The young married couple was **surviving on a meager income**.   9. _____

10. She earnestly desires **to increase the membership**.   10. _____

21. SENTENCES AND GRAMMAR: Verbal Phrases

(Study 124B, The Verbal Phrase)

Part 1

In each sentence, find a verbal phrase. **Circle** it, and in the small blank at the right, tell how it is used: as adjective (write **adj**), adverb (write **adv**), or **noun**.

Example: A study conducted by the Yale Medical School found that smoking is addictive.   ___adj___

1. Dressed in a pale yellow gown, the bride walked out of the church with her new husband.   1. _____

2. Keeping up with his assigned reading helped Jim with his biology course.   2. _____

3. Having a research question can help a student begin on a paper.   3. _____

4. After she fell hopelessly in love, Jill neglected to complete her assignments.   4. _____

5. Maurice Jones, realizing he hadn't received mail in several days, contacted the post office.   5. _____

6. To boost the student's confidence, the teacher gave her several simple problems.   6. _____

7. John tried cooking dinner for Melissa's parents.   7. _____

8. Irene, elated by earning a perfect score on the algebra quiz, bought herself a cashmere sweater set as a gift to herself.   8. _____

9. Unloading the dishwasher is a task I despise.   9. _____

10. Our lacrosse team, beaten in the playoffs, congratulated the winners.   10. _____

11. To feel more safe, they changed all the locks.   11. _____

12. After the teacher told them to be quiet, the kindergartners listened to the story about Paddington Bear.   12. _____

13. John found repairing the very top of the roof difficult.   13. _____

14. Josh passed the course in grammar by rereading confusing parts of the textbook.   14. _____

15. The hunter put down his gun, saying that he could no longer take the life of a living creature.   15. _____

Part 2

Complete each sentence with a verbal phrase of your own. Then, in the small blank at the right, tell how you used it: **adj**, **adv**, or **noun**.

1. To take the test without _____ was not wise at all.   1. _____

2. Alison organized a group of senior citizens [hint: for what purpose?] _____   2. _____

   _____.

3. Worried about her children, the young mother decided _____   3. _____

   _____.

4. _____ may be

    linked to increased risk of infection.   4. _____

5. She tried to obtain the information without _____

    _____.   5. _____

6. The student _____ is here to

    select a major.   6. _____

7. The best book _____ is one

    that helps you escape daily tension.   7. _____

8. _____, he found an article

    that was easy to understand.   8. _____

9. Physicians recommend that patients _____

    donate their own blood.   9. _____

10. _____ has been

    the cause of too many fires.   10. _____

22. SENTENCES AND GRAMMAR: Review of Phrases

(Study 124, Phrases; also suggested: 128E, Use Reduction)

Part 1

Classify each boldfaced phrase (use the abbreviations in parentheses):

prepositional phrase (**prep**)   gerund phrase (**ger**)
infinitive phrase (**inf**)   absolute phrase (**abs**)
participial phrase (**part**)

Example: The economies **of Asian countries** grew shaky.   ____prep____

1. Although cooked potatos are safe to eat, the stems and leaves **of potato plants** contain a poison called Solanine.   1. _____

2. The large strange insect **hiding among the weeds** is a praying mantis.   2. _____

3. The first home computers had green letters **on a small black screen.**   3. _____

4. **His insisting that he was right** made him unpopular with his associates.   4. _____

5. The committee voted **to adjourn immediately.**   5. _____

6. **Because of the storm**, the excursion around the lake had to be postponed.   6. _____

7. **To watch a television program in the 1950s** required letting the set warm up for about five minutes.   7. _____

8. **During early television programming**, nightly news shows were fifteen minutes long.   8. _____

9. **Modeling for fashion magazines** has been Sally's dream since childhood.   9. _____

10. We were obliged to abandon our plans, **the boat having been damaged in a recent storm.**   10. _____

11. **Realizing that her mother's illness was getting worse**, Christine decided to postpone her vacation.   11. _____

12. **To buy the new hybrid car,** Ben borrowed the down payment from his father.   12. _____

13. The children were successful in **developing their own lawn-mowing company.**   13. _____

14. **The semester completed**, the teachers planned to have a crab feast at Druid Hill Park.   14. _____

15. The distinguished-looking man **in the blue suit** is the head of the company.   15. _____

16. **Earning a college degree** requires that you make sacrifices.   16. _____

17. *The Wonderful Wizard of Oz* is one of the most popular books **in American children's literature**.   17. _____

18. On August 12, 1939, the film *The Wizard of Oz* premiered at the Strand Theatre **in Oconomowoc, Wisconsin.**   18. _____

19. W. W. Denslow was hired **to illustrate *The Wonderful Wizard of Oz*, the book on which the film was based.**   19. _____

20. Two crates **of lemons** were delivered to the backdoor of the restaurant.   20. _____

21. **Preparing for a dinner of barbecued ribs**, Mary put stacks of napkins in the middle of the table.   21. _____

22. A car **filled with students** left early this morning to attend the class picnic.   22. _____

23. The tall woman **wearing an apron** is the one to see about your dinner orders.   23. _____

24. **Her mind going blank at the last minute,** Madeline could not answer the quizmaster's million-dollar question.   24. _____

25. **Frequently checking one's bank-account balance** can prevent embarrassing "insufficient funds" check returns.   25. _____

Part 2

Combine the following pairs of sentences by reducing one of the sentences to a phrase.

Examples: The new furniture arrived yesterday. It was for the den.
The new furniture for the den arrived yesterday.

Professor Hughes gave us an assignment. We had to find five library references on the Depression.
Professor Hughes gave us an assignment to find five library references on the Depression.

(Collaborative option: Students work in pairs or small groups to suggest ways of combining.)

1. Martina flipped through the channels. She decided that watching paint dry would be more exciting than watching television.

   _____

   _____

   _____

2. The tulip was introduced to Holland in 1593 by Carolus Clusius, a botanist. He brought it from Constantinople.

   _____

   _____

   _____

3. Carolus Clusius planted tulips in his garden. He intended to research the plant for medicinal purposes.

   _____

   _____

   _____

4. The cost of international flights has increased more over the past two years than during any other period. This increase has been caused by skyrocketing fuel costs.

   _____

   _____

   _____

5. In the 1920s, Americans often used homemade crystal radio sets. They did this so that they could listen to radio broadcasts.

_____

_____

_____

6. Annabelle forgot to pick up her dress from the drycleaners. She panicked and then borrowed one from her sister.

_____

_____

_____

7. The white potato plant was grown strictly as an ornament in Europe. This was before the 1700s.

_____

_____

_____

8. Scientists are using artificial life simulation programs. They are doing this for futuristic experimentation.

_____

_____

_____

23. SENTENCES AND GRAMMAR: Recognizing Clauses

(Study 125, Clauses)

Classify each boldfaced clause (use the abbreviations in parentheses):

independent [main] clause (**ind**)
dependent [subordinate] clause: adjective clause (**adj**)
                                      adverb clause (**adv**)
                                      noun clause (**noun**)

Example: The program will work **when the disk is inserted**.   ____adv____

1. The Appalachian National Scenic Trail, **which is generally known as the Appalachian Trail**, is a marked hiking trail in the eastern United States.   1. _____

2. The restaurant owner bought a new refrigerator because the staff complained about the old one, **which had by then been used for nearly eight years**.   2. _____

3. The foreign tourists asked **whether New York City was the state capital.**   3. _____

4. The woman **who painted her house purple and pink** is my neighbor.   4. _____

5. **Whether Carmen will go skiing with us** depends on whether she can find someone to substitute for her at work.   5. _____

6. Mildred learned to knit **when she spent six weeks in bed with a broken leg.**   6. _____

7. **The Appalachian Trail is approximately 2175 miles long**; its path is maintained by thirty trail clubs and multiple partnerships.   7. _____

8. The grocery store near my house offers free shopping and delivery to senior citizens **who are too sick to leave their homes.**   8. _____

9. **Whenever Mother makes a cherry cheesecake,** everyone in the family is home for dinner.   9. _____

10. The detective listened carefully to the suspect's answers, but **she couldn't find a reason to charge the suspect.**   10. _____

11. Few people realize **that their mattresses are full of tiny dust mites.**   11. _____

12. My first impression was **that someone had been in my room quite recently.**   12. _____

13. The actor **who had lost the Oscar** declared through clenched teeth that she was delighted just to have been nominated.   13. _____

14. Laura took the grammar test; **then she checked the textbook to see how subordinate conjunctions are used.**   14. _____

15. The candidate decided to withdraw from the city council race **because she didn't approve of the media's treatment of her family**.   15. _____

16. Why don't you sit here **until the rest of the class arrives**?   16. _____

17. The real estate mogul, **who is not known for his modesty**, has named still another building after himself.   17. _____

18. **Although she is sixty-two years old**, she can ride a horse like a teenager.   18. _____

19. The Battle of Saratoga is more famous, yet **the Battle of Brandywine involved more soldiers**.   19. _____

20. **What Jeff wanted for his birthday** was dinner and a movie with his girlfriend.   20. _____

21. **Don't begin the assignment** until you know how many sources the instructor requires for it. 21. _____

22. She is a person **whom everyone respects and admires**. 22. _____

23. The weather is surprisingly warm **even though it is December**. 23. _____

24. My answer was **that I had been unavoidably detained**. 24. _____

25. The cat loved to sleep in the boys' room **because it could stalk their goldfish at night.** 25. _____

26. The trophy will be awarded to **whoever wins the contest**. 26. _____

27. The nurse walked up the stairs; **she peeked into the invalid's room.** 27. _____

28. Is this the book **that you asked us to order for you**? 28. _____

29. The congregation could not believe **that the sermon lasted three hours.** 29. _____

30. Zora Neale Hurston, the African American woman **who wrote** *Their Eyes Were Watching God*, died penniless. 30. _____

31. **Because students are prone to resolving conflicts by fighting with one another**, the principal is working on developing conflict resolution groups. 31. _____

32. The log cabin **where my father was born** is still standing. 32. _____

33. Many Americans do not realize **that dual-income families are a result of a declining economy rather than gender equality**. 33. _____

24. SENTENCES AND GRAMMAR: Dependent Clauses

(Study 125B, Kinds of Dependent Clauses; also suggested: 128D, Use Subordination)

Part 1

Circle the dependent clause in each item. Then, in the blank, **classify** it as an adjective (**adj**), adverb (**adv**), or **noun**.

Example: The textbook explained fully what the instructor had outlined.   _____noun_____

1. Although she was an experienced tailor, her incorrect measurements made the wedding
   dress four inches too short.   1._____

2. The couple searched the Internet for a vacation spot where they could improve their bridge game.   2._____

3. The early bicycles weren't comfortable because they had wooden wheels and wooden seats.   3._____

4. The debutante who wore a gown trimmed in white feathers was told to leave the ballroom.   4._____

5. Whether Doris had plastic surgery remains a mystery.   5._____

6. When Elvis left the building, his fans ran to his limousine to catch a glimpse of him.   6._____

7. Whoever prepared the pumpkin pie for Thanksgiving should be a professional baker.   7._____

8. The karate instructor gave extra help to anyone who asked for it.   8._____

9. There is always much anxiety whenever final exams are held.   9._____

10. Some people believe that sunscreen does more harm than good.   10._____

Part 2

In each long blank, write a dependent clause of your own. Then, in the small blank, **identify** your clause as adjective (**adj**), adverb (**adv**), or **noun**.

Example: The noted author, *who was autographing her books*, smiled at us.   _____adj_____

(Collaborative option: Students work in pairs, alternating: one writes the clause, the other tells how it is used.)

1. Dr. Jackson,_____,
   declared Burton the winner.   1._____

2. The award went to the actor _____.   2._____

3. _____,
   vacationing families are staying closer to home.   3._____

4. Lucille remarked _____.   4._____

5. _____,
   Congress voted against the bill.   5._____

6. It was the only mistake _____.   6._____

7. During his acceptance speech, the new class president said _____
_____.   7. _____

8. Most of the audience had tears in their eyes _____
_____.   8. _____

9. The United States, _____,
   is still the preferred destination of millions of immigrants.   9. _____

10. The candidate told her followers _____.   10. _____

25. SENTENCES AND GRAMMAR: Noun and Adjective Clauses

(Study 125B, Kinds of Dependent Clauses; also suggested: 128D, Use Subordination)

Combine each of the following pairs of sentences into one sentence. Do this by reducing one of the pair to a noun or adjective clause.

Examples: Something puzzled the police. What did the note mean?
> What the note meant puzzled the police.

The X-Files became immensely popular in the late 1990s. It appeared on the Fox TV network.
> The X-Files, which appeared on the Fox TV network, became immensely popular in the late 1990s.

(Collaborative option: Students work in pairs or small groups to suggest ways of combining.)

1. One thing remained unresolved. Who was the more accomplished chef? [Hint: try a noun clause.]

   _____

   _____

2. The programmer retired at age twenty. She had written the new computer game. [Hint: try an adjective clause.]

   _____

   _____

3. I do not see how anyone could object to that. The senator said it.

   _____

   _____

4. The laboratory assistant gave the disk to Janine. He had helped Janine learn the word-processing software.

   _____

   _____

5. They planned something for the scavenger hunt. It seemed really bizarre.

   _____

   _____

6. We should donate the money to a charity. You choose one.

   _____

   _____

7. Large classes and disruptive students are problems. Most school districts are seeking ways to correct these problems.

_____

_____

8. Every teacher has a worst fear. Her students may hate to read.

_____

_____

9. Marjorie was an excellent employee. She seemed to thrive on working well with others and completing all her tasks.

_____

_____

10. Animal rights activists demonstrated in certain states. In these states grizzly bear hunting is allowed.

_____

_____

11. Samuel F. B. Morse is famous for pioneering the telegraph. He was also a successful portrait painter.

_____

_____

12. Something could no longer be denied. The war was already lost.

_____

_____

13. The long black limousine had been waiting in front of the building. It sped away suddenly.

_____

_____

14. When Columbus reached America, there were more than three hundred Native American tribes. Together these tribes contained more than a million people.

_____

_____

_____

15. You must decide something now. That thing is critically important.

_____

_____

16. My English professor has written a biography of Bret Harte. She is obviously enthralled by this nineteenth-century writer.

_____

_____

17. The lottery will be won by someone. That person holds the lucky numbers.

_____

_____

18. Juan has a friendly disposition. It has helped him during tense negotiations at work.

_____

_____

19. The TV news reported things regarding the episode. We were appalled by them.

_____

_____

20. Paleontologists have unearthed a set of bones. They make up the most nearly complete Tyrannosaurus Rex ever found.

_____

_____

_____

26. SENTENCES AND GRAMMAR: Adverb Clauses

(Study 125B, Kinds of Dependent Causes; also suggested: 128D, Use Subordination)

Combine each of the following pairs of sentences into one sentence by reducing one sentence to the kind of adverb clause specified in brackets.

___

Examples: The sun set. Then the lovers headed home. [time]
  When the sun set, the lovers headed home.
  Students must score 1700 on their College Boards. Otherwise they will not be admitted. [condition]
  Students will not be admitted unless they score 1700 on their College Boards.

(Collaborative option: Students work in pairs or small groups to suggest ways of combining.)

1. [cause] Four hundred thousand Americans each year get skin cancer. Therefore, many parents are teaching their children to avoid overexposure to sunlight.

   _____

   _____

   _____

2. [place] The candidate was willing to speak anywhere. But she had to find an audience there.

   _____

   _____

3. [manner] Carl ran the race. He seemed to think his life depended on it.

   _____

   _____

4. [comparison] Her brother has always been able to read fast. She has always been able to read faster.

   _____

   _____

5. [purpose] This species of tree has poisonous leaves. That way, insects will not destroy it.

   _____

   _____

6. [time] The concert was half over. Most of the audience had already left.

   _____

   _____

7. [comparison] I worked hard on that project. I could not have worked harder.

_____

_____

8. [purpose] He read extensively. His purpose was to be well prepared for the test.

_____

_____

9. [condition] American attitudes must change. Otherwise small family farms will disappear.

_____

_____

10. [concession] Her grades were satisfactory. But she did not qualify for the scholarship.

_____

_____

11. [result] She worried very much. The result was that she could no longer concentrate in her classes.

_____

_____

12. [condition] You may accept the position, or you may not. Either way, you should write a thank-you note to the interviewer.

_____

_____

13. [cause] Frosts destroyed Florida's citrus crops this year. So citrus prices will increase significantly.

_____

_____

14. [condition] Do not complete the rest of the registration form. You have to see your advisor first.

_____

_____

15. [concession] Marina was only 5 feet 5 inches tall. But she was determined to be a basketball star.

_____

_____

16. [place] Ms. Bellamy preferred one kind of grocery store. No one stood in line for anything there.

   _____

   _____

17. [condition] The substance may be an acid. Then the litmus paper will turn red.

   _____

   _____

18. [cause] Ethnic jokes can be particularly harmful. Such humor subtly reinforces stereotypes.

   _____

   _____

19. [manner] Harvey smiled in a certain way. Maybe he knew something the rest of us didn't.

   _____

   _____

20. [comparison] Jose received good grades. But George usually received better ones.

   _____

   _____

27. SENTENCES AND GRAMMAR: Kinds of Sentences

(Study 125C, Clauses in Sentences; also suggested: 128B–E, Use Coordination, Compounding, Subordination, and Reduction)

Part 1

Classify each sentence (use the abbreviations in parentheses):

simple (**sim**)   complex (**cx**)
compound (**cd**)   compound-complex (**cdcx**)

Example: Liza baked a yellow cake, but she had no chocolate for the icing.   ___cd___

1. Geraldine's friends didn't know that she couldn't swim.   1. _____

2. Bob, Jimmy, Luis, and Ben invited Mary, Juanita, Doreen, and Margie to go to the dinner dance with them next weekend.   2. _____

3. Unless funds become available, completion of the new library will be delayed.   3. _____

4. Consider your yard space carefully before you decide on a landscaping plan; your choices will be difficult to change.   4. _____

5. This year, either medical companies or discount store chains are a good investment for the small investor.   5. _____

6. *My Fair Lady*, which is a 1956 musical based upon George Bernard Shaw's *Pygmalion*, continues to be popular with audiences.   6. _____

7. The storm, which had caused much damage, subsided; we then continued on our hike.   7. _____

8. We gave instructions to the new babysitter before we left for the movies.   8. _____

9. The jury's verdict having been given, the prisoner feared his sentencing.   9. _____

10. The ointment was supposed to cure my rash; instead, it made my condition worse.   10. _____

11. In the novelette *Metamorphoses*, Gregor Samsa awakes to discover that he has become a giant beetle.   11. _____

12. When the wily fox left the henhouse through a hole in the floor, the chickens gave a cluck of relief.   12. _____

13. Insurance cannot cover everything; however, it does cover the big expenses accrued during pregnancy.   13. _____

14. Wearing a slinky dress with sequins, Joan went to the opening of the new nightclub.   14. _____

15. John and Elsie sang and danced at the celebration.   15. _____

16. After he itemized the latest catastrophes in his life, the millionaire became depressed.   16. _____

17. By 2080, over one million Americans will be one hundred years old or older; this significant increase of centenarians will profoundly affect the health care system.   17. _____

18. Seeing everyone already seated at the long table, the host proposed a toast to the couple.   18. _____

19. If Stephen changes his mind, we shall know for sure that Mary has learned her lesson, but only time will tell.   19. _____

20. At a picnic near the river in that sunny field, Matthew and Elizabeth had fried chicken for lunch.   20. _____

21. The play, which was written by Tom, was well received by the audience.   21. _____

22. His worry was that he might reveal the secret by talking in his sleep.   22. _____

23. The story appearing in the newspaper contained several inaccuracies.   23. _____

24. Many people are surprised to learn that animal crackers were originally designed as a
Christmas treat.   24. _____

25. The television special accurately portrayed life in the early twentieth century.   25. _____

Part 2

In the long blank, **combine** each set of sentences into one sentence. Then, in the small blank, **classify** your new sentence as simple (**sim**), compound (**cd**), complex (**cx**), or compound-complex (**cdcx**).

Examples: The President flew to Gibraltar. From there she cruised to Malta.
The President flew to Gibraltar and from there cruised to Malta.   _____sim_____

The ballerina's choreography won praise that night. She was not satisfied with it.
She spent the next morning reworking it.
Although the ballerina's choreography won praise that night, she was not satisfied
with it and spent the next morning reworking it.   _____cx_____

(Collaborative option: Students work in pairs or small groups to suggest ways of combining.)

1. The suspect went to the police station. He turned himself in.   1. _____

   _____

   _____

   _____

2. Maria has always had a garden. She plans to earn a degree in botany.   2. _____

   _____

   _____

   _____

3. Andy wanted that puppy. It was already sold. So he had to look for another one.   3. _____

   _____

   _____

   _____

4. Batik is a distinctive and complex method of dyeing cloth. It was created on the island of Java.   4. _____

   _____

   _____

   _____

5. Scientists convened. They came from all over the world. They wanted to discuss finding other forms of fuel. This was a serious problem.

5. _____

_____

_____

_____

6. In the 1920s, there were three favorite amusements. They were mahjong, ouija, and crossword puzzles.

6. _____

_____

_____

_____

7. Only one country has a lower personal income tax than the United States. That is Japan. This is among the wealthy nations.

7. _____

_____

_____

_____

8. The American Dream seems inaccessible to many Americans. These Americans have difficulty even making ends meet.

8. _____

_____

_____

_____

9. Some couples marry before age thirty. These couples have a high divorce rate.

9. _____

_____

_____

_____

10. Banks make this promise to their customers. Banking will become more convenient. It will happen through computer technology.

10. _____

_____

_____

_____

11. Janelle rolled up her sleeves. She planned to spend the afternoon making bread and cinnamon rolls. She was going to use several sticks of butter in each recipe.

11. _____

_____

_____

_____

12. The Middle East is the birthplace of three major world religions. One is Judaism. Another is Christianity. The third is Islam.

12. _____

_____

_____

_____

13. The women sat up talking. They did this late one night. They talked about their first dates. Most laughed about their teenage years. Those years had been awkward.

13. _____

_____

_____

_____

28. SENTENCES AND GRAMMAR: Subject-Verb Agreement

(Study 126, Subject-Verb Agreement)

Write the number of the **correct** choice.

Example: One of the network's best programs (1)**was** (2)**were** canceled. _____1_____

1. Neither the men's nor the women's room (1)**has** (2)**have** been cleaned today. 1._____

2. Economics (1)**is** (2)**are** among the hardest majors in the curriculum. 2._____

3. Working a second job to pay off his school loans (1)**has** (2)**have** become a priority for Jason. 3._____

4. Not one of the new players on the team (1)**has** (2)**have** impressed me. 4._____

5. (1)**Does** (2)**Do** each of the questions count the same number of points? 5._____

6. The number of jobs lost in the furniture industry in North Carolina (1)**has** (2)**have** increased significantly in the past four years. 6._____

7. *Twenty-two* (1)**is** (2)**are** hyphenated because it is a compound number. 7._____

8. The college president, along with five deans, (1)**was** (2)**were** ready for the annual meeting. 8._____

9. Both the secretary and the treasurer (1)**was** (2)**were** asked to submit their expense accounts for the audit. 9._____

10. Everyone in the audience (1)**was** (2)**were** stunned by the new governor's policy regarding the death penalty. 10._____

11. *Women* (1)**is** (2)**are** spelled with an *o* but pronounced with an *i* sound. 11._____

12. Every junior and senior (1)**was** (2)**were** expected to attend the memorial ceremony. 12._____

13. There (1)**was** (2)**were** an advisor, two English professors, four students, and a representative from the Honors Council at the meeting on the new plagiarism policy. 13._____

14. Twenty dollars (1)**is** (2)**are** too much to pay for that book. 14._____

15. (1)**Is** (2)**Are** there any doughnuts left on the kitchen table? 15._____

16. Neither the neighbors nor the police officer (1)**was** (2)**were** surprised by the graffiti found on the garage doors along the street. 16._____

17. Each of the crises actually (1)**needs** (2)**need** the President's immediate attention. 17._____

18. (1)**Is** (2)**Are** your father and brother coming to see you play in the championship tomorrow? 18._____

19. A good book and a cup of tea (1)**was** (2)**were** all she needed to relax. 19._____

20. There (1)**is** (2)**are** one coat and two hats in the hallway. 20._____

21. (1)**Does** (2)**Do** Coach Alonzo and the players know about the special award? 21._____

22. My two weeks' vacation (1)**was** (2)**were** filled with swimming, surfing, and sunning. 22._____

23. The only thing that annoyed me more (1)**was** (2)**were** the boys' making airplanes out of their homework. 23._____

24. (1)**Hasn't** (2)**Haven't** either of the roommates looked for the missing ring? 24._____

25. There (1)**is** (2)**are** a bird and a squirrel fighting over the birdseed in the feeder. 25._____

26. On the table (1)**was** (2)**were** a key, a note, and two dollars. 26._____

27. It is remarkable that the entire class (1)**is** (2)**are** visiting the museum.   27. _____

28. It (1)**was** (2)**were** a book and a flashlight that disappeared from the desk.   28. _____

29. There (1)**is** (2)**are** many reasons to thank the teachers who helped you in elementary school.   29. _____

30. (1)**Is** (2)**Are** algebra and chemistry required courses?   30. _____

31. One of his three instructors (1)**has** (2)**have** offered to write a letter of recommendation.   31. _____

32. (1)**Does** (2)**Do** either of the books have a section on citing sources?   32. _____

33. Neither my parents' car nor our old Jeep (1)**is** (2)**are** reliable enough to make the trip.   33. _____

34. Marbles, stones, and string (1)**is** (2)**are** my son's favorite playthings.   34. _____

35. Each of the books (1)**has** (2)**have** an introduction written by the author's mentor.   35. _____

36. The essay on *Hamlet*, in addition to several short papers, (1)**was** (2)**were** due immediately after spring break.   36. _____

37. Neither the teacher nor the parents (1)**understands** (2)**understand** why Nathan does so well in math but can barely read first-grade books.   37. _____

38. The old woman who walks the twin Scottish terriers (1)**has** (2)**have** a garden filled with hydrangea bushes.   38. _____

39. At the Boy Scout camp-out, eggs and bacon (1)**was** (2)**were** the first meal the troop attempted to prepare on an open fire.   39. _____

40. (1)**There's** (2)**There are** more pickles and mustard in the refrigerator.   40. _____

41. Everyone (1)**was** (2)**were** working hard to finish planting the crops before the rainy season.   41. _____

42. The children, along with their teacher, (1)**is** (2)**are** preparing a one-act play for the spring open house.   42. _____

43. Minnie Olson is one of those people who always (1)**volunteers** (2)**volunteer** to help the homeless.   43. _____

44. Lucy announced that *The Holy Terrors* (1)**is** (2)**are** the title of her next book, which is about raising her three sons.   44. _____

45. The class, along with the teacher, (1)**was** (2)**were** worried about the ailing class pet.   45. _____

46. Five dollars (1)**does** (2)**do** not seem like much to my eight-year-old son.   46. _____

47. Either the choir members or the organist (1)**was** (2)**were** constantly battling with the minister about purchasing fancy new choir robes.   47. _____

48. In the last 200 years, over 50 million people from 140 countries (1)**has** (2)**have** left their homelands to immigrate to the United States.   48. _____

49. Food from different geographic locations and ethnic groups often (1)**helps** (2)**help** distinguish specific cultural events.   49. _____

50. Virtually every painting and every sculpture Picasso did (1)**is** (2)**are** worth over a million dollars.   50. _____

51. There on the table (1)**was** (2)**were** my lipstick and my keys.   51. _____

52. Neither the documentary about the history of candles nor the two shows about New Guinea (1)**was** (2)**were** successful in the ratings.   52. _____

53. Each of the new television series (1)**is** (2)**are** about teenagers taking responsibility for their actions.   53. _____

54. Snowboarding at Mount Kisco (1)**was** (2)**were** Evan and his three best friends.   54. _____

55. The Oberammergau Passion Play, which began in 1633, (1)**is** (2)**are** about the crucifixion of Jesus Christ and is performed every 10 years in Germany.

55. _____

56. A political convention, with its candidates, delegates, and reporters, (1)**seems** (2)**seem** like bedlam.

56. _____

57. In the auditorium (1)**was** (2)**were** assembled the orchestra members who were ready to practice for the upcoming concert.

57. _____

58. Each of the art historians (1)**has** (2)**have** given an example of how Africa influenced European art in the late nineteenth century.

58. _____

59. (1)**Was** (2)**Were** either President Smith or Dean Nicholson asked to speak at the awards ceremony?

59. _____

60. Baking fancy wedding and birthday cakes (1)**has** (2)**have** become Joan's favorite weekend activity.

60. _____

61. A pad and pencil (1)**was** (2)**were** all Gail was permitted to take into the rare-book collection.

61. _____

62. Neither my friend nor I (1)**expects** (2)**expect** to go to Paris this summer.

62. _____

63. My coach and mentor (1)**is** (2)**are** Gwen Johnson.

63. _____

64. Cable television, along with the Internet and DVDs, (1)**has** (2)**have** drawn millions of viewers away from traditional network television.

64. _____

65. She is the only one of eleven candidates who (1)**refuses** (2)**refuse** to speak about environmental issues on live television.

65. _____

66. Neither the systems analyst nor the accountants (1)**was** (2)**were** able to locate the problem in the computer program.

66. _____

29. SENTENCES AND GRAMMAR: Pronoun-Antecedent Agreement

(Study 127, Pronoun-Antecedent Agreement)

Write the number of the **correct** choice.

Example: One of the women fell from (1)**her** (2)**their** horse.   _____1_____

1. Alfred Hitchcock is the kind of director who loves to keep (1)**his** (2)**their** viewers guessing until nearly the final scene.   1. _____

2. Many tourists traveling in the West enjoy stopping at roadside attractions because (1)**you** (2)**they** never know what to expect.   2. _____

3. When Lucia found that her young son had caught the measles, she became concerned that (1)**it** (2)**they** would leave marks on his face.   3. _____

4. He majored in mathematics because (1)**it** (2)**they** had always been of interest to him.   4. _____

5. Martha edited the news because (1)**it was** (2)**they were** often full of inaccuracies.   5. _____

6. He assumed that all of his students had done (1)**his** (2)**their** best to complete the test.   6. _____

7. Both Ed and Luis decided to stretch (1)**his** (2)**their** legs when the bus reached Philadelphia.   7. _____

8. Ironically, neither woman had considered how to make (1)**her** (2)**their** job easier.   8. _____

9. Each of the researchers presented (1)**a** (2)**their** theory about the age of the solar system.   9. _____

10. He buys his books at an online site because (1)**it has** (2)**they have** low prices.   10. _____

11. Electronics can be a rewarding field of study because (1)**it** (2)**they** can lead to good jobs in a number of areas.   11. _____

12. Every member of the men's soccer team received (1)**his** (2)**their** individual trophy.   12. _____

13. All in the class voted to have (1)**its** (2)**their** term papers due a week earlier.   13. _____

14. I like swimming because it develops (1)**one's** (2)**your** muscles without straining the joints.   14. _____

15. Neither Aaron nor Andrew has declared (1)**his** (2)**their** major.   15. _____

16. Citizens who still do not recycle (1)**your** (2)**their** garbage need to read this news article.   16. _____

17. The HAL Computer Company has just introduced (1)**its** (2)**their** new 100-terabyte computer.   17. _____

18. Neither the guide nor the hikers seemed aware of (1)**her** (2)**their** danger on the trail.   18. _____

19. The faculty has already selected (1)**its** (2)**their** final candidates.   19. _____

20. Critics argue that (1)**those kind** (2)**those kinds** of movies may promote violent tendencies in children.   20. _____

21. One has to decide early in life what (1)**one wants** (2)**they want** out of life.   21. _____

22. Neither the coach nor the players underestimated (1)**her** (2)**their** opponents.   22. _____

23. The corporation insists that (1)**its** (2)**their** financial statements have been completely honest. 23. _____

24. Students should take accurate and complete notes so that (1)**they** (2)**you** will be prepared for the exam.   24. _____

25. Some people prefer trains to planes because trains bring (1)**you** (2)**them** closer to the scenery. 25. _____

26. In the next five years, owners of older vehicles polluting the environment can sell (1)**their** (2)**your** cars or trucks for scrap.

26. _____

27. If a stranger tried to talk to her, she would just look at (1)**him** (2)**them** and smile.

27. _____

28. Every one of the trees in the affected area had lost most of (1)**its** (2)**their** leaves.

28. _____

29. Some women can understand (1)**herself** (2)**themself** (3)**themselves** better through reading feminist literature.

29. _____

30. The medical committee was surprised to learn that (1)**its** (2)**their** preliminary findings had been published in the newspaper.

30. _____

31. The campus disciplinary board determined that (1)**its** (2)**their** process for reviewing student complaints was too cumbersome and slow.

31. _____

32. None of the boys should blame (1)**himself** (2)**themself** (3)**themselves** (4)**yourself** for misfortunes that cannot be prevented.

32. _____

33. Rita is a person who cannot control (1)**her** (2)**their** anger when under stress.

33. _____

34. Professor Brown is one of those teachers who really love (1)**his** (2)**their** profession.

34. _____

35. Everyone in the men's locker room grabbed (1)**his** (2)**their** clothes and ran when the cry of "Fire!" came from the hallway.

35. _____

36. Rita is the only one of the singers who writes (1)**her** (2)**their** own music.

36. _____

37. Each of the singers in the newly formed Irish band dreamed of earning (1)**her** (2)**their** first million dollars.

37. _____

38. As part of the Kim family's Vietnamese New Year celebration, each wrote *cau doi*. Memories of home and family are the subject of (1)**this kind of poem** (2)**these kind of poems**.

38. _____

39. During the Christmas season, many Latin American families serve (1)**its** (2)**their** favorite dish—tortillas spread with mashed avocado and roast chicken.

39. _____

40. If everyone in the Women's Club would contribute a small portion of (1)**her** (2)**their** January 1 paycheck, we should be able to purchase the microwave for the staff luncheon room.

40. _____

41. Each cat claimed (1)**its** (2)**their** specific area of the bedroom for long afternoon naps.

41. _____

42. Hearing-impaired people now have a telecommunication device to allow (1)**him** (2)**them** to make phone calls to a hearing person.

42. _____

43. When my professors complain that Americans don't support local school districts, I remind (1)**her** (2)**them** that most families view education as extremely important.

43. _____

44. Drivers of the new Mercolet sedan know that Mercolet has produced the most stylish car that (1)**its** (2)**their** engineers could design.

44. _____

45. If viewers are not happy with public television programming, (1)**you** (2)**they** should write letters to local television stations.

45. _____

46. Researchers have found that the type of relationship couples have can affect (1)**your** (2)**their** overall immune system.

46. _____

47. When climbing a mountain in autumn, amateurs had better take warm clothing in (1)**your** (2)**their** packs to guard against hypothermia.

47. _____

48. Unfortunately, Sid was one of those climbers who neglected to pack (1)**his** (2)**their** winter gear.

48. _____

49. A neighborhood organization of young people is meeting to determine how (1)**it** (2)**they** can help elderly neighbors in the community.

49. _____

50. Either the lead actor or the chorus members missed (1)**his** (2)**their** cue.

50. _____

30. SENTENCES AND GRAMMAR: Agreement Review

(Study 126–127, Agreement)

Write **C** if the sentence is **correct**.
Write **X** if it is **incorrect**.

Example: Nobody in the first two rows were singing.   ___X___

1. The orange sunset over the trees remind me of nights in Texas.   1. _____
2. All of the sheep grazes in the back pasture.   2. _____
3. All of the fish tastes good if you grill it properly.   3. _____
4. The strength of these new space-age materials have been demonstrated many times.   4. _____
5. The high grades on my English papers, along with my successes at biology, has shown me that I can succeed if I believe in myself.   5. _____
6. Evan's pants are ripped beyond repair.   6. _____
7. A northbound bus and a southbound bus leaves here every hour.   7. _____
8. According to a recent survey, almost every American believes their vote is important.   8. _____
9. The management now realizes that a bigger budget is needed; they plan to ask for federal assistance.   9. _____
10. When an older student senses that an institution understands nontraditional students, she generally works to her academic potential.   10. _____
11. I found that the thrill of attending college soon leaves when you have to visit the bursar's office.   11. _____
12. Everyone who read the letter stated that they were surprised by the contents.   12. _____
13. You should hire one of those experts who solves problems with computers.   13. _____
14. Two hundred miles was too much for a day trip.   14. _____
15. At school, there are always pizza and tacos for lunch.   15. _____
16. Cleveland or Cincinnati are planning to host the statewide contests.   16. _____
17. Bacon and eggs are no longer considered a healthy breakfast.   17. _____
18. Probably everybody in the computer center, except Colleen and Aaron, know how to run the scanner.   18. _____
19. Neither Leslie nor Carol are as good at math as Cynthia.   19. _____
20. *Powerpuff Girls* was described as "comic book stuff" by the newspaper's television critic.   20. _____
21. The researcher, as well as his assistants, are studying how red ants are related to black ants.   21. _____
22. Neither criticism nor frequent failures were enough to retard his progress.   22. _____
23. Where are the end of the recession and the revival of consumer confidence?   23. _____
24. Mathematics have been the most difficult subject I've ever studied.   24. _____
25. Has either of your letters appeared in the newspaper?   25. _____
26. It were the general and the Secretary of State who finally convinced the President to end the war.   26. _____

27. Neither Janet nor her parents want to attend the new production of *Hamlet*.   27. _____

28. He was one of those employees who was always late for work on Monday mornings.   28. _____

29. She is the only one of the experts who solves problems with computers.   29. _____

30. The faculty are squabbling among themselves, disagreeing vehemently about Faculty Senate bylaws.   30. _____

31. Such was the hardships of the times that many were forced into begging or stealing to survive.   31. _____

32. The special scissors that was needed for the repair could not be found.   32. _____

33. Checkers were becoming a popular game at the summer camp.   33. _____

31. SENTENCES AND GRAMMAR: Effective Sentences

(Study 128, Creating Effective Sentences)

Choose the **most effective** way of expressing the given ideas. Write the letter of your choice (**A**, **B**, or **C**) in the blank.

Example: A. The floods came. They washed away the roadway. They also uprooted trees.

      B. The floods came, and they washed away the roadway and uprooted trees.

      C. The floods came, washing away the roadway and uprooting trees.   C

1. A. There was a company in Baltimore. It shortened its work week from 40 hours to 36 hours. The company's output increased.

  B. A company in Baltimore shortened its work week from 40 hours to 36 hours, and this company found out the company's output increased.

  C. When a Baltimore company shortened its work week from 40 to 36 hours, its output increased.   1._____

2. A. Broadway has been revived by a new band of actors. These new actors are from Hollywood. They find it refreshing and challenging to perform before a live audience.

  B. Broadway has been revived by a new breed of actors—Hollywood stars, who find it refreshing and challenging to perform before a live audience.

  C. Broadway has been revived by this new breed of actors, which has seen actors coming from Hollywood; they have found it refreshing and challenging to perform before a live audience.   2._____

3. A. Recreational tree climbing has become popular. Ecologists hope that a code of tree-climbing ethics will be developed. Such a code may help to prevent damage to the delicate forest ecosystems.

  B. Recreational tree climbing has become popular and ecologists hope that a code of tree-climbing ethics will be developed, and such a code may help to prevent damage to the delicate forest ecosystems.

  C. Before recreational tree climbing becomes any more popular, ecologists hope that a code of tree-climbing ethics will be developed to prevent permanent damage to delicate forest ecosystems.   3._____

4. A. Harry Truman, who woke up the next morning to find himself elected President, had gone to bed early on election night.

   B. Harry Truman, who had gone to bed early on election night, woke up the next morning to find himself elected President.

   C. Harry Truman went to bed early on election night, and he woke up the next morning and found himself elected President.

   4. _____

5. A. The papers were marked "Top Secret." The term *Top Secret* indicates contents of extraordinary value.

   B. The papers were of extraordinary value, and therefore they were marked "Top Secret."

   C. The papers were marked "Top Secret," indicating their extraordinary value.

   5. _____

6. A. The university was noted for its outstanding faculty, its concern for minorities, and the quality of its graduates.

   B. The university was noted for its outstanding faculty, it showed concern for minorities, and how well its graduates did.

   C. The university was known for three things: it had an outstanding faculty, it showed concern for minorities, and the quality of its graduates.

   6. _____

7. A. The Broadway theater, which has survived many changes, is changing rapidly again, the change being that wealthy entertainment corporations, which include, for example, Disney's company, are taking over the big theaters as they bring in huge musicals that have vapid content, high prices, and draw audiences away from more challenging plays.

   B. The Broadway theater, having survived many changes, is again changing rapidly as wealthy entertainment corporations such as Disney take over the big theaters with vapid, high-priced musicals, drawing audiences away from more challenging plays.

   C. The Broadway theater has survived many changes. Once again, it is changing rapidly. Wealthy entertainment corporations are taking over the big theaters. One example is Disney. These corporations bring in huge musicals that prove to be vapid as well as high priced. The result is that they draw audiences away from more challenging plays.

   7. _____

8. A. Nick moves to Long Island and rents a house, and it is next to Gatsby's, but he does not know Gatsby. One night he sees a shadowy figure on the lawn, and he concludes that it must be Gatsby himself.

   B. Moving to Long Island, Nick rents a house next to Gatsby's. Though he does not know Gatsby, one night he concludes that the shadowy figure he sees on the lawn must be Gatsby himself.

   C. Nick, who moves to Long Island, rents a house that is next to Gatsby's, whom he does not know; one night he concludes that the shadowy figure that he sees on the lawn must be Gatsby himself.

8. _____

9. A. A fungus struck one plant and then another until it had killed nearly all of them, but one of them survived.

   B. A fungus that killed nearly all the plants spread from one to another, yet only one survived.

   C. A fungus spread among the plants, killing all but one.

9. _____

10. A. One family in a heatless building called the welfare office for money to buy an electric heater.

    B. One family lived in a building that had no heat, and so they called the welfare office to get money to buy an electric heater.

    C. One family, calling the welfare office for money to buy an electric heater, lived in a building that was heatless.

10. _____

32. SENTENCES AND GRAMMAR: Effective Sentences

(Study 128B–E, Use Coordination, Compounding, Subordination, Reduction)

Rewrite each of the following sets of sentences in the **most effective** way. Your result may contain one sentence or more. You may add, drop, or change words, but do not omit any information.

Example: The Lions had the ball on the Broncos' ten-yard line, and they attempted four passes, but they could not score, and so they lost the game.

Though the Lions had the ball on the Broncos' ten-yard line, they lost the game because they could not score in four pass attempts.

(Collaborative option: Students work in pairs or small groups to suggest different ways of rewriting.)

1. The Washington Monument was closed to the public. This happened in the spring and fall of 1998. The National Park Service had to repair the structure. That was the reason for the closing.

   _____

   _____

   _____

   _____

2. One airline charges an unrestricted fare of $1,734 from Boston to Reykjavik. Reykjavik is in Iceland. The same airline will fly you between the same cities for $298.

   _____

   _____

   _____

   _____

3. Many college students have a choice. This is what car-leasing companies report. These college students are the ones who do not have much in savings. One choice is that they can drive an old used car. The other is that they can lease a new car.

   _____

   _____

   _____

   _____

4. Computers have become less expensive. They have also become easier to use. And you can get free software. With this you can browse the Internet.

_____

_____

_____

_____

5. More bodies were pulled from the floodwaters in central Texas. This happened as storms continued their eastward march across the Southwest. The storms were torrential, and the march was deadly. One man was killed. This was because his home was swept away in the floods.

_____

_____

_____

_____

6. A new report has come out. It states that girls now outnumber boys in secondary schools. This is true in eighteen countries. Most of these countries are in Latin America.

_____

_____

_____

_____

7. But fifty-one countries still have serious gender gaps in education. In these countries there are 75 million fewer girls than boys in schools. This figure comes from a report by a population research group. The report was released on October 18.

_____

_____

_____

_____

8. The Surgeon General has announced new plans. The plans unveil the first national strategy for suicide prevention. The Surgeon General says that suicide is a serious public health problem, and it can no longer be ignored.

_____

_____

_____

_____

9. Gardeners are dealing with an increasingly serious pest. These gardeners are on both sides of the Rocky Mountains. The pest is hungry deer. Some gardeners are spraying odors. The deer do not like these odors. Other gardeners are covering their plants with plastic.

_____

_____

_____

_____

10. Kidnappings have reached record levels around the world. The global economic turmoil is likely to push the figure still higher. A leading institution states this.

_____

_____

_____

_____

33. SENTENCES AND GRAMMAR: Parallel Structure

(Study 128F, Use Parallel Structure)

Part 1

For each sentence: in the first three blanks, **identify** each of the boldfaced elements (use the abbreviations in parentheses):

gerund or gerund phrase (**ger**)   participle or participial phrase (**part**)
prepositional phrase (**prep**)   infinitive or infinitive phrase (**inf**)
clause (**cl**)   adjective (**adj**)
noun [with or without modifiers] (**noun**)
verb [with or without modifiers or complements] (**verb**)

Then, in the last blank, write **P** if the sentence contains **parallel structure**, or **NP** if it does **not**. (If the sentence is parallel, the first three blanks will all have the same answer.)

Examples: Congress rushed **to pass the tax bill, the Medicare bill,**
and **to adjourn.**   _inf_   _noun_   _inf_   _NP_
Shakespeare was **a poet, a playwright, and an actor.**   _noun_   _noun_   _noun_   _P_

1. The job required some knowledge of **word processing, desktop
   publishing, and to write.**   1. _____ _____ _____ _____

2. Hector fought with **great skill, epic daring, and superb intelligence.**   2. _____ _____ _____ _____

3. The mosques of ancient Islamic Spain typically contained **ornate
   stone screens, long hallways, and the columns looked like
   spindles.**   3. _____ _____ _____ _____

4. To help the environment, you should **separate glass and plastic,
   stop faucets from leaking, and taking public transportation
   is good.**   4. _____ _____ _____ _____

5. A newly discovered primate from the Amazon has **wide-set eyes,
   a broad nose, and the fur is striped like a zebra.**   5. _____ _____ _____ _____

6. By morning, we were **awake, ready, and starving.**   6. _____ _____ _____ _____

7. The monkeys **jumped from tree to tree, ate bananas, and the
   children laughed at them.**   7. _____ _____ _____ _____

8. Keisha did not know **where she had come from, why she was
   there, or the time of her departure.**   8. _____ _____ _____ _____

9. Her favorite pastimes remain **designing gardens, riding her
   unicycle, and playing in a rock band.**   9. _____ _____ _____ _____

10. Eliot's poetry is **witty, complex, and reveals his belief in God.**   10. _____ _____ _____ _____

Rewrite each sentence in parallel structure.

Example: The apartment could be rented by the week, the month, or you could pay on a yearly basis.
The apartment could be rented by the week, month, or year.

(Collaborative option: Students work in pairs or small groups to explore possible different parallel options. Each student writes a different version—where possible—in the blanks.)

1. Before 8 a.m., my youngest son had made himself breakfast, a snow fort in the front yard, and tormented his brothers.

   _____

   _____

   _____

2. Our new wood-burning stove should keep us warm, save us money, and should afford us much pleasure.

   _____

   _____

   _____

3. Christopher Columbus has been remembered as an entrepreneur, an explorer, a sailor, and now perhaps for how he exploited native populations.

   _____

   _____

   _____

4. The chief ordered Agent 007 to break into the building, crack the safe, and to steal the plans.

   _____

   _____

   _____

5. A good batter knows how to hit to the opposite field and staring down the pitcher.

   _____

   _____

   _____

6. When kindergartners were asked how the U.S. President should behave, they said someone who was fair, who shares, and not a hitter.

_____

_____

_____

7. The scouts marched briskly off into the woods, trekked ten miles to Alder Lake, and tents were erected by them.

_____

_____

_____

8. Dean has three main strengths: his ability to listen, he likes people, and his interest in cultural awareness.

_____

_____

_____

9. Global warming may not only increase air and ocean temperatures but also the force of storms.

_____

_____

_____

10. Neither regulating prices nor wages will slow inflation enough.

_____

_____

_____

11. During its early years, Sears, Roebuck and Company sold not only clothes, furniture and hardware, but also customers could buy cars and houses.

_____

_____

_____

12. Charlene practiced shooting from the top of the key as well as how to dribble with either hand.

_____

_____

_____

13. The new ambassador impressed everyone with her wit, charm, her grace, and they liked her intelligence.

_____

_____

_____

14. The experimental group either consisted of white rats or gray ones.

_____

_____

_____

15. But in a larger sense we cannot dedicate this ground, we cannot consecrate it either, nor can it be hallowed by us.

_____

_____

_____

34. SENTENCES AND GRAMMAR: Fragments

(Study 129A, Fragments)

Part 1

Write **S** after each item that is one or more **complete sentences.**
Write **F** after each item that contains a **fragment.**

Example: Luis was offered the job. Having presented the best credentials.   _____F_____

1. When people enter a theater or house of worship. It is important for them to turn off
    their cell phones.   1._____

2. Being coached in what is appropriate to do and say in a job interview, so as not to make
    a disastrous mistake.   2._____

3. The manuscript having been returned, Johanna sat down to revise it.   3._____

4. Harrison desperately wanted the part. Because he believed that this was the film that would
    make him a star.   4._____

5. The old-fashioned clock stopped ticking. Renée had forgotten to wind it.   5._____

6. He admitted to being a computer nerd. As a matter of fact, he was proud of his computing skills.   6._____

7. More than 50 percent of Americans surveyed felt guilty. About their child-care arrangements.   7._____

8. I read all the articles. Then I wrote the first draft of my paper.   8._____

9. Many Americans prefer indirect business levies rather than direct taxation. Where do you stand
    on this issue?   9._____

10. Maurice kept nodding his head as the coach explained the play. Thinking all the time that it
    would never work.   10._____

11. Because she was interested in studying ancient cultures. She majored in geology.   11._____

12. I argued with two of my classmates. First with Edward and then with Harry.   12._____

13. Scientists are seeking a cure for muscular dystrophy. By studying the effects of protein on mice.   13._____

14. William was certain he had passed the course. Even though he had not turned in four of the six
    required English papers.   14._____

15. Jason won the tennis match. His wife, however, always beats him when they play against
    each other.   15._____

16. Clarice was seen as the best detective in the force. For example, going undercover for two years
    to catch a car-theft ring.   16._____

17. When was the Declaration of Independence written?   17._____

18. She went to the supermarket. After she had made a list of groceries that she needed.   18._____

19. Janice went to see Dr. Toomey. The dentist whom all her family had visited for years.   19._____

20. After the tornado moved over the land. The family worried about the crops planted last spring.   20._____

Rewrite each item in one or more sentences, eliminating any **fragment(s)**. You may add information, but do not omit any.

Examples: Chief Joseph led his Native Americans on a desperate flight to freedom. A flight doomed to failure.
Chief Joseph led his Native Americans on a desperate flight to freedom, a flight doomed to failure.

Because the patient was near death.
Because the patient was near death, the doctors operated immediately.

1. Two days before the competition, he felt nervous. However, much more at ease just before the contest.

2. She was a star athlete. A brilliant student besides.

3. If there is no change in the patient's condition within the next twenty-four hours.

4. The Scottish and Irish farmers forced from their land so it could be turned into sheep pastures. More profitable for the landowners.

5. When it becomes too hot to work in the fields. The workers taking a welcomed rest.

35. SENTENCES AND GRAMMAR: Comma Splices and Fused Sentences

(Study 129B, Comma Splices and Fused Sentences)

Part 1

Write **S** after any item that is a **complete sentence**.
Write **Spl** after any item that is a **comma splice**.
Write **FS** after any item that is a **fused sentence**.

Example: The mission was a success, everyone was pleased.   ___Spl___

1. We remodeled the kitchen the bathroom is our next project.   1._____

2. Sheila couldn't stay late, her plane was leaving early the next morning.   2._____

3. Stunned by the high price of gasoline, the family took the hybrid car to the beach.   3._____

4. The moon enters the earth's shadow, a lunar eclipse occurs, causing the moon to turn a deep red. 4._____

5. When I saw what he had done, I couldn't believe my eyes he had repainted the whole room while I was gone.   5._____

6. The film ended no one noticed.   6._____

7. The ticket agent had sold eighty-one tickets to boarding passengers, only eleven seats were left on the train.   7._____

8. Because she was in the mood for an old Walt Disney film, she hired a babysitter and went to see *Bambi*.   8._____

9. They didn't try to fix the car, they just abandoned it.   9._____

10. Sheer exhaustion having caught up with me, I had no trouble falling asleep.   10._____

11. The restaurant check almost made me faint, because I had left my wallet home, I couldn't pay for the meal.   11._____

12. Those of us who lived in off-campus housing ignored the rule, because we were seniors, we never worried about campus regulations.   12._____

13. On a dark, damp, and dreary night in 1845, Edgar Allen Poe wrote his strange poem "The Raven," which ensured his fame.   13._____

14. When the peace treaty was signed, the people rejoiced; however, they were painfully aware of the damage to the town.   14._____

15. The author demonstrated twenty ways to arrange flowers for a table setting in my favorite arrangement she used purple irises and pink roses.   15._____

16. The three major television networks face stiff competition for ratings, because of cable networks, viewers can decide from among four hundred programs.   16._____

17. In the film, a lawyer reopens an investigation on behalf of a woman imprisoned for murder she convincingly claims that she is innocent.   17._____

18. Though the teacher believed that it was important for her students to write every day, she did not enjoy grading so many papers.   18._____

19. Fearing for her safety, the elderly woman locked the car doors she then hid her purse under the seat.

19. _____

20. We can't go camping this week; heavy thunderstorms are predicted.

20. _____

Part 2

Rewrite each item in one or more **correct sentences,** eliminating any **comma splices** or **fused sentences**. Add or change words as needed. Do not omit any information.

Example: The software game was full of violent scenes, thus it was banned from the school's computer center.
The software game was banned from the school's computer center because it was full of violent scenes.

(Collaborative option: Students work in pairs or small groups to suggest different ways of rewriting.)

1. Some Americans are still buying sport-utility vehicles, however, they are finding the insurance premiums unexpectedly high.

_____

_____

_____

2. Crime is still a major concern for many Americans so many teenagers are arrested for violent crimes.

_____

_____

_____

3. I waited in line for my turn at the automatic teller machine, I balanced my checkbook.

_____

_____

_____

4. Over 30 percent of children from rural America live in mobile homes, therefore, Congress has established a commission to study mobile home safety and construction standards.

_____

_____

_____

5. A shortage of licensed contractors often exists in the areas hit by natural disasters homeowners quickly learn to wait for a work crew with the proper credentials.

_____

_____

_____

6. The largest Native American reservation is the Navajo it is located mostly in Arizona and covers 16 million acres.

_____

_____

_____

7. According to some researchers, little boys may have different educational experiences from little girls, in other words, even though it may be unintentional, teachers often have subtly different expectations based on the gender of their students.

_____

_____

_____

_____

8. Tarantulas are large spiders with powerful fangs and a mean bite, they live not only in the tropics but also in the United States.

_____

_____

_____

9. Jogging can reduce fatal heart attacks because it is an aerobic activity, it keeps the arteries from clogging.

_____

_____

_____

10. The software game was full of violent scenes, therefore, it was banned from the school's computer center. [Correct this in a different way from that shown in the example.]

_____

_____

_____

36. SENTENCES AND GRAMMAR: Fragments, Comma Splices, and Fused Sentences

(Study 129, Conquering the "Big Three" Sentence Errors)

Rewrite any item that contains a **fragment**, **comma splice**, or **fused sentence**, so that it contains none of these. You may add words or information as needed, but do not omit any information. If an item is already correct, leave the blank empty.

Examples: When she saw the full moon rising over the hill.
     When she saw the full moon rising over the hill, she thought of the night they had met.
     When Peary and Henson reached the Pole, they rejoiced.
     _____

(Collaborative option: Students work in pairs or small groups to suggest different ways of rewriting.)

1. When Nora leaves the house at the end of the play.

     _____

     _____

     _____

2. When a tennis match is over, the opponents shake hands over the net.

     _____

     _____

     _____

3. Which should not bake for more than two hours.

     _____

     _____

     _____

4. *Othello* and *Hamlet*, two of Shakespeare's greatest plays.

     _____

     _____

     _____

5. Whereas older cars run on leaded gas and lack complex pollution controls.

     _____

     _____

     _____

6. Because she was not prepared for the interviewer's questions and felt she would never get the job.

_____

_____

_____

7. By installing smoke detectors, families may someday save family members from perishing in a fire.

_____

_____

_____

8. Watching from the seventh floor during the parade.

_____

_____

_____

9. Which could strengthen your immune system.

_____

_____

_____

10. Stay.

_____

_____

_____

11. We planned the trip carefully, yet we still had a series of disasters.

_____

_____

_____

12. The quarterback signed the largest professional football contract to date, he will earn $120 million over a six-year period.

_____

_____

_____

13. Native American dances and music for every tribal ceremony and social occasion celebrated.

    _____

    _____

    _____

14. Scientists are currently interested in studying polar bears. Because the bears' body chemistry may reveal how pollution has affected the Arctic.

    _____

    _____

    _____

15. Americans, for the moment, may be less concerned about taxes. Polls indicate that Americans would rather balance the federal budget than lower taxes.

    _____

    _____

    _____

16. Until all the workers were able to present their points of view.

    _____

    _____

    _____

17. The community was unaware of the city's plan to tear down a playground, therefore, few citizens attended the City Council meetings.

    _____

    _____

    _____

18. Since 1975, over 1.5 million Vietnamese have left their homeland in search of a peaceful life, many have settled in Australia, Canada, Europe, and the United States.

    _____

    _____

    _____

19. Because the founder of a popular fast-food restaurant chain has encouraged corporations to provide financial support for employees adopting children.

   _____

   _____

   _____

20. All my coworkers are on diets and won't eat any cookies or cake.

   _____

   _____

21. What happened to Clyde, Roberta, and Sondra is told in the novel *An American Tragedy* it was written by Theodore Dreiser.

   _____

   _____

   _____

22. He wore a pair of mud-encrusted, flap-soled boots they looked older than he did.

   _____

   _____

   _____

23. The agency wanted to know how and when its money was spent.

   _____

   _____

   _____

24. Enrique reread his assignment a dozen times before handing it in. To be absolutely sure his ideas were clear.

   _____

   _____

   _____

25. The executive waited, however, until every worker at the meeting presented a point of view.

   _____

   _____

   _____

26. That she is dead is beyond dispute.

   _____

   _____

   _____

27. "I believe," declared the headmaster. "That you deserve expulsion."

   _____

   _____

   _____

28. The scouts hiked two miles until they reached the falls then they had lunch.

   _____

   _____

   _____

29. The police having been warned to expect trouble, every available officer lined the avenue of the march.

   _____

   _____

   _____

30. In the 1800s, Ireland's vital crop was wiped out by the potato blight, Irish people who owned ten acres of land were disqualified from poor relief.

   _____

   _____

   _____

31. The Irish immigrants did not settle on farms for fear that the potato blight would strike again, but the German immigrants did go into farming they had no fear of this blight.

   _____

   _____

   _____

32. In the first George Bush's administration the Gulf War, and in George W. Bush's the war against terrorism.

   _____

   _____

   _____

33. A victory that is unmatched in the history of amateur sports.

_____

_____

_____

37. SENTENCES AND GRAMMAR: Placement of Sentence Parts

(Study 130A, Needless Separation of Related Sentence Parts and 130B, Misplaced and Dangling Modifiers)

If the boldfaced words are **in the wrong place**, draw an arrow from these words to the place in the sentence where they should be.

If the boldfaced words are **in the right place**, do nothing.

Examples: Never give a toy to a child **that can be swallowed**.

People who buy cigars **made in Cuba** violate U.S. laws.

1. He always ate peanut butter sandwiches **for his lunch**.

2. **When Helen was a child,** she wanted a pet bird like the one her friend had.

3. Michael Phelps returned to his home after winning the Olympic medals **in Baltimore**.

4. After failing the math exam, the students decided **more thoroughly** to study for the next one.

5. They watched the rocket leave the launch pad **that would soon be going to Mars**.

6. I **only** have eyes for you.

7. The police captain ordered the force to clean up the graffiti **from his patrol car**.

8. Unfortunately, the thrift shop has many **wrinkled** little girls' dresses.

9. The Albertsons rushed to buy a card table from a clerk **with folding legs.**

10. We learned that no one could discard anything at the municipal dump **except people living in the community.**

11. The only dress left on the rack was a **pink ruffled** girl's dress.

12. **Wearing a lavender pinafore**, the father took his young daughter to the wedding.

13. **Seeing the danger**, the captain told the crew to go below deck as the boat filled with water.

14. Despite her sincerity and honesty, the candidate failed to **carefully, completely, and candidly** explain why she dropped out of the campaign.

15. The two scientists, **working independently,** achieved the same results.

16. Send, **after you have received all the donations,** the total amount to the organization's headquarters.

17. One coach **only** seems able to convince Beverly that she should practice.

18. Only a few Olympic athletes can expect lucrative endorsement contracts **with gold medals**.

19. The Santiagos watched the yacht as she slowly sailed out to sea **from their car.**

20. Indicate whether you are going to the class picnic **on the enclosed sheet.**

21. A **moth-eaten** woman's wool suit was found in the back of the closet.

22. The warning label said to dispense the medication **with the enclosed patient's instructions for use.**

23 Jim Schreiber, who was recovering from a twisted ankle, met with the football team **on crutches**.

24. Marcia Simpson discovered that the pansies she planted last fall had survived through the winter **while she was working in the garden**.

25. The wealthy couple **usually** stated that they went to Rome in the spring to buy their fall wardrobes.

38. SENTENCES AND GRAMMAR: Dangling and Misplaced Modifiers

(Study 130A, Needless Separation of Related Sentence Parts, and 130B, Misplaced and Dangling Modifiers)

Part 1

If the boldfaced words are a dangling or misplaced modifier, **rewrite** the sentence correctly in the blanks below it. If the sentence is correct, do nothing.

Examples: Returning the corrected essays, most students were disappointed by their marks.
When the instructor returned their corrected essays, most students were disappointed by their marks.

Roosevelt and Churchill, **meeting at sea**, drafted the Four Freedoms.
_____
_____

(Collaborative option: Students work in pairs to suggest different ways of rewriting.)

1. **Reading a mystery novel and eating bonbons,** Jen's cat curled up next to her.

_____

_____

2. **While cleaning out the basement,** my cheerleader outfit was found by my mother.

_____

_____

3. **Having worked on my paper for three hours,** the network went down and my paper was lost in cyberspace.

_____

_____

4. **When put inside the turkey,** Connie's father saw that she had prepared cornbread dressing for Thanksgiving.

_____

_____

5. **Worried about what books their children are borrowing from libraries,** the library finally agreed to develop an on-line rating system for families.

_____

_____

_____

6. **Upon entering the church,** the new statues of Mary and Joseph, which were stunning, caught the attention of the parishioners.

    _____

    _____

7. **Practicing every day for five hours,** Margie's expensive saxophone lessons really paid off.

    _____

    _____

8. **Sleeping in late,** the house seemed incredibly quiet with the boys still in bed.

    _____

    _____

9. **After sleeping in until noon,** the day seemed to go by too quickly.

    _____

    _____

10. **When five years old,** my mother took my sister and me to the circus.

    _____

    _____

11. **At the age of ten,** I was permitted to go to a summer camp for the first time.

    _____

    _____

12. **After working in the paper mill for twelve hours,** the children greeted their father with hugs and kisses.

    _____

    _____

13. **Screeching from their cages,** the children stood in front of the monkeys and threw in peanuts.

    _____

    _____

14. **To achieve a goal,** a person must expect to work and to make sacrifices.

    _____

    _____

15. **Suggesting that the American standard of living has declined,** some American economists predict a gloomy financial status for the next generation.

_____

_____

16. **Jogging along Monument Avenue,** the burning house caught the attention of the marathon runners.

_____

_____

17. **A hamburger in his hand,** the dog barked at the thought of eating it.

_____

_____

18. **While biking in the local race,** I found the weather was quite uncooperative.

_____

_____

19. **Relieved by her high grade on the first paper,** her next paper seemed less difficult.

_____

_____

20. **While brushing her cat's coat,** the cake in the oven began to burn.

_____

_____

21. **As a teenager,** Evangeline worked two jobs to help her family financially.

_____

_____

22. **After eating so many sticky buns over the past month,** my scale revealed that I had gained ten pounds.

_____

_____

23. Finally, **after working for days,** the garden was free of weeds.

_____

_____

24. **To proofread my paper,** I reread it several times and used the grammar- and spell-checking functions of my word-processing software.

_____

_____

25. **After finishing my assignment,** the dog ate it.

_____

_____

26. **To get ready for summer vacation,** camp registrations had to be completed this week.

_____

_____

27. **Realizing that the unemployment rate was still over 10 percent,** most workers were not changing jobs.

_____

_____

28. **To get a passing grade in this course,** the professor's little quirks must be considered.

_____

_____

Part 2

In the first set of blanks, write a sentence of your own containing a humorous dangling or misplaced modifier. In the second set of blanks, **rewrite** the sentence correctly.

_____

Example: _Hanging stiffly from the clothesline, Mother saw that the wash had frozen overnight._
Mother saw that the wash, hanging stiffly from the clothesline, had frozen overnight.

(Collaborative option: Students work in pairs or small groups to invent and correct sentences.)

1. _____

_____

_____

_____

_____

_____

2. _____

3. _____

4. _____

5. _____

39. SENTENCES AND GRAMMAR: Effective Sentences Review

(Study 128–130, Effective Sentences)

If an item is **incorrect** or **ineffective** in any of the ways you learned in sections 128–130, **rewrite** it correctly or more effectively in the blanks below it.

If an item is **correct** and **effective** as is, do nothing.

_____

Examples: The lakes were empty of fish. Acid rain had caused this.
             Acid rain had left the lakes empty of fish.
             Working in pairs, the students began to edit the practice exercise.
             _____

(Collaborative option: Students work in pairs to suggest ways of rewriting incorrect or ineffective sentences.)

1. If one drives a car without thinking, you are more than likely to have an accident.

   _____

   _____

2. The entire class was pleased at learning that Dr. Turner has rescheduled the quiz.

   _____

   _____

3. The author decided to forthrightly, absolutely, unequivocally, and immediately deny the allegations of plagiarism.

   _____

   _____

4. A study revealed that vigorous exercise may add only one or two years to a person's life. This study used Harvard graduates.

   _____

   _____

5. The film director, thinking only about how he could get the shot of the erupting volcano, endangered everyone.

   _____

   _____

6. With her new auditory implant, Audrey heard so much better.

   _____

   _____

7. Watching the star hitter blast a home run over the fence, the ball smashed a windshield of an expensive sports car.

   _____

   _____

8. The owner of the team seems to insult her players and fans and mismanaging the finances.

   _____

   _____

9. The witness walked into the courtroom, and then she wishes she could avoid testifying.

   _____

   _____

10. An increase in energy taxes causes most people to consider carpooling and improving energy-conservation practices in their homes.

    _____

    _____

    _____

11. According to historians, settlers traveling westward used prairie schooners, not Conestoga wagons, and they used oxen and mules instead of horses to pull the wagons, and they did not pull their wagons into a circle when under an attack.

    _____

    _____

    _____

    _____

12. He told me that he was going to write a letter and not to disturb him.

    _____

    _____

13. Ajay Smith is a senior, and he just won national recognition for his poetry.

    _____

    _____

14. In the 1400s, many English villages held football competitions, an inflated animal bladder was kicked or shoved between two distant points by opposing teams.

_____

_____

_____

15. If a student knows how to study, you should achieve success.

_____

_____

16. He went to his office. He sat down. He opened his briefcase. He read some papers.

_____

_____

17. Summer is a time for parties, friendships, for sports, and in which we can relax.

_____

_____

18. I met the new dorm counselor in my oldest pajamas.

_____

_____

19. Being a ski jumper requires nerves of steel, you have to concentrate to the utmost, and being perfectly coordinated.

_____

_____

_____

20. The plane neither had enough fuel nor proper radar equipment.

_____

_____

21. The instructor wondered when did the students begin sneaking out of class.

_____

_____

22. Because they would not worship the Roman gods meant that Christians might be thrown to the lions.

_____

_____

115

23. In baseball, a sacrifice is when the batter allows himself to be put out in order to advance a base runner.

_____

_____

24. Saddened by the collapse of his marriage, Norton's mansion now seemed an ugly, echoing cavern.

_____

_____

25. By the coach putting Robinson at quarterback would have given the team a chance at the title.

_____

_____

40. SENTENCES AND GRAMMAR: Review

(Study 101–130, Sentences and Grammar)

Part 1

Write **T** for each statement that is **true**.
Write **F** for each statement that is **false**.

Example: A **present participle** ends in -*ing* and is used as an adjective.	____T____
1. Both a **gerund** and a **present participle** end in -*ing*.	1._____
2. The greatest number of words ever used in a **verb phrase** is four.	2._____
3. **Parallel structure** is used to designate ideas that are unequal in importance.	3._____
4. A **dangling participle** may be corrected by being changed into a dependent clause.	4._____
5. *It's* is a contraction of *it is; its* is the **possessive** form of the pronoun *it*.	5._____
6. The **verb precedes the subject** in a sentence beginning with the expletive *there*.	6._____
7. A **preposition** may contain two or more words; *because of* is an example.	7._____
8. The **principal parts of a verb** are the *present tense*, the *future tense,* and the *past participle*.	8._____
9. A **collective noun** may be followed by either a singular or plural verb.	9._____
10. A **prepositional phrase** may be used only to modify an adjective.	10._____
11. A **compound sentence** is one that contains two or more independent clauses.	11._____
12. Not all **adverbs** end in -*ly*.	12._____
13. The verb **be** is often like an equal sign in mathematics.	13._____
14. A **noun clause** may be introduced by the subordinating conjunction *although*.	14._____
15. An **adjective clause** may begin with *when* or *where*.	15._____
16. Both **verbals** and **verbs** may have modifiers and complements.	16._____
17. The terminal punctuation of a declarative sentence is the **exclamation point.**	17._____
18. *Without* is a **subordinating conjunction**.	18._____
19. A sentence may begin with the word *because.*	19._____
20. The **verb** of a sentence can consist of a past participle alone.	20._____
21. A **subject complement** may be a noun, a pronoun, or an adverb.	21._____
22. A **direct object** may be a noun or a pronoun.	22._____
23. When there is an **indirect object**, it normally precedes the direct object.	23._____
24. When there is an **object complement**, it must precede the direct object.	24._____
25. *Self*-pronouns used as appositives are called **intensive pronouns.**	25._____
26. The word *scissors* takes a **singular verb**.	26._____
27. An **antecedent** is the noun for which a pronoun stands.	27._____

28. A **simple sentence** contains two or more independent clauses.   28._____

29. A pronoun following the verb *be* should be in the **objective case**.   29._____

30. A **complex sentence** contains at least one independent clause and one dependent clause.   30._____

31. A **sentence fragment** is not considered a legitimate unit of expression; a **nonsentence** is.   31._____

32. **Adjectives** never stand next to the words they modify.   32._____

33. Not all words ending in *-ly* are **adverbs**.   33._____

34. An **indefinite pronoun** designates no particular person.   34._____

35. The words *have* and *has* identify the **present perfect tense** of a verb.   35._____

36. A statement with a subject and a verb can be a fragment if it follows a **subordinating conjunction.**   36._____

37. An **adverb** may modify a noun, an adjective, or another adverb.   37._____

38. **Verbs** are words that assert an action or a state of being.   38._____

39. The **indicative mood** of a verb is used to express a command or a request.   39._____

40. The function of a **subordinating conjunction** is to join a dependent clause to a main clause.   40._____

41. The **subjunctive mood** expresses doubt, uncertainty, a wish, or a supposition.   41._____

42. An **adjective** may modify a noun, a pronoun, or an adverb.   42._____

43. A **gerund** is a verb form ending in *-ing* and used as a noun.   43._____

44. A **clause** differs from a **phrase** in that a clause always has a subject and a predicate.   44._____

45. **Adjectives** tell *what kind, how many,* or *which one;* **adverbs** tell *when, where, how,* and *to what degree.*   45._____

46. A **comma splice** is a grammatical error caused by joining two independent clauses with a comma.   46._____

47. **Coordinating conjunctions** *(and, but, or, nor, for, yet, so)* join words, phrases, and clauses of equal importance.   47._____

48. **Pronouns in the objective case** *(him, me . . .*) should be used as direct objects of verbs and verbals.   48._____

49. **Mixed construction** occurs when two sections of a sentence that should be grammatically compatible are not.   49._____

50. A **simple short sentence** can be a forceful expression in a passage.   50._____

51. A **compound sentence** always has a compound subject in each clause.   51._____

52. **Coordinating conjunctions** open dependent clauses.   52._____

53. **Pronouns** in the subjective case (*I, he*, and *they*, for example) are always used as the objects of prepositions.   53._____

54. The **past perfect tense** uses *had* as an auxiliary verb.   54._____

55. **Coordinating conjunctions** are not considered part of the clauses they join.   55._____

56. The **imperative mood** is used for commands.   56._____

57. A **subject complement** can be an adverb.   57._____

58. *However* is a **subordinating conjunction**.   58._____

59. *Which* usually opens **essential clauses**.   59._____

60. A **compound sentence** has at least two independent clauses.   60. _____

61. A **complex sentence** can have a relative clause.   61. _____

62. A **gerund** is a verbal.   62. _____

Part 2

Write **C** if the item is **free of faults**.
Write **X** if it **has one or more faults**.

Example: Was that letter sent to Paul or **I**?   __X__

1. **Having been notified to come at once,** there was no opportunity to call you.   1. _____

2. I suspected that his remarks were directed to Larry and **me**.   2. _____

3. He, **thinking that he might find his friends on the second floor of the library,** hurried.   3. _____

4. If a student attends the review session, **they** will do well on the first exam.   4. _____

5. In the cabin of the boat **was** a radio, a set of flares, and a map of the area.   5. _____

6. The Queen, standing beside her husband, children, and grandchildren, **were** waving regally at the crowd.   6. _____

7. She is a person **who** I think is certain to succeed as a social worker.   7. _____

8. **Is** there any other questions you wish to ask regarding the assignment?   8. _____

9. The driver had neglected to fasten his seat belt, **an omission that cost him a month in the hospital.**   9. _____

10. He particularly enjoys **playing softball** and **to run** a mile every morning.   10. _____

11. Forward the complaint to **whoever** you think is in charge.   11. _____

12. Every girl and boy **was** to have an opportunity to try out for the soccer team.   12. _____

13. Neither the bus driver nor the passengers **were** aware of their danger.   13. _____

14. Within the next five years, personal computers will be **not only** smaller **but also** more affordable.   14. _____

15. Not everyone feels that **their** life is better since the 1960s civil rights movement.   15. _____

16. Homemade bread tastes **differently** from bakery bread.   16. _____

17. Not **having had** the chance to consult his lawyer, Larry refused to answer the officer's questions.   17. _____

18. **Is** either of your friends interested in going to Florida over spring break?   18. _____

19. He enrolled in economics because **it** had always been of interest to him.   19. _____

20. The snow fell **steady** for two days.   20. _____

21. Burt paced nervously up and down the corridor. **Because he was concerned about the weather.**   21. _____

22. **A heavy rain began without warning,** the crew struggled with the tarpaulin.   22. _____

23. **To have better control over spending,** the checkbook is balanced each week.   23. _____

24. Casey **asked for time, stepped out of the batter's box, and his finger was pointed toward the bleachers**.

24. _____

25. **By investing in real estate at this time** can earn you a substantial profit in several years.

25. _____

41. SENTENCES AND GRAMMAR: Review

(Study 101–130, Sentences and Grammar)

On your own paper, **rewrite** each of the following paragraphs so that it is **free of errors** and more **effective**. You may change or reduce wording, combine sentences, and make any other necessary changes, but do not omit any information.

(Collaborative option: Students work in pairs or small groups to suggest ways of improving the paragraphs. They evaluate or edit each other's work.)

1. Neither the strength nor the wisdom of Clyde Griffiths' parents were sufficient to bring up their family properly. He grew ashamed of his parents, his clothes, and he had to live in ugly surroundings. Clyde grew older, he dreamed of a life of wealth and elegance. Spending most of his money on clothes and luxuries for himself, his parents were neglected by him. One night when Clyde's uncle invited him to dinner. He met beautiful, wealthy Sondra Finchley. Determined to have her, she was too far above his social position. So Clyde starts going with a factory worker, her name was Roberta, and she became pregnant by him, but it was decided by Clyde that just because of Roberta was no reason he had to give up his pursuit of Sondra.

2. The novel *Slaughterhouse-Five* tells of a man named Billy Pilgrim, who is a prisoner in World War II and later traveled to the planet Tralfamadore. In one particularly amusing episode, the Tralfamadoreans throw Billy into a cage in one of their zoos, along with a sexy Earthling actress named Montana Wildhack. The Tralfamadoreans crowd around the cage to watch the lovemaking between he and her. The less interesting sections of the novel depict the middle-class civilian life of Billy. Who grows wealthy despite having little awareness of what is going on. Billy acquires his wealth by becoming an optometrist, he marries his employer's daughter, and giving lectures on his space travels. I like most of the book because its the most unique novel I have ever read and because it makes you realize the horrors of war and the hollowness of much of American life. However, after reading the entire book, Kurt Vonnegut, Jr., the author, disappointed me because I, enjoying science fiction, wish they had put more about space travel into it.

3. In reading, critical comprehension differs from interpretive comprehension. Critical comprehension adds a new element. That element was judgment. On the interpretive level a student may understand that the author of a poem intends a flower to represent youth, on the critical level they evaluate the author's use of this symbol. The student evaluate the quality of the poem too. For example. On the interpretive level a student would perceive that the theme of a story is "If at first you don't succeed, try, try again"; on the critical level the student judges whether the saying is valid. Critical comprehension includes not only forming opinions about characters in stories but also judgments about them. By learning to comprehend critically, the student's overall reading ability will increase markedly.

4. Studying the woodland ground with my magnifying glass, I grew astonished. First I saw a column of tiny leaves marching along a two-inch-wide road. Peering through the glass, each leaf was being carried like an umbrella in the jaws of an ant far more smaller than the leaf itself. I began to notice other ant trails, all leading to tiny mounds of earth, they looked like miniature volcanoes. Up the mounds and into the craters trod endless parades of ants, each holding aloft its own parasol, which made my spine tingle with excitement. When I heard a faint buzzing made me look around. Above the ant-roads swarmed squadrons of tiny flies. As if on signal they dived straight down to attack the ants. If a person saw this, they would not have believed it. The ants, their jaws clamped upon the giant leaves, had no means of defense. Yet, as if answering air-raid sirens, you could see an army of smaller ants racing toward the leaf-carriers, who they strove to protect.

5. Because the leaf-carrying ants now had some protection did not mean that the attack was over by the flies. As the first attacking fly dived upon a leaf-carrier, the tiny protector ants reached and snapped at the aerial raider with their formidable jaws and they drove it away, but then all along the leaf-carrying column other flies joined the attack. Now I could see that atop each moving leaf a tiny protector ant was "riding shotgun" through my magnifying glass. Whenever a fly dive-bombed a leaf-carrier was when the shotgun ant on the leaf reached out and bit the fly. One shotgun ant grasped a fly's leg in its jaws and sends the winged enemy spinning to the ground. The ant's comrades swarmed all over the helpless fly, and it was soon reduced to a lifeless shell by them. Similar scenes were taken place all over the miniature battlefield. Finally the squadrons of flies, unable to penetrate the ants' defenses, rised, seemingly in formation, and droned back to their base. Would they mourn their casualties, I wondered. Will their leader have to report the failed attack to an angry insect general?

42. SENTENCES AND GRAMMAR: Review for Non-Native English Speakers

**(Study 107, Words that Connect; 115, Principal Parts of Verbs;
and 120, Using Articles and Determiners Correctly)**

Part 1

In each ⬚box , write the **correct** preposition: **at**, **in**, or **on**.

On each blank line, write the **correct** verb ending: **ed** (or **d**), **s** (or **es**), or **ing**. If no ending is needed, leave the line empty.

In each set of brackets [   ], write the correct **article**: **a**, **an**, or **the**. If no article is needed, leave the brackets empty.

Example: [The] newest building ⬚in our city is [an] apartment house. It was constru<u>ct</u>ed for senior citizens.

1. Living ⬚ [   ] large city requires strong nerves and [   ] outstanding sense of humor. This is especially true ⬚ Mondays. When I wait ⬚ my corner for [   ] bus that take____ me to work, I hear [   ] screams of ambulances and fire engine____ as they speed by. When I am finally ⬚ my office building, I am push____ into [   ] elevator by [   ] crowd. I manage to get off ⬚ [   ] twelfth floor. But when I give [   ] cheery "Good morning!" to [   ] first coworker I meet, I am often answer____ with [   ] grouchy remark. The people at my former job, ⬚ 2007, treat____ me much better. I stay____ there only a year, but it was [   ] best job I have had since be____ [   ] America.

2. In [   ] depth of winter ⬚ 1925, ⬚ [   ] small Alaskan town called Nome, [   ] epidemic of [   ] deadly disease diphtheria start____. The people were shock____ to hear that there was no medicine available to stop [   ] disease from spread____. The ice-locked town was completely block____ off from the outside world: no boat or plane could reach____ it, and no roads or rail lines had yet been construct____ there. Only [   ] dogsleds might possibly rush____ the medicine to Nome in time. But [   ] nearest supply of medicine was ⬚ the city of Anchorage, a thousand miles away. ⬚ Nome's tiny telegraph office, the town's doctor transmitt____ [   ] desperate message: "Nome need____ diphtheria medicine at once!"

3. Officials in Anchorage round____ up all the available medicine and had it shipped [   ] [   ] train to the end

of the line [   ] Nenana, still 674 miles from Nome. From there relays of dogsled teams took over. The first

team's drivers trudge____ through the white wilderness to [   ] tiny hamlets of Tolovana and Bluff. [   ]

Bluff, Gunnar Kaasen's team, headed by the dog Balto, began [   ] next leg of [   ] journey. Through raging

blizzards, thirty-below-zero cold, and missed relay stations, [   ] Balto led Kaasen's team all the way to Nome.

[   ] just 5½ days the dog teams had cover____ what was normally [   ] month's journey. Nome had been

save____ .

Part 2

In each blank, write any correct determiner (limiting adjective) from the list. Try not to use any word on the
list more than once.

every	many	other	more	some	several
each	most	such	(a) little	another	all
(n) either	(a) few	both	much	enough	any

Example: They needed _another_ person to help lift the car.

_____ day last week there were _____ alarming stories in the newspapers.

_____ of them made _____ sense. One story said that soon there would not be

_____ fish left in the oceans or lakes. _____ story warned that global warming would

soon drown or boil us all. _____ of these stories gave me nightmares.

43. PUNCTUATION: The Comma

(Study 201–203, The Comma)

Part 1

If **no comma** is needed in the bracketed space(s), leave the blank empty. If **one or more commas** are needed, write in the **reason** from the list below (only one reason per blank; use the abbreviations in parentheses).

independent clauses joined by conjunction (**ind**)	appositive (**app**)
	absolute phrase (**abs**)
introductory adverb clause (**intro**)	direct address (**add**)
series (**ser**)	mild interjection (**inter**)
parenthetical expression (**par**)	direct quotation (**quot**)
nonessential clause (**ne**)	

Examples: The Appalachian states include Kentucky[ ] West Virginia[ ] and Tennessee.   _____ser_____
The Secretary of State[ ] held a press conference.   _____

1. *To Kill a Mockingbird,* a novel by Harper Lee[ ] recounts a trial in which a white southern lawyer defends a young black man.   1._____

2. English professors[ ] who expect a long paper each week[ ] might be considered too demanding.   2._____

3. Well[ ] we'll just have to buy more ice cream for the party.   3._____

4. If the submarine descends deep enough[ ] the crew might be able to see a giant squid.   4._____

5. Indeed[ ] Monsieur Profiterole[ ] mice have been nibbling your pastries.   5._____

6. Jane's mother[ ] who is a yoga instructor[ ] does not allow foods made with refined sugar in her house.   6._____

7. Will and Sam[ ] however[ ] are planning a victory party after the election.   7._____

8. Barack Obama[ ] the first black President[ ] was elected on November 4, 2008.   8._____

9. All things being equal[ ] the active voice tends to be correct more often than the passive on standardized tests.   9._____

10. Before you go to a job interview[ ] learn all that you can about the company.   10._____

11. Wendy spread the family silver out on the table[ ] and slowly began to polish it for dinner on Thanksgiving Day.   11._____

12. The young boys bravely walked into the haunted house[ ] but they quickly ran out a few minutes later.   12._____

13. Lincoln spoke eloquently about government of the people[ ] by the people[ ] and for the people.   13._____

14. After Ben had recharged his iPod[ ] he called his girlfriend to see if she could go out that evening.   14._____

15. The candidate gave a number of speeches in Illinois[ ] where she hoped to win support.   15._____

16. She always wanted to visit the small village[ ] where her father had lived, but she knew neither its name nor its location.   16._____

17. My biology professor[ ] Dr. Julia Johnson[ ] handed out the syllabus on the first day of class.   17._____

independent clauses joined by
   conjunction (**ind**)
introductory adverb clause (**intro**)
series (**ser**)
parenthetical expression (**par**)
nonessential clause (**ne**)

appositive (**app**)
absolute phrase (**abs**)
direct address (**add**)
mild interjection (**inter**)
direct quotation (**quot**)

_____

18. You must plant tulips now[ ] Louise[ ] if you want a colorful garden in the spring. 18. _____

19. "Get out of my yard[ ]" the elderly man cried[ ] "or I'll chase you out with a broom." 19. _____

20. Castles were cold and filthy[ ] according to historians[ ] because castles were built more for protection than convenience. 20. _____

21. His soda cans piled to the ceiling[ ] Ernesto knew it was time to clean out his room. 21. _____

22. Both potato and corn crops had a major impact on the life expectancy of Europeans[ ] living in the eighteenth century. 22. _____

23. Ford's first Model T sold for $850 in 1908[ ] but the price dropped to $440 in 1915 because of mass production. 23. _____

24. We were required to read _Frankenstein_[ ] which was written by Mary Shelley when she was only nineteen years old. 24. _____

25. Willis Richardson[ ] an African American writer[ ] wrote 46 plays by 1955, yet few people have heard of him. 25. _____

Part 2

If **no comma** is needed in the bracketed space(s), leave the blank empty. If **one or more commas** are needed, write in the **reason** from the list below (only one reason per blank; use the abbreviations in parentheses).

parenthetical expression (**par**)
after yes and no (**y/n**)
examples introduced by _such as_,
   especially, or _particularly_ (**examp**)
contrast (**cont**)
nonessential clause (**ne**)

omission (**om**)
confirmatory question (**ques**)
direct address (**add**)
date (**date**)
state or country (**s/c**)

_____

Examples: He came from New York; she[   ] from Maine.   __om__
       The Secretary of State[   ] held a press conference. _____

1. On New York's number 7 subway line[ ] which runs through Queens[ ] one can hear more languages spoken than almost anywhere in the world. 1. _____

2. Senator[ ] please comment on the rumors that you plagiarized as an undergraduate? 2. _____

3. Latrobe[ ] Pennsylvania[ ] is thought to be the site of the first professional football game. 3. _____

4. Seashells are an exquisite natural sculpture[ ] aren't they? 4. _____

5. The decision to have the surgery[ ] of course[ ] should be based on several doctors' opinions. 5. _____

6. Mary's triplets[ ] who jumped on my new furniture[ ] need a lesson in manners! 6. _____

7. The children[ ] who jumped on my new furniture[ ] need a lesson in manners! 7. _____

8. For this production, Bill will play Hamlet; Judith[ ] Ophelia. 8. _____

parenthetical expression (**par**)   omission (**om**)
after yes and no (**y/n**)   confirmatory question (**ques**)
examples introduced by *such as*,   direct address (**add**)
   especially, or *particularly* (**examp**)   date (**date**)
contrast (**cont**)   state or country (**s/c**)
nonrestrictive clause (**nr**)   series (**ser**)

9. Is it true[ ] sir[ ] that you are unwilling to be interviewed by the press?   9. _____

10. Marisa Martinez came all the way from San Antonio[ ] Texas[ ] to attend college in Cleveland.   10. _____

11. Frank graduated from the University of Michigan; Esther[ ] from Columbia University.   11. _____

12. Students[ ] who work their way through college[ ] learn to value their college training.   12. _____

13. She said, "No[ ] I should no be punished for stealing bread to feed my children."   13. _____

14. Latin America has many types of terrain[ ] such as lowlands, rain forests, vast plains, high
plateaus, and fertile valleys.   14. _____

15. On September 11[ ] 2001[ ] people throughout the world were horrified by what they saw
on television.   15. _____

16. I respect my parents, Mother Theresa[ ] and Albert Einstein.   16. _____

17. We were fortunate[ ] nevertheless[ ] to have recovered all of our luggage.   17. _____

18. The average person in the Middle Ages never owned a book[ ] or even saw one.   18. _____

19. I do believe a flying saucer landed in Siberia in 1908[ ] don't you?   19. _____

20. I've already told you[ ] little boy[ ] that I'm not giving back your ball.   20. _____

21. Frank Baum[ ] who wrote *The Wizard of Oz*[ ] had nine pseudonyms under which he wrote
other books.   21. _____

22. Not everyone[ ] who objected to the new ruling[ ] signed the petition.   22. _____

23. It was[ ] on the other hand[ ] an opportunity that he could not turn down.   23. _____

24. William Clinton[ ] who was our forty-second President[ ] was only the third to face
impeachment hearings.   24. _____

25. She enjoys several hobbies[ ] especially collecting coins and writing verse.   25. _____

44. PUNCTUATION: The Comma

(Study 201–203, The Comma)

Part 1

If **no comma** is needed in the bracketed space(s), leave the blank empty. If **one or more commas** are needed, write in the **reason** from the list below (only one reason per blank; use the abbreviations in parentheses).

independent clauses joined by
   conjunction (**ind**)
introductory clause or phrase(s) (**intro**)
series (**ser**)
contrast (**cont**)

appositive (**app**)
absolute phrase (**abs**)
coordinate adjectives (**adj**)
mild interjection (**inter**)
direct quotation (**quot**)

Examples: The New England states include Vermont[   ] Maine[   ] and New Hampshire. _____ser_____
    The Secretary of State[   ] held a press conference. _____

1. In China one can be treated for dental problems in an office[ ] or on a sidewalk along a busy street. 1. _____
2. Oh[ ] I forgot to give my parakeet its vitamins. 2. _____
3. F. Scott Fitzgerald[ ] author of *The Great Gatsby*[ ] often wrote novels about doomed relationships. 3. _____
4. Confused by the jumble of direction signs at the intersection[ ] Lomanto pulled into a gas station to ask for help. 4. _____
5. The snow having been shoveled from the sidewalk[ ] Mrs. Martin felt much safer walking on it. 5. _____
6. I lost ten pounds[ ] had my hair done[ ] and bought a dress so I could go to the holiday party. 6. _____
7. If the rain continues[ ] we'll play Monopoly instead of hiking. 7. _____
8. Many people had tried to reach the top of the mountain[ ] yet only a few had succeeded. 8. _____
9. Equipped with only an inexpensive camera[ ] she succeeded in taking a prize-winning picture. 9. _____
10. During times of emotional distress and heightened tensions[ ] Lee remains calm. 10. _____
11. To make an argyle sweater for her husband[ ] Miranda had to buy special yarn and instructions. 11. _____
12. Recognizing that his position was hopeless[ ] James resigned. 12. _____
13. Airbags in cars have saved many lives during crashes[ ] but they can be dangerous for children under twelve. 13. _____
14. Mr. Novak found himself surrounded by noisy[ ] exuberant students. 14. _____
15. "We are[ ]" she said[ ] "prepared to serve meals to a group of considerable size." 15. _____
16. The study found that the experimental medication did not significantly reduce blood pressure[ ] nor did it lower patients' heart rates. 16. _____
17. To improve a child's diet[ ] add more beans and green vegetables to the meal. 17. _____
18. Although Derek was an excellent driver[ ] he still had difficulty finding a sponsor for the race. 18. _____
19. We went to the ice rink[ ] and my parents went skiing. 19. _____
20. Betsy Johnson[ ] the sophomore class president[ ] campaigned for better food in the cafeteria. 20. _____

21. I could not decide whether to attend college[ ] or to travel to Norway with my uncle.

21._____

22. Built on a high cliff[ ] the house afforded a panoramic view of the valley below.

22._____

23. Our phone constantly ringing[ ] we decided to rely on the answering machine to avoid interruptions during supper.

23._____

24. The professor raised his voice to a low roar[ ] the class having apparently dozed off.

24._____

25. Her courses included Latin[ ] inorganic chemistry[ ] and technical writing.

25._____

Part 2

Write **C** if the punctuation in brackets is **correct**.
Write **X** if it is **incorrect**.
(Use only one letter for each answer.)

Example: The New England states include Vermont[,] Maine[,] and Rhode Island.

____C____

1. All the art classes visited the Museum of Modern Art[,] when it held its long-awaited Matisse retrospective.

1._____

2. We traveled to Idaho[,] and went down the Snake River.

2._____

3. "The records show," the clerk declared[,] "that there is a balance due of $38.76."

3._____

4. As they trudged deeper into the woods[,] they recalled hearing about Bigfoot and became frightened at the prospect of encountering the creature.

4._____

5. You expect to graduate in June[,] don't you?

5._____

6. O'Connor started the second half at linebacker[,] Bryant having torn his knee ligaments.

6._____

7. O'Connor started the second half at linebacker[,] Bryant had torn his knee ligaments.

7._____

8. Trying to concentrate[,] Susan closed the door and turned off the television set.

8._____

9. "My fellow Americans[,] I look forward to the opportunity to serve this country," he said.

9._____

10. The newly elected President, on the eve of his inauguration, declared[,] "The environment and peace with the Middle East are priorities in my administration."

10._____

11. Helen, who especially enjoys baseball, sat in the front row[,] and watched the game closely.

11._____

12. "Are you going to a fire?"[,] the police officer asked the speeding motorist.

12._____

13. Two of the students left the office[,] the third waited to see the dean.

13._____

14. Angela and two of her friends[,] recently performed at the student talent show.

14._____

15. "I won't wait any longer," she said[,] picking up her books from the bench.

15._____

16. His tough[,] angry attitude was only a way to prevent others from knowing how scared he was about failing.

16._____

17. The relatively short drought[,] nonetheless[,] had still caused much damage to the crops.

17._____

18. The cake in the oven[,] smells wonderful.

18._____

19. According to the polls, the candidate was losing[,] he blamed the media for the results.

19._____

20. The challenger[,] said the incumbent[,] was a tax evader. [The incumbent was making a statement about the challenger.]

20._____

21. The challenger[,] said the incumbent[,] was a tax evader. [The challenger was making a statement about the incumbent.]

21. _____

22. "Did you know," the financial aid officer replied[,] "that each year thousands of scholarships go unclaimed?"

22. _____

23. Her English professor[,] who was having difficulty getting to class on time[,] requested that the class move to a different building.

23. _____

24. She said [,] that she couldn't believe the Girl Scouts had raised so much money in one week.

24. _____

25. Next summer she hopes to fulfill her dearest lifelong wish[,] to visit Roslyn Chapel in Edinburgh.

25. _____

45. PUNCTUATION: The Comma

(Study 201–203, The Comma)

Part 1

Write **C** if the punctuation in brackets is **correct**.
Write **X** if it is **incorrect**.
(Use only one letter for each blank.)

Example: Since they had no further business there[,] they left. _____C_____

1. Tomorrow afternoon[,] Tom told Margaret[,] we'll go to the modern art exhibit at the Baltimore Museum of Art. 1._____

2. When she saw the puppies[,] at the dog pound Portilla knew she would take one home. 2._____

3. In the haste of the evacuation[,] from New Orleans many citizens left everything they owned behind. 3._____

4. Marlene cannot resist chocolate[,] which is why she left her job at the candy store. 4._____

5. You do not understand the temperament of a star[,] the diva told her agent. 5._____

6. First-graders now engage in writing journals[,] in problem-solving activities[,] and in brief science experiments. 6._____

7. Shaking hands with his patient, the physician asked[,] "Now what kind of surgery are we doing today?" 7._____

8. Peter's goal was to make a short film in graduate school[,] and not worry about a future career. 8._____

9. Aaron and Natasha decided to find a less painful[,] but more effective diet. 9._____

10. The American cowboys' hats actually had many purposes besides shielding their faces from the sun and rain[,] for many cowboys used their hats as pillows and drinking cups. 10._____

11. During conversations about controversial topics[,] our faces often communicate our thoughts, especially our emotional responses. 11._____

12. Harry Rosen[,] a skilled, polished speaker[,] effectively used humor during his speeches. 12._____

13. To understand how living arrangements affect student relationships[,] the psychology department completed several informal observational studies on campus. 13._____

14. Many music lovers insist[,] that the now-obsolete vinyl LP record produces better sound quality than the currently popular CD. 14._____

15. The states with the greatest numbers of dairy cows are Wisconsin[,] and California. 15._____

16. Mincemeat[,] a mixture of apples, raisins, sugar, and rum[,] is a traditional dessert at Christmas dinner. 16._____

17. Having friends must be an important aspect of our culture[,] for many popular television series focus on how a group of characters care for their friendships with one another. 17._____

18. People beginning an intimate relationship use a significant number of affectionate expressions[,] but the frequency of these expressions drops as the relationship matures. 18._____

19. Working hard to pay the mortgage, to educate their children, and to save money for retirement[,] many of America's middle class now call themselves the "new poor." 19._____

20. The children tiptoed while in the library[,] they heard that librarians are upset by any noise. 20. _____

21. Now only 68 percent of American children live with both biological parents[,] 20 percent of children live in single-parent families[,] and 9 percent live with one biological parent and a stepparent. 21. _____

22. Jeff was hungry for a rich[,] gooey brownie smothered in whipped cream and chocolate sauce. 22. _____

23. His thoughts dominated by grief[,] Jack decided to postpone his vacation for another month. 23. _____

24. "Oh[,] I forgot to bring my report home to finish it tonight," sighed Mary. 24. _____

25. People exercise because it makes them feel good[,] they may even become addicted to exercise. 25. _____

Part 2

In each sentence the brackets show where a comma may or may not be needed. In the blank, write the **number of commas** needed. If none, write **0**.

Example: Lucy ordered crab cakes[ ] a salad[ ] and an iced tea[ ] with plenty of ice. _____2_____

1. In addition to your completed honors application form[ ] you will need to submit[ ] an official high school transcript[ ] three letters of recommendation[ ] and two essays. 1. _____

2. Although it is not required[ ] by state law[ ] the presence of a lifeguard would have prevented[ ] the nearly fatal accident. 2. _____

3. According to research[ ] "Cinderella[ ]" is based on a Chinese[ ] folk tale[ ] that was first told around 850; the young woman in the story is named Yeh-Shen. 3. _____

4. Citizens[ ] do not vote[ ] unless you understand each candidate's position[ ] on the issues. 4. _____

5. I wanted[ ] to go[ ] to Harvard; Terry[ ] to Yale. 5. _____

6. I[ ] didn't realize[ ] that four Latin American writers[ ] have won the Nobel Prize for Literature. 6. _____

7. Unlike the Maya[ ] and Aztecs[ ] the Incas had no written language; instead[ ] they kept records on *quipus*[ ] which are knotted strings. 7. _____

8. The chairman[ ] who had already served two terms in Congress[ ] and one in the State Assembly[ ] declared his candidacy again. 8. _____

9. Matthew was born on March 16[ ] 1969[ ] in Fargo[ ] North Dakota[ ] during a blizzard. 9. _____

10. I consider him[ ] to be[ ] a hard-working student[ ] but[ ] I may be wrong. 10. _____

11. Audrey Starke[ ] a woman[ ] whom I met last summer[ ] is here[ ] to see me. 11. _____

12. Having an interest[ ] in anthropology[ ] she frequently audited[ ] Dr. Irwin's class[ ] that met on Saturdays. 12. _____

13. Native Americans were the first to grow corn[ ] potatoes[ ] squash[ ] pumpkins[ ] and avocados. 13. _____

14. Well[ ] I dislike her intensely[ ] but[ ] she is quite clever[ ] to be sure. 14. _____

15. To solve[ ] her legal problems[ ] she consulted an attorney[ ] that she knew[ ] from college. 15. _____

16. "To what[ ]" he asked[ ] "do you attribute[ ] your great popularity[ ] with the students?" 16. _____

17. From Native Americans[ ] the world learned about cinnamon[ ] and chocolate[ ] and chicle[ ] the main ingredient in chewing gum. 17. _____

18. "Fire and Rain[ ]" a song written by James Taylor[ ] in 1968[ ] is thought [ ] to be about a girlfriend [ ] who died.   18. _____

19. Many filmmakers are creating[ ] serious movies[ ] about their cultural heritage; however, there are[ ] few commercially successful movies about Asian American cultures.   19. _____

20. "You haven't seen my glasses[ ] have you?" Granny asked[ ] the twins[ ] thinking they had hidden them[ ] somewhere in the living room.   20. _____

21. The car having broken down[ ] because of a dirty carburetor[ ] we missed the first act[ ] in which[ ] Hamlet confronts his father's ghost.   21. _____

22. After she had paid her tuition[ ] she checked in at the residence hall[ ] that she had selected[ ] and soon began[ ] unloading her suitcases and boxes.   22. _____

23. The space launch went so punctually[ ] and smoothly[ ] that the astronauts began their voyage[ ] relaxed[ ] and confident.   23. _____

24. Chinese porcelain[ ] which is prized for its beauty[ ] and its translucence[ ] was copied[ ] by seventeenth-century Dutch potters.   24. _____

25. The road to Brattleboro[ ] being coated with ice[ ] we proceeded[ ] slowly[ ] and cautiously.   25. _____

46. PUNCTUATION: The Comma

(Study 201–203, The Comma)

Part 1

Either **insert** or **cross out a comma** to make the sentence correct. In the blank, write the word that comes just **before** the inserted or crossed-out comma.

Examples: When the soldiers looked around, the stranger had vanished.   <u>around</u>
           The cloud-hidden sunX gave us no clue as to which way was south.   <u>sun</u>

1. As the mother knelt in the chapel, she prayed that her son would return safely from Iraq.   1._____

2. The 1990s will be remembered by most Americans, as a decade of rising prosperity.   2._____

3. Having examined and reexamined the ancient tomb the committee of scholars declared it to be a genuine Viking burial site.   3._____

4. If we go to Ireland in the spring then we cannot go to Germany in the fall.   4._____

5. Amanda has decided to write a cookbook, remodel her kitchen and travel through California.   5._____

6. Many Americans now prefer news sources, that offer human interest stories.   6._____

7. The country that receives the most media attention, is often the recipient of the most aid from the United Nations.   7._____

8. Coaching soccer, and teaching part-time at a local college keep me quite busy.   8._____

9. George and Robert thoroughly and painstakingly considered, what had to be done to defuse the bomb.   9._____

10. If ever there was the law on one side, and simple justice on the other, here is such a situation.   10._____

11. According to the College Board, Advanced Placement exams are always given in May and scored in June.   11._____

12. President Barack Obama chose Hillary Clinton, to be the Secretary of State.   12._____

13. My corgi Albert lets me know, when he wants to take a walk.   13._____

14. What gave Helen the inspiration for her short story, was her mother's account of growing up on a farm.   14._____

15. Owen's baseball cards included such famous examples as Willie Mays's running catch in the 1954 World Series, and Hank Aaron's record-breaking home run.   15._____

16. The volume that was the most valuable in the library's rare book collection, was a First Folio edition of Shakespeare's plays.   16._____

17. *Gone with the Wind*, a film enjoyed by millions of people throughout the world was first thought unlikely to be a commercial success.   17._____

18. Because the material was difficult to understand Monica decided to hire a tutor.   18._____

19. The study asserted that parents in sending their infant children to daycare, may be slowing their youngsters' mental development.   19._____

20. When Professor Smith canceled the trigonometry test no one in the math class complained.   20._____

Write an original sentence that contains an example of the comma used as stated in the brackets. **Circle** the comma(s) used.

___

Example: [Setting off a parenthetical expression] <u>This course‚ it seems to me‚ requires too much work.</u>

(Collaborative option: Students work in pairs or small groups to suggest and comment on different examples.)

1. [between two independent clauses] _____

   _____

   _____

2. [with an introductory adverb clause] _____

   _____

   _____

3. [with coordinate adjectives] _____

   _____

   _____

4. [with a long introductory prepositional phrase or a series of introductory prepositional phrases or an introductory verbal phrase] _____

   _____

   _____

5. [with an absolute phrase] _____

   _____

   _____

6. [with a parenthetical expression] _____

   _____

   _____

7. [with an expression of contrast]_____

_____

_____

8. [with a date or address] _____

_____

_____

9. [with a nonessential (nonrestrictive) clause or phrase] _____

_____

_____

10. [with a direct quotation]_____

_____

_____

11. [to prevent misreading] _____

_____

_____

12. [in direct address]_____

_____

_____

13. [Write a sentence with an essential (restrictive) clause—one that does **not** use commas.] _____

_____

_____

47. PUNCTUATION: The Period, Question Mark, and Exclamation Point

(Study 204–205, The Period; 206–207, The Question Mark; and 208–209, The Exclamation Point)

Write **C** if the punctuation in brackets is **correct**.
Write **X** if it is **incorrect**.

Example: Is there any word from the Awards Committee yet[?]   _____C_____

1. The judge would never hold me in contempt, would she[?]   1._____
2. "Move back; the fire's advancing!" shouted the forest ranger[!]   2._____
3. Sally asked her parents if she could go to the beach for a week with Marisa and her familiy[?]   3._____
4. Mr. Hall and Miss[.] James will chair the committee.   4._____
5. The chem[.] test promises to be challenging.   5._____
6. Where is the office? Down the hall on the left[.]   6._____
7. Good afternoon, ma'am[.] May I present you with a free scrub brush?   7._____
8. "How much did the owners spend on players' salaries?" the reporter asked[?]   8._____
9. His next question—wouldn't you know[?]—was, "What do you need, ma'am?"   9._____
10. "Wow! Does your computer have a video camera too[!]"   10._____
11. "What a magnificent view you have of the mountains[!]" said he.   11._____
12. Who said, "If at first you don't succeed, try, try again" [?]   12._____
13. Would you please check my computer for viruses[?]   13._____
14. HELP WANTED: Editor[.] for our new brochure.   14._____
15. Jeannette, would you buy some chocolate ice cream on your way home[.]   15._____
16. What? You lent that scoundrel Snively $10,000[?!]   16._____
17. I asked her why, of all the men on campus, she had chosen him[?]   17._____
18. Why did I do it? Because I respected her[.] Jackie worked hard to finish her degree.   18._____
19. "Footloose and Fancy Free[.]" [title of an essay]   19._____
20. Would you please send me your reply by e-mail[.]   20._____
21. "The Lakers win[!!]" the announcer screamed as Bryant's jump shot slipped through the net at the buzzer.   21._____
22. She asked me if I knew that the Queen of England was the head of the Church of England[?]   22._____
23. My supervisor asked how much equipment I would need to update the computer center[.]   23._____
24. My essay's title was "Computers: Can We Live Without Them[?]"   24._____
25. I heard the news on station W[.]I[.]N[.]K.   25._____
26. The postmark on the package read "Springfield, MA[.] 01102."   26._____
27. The monarch who followed King George VI[.] was Queen Elizabeth II.   27._____
28. According to Ramsey, "The election drew a light turnout[.] . . . Predictably, the Socialist Party won."   28._____

29. You lost your wallet again[?] I don't believe it.   29. _____

30. The duke was born in 1576[(?)] and died in 1642.   30. _____

31. What[!?] What did you just call me?   31. _____

32. You didn't drive all the way from Wilmington, Delaware, to Los Angeles, did you[.]   32. _____

33. Could I have committed the crime? Never[.] I was on a business trip to St. Louis at the time.   33. _____

48. PUNCTUATION: The Semicolon

(Study 210, The Semicolon)

Part 1

Write the **reason** for the semicolon in each sentence (use the abbreviations in parentheses). Use only one reason for each sentence.

between clauses lacking a coordinating conjunction (**no conj**)
between clauses joined by a conjunctive adverb (**conj adv**)
between clauses having commas within them (**cl w com**)
in a series having commas within the items (**ser w com**)

Example: It was a glorious day for the North; it was a sad one for the South.   ___no conj___

1. Pressure-treated wood has been popular for decks because it resists the elements for years; however, its arsenic content has made it environmentally undesirable.   1._____

2. The farmers are using an improved fertilizer; thus their crop yields have increased.   2._____

3. Still to come were Perry, a trained squirrel; Arnold, an acrobat; and Mavis, a magician.   3._____

4. "Negotiations," he said, "have collapsed; we will strike at noon."   4._____

5. Tacoma's Museum of Glass is one of only two museums in the country dedicated to exhibiting glass; the other is the Corning Museum of Glass in upstate New York.   5._____

6. The average Internet user spends about six hours a week online; the majority of these users reach the Internet from work.   6._____

7. Joyce grows her own vegetables; however, John, her neighbor, would rather spend the money to buy them at the grocery store.   7._____

8. Every Sunday afternoon, Jane planned what she would wear to school the following week; she found that this planning saved her time on weekday mornings.   8._____

9. The play was performed in Altoona, Pennsylvania; Buckhannon, West Virginia; and The Woodlands, Texas.   9._____

10. Flight 330 stops at Little Rock, Dallas, and Albuquerque; but Flight 440, the all-coach special, is an express to Phoenix.   10._____

Part 2

If a **semicolon is needed** in the brackets, write the **reason** in the blank, as you did in part 1 (**no conj, conj adv, cl w com, ser w com**). If **no semicolon** is needed, leave the blank empty.

Examples: He would not help her get the job[   ] moreover, he could not.   ___conj adv___
     After the rap concert[   ] we drove to Salty's.   _____

1. The Puritans banned the Christmas holiday when they settled in North America[   ] the holiday was not revived until the 1880s.   1._____

2. Maureen took her violin to the auditorium[   ] she planned to practice with the other violinists.   2._____

between clauses lacking a coordinating conjunction (**no conj**)
between clauses joined by a conjunctive adverb (**conj adv**)
between clauses having commas within them (**cl w com**)
in a series having commas within the items (**ser w com**)

---

3. A recent study indicates that saccharin does not cause cancer in humans[ ] the only consumers who should worry are laboratory rats.

3. _____

4. The lake suffered from a buildup of stream-borne silt[ ] until it became so shallow that it had to be dredged.

4. _____

5. The lake suffered from a buildup of stream-borne silt[ ] it became so shallow that it had to be dredged.

5. _____

6. Jane, bring the paper items[ ] Bill, the hot dogs and rolls[ ] Jessie the cole slaw and chips[ ] Florence, the desserts.

6. _____

7. The national public education system needs to redefine its expectations[ ] because most schools do not expect all of their students to succeed.

7. _____

8. Hollywood has always portrayed the Union soldiers as dressed in blue and the Confederate troops in gray[ ] however, for the first year of the Civil War, most soldiers wore their state militia uniforms, which came in many colors.

8. _____

9. Soft drinks are a traditional beverage in the United States[ ] flavored soda water first appeared in 1825 in Philadelphia.

9. _____

10. Orville and Wilbur Wright ran a bicycle shop in Dayton, had no scientific training, and never finished high school[ ] yet, by inventing the airplane, they revolutionized transportation worldwide.

10. _____

11. She is very bright[ ] at twenty, she is the owner of a successful small business.

11. _____

12. John uses a video conferencing network to conduct business[ ] instead of spending time flying all over the world for meetings.

12. _____

13. Exercising is quite beneficial[ ] because it helps to reduce physical and psychological stress.

13. _____

14. Our representatives included Will Leeds, a member of the Rotary Club[ ] Augusta Allcott, a banker[ ] and Bill Rogers, president of the Chamber of Commerce.

14. _____

15. Peter lives in Minnesota[ ] Howard, in Maryland.

15. _____

49. PUNCTUATION: The Semicolon and the Comma

(Study 201–203, The Comma, and 210, The Semicolon)

Write **com** if you would insert a **comma** (or commas) in the brackets.
Write **semi** if you would insert a **semicolon** (or semicolons).
If you would insert nothing, leave the blank empty.
Write only one answer for each blank.

Example: The milk had all gone sour[   ] we could not have our cappucino. _____semi_____

1. Because the Johnsons' neighbor had borrowed the ladder[ ] Mr. Johnson was not able to clean the gutters before the storm.   1. _____

2. Many Americans have financial plans for retirement[ ] but stock-market turmoil has made them rethink those plans.   2. _____

3. Professor Nicholas[ ] who teaches chemistry[ ] graduated from MIT.   3. _____

4. The Profeessor Nicholas[ ] who teaches chemistry[ ] graduated from MIT.   4. _____

5. Marcia Simpson[ ] who is to be president of the new community college[ ] spoke at the reception for new honors students.   5. _____

6. She likes working in Washington, D.C.[ ] she hopes to remain there permanently.   6. _____

7. To the east we could see the White Mountains[ ] to the west, the Green.   7. _____

8. Find the allusions in the sonnet[ ] then examine its meter and rhyme.   8. _____

9. One of my grandmother's most prized possessions is an antique glass bowl[ ] that was made in Murano, Italy.   9. _____

10. Ruth uses chopsticks at lunch[ ] no matter what she's eating.   10. _____

11. We're going on a cruise around the bay on Sunday[ ] and we'd like you to come with us.   11. _____

12. If Amy decides to become a lawyer[ ] you can be sure she'll be a good one.   12. _____

13. The election officials made the students move their posters[ ] away from the entrance to the polling place.   13. _____

14. Li-Young registered for an advanced biology course[ ] otherwise, she might not have been admitted to medical school.   14. _____

15. The newest computers[ ] moreover[ ] are cheaper than last year's less powerful models.   15. _____

16. Cell phones are here to stay[ ] even my great-grandmother has one.   16. _____

17. He began his speech again[ ] fire engines having drowned out his opening remarks.   17. _____

18. The best day of the vacation occurred[ ] when we took the children sledding.   18. _____

19. Let me introduce the new officers: Phillip Whitaker, president[ ] Elaine Donatelli, secretary[ ] and Pierre Northrup, treasurer.   19. _____

20. We thought of every possible detail when planning the dinner party[ ] yet we didn't anticipate our cat's jumping into the cake.   20. _____

21. The high-school teacher was delighted[ ] because her class had learned how to catch and correct sentence fragments.   21. _____

22. Melissa thought that if people realized how the trash from storm drains affected the Chesapeake Bay[ ] they would dispose of trash more carefully.   22. _____

23. The drama coach was a serene person[ ] not one to be worried about nervous amateurs. 23._____

24. To turn them into professional performers was[ ] needless to say[ ] an impossible task. 24._____

25. "When you plan a meeting," Jack said, "always have an agenda and stick to it[ ] or people will think you've wasted their time." 25._____

26. Call the security office[ ] if there seems to be any problem with the locks. 26._____

27. Couples with severe disabilities may have difficulty raising a family[ ] there are few programs to help disabled parents with their children. 27._____

28. Britain was the first Common Market country to react[ ] others quickly followed suit. 28._____

29. The American troops stormed ashore at Omaha and Utah beaches[ ] the British, at Sword, Gold, and Juno. 29._____

30. Perhaps because the weather was finally warm again[ ] I didn't want to stay inside. 30._____

31. American couples are examining their lifestyles[ ] many are cutting back in their work schedules to spend more time with their children. 31._____

32. The World Series hadn't yet begun[ ] however, he had equipped himself with a new radio. 32._____

33. I could not remember ever having seen her as radiantly happy[ ] as she now was. 33._____

34. No, I cannot go to the game[ ] I have a term paper to finish. 34._____

35. Kristi Yamaguchi[ ] in fact, is a fourth-generation Japanese American. 35._____

36. Victor, on the other hand[ ] played the best game of his career. 36._____

37. Home-grown products are common in rural farming communities[ ] on the other hand, such products can command high prices in urban areas. 37._____

38. "There will be no rain today[ ]" she insisted. "The weather forecaster says so." 38._____

39. Swimming is an excellent form of exercise[ ] swimming for twenty-six minutes consumes 100 calories. 39._____

40. Though the American flag had only forty-eight stars in 1944[ ] the war movie mistakenly showed a fifty-star flag. 40._____

41. The short story[ ] that impressed me the most[ ] was written by a thirty-five-year-old police officer. 41._____

42. Mary constantly counts calories and fat content in the food she eats[ ] yet she never loses more than a pound. 42._____

43. Many cultures follow different calendars[ ] for example, the Jewish New Year is celebrated in the fall, the Vietnamese and Chinese New Year at the beginning of the year, and the Cambodian New Year in April. 43._____

44. "My fraternity[ ]" stated Travis, "completes numerous community service projects throughout the school year." 44._____

45. All the students were present for the final, but[ ] most were suffering from the flu. 45._____

46. Muslim students on campus asked the administration for a larger international student center[ ] and a quiet place for their daily prayers. 46._____

47. Whenever Sam is feeling sad and discouraged about his job[ ] he puts on a Tony Bennett record and dances with the dog. 47._____

48. Barry and I were planning a large farewell party for Eugene within the next month[ ] but certainly not next week. 48._____

49. To read only mysteries and novels[ ] was my plan for the holiday break. 49._____

50. Most Amish reside in Pennsylvania[ ] however, there are settlements also in Ohio and upstate New York. 50._____

50. PUNCTUATION: The Semicolon and the Comma

(Study 201–203, The Comma, and 210, The Semicolon)

Write an **original sentence** illustrating the use of the semicolon or comma stated in brackets.

_____

Example: [two independent clauses with no coordinating conjunction between them]
   Five students scored A on the exam; four scored D.

(Collaborative option: Students work in pairs or small groups to suggest and comment on different examples.)

1. [two independent clauses with *furthermore* between them] _____

   _____

   _____

2. [two independent clauses joined by *and*, with commas within the clauses]_____

   _____

   _____

3. [two independent clauses joined by *yet*] _____

   _____

   _____

4. [three items in a series, with commas within each of the items] _____

   _____

   _____

5. [two independent clauses with *then* between them] _____

   _____

   _____

6. [two independent clauses with no word between them] _____

   _____

   _____

7. [an introductory adverb clause] _____

   _____

   _____

8. [a nonessential (nonrestrictive) clause] _____

    _____

    _____

9. [two independent clauses with *in fact* or *also* between them]_____

    _____

    _____

10. [two independent clauses with *however* inside the second clause (not between the clauses)] _____

    _____

    _____

51. PUNCTUATION: The Apostrophe

(Study 211–213, The Apostrophe)

In the first blank, write the number of the **correct** choice (**1** or **2**). In the second blank, write the **reason** for your choice (use the abbreviations in parentheses; if your choice for the first blank has no apostrophe, leave the second blank empty).

singular possessive (**sing pos**)   contraction (**cont**)
plural possessive (**pl pos**)   plural of letter or symbol used as a word (**let/sym**)

Examples: The fault was (1) **Jacob's** (2) **Jacobs'**.   __1__ sing pos
          The fault was (1) **your's** (2) **yours**.   __2__ _____

1. It (1)**wasn't** (2)**was'nt** the weather that caused the delay; it was an electrical failure.   1. ____ _____

2. The (1)**Smith's** (2)**Smiths** have planned a murder-mystery party.   2. ____ _____

3. The (1)**James'** (2)**Jameses** are moving to Seattle.   3. ____ _____

4. My (1)**brother-in-law's** (2)**brother's-in-law** medical practice is flourishing.   4. ____ _____

5. The (1)**Novotny's** (2)**Novotnys'** new home is spacious.   5. ____ _____

6. (1)**Its** (2)**It's** important to exercise several times a week.   6. ____ _____

7. (1)**Who's** (2)**Whose** responsible for the increased production of family-oriented movies?   7. ____ _____

8. The two (1)**girl's** (2)**girls'** talent was quite evident to everyone.   8. ____ _____

9. Some economists fear that the Social Security system may be bankrupt by the (1)**2020s**
    (2)**2020's**.   9. ____ _____

10. It will be a two-(1)**day's** (2)**days'** drive to Galveston.   10. ____ _____

11. The dispute over the last clause caused a (1)**weeks** (2)**week's** delay in the contract signing. 11. ____ _____

12. Mary accidentally spilled tea on her (1)**bosses** (2)**boss's** report.   12. ____ _____

13. After the long absence, they fell into (1)**each others'** (2)**each other's** arms.   13. ____ _____

14. Each woman claimed that the diamond ring was (1)**her's** (2)**hers**.   14. ____ _____

15. Geraldine uses too many (1)*and*s (2)*and*'s in most of her presentations.   15. ____ _____

16. Bumstead never dots his (1)**I's** (2)**Is**.   16. ____ _____

17. (1)**Wer'ent** (2)**Weren't** you surprised by the success of her book?   17. ____ _____

18. Which is safer, your van or (1)**ours** (2)**our's**?   18. ____ _____

19. Georgiana insisted, "I (1)**have'nt** (2)**haven't** seen Sandy for weeks."   19. ____ _____

20. He bought fifty (1)**cents** (2)**cents'** worth of bubblegum.   20. ____ _____

21. The back alley was known to be a (1)**thieve's** (2)**thieves'** hangout.   21. ____ _____

22. (1)**Paul's and David's** (2)**Paul and David's** senior project was praised by their advisor.   22. ____ _____

23. The (1)**children's** (2)**childrens'** kitten ate our goldfish.   23. ____ _____

24. "The (1)**evenings** (2)**evening's** been delightful," Lily said. "Thank you."   24. ____ _____

25. The local (1)**coal miner's** (2)**coal miners'** union was the subject of Bill's documentary.   25. ____ _____

52. PUNCTUATION: The Apostrophe

(Study 211–213, The Apostrophe)

For each bracketed apostrophe, write **C** if it is **correct**; write **X** if it is **incorrect**. Use the first column for the first apostrophe, the second column for the second apostrophe.

Example: Who[']s on first? Where is todays['] lineup?

                C   X

1. Everyone else[']s opinion carries less weight with me than your[']s. 1. ____ ____

2. Mrs. Jackson[']s invitation to the William[']s must have gone astray. 2. ____ ____

3. He would[']nt know that information after only two day[']s employment. 3. ____ ____

4. Were[']nt they fortunate that the stolen car wasn't their[']s? 4. ____ ____

5. It[']s a pity that the one bad cabin would be our[']s. 5. ____ ____

6. We[']re expecting the Wagner[']s to meet us in Colorado for a ski trip. 6. ____ ____

7. Home-baked pizza[']s need an oven temperature in the upper 400[']s. 7. ____ ____

8. Does[']nt the governor see that most voters won[']t support her cuts in farm aid? 8. ____ ____

9. The two sisters had agreed that they[']d stop wearing each others['] shoes. 9. ____ ____

10. She[']s not going to accept anybody[']s advice, no matter how sound it might be. 10. ____ ____

11. The three students['] complaints about the professor[']s attitude in class were finally addressed by the administration. 11. ____ ____

12. He[']s hoping for ten hours['] work a week in the library. 12. ____ ____

13. The idea of a cultural greeting card business was not our[']s; it was Lois[']s. 13. ____ ____

14. There are three *i*[']s in the word *optimistic;* there are two *r*[']s in the word *embarrass.* 14. ____ ____

15. The computer printout consisted of a series of *1*[']s and *0*[']s. 15. ____ ____

16. Their advisor sent two dozen yellow rose[']s to the Women Student Association[']s meeting. 16. ____ ____

17. I really did[']nt expect to see all of the drivers['] finish the race. 17. ____ ____

18. Hav[']ent you heard about the theft at the Jone[']s house? 18. ____ ____

19. The popular mens['] store, established in 1923, was[']nt able to compete with the large discount stores in the nearby mall. 19. ____ ____

20. I'm sure that, if he[']s physically able, he[']ll be at the volunteer program. 20. ____ ____

21. The responsibility for notifying club members is her[']s, not our[']s. 21. ____ ____

22. Can[']t I persuade you that you[']re now ready to move out of the house? 22. ____ ____

23. Both lawyers['] used hard-hitting tactic[']s to explain why their company should not be required to pay damages. 23. ____ ____

24. Everyones['] agreeing that in the 1990[']s too many stocks were overvalued. 24. ____ ____

25. Marie Stockton sought her sister-in-law[']s advice when she considered opening a women[']s fitness salon. 25. ____ ____

53. PUNCTUATION: The Apostrophe

(Study 211–213, The Apostrophe)

In the paragraphs below, most words ending in **s** are followed by a small number. At the right are blanks with corresponding numbers. In each blank, write the **correct ending** for the word with that number: **'s** or **s'** or **s**.

Example: We collected our days$_{51}$ pay after cleaning the tables$_{52}$.   51. _'s_ 52. _s_

All young performers$_1$ dream of gaining recognition from their audiences$_2$ and of seeing   1.____ 2.____

their names in lights$_3$ on Broadway. These were Annie Smiths$_4$ dreams when she left her   3.____ 4.____

parents$_5$ home and ran off to New York City. At age eighteen, however, Annie was not prepared   5.____

for the difficulties$_6$ of living alone and working in a large city. Her wages$_7$ as a waitress barely   6.____ 7.____

covered a months$_8$ rent. And she still needed to buy groceries$_9$ and pay her utilities$_{10}$. It took   8.____ 9.____ 10.____

Annie several months$_{11}$ time to find two suitable roommates, who would share the rent and   11.____

other bills. However, the roommates$_{12}$ also helped in other important ways, for when Annie   12.____

felt that she couldn't go for another audition, her roommates$_{13}$ encouragement to continue   13.____

helped bolster Annies$_{14}$ determination. Annie realized that for anyones$_{15}$ dream to happen, a   14.____ 15.____

great deal of hard work had to come first.

One evening in the late 1990s$_{16}$, as she was clearing away the last two customers$_{17}$ 16.____ 17.____

dishes at Carusos$_{18}$ Restaurant, she heard a distinguished-looking woman asking the head   18.____

waiter, "Whos$_{19}$ that young lady? She moves$_{20}$ with such grace, and shes$_{21}$ got the poise   19.____ 20.____ 21.____

and features$_{22}$ of a movie star; I'm a film director, and I'd like to speak to her."   22.____

This storys$_{23}$ ending is a happy one, for in a years$_{24}$ time Annie became a star.   23.____ 24.____

All that she had dreamed of was now hers$_{25}$.   25.____

54. PUNCTUATION: Italics

(Study 214, Italics [Underlining])

Part 1

Write the **reason** for each use of italics (use the abbreviations in parentheses):

title of printed, performed, or electronic work (**title**)
name of ship, train, plane, or spacecraft (**craft**)
title of painting or sculpture (**art**)
foreign word not Anglicized (**for**)
word, letter, symbol, or figure referred to as such (**wlsf**)
emphasis (**emph**)

Example: Does this library subscribe to
Smithsonian?   title

1. On May 6, 1937, in Lakehurst, New Jersey, the *Hindenburg*, a German airship, caught fire and was destroyed within one minute.   1. ____

2. Channel 8 seems to show nothing but reruns of *Raymond* and *Seinfeld*.   2. ____

3. For many years, the *Manchester Guardian* has been a leading newspaper in England.   3. ____

4. Norman Rockwell painted *The Four Freedoms* during World War II.   4. ____

5. The directions on the test indicated that all questions were to be answered with *1*s or *2*s. 5. ____

6. Dozens of English words connected with dining come from the French—*cuisine, à la mode,* and *hors d'oeuvres,* to name just a few.   6. ____

7. Susan learned to spell the word *villain* by thinking of a "villa in" Italy.   7. ____

8. "Are you sure you won't *ever* cheat on me?" she asked.   8. ____

9. The statue *The Women of Belfast* is on loan from the Ulster Museum.   9. ____

10. An article had been written recently about the submarine *Nautilus*.   10. ____

11. N. Scott Momaday's *1969: The Way to Rainy Mountain* recounts the Kiowa Indians' migration to the American plains.   11. ____

12. How many *s*'s and *i*'s are there in your last name?   12. ____

13. Though *Oklahoma!* was first performed more than sixty years ago, it is still a favorite of local theater groups.   13. ____

14. The American pronunciation of *vase* is *vayss* or *vaze*; the British pronunciation is *vahz*.   14. ____

15. Richard Rodriguez's autobiography, *Hunger of Memory*, helped me understand some of the issues surrounding bilingual education. 15. ____

16. American women are learning to say a strong *no* to many professional demands so that they have time for family and friends.   16. ____

17. Aboard the *Enterprise*, the captain made plans to return to the planet Zircon to rescue Mr. Spock.   17. ____

18. Michelangelo's *David* was originally mounted outdoors but was moved into a museum to protect the stone from erosion.   18. ____

19. Now that I have *Ace Anti-virus Protector* software installed on my hard drive, I have no worries about computer viruses.   19. ____

20. The first American to orbit the earth was John Glenn in *Friendship 7*.   20. ____

21. Her printed *R*'s and *B*'s closely resemble each other.   21. ____

22. Although he never held office, Lopez was the *de facto* ruler of his country.   22. ____

23. Some people spell and pronounce the words *athlete* and *athletics* as if there were an *e* after *th* in each word.   23. ____

24. The movie *A Family Thing* addresses racial issues in the United States in a thought-provoking and sensitive manner.   24. ____

25. The original meaning of the word *mad* was "disordered in mind" or "insane."   25. ____

155

Part 2

In each sentence, **underline** the word(s) that should be in italics.

Example: The cover of <u>Newsweek</u> depicted African refugees.

1. Dave Matthews and his group performed items from their new CD, Busted Stuff.

2. Deciding to come home by ship, we made reservations on the Queen Elizabeth II.

3. Geraldine went downtown to buy copies of Esquire and Field and Stream.

4. "It's time for a change!" shouted the candidate during the debate.

5. Proof, David Auburn's drama about love, fear, genius, and madness, won both the Pulitzer Prize and a Tony Award.

6. The New York Times must have weighed ten pounds last Sunday.

7. The Mystery! series on public television promises amateur sleuths a weekly escape into murder and intrigue.

8. Browsing through recent fiction at the library, Ms. Kovalchik came across The Red Tent, by Anita Diamant.

9. Among the magazines scattered in the room was a copy of Popular Mechanics.

10. Maya Angelou's first published work, I Know Why the Caged Bird Sings, is an autobiography describing her first sixteen years.

11. When I try to pronounce the word statistics, I always stumble over it.

12. I still have difficulty remembering the difference between continual and continuous.

13. "I'll never stop fighting for my rights," Megan Morton thundered. "And I mean never."

14. Picasso's Guernica depicts the horrors of war.

15. The Thinker is a statue that many people admire.

16. Spike Lee's film Malcolm X inspired me.

17. You'll enjoy reading "The Man of the House" in the book Fifty Great Short Stories.

18. The British spelling of the word humor is h-u-m-o-u-r.

19. "How to Heckle Your Prof" was an essay in John James's How to Get Thrown Out of College.

20. Michelangelo's Last Judgment shows "the omnipotence of his artistic ability."

21. The source of the above quotation is the Encyclopaedia Britannica.

22. They were able to download the entire program Master Chess from the Internet.

23. He had been a noted braumeister in Germany.

24. Perry won the spelling bee's award for creative expression with his rendition of antidisestablishmentarianism.

25. The instructor said that Sam's 7s and his 4s look very much alike.

55. PUNCTUATION: Quotation Marks

(Study 215–219, Quotation Marks)

Insert quotation marks at the proper places in each sentence.

Example: She wrote "Best Surfing Beaches" for *Outdoor* magazine.

1. Readers were mesmerized by the article Halle Berry: A True Survivor Story in *Good Housekeeping*.

2. The young couple read the *Better Homes and Gardens* article No Need to Cook.

3. W. C. Fields's dying words were, I'd rather be in Philadelphia.

4. The poem The Swing was written by Robert Louis Stevenson.

5. Be prepared, warned the weather forecaster, for a particularly harsh winter this year.

6. Childhood Memories is a chapter in the reader *Growing Up in the South*.

7. In Kingdom of the Skies, in the magazine *Arizona Highways*, Joyce Muench described the unusual cloud formations that enhance Arizona's scenery.

8. The word *cavalier* was originally defined as a man on a horse.

9. One of the most famous American essays is Emerson's Self-Reliance.

10. One of my favorite short stories is Eudora Welty's A Worn Path.

11. The song The Wind Beneath My Wings was sung to inspire mentors to stay with the literary program.

12. The World Is Too Much with Us is a poem by William Wordsworth.

13. The New Order is an article that appeared in *Time* magazine.

14. An article that appeared in the *Washington Post* is Can We Abolish Poverty?

15. Cousins' essay The Right to Die poses the question of whether suicide is ever an acceptable response to life circumstances.

16. The Love Song of J. Alfred Prufrock is a poem by T. S. Eliot.

17. The dictionary of slang defines *loopy* as slightly crazy.

18. The concluding song of the evening was Auld Lang Syne.

19. We read a poem by Alice Walker entitled Women.

20. Today's local newspaper ran an editorial titled Save the Salmon.

21. What we have here, the burly man said, is a failure to communicate.

22. Never in the field of human combat, said Winston Churchill, has so much been owed by so many to so few.

23. She read Julio Cortazar's short story The Health of the Sick.

24. *Discography* means a comprehensive list of recordings made by a particular performer or of a particular composer's work.

25. How rude of him to say, I don't care to see you!

56. PUNCTUATION: Quotation Marks

(Study 215–219, Quotation Marks)

Write **C** if the punctuation in brackets is **correct**.
Write **X** if it is **not**.

Example: "What time is it["?] wondered Katelyn.   _____X_____

1. The stadium announcer intoned[, "]Ladies and gentlemen, please rise for our national anthem."   1. _____

2. The television interviewer shoved a microphone in the mother's face and demanded, "How did you feel when you heard that your little girl had been kidnapped[?"]   2. _____

3. In the first semester, we read Gabriel García Márquez's short story "Big Mama's Funeral[".]   3. _____

4. "Where are you presently employed?[",] the interviewer asked.   4. _____

5. "When you finish your rough draft," said Professor Grill[, "]send it to my e-mail address."   5. _____

6. Who was it who mused, "Where are the snows of yesteryear[?"]   6. _____

7. Dr. Nelson, our anthropology teacher, asked, "How many of you have read *The Autobiography of Malcolm X*["?]   _____

8. "We need more study rooms in the library[,"] declared one presidential candidate in the student government debate.   8. _____

9. "Write when you can[,"] Mother said as I left for the airport.   9. _____

10. To *dissuade* means "to persuade someone not to do something[."]   10. _____

11. "Ask not what your country can do for you[;"] ask what you can do for your country."   11. _____

12. He said, "Our language creates problems when we talk about race in America.[" "]We don't have enough terms to explain the complexities of cultural diversity."   12. _____

13. "Do you remember Father's saying, 'Never give up['?"] she asked.   13. _____

14. She began reciting the opening line of one of Elizabeth Barrett Browning's sonnets: "How do I love thee? Let me count the ways[."]   14. _____

15. Gwendolyn Brooks's poem ["]The Bean Eaters["] is one of her best.   15. _____

16. ["]*The Fantasticks*,["] which ran for more than forty years, is the longest-running musical play in American theater.   16. _____

17. As her final words, Lady Nancy Astor said, "Am I dying or is this my birthday["?]   17. _____

18. "Shall I read aloud Whitman's poem 'Out of the Cradle Endlessly Rocking['?"] she asked.   18. _____

19. Have you read Adrienne Rich's poem "Necessities of Life[?"]   19. _____

20. When Susan saw the show about America's homeless, she exclaimed, "I have to find a way to help[!"]   20. _____

21. The noun *neurotic* is defined as "an emotionally unstable individual["．]   21. _____

22. "I'm going to the newsstand," he said[, "]for a copy of *Sports Illustrated*."   22. _____

23. "Do you believe in fairies[?"] Peter Pan asks the children.   23. _____

24. How maddening of her to reply calmly, "You're so right["!]   24. _____

25. "I need you in my office right away," the comptroller barked over the phone[. "]The FBI has subpoenaed our books."   25. _____

26. The city's Department of Investigation used hotel rooms specially ["]salted["] with money and jewelry to bait their traps for the criminals.   26. _____

27. "The Lottery[,"] a short story by Shirley Jackson, was discussed in Janet's English class.   27. _____

28. The reporter said[, "]Thank you for the lead on the story," and ran off to track down the source.   28. _____

29. "Was the treaty signed in 1815[?"] the professor asked, "or in 1814?"   29. _____

30. The mayor said, "I guarantee that urban renewal will move forward rapidly[;"] however, I don't believe him.   30. _____

31. The book reviewer stated, "The essays collected in this volume explore encounters with the mysterious and the foreign["].   31. _____

32. "Have you seen the rough draft of the article?" asked Jackie[?]   32. _____

33. "You blockhead," screamed Lucy[!]   33. _____

57. PUNCTUATION: Italics and Quotation Marks

(Study 214, Italics, and 215–219, Quotation Marks)

Write the number of the **correct** choice.

_____

Example: A revival of Lerner and Lowe's show (1)*My Fair Lady* (2)"My Fair Lady" is playing
at Proctor's Theater. ___1___

1. The Broadway hit play (1)*Rent* (2)"Rent" is based on a Puccini opera. 1. _____

2. That opera was (1)*La Boheme* (2)"La Boheme." 2. _____

3. Keats's poem (1)"Ode on a Grecian Urn" (2) *Ode on a Grecian Urn* is required reading. 3. _____

4. Paul Kennedy's book (1)*The Rise and Fall of the Great Powers* (2)"The Rise and Fall of the
Great Powers" discusses how nations become politically and militarily dominant. 4. _____

5. I just remembered the title of that article in *Prevention* magazine. It is (1)*The New Science of
Eating to Get Smart* (2)"The New Science of Eating to Get Smart." 5. _____

6. The closing song of the concert was (1)"R-e-s-p-e-c-t" (2)*R-e-s-p-e-c-t.* 6. _____

7. (1)*A Haunted House* (2)"A Haunted House" is a short story by Virginia Woolf. 7. _____

8. The brevity of Carl Sandburg's poem (1)*Fog* (2)"Fog" appealed to her. 8. _____

9. Jack received (1)*A*'s (2) "A's" in three of his classes this fall. 9. _____

10. She used too many (1)*and*s (2)"ands" in her introductory speech. 10. _____

11. (1)*Science and Religion* (2)"Science and Religion" is an essay by Albert Einstein. 11. _____

12. He has purchased tickets for the opera (1)"Faust" (2)*Faust.* 12. _____

13. Sharon didn't use a spell-check program and, therefore, unfortunately misspelled (1)*psychology*
(2)"psychology" throughout her paper. 13. _____

14. Dr. Baylor spent two classes on Wallace Stevens's poem (1)"The Idea of Order at Key West"
(2)*The Idea of Order at Key West.* 14. _____

15. His favorite newspaper has always been the (1)*Times* (2)"Times." 15. _____

16. (1)"Our Town" (2)*Our Town* is a play by Thornton Wilder. 16. _____

17. The word *altogether* means (1)"wholly" or "thoroughly." (2)*wholly* or *thoroughly.* 17. _____

18. (1)*What Women Want* (2)"What Women Want" is an essay by Margaret Mead. 18. _____

19. James Thurber's short story (1)*The Secret Life of Walter Mitty* (2)"The Secret Life of Walter
Mitty" amused her. 19. _____

20. The Players' Guild will produce Marlowe's (1)*Dr. Faustus* (2)"Dr. Faustus" next month. 20. _____

21. Who do you think will ever publish your article (1)*The Joy of Fried Earthworms* (2)"The Joy
of Fried Earthworms"? 21. _____

22. (1)*Biology: Science of Life* (2)"Biology: Science of Life" is our very expensive textbook for
biochemistry class. 22. _____

23. One of the first assignments for our African American history classes was to read James
Baldwin's book (1)*Notes of a Native Son* (2)"Notes of a Native Son." 23. _____

24. Our film class saw Truffaut's (1)*Shoot the Piano Player* (2)"Shoot the Piano Player" last week. 24. _____

25. She read (1)*Dover Beach,* (2)"Dover Beach," a poem by Matthew Arnold. 25. _____

26. (1)*Pygmalion* (2)"Pygmalion" is a play by George Bernard Shaw. 26. _____

27. You fail to distinguish between the words (1)*range* and *vary.* (2)"range" and "vary." 27. _____

28. I read a poem by Yeats titled (1)"The Cat and the Moon." (2)*The Cat and the Moon.* 28. _____

29. Madeline decided to treat herself by ordering a subscription to (1)*Vogue* (2)"Vogue." 29. _____

30. (1)*Fragmented* (2)"Fragmented" is a play by my colleague Prester Pickett. 30. _____

31. I used (1)"Do Lie Detectors Lie?" (2)*Do Lie Detectors Lie?* from *Science* magazine to write my report on famous murder trials. 31. _____

32. Through Kevin Coyne's book (1)"A Day in the Night of America," (2)*A Day in the Night of America*, readers have a chance to see how 7.3 million Americans spend their time working a night shift. 32. _____

33. The last section of the textbook is titled (1)*Paragraphs and Papers.* (2)"Paragraphs and Papers." 33. _____

58. PUNCTUATION: Colon, Dash, Parentheses, and Brackets

(Study 220–221, The Colon; 222, The Dash; 223–224, Parentheses; and 225, Brackets)

Part 1

Write **C** if the colon is used **correctly**.
Write **X** if it is used **incorrectly**.

Example: This bus runs via: Swan Street, Central Avenue, and North Main.   <u>   X   </u>

1. The President of the International Olympic Committee stepped to the podium and declared:
   "Let the games begin."   1. _____

2. The coach signaled the strategy: we would try a double steal on the next pitch.   2. _____

3. Dear Sir:
   My five years' experience as a high school English teacher qualifies me to be the editor of
   your newsletter.   3. _____

4. Dearest Rodney:
   My heart yearns for you so greatly that I can hardly bear the days until we're in each
   other's arms again.   4. _____

5. The following soldiers will fall out for guard duty: Pierce, Romano, Foster, and Sanchez. 5. _____

6. The carpenter's tools included: saw, hammer, square, measuring tape, and nails.   6. _____

7. College students generally complain about things such as: their professors, the cafeteria food,
   and their roommates.   7. _____

8. She began her letter to Tom with these words: "I'll love you forever!"   8. _____

9. Her train reservations were for Tuesday at 3:30 p.m.   9. _____

10. The dean demanded that: the coaches, the players, and the training staff meet with him
    immediately.   10. _____

11. Tonight's winning numbers are: 169, 534, and 086.   11. _____

12. She was warned that the project would require two qualities: creativity and perseverance. 12. _____

13. The project has been delayed: the chairperson has been hospitalized for emergency
    surgery.   13. _____

14. If Smith's book is titled *The World Below the Window: Poems 1937–1997*, must I include
    both the title and subtitle in my Works Cited list?   14. _____

15. I packed my backpack with: bubble bath, a pair of novels, and some comfortable clothes.   15. _____

Set off the boldfaced words by inserting the correct punctuation: **dash(es)**, **parentheses**, or **brackets**.

Example: Senator Aikin (**Dem., Maine**) voted for the proposal.

1. In my research paper, I quoted Wilson as observing, "His **Fitzgerald's** last years became a remarkable mix of creative growth and physical decline." [Punctuate to show that the boldfaced expression is inserted editorially by the writer of the research paper.]

2. Holmes had deduced **who knew how?** that the man had been born on a moving train during the rainy season. [Punctuate to indicate a sharp interruption.]

3. He will be considered for **this is between you and me, of course** one of the three vice-presidencies in the firm. [Punctuate to indicate merely incidental comment.]

4. I simply told her **and I'm glad I did!** that I would never set foot in her house again. [Punctuate to indicate merely incidental comment.]

5. Campbell's work on *Juvenal* **see reference** is an excellent place to start.

6. At Yosemite National Park we watched the feeding of the bears **from a safe distance, you can be sure**. [Punctuate to achieve a dramatic effect.]

7. Her essay was entitled "The American Medical System and It's **sic** Problems."

8. The rules for using parentheses **see page 7** are not easy to understand.

9. We traveled on foot, in horse-drawn wagons, and occasionally **if we had some spare cash to offer, if the farmers felt sorry for us, or if we could render some service in exchange** atop a motorized tractor. [Punctuate to indicate that this is *not* merely incidental comment.]

10. The statement read: "Enclosed you will find one hundred dollars **$100** to cover damages."

11. David liked one kind of dessert **apple pie.**

12. **Eat, drink, and be merry** gosh, I can hardly wait for senior week.

13. The essay begins: "For more than a hundred years **from 1337 until 1453** the British and French fought a pointless war." [Punctuate to show that the boldfaced expression is inserted editorially.]

14. The concert begins at **by the way, when does the concert begin**?

15. Getting to work at eight o'clock every morning **I don't have to remind you how much I dislike getting up early** seemed almost more than I cared to undertake. [Punctuate to indicate merely incidental comment.]

16. She said, "Two of my friends **one has really serious emotional problems** need psychiatric help." [Punctuate to achieve a dramatic effect.]

17. Within the last year, I have received three **or was it four?** letters from her. [Punctuate to indicate merely incidental comment.]

18. Julius was born in 1900 **?** and came west as a young boy.

59. PUNCTUATION: The Hyphen and the Slash

(Study 226, The Hyphen, and 227, The Slash)

Write **C** if the use or omission of a hyphen or slash is **correct**.
Write **X** if it is **incorrect**.

Example: Seventy six trombones led the big parade.	___X___
1. Emily Dickinson wrote, "Because I could not stop for **Death, / He** kindly stopped for me."	1._____
2. "I've **n-n-never** been so **c-c-cold**," stammered Neil, stumbling to shore after the white-water raft overturned.	2._____
3. He's a true **show-must-go-on** kind of actor.	3._____
4. One refers to the monarch of Britain as "**His/Her** Majesty."	4._____
5. The speaker was **well known** to everyone connected with administration.	5._____
6. The **well-known** author was autographing his latest novel in the bookstore today.	6._____
7. The team averaged over **fifty-thousand** spectators a game.	7._____
8. The contractor expects to build many **five-** and **six-room** houses this year.	8._____
9. The senator composed a **carefully-worded** statement for a press conference.	9._____
10. I sent in my subscription to a new **bi-monthly** magazine.	10._____
11. Sam's **brother-in-law** delighted in teasing his sister by belching at family dinners.	11._____
12. We'll have a chance to see two top teams in action at tonight's **Spurs/Pistons** game.	12._____
13. He made every effort to **recover** the missing gems.	13._____
14. After the children spilled blueberry syrup on her white sofa, Letitia had to **recover** it.	14._____
15. At **eighty-four**, Hartley still rides his motorcycle in the mountains on sunny days.	15._____
16. Charles will run in the **hundred yard** dash next Saturday.	16._____
17. "The children are not to have any more **c-a-n-d-y**," said Mother.	17._____
18. After he graduated from college, he became a manager of the **student-owned** bookstore.	18._____
19. The idea of a **thirty hour** week appealed to the workers.	19._____
20. Baird played **semi-professional** baseball before going into the major leagues.	20._____
21. Customers began avoiding the **hot-tempered** clerk in the shoe department.	21._____
22. Al's main problem is that he lacks **self-confidence**.	22._____
23. The **brand-new** vacuum cleaner made a loud squealing noise every time we turned it on.	23._____
24. The word-processing software was **brand new**.	24._____
25. Mr. Pollard's major research interest was **seventeenth-century** French history.	25._____

60. PUNCTUATION: Review

(Study 201–227, Punctuation)

Write **T** for each statement that is **true**.
Write **F** for each that is **false**.

Example: A period is used at the end of a declarative sentence.   ____T____

1. **Three spaced periods** are used to indicate an omission (ellipsis) in quoted material.   1. _____

2. **Possessive personal pronouns** contain an apostrophe.   2. _____

3. The **question mark** is always placed inside closing quotation marks.   3. _____

4. The sentence "Dellene searched for her friend, Mitch," means that Dellene has only one friend.   4. _____

5. A **dash** is used before the author's name on the line below a direct quotation.   5. _____

6. **Parentheses** are used to enclose editorial remarks in a direct quotation.   6. _____

7. An **essential (restrictive) clause** is not set off within commas.   7. _____

8. A **semicolon** is used to set off an absolute phrase from the rest of the sentence.   8. _____

9. The use of **brackets** around the word *sic* indicates an error occurring in quoted material.   9. _____

10. Mild interjections should be followed by an **exclamation point**; strong ones, by a **comma**.   10. _____

11. An indirect question is followed by a **period**.   11. _____

12. A **semicolon** is used after the expression *Dear Sir*.   12. _____

13. The title of a magazine article should be underlined to designate the use of **italics**.   13. _____

14. *Ms.* may take a **period** but *Miss* does not.   14. _____

15. **Single quotation marks** are used around a quotation that is within another quotation.   15. _____

16. Both *Mr. Jones'* and *Mr. Jones's* are acceptable **possessive forms** of *Mr. Jones*.   16. _____

17. The title at the head of a composition should be enclosed in **double quotation marks**.   17. _____

18. **No apostrophe** is needed in the following greeting: "Merry Christmas from the Palmers."   18. _____

19. The **possessive** of *somebody else* is *somebody's else*.   19. _____

20. The **possessive** of *mother-in-law* is *mother's-in-law*.   20. _____

21. A **semicolon** is normally used between two independent clauses joined by *and* if one or both clauses contain internal commas.   21. _____

22. A quotation consisting of several sentences takes **double quotation marks** at the beginning of the first sentence and at the end of the last sentence.   22. _____

23. A quotation consisting of several paragraphs takes **double quotation marks** at the beginning and end of each paragraph.   23. _____

24. Generally, a **foreign word** is not italicized if it can be found in a reputable American dictionary.   24. _____

25. The word *the* is **italicized** in the name of a newspaper or a magazine.   25. _____

26. A polite request in the form of a question is followed by a **period**.   26. _____

27. **Single quotation marks** may be substituted for double quotation marks around any quoted passage.   27. _____

28. The **comma** is always placed outside quotation marks.   28. _____

29. The **colon** and **semicolon** are always placed outside quotation marks.   29. _____

30. A **comma** is always used to separate the two parts of a compound predicate.   30. _____

31. The expression *such as* is normally followed by a **comma**.   31. _____

32. The **nonsentence** is a legitimate unit of expression and may be followed by a **period**.   32. _____

33. An **exclamation point** and a **question mark** are never used together.   33. _____

34. **Parentheses** are used around words that are to be deleted from a manuscript.   34. _____

35. A **comma** is used between two independent clauses not joined by a coordinating conjunction.   35. _____

36. A **semicolon** is used after the salutation of a friendly letter.   36. _____

37. The subject of a sentence should be separated from the predicate by a **comma**.   37. _____

38. An overuse of **underlining** (italics) for emphasis should be avoided.   38. _____

39. The **contraction** of the words *have not* is written thus: *hav'ent*.   39. _____

40. Nonessential (nonrestrictive) clauses are always set off with **commas**.   40. _____

41. **Double quotation marks** are used around the name of a ship.   41. _____

42. A **comma** is used before the word *then* when it introduces a second independent clause.   42. _____

43. The prefix *semi* always requires a **hyphen**.   43. _____

44. **No comma** is required in the following sentence: "Where do you wish to go?" he asked.   44. _____

45. A **dash** is a legitimate substitute for all other marks of punctuation.   45. _____

46. A **slash** is used to separate two lines of poetry quoted in a running text.   46. _____

47. A **dash** is placed between words used as alternatives.   47. _____

48. Every introductory prepositional phrase is set off by a **comma**.   48. _____

49. An introductory adverbial clause is usually set off with a **comma**.   49. _____

50. A **colon** may be used instead of a **semicolon** between two independent clauses when the second clause is an explanation of the first.   50. _____

61. PUNCTUATION: Review

(Study 201–227, Punctuation)

Part 1

Write **C** if the punctuation in brackets is **correct**.
Write **X** if it is **incorrect**.

Example: The last question on the test [,] counted 30 points.   _____X_____

1. Abner Fenwick found, to his chagrin, that Physics 101 was quite difficult[;] but, because he put in maximum effort, he earned a *B*.   1. _____

2. Pritchett left the casino in despair[,] his last hundred dollars lost on a wrong call in blackjack.   2. _____

3. I wondered why we couldn't get rid of the computer virus[?]   3. _____

4. Dear Dr. Stanley[;] Thank you for your letter of May 10.   4. _____

5. Rafael enjoyed inviting his friends[,] and preparing elaborate meals for them; however, most of his attempts were disasters.   5. _____

6. When the benefits officer described the new medical insurance package, everyone asked, "How much will this new policy cost us["?]   6. _____

7. I remembered the job counselor's remark: "If you send out three hundred inquiry letters in your hometown without even one response, relocate[."]   7. _____

8. "Despite the recession," explained the placement counselor[,] "health care, construction, and teaching still promise an increase in employment opportunities."   8. _____

9. A novella by Conrad, a short story by Lawrence, and some poems of Yeats[,] were all assigned for the last week of the semester.   9. _____

10. Despite the population loss in many Great Plains towns, Fargo, North Dakota[,] is thriving.   10. _____

11. Why is it that other children seem to behave better than our[']s?   11. _____

12. The relief workers specifically requested food, blankets, and children['s] clothing.   12. _____

13. Approximately seven million Americans visit their doctor each year[;] seeking an answer for why they feel so tired.   13. _____

14. Whenever he speaks, he's inclined to use too many *and-uh*[']s between sentences.   14. _____

15. The auditor requested to review[:] the medical receipts, our child-care expenses, and any deductions for home improvement.   15. _____

16. The last employee to leave the office is responsible for the following[,] turning off the machines, extinguishing all lights, and locking all executives' office doors.   16. _____

17. Everywhere there were crowds shouting anti[-]American slogans.   17. _____

18. Private colleges and universities are concerned about dwindling enrollment[;] because their tuition costs continue to climb while requests for substantial financial aid are also increasing.   18. _____

19. During the whole wretched ordeal of his doctoral exams[;] Charles remained outwardly calm.   19. _____

20. More than twenty minutes were cut from the original version of the film[,] the producers told neither the director nor the writer.   20. _____

21. The mock-epic poem "Casey at the Bat" was first published June 3, 1888[,] in the *Examiner*.   21. _____

22. We were married on June 5, 2003[,] in Lubbock, Texas.

23. The temperature sinking fast as dusk approached[;] we decided to seek shelter for the night.

24. By the year 2000, only about half of Americans entering the workforce were native born and of European stock[;] thus this country is truly becoming a multiracial society.

25. My only cousin[,] who is in the U.S. Air Force[,] is stationed in the Arctic.

26. Any U.S. Air Force officer[,] who is stationed in the Arctic[,] receives extra pay.

27. Hey! Did you find a biology book in this classroom[?!]

28. Charles Goodyear, the man who gave the world vulcanized rubber, personified the qualities of the classic American inventor[:] he spent nine years experimenting to find a waterproof rubber that would be resistant to extreme temperatures.

29. To reach the Museum of Natural History you take the D train to Columbus Circle[;] then you transfer to the C train.

30. The first well-known grocery store group was[,] the Atlantic and Pacific Tea Company, founded in 1859.

31. Fernando jumped and squealed with delight[,] because he found a new pair of roller blades under his bed as a present from his family's Three Kings celebration.

32. The movies[,] that I prefer to see[,] always have happy endings.

33. At the powwow, Anna and her friends entered the Fancy Shawl Dance competition[;] for they wanted to dance in their new dresses and moccasins.

In the following paragraphs, **insert** the correct punctuation mark(s) in each set of brackets. If no punctuation

22. _____

23. _____

24. _____

25. _____

26. _____

27. _____

28. _____

29. _____

30. _____

31. _____

32. _____

33. _____

Part 2

is needed, leave the brackets empty.

Example: Shawaun said[, "]Do it yourself[,"] and stormed out.

1. The published writings of F. Scott Fitzgerald[ ] range from youthful short stories[ ] such as [ ]Bernice Bobs Her Hair[ ] to novels of well[ ]to[ ]do Long Islanders[ ] American expatriates[ ] and Hollywood movie moguls. His most famous novel[ ] [The Great Gatsby][ ] set on Long Island[ ] depicts the rise and fall[ ] of a [nouveau-riche] young man[ ] who was born James Gatz[ ] in the Midwest. Gatsby[ ]s failed attempt to recapture his past has captivated Americans[ ]it also became a play and a film[ ].

2. Kidnapped in Africa[ ] brought to America, and sold to a white man in 1761[ ] Phillis Wheatley (1753–1784) is among the earliest African American poets. Despite her humble childhood and youth[ ] she learned Greek and Latin and wrote poems. In 1773 a collection of her poems was published[ ] which caused great concern among many of her owner's educated friends[ ] who did not believe that Wheatley wrote the poetry attributed to her. [ ]How[ ][ ] they asked[ ] could a slave write such beautiful lines[ ] [ ] Recent scholarship[ ] however[ ] has shown that Wheatley did[ ] indeed[ ] write the poetry. Although Wheatley eventually[ ] received her freedom[ ] her life did not end well. In 1778 she married a free black man[ ] who later abandoned her. To support herself and her three children[ ] she worked as a scullery maid in a boardinghouse. Although she died unknown and in complete poverty[ ] later generations would recognize and value the work of Phillis Wheatley[ ] the first major black American poet.

62. MECHANICS: Capitals

(Study 301–303, Capitalization)

Write **C** if the boldfaced word(s) are **correct** in use or omission of capital letters.
Write **X** if the word(s) are **incorrect**.

Example: Cajuns speak a dialect of **french**. ___X___

1. Hundreds attended the **greek orthodox** prayer vigil. 1.____
2. June's mother attended an expensive **College** in 1944. 2.____
3. The bed linens we splurged on were made of **egyptian** cotton. 3.____
4. Matthew married **a Norwegian** woman. 4.____
5. When will **Congress** convene? 5.____
6. He is now a **Freshman** at the University of Maryland. 6.____
7. Thea and Gus went to Dallas to visit his **Mother**. 7.____
8. Gilbert played **Basketball** well in high school. 8.____
9. Joe constantly reads about the **Civil War.** 9.____
10. A **civil war** in Bangladesh lasted five years. 10.____
11. Two **Professors** were chosen to serve on the committee. 11.____
12. "Did you save your essay on the flash stick?" **she** asked. 12.____
13. Every **Winter** I go to Vermont to ski. 13.____
14. The deaths were reported in the *Times*. 14.____
15. I worked in the **Southwest**. 15.____
16. Her **Mother** returned from Miami this morning. 16.____
17. He was late for today's **Grammar** class. 17.____
18. La Keisha was elected **president** of her class 18.____
19. Tina Woods was promoted to **Major**. 19.____
20. The bookstore has a special sale on Hewlett-Packard **Computers**. 20.____
21. I enrolled in **english** and physics. 21.____

22. Marcia signed the letter "**very truly yours**." 22.____
23. He ended the note with "Yours **Truly**." 23.____
24. We once lived in the **Northwest**. 24.____
25. Sally excels in **Biology** but is confused by her course in German. 25.____
26. Shirley plans to become a **Medical Researcher** after graduation. 26.____
27. Is **jupiter** the planet with the moons? 27.____
28. I asked **Mother** for some advice on stuffing a turkey. 28.____
29. He goes to **Roosevelt High School**. 29.____
30. How will the **senate** in Washington react to President Obama? 30.____
31. The year that actually began the **Twenty-First Century** was 2001, not 2000. 31.____
32. I listen to **wmar** every morning. 32.____
33. We are planning a picnic for Memorial **day**. 33.____
34. I spent Thanksgiving with my **Uncle**. 34.____
35. Her favorite subject is **latin**. 35.____
36. The tourists visited **Niagara Falls**. 36.____
37. Did you know that the **everglades** has an alligator farm? 37.____
38. He enrolled in **Physics 215**. 38.____
39. Is that **synagogue** named Beth Tfiloh**?** 39.____
40. I am writing a book; **My** editor wants the first chapter soon. 40.____
41. Maryland was one of the first **catholic** states. 41.____
42. Maryland was one of the key destinations of tens of thousands of **British** convicts. 42.____
43. I think **mother nature** was particularly cruel this winter 43.____

44. The **Championship Fight** was a disappointment.   44.____

45. It is a **Jewish** custom for men to wear skullcaps, called yarmulkes, during worship.   45.____

46. I made an appointment with my **biology** professor.   46.____

47. The chairperson of the **Department of History** is Dr. McDonald.   47.____

48. He said simply, "**my** name is Bond."   48.____

49. "**Sexual Harassment: The Price of Silence**" is a chapter from my composition reader.   49.____

50. Kenny spent his **Thanksgiving** break in Puerto Rico on a vacation with his family.   50.____

63. MECHANICS: Capitals

(Study 301–303, Capitalization)

In the first blank write the number of the **first** correct choice (**1** or **2**).
In the second blank write the number of the **second** correct choice (**3** or **4**).

Example: Wandering (1)**West** (2)**west**, Max met (3)**Milly** (4)**milly**.   <u>2</u>   <u>3</u>

1. Investors lost millions in accounting scandals at the Megabux (1)**Company** (2)**company**, which produces Zoomfast (3)**Cars** (4)**cars**.   1. ____ ____

2. Her (1)**Father** (2)**father** went (3)**North** (4)**north** on business.   2. ____ ____

3. The new (1)**College** (2)**college** is seeking a (3)**Dean** (4)**dean**.   3. ____ ____

4. Children are taught to begin letters with "My (1)**Dear** (2)**dear** (3)**Sir** (4)**sir**."   4. ____ ____

5. Business letters often end with "Very (1)**Truly** (2)**truly** (3)**Yours** (4)**yours**."   5. ____ ____

6. After (1)**Church** (2)**church**, we walked across the Brooklyn (3)**Bridge** (4)**bridge**.   6. ____ ____

7. The (1)**Politician** (2)**politician** declared that the protester was (3)**Un-American** (4)**un-American**.   7. ____ ____

8. The young (1)**Lieutenant** (2)**lieutenant** prayed to the (3)**Lord** (4)**lord** for courage in the battle.   8. ____ ____

9. My (1)**Cousin** (2)**cousin** now lives (3)**East** (4)**east** of the city.   9. ____ ____

10. The (1)**President** (2)**president** addresses (3)**Congress** (4)**congress** tomorrow.   10. ____ ____

11. Cathy Peterson, (1)**M.D.**, (2)**m.d.**, once taught (3)**Chemistry** (4)**chemistry**.   11. ____ ____

12. Dr. McCampbell, (1)**Professor** (2)**professor** of (3)**English** (4)**english**, is writing a musical set in the last century.   12. ____ ____

13. The (1)**Comet** (2)**comet** can be seen just below (3)**The Big Dipper** (4)**the Big Dipper**.   13. ____ ____

14. "I'm also a graduate of North Harris (1)**College** (2)**college**," (3)**She** (4)**she** added.   14. ____ ____

15. The (1)**Rabbi** (2)**rabbi** of (3)**Temple** (4)**temple** Beth Emeth is a leader in interfaith cooperation.   15. ____ ____

16. Janelle disagreed with the review of "(1)**The** (2)**the** War Chronicles" in (3)*The* (4)**the** New York *Times*.   16. ____ ____

17. The club (1)**Treasurer** (2)**treasurer** said that the financial report was "(3)**Almost** (4)**almost** complete."   17. ____ ____

18. The (1)**Girl Scout** (2)**girl scout** leader pointed out the (3)**Milky Way** (4)**milky way** to her troop.   18. ____ ____

19. Students use the textbook *Writing (1)For (2)for Audience (3)And (4)and Purpose*.   19. ____ ____

20. Educational Support Services is in (1)**Room** (2)**room** 110 of Yost (3)**Hall** (4)**hall**.   20. ____ ____

21. At the (1)**Battle** (2)**battle** of Gettysburg, Confederate troops actually approached from (3)**North** (4)**north** of the town.   21. ____ ____

22. I think it's never (1)**O.K.** (2)**o.k.** to ignore a summons from the (3)**Police** (4)**police**.   22. ____ ____

23. The correspondent described the (1)**Pope** (2)**pope** as looking "(3)**Frail** (4)**frail** and unsteady."   23. ____ ____

24. "Maria, look up at the (1)**Moon** (2)**moon**," Guido said softly, "(3)**And** (4)**and** drink in its beauty."   24. ____ ____

25. "Maria, look up at (1)**Venus** (2)**venus**," Guido said softly. "(3)**Drink** (4)**drink** in its beauty."   25. ____ ____

64. MECHANICS: Numbers and Abbreviations

(Study 305–307, Numbers, and 308–309, Abbreviations)

Write the number of the **correct** choice.

_____

Example: The book was (1)**3** (2)**three** days overdue.   _____2_____

1. (1)**135** (2)**One hundred thirty-five** votes was the official margin of victory.   1._____

2. The odometer showed that the apartment was (1)**5½** (2)**five and one-half** miles from the campus. 2._____

3. (1)**Prof.** (2)**Professor** Hilton teaches Asian philosophy.   3._____

4. The Johnson family went to (1)**Ala.** (2)**Alabama** over Thanksgiving.   4._____

5. Builders are still reluctant to have a (1)**thirteenth** (2)**13th** floor in any new buildings.   5._____

6. The exam will be held at noon on (1)**Fri.** (2)**Friday**.   6._____

7. The (1)**P.O.** (2)**post office** on campus always has a long line of international students mailing letters and packages to their friends and families.   7._____

8. Judd has an interview with the Sherwin Williams (1)**Co.** (2)**Company**.   8._____

9. Nicole will study in Germany, (1)**Eng.** (2)**England**, and Sweden next year.   9._____

10. Daniel Levy, (1)**M.D.**, (2)**medical doctor,** is my physician.   10._____

11. Frank jumped 22 feet, (1)**3** (2)**three** inches at the Saturday meet.   11._____

12. For the laboratory, the department purchased permanent markers, legal pads, pencils, (1)**etc.** (2) **and other office supplies**.   12._____

13. For (1)**Xmas** (2)**Christmas**, the Swansons planned a family trip to Disneyland rather than their usual ski holiday.   13._____

14. Travis needed to leave for work at exactly 8:00 (1)**a.m.** (2)**o'clock**.   14._____

15. For her travel expenses, Professor Joseph received (1)**$2,145** (2)**two thousand one hundred forty-five dollars**.   15._____

16. Lenore will graduate from dental school June (1)**2**, (2)**2nd**, 2011.   16._____

17. Did Mary MacDonald move to Vermont last (1)**Feb.** (2)**February**?   17._____

18. Over (1)**800** (2)**eight hundred** students attend Woodlawn High School.   18._____

19. Brenda enjoyed all of her (1)**phys. ed.** (2)**physical education** courses.   19._____

20. Next year, the convention will be held on March (1)**19**, (2)**19th**, (3)**nineteenth**, in Baltimore.   20._____

21. The session included an inspiring lecture by (1)**Dr.** (2)**Doctor** Bauer.   21._____

22. The lottery prize has reached an astonishing (1)**twenty-four million dollars** (2)**$24 million**.   22._____

23. The family next door adopted a (1)**two-month-old** (2)**2-month-old** baby girl from China.   23._____

24. We had an opportunity to meet (1)**Sen.** (2)**Senator** Lester at the convention.   24._____

25. The chart on verb tenses is on (1)**pg.** (2)**page** 44.   25._____

26. Arlene Riley will do her student teaching in (1)**TN.** (2)**Tennessee** this spring.   26._____

27. When we offered tickets to a baseball game for our raffle, we had (1)**one-third** (2)**1/3rd** of the employees purchase tickets.   27. _____

28. Jack's dissertation was (1)**two hundred fifty** (2)**250** pages.   28. _____

29. The plane expected from (1)**LA early this a.m.** (2)**Los Angeles early this morning** is late. 29. _____

30. The bus arrives at 10:45 a.m. and leaves at (1)**11:00** (2)**eleven** a.m.   30. _____

31. The Elks Club raised $265, The Moose $126, and the Beavers Lodge (1)**ninety dollars** (2)**$90**. 31. _____

32. Rachel's name was (1)**twenty-sixth** (2)**26th** on the list of high-school graduates.   32. _____

33. Lieutenant Marshall requested a (1)**3-day** (2)**three-day** pass to visit his sick mother.   33. _____

65. MECHANICS: Capitals, Numbers, and Abbreviations

(Study 301–303, Capitalization; 305–307, Numbers; and 308–309, Abbreviations)

In the first blank write the number of the **first** correct choice (**1** or **2**).
In the second blank write the number of the **second** correct choice (**3** or **4**).

Example: I have only (1)**three and one-half** (2)**3½** years until (3)**Graduation** (4)**graduation**.   <u> 2 </u>   <u> 4 </u>

1. After much discussion, the (1)**Arab** (2)**arab** leaders signed the Global Warming (3)**Pact** (4)**pact.** 1. ____ ____

2. Many of those who died when (1)*The Titanic* (2)the *Titanic* went down are buried in a (3)**Cemetery** (4)**cemetery** in Halifax, Nova Scotia. 2. ____ ____

3. My (1)**Supervisor** (2)**supervisor** said our presentation was (3)**"Insightful!"** (4)**"insightful."** 3. ____ ____

4. "I expect," he said, (1)**"To** (2)**"to** get an *A* in my (3)**Chem.** (4)**chemistry** class." 4. ____ ____

5. On June (1)**6,** (2)**6th,** 2009, she spoke at her former (3)**high school** (4)**High School.** 5. ____ ____

6. The new college (1)**President** (2)**president** greeted the (3)**Alumni** (4)**alumni** during the graduation ceremonies. 6. ____ ____

7. An American flag from the World Trade (1)**Center** (2)**center** was flown at the (3) **memorial service** (4)**Memorial Service.** 7. ____ ____

8. The (1)**Community College** (2) **community college** (3)**North** (4)**north** of the city won an award for the greenest campus in the state. 8. ____ ____

9. (1)**308** (2)**Three hundred eight** students passed the test out of (3)**427** (4)**four hundred twenty-seven** who took it. 9. ____ ____

10. She likes her (1)**english** (2)**English** and (3)**science** (4)**Science** classes. 10. ____ ____

11. I soon realized that (1)**spring** (2)**Spring** means rain, rain, and more rain in northeastern (3)**Ohio** (4)**ohio.** 11. ____ ____

12. The (1)**Special Focus** (2)**special focus** of this week's *Newsweek* magazine is the (3)**election** (4)**Election.** 12. ____ ____

13. Maureen is taking a (1)**chinese** (2)**Chinese** course this semester instead of one in (3) **History** (4)**history.** 13. ____ ____

14. She was ecstatic; (1)**Her** (2)**her** boyfriend had just bought her a 2009 Toyota (3)**Pickup Truck** (4)**pickup truck.** 14. ____ ____

15. The new (1)**dentist** (2)**Dentist** has opened a small office on Elm (3)**Street** (4)**street.** 15. ____ ____

16. The (1)**korean** (2)**Korean** students have planned their (3)**3rd** (4)**third** annual International Dinner. 16. ____ ____

17. I spent (1)**New Year's Day** (2)**new year's day** with (3)**mother** (4)**Mother.** 17. ____ ____

18. Her (1)**Japanese** (2)**japanese** instructor is touring the American (3)**Midwest** (4)**midwest** over the summer. 18. ____ ____

19. This morning, Marta's (1)**Journalism** 2)**journalism** class had a research session at the (3)**Library** (4)**library.** 19. ____ ____

20. The (1)**class** (2)**Class** of '09 honored the (3)**Dean of Men** (4)**dean of men.** 20. ____ ____

21. When Leslie decided to major in (1)**social science** (2)**Social Science**, she knew she'd have to take (3)**Professor** (4)**Prof**. Pickard's dreaded statistics course. 21. ____ ____

22. For years, Georgia had dreamt of dancing in a (1)**Broadway** (2)**broadway** show; she would even be happy with only a small role in the back of the **(3)chorus line (4)Chorus Line**. 22. ____ ____

23. She knows (1)**four** (2)**4** graduates who are going to teach at (3)**Elementary Schools** (4)**elementary schools** this fall. 23. ____ ____

24. Although Josh thinks (1)**latin** (2)**Latin** is very difficult, Linda finds the (3)**course** (4)**Course** exciting and challenging. 24. ____ ____

25. In (1)**Chapter four** (2)**chapter 4**, (3)**Chief Inspector Morse** (4)**chief inspector Morse** discovers the magician's body. 25. ____ ____

66. SPELLING

(Study 310–314, Spelling)

Write the number of the **correctly spelled** word.

Example: A knowledge of (1)**grammar** (2)**grammer** is helpful.   _____1_____

1. A large (1)**quantity** (2)**quanity** of illegal drugs was seized by customs inspectors at the border.   1. _____

2. The company's lawyers said that it was (1)**alright** (2)**all right** to sign the contract.   2. _____

3. No one thought that a romance would (1)**develope** (2)**develop** between those two.   3. _____

4. Mrs. Smith will not (1)**acknowlege** (2)**acknowledge** whether she received the check.   4. _____

5. I love to (1)**surprise** (2)**suprize** the children with small presents.   5. _____

6. After three well-played quarters, the Steelers had a (1)**disasterous** (2)**disastrous** fourth quarter.   6. _____

7. The oldest fireman has worked for (1)**forty** (2)**forety** (3)**fourty** years.   7. _____

8. The salary will depend on how (1)**competant** (2)**competent** the employee is.   8. _____

9. I love listening to Grandpa's tales about his childhood because he always (1)**exagerates** (2)**exaggerates**.   9. _____

10. It's important to accept valid (1)**criticism** (2)**critcism** without taking the comments personally.   10. _____

11. It was (1)**ridiculous** (2)**rediculous** to expect Fudgley to arrive on time.   11. _____

12. (1)**Approximately** (2)**Approximatly** fifty families attended the adoption support group meeting.   12. _____

13. The murder was a (1)**tradegy** (2)**tragedy** (3)**tradgedy** felt by the entire community.   13. _____

14. The Statue of Liberty is a (1)**symbel** (2)**symbol** of the United States.   14. _____

15. Everyone could hear the (1)**argument** (2)**arguement** between the two young lovers.   15. _____

16. Tim asked several questions because he wasn't sure what the professor (1)**ment** (2)**meant** by a "term paper of reasonable length."   16. _____

17. The professor deducted points for Mary's (1)**ommission** (2)**omission** of her Works Cited section.   17. _____

18. Having a cell phone is (1)**necessary** (2)**neccessary** in today's busy world.   18. _____

19. Every time I visit Uncle Bob, he (1)**reminisces** (2)**reminices** about his youth.   19. _____

20. Going to the Writing Center an hour before the paper was due was a 1)**desperate** (2)**desparate** attempt by Tom to submit a good essay.   20. _____

21. Susan was excited about her (1)**nineth**- (2)**ninth**-grade graduation ceremony.   21. _____

22. The play's director told each student that (1)**repetition** (2)**repitition** was the key to memorizing a part in the production.   22. _____

23. How (1)**definite** (2)**defenite** is their decision to return to Texas?   23. _____

24. The salesperson said the (1)**guarantee** (2)**garantee** was good only if a paint primer was used first.   24. _____

25. Virginia used a (1)**permenent** (2)**permanent** marker to label all her sports gear.   25. _____

26. Cindy always buys a (1)**souvenir** (2)**suvinir** for her son when she travels to Florida.   26. _____

27. We were glad that the (1)**auxilary** (2)**auxiliary** lights came on during the severe thunderstorm.   27. _____

28. Jerry had (1)**fulfilled** (2)**fullfilled** the requirements for graduation.   28. _____

29. In our state, students in the (1)**twelf** (2)**twelfth** grade must pass a basic skills test.   29. _____

30. This year, our five-year-old son began to question the (1)**existance** (2)**existence** of the tooth fairy.   30. _____

31. When my great grandmother turned (1)**ninety** (2)**ninty**, her neighbors gave her a surprise party.   31. _____

32. (1)**Suppression** (2) **Suppresion** of religious activity often occurs when a government fears loss of control.   32. _____

33. Beverly (1)**use to** (2)**used to** run two miles five mornings a week.   33. _____

34. Unfortunately, I find chocolate—any chocolate—(1)**irresistable** (2)**irresistible**.   34. _____

35. All three of my children are heading towards (1)**adolescence** (2)**adolesence**.   35. _____

36. The (1)**phychologist** (2)**psychologist** arranged a group program for procrastinators.   36. _____

37. My mother's suggestion actually seemed quite (1)**sensible** (2)**sensable**.   37. _____

38. The (1)**Sophomore** (2)**Sophmore** Class voted to sponsor a dance next month.   38. _____

39. After the study session, Martin and his friends went to a restaurant that had a (1)**drive-thru** (2)**drive-through** window.   39. _____

40. The high school's star athlete was a (1)**conscientous** (2)**conscientious** student.   40. _____

41. The (1)**rythm** (2)**rhythm** of the song was perfect for our skating routine.   41. _____

42. My doctor (1)**recommended** (2)**reccommended** a daily aspirin.   42. _____

43. I don't have time for (1)**questionaires** (2)**questionnaires**.   43. _____

44. Robert's (1)**perseverance** (2)**perserverence** led to his ultimate success in the theater.   44. _____

45. Gerald's (1)**conscience** (2)**conchance** bothered him after he told a lie.   45. _____

46. Her services had become (1)**indispensible** (2)**indispensable** to the firm.   46. _____

47. Ridgely considered (1)**writing** (2)**writting** a letter to his state senator.   47. _____

48. Glen hopes to add (1)**playright** (2)**playwright** (3)**playwrite** to his list of professional credits.   48. _____

49. You will find no (1)**prejudice** (2)**predjudice** in our organization.   49. _____

50. Kenny is (1)**suppose to** (2)**supposed to** turn in his project report sometime today.   50. _____

67. SPELLING

(Study 310–314, Spelling)

If the word is spelled **incorrectly**, write the **correct spelling** in the blank.
If the word is spelled **correctly**, leave the blank empty.

Examples: hindrance _____
vaccum _____vacuum_____

1. unusualy	1._____	26. sincereley	26._____
2. oppinion	2._____	27. saftey	27._____
3. criticize	3._____	28. synonim	28._____
4. familar	4._____	29. catagory	29._____
5. proceedure	5._____	30. imaginery	30._____
6. thru	6._____	31. managment	31._____
7. pursue	7._____	32. amateur	32._____
8. accross	8._____	33. reguler	33._____
9. confident	9._____	34. hygiene	34._____
10. maneuver	10._____	35. cemetery	35._____
11. relieve	11._____	36. heros	36._____
12. absense	12._____	37. bookkeeper	37._____
13. sacrefice	13._____	38. monkeys	38._____
14. mischievious	14._____	39. persistant	39._____
15. prevalent	15._____	40. curiosity	40._____
16. parallel	16._____	41. stimulent	41._____
17. noticeable	17._____	42. villian	42._____
18. disasterous	18._____	43. knowledge	43._____
19. indepindent	19._____	44. optimism	44._____
20. bussiness	20._____	45. embarass	45._____
21. acquire	21._____	46. eighth	46._____
22. truly	22._____	47. maintenence	47._____
23. government	23._____	48. father-in-laws	48._____
24. appologize	24._____	49. happyness	49._____
25. controlling	25._____	50. crisises	50._____

68. SPELLING

(Study 310–314, Spelling)

Part 1

In the blank, write the **missing letter(s)** (if any) in the word.
If no letter is missing, leave the blank empty.

Examples: gramm_*a*_r
ath____lete

1. suppr____ssion
2. piano____s
3. kni____s [sharp instruments]
4. bus____ly
5. defin____te
6. permiss____ble
7. perm____nent
8. guid____nce
9. d____scription
10. fascinat____ing
11. gu____rantee
12. abs____nce
13. appar____nt
14. hindr____nce
15. crit____cism
16. benefit____ed
17. confer____ed
18. am____teur
19. argu____ment
20. me____nt

21. math____matics
22. pre____judice
23. par____llel
24. erron____ous
25. prev____lent
26. rest____urant
27. rep____tition
28. nec____ssary
29. sacr____fice
30. compet____nt
31. com____ing [arriving]
32. tru____ly
33. chimn____s
34. excell____nt
35. sch____dule
36. independ____nt
37. immediat____ly
38. consc____entious
39. op____ortunity
40. dis____atisfied

Part 2

In the blank, write the **missing letters** in each word: **ie** or **ei**.

Example: bel _ie_ ve

1. h____r
2. ach____ve
3. rec____ve
4. c____ling
5. w____rd

6. v____n
7. ch____f
8. l____sure
9. hyg____ne
10. w____gh

69. MECHANICS, WITH SPELLING: Review

(Study 301–314, Mechanics, with Spelling)

In each of the following paragraphs, correct all errors in **capitalization**, **number form**, **abbreviations**, **syllabication**, and **spelling**. (You may also find some errors covered in previous sections.) Cross out the incorrect form and write the correct form above it.

(Collaborative option: Students work in pairs or small groups to find and correct errors.)

1. In june of sixteen 06, king James I granted a charter to a group of London entrepreneurs, the Virginia company, to establish a permanant english settlement in the Chesapeake region of north America. By December, one hundred and four settlers sailed from London; they had been instructed to settle VA, find gold and seek a water route to the orient. Some scholars of early Jamestown history believe that those pioneers were ameteurs and not well prepared for the task. With about ½ of this group identified as "gentlemen" by capt. John Smith, historians researching these explorers found that they knew little about how to tame a wilderness. Recent archeological reserach at the site of Jamestown suggests that at least some of the gentlemen and certainly many of the laborers who accompanied Captain Smith were conschiensus. The men had no time for leesure and took every oportunity to overcome hindrences and help the Colony succeed.

2. Lewis Carroll, who's actual name was Charles Lutwidge Dodgson, wrote sevral books in the 19th century. Today, he is known for the childrens' classics *alice's Adventures in Wonderland* and *Thorough the Looking-Glass and What Alice found There.* In the first book, Alice, a young girl, grows and shrinks, animals talk, and characters speak nonsense. She gets into an arguement with a pipe-smoking caterpillar, and meets a truely strange bird, and a smiling cat. The Queen that Alice meets in his parelel world is actually a playing-card Queen of Hearts. Alice is definately fasinated. In *Through the Looking-Glass*, Alice steps through a looking-glass, or mirror, and into a strange World that resembles the chess game Alice had been playing. She meets live chess pieces, a garden of talking flowers, and odd insects—all garantees that she is in a strange place. She is interduced to Tweedledum, Tweedledee, and Humpty Dumpty, who offers her guidence. These 2 books were very popular in Eng. when they were published; today, people worldwide have read Carroll's novels, which are in the permenent colections of many libaries. Far less famous than Carroll's books for children are his books on Mathematics. They include his *Syllabus of Plane Algebraical Geometry* & his *Elementary Treatise*.

3. Turkey is a unique Country. Though partly in Europe, it is ninety seven % in Asia; thus it combines elements of European, middle eastern, and Asiatic cultures. Though the country's Capital is Ankara, its most-famous city is Istanbul, which was for 100s of yrs. called Constantinople and before that Byzantium. To the west of Turkey lies the Aegean sea; to the s.e. lie Iran, Iraq, & Syria. The vast majority of Turks are Muslim, but there are also small numbers of christians and Spanish-Speaking Jews. Modern Turkey came into being after the downfall of the Ottoman empire in world war I; it's present boundaries were established by the treaty of Lausanne in nineteen twenty-three. 17 years later the nation switched from the arabic to the roman Alphabet. In Government Turkey has a 2 house Legislature and a head of State.

70. WORD CHOICE: Conciseness, Clarity, and Originality

(Study 401, Conciseness, Clarity, and Originality)

Rewrite each sentence in the space below it, **replacing** or **eliminating** all redundant, overblown, vague, or clichéd expressions. You may use a dictionary, and you may invent specifics if necessary.

Examples: We find our general consensus of opinion to be that the governor should resign.
  Our consensus is that the governor should resign.

  She looked really nice.
  She wore jet-black jeans and a trim white blouse, and her broad smile would melt an iceberg.

(Collaborative option: Students work in pairs or small groups to examine sentences and suggest improvements.)

1. Medical Terminology 101, is a course that is designed to help the student understand and learn the medical terms, abbreviations, and different types of hospitals where you can receive care.

  _____

  _____

2. Speech has been John's most challenging academic subject because of the fantastic anxiety he feels when he is speaking in front of a group of people, who are his classmates, in the speech class.

  _____

  _____

3. Lady Macbeth returned back to the deadly fatal murder scene to leave the daggers beside the grooms.

  _____

  _____

4. In the Bible it says that we should not make a judgment about others as to whether they are good or bad.

  _____

  _____

5. Except for the fact that my grandmother is on Medicaid, she would not be able to afford living in her totally unique senior citizens' residential facility home.

  _____

  _____

6. The deplorable condition of business is due to the nature of the current conditions relevant to the economic situation.

  _____

  _____

7. The thing in question at this point in time is whether the first initial phase of the operation is proceeding with a sufficient degree of efficiency.

_____

_____

8. Jennifer waited for me after class so that she could walk with me to my domicile.

_____

_____

9. The carving knife instrument, which is silver in color and is stored in a box rectangular in shape, has been in our family's possession for several generations.

_____

_____

10. She couldn't hardly lose her way, due to the fact that the road was intensely and brightly illuminated by the street lamp that was on and shining.

_____

_____

11. On the basis of this report, it leads me to come to the final conclusion that the recruitment process at this office is in need of amelioration.

_____

_____

12. The next thing our speaker will speak about is the topic of the problem of the transportation situation.

_____

_____

13. The reason why mathematics is so awesomely challenging for me is because for many years for some time now I have been unable to grasp working with numbers and fractions, which has made that subject difficult for me.

_____

_____

14. In this day and age, things can happen out of a clear blue sky, quick as a wink, to upset one's apple cart.

_____

_____

15. The patient fell on his gluteus maximus when we IV'd him in pre-op.

   _____

   _____

16. We have reached the final conclusion that the men and women who fly our planes need further training in learning how to find their way from one location to another.

   _____

   _____

17. My Uncle Harry always makes future plans before the holidays so he can go shopping without telling the family that he's going shopping for them in secret because he doesn't want them to know.

   _____

   _____

18. It is a known true fact that people who have undergone the training process in emergency rescue procedures necessarily have to know how to take over in a crisis situation that is dangerous.

   _____

   _____

19. Janice and Tim, who thought their new puppy was as cute as a button, were surprised by the fact that he could eat like a horse.

   _____

   _____

20. We have lost our way, but however, we may connect up with our friends if we utilize our noggins to find the right road.

   _____

   _____

71. WORD CHOICE: Standard, Appropriate English

(Study 402, Standard, Appropriate English: Review 401.)

Part 1

Write the number of the **correct** choice (use standard, formal American English).

_____

Example: Lincoln had no doubt (1)**but that** (2)**that** the South would secede.   _____2_____

1. The driving instructor let the student driver take the car on the beltway (1)**irregardless** (2)**regardless** of the consequences.   1. _____

2. That year Einstein conceived his most (1)**revolutionary** (2)**terrific** theory, that of general relativity.   2. _____

3. (1)**Hopefully**, (2)**We hope that** the city will pass the law requiring animal shelters to provide fresh air for the dogs and cats there.   3. _____

4. Mark used (1)**these kind of tools** (2)**these kinds of tools** to repair the bicycle.   4. _____

5. We were disappointed (1)**somewhat** (2)**some** at the quality of the photo.   5. _____

6. The Nelsons heard about the predicted hurricane (1)**everywhere** (2)**everywheres** they traveled.   6. _____

7. Eileen and Bob (1)**got married** (2)**were married** on a beach at sunrise.   7. _____

8. Do (1)**try to** (2)**try and** visit Disney World when you are in Florida.   8. _____

9. The piano teacher was (1)**most** (2)**almost** at the end of her patience with her young students.   9. _____

10. Mark (1)**had ought** (2)**ought** to have let us know that he was a vegetarian.   10. _____

11. Will you be sure to (1)**contact** (2)**telephone** me tomorrow?   11. _____

12. He (1)**seldom ever** (2)**hardly ever** writes to his sister.   12. _____

13. The (1)**children** (2)**kids** in my class are interested in the field trip.   13. _____

14. My parents weren't (1)**enthused** (2)**enthusiastic** about the new French restaurant.   14. _____

15. The supervisor (1)**should of** (2)**should have** rewritten the memo.   15. _____

16. The van needed a new battery (1)**besides** (2)**plus** an oil change   16. _____

17. Sherry asked where the car was (1)**parked** (2)**parked at**.   17. _____

18. We might (1)**could** (2)**be able to** drive you to the station tomorrow.   18. _____

19. By the time we arrived at the picnic, everyone had (1)**hightailed** (2)**gone** home.   19. _____

20. Mr. Robertson's diet was very (1)**real** (2)**truly**.   20. _____

Write **C** if the boldfaced expression is **correct**.
Write **X** if it is **incorrect**.

___

Example: Lincoln had no doubt **but that** the
South would secede.   X___

1. You **hadn't ought** to sneak into the show.   1.____

2. We were **plenty** surprised by the outcome
    of our survey.   2.____

3. Karen studied **a lot** for the psychology exam. 3.____

4. Jessica was **totally** happy with her math
    grade.   4.____

5. Arthur **sure** was happy to see his girlfriend. 5.____

6. He **better** get here before noon.   6.____

7. Bill earned **alot** of money this weekend.   7.____

8. I admire **that kind** of initiative.   8.____

9. He has **plenty** of opportunities for earning
    money.   9.____

10. Where did Maureen park her new car **at**?   10.____

11. **Seeing as how** he was a good waiter, I left
    him a large tip.   11.____

12. **Due to** the pollution levels, the city
    banned incinerators.   12.____

13. The litter in the park made him **mad**.   13.____

14. She was **terribly** pleased at winning
    the contest.   14.____

15. Be sure **and** review your class notes before
    the examination.   15.____

16. The chocolate cookies are **totally
    awesome**.   16.____

17. He wrote essays, short stories, **etc.**   17.____

18. There was a **bunch** of people in the
    waiting room.   18.____

19. Sue's balloon had **bursted**.   19.____

20. Jake **got to get** a bonus for his hard work. 20.____

21. The students **theirselves** created a
    mock debate.   21.____

22. Their travel will take them to Rome,
    Florence, **and/or** Vatican City.   22.____

23. **Being as how** the bank was closed, Sonya
    could not withdraw her money.   23.____

24. She needed the money so **bad** that she cried. 24.____

25. This has been an auspicious day for you
    and **me**.   25.____

26. He **busted** his foot on the camping trip.   26.____

27. Bill was **all amped up** about the game.   27.____

28. Her **weird** way of speaking made them
    wonder where she had grown up.   28.____

29. The housing crisis in the fall of 2008
    impacted employment and the stock
    market.   29.____

30. **Basically**, John's proposal made Marsha
    happy.   30.____

31. Do you plan to go to **that there** party?   31.____

32. Carmen **might can** help wash the car
    this afternoon.   32.____

33. The guide **can't hardly** unlock the door
    for the tour bus.   33.____

34. John **has got** the answers to the crossword
    puzzle.   34.____

35. They **had drove** all night to get to the beach
    before dawn.   35.____

36. Have you ever **swum** in this lake?   36.____

37. The **fuzz** directed traffic at the accident
    scene.   37.____

38. **Whose** Ben's doctor?   38.____

39. I think I did **incredible** on the grammar test. 39.____

40. Anita **can't barely** reach the top of
    the cupboard.   40.____

72. WORD CHOICE: Standard, Appropriate English

(Study 402, Standard, Appropriate English: Review 401.)

Most of the following sentences contain one or more lapses from standard formal English. In the blanks below, **rewrite** the sentence in standard, formal English. If a sentence needs no change, leave the blanks empty.

Example: You better not bring drugs to campus, seeing as how this is a drug-free school.
You had better not bring drugs to campus, because this is a drug-free school.

(Collaborative option: Students work in pairs to discuss ways sentences could be rewritten.)

1. It was totally awesome that Martin couldn't scarcely outrun the little kid.

   _____

   _____

2. Just between you and I, she needs to lose a whole lotta weight before she enters that there beauty contest.

   _____

   _____

3. If and when they would have had kids, they would of been a lot happier.

   _____

   _____

4. They considered it okay for him to drive hisself home, being that he had not gotten sloshed.

   _____

   _____

5. Irregardless of what the critics think, the new CD by the Pink Rabbits will sell a half a million copies.

   _____

   _____

6. Clara was sort of hungry after them guests had got to eat all her food.

   _____

   _____

7. Hopefully, this new tax will not impact on the poor an awful lot.

_____

_____

8. If he had of known that the authorities had contacted a bunch of his friends, he would of left town without waiting on a bus.

_____

_____

9. George might could of met up with more college girls if he'd of gone to the local coffee joint.

_____

_____

10. They had not hardly ever seen the manager so awful mad at anyone any wheres.

_____

_____

11. If Grace's appendix busts, there will be no doubt but that the family better rush her to a hospital.

_____

_____

12. The diplomats agreed that if they signed the treaty, you could be sure they'd avoid a confrontation in the Congo.

_____

_____

13. After she's been shopping and buying stuff and had returned back to her car, Marcy exclaimed, "This is horrible!" She had just saw that she'd gotten a ticket for where she'd parked her car at.

_____

_____

14. Bobby said that yoga is a bunch of stuff where you try and meditate on peaceful things or move your body every which way.

_____

_____

15. The generals read in the intelligence reports where the enemy forces had spread themselves every which way across the battlefront; plus, their troops must have been some fatigued after a couple days of forced marches.

_____

_____

_____

_____

73. WORD CHOICE: Nondiscriminatory Terms

(Study 403, Nondiscriminatory Terms)

Each sentence contains a sexist or other discriminatory term. **Circle** that term. Then, in the blank, write a nondiscriminatory replacement. (If the circled term should be deleted without a replacement, leave the line empty.)

Example: (Every citizen must use his) right to vote.

All citizens must use their

1. Professor Johnson said, "OK, girls, you stand on this side of the room. Men, you stand over there."

   _____

2. Every student must bring his textbook to class.

   _____

3. I certainly hope that the best man is elected.

   _____

4. Has mankind really progressed over the past several thousand years?

   _____

5. The speaker asserted that every gal in his audience should make her husband assume more household responsibilities.

   _____

6. The waitress carefully balanced the tray with our order of eight desserts.

   _____

7. The female truck driver stopped and asked us for directions.

   _____

8. "When I grow up, I want to be a stewardess," the little girl said.

   _____

9. The repairman's estimate was much lower than we had expected.

   _____

10. Everyone hoped that his or her proposal would be accepted.

_____

11. The spinster who lives upstairs never attends the block parties.

_____

12. The victim was shot by an unknown gunman.

_____

13. The new lady mathematics professor has published several textbooks.

_____

14. The college has a large ratio of Oriental students.

_____

15. The ecumenical worship service was open to all faiths, Christian and non-Christian.

_____

16. All kinds of persons with disabilities were there, including the mentally deficient.

_____

17. Our South Side neighborhood was home to many Italians and colored people.

_____

18. Why would you want to blacken your reputation by doing something like that?

_____

19. In our country, people may attend whatever church they choose.

_____

20. Early in the fall, the senior men began inviting girls to the graduation dance.

_____

74. WORD CHOICE: Similar Words Often Confused

(Study 404, Similar Words Often Confused)

Write the number of the **correct** choice.

Example: He sought his lawyer's (1)**advise** (2)**advice**.   _____2_____

1. I (1)**advice** (2)**advise** you to take Latin to fulfill your language requirement.   1._____

2. If you (1)**break** (2)**brake** the car gently, you won't feel a jolt.   2._____

3. Did you (1)**canvas** (2)**canvass** the neighborhood to get everyone's opinion?   3._____

4. The diamond tiara stolen from the museum exhibit weighed more than three (1)**carets** (2)**carats**.   4._____

5. The dean of student affairs doubted whether the young man was a (1)**credible** (2)**creditable** witness to the fight in the dining hall.   5._____

6. Over the (1)**course** (2)**coarse** of the next month, the committee will review the sexual harassment policy.   6._____

7. Helping Allie with history was quite a (1)**descent** (2)**decent** gesture, don't you agree?   7._____

8. This little (1)**device** (2)**devise** will revolutionize the personal computer industry.   8._____

9. The professor made an (1)**illusion** (2)**allusion** to a recent disaster in Tokyo when describing crowd behavior.   9._____

10. She was one of the most (1)**eminent** (2)**imminent** educators of the decade.   10._____

11. We knew that the offense would try to (1)**envelop** (2)**envelope** our defense.   11._____

12. Go (1)**fourth** (2)**forth**, graduates, and be happy as well as successful.   12._____

13. Despite their obvious differences, the five students in Suite 401 had developed real friendships (1) **among** (2)**between** themselves.   13._____

14. The software game created by Frank really was (1)**ingenious** (2)**ingenuous**.   14._____

15. She tried vainly to (1)**lesson** (2)**lessen** the tension in the house.   15._____

16. The style of furniture is actually a matter of (1)**personal** (2)**personnel** taste.   16._____

17. By the way the new instructor entered the room and impatiently told the students to be quiet, the class (1)**inferred** (2)**implied** that this class would be stressful.   17._____

18. The judge (1)**respectfully** (2)**respectively** called for the bailiff to read the jury's questions.   18._____

19. When the grand marshal gave the signal, the parade (1)**preceded** (2)**proceeded.**   19._____

20. Middle-aged professionals are forsaking their high-powered lifestyles for a (1)**quiet** (2)**quite** existence in the country.   20._____

21. Arnold and Jan couldn't decide (1)**weather** (2)**whether** (3)**wether** to paint the house dark purple or beige.   21._____

22. Katie was so overweight that we bought a (1)**stationary** (2)**stationery** bicycle for our fifth anniversary.   22._____

23. The laser printer produces a much sharper image (1)**than** (2)**then** the older dot-matrix printer.   23._____

24. The computer operator read (1)**thorough** (2)**through** most of the manual before finding a possible solution.   24._____

25. The ability to pass doctoral qualifying exams is essentially a (1)**rite** (2)**right** of passage.   25. _____

26. Every (1)**women** (2)**woman** likes to be admired.   26. _____

27. (1)**Your** (2)**You're** aware, aren't you, that the play is sold out?   27. _____

28. This scanner will (1)**complement** (2)**compliment** your computer.   28. _____

29. After missing class four times, the student sat (1)**anxiously** (2)**eagerly** outside the principal's office.   29. _____

30. Marilyn feared that her sprain might (1)**effect** (2)**affect** her performance.   30. _____

31. The best advice is to take a long walk if you (1)**lose** (2)**loose** your temper.   31. _____

32. Parents rallied outside the movie theater to have the film (1)**censored** (2)**censured** because of its violence against animals.   32. _____

33. Nobody (1)**accept** (2)**except** Gloria would stoop so low.   33. _____

34. Although the machinist didn't understand it, the engine ran (1)**continuously** (2)**continually.**   34. _____

35. Her approach for preparing for the history final was (1)**different from** (2)**different than** my strategy.   35. _____

36. (1)**Everyone** (2)**Every one** of the computers was destroyed by the flood.   36. _____

37. If John (1)**passed** (2)**past** the physics final, it must have been easy.   37. _____

38. The dog had eaten (1)**its** (2)**it's** food and begged for more.   38. _____

39. The judge listened for an (1)**instance** (2)**instant** before deciding that the kitten thief was guilty.   39. _____

40. The company is (1)**already** (2)**all ready** for any negative publicity from the outcome of the lawsuit.   40. _____

41. Did you know that Annapolis, Maryland, was the first (1)**capital** (2)**capitol** of the United States?   41. _____

42. I've often heard that rainy weather (1)**affects** (2)**effects** the sleep of animals.   42. _____

43. Dressed in a yellow chiffon gown, Natasha was (1)**eager** (2)**anxious** to go to the party.   43. _____

44. Shall we dress (1)**formally** (2)**formerly** for the Senior Ball?   44. _____

45. The 1)**principal** (2)**principle** has the high school practice a fire drill monthly.   45. _____

46. More than a million people (1)**emigrated** (2)**immigrated** from Ireland during the nineteenth-century potato famine.   46. _____

47. The Berger family sat (1)**altogether** (2)**all together** in the living room to watch the election results.   47. _____

48. The student (1)**inferred** (2)**implied** from the professor's expression that the final exam would be challenging.   48. _____

49. "I, (1)**to** (2)**too** (3)**two**, have a statement to make," she said.   49. _____

50. The financial crisis—(1)**its** (2)**it's** affecting every country in the world.   50. _____

75. WORD CHOICE: Similar Words Often Confused

(Study 404, Similar Words Often Confused)

Write the number of the **correct** choice.

Example: He sought his lawyer's (1)**advise** (2)**advice**.   __2__

1. I think I did (1)**good** (2)**well** on the chemistry test.   1._____

2. He said, "(1)**Their** (2)**There** (3)**They're** is no reason for you to wait."   2._____

3. "(1)**Whose** (2)**Who's** there?" she whispered.   3._____

4. The cat ran behind my car, and I accidentally ran over (1)**its** (2)**it's** tail.   4._____

5. The consultant will (1)**ensure** (2)**insure** that the audit is completed on time.   5._____

6. My grandmother has a difficult time getting a thread to go (1)**through** (2)**thru** (3)**thorough** (4)**threw** the eye of a needle.   6._____

7. The mere (1)**cite** (2)**site** (3)**sight** of Julia made his heart soar.   7._____

8. Will people be standing in the (1)**aisles** (2)**isles** at the dedication ceremony?   8._____

9. Dr. Smith is (1)**famous** (2)**notorious** for her educational research.   9._____

10. "Sad movies always (1)**affect** (2)**effect** me that way," lamented Kay.   10._____

11. The (1)**thorough** (2)**through** commission report indicated that approximately forty percent of American schools do not have enough textbooks in their classrooms.   11._____

12. Jonathon had the (1)**presence** (2)**presents** of mind to make a sharp right turn and to step on the accelerator.   12._____

13. The principal expected the students' behavior to (1)**correspond to** (2)**correspond with** the school district's expectations.   13._____

14. If you rehearse enough, you're (1)**likely** (2)**liable** to get the lead role in the play.   14._____

15. The family has (1)**born** (2)**borne** the noise and dust of the nearby highway construction for several months.   15._____

16. (1)**Their** (2)**They're** (3)**There** leasing a truck because they can't afford the down payment to purchase a new one.   16._____

17. The time capsule (1)**may be** (2)**maybe** the best way for the general public to understand how people lived one hundred years ago.   17._____

18. Some (1)**individual** (2)**person** dropped off a package at the mailroom.   18._____

19. The track coach told me that he wanted to (1)**discuss** (2)**discus** my performance at the last meet.   19._____

20. The voters are (1)**apt** (2)**likely** to vote for a candidate who promises to reduce unemployment.   20._____

21. (1)**Who's** (2)**Whose** theory do you believe regarding the geographical origin of humankind?   21._____

22. The (1)**council** (2)**counsel** (3)**consul** met to decide the fate of the student who cheated on the psychology final.   22._____

23. A tall tree has fallen and is (1)**laying** (2)**lying** across the highway.   23._____

24. A significant (1)**percent** (2)**percentage** of Americans still smoke.   24._____

25. In *The Oxbow Incident*, the wrong man is (1)**hung** (2)**hanged**. 25. _____

26. Did you ask if he will (1)**let** (2)**leave** you open a charge account? 26. _____

27. The new dance had (1)**to** (2)**too** (3)**two** many steps to remember. 27. _____

28. Sarah promised to (1)**learn** (2)**teach** me some gardening techniques. 28. _____

29. Shooting innocent bystanders is one of the most (1)**amoral** (2)**immoral** street crimes committed. 29. _____

30. The alfalfa milkshake may taste unpleasant, but it is (1)**healthy** (2)**healthful**. 30. _____

31. The tennis player always (1)**lays** (2)**lies** down before an important match. 31. _____

32. When (1)**your** (2)**you're** in love, the whole world seems beautiful. 32. _____

33. On high-school basketball courts, Sam was often (1)**compared to** (2)**compared with** the young Michael Jordan. 33. _____

34. The (1)**amount** (2)**number** of trees needed to produce a single book should humble any author. 34. _____

35. This medication will (1)**lessen** (2)**lesson** the pain until we reach the emergency room. 35. _____

36. The newspaper was soggy because it had (1)**laid** (2)**lain** in a rain puddle all morning. 36. _____

37. After spending $1,000 on repairs, we hope that the van finally works (1)**like** (2)**as** it should. 37. _____

38. The couple (1)**adapted** (2)**adopted** a baby girl from Bulgaria. 38. _____

39. Cindy was (1)**besides** (2)**beside** herself with anger. 39. _____

40. The agreement was (1)**among** (2)**between** Harry, Justine, and me. 40. _____

41. Do not (1)**set** (2)**sit** the disk on top of the computer monitor. 41. _____

42. The play was from (1)**classical** (2)**classic** Rome. 42. _____

43. The curtain was about to (1)**raise** (2)**rise** on the last act of the senior play. 43. _____

44. The camp is just a few miles (1)**farther** (2)**further** along the trail. 44. _____

45. The news report (1)**convinced** (2)**persuaded** me to join a volunteer organization that renovates homes in low-income neighborhoods. 45. _____

46. The author of that particular book was (1)**censored** (2)**censured** for his views by a national parenting group. 46. _____

47. Do (1)**as** (2)**like** I told you during the game. 47. _____

48. Compared (1)**to** (2)**with** the Steelers, the Ravens have a weaker defense but a stronger offense. 48. _____

49. The line backing unit was (1)**composed** (2)**comprised** of Taylor, Marshall, and Burt. 49. _____

50. The three children tried to outrun (1)**each other** (2)**one another**. 50. _____

76. WORD CHOICE: Review

(Study 401–404, Word Choice)

Each sentence may contain an inappropriate or incorrect expression. **Circle** that expression, and in the blank write an appropriate or correct replacement. Use standard, formal American English. If the sentence is correct as is, leave the blank empty.

Examples: He sought his lawyer's (advise.) ____advice____

The director reported that the company (was fine and dandy.) ____had doubled its profits.____

Whose idea was it? _____

1. I strongly dislike those sort of films, no matter how sophisticated they are supposed to be. _____

2. Barbara said, "Aunt Mary, your peach pie tastes good, just like I thought it would." _____

3. We were supposed to have the class picnic today; the wether, however, changed our plans. _____

4. I was surprised that the banquet was attended by alot of people. _____

5. Its time for class. _____

6. You to can afford such an apartment. _____

7. I can't hardly hear the speaker. _____

8. I think you should of cooked the pasta longer; it's nearly crunchy. _____

9. Irregardless of the result, you did your best. _____

10. Will he raise your salary? _____

11. Try and keep the puppies off the new chair. _____

12. I usually always stop at this meat market when I am having dinner guests. _____

13. You are selling vanilla, chocolate, and black cherry? I'll take the latter. _____

14. His efforts at improving communication among all fifty staff members will determine his own success. _____

15. Her success was due to hard work and persistence. _____

16. They should have done that by themself. _____

17. Their house is now for sale. _____

18. Henry and myself decided to start a small business together. _____

19. The reason why Jose can't go is because he has to clean out the garage. _____

20. Did he lay awake last night? _____

21. The professor's opinion differed with the teaching assistant's perspective. _____

22. Bob laid the carpet in the hallway. _____

23. The cat has been laying on top of the refrigerator all morning. _____

24. He has plenty of opportunities for earning money. _____

25. San Francisco offers many things for tourists to do. _____

26. We hanged the paintings over the mantelpiece last night. _____

27. He always did good in English courses. _____

28. The low price of the printer plus the modem prompted me to buy both. _____

29. Because her supervisor seemed unreasonable, Sue finally decided to resign. _____

30. Max has less enemies than Sam. _____

31. The speaker inferred that time management depended more on attitude than skill. _____

32. Glenn has a long way to travel each week. _____

33. Did he loose his wallet and credit cards? _____

34. She looked like she was afraid. _____

35. Walking to school was a rite of passage in our home. _____

36. "What principals do you live by?" the politician asked the crowd. _____

37. Have you written in regards to an appointment? _____

38. Elaine adopted her novel for television. _____

39. Damp weather affects her sinuses. _____

40. A lion hunting its prey is immoral. _____

41. The troop was already to leave for camp. _____

42. The men and girls on the team played well. _____

43. We split the bill between the three of us. _____

44. Be sure to wear causal clothes to tonight's party. _____

45. The hum of the air conditioner was continual. _____

46. The informer was hanged. _____

47. The air conditioner runs good now. _____

48. The child is too young to understand. _____

49. Regardless of his shortcomings, she loves him. _____

50. Where is the party at? _____

51. Please bring these plans to the engineering department. _____

52. The salesman was looking forward to the sale. _____

53. The sun will hopefully shine today. _____

54. Their political strategy failed in the end. _____

55. The workmen complained that the work site was unsafe. _____

56. His chances for a promotion looked good. _____

57. The twins frequently wear one another's clothing. _____

58. A twisted branch was laying across our path. _____

59. She was disinterested in the boring play. _____

60. Send a cover letter to the chair of the department. _____

61. This line is for shoppers with ten items or fewer. _____

62. The hostile countries finally effected a compromise. _____

63. The professor was somewhat annoyed at the girls in his class. _____

64. Sam differed from Gina about the issue of increasing social services. _____

65. I meant to lay down for just an hour. _____

66. She asked me whether I worked in the personnel department. _____

67. He is the most credible person I have ever met. He will believe anything. _____

68. He enjoys the healthy food we serve. _____

69. Paul's conversation was sprinkled with literary illusions. _____

70. The husband and wife were both pursuing law degrees. _____

71. Her position in the company was most unique. _____

72. He has already departed. _____

73. I will have to rite a letter to that company. _____

74. There's was an informal agreement. _____

75. Albert is a student which always puts his studies first. _____

76. Their is always another game. _____

77. The gold locket had lain on the floor of the attic for ten years. _____

78. Foyt lead the race from start to finish. _____

79. By the tone of her writing, the news reporter implied that the politician was guilty of fraud. _____

80. To find the missing watch, we ventured further into the crowd. _____

77. WORD CHOICE: Review

(Study 401–404, Word Choice)

On your own paper, **rewrite** each paragraph below so that it displays all the word-choice skills you have learned, but none of the word-choice faults you have been cautioned against. Use standard, formal English.

(Collaborative option: Students work in pairs or small groups to discuss each paragraph, suggest new wording, and edit one another's work.)

1. It has been brought to our attention that company personnel have been engaging in the taking of unauthorized absences from their daily stations. The affect of this action is to leave these stations laying unattended for durations of time extending up to a quarter of an hour. In this day and age such activity is inexcusable. Therefore the management has reached the end conclusion that tried and true disciplinary measures must necessarily be put into effect. Thus, commencing August 5, workmen who render theirselves absent from their work station will have a certain amount of dollars deducted from the wages they are paid.

2.   Needless Required College Courses [title of essay]

   The topic of which I shall write about in this paper is needless required college courses. I will show in the following paragraphs that many mandatory required courses are really just not necessarily needed. They have no purpose due to the fact that they are not really needed or wanted but exist just to provide jobs for professors which cannot attract students by themselfs on there own. It is this that makes them meaningless and not worth anything.

3. In my personal opinion, I think that the general consensus of opinion is usually always that the reason why lots of people fail to engage in the voting procedure today is because they would rather set around home then get off of they're tails and get down to the nearest voting facility. In regards to this matter some things ought to be done to get an O.K. percent of the American people to vote, irregardless of why they don't want to do so.

4. Each and every day we learn, verbally or from newspapers, about business executives having heart attacks and every so often ending up fatally dead. The stress of high management-type positions is said to be the principle casual factor in causing such attacks. But a search threw available data shows that this is a unfounded belief. For awhile it was universally expected that persons in high-level jobs experienced the most stress. But yet however this is such a wrong misconception. It is in the low-echelon jobs that more strain and consequently more heart attacks usually often occur.

5. In the Bible's Book of Exodus, it relates the flight of the ancient Jews from Egypt to Israel. The narrative says where God sent ten plagues upon the land, the reason why being to punish the rulers for not letting the Jewish people go and letting them be free. Moses than lead his people across the Red Sea, who's waves parted to leave them go through the water. There trek thorough the dessert lasted weaks, months, and than years and years. The people's moral began to sag. However, Moses then brought them the Ten Commandments from Mt. Sinai, and they

emigrated safely into the Promised Land. Moses, though, died before he could enter this very fine country. Some question the historic accuracy of the narrative, but others find it entirely believably credulous. If you except it fully or not, its one of the world's most engrossing stories.

78. PARAGRAPHS AND PAPERS: Topic Sentences and Paragraph Unity

(Study 503A, The Topic Sentence, and 503D, Unity and Emphasis)

First, **circle** the topic sentence of each paragraph. Then find one or more sentences that violate the **unity** of the paragraph (that do not relate directly to the topic). Write the number(s) of the sentence(s) in the blank at the end of the paragraph.

_____

1. (1)From a pebble on the shore to a boulder on a mountainside, any rock you see began as something else and was made a rock by the earth itself. (2)Igneous rock began as lava that over hundreds of years hardened far beneath the earth's surface. (3)Granite is an igneous rock that is very hard and used for buildings and monuments. (4)Sedimentary rock was once sand, mud, or clay that settled to the bottom of a body of water and was packed down in layers under the ocean floor. (5)All rocks are made up of one or more minerals. (6)Metamorphic rock began as either igneous rock or sedimentary rock whose properties were changed by millions of years of exposure to the heat, pressure, and movement below the earth's crust.

   1. _____

2. (1)Although we normally associate suits of armor with the knights of medieval Europe, the idea of such protective coverings is much older and more pervasive than that. (2)Some knights even outfitted their horses with metal armor. (3)As long as 3,500 years ago, Assyrian and Babylonian warriors sewed pieces of metal to their leather tunics to repel enemy arrows. (4)A thousand years later, the Greeks wore metal helmets, in addition to large metal sheets over their chests and backs. (5)Native Americans of the Northwest wore both carved wooden helmets and chest armor made from wood and leather. (6)Nature protects the turtle and the armadillo with permanent armor. (7)Even with body armor largely absent from the modern soldier's uniform, the helmet still remains as a reminder of the vulnerability of the human body.

   2. _____

3. (1)Mention the name of George Washington and most Americans envision a larger-than-life hero, who, even as a little boy, could not tell a lie. (2)However, it turns out that Washington was more human than his biographers would have us believe. (3)His contemporaries described Washington as moody and remote. (4)He was also a bit vain, for he insisted that his fellow officers address him as "Your Excellency." (5)He refused to allow himself to be touched by strangers. (6)Washington was also known to weep in public, especially when the Patriots' war effort was sagging. (7)Washington was even plagued with traitors, who gave the British advice on how to beat the Americans. (8)He was not even a gifted military officer. (9)Rather than being a hero of the French and Indian War, Washington may have provoked the French to go to war by leading an unnecessary and irrational attack against a group of Frenchmen. (10)While Washington was certainly a brave man, dedicated to freeing the colonists from British tyranny, he was not the perfect man that early biographers described.

   3. _____

4. (1)In the mid-1800s, an apple or a pear was considered too dangerous to eat. (2)In fact, any fresh vegetable or fruit was considered too risky because one bite might lead to cholera, dysentery, or typhoid. (3)During cholera epidemics, city councils often banned the sale of fruits and vegetables. (4)The only safe vegetable was a boiled potato. (5)A typical breakfast might include black tea, scrambled eggs, fresh spring shad, wild pigeons, pig's feet, and oysters. (6)Milk was also considered a perilous beverage because many people died from drinking spoiled milk. (7)Milk really was a threat to people's health, because it was processed and delivered to home with little regard for hygiene. (8)Children and those who were ill were often malnourished because the foods with the most nutrients were also the most deadly. (9)Until the invention of the icebox in the 1840s, rich and poor people alike risked their health and even their lives every time they ate a meal.

4. _____

5. (1)There are many more kinds of insects on earth than there are of any other kind of living creature! (2)It is estimated that approximately 10 quintillion (10,000,000,000,000,000,000) individual insects are alive. (3)Some experts estimate that as many as 10 million species of insects exist. (4)In fact, you could spend your entire life looking at different kinds of insects and you would never see them all. (5)It's hard to imagine, but 95% of all the animal species on the earth are insects! (6) Spiders are not really insects. (7)Did you know that on average one million insects live on every single acre of land? (8)Many people are scared of moths. (9)Over one million species have been discovered by scientists and entomologists, who think there might be more than ten times as many insects than we currently know about that haven't even been named yet! (10)Insects are an extremely diverse type of animal.

5. _____

79. PARAGRAPHS AND PAPERS: Paragraph Development

(Study 503B, Adequate Development)

Each paragraph below is inadequately developed. Choose **one**, and, on the back of this page or on your own paper, **rewrite** it to develop the topic sentence (boldfaced) adequately. Use six to nine sentences, adding your own facts and ideas as needed. (You may change the topic sentence to express a different viewpoint.) Some paragraphs may have repeated or unrelated material.

(Collaborative option: Students work in pairs or small groups to pool information, discuss how to develop paragraphs, and review or edit one another's work.)

1. Young people today see how their parents act and how they feel about the world today. Because they feel their parents are wrong, young people rebel because they do not want to become a carbon copy of their elders. Young people want to be treated as persons, not just kids who do not know what they are talking about and who should not express their own ideas because they are too young to understand. **Young people today want to do and think as they please.**

2. **Everyone would like to have lower prices at the gas pump and at the same time be less reliant upon foreign energy.** The carbon from the burning of the gasoline makes it difficult to breathe. Many Americans think we can solve both problems by drilling for oil in the United States. Others, however, disagree, fearing the damage drilling would cause to fragile ecosystems. The emissions hurt the environment and the use of gasoline requires our dependence on other countries for oil resources. The United States has reserve oil, but we seem to be waiting for the correct time to release it to the public. Carbon also damages the paint on cars as well as plant life and the ozone layer.

3. **I like the old movies shown on TV better than the recent releases shown in theaters.** The old films contain more-dramatic plots and more-famous actors. They are exciting and fast paced. The actors are widely known for their acting ability. Today's films are boring or mindless and have less-famous actors.

80. PARAGRAPHS AND PAPERS: Paragraph Coherence

(Study 503C, Coherence)

In each blank, write the transitional expression from the list below that fits most logically. For some blanks there is more than one correct answer. Try not to use any expression more than once.

afterward	meanwhile	more important	however
consequently	nevertheless	therefore	likewise
even so	on the other hand	thus	in particular
formerly	finally	as a result	that is

Example: Thousands of workers were heading home by car, bus, and train. <u>Meanwhile,</u> at home, their spouses were readying supper.

1. Yesterday afternoon, the third-grade teachers met for four hours with all the parents of their students; _____, as they prepared to go home, they spoke about how successful the meetings had been.

2. Out on the prairie, the cowpokes were rounding up the herds of cattle; _____, back at the ranch, the sheep had gotten out of the pens and were wandering in the fields.

3. Today we take cell phones for granted. Early mobile phones, _____, filled the entire trunk of a large automobile.

4. In the 1950s, American people were enjoying a strong economy, which provided plenty of jobs and high wages; _____, life seemed secure and promising.

5. The term *teenager* entered the language only as recently as 1941; _____, teenagers were not really a recognized presence in American society.

6. In late 19th century America, men made out of various pieces of tin were used in advertising and political cartoons; _____, the figure of a man made of tin had been part of European folk art for 300 years.

7. In Frank Baum's classic 1900 book *The Wonderful Wizard of Oz*, the Tin Woodman is made completely out of tin; _____, he had been an ordinary man by the name of Nick Chopper, who made his living chopping down trees in the forests of Oz.

8. The Wizard could provide the Tin Woodman with only a heart made of velvet and filled with sawdust; _____, this was enough to please the Tin Woodman, who was the most tender and emotional of Dorothy's companions.

9. *The Wonderful Wizard of Oz* is said to have many symbols; the Tin Woodman, _____, is described as a worker dehumanized by industrialization in early twentieth-century America.

10. The Cowardly Lion, Scarecrow, and Tin Woodman each wished to get something from the Wizard; _____ so did Dorothy; she wanted to go home.

11. For her to go home, the wizard told Dorothy that she had to click together the heels of her ruby slippers, which she did; _____, Dorothy found herself at home in her own bed.

12. Jonah's stock tripled in value in one week; _____, he felt that he should continue to be a cautious investor.

13. A seven-hundred pound microwave oven, called the Radarange, was first produced by Tappan in 1955. _____, Americans were not interested in purchasing a microwave oven until the late 1960s, when the appliance was much smaller and more reliable.

14. Franklin Roosevelt's third term began in 1941; _____, it was the year that the U.S. was plunged into World War II.

81. PARAGRAPHS AND PAPERS: Paragraph Review, Netiquette

(Study 503C, Coherence, and 504, Netiquette)

Part 1

Go back to the paragraph you wrote in exercise 79.

On your own paper or in the space below, **rewrite** it, being sure that it has a controlling structure, appropriate transitions, and repeated key words or phrases as needed to give it coherence. **Circle** your transitions and repeated key words or phrases. At the end, skip a line and **write a sentence** briefly stating what your controlling structure is.

_____

(Collaborative option: Students work in pairs or small groups to assist one another in revising.)

A student sent the following e-mail in response to an online job offer. On the lines below, **rewrite** the e-mail in appropriate English, changing, deleting or adding text as necessary. (This is a preliminary contact, not a full application letter.)

FROM: Silvia Moss

TO: Online Services Company

SUBJECT: Your Website

DATE: August 18, 2009

Howdy!

I got real enthused when I saw your job offer on your Website June 4. In this day and age you won't find many as UNIQUE as me. Being as how I have taken a lot of computer courses and plan on taking more in the future, I can, IMHO, handle ANY THING I could meet up with in your service department. If you can utilize my services, contact me. I'll be waiting anxiously. Gotta go now. See ya! ☺

Silvia

FROM: _____

TO: _____

SUBJECT: _____

DATE: _____

_____

_____

_____

_____

_____

_____

_____

_____

_____

_____

_____

_____

_____

_____

_____

_____

82. PARAGRAPHS AND PAPERS: The Thesis Sentence

(Study 505C, Forming a Thesis)

First, from the list below, **identify** the main weakness in each thesis sentence, and write the letter of that weakness in the short blank. Then, in the long blanks, **rewrite** the thesis sentence so that it is usable for an essay. (For the purposes of this exercise, you may invent facts or ideas as needed.)

A–no assertion   C–too broad, too vague, or unsupportable
B–split focus   D–stale, uninteresting to U.S. collegians

Examples: Our nation's social problems need solving now.   __C__
Our college has a moral obligation to use part of its endowment to relieve local poverty.

The Antarctic is one of the coldest places on earth.   __A__
Despite its inhospitable climate, new scientific advances hold promise for making the Antarctic a desirable place for people to live.

(Collaborative option: Students work in pairs or small groups to evaluate thesis sentences and compose new ones.)

1. Canada is actually larger than the United States.   1._____

_____

_____

2. CNN is the best cable channel for news.   2._____

_____

_____

3. Breastfeeding in public is discouraged by many people in the United States, yet it provides the best nutrition for an infant.   3._____

_____

_____

4. Studying the calls of birds in the hills of Vietnam can be rewarding.   4._____

_____

_____

5. The history of China is very interesting.   5._____

_____

_____

6. The state's welfare system is inhumane, and its housing rehabilitation program is in shambles. 6. _____

_____

_____

7. Fatherhood changed my life. 7. _____

_____

_____

8. I have strong feelings about abortion. 8. _____

_____

_____

9. Global warming is killing us. 9. _____

_____

_____

10. We must stop eating fast food. 10. _____

_____

_____

83. PARAGRAPHS AND PAPERS: Planning the Essay

(Study 505A–D, Before Starting to Write)

Follow the directions below.

_____

(Collaborative option: Students work in pairs or small groups to share knowledge and ideas and to offer suggestions.)

A. Assume that you have been assigned to write an essay in one of these broad subject areas: popular culture, environmental problems, or improving this college. Choose one. On your own paper, **brainstorm, freewrite,** or **cluster** whatever ideas you can generate on this subject. From those ideas, produce **three** limited topics suitable for a 2- to 4-page essay. List those topics here:

1._____

2._____

3._____

B. From each of these topics, develop the best tentative thesis sentence you can for this 2- to 4-page essay:

Topic 1:_____

_____

Topic 2:_____

_____

Topic 3:_____

_____

From these three, choose the one that, considering your knowledge, ideas, and interests, you can best develop into an essay. Refine that thesis sentence and write it here:

Topic #____: _____

_____

C. Consider which approach seems most workable for this topic and thesis: narration, description, explanation, persuasion, problem-solution, effect-cause (or vice versa), comparison/contrast. State your most likely approach:

_____

D. List below the major divisions (subtopics) you see for your essay (three is the most common number, but others may work better for your topic). If you chose the persuasive approach, for example, each division would probably be a separate reason.

Divisions:

_____

_____

_____

_____

84. PARAGRAPHS AND PAPERS: The Essay Outline

(Study 505E, Outlining)

In the space below, write a detailed **outline** for the essay you began preparing in exercise 83. Continue on the back or on your own paper if necessary. Use any of the methods mentioned in section 505E. Make it detailed enough so that you can write an essay from it.

_____

(Collaborative option: Students work in pairs or small groups to construct the outline or evaluate one another's outlines.)

85. PARAGRAPHS AND PAPERS: The Essay Introduction and Conclusion

(Study 506, Writing and Revising the Essay; Review 502–503, Paragraphs)

Part 1

Each sentence is the opening of an essay. In the blank, write **Y** (for **yes**) if the sentence is an **effective interest-arouser**. Write **N** (for **no**) if it is **not**.

Example: The United States faces many problems today.   _____N_____

(Collaborative option: Students in pairs or small groups discuss the effectiveness of each sentence.)

1. The background of the Civil War is interesting.   1._____

2. It is 7 a.m. this bitter cold December day, and the line outside the employment agency has grown bigger since I arrived two hours ago.   2._____

3. There are both similarities and differences between cell phones and landline phones   3._____

4. One of the biggest-selling items in this city's public housing project supermarkets is dog food—yet no dogs are allowed in the projects.   4._____

5. That little gadget ding-a-linging in your pocket—the cell phone—has altered American culture dramatically.   5._____

6. The United States is a very different place from what it was a hundred years ago, or even fifty, all because of different circumstances that have surrounded people in each era.   6._____

7. What would you do if your life savings were suddenly wiped out, and you and all your family lost their jobs, as happened to our great-grandparents in the Depression?   7._____

8. The potato salad at the picnic looked fine and even tasted good. But later that day I learned that food that looks and tastes good can still harbor bacteria.   8._____

9. The figures are awesome: a world population today of more than 6 billion, with more than a million newcomers born every week.   9._____

10. In my short but checkered career, I have worked at a wide variety of jobs, some indoors and some out, some easy and some hard.   10._____

Part 2

Each item contains the closing sentence(s) of an essay. In the blank, write **Y** (for **yes**) if the sentence is an **effective closing**. Write **N** (for **no**) if it is **not**.

Example: And so we must do something about this problem.   _____N_____

(Collaborative option: Students in pairs or small groups discuss the effectiveness of each sentence.)

1. On the whole, as I said before, my experience was one of the many things I remember as significant in my life.   1._____

2. So, the next time you're broke, don't do what I did. Or you'll regret it.   2._____

3. In my personal opinion, the time has come to start doing something about all the gas guzzlers on the road. Those vehicles are using too much gasoline and their owners should be fined.   3. _____

4. This experience changed my whole attitude toward money, making me ruthlessly determined never again to be embarrassed by lack of funds. We all seem to suffer more from such humiliations than from any other kind of defeat, even a physical beating, a job lost, or a romance gone sour. Along with hunger and sex, the fear of looking bad in the eyes of others is one of the most basic of human motives.   4. _____

5. Therefore, every citizen should go to the polls this election day and vote for Maryann Rivera for governor. Another reason is that her opponent is old and may die in office.   5. _____

6. The federal government, then, must cut the money supply before it is too late; otherwise, as in Germany in the 1920s, our money may literally not be worth the paper on which it is printed.   6. _____

7. Every spring since that day my parents first took me to Wrigley Field, my heart pounds with anticipation when I hear the cry "Play ball!" Keep your football, basketball, and hockey; baseball will always be America's game.   7. _____

8. Thus, since there are more people in the world today than can be fed, and a million more arriving weekly, it is up to the United Nations to take the bull by the horns and find a solution to the problem.   8. _____

9. Because poverty will never disappear, it is up to leaders of the prosperous nations, particularly the United States, to shift their focus from assuring middle-class comfort to making laws and programs that will create a vast new Marshall Plan to feed the hungry at home and worldwide. Perhaps then those in our housing projects will not have to subsist on dog food.   9. _____

10. [For this item, supply your own effective conclusion.]

    I, then, am one of those who have grown up as a so-called victim of society. _____

    _____

    _____

    _____

Part 3

On your own paper: First, write an effective **introductory paragraph** for the essay you outlined in exercise 84. Then write an effective **concluding paragraph** for the same essay. (These may be considered drafts until you complete exercise 86. Or your instructor may have you defer writing the conclusion until you have completed exercise 86.)

_____

(Collaborative option: Students in pairs or small groups critique one another's paragraphs.)

86. PARAGRAPHS AND PAPERS: The Essay Body

(Study 506, Writing and Revising the Essay; Review 502–503, Paragraphs)

Part 1

In the blanks, write an effective **topic sentence** for each body paragraph of the essay you have been planning and writing in exercises 83, 84, and 85. (You do not have to use all five sets of blanks; use as many body paragraphs as the structure of your essay demands.) Include a transitional expression or sentence that links each paragraph to the preceding one.

Example: <u>In the late 1970s and early '80s, mobile phones were incredibly primitive by today's standards.</u>

(Collaborative option: Students in pairs or small groups discuss the effectiveness of each sentence.)

1. _____

   _____

   _____

2. _____

   _____

   _____

3. _____

   _____

   _____

4. _____

   _____

   _____

5. _____

   _____

   _____

Part 2

On your own paper, complete the **body paragraphs** of your essay. Remember what section 503B stated about supporting evidence.

(Collaborative option: Students in pairs or small groups critique one another's work.)

Part 3

Bring your introductory, body, and concluding paragraphs together. On your own paper, **revise**, **edit**, and **proofread** your essay until you are satisfied with its quality. Submit a clean copy.

(Collaborative option: Students in pairs or small groups critique, edit, and proofread one another's work.)

87. PARAGRAPHS AND PAPERS: Research Paper Topics and Theses

(Study 507A, Choosing and Limiting a Topic, and 507B, Forming a Thesis)

Part 1

If the topic is **suitable** for a research paper, write **Y** (for **Yes**) in the blank. If the topic is **not suitable**, write the **letter of the reason** in the blank. (For some items there is more than one possible correct answer.)

A—too broad, vague, or speculative
B—not researchable or completable with available resources
C—unable to be treated objectively

Example: Poland's transition from communism to capitalism, 1985–1995   ____Y____

1. Ice cream is the best dessert   1._____
2. Did prehistoric people enjoy music?   2._____
3. Imagery in *The Prelude*, by William Wordsworth   3._____
4. How cell phones will change the world   4._____
5. The torch is passed: the effects of the 1960 presidential election on the Cold War   5._____
6. The role of women in the Union Army during the Civil War   6._____
7. New treatments of athletic knee injuries in girls and women   7._____
8. Animal worship: the one true religion   8._____
9. Voting patterns of current freshmen at this college in public elections   9._____
10. The collapse of communism as seen through the eyes of selected average Russians   10._____
11. How John McCain could have been elected in the 2008 presidential election   11._____
12. The decline in foreign trade as a cause of the Great Depression   12._____
13. Will humans ever live on Mars?   13._____
14. The interstate highway system in our state, 1955–1975: boon or boondoggle?   14._____

Part 2

In the short blank, write **Y** (for **yes**) if the thesis sentence is a **workable** one for a research paper. Write **N** (for **no**) if it is **not**. Then, after each sentence for which you wrote **N**, write in the long blank a workable thesis sentence on the same topic.

Example: Roosevelt's China policy before World War II was bad.   ____N____
      Roosevelt's China policy helped draw the U.S. into World War II.

(Collaborative option: Students in pairs or small groups suggest workable thesis sentences.)

1. In his story "The Rich Boy," F. Scott Fitzgerald conveys ambivalent attitudes toward wealth. 1. _____

_____

_____

_____

2. The U.S. presidential election of 2008 has many parallels to that of 1932. 2. _____

_____

_____

_____

3. *Huckleberry Finn* is the most important novel written by an American. 3. _____

_____

_____

_____

4. The lost continent of Atlantis lies just off the sea in the Bermuda Triangle, waiting to be discovered. 4. _____

_____

_____

_____

5. The Second Vatican Council played only a secondary role in the widespread defection of U.S. Catholics in the 1960s and '70s. 5. _____

_____

_____

_____

6. Despite being maligned by critics, current afternoon TV talk shows tend to raise the cultural level of all their viewers. 6. _____

_____

_____

_____

7. The present family court system in this county often harms the very people it is intended to help. 7. _____

_____

_____

_____

8. The U.S. Electoral College should be replaced by direct popular vote because the College system distorts vote totals.

8. _____

_____

_____

_____

9. Shakespeare's works really had to have been written by Francis Bacon because Bacon was educated and Shakespeare was not.

9. _____

_____

_____

_____

10. The E-waste, electronic products containing hazardous materials, that is routinely sold and shipped from the industrialized world to developing countries in Asia for recycling can be deadly to the people of those countries.

10. _____

_____

_____

_____

11. Massive urban renewal projects in the 1960s and 1970s failed throughout the nation; I know because I grew up in one of them.

11. _____

_____

_____

_____

88. PARAGRAPHS AND PAPERS: Locating and Evaluating Sources

(Study 507C and E, Locating and Evaluating Sources, and 509, Works Cited/References)

Part 1

Choose one of the subjects below. In the library, **locate** five useful printed (not electronic) sources on your subject. In the space on this page, **list** the needed bibliographical information for each, in either **MLA** or **APA** form, as your instructor directs. (For books, also make a note of the call number.)

The Nuremburg Trials	U.S. wheat production since 1970
The growth of the technology industry in India since 1990	Bluegrass music
	T. S. Eliot's early poetry (up to 1930)
The World's Columbian Exposition	L. Frank Baum

(Collaborative option: Students in pairs or small groups share research tasks and findings.)

Follow the directions for part 1, using the same topic you chose there. This time use electronic instead of printed sources. Be sure to include Internet addresses or other needed information for retrieval, where necessary.

Evaluate the usability of each of the following sources for a research paper titled "The Choosing of U.S. Vice-presidential Candidates, 1988–2008." In the blank, write the number of your evaluation:

1—source is unquestionably usable

2—source is usable but needs to be balanced with a source giving a different viewpoint

3—source is not usable

Example: A 1988 pamphlet urging people to boycott the election   <u> 3 </u>

1. The *Congressional Record*, published regularly by the U.S. Congress, including speeches of several future Vice-presidents   1. _____

2. Your grandmother's high school history textbook   2. _____

3. The biography of Adolf Hitler by a noted German historian, published in 1940   3. _____

4. An article, "A Day with the Vice-president," in the current issue of a magazine sold at your supermarket checkout   4. _____

5. An article on the American political press in *PMLA* (*Publications of the Modern Language Association*)   5. _____

6. A Web site sponsored by the Republican National Committee   6. _____

7. A book, *The American Vice-presidency*, published by Yale University Press in 2008   7. _____

8. An e-mail message from a friend who is a Washington intern in the Vice-president's secretary's office   8. _____

9. A 2004 article in the *Nation* magazine, titled "A Liberal's-eye View of Recent Vice-presidents"   9. _____

10. A Web site named "Traitorous Capitalist Pigs in the White House"   10. _____

89. PARAGRAPHS AND PAPERS: Taking Notes, Citing, Avoiding Plagiarism

(Study 507F, Taking Notes; 508A, Citing Within the Paper; and 508B, Avoiding Plagiarism)*

Part 1

Each item below contains an original passage from a source, followed by a student's note card on the passage. The student has done one or more of the following:

(1) incorrectly or inadequately keyed the note card to its corresponding bibliography card,

(2) misrepresented or distorted what the source said,

(3) come too close to the source's wording (plagiarized).

In the blank note card, **write** a correctly keyed, accurate, unplagiarized note on the passage.

Example: [From page 197 of a book by Antonia Fraser called *The Wives of Henry VIII*. (Catherine is the former Queen; Henry's new Queen is Anne.)]

ORIGINAL: Meanwhile at the court these days, there were indications to encourage Catherine's supporters that all was not well between the King and the new Queen.

STUDENT:

```
Wives of Hen. 8th—197

At this time in the palace, indications
encouraged Catherine's supporters that
things were not well between the King and
his new Queen.
```

YOUR CORRECTED NOTE CARD:

```
Fraser 197

Those who favored the former Queen noticed
and were heartened by signs of friction
between Henry and Anne.
```

*APA-based material in exercises 89 and 90 copyright © 2001, 2007 by the American Psychological Association. Adapted with permission.

1. [From page 334 of a book by Walter Cronkite titled *A Reporter's Life*]

ORIGINAL: He [Daniel Ellsberg] had worked on the Pentagon's detailed history of our involvement in the Vietnam War. He became so incensed over what he considered the dirty secrets therein that he made off with hundreds of pages of papers and offered them to the news media.

STUDENT:

Cronkite, chap. 7

Daniel Ellsberg, who had worked on the Pentagon's involvement in Vietnam, became incensed over the dirty secrets he found and stole hundreds of papers, which he offered to the news media.

2. [From page 2 of an anonymous online article from the Sierra Club, "Endangered Species and Their Habitats"; last update, 4 Nov. 2003, retrieved 8 May 2007]

ORIGINAL: In fact, it is massive overcutting—along with automation and the industry's practice of exporting logs for processing with cheap, non-U.S. labor—that has wiped out over 90 percent of America's ancient forests.

STUDENT:

Sierra Club 2

"Massive overcutting" has caused the destruction of nine-tenths of our old-growth forests.

3. [From page 1319 of an article in the October 29, 1998, issue of the *New England Journal of Medicine*. The article is "Therapeutic Strategies for HIV Infection—Time to Think Hard" by David A. Cooper and Sean Emery. You may need a dictionary to rephrase medical jargon.]

ORIGINAL: We must think hard about the implications and practicalities of a medical strategy based on aggressive early intervention with lifelong, complex regimens of antiretroviral therapy to preserve immunocompetence after the suppression of a cytopathic virus.

STUDENT:

Emery, p. 1319

We must think hard about the implications and practical effects of a medical approach based on early aggressive intervening with "lifelong, complex regimens of antiretroviral therapy to preserve immuno-competence" after a cytopathic virus is suppressed.

4. [From a newspaper article by Jane Brody on page 18 of section A of the late edition of the *New York Times* of 6 September 2002. The article is "U.S. Panel Urges Hour of Exercise Each Day."]

ORIGINAL: As for carbohydrates, there is again a wide range of recommended intakes—45 to 65 percent of calories—to allow for dietary flexibility. This range recognizes that both the high-carbohydrate, low-fat diet of many Asian peoples and the higher-fat diet of Mediterranean peoples . . . are . . . associated with good health.

STUDENT:

Good health

When you eat carbohydrates, a wide range of intakes is recommended, from half to 3/4 of your calories. This gives your diet flexibility. This range takes into account that high fat Asian diets and low fat Mediterranean diets both lead to good health.

5. [From page 13 of a book by Philip Zelikow and Condoleezza Rice titled *Germany Unified and Europe Transformed: A Study in Statecraft*, published in 1995. (Gorbachev was the leader of the Soviet Union.)]

ORIGINAL: By far the most important man in Gorbachev's entourage was, like him, an outsider, with no foreign policy expertise. Eduard Shevardnadze, the foreign minister, had been too young to serve in World War II.

STUDENT:

Rice and Zelikov 1995

It is my belief that both Gorbachev and his foreign minister, Eduard Shevardnadze, had very little experience in foreign policy. Shevardnadze had been even too young for World War II military service.

Write the material from each of your note cards in part 1, as you would write it in an actual research paper. Use MLA or APA style as indicated or as your instructor directs. Be accurate, cite correctly, and do not plagiarize.

Example (MLA): *According to Fraser, those who favored the former Queen noticed and were heartened by signs of friction between Henry and Anne (197).*

1. (MLA) _____

_____

_____

_____

_____

_____

2. (MLA) _____

_____

_____

_____

_____

_____

3. (APA) _____

_____

_____

_____

_____

_____

4. (APA) _____

_____

_____

_____

_____

_____

5. (MLA) _____

_____

_____

_____

_____

_____

90. PARAGRAPHS AND PAPERS: The Works Cited/Reference List

(Study 509, The Works Cited/Reference List)

(Open book) Write a **correct** bibliographical entry for each item. Use **MLA** or **APA** style, or both, as your instructor directs. (If both, make a copy of this page before starting, or use your own paper for the APA entries.)

Example (MLA): Book: The Essential Heart Book for Women, by Morris Notelovitz and Diana Tonnessen, published in New York in 1996 by St. Martin's Griffin Press.

Notelovitz, Morris, and Diana Tonnessen. The Essential Heart Book for Women. New York: St. Martin's, 1996.

1. Book: In the Beginning: The Story of the King James Bible. Published: 2001 by Holder & Stoughton in London. Author: Alister McGrath

   _____

   _____

   _____

   _____

2. Journal article: Therapeutic Strategies for HIV Infection—Time to Think Hard. Authors: David A. Cooper and Sean Emery. Journal: New England Journal of Medicine. Published: October 29, 1998, on pages 1319–1321 (pages consecutive throughout volume) of volume 339, number 18.

   _____

   _____

   _____

   _____

3. Online article by Linda Greenhouse in the New York Times Online. It is entitled Citizens' Rights: Justices Ban Two-Tiered Welfare. It was in the issue of May 18, 1999, and was retrieved (accessed) on June 3, 2004. There are no page or edition numbers. The Web address is http://www.nytimes.com/library/politics/scotus/articles/051899welfare-benefits.html

   _____

   _____

   _____

   _____

4. Encyclopedia article: Title: Honoré de Balzac [a writer]. No author of article given. Published on pages 851–852 of vol. 1 of The New Encyclopaedia Britannica: Micropaedia, A very interesting book. 15th edition. The publisher is Encyclopaedia Britannica, Inc., of Chicago, and the date is 1998.

_____

_____

_____

_____

5. Magazine article: Why Jamestown Matters. Magazine: American Heritage. Published: Winter 2008 on pages 52–53 of volume 58, number 3. James Horn wrote this article.

_____

_____

_____

_____

6. Online article from personal Web site: Article title: The Mythic Role of Space Fiction. Name of site: Welcome from Sylvia Engdahl. Author: Sylvia Engdahl. Written August 17, 1998. No pages. No publishing organization given. Retrieved September 30, 2002. Web address: http://www.teleport.com/~sengdahl/spacemyth.htm

_____

_____

_____

_____

7. Newspaper article: Title: That Money Isn't Leaving the Vault. Author: Gretchen Morgenson. Published on page 1H of the business section in the late edition of the New York Times on November 23, 2008.

_____

_____

_____

_____

8. Compact disk: Title: Overtures. Composer: Ludwig van Beethoven. Performed by the Philharmonia Orchestra conducted by Otto Klemperer. Recorded by EMI Records of Hayes Middlesex, England, in 1990.

_____

_____

_____

_____

9. Story in collection: Story title: Girls Like You. Author: Jennifer Moses. Collection title: New Stories from the South: The Year's Best, 1998. Editor of collection: Shannon Ravenel. This story is on pages 143–152 of collection. Collection published by Algonquin Books of Chapel Hill, Chapel Hill, North Carolina, in 1998.

    _____

    _____

    _____

    _____

10. Book: Title: The Universe Unveiled: Instruments and Images Through History. Authors: Bruce Stephenson, Marvin Bolt, and Anna Felicity Friedman. Published by Cambridge University Press in New York City in 2001.

    _____

    _____

    _____

    _____

91. REVIEW: Proofreading

(Study 201–314, Punctuation; Mechanics, with Spelling)

Proofread the following paragraphs, focusing on **typographical errors, omitted** or **doubled words,** and errors in **punctuation, capitalization, number form, abbreviations,** and **spelling.** You may find other errors as well. (You may use a dictionary.) Make all corrections neatly above the line.

(Collaborative option: Students work in pairs to detect and correct errors.)

1. It all began when I joined the U.S. Army. My atittude toward life changed completely. I had just truned twenty one and in the prime of my life. I had every thing, that I had always wanted when I was a Teenager. My parents had given me: no responsibility, no realistic outlook on life and I didn't understand what it meant to go form a small country town into a huge army Camp.

2. I came to know what predjudice really means when I lived in China for one year. When I visited small towns, young children would often ran away from me, or they call me the women with the big nose, I could'nt figure out why until my Guide tells me they only saw a few white person before and that they think white people have big noses. I remembered one time I had went to a small grocery store to buy some rice. The clerk said, "because your an American, you must buy 2 packages. American are rich. Another time I couldl not enter a chinese restirant because I was not Chinese. During my time in china I learned how it feels to be discriminated against. Since return to America, I've made sure that I treated everyone Equal.

3. The word grammer strikes fear or loathing into some students hearts, but, such need not be the case. It's concepts can be simplifyed. For example take the 8 parts of speech; If you except Interjections which are grammatically unconnected to the rest of the sentence there are only 4 kinds of words; naming words (nouns), doing-being word's (verb's), modifiers (adjs. and advs.) and connectors [prepositions and conjunctions.]

4. When we wear silk, we are actualy wearing cocoons spun by silkworms. Think about the silk scarves, ties, or blouses we wear—they all originated with the silkworm, without which we would not have this prized fabric. Mulberry silk which is the highest qualty silk avalable, is the most expensive type of silk. It is made from silkworms that is raise in captivity under exacting conditions. The Chinese developed the method of making mulberry silk thousands of years ago; having perfected this technique, the Orientals are the Worlds experts in producing the

finest silk. The silkworms of the *Bombyx mori* moth, from which mulberry silk was made, has only one job to do: lay eggs. After it lays about 500 eggs, it's job is finished and it dies. The tiny eggs are kept at a low temprature, which is slowly raised until they hatched. Once hatched, the tiny silkworms are fed mulberry leaves, which is the only food these moths will eat. After about a month of gorging on the leaves, the silkworms would spin their cocoons with filament long threads, that they produce. This filament is what we called silk, the strongest natural fiber in the World.

5.   Darlene gazed lovingley at Michael. "Oh, Michael I can't bear the though that you have to leave", she whispered. "must you go back to So. Hadleyville so soon."

"It's a 2 & one half hour trip," Michael replied. "and a snowstorm is blowing in from the North."

"If you go there is my ring!" she cried, pulling the gold band from her finger, and hurling it to the floor. Michael wandered weather she was serious?

92. REVIEW: Editing and Proofreading

(Review 101–404: Grammar and Sentences; Punctuation; Mechanics, with Spelling; Word Choice)

Edit and proofread the paragraphs below. Look not only for **mechanical errors** as in exercise 91, but also for **weak or faulty sentence structure**, and for **grammatical** and **word-choice errors**. Use standard formal English. Rewrite the paragraphs on your own paper.

(Collaborative option: Students work in pairs to detect and correct errors and weaknesses; students critique each other's rewrites.)

1. The birth of my son changed my whole life, I found myself for the first time responsable for another human being. Because of complications in my pregnancy, I had to have a Cesarean, but everything work out without to much difficulty. Since then Roger has made me forget that pain. Being a healthy boy of 5 today, I find him a joy, even thorough he can occasionally be annoying. Everyone of his friends have a delightful time when playing with him. Because he has such a sunny disposition. Whenever a new child moved into the neighborhood, Roger is the first to run over and offer them his toys to play with.

2. The high pay earned by many athletes are ruining professional sports. These jerks are being paid outrageous amounts of money just to run around a field or a court for a few months. For example, Alex Rodriguez, the Yankee's star, has a salary of $28 million, and LeBron James will earn more than he can ever count. Most players' salarys exceed a million dollar's. In baseball, ever since the players became free agents, they have recieved exorbitant paychecks. I believe such sums are being award to the players without regard to we fans. How many of us can afford to pay a price that amounts to a total of $100 for a seat at a basketball game. Moreover, the players are rarely exerting maximum effort to justify their seven-figure incomes. I, for one, will not return back to Municipal Stadium or Central coliseum unless they have scheduled a good college game there. It is up to we fans to reverse this thing by boycotting professionel game.

3. Most Americans are woefully ignorant of the World's geography. Where a country is located, what kind of resources does it have, and how far away it is are questions that bring a puzzled frown to many? Angola, for example. Where is it? Is it an island? What do they produce there? What are it's people like, do they think and act like we do? Just because a land is distant from us doesn't mean that it's not importent. Being so far from our shores, Americans should not ignore other countries.

4. Commuting to a city College from your home may seam less attractive then to live on a rolling green campus in the hills. Yet they have many advantages. Lower cost is an obvious one, home cooked meals is another. It gives a student the freedom to go wherever they want after classes: to movies or shows, museums, or even get a part-time job. Citys are full of exciting places to find excitement in, therefore they form a welcome break from a boring classes.

5. There are a right way and a wrong way to walk when hiking. First of all, stay relaxed and no slouching. Swing you're arms, this will help relaxation and momentum it will also make you feel good. You should maintain straightness in your shoulders & hips to. When carrying a pack, leaning a bit forward will help a person center their weight over their feet. Carry plenty of water, and stop to rest after a half an hour.

93. REVIEW: Revising, Editing, and Proofreading

(Study 101–503: Grammar and Sentences; Punctuation; Mechanics, with Spelling; Word Choice; Paragraphs)

On your own paper, **revise**, **edit**, and **proofread** the paragraphs below. Correct **all errors** and make any necessary **improvements**, including strengthening **paragraph structure**. Use all the skills and knowledge you have learned in *English Simplified.*

(Collaborative option: Students work in pairs to detect and correct errors and weaknesses; students critique each other's rewrites.)

1. The government must take strong action against polluters, it is slowly killing us all. By poisoning our air and our water. The big business lobbies control Congress, and so they pass less antipollution laws. Its frightening, for example to find that Midwest smokestacks fill the air with acid. Rain become's filled with this acid. It is killing fish in Adirondack Mountain lakes. These lakes are hundreds of miles to the east. Elsewhere, pesticides are being used. They are been sprayed on potatoe fields. The chemicals seeped underground, and then the local well water becomes contaminated. In Texas, they have polluted water almost kill ten thousand cattles. The corpses of these cattle had to be burned to prevent the spread of the poison. The government is responding far too weak to this pollution crisis situation. Congress must resist the lobbyists, and strong antipollution laws must be passed by it. I hope they have a future plan for it.

2. "Warning: The surgion general has determined that cigarette smoking is dangerous to your health," or a similar message printed on all packs of cigaretes but people still smoke. Did you ever wonder why? Every smoker know that cigarettes are harmful to their lungs, but this doesn't stop them. I beleive that people just don't care any more about their selve's. Years ago people they tried to live longer and not to do any thing that would damage their Health now things have changed. I feel that people feel that their is nothing to live for and if your going to die it has to be from something even if its not cancer. Also people relizing that life is not to easy. Price's are going up jobs are hard to find and who wants to live in a world where many things are difficult to get. Being a non smoker, Cigarettes should be banned from society. If they were baned from Society, smokers will live longer. In spite of themself.

3. Enlisting in the army was an experience that changed my life. June 10, 2001 was the day it began. The plane left Boston for Georgia. The plane arrived 3 hour's later. A group of we recruits waited for 4 more hour for the bus to come to take us to Ft. Gordon. The bus came and took us to Camp. We were processed in, and we was given sleeping quarters. They were cold and drafty. The 1st week was spent in a reception Center. It was nice there, too nice. The next week we were transfered to our duty stations to start the armys new basic training program. The sergents appeared to look nice but that was just a dream, For five weeks we did the same grueling thing everyday. At 4 o'clock we woke up, did lots of exercises, etc, and did the things that had to be done that day. The training was easy but the sergent's made it hard. Some of the other guys were there made it worst. They resisted the discipline. The last week had came and I was a new person. I have learned that, I will never join anything with out thinking twice about it.

4. Cross-country skiing is not as popular as downhill skiing. But it has been slowly but steadily gaining in popularity in the United States, and this is a good thing because it is a much more aerobic sport that is, it gives the skier a better cardiovascular workout and is therefore better for your all-around health, which, in turn, can lead to a person having a longer life because it is healthy for you. Cross-country skiing will burn up to 9 hundred calories an hour, moreover the upper body muscles are developed as well as the lower body, which is the only part that running or cycling develop. Beside this it developes coordination. And they have less risk of injury then downhill skiers.

5. One of the biggest dangers in writing a paragraph is straying from the topic. It drives me crazy when my history professor does this often when lecturing. Another is fused sentences they can be tricky, so do comma splices. By dangling a modifier, your Composition can sound silly. Do not shift voice or mood for your essay can be made confusing by it. Lack of agreement between subjects and verbs reveal a careless writer at work who isn't paying attention to what he is doing when he writes. You have to know wear to put the verb at. Worst of all, is to have no topic sentence or cohesion.

94. ACHIEVEMENT TEST: Grammar, Sentences, and Paragraphs

Part 1: Sentence Errors

Write **S** if the boldfaced expression is one complete, correct **sentence**.
Write **F** if it is a **fragment** (incorrect: less than a complete sentence).
Write **Spl** or **FS** if it is a **comma splice** or **fused sentence** (incorrect: two or more sentences written as one).

Example: The climbers suffered from hypothermia. **Having neglected to bring warm clothing.** _____F_____

1. Sarah cut roses for the dining-room table. **After waiting months for them to bloom.** 1. _____

2. Sue took me shopping with her; she bought items I could never afford. **Such as a diamond bracelet, a pair of dangling gold earrings, Italian leather flats, and a cashmere coat.** 2. _____

3. **Shawna always eats a good breakfast she isn't hungry until noon.** 3. _____

4. The rancher sold most of his livestock. **Then he turned his property into a profitable dude ranch.** 4. _____

5. **Shocked at her surprise birthday party, Emily began crying.** 5. _____

6. **When does abstract art become just scribbles?** 6. _____

7. **The team having arrived.** The swim meet competition began. 7. _____

8. Nine families joined the pollution study. **They will wear carbon-filter badges, this device will monitor the air that they are breathing** 8. _____

9. **The horse having escaped from the pasture.** The rancher drove his truck across the fields to find him. 9. _____

10. Curling is a sport played on ice with stones and brooms. **A game I had never even heard of until recently.** 10. _____

11. **The high temperature made the snow melt we had to cancel our plans for sledding.** 11. _____

12. **The woman who is wearing the black velvet suit with gold buttons.** 12. _____

13. **Joanne and Dante danced at Rootie Kazootie's until midnight even though they had not begun to write their history essays, which were due the next day.** 13. _____

14. Elaine went skiing in Vermont for ten days. **Because she had planned and saved for two years to make this dream come true.** 14. _____

15. **Children in the experimental group improved their reading scores by nearly a full grade, however, six-month follow-up studies showed that the gains did not last.** 15. _____

16. **Though armed and considered dangerous, the thief surrendered without a struggle.** 16. _____

In the blank, write **C** if the boldfaced expression is used **correctly**.
Write **X** if it is used **incorrectly**.

Example: There **was** dozens of dinosaur bones on the site. _____X_____

1. The secret of their elopement was between Cathy and **myself**. 1. _____
2. During the summer, she trained horses, **which** assisted her financially. 2. _____
3. On the front porch, there **were** cans of paint, brushes, scrapers, and primer. 3. _____
4. Julie Diver, along with her three cats, **were** waiting at my front door. 4. _____
5. The interviewer asked each of the politicians to explain **their** position on taxation. 5. _____
6. Copies of the test **was** left on the secretary's desk. 6. _____
7. The gift my parents gave to Josh and **I** on our wedding day stunned us: it was a trip to Paris. 7. _____
8. The ticket agent gave Ed and **me** concert seats that were in the front row. 8. _____
9. Each of the cabinet members **were** given a copy of the president's speech. 9. _____
10. **Nervous about the state of the economy**, people are spending less money on luxury items. 10. _____
11. Parking restrictions apply to **not only** students **but also** to visitors. 11. _____
12. His mother wanted him to become a corporate lawyer, move to New York, and marry a celebrity. **This** kept Joshua in college. 12. _____
13. Students should meet their professors, so that if **you** have questions about class, **you** will feel comfortable approaching a professor during office hours. 13. _____
14. **Having an afternoon off**, there was time to do the laundry and go shopping. 14. _____
15. She wanted to model in New York and **earning** money for a large apartment. 15. _____
16. **Being anxious about the speech**, the microphone amplified my quavering voice. 16. _____
17. We wondered why the list of courses **was** not posted yet. 17. _____
18. Few people enjoy playing the piano as much as **him**. 18. _____
19. I like swimming in icy lakes as well as **to relax in the warm sunshine**. 19. _____
20. Aggression **is when** one nation attacks another without provocation. 20. _____
21. **Is** either of the two bands ready to go on? 21. _____
22. Was it you **who** wrote the editorial titled "Ban Smoking on Campus"? 22. _____
23. Everyone who plays the lottery hopes that **their** ticket will win the million-dollar jackpot. 23. _____
24. It is up to **us** parents to insist on better textbooks for our children. 24. _____
25. All of **we** residents living in the Hampden neighborhood were upset when a pawn shop was planned for the main shopping area. 25. _____
26. The man **who** I met in the park was there to watch the birds. 26. _____
27. Every parent of young children should understand that it is up to **you** to attend the PTA meetings at their elementary school. 27. _____
28. He coached Little League and joined two service clubs. **It** was expected of him by his associates. 28. _____
29. Harry and **myself** tried snorkeling in his swimming pool. 29. _____
30. **Whom** do you think will apply for the position of dean of students? 30. _____

31. There **was** a Buick, a Toyota, and a Mercedes parked in the lot. 31._____

32. Madeline said she gave her password to only you and **I.** 32._____

33. **Is** there any objections to your opening a nightclub on campus? 33._____

34. My advisor suggested that I take Russian and that I should get a part-time job. **That** was
fine with me. 34._____

35. Each of the players **has** two passes for all home games. 35._____

36. Neither Joan nor her two attendants **was** asked to appear on television. 36._____

37. He is one of the engineering students who **are** interning this summer. 37._____

38. You will never find anyone more responsible than **her**. 38._____

39. Jennifer is the **healthiest** of the two trainers at the fitness center. 39._____

40. When the Baltimore Ravens and the Pittsburgh Steelers play, I know **they** will win. 40._____

41. Why not give the books to **whomever** you think will be going to the library. 41._____

42. Did the committee approve of **his** assuming the chair position? 42._____

43. The children wanted **not only** longer recesses **but also** new playground equipment. 43._____

44. On her kitchen counter **were** a cake mix, a bowl, two eggs, and a cup of milk; Maureen
planned to make a cake that afternoon. 44._____

45. The coach, as well as the players and manager, **was** sure of winning. 45._____

46. **Knowing of his parents' disapproval**, it seemed wise for him to reconsider his plan to drop
out of school to become a magician in a coffee shop. 46._____

47. Daniel decided to **only** purchase three new fish for his aquarium. 47._____

48. If he **were** more tactful, he would have fewer enemies. 48._____

49. **If you submit your paper late,** does not mean that it will be graded *F*. 49._____

50. Neither the camp director nor the hikers **was** aware of their danger. 50._____

Part 3: Paragraphs (not included in scoring)

On the back of this page, write a **paragraph** of six to eight sentences on **one** of the following
topics (you may use scrap paper also):

_____

The thrill of _____ (something you have done)

A friend I will never forget

If I could run the country for one month

The best (or worst) movie I have seen in the past year

A sorely needed law

95. ACHIEVEMENT TEST: Punctuation

Write **C** if the punctuation in brackets is **correct**.
Write **X** if it is **incorrect**.
(Use only one number in each blank.)

Example: Regular exercise[,] and sound nutrition are essential for good health.   _____X_____

1. Potomac Mills, Virginia[,] is the site of a huge outlet mall.   1._____

2. Residents[,] who own barking dogs[,] refuse to do anything about the noise.   2._____

3. Bill thought the bicycle was mine, but it was her[']s.   3._____

4. The strike having been averted[,] the workers returned to their jobs.   4._____

5. He asked me where I had bought my surfboard[?]   5._____

6. When I open it[']s favorite cat food, the cat races into the kitchen.   6._____

7. Haven't you often heard it said, "Haste makes waste["?]   7._____

8. Wouldn't you like to go to the rally with us?"[,] asked the girl across the hall.   8._____

9. He said, "Let's walk across the campus.[" "]It's such a warm evening."   9._____

10. Enrollment is up to three[-]thousand students this quarter.   10._____

11. Twenty[-]six students have volunteered to serve on various committees.   11._____

12. Dear Sir[;] I have enclosed my application and résumé.   12._____

13. After you have finished your sociology assignment[,] let's go to a movie.   13._____

14. The happy little girls jumped up and down[;] because they were going to get a puppy.   14._____

15. Melanie isn't going to the movies again[,] is she?   15._____

16. We were early[;] as a matter of fact, we were the first guests to arrive.   16._____

17. "If you really look closely," the art critic commented[,] "you'll see a purple turtle in the middle of the painting."   17._____

18. Dr. Johnson had little praise for the current health care system[;] calling it an elitist structure.   18._____

19. The band recorded its first album in the spring[,] and followed it with a summer concert tour.   19._____

20. She had hoped to arrange a two month[']s tour of Korea and Japan.   20._____

21. We hope[,] Ms. Foster[,] that your office will be satisfactory.   21._____

22. The next stockholders' meeting is scheduled for August 9, 2012[,] but it will be open only to major investors.   22._____

23. My youngest sister[,] who is fourteen[,] is already looking at colleges.   23._____

24. Because she played cards until midnight[;] she overslept.   24._____

25. Jane Cox[,] a biochemistry major[,] won the top scholarship.   25._____

26. Professor Thomas was asked to create a course for the Women[']s Studies Department.   26._____

27. The little boy in the center of the old photograph[,] would later write five novels.   27._____

28. "As for who has written the winning essay[—]well, I haven't as yet heard from the judges," said Mr. Hawkins.   28. _____

29. What he described about the massive oil spill[,] filled us with horror.   29. _____

30. I asked Elizabeth what we should do about our vacation plans[?]   30. _____

31. The newly elected officers are Dan Sullivan, president[;] Ruby Pillsbury, vice president[;] and Maria Garcia, secretary.   31. _____

32. Before the radical group surrendered[;] they attempted to negotiate their freedom.   32. _____

33. We followed the trail over several ridges[,] and along the edge of two mountain lakes.   33. _____

34. Before touring Europe, I had many matters to attend to[;] such as making reservations, buying clothes, and getting a passport.   34. _____

35. Having a good sense of humor helps one put problems into perspective[;] certainly it's better than brooding.   35. _____

36. The ticket agent inquired ["]if we were planning to stop in Paris.["]   36. _____

37. Once retired, Ensel painted portraits of family pets[,] and played bingo every Thursday and Saturday.   37. _____

38. Marcia learned that all foods[,] that are high in fat[,] should be eaten in moderation.   38. _____

39. We were told to read ["]Ode to a Nightingale,["] a poem by Keats.   39. _____

40. The alumni magazine had a column cleverly entitled ["]Grad-Tidings.["]   40. _____

41. A civilian conservation corps could provide[:] education, training, and work for thousands of unemployed teenagers.   41. _____

42. Some people wish to have ["]America, the Beautiful["] become our national anthem.   42. _____

43. She hurried towards us[,] her books clasped under her arm[,] to tell us the good news.   43. _____

44. The audience wanted him to sing one more song[;] however, he refused.   44. _____

45. They must be the only ones who have visited New York in recent years and not seen the show ["]The Lion King[."]   45. _____

46. She found a note in her mailbox: "Sorry to have missed you. The Lawson[']s."   46. _____

47. His mother wanted him to major in chemistry[;] he wanted to major in music.   47. _____

48. Chris decided that he wanted a quiet vacation[,] not one full of schedules and guided tours.   48. _____

49. He had gone to the library[. B]ecause he wanted to borrow some videos.   49. _____

50. Her program included courses in English[,] social science[,] and chemistry.   50. _____

51. Every child knows "Twinkle, twinkle, little star[/]How I wonder what you are."   51. _____

52. To prepare for the baseball tryouts[,] Sam practiced every night.   52. _____

53. Ms. Whitney, who is a physical education instructor, came to the rally[;] with Mr. Martin, who is the football coach.   53. _____

54. When the tornado hit eastern Ohio[,] it caused millions of dollars of damage.   54. _____

55. "Some of the seniors wer[']ent able to pay their dues," she said.   55. _____

56. Frank Anderson[,] who is on the tennis team[,] is an excellent athlete.   56. _____

57. "All motorists[,] who fail to stop at the crosswalk[,] should be put in jail!" declared an angry parent.   57. _____

58. Looking at Susan sweetly, Mark replied, "No[,] I will not lend you a thousand dollars."   58. _____

59. George enrolled in a course in home economics; Elsa[,] in woodworking.   59. _____

60. "Haven't I met you somewhere before?"[,] he asked.   60. _____

61. "It's most unlikely["!] she said, turning away.   61. _____

62. A student[,] whom I met at the banquet[,] would like to work in our department next semester.   62. _____

63. It is a monumental task to build a highway[,] where 10,000-foot mountains block the way.   63. _____

64. He moved to Denver[,] where he worked as a freelance photographer.   64. _____

65. We were[,] on the other hand[,] not surprised by his decision.   65. _____

66. I bought a special type of paintbrush to reach those hard[-]to[-]reach spots near the rain gutters.   66. _____

67. Listen to the arguments of both speakers[,] then decide which side you favor.   67. _____

68. Four generations of Spencer[']s will attend the family reunion.   68. _____

69. Susannah is familiar with many customs of Sweden [(]her father's homeland[)] and can prepare many Swedish dishes.   69. _____

70. Our ex[-]mayor pleaded guilty to a speeding ticket.   70. _____

71. The conference sponsored by our fraternity was successful[,] especially the sessions concerning community-service projects.   71. _____

72. Liberty University scored ten points in the last minute but[,] the Sparks held on for the win.   72. _____

73. Jack displayed a unique [(?)] talent when he created a collage of spaghetti sauce, pickles, and pancakes.   73. _____

74. The children[,] on the other hand[,] were content to wear last year's coats and boots.   74. _____

75. The teenager used the word [*like*] throughout her conversation.   75. _____

96. ACHIEVEMENT TEST: Mechanics, Spelling, and Word Choice

Part 1: Capitalization

In each blank, write **C** if the boldfaced word(s) **follow** the rules of capitalization.
Write **X** if the word(s) **do not follow** the rules.

Example: The Mormons settled in what is now **Salt Lake City**.   _____C_____

1. Please meet Charles Ebbings, **Professor** of psychology at Yale.   1. _____
2. It was relaxing to spend a few days away from **college**.   2. _____
3. She is **President** of her class.   3. _____
4. I belong to a **Science Club.**   4. _____
5. He plays for Ohio **State**.   5. _____
6. We saluted the **american** flag.   6. _____
7. We flew over the **french Alps**.   7. _____
8. I asked **Grandmother** to lend me the family photo album.   8. _____
9. He enjoys living in the **Southwest**.   9. _____
10. The **East** side of the house needs to be repainted.   10. _____
11. I visited an **indian** village while on vacation.   11. _____
12. He naps in his **history** class.   12. _____
13. We heard that **Aunt Harriet** had eloped with the butcher.   13. _____
14. The note ended, "**sincerely yours**."   14. _____
15. I am going to be a **Medical Anthropologist**.   15. _____
16. The magazine recommended buying a Dell **Computer**.   16. _____
17. Professor Balkan let me borrow a copy of **Science Journal** for my research project. refused to change my grade.   17. _____
18. History 303 studies the Russian **Revolution**.   18. _____
19. We toured the marshes of the Thames River, where part of the novel *Great Expectations* is set.   19. _____
20. Walter prayed that **god** would let him win the lottery.   20. _____

Part 2: Abbreviations and Numbers

Write **C** if the boldfaced abbreviation or number is used **correctly**.
Write **X** if it is used **incorrectly**.

Example: They drove through **Tenn.**   _____X_____

1. **Fifty million** voters went to the polls in November 2008.   1. _____

2. We'll meet you on **Thurs.** afternoon.   2. _____

3. My cat named Holiday is **5** years old.   3. _____

4. The Jenkins live on Sutherland **Rd**.   4. _____

5. She was born on July **6th**, 1990.   5. _____

6. Please meet me at **10** o'clock.   6. _____

7. He released **two hundred** doves after the wedding.   7. _____

8. After a brief investigation, we discovered that **13** students were involved in the prank.   8. _____

9. The train leaves at **7** p.m.   9. _____

10. Dinner was served at **six** o'clock.   10. _____

11. Joan Allen, **Ph.D.,** spoke first.   11. _____

12. Lunch cost **17** dollars!   12. _____

13. **Ms**. Martin, please chair the meeting today.   13. _____

14. Lloyd's monthly salary is now **$3,200.50.**   14. _____

15. They lived at **six seventy-four** Ninth Avenue.   15. _____

Part 3: Spelling

In each sentence, one boldfaced word is **misspelled**. Write its number in the blank.

Example: (1)**Its** (2)**too** late (3)**to go**.   _____1_____

1. Horace's (1)**peculiar** expression of boredom was his way of making a (2)**statment** about the quality of the (3)**equipment**.   1. _____

2. The open (1)**cemetary** gates permitted an (2)**excellent** (3)**opportunity** for Karloff's laboratory assistant.   2. _____

3. My (1)**psychology** (2)**proffessor** assigns a weekly (3)**written** report.   3. _____

4. He needed (1)**permission** from the (2)**commitee** to participate in the (3)**competition**.   4. _____

5. The (1)**bookkeeper** learned that a (2)**knowledge** of (3)**grammer** is helpful.   5. _____

6. A (1)**fourth** such disaster threatens the very (2)**existance** of the Alaskan (3)**environment.**   6. _____

7. Arthur (1)**definately** considered it a (2)**privilege** to help write the (3)**article**.   7. _____

8. The (1)**principal** (2)**complimented** her for her (3)**excellant** performance.   8. _____

9. It was (1)**apparent** that she was (2)**desparate** because she was listening to his (3)**advice**.   9. _____

10. We (1)**imediately** became (2)**familiar** with the requirements for a (3)**license**.   10. _____

11. Is it (1)**permissable** to ask him to (2)**recommend** me for a (3)**government** position?   11. _____

12. (1)**Personaly**, I didn't believe his (2)**analysis** of the result of the (3)**questionnaire**.   12._____

13. The test pilot felt enormous (1)**optimism** after her third (2)**repitition** of the dangerous (3) **maneuver**.   13._____

14. It's (1)**ridiculus** that Sue became so angry about the (2)**criticism** of her friend, the (3) **playwright**.   14._____

15. She was not (1)**conscious** of being (2)**unnecessarily** (3)**persistant** about the matter.   15._____

Part 4: Word Choice

To be correct, the boldfaced expression must be standard, formal English and must not be sexist or otherwise discriminatory.
Write **C** if the boldfaced word is used **correctly**.
Write **X** if it is used **incorrectly**.

Examples: The counsel's **advice** was misinterpreted.   C
They **could of** made the plane except for the traffic.   X

1. I was not **altogether** amused.   1._____

2. Aaron looked **sort of** tired after the test.   2._____

3. They are all old; for **instants**, Grayson is eighty-six.   3._____

4. Billy cried when his balloon **burst**.   4._____

5. Next time, plan to invite **fewer** guests.   5._____

6. He earned no interest on his **principal**.   6._____

7. **Can** I add your name as a contributor to the scholarship fund?   7._____

8. The judge would hear no **farther** arguments.   8._____

9. I am in real trouble, **aren't I**?   9._____

10. The team was **plenty** angry.   10._____

11. The parent **persuaded** her child to take out the garbage.   11._____

12. He notified **most** of his creditors.   12._____

13. She knows **less** people than I.   13._____

14. Saul made an **illusion** to *Hamlet*.   14._____

15. Was the murderer **hanged**?   15._____

16. The team **would of** done much better with a different quarterback.   16._____

17. The old **codgers** shouldn't be driving.   17._____

18. I had **already** signed the check.   18._____

19. John sounds **like** he needs a vacation.   19._____

20. I can't stand **those kind** of jokes.   20._____

21. He is **real** happy about winning the contest.   21._____

22. The sleepy dog is **laying** by the fire.   22._____

23. She **generally always** works hard.   23._____

24. He does **good** in math courses.   24. _____

25. His speech **implied** that he would raise taxes.   25. _____

26. We took the tour because of its awesome **things to see**.   26. _____

27. On the bus were city people, suburbanites, and **hillbillies**.   27. _____

28. The chair was about **thirty inches in width**.   28. _____

29. **Due to the fact of his escape**, the police have set up roadblocks.   29. _____

30. Our vacation was even **more perfect** than you can imagine.   30. _____

31. The road through the mountains was **pretty crooked**.   31. _____

32. Thank you for the **most unique** gift I've ever received.   32. _____

33. The Sherrill family did **lots of stuff** on vacation.   33. _____

34. The **advise** the counselor gave Betsy was very helpful   34. _____

35. She **advised** the students to go to class before buying their textbooks.   35. _____

97. ACHIEVEMENT TEST: General Review

Part 1: Punctuation Errors

Most of the following sentences have several errors with punctuation and sentence structure. The following errors will be found throughout this exercise: fused sentences, commas, semicolons, quotation marks, hyphens, apostrophes, semicolons, colons, and dashes. Some sentences might be correct as they are. After reading each sentence carefully, correct the errors so that the sentence is in standard, formal English.

1. For dinner, Mother prepared her spinach and lima bean casserole with liver Father and us children decided to go out for pizza.

   _____

   _____

2. The animal trainer asked the students to bring to the session a cats collar a dogs toy a hamsters cage and a parakeets perch.

   _____

   _____

3. Youre wondering why I called you here aren't you? the leader asked.

   _____

   _____

4. You're out of your mind! exclaimed Lydia slamming down her books.

   _____

   _____

5. As I left for the airport Mother said write when you can.

   _____

   _____

6. The twin sisters agreed that they would not wear matching clothes.

   _____

   _____

7. Shes the sort of person who wont listen to anybodys opinion.

   _____

   _____

8. Do you remember Fathers favorite saying Never give up she asked.

_____

_____

9. She began reciting the opening lines of Elizabeth Barrett Browning's sonnet How do I love thee?/Let me count the ways.

_____

_____

10. Dear Coach Hope The whole group all eight of us plans to spend the weekend with you.

_____

_____

11. Johns shopping list included these items truffles caviar champagne and a dozen hot dogs.

_____

_____

12. The lead runner crested the hill and glanced back at the others struggling far behind.

_____

_____

13. The rules for using semicolons see page 7 are not difficult to master.

_____

_____

14. Only one thing stood in the way of his buying the yellow Cadillac money.

_____

_____

15. The statement read enclosed you will find one hundred dollars $100 to cover damages.

_____

_____

16. The score was tied the game would go into overtime.

_____

_____

17. Spencer studied all night but failed the test.

_____

_____

18. Do you know Ms. Lane how we can get in touch with Supermans girlfriend the one who has kryptonite?

_____

_____

19. The oldest building on campus is now a dilapidated three story structure.

_____

_____

20. Time having run out I was obliged to hand in my test paper before I had finished Mary said.

_____

_____

Part 2: Sentence Design

At the bottom and back of this page, design sentences that contain all the elements listed. These elements do not have to be in any order. You will probably need to add words to design a sentence in Standard English. [Hint: choose the verb and put it in the requested tense first.]

_____

1. A simple sentence with compound subject, a verb in the present tense, and two adjectives

2. A simple sentence with a compound verb in the simple past tense and two prepositional phrases

3. A compound sentence with both verbs in the future tense, two prepositional phrases, and three adjectives

4. A compound sentence with the two independent clauses joined with *but*, both verbs as transitive, two adverbs, and two prepositional phrases

5. A complex sentence with a verb in the simple past tense, a verb in the past perfect tense, and one adjective

The following chart gives brief definitions and examples of the grammatical terms you will read about most often in these exercises. Refer to *English Simplified* for more information.

Term	What It Is or Does	Examples
Adjective	Describes a noun	a **fast** runner (describes the noun **runner**)
Appositive	A noun that renames another	Tom Wolfe, **the writer**, lives in New York. (The appositive follows the man's name.)
Adverb	Describes a verb, adjective, or another adverb	He runs **fast** (describes the verb **run**). He runs **very** fast (describes the adverb **fast**). He is an **extremely** fast runner (describes the adjective **fast**).
Clause	A group of words with a subject and a predicate. An independent clause can stand by itself and make complete sense; a dependent clause must be attached to an independent clause.	**He is a fast runner.** (An independent clause) **if he is a fast runner** (A dependent clause that must be attached to some independent clause, such as **He will win.**)
Complement	Completes the meaning of the verb	Direct Object: He threw the **ball.** (Says what was thrown.) Indirect Object: He threw **me** the ball. (Says to whom the ball was thrown.) Subjective Complement: He is a **pitcher.** (Renames the subject **He** after the linking verb **is.**) Objective Complement: The team named Rodgers **coach.** (Follows the direct object **Rodgers** and renames it.)
Conjunction	A word that joins	Coordinating Conjunction: Joins things of equal importance: Men **and** women. Poor **but** honest. Subordinating Conjunction: Joins a dependent clause to a main clause: I left **when** she arrived.
Fragment	A group of words that cannot stand by itself as a sentence	**when I saw them** (a dependent clause); **from Maine to California** (a prepositional phrase)
Noun	Names a person, place, animal, thing, or idea	**Tom, Denver, cat, book, love, truth**
Phrase	A group of related words without a subject and a verb	**from California** (a prepositional phrase); **to see the king** (an infinitive phrase); **built of bricks** (a participial phrase); **building houses** (a gerund phrase)
(Complete) Predicate	The part of the sentence that speaks about the subject	The man **threw the ball.** (says what the subject did)
Pronoun	A word that replaces a noun (or replaces a word group acting as a noun)	**He** will be here soon. (**He** takes the place of the man's name.)
Subject	The person or thing about whom the sentence speaks	**Polly** writes children's books.
Verb	Says what the subject either does or is	She **buys** seashells. She **is** a doctor.

P9-EJH-361

ANNUAL EDITIONS

American Foreign Policy 09/10

Fourteenth Edition

EDITOR

Glenn P. Hastedt

James Madison University

Glenn Hastedt received his PhD from Indiana University. He is professor of political science at James Madison University, where he teaches courses on U.S. foreign policy, national security policy, and international relations. His special area of interest is on the workings of the intelligence community and the problems of strategic surprise and learning from intelligence failures. In addition to having published articles on these topics, he is the author of *American Foreign Policy: Past, Present, Future;* coauthor of *Dimensions of World Politics;* and editor and contributor to *Controlling Intelligence.* He has also published two volumes of readings, *Toward the Twenty-First Century* and *One World, Many Voices.*

Boston   Burr Ridge, IL   Dubuque, IA   New York   San Francisco   St. Louis
Bangkok   Bogotá   Caracas   Kuala Lumpur   Lisbon   London   Madrid   Mexico City
Milan   Montreal   New Delhi   Santiago   Seoul   Singapore   Sydney   Taipei   Toronto

ANNUAL EDITIONS: AMERICAN FOREIGN POLICY, FOURTEENTH EDITION

1 2 3 4 5 6 7 8 9 0 QPD/QPD 0 9 8

ISBN 978–0–07339764–1
MHID 0–07–339764–4
ISSN 1075–5225

Managing Editor: *Larry Loeppke*
Senior Managing Editor: *Faye Schilling*
Developmental Editor: *Debra Henricks*
Editorial Coordinator: *Mary Foust*
Editorial Assistant: *Nancy Meissner*
Production Service Assistant: *Rita Hingtgen*
Permissions Coordinator: *Lenny Behnke*
Senior Marketing Manager: *Julie Keck*
Marketing Communications Specialist: *Mary Klein*
Marketing Coordinator: *Alice Link*
Project Manager: *Sandy Wille*
Design Specialist: *Tara McDermott*
Senior Production Supervisor: *Laura Fuller*
Cover Graphics: *Kristine Jubeck*

Compositor: Laserwords Private Limited
Cover Image: Department of Defense/U.S. Air Force Tech. Sgt. Jerry Morrison (both)

Library in Congress Cataloging-in-Publication Data
Main entry under title: Annual Editions: American Foreign Policy, 2009/2010.
  1. U.S. Foreign Relations—Periodicals. I. Hastedt, Glenn P., *comp.* II. Title: American Foreign Policy.
658'.05

www.mhhe.com

Editors/Advisory Board

Members of the Advisory Board are instrumental in the final selection of articles for each edition of ANNUAL EDITIONS. Their review of articles for content, level, currentness, and appropriateness provides critical direction to the editor and staff. We think that you will find their careful consideration well reflected in this volume.

Preface

In publishing ANNUAL EDITIONS we recognize the enormous role played by the magazines, newspapers, and journals of the public press in providing current, first-rate educational information in a broad spectrum of interest areas. Many of these articles are appropriate for students, researchers, and professionals seeking accurate, current material to help bridge the gap between principles and theories and the real world. These articles, however, become more useful for study when those of lasting value are carefully collected, organized, indexed, and reproduced in a low-cost format, which provides easy and permanent access when the material is needed. That is the role played by ANNUAL EDITIONS.

This fourteenth edition of *Annual Editions: American Foreign Policy* presents an overview of American foreign policy. Prior to September 11, 2001, the debate over the future of American foreign policy proceeded at a measured pace since few pressing threats to American national security seemed to exist. The foreign policy debate centered on selection strategies and tactics that could guide the United States in the transition period between the end of the Cold War and the emergence of a post–Cold War era. It was a debate largely conducted in the language of academics and it was one that did not engage large numbers of the American public. All of that has changed. After September 11, the conduct and content of American foreign policy is seen as important by virtually all Americans.

The immediate issue was combating and eradicating terrorism; the geographic focal point was Afghanistan; and the target was the Taliban government and Osama bin Laden's al Qaeda terrorist organization. Few quarreled with the merits of this military undertaking, either in the United States or abroad. This was not true for the Bush administration's next major foreign policy initiative when the war against terrorism was expanded to Iraq with the objective of removing Saddam Hussein from power. This successful military action was followed by an occupation marked by violence and political turmoil. Additional international challenges surfaced in short order. The most noteworthy being revelations concerning the North Korean and Iranian nuclear programs, and growing conflict over trade and monetary matters with China. As a consequence, we are now witnessing a wide-ranging debate over the strategic and tactical choices open to the United States in an era when it is the dominant (and some would say unchallenged) world power. To date, this debate has produced far more questions than answers, and it extends beyond questions of responding to terrorism and Iraq.

Annual Editions: American Foreign Policy 09/10 is divided into eight units. The first unit addresses questions of grand strategy. The second unit focuses on selected regional and bilateral relations. In the third unit, our attention shifts inward to the ways in which domestic forces affect the content of American foreign policy. The fourth unit looks at the institutions that make American foreign policy. In the fifth unit, the process by which American foreign policy is made is illustrated through accounts of recent foreign policy decisions. The sixth and seventh units provide an overview of the economic and military issues confronting the United States today. The final unit looks in depth at the issues surrounding the war in Iraq and its aftermath from a variety of different perspectives.

Together the readings in these eight units provide students with an up-to-date overview of key events in American foreign policy, the forces that shape it, and the policy problems on the agenda. The essays were chosen for their ability to inform students and spark debate. They are not designed to advance any particular interpretation of American foreign policy.

I would like to thank Ian Nielsen for supporting the concept of an *Annual Editions: American Foreign Policy* many years ago. Also deserving of thanks are the many people at McGraw-Hill/Contemporary Learning Series who worked to make the project a success and those faculty on the Advisory Board who provided input on the selection of articles. In the end, the success of *Annual Editions: American Foreign Policy* depends upon the views of the faculty and students who use it. I encourage you to let me know what worked and what did not so that each successive volume will be better than its predecessor. Please complete and return the postage-paid *article rating form* at the end of this book.

Glenn Hastedt
Editor

Contents

UNIT 1
The United States and the World: Strategic Choices

The concepts in bold italics are developed in the article. For further expansion, please refer to the Topic Guide.

UNIT 2
The United States and the World: Regional and Bilateral Relations

The concepts in bold italics are developed in the article. For further expansion, please refer to the Topic Guide.

UNIT 3
The Domestic Side of American Foreign Policy

UNIT 4
The Institutional Context of American Foreign Policy

The concepts in bold italics are developed in the article. For further expansion, please refer to the Topic Guide.

UNIT 5
The Foreign Policy Making Process

The concepts in bold italics are developed in the article. For further expansion, please refer to the Topic Guide.

UNIT 6
U.S. International Economic Strategy

UNIT 7
U.S. Military Strategy

The concepts in bold italics are developed in the article. For further expansion, please refer to the Topic Guide.

UNIT 8
The Iraq War and Beyond

The concepts in bold italics are developed in the article. For further expansion, please refer to the Topic Guide.

The concepts in bold italics are developed in the article. For further expansion, please refer to the Topic Guide.

Correlation Guide

The *Annual Editions* series provides students with convenient, inexpensive access to current, carefully selected articles from the public press. **Annual Editions: American Foreign Policy 09/10** is an easy-to-use reader that presents articles on important topics such as *diplomacy, globalization, military power,* and many more. For more information on *Annual Editions* and other *McGraw-Hill Contemporary Learning Series* titles, visit www.mhcls.com.

This convenient guide matches the units in **Annual Editions: American Foreign Policy 09/10** with the corresponding chapters in two of our best-selling McGraw-Hill Political Science textbooks by Boyer and Rourke.

Annual Editions: American Foreign Policy 09/10	International Politics on the World Stage, Brief, 8/e by Boyer/Rourke	International Politics on the World Stage, 12/e by Rourke
Unit 1: The United States and the World: Strategic Choices	**Chapter 1:** Thinking and Caring about World Politics **Chapter 2:** The Evolution of World Politics **Chapter 10:** Globalization in the World Economy	**Chapter 1:** Thinking and Caring about World Politics **Chapter 2:** The Evolution of World Politics **Chapter 12:** National Economic Competition: The Traditional Road **Chapter 13:** International Economic Cooperation: The Alternative Road
Unit 2: The United States and the World: Regional and Bilateral Relations	**Chapter 1:** Thinking and Caring about World Politics **Chapter 6:** Power and the National States: The Traditional Structure **Chapter 7:** International Organization: An Alternative Structure	**Chapter 7:** Intergovernmental Organization: Alternative Governance **Chapter 8:** National Power and Statecraft: The Traditional Approach
Unit 3: The Domestic Side of American Foreign Policy	**Chapter 1:** Thinking and Caring about World Politics **Chapter 10:** Globalization in the World Economy	**Chapter 1:** Thinking and Caring about World Politics **Chapter 12:** National Economic Competition: The Traditional Road
Unit 4: The Institutional Context of American Foreign Policy	**Chapter 8:** International Law and Human Rights: An Alternative Approach	**Chapter 9:** International Law and Justice: An Alternative Approach **Chapter 14:** Preserving and Enhancing Human Rights and Dignity
Unit 5: The Foreign Policy Making Process	**Chapter 3:** Level of Analysis **Chapter 8:** International Law and Human Rights: An Alternative Approach	**Chapter 3:** Levels of Analysis and Foreign Policy **Chapter 14:** Preserving and Enhancing Human Rights and Dignity
Unit 6: U.S. International Economic Strategy	**Chapter 11:** Global Economic Competition and Cooperation	**Chapter 8:** National Power and Statecraft: The Traditional Approach
Unit 7: U.S. Military Strategy	**Chapter 9:** Pursuing Security	**Chapter 8:** National Power and Statecraft: The Traditional Approach **Chapter 10:** National Security: The Traditional Road **Chapter 11:** International Security: The Alternative Road
Unit 8: The Iraq War and Beyond	**Chapter 5:** Globalization and Transnationalism: The Alternative Orientation **Chapter 9:** Pursuing Security	**Chapter 5:** Globalism: The Alternative Orientation **Chapter 10:** National Security: The Traditional Road **Chapter 11:** International Security: The Alternative Road

Topic Guide

This topic guide suggests how the selections in this book relate to the subjects covered in your course. You may want to use the topics listed on these pages to search the Web more easily.

On the following pages a number of Web sites have been gathered specifically for this book. They are arranged to reflect the units of this Annual Editions reader. You can link to these sites by going to *http://www.mhcls.com*.

All the articles that relate to each topic are listed below the bold-faced term.

Internet References

The following Internet sites have been selected to support the articles found in this reader. These sites were available at the time of publication. However, because Web sites often change their structure and content, the information listed may no longer be available. We invite you to visit *http://www.mhcls.com* for easy access to these sites.

Annual Editions: American Foreign Policy 09/10

General Sources

Avalon Project at Yale Law School
http://www.yale.edu/lawweb/avalon/terrorism/terror.htm

The Avalon Project website features documents in the fields of law, history, economics, diplomacy, politics, government, and terrorism.

Center for Strategic and International Studies (CSIS)
http://www.csis.org

The Center for Strategic and International Studies (CSIS), which is a nonpartisan organization, has been dedicated to providing world leaders with strategic insights on, and policy solutions to, current and emerging global issues for 40 years. Currently, CSIS has responded to global terrorism threats by developing a variety of well-defined projects and responses that are available at this site.

The Federal Web Locator
http://www.lib.auburn.edu/madd/docs/fedloc.html

Use this handy site as a launching pad for the Web sites of federal U.S. agencies, departments, and organizations. It is well organized and easy to use for informational and research purposes.

Foreign Affairs
http://www.foreignaffairs.org

The *Foreign Affairs* site allows users to search the magazine's archives and provides access to the field's leading journals, documents, online resources, and so on. Links to dozens of other related Web sites are possible from here.

International Information Programs
http://www.america.gov/

This wide-ranging page offered by the State Department provides definitions, related documentation, and a discussion of topics of concern to students of foreign policy and foreign affairs. It addresses today's hot topics as well as ongoing issues that form the foundation of the field. Many Web links are provided.

Oneworld.net
http://www.oneworld.net/section/partners/

Search this site for information and news about issues related to human sustainable development throughout the world. Information is available by topic or by country.

United Nations Home Page
http://www.un.org

Here is the gateway to information about the United Nations.

U.S. International Affairs
http://www.state.gov/www/regions/internat.html

Data on U.S. foreign policy around the world are available here. Some of the areas covered are arms control, economics and trade, international organizations, environmental issues, terrorism, current treaties, and international women's issues.

UNIT 1: The United States and the World: Strategic Choices

The Bulletin of the Atomic Scientists
http://www.bullatomsci.org

This site allows you to read more about the Doomsday Clock and other issues as well as topics related to nuclear weaponry, arms control, and disarmament.

The Henry L. Stimson Center
http://www.stimson.org

The Stimson Center, a nonprofit and (self-described) nonpartisan organization, focuses on issues where policy, technology, and politics intersect. Use this site to find assessments of U.S. foreign policy in the post-cold war world and to research many other topics.

International Network Information Center at University of Texas
http://inic.utexas.edu

This gateway has many pointers to international sites, organized into African, Asian, Latin American, Middle East, and Russian and East European subsections.

ISN International Relations and Security Network
http://www.isn.ethz.ch

Maintained by the Center for Security Studies and Conflict Research, this site is a clearinghouse for information on international relations and security policy. The many topics are listed by category (Traditional Dimensions of Security and New Dimensions of Security) and by major world regions.

UNIT 2: The United States and the World: Regional and Bilateral Relations

Inter-American Dialogue (IAD)
http://www.iadialog.org

This IAD Web site provides data on U.S. policy analysis, communication, and exchange in Western Hemisphere affairs. The organization has helped to shape the agenda of issues and choices in hemispheric relations.

Political Science RESOURCES
http://www.psr.keele.ac.uk/psr.htm

This is a link to sources available via European addresses. Listed by country name, it includes official government pages, official documents, speeches, elections, and political events.

Russian and East European Network Information Center
http://reenic.utexas.edu/reenic/index.html

Information ranging from women's issues to foreign relations and coverage of more than two dozen countries in Central and Eastern Europe and western Asia may be found here. Also check out University of Texas/Austin's site on Broader Asia (http://asnic.utexas.edu/asnic/index.html) for more insight into bilateral/regional relations.

World Wide Web Virtual Library: International Affairs Resources
http://www.etown.edu/vl/

Extensive links are available here to help you learn about specific countries and regions, to research for various think tanks, and to study such vital topics as international law, development, the international economy, human rights, and peacekeeping.

UNIT 3: The Domestic Side of American Foreign Policy

American Diplomacy
http://www.unc.edu/depts/diplomat/

American Diplomacy is an online journal of commentary, analysis, and research on U.S. foreign policy and its results around the world. It provides discussion and information on current news, such topics as Life in the Foreign Service, and A Look Back.

Internet References

Carnegie Endowment for International Peace (CEIP)
http://www.ceip.org

One of the most important goals of CEIP is to stimulate discussion and learning among both experts and the public on a range of international issues. This site provides links to the magazine *Foreign Policy,* to the Carnegie Moscow Center, and to descriptions of various programs.

RAND
http://www.rand.org

RAND, a nonprofit institution that works to improve public policy through research and analysis, offers links to certain topics and descriptions of RAND activities as well as major research areas (such as international relations and strategic defense policy).

UNIT 4: The Institutional Context of American Foreign Policy

Central Intelligence Agency (CIA)
http://www.cia.gov

Use this official CIA page to learn about many facets of the agency and to connect to other sites and resources.

The NATO Integrated Data Service (NIDS)
http://www.nato.int/structur/nids/nids.htm

NIDS was created to bring information on security-related matters within easy reach of the widest possible audience. Check out this Web site to review North Atlantic Treaty Organization documentation of all kinds, to read *NATO Review* magazine, and to explore key issues in the field of European security and transatlantic cooperation.

U.S. Department of State
http://www.state.gov/index.html

This State Department page is a must for any student of foreign affairs. Explore this site to find out what the department does, what services it provides, what it says about U.S. interests around the world, and much more.

United States Institute of Peace (USIP)
http://www.usip.org

The USIP, which was created by Congress to promote peaceful resolution of international conflicts, seeks to educate people and disseminate information on how to achieve peace.

U.S. White House
http://www.whitehouse.gov

This official Web page for the White House includes information on the President and Vice President and What's New. See especially The Virtual Library and Briefing Room for Hot Topics and latest Federal Statistics.

UNIT 5: The Foreign Policy Making Process

Belfer Center for Science and International Affairs (BCSIA)
http://belfercenter.ksg.harvard.edu/

BCSIA is the hub of the John F. Kennedy School of Government's research, teaching, and training in international affairs and is related to security, environment, and technology. This site provides insight into the development of leadership in policy making.

The Heritage Foundation
http://www.heritage.org

This page offers discussion about and links to many sites of the Heritage Foundation and other organizations having to do with foreign policy and foreign affairs.

National Archives and Records Administration (NARA)
http://www.archives.gov/index.html

This official site, which oversees the management of all federal records, offers easy access to background information for students interested in the policy-making process, including a search of federal documents and speeches, and much more.

U.S. Department of State: The Network of Terrorism
http://usinfo.state.gov/products/pubs/

This Web site offers complete coverage from the American government's viewpoint regarding the war against terrorism. It provides a wealth of first-hand documentation and evidence.

UNIT 6: U.S. International Economic Strategy

International Monetary Fund (IMF)
http://www.imf.org

This Web site is essential reading for anyone wishing to learn more about this important body's effects on foreign policy and the global economy. It provides information about the IMF, directs readers to various publications and current issues, and suggests links to other organizations.

United States Agency for International Development
http://www.usaid.gov/

Information is available here about broad and overlapping issues such as agriculture, democracy and governance, health, economic growth, and the environment in many regions and countries around the world.

United States Trade Representative
http://www.ustr.gov

The mission of the U.S. Trade Representative is presented on this site. Background information on international trade agreements and links to other sites may be accessed.

World Bank
http://www.worldbank.org

News (including press releases, summaries of new projects, and speeches), publications, and coverage of numerous topics regarding development, countries, and regions are provided at this Web site. It also contains links to other important global financial organizations.

UNIT 7: U.S. Military Strategy

Arms Control and Disarmament Agency (ACDA)
http://dosfan.lib.uic.edu/acda/

This archival ACDA page provides links to information on arms control and disarmament. Researchers can examine texts of various speeches, treaties, and historical documents. For further current information, go to the Bureau of Arms Control page at http://state.gov/t/ac/.

Counterterrorism Page
http://counterterrorism.com

A summary of worldwide terrorism events, groups, and terrorism strategies and tactics, including articles from 1989 to the present of American and international origin, plus links to related Web sites and graphs are available on this site.

DefenseLINK
http://www.defenselink.mil/news/

Learn about the Department of Defense at this site. News, publications, photos, and other related sites of interest are noted.

Federation of American Scientists (FAS)
http://www.fas.org

FAS, a nonprofit policy organization, maintains this site to provide coverage of such topics as terrorism and weapons of mass destruction.

Human Rights Web
http://www.hrweb.org

The history of the human rights movement, text on seminal figures, landmark legal and political documents, and ideas on how individuals can get involved in helping to protect human rights around the world can be found here.

UNIT 8: The Iraq War and Beyond

White House: Renewal in Iraq
http://www.whitehouse.gov/infocus/iraq/

View official White House reports, including presidential remarks, on this site.

UNIT 1

The United States and the World: Strategic Choices

Unit Selections

Key Points to Consider

• Make a scorecard of the successes and failures of the Bush administration's foreign policy to date. Defend your choices and explain why these policies turned out the way they did.

• How powerful is the United States today? How should it use its power?

• Make a list of the five most important foreign policy problems facing the United States today. Defend your choices and explain why you ranked them in this order.

• Has the United States become a rogue superpower? Defend your answer.

• What principles do you think should guide American foreign policy in the future?

• How much and what type of responsibility does the United States have for maintaining world order?

• How helpful is the past as a guide in constructing foreign policy strategies for the future?

Student Web Site

www.mhcls.com/online

Internet References

The Bulletin of the Atomic Scientists
   http://www.bullatomsci.org
The Henry L. Stimson Center
   http://www.stimson.org
International Network Information Center at University of Texas
   http://inic.utexas.edu
ISN International Relations and Security Network
   http://www.isn.ethz.ch

Choice in foreign policy is always present. The September 11, 2001, terrorist attacks on the World Trade Center and the Pentagon did not change this reality. The strong sense of national unity that followed these attacks momentarily quieted the debate on the proper conduct and content of American foreign policy but it did not end it. This debate was renewed as the Bush administration moved toward war with Iraq and it emerged with new force as the United States entered into a period of occupation and reconstruction in Iraq. While much of the current debate is highly politicized, we also see the outlines of a more far reaching conceptual discussion about the shape of the future world that the United States wishes to see come into existence, and how to bring it about.

The strategic debate today is different from that which long dominated the scene. For much of the period of the Cold War the foreign policy debate focused on tactics. A consensus had been formed on the policy of containment. But there were still choices. Rolling back the iron curtain was a minority view during the 1950s and cooperation with the Soviet Union was advocated by some during the immediate post–World War II period. In the late 1960s, a period of détente emerged as a serious competitor to containment and succeeded in supplanting it for a brief period of time.

No single vision of American foreign policy emerged as dominant in the first decade of the post–Cold War era. For some, the 1990s provided the United States with the long-awaited opportunity to walk away from the distracting and corrupting influence of international affairs and focus instead on domestic concerns and embrace traditional American values. For others, the 1990s represented a moment to be seized. Adherents to this perspective were divided over how to proceed. One group advocated replacing the strategies of conflict and confrontation of the cold war with ones designed to foster cooperation among states and to lift the human condition. A second group saw it as an opportunity to reorder the world in America's image, for it had won the Cold War.

When he entered office, George W. Bush's early initiatives suggested his administration would pursue a foreign policy based on unilateralist principles, favoring disengagement from global problem-solving efforts. This was evidenced in its withdrawal from the Kyoto protocol, its stated desire to extract the United States from involvement in the Balkans, the negotiations with North Korea, and the brokering of a Middle East peace accord. Pursuit of a national ballistic missile defense system, in face of global opposition, further reinforced this perception.

The terrorist attacks on September 11 forced the Bush administration to reexamine its approach to foreign policy. Still pragmatic, there now was also present a strong sense of missionary zeal. Yet being unilateralist at heart, the administration now confronts demands that it works with the broader international community in order to achieve its foreign policy goals. Still reluctant

U.S. Army photo by Sgt. Micah E. Clare

to play the role of global policeman, it finds itself drawn much more deeply into regional and global disputes. The result has been a foreign policy that often seems at war with itself. It is self-confident, if not defiant, yet often appears to stumble as it moves forward. Deciding how to reconcile these competing tendencies and what new directions American foreign policy should take, if any, will be one of the most challenging tasks facing George W. Bush's successor.

The essays in this unit introduce us to the scope of the contemporary debate over the strategic choices open to the United States. The first two articles, "The Day Nothing Much Changed" and "How Globalization Went Bad," provide interpretive surveys of the global context facing American foreign policy today. The first essay stresses continuity with the past while the second focuses on the new, most pronounced aspect of world politics: globalization. The other essays in this section provide critiques of the Bush administration's strategy and suggestions for how to go forward. In "Hegemony on the Cheap," Colin Dueck criticizes Bush's pursuit of an ambitious Wilsonian agenda without adequate resources. Bush is not the first Wilsonian to error in this regard argues Dueck. The next article, "The Eagle Has Crash Landed," raises the possibility that the United States has become a powerless superpower. "Grand Strategy for a Divided America" and "The Palmerstonian Moment" provide alternative recommendations for how to proceed in fixing American foreign policy. They proceed from different points of view. "Grand Strategy for a Divided America" looks inward to divisions in American society for its inspiration while "The Palmerstonian Moment" looks outward to the fundamental nature of world politics. The final essay, "Strategic Fatigue," argues that a universal problem has befallen the Bush administration and if not addressed will result in imperial overreach and self-inflicted wounds that will undermine the ability of American foreign policy to achieve its objectives.

The Day Nothing Much Changed

We were told the world would never be the same. But did 9/11 actually alter the state of global affairs? For all the sound and fury, the world looks much like it did on September 10.

WILLIAM J. DOBSON

At 8:45 A.M., Sept. 11, 2001, we were living in the post-Cold War era. At 9:37 A.M., just 52 minutes later, as the third hijacked airliner careened into the Pentagon, the post-9/11 era had begun. Everyone told us that everything had changed.

It was the beginning of a new chapter in history. The image of thousands of people perishing as the Twin Towers collapsed in a cascade of fire and dust, live on television, was a bookmark for the ages. There was a world before this tragedy, and then there was something very different that was about to follow. It is tempting to assume that this attitude was just another example of American narcissism. (The United States was attacked, so the world had changed.) But that wasn't the case. A poll taken shortly after the attacks by the Pew Research Center found a remarkable degree of agreement among opinion leaders around the world about what the September 11 attacks represented. In Western Europe, 76 percent of those polled said the events of that day had amounted to a turning point in world history. In Russia and Asia, 73 and 69 percent of people agreed. In the Middle East and Latin America, the percentage of opinion leaders who believed 9/11 marked the beginning of a new era rose to 90 percent. Rarely have so many agreed about the meaning of a single moment.

Five years on, this response must be understood as one being born out of shock. Certainly, for some, there could not have been a more life-changing moment. Collectively, we feared what was about to end. Globalization would surely grind to a halt. Borders—in particular, the need to maintain them—would undergo a renaissance as governments looked to shield themselves from the next attack. Global trade, capital flows, and immigration could no longer be what they once were. National economies would cool, as the realization of a "clash of civilizations" grew hot. Industries like tourism and air travel would be crippled.

Yet, if you look closely at the trend lines since 9/11, what is remarkable is how little the world has changed. The forces of globalization continue unabated; indeed, if anything, they have accelerated. The issues of the day that we were debating on that morning in September are largely the same. Across broad measures of political, economic, and social data, the constants outweigh the variations. And, five years later, the United States' foreign policy is marked by no greater strategic clarity than it had on Sept. 10, 2001.

The attacks on the World Trade Center and the Pentagon were theatrical terrorism of the worst kind. But, even in an age when image usually trumps substance, the tragic drama of that day did not usher in a new era. No, if there was a day that changed the world forever, it was 15 years ago, not five. New Year's Eve, 1991. It was on that day, far away from any cameras, that the Soviet Union finally threw in the towel, dissolving itself and officially bringing an end to the Cold War. From that moment on, the United States reigned supreme— "the sole superpower," "the hyperpower," "the global hegemon," call it what you like. And from that moment on, the world was out of balance—and it still is. The tragedy of 9/11 was a manifestation of the unipolar disorder the world had already entered a decade earlier. A day after 9/11, we were still living in the post-Cold War era, we still are today, and that is precisely the problem.

Where We Left Off

If you were in either of the two cities that were attacked on September 11, you might have picked up a copy of one of the daily newspapers. The headline of one story in the *Washington Post* read, "Israeli Tanks Encircle a City in West Bank." The front page of the *New York Times* led with a story headlined, "Scientists Urge Bigger Supply of Stem Cells." Inside the paper, readers might have also noticed a small item that read, "Iran: Denial on Nuclear Weapons." The headlines on that morning—before the world learned of the attacks—suggest that our pre-9/11 preoccupations are certainly not that different from those we carry today.

The global economy offered the first sign that a new, darker day hadn't dawned. On September 10, the Dow Jones Industrial Average closed at 9,605.51. Once markets reopened on September 17, it took only 40 days for the market to close above that level again. The value of the United States' monthly exports has continued to rise steadily from $60 billion to more than $75 billion between 2001 and 2005. The value of global trade dipped slightly in 2001 from $8 trillion to $7.8 trillion. Then, once markets found their footing, they came racing back, increasing every subsequent year, topping $12 trillion in 2005. Hard-hit businesses such as the tourist industry bounced back remarkably fast. In 2001, more than 688 million tourists traveled abroad; by 2005, that number had climbed to 808 million—a

17 percent increase in four years. Confidence returned so quickly that we are not even shying away from building skyscrapers. Fourteen buildings taller than the World Trade Center have either been built, proposed, or began construction since 9/11.

The United States' openness to the immigrants of the world was supposed to be another unfortunate casualty of September 11. University presidents, CEOs, and, of course, those seeking to immigrate for work or study, have complained loudly that the United States has fallen into a "Fortress America" mentality. It's a legitimate concern, but the picture is far less dire than they claim. For example, the United States granted far more worker visas in 2005 than in 1998, the heyday of America's triumphant, open-for-business dot-com boom. Last year, 255,993 student visas were handed out—only 541 fewer than in 2002. Also in 2005, the United States rejected fewer foreigners for H1B visas—the work permit given to those who have a special occupational expertise in, say, medicine, engineering, or science—than in 2001; in fact, last year was the lowest refusal rate of the past 5 years. The number of people becoming American citizens is also on the rise. More foreigners were naturalized in 2005 than in 1998, and the number of naturalizations leapt 12 percent from 2004 to 2005. Overall levels of legal immigration may have fallen off somewhat since 2001, which was a high-water mark, but it's hardly the case that the United States is cutting itself off from the world's best and brightest.

Surely, though, there is a growing gulf between America and the world. Otherwise, how could anyone explain the mounting anti-Americanism in recent years? It is true that anti-American sentiment runs wide and deep today, but it is also true that it is not new. Europeans had only slightly more confidence in President George W. Bush than in Russian President Vladimir Putin on the eve of 9/11. In an August 2001 poll conducted by the Pew Research Center, strong majorities—more than 70 percent—of four West European nations characterized the Bush administration as unilateralist. They held this opinion before the war on terror or the invasions of Afghanistan and Iraq, which in their execution are far more responsible for the current antipathy toward the United States than anything else.

Anti-Americanism, however, has a far longer lineage than the Bush administration. Its roots are in the world's collective fear that U.S. preeminence would become so great that the United States would come to dominate others. In 1983, a *Newsweek* poll conducted by the Gallup Organization found that in six countries, Brazil, Britain, France, Japan, Mexico, and West Germany, only the Brazilians approved of U.S. government policy. In the same poll, a majority in Brazil, Japan, and Mexico believed that a strong U.S. military presence around the world increased the chance of war.

Sensibly, those fears grew with the end of the superpower contest. In 1995, in a survey conducted by the United States Information Agency, majorities around the world said that the United States was intent on dominating them. Even with a president as beloved abroad as Bill Clinton, America was considered a bully by 83 percent of people polled in Israel, 77 percent in Morocco, 71 percent in Colombia, and 61 percent in Britain. In December 2001, resentment of U.S. power was still the leading reason for disliking the United States in Europe, Russia, and Latin America, and a close second everywhere else. But the fact that anti-Americanism has spiked since the U.S. invasion of Iraq is, again, entirely sensible.

For the rest of the world, it is the realization of the fears of American dominance that they have long harbored.

What Has Changed

In 2002, then National security Advisor Condoleezza Rice said of the time following September 11: "I really think this period is analogous to 1945 to 1947 in that the events . . . started shifting the tectonic plates in international politics." Of course, it is tempting to see 9/11 as the beginning of a new era. Destruction as unexpected and dramatic as occurred on that day almost demands a label or name all its own. But the plates had already shifted 10 years earlier. The United States was a target on September 11 because it was perceived to be the global hegemon. Al Qaeda's efforts to overthrow the Arab regimes had been an abysmal failure in the 1990s. Unable to accomplish his objectives in the Arab world, Osama bin Laden plotted to strike the "faraway enemy," the United States. By striking at the colossus, which for decades had helped shore up the bedrock of Arab regimes, bin Laden hoped to remake the world. What Rice saw on September 11 was an explosion that had been building for some time.

The attacks of September 11 have not altered the balance of power. Instead, they only aggravated differences in the imbalance that already existed. Perhaps the truest thing that changed because of 9/11 was the way in which the Pentagon's budget soared. The American military's budgeted defense spending grew 39 percent between 2001 and 2006. Put another way, in 2001, the United States' military expenditure of $325 billion was the same as the next 14 biggest militaries combined. By 2005, the Pentagon was outspending the next 14 militaries by $116 billion.

This monumental increase in military spending has helped finance the U.S. war on terror and the invasions of Afghanistan and Iraq. And some would argue that these campaigns, and the general American foreign policy that has undergirded them, have made the world a far more dangerous place for everyone—everyone, that is, except Americans. Consider that between Sept. 12, 2001, and Dec. 31, 2005, 18,944 people around the world died in acts of terrorism. Only eight of those deaths were on American soil.

The attacks of September 11 have not altered the balance of power. Instead, they only aggravated differences in the imbalance that already existed.

If the world resented the imbalance between the United States and everyone else before September 11, you can understand how that resentment could be so much greater today. The gulf between the United States and the rest of the world has only grown wider. For better or worse, only when the international system achieves some sort of balance—whether it happens because of others' progress, American decline, or both—will the post-Cold War era come to a close. Until then, 1991 will remain the year that matters most.

WILLIAM J. DOBSON is managing editor of *Foreign Policy*.

How Globalization Went Bad

From terrorism to global warming, the evils of globalization are more dangerous than ever before. What went wrong? The world became dependent on a single superpower. Only by correcting this imbalance can the world become a safer place.

Steven Weber, et al.

The world today is more dangerous and less orderly than it was supposed to be. Ten or 15 years ago, the naive expectations were that the "end of history" was near. The reality has been the opposite. The world has more international terrorism and more nuclear proliferation today than it did in 1990. International institutions are weaker. The threats of pandemic disease and climate change are stronger. Cleavages of religious and cultural ideology are more intense. The global financial system is more unbalanced and precarious.

It wasn't supposed to be like this. The end of the Cold War was supposed to make global politics and economics easier to manage, not harder. What went wrong? The bad news of the 21st century is that globalization has a significant dark side. The container ships that carry manufactured Chinese goods to and from the United States also carry drugs. The airplanes that fly passengers nonstop from New York to Singapore also transport infectious diseases. And the Internet has proved just as adept at spreading deadly, extremist ideologies as it has e-commerce.

The conventional belief is that the single greatest challenge of geopolitics today is managing this dark side of globalization, chipping away at the illegitimate co-travelers that exploit openness, mobility, and freedom, without putting too much sand in the gears. The current U.S. strategy is to push for more trade, more connectivity, more markets, and more openness. America does so for a good reason—it benefits from globalization more than any other country in the world. The United States acknowledges globalization's dark side but attributes it merely to exploitative behavior by criminals, religious extremists, and other anachronistic elements that can be eliminated. The dark side of globalization, America says, with very little subtlety, can be mitigated by the expansion of American power, sometimes unilaterally and sometimes through multilateral institutions, depending on how the United States likes it. In other words, America is aiming for a "flat," globalized world coordinated by a single superpower.

That's nice work if you can get it. But the United States almost certainly cannot. Not only because other countries won't let it,

but, more profoundly, because that line of thinking is faulty. The predominance of American power has many benefits, but the management of globalization is not one of them. The mobility of ideas, capital, technology, and people is hardly new. But the rapid advance of globalization's evils is. Most of that advance has taken place since 1990. Why? Because what changed profoundly in the 1990s was the polarity of the international system. For the first time in modern history, globalization was superimposed onto a world with a single superpower. What we have discovered in the past 15 years is that it is a dangerous mixture. The negative effects of globalization since 1990 are not the result of globalization itself. They are the dark side of American predominance.

> **The world is paying a heavy price for the instability created by globalization and unipolarity, and the United States is bearing most of the burden.**

The Dangers of Unipolarity

A straightforward piece of logic from market economics helps explain why unipolarity and globalization don't mix. Monopolies, regardless of who holds them, are almost always bad for both the market and the monopolist. We propose three simple axioms of "globalization under unipolarity" that reveal these dangers.

Axiom 1. Above a certain threshold of power, the rate at which new global problems are generated will exceed the rate at which old problems are fixed.

Power does two things in international politics: It enhances the capability of a state to do things, but it also increases the number of things that a state must worry about. At a certain point, the latter starts to overtake the former. It's the familiar law of diminishing returns. Because powerful states have large spheres of influence and their security and economic interests touch every region of the world, they are threatened by the risk of things going wrong—anywhere. That is particularly true for the United States, which leverages its ability to go anywhere and do anything through massive debt. No one knows exactly when the law of diminishing returns will kick in. But, historically, it starts to happen long before a single great power dominates the entire globe, which is why large empires from Byzantium to Rome have always reached a point of unsustainability.

That may already be happening to the United States today, on issues ranging from oil dependency and nuclear proliferation to pandemics and global warming. What Axiom 1 tells you is that more U.S. power is not the answer; it's actually part of the problem. A multipolar world would almost certainly manage the globe's pressing problems more effectively. The larger the number of great powers in the global system, the greater the chance that at least one of them would exercise some control over a given combination of space, other actors, and problems. Such reasoning doesn't rest on hopeful notions that the great powers will work together. They might do so. But even if they don't, the result is distributed governance, where some great power is interested in most every part of the world through productive competition.

Axiom 2. In an increasingly networked world, places that fall between the networks are very dangerous places—and there will be more ungoverned zones when there is only one network to join.

The second axiom acknowledges that highly connected networks can be efficient, robust, and resilient to shocks. But in a highly connected world, the pieces that fall between the networks are increasingly shut off from the benefits of connectivity. These problems fester in the form of failed states, mutate like pathogenic bacteria, and, in some cases, reconnect in subterranean networks such as al Qaeda. The truly dangerous places are the points where the subterranean networks touch the mainstream of global politics and economics. What made Afghanistan so dangerous under the Taliban was not that it was a failed state. It wasn't. It was a partially failed and partially connected state that worked the interstices of globalization through the drug trade, counterfeiting, and terrorism.

Can any single superpower monitor all the seams and back alleys of globalization? Hardly. In fact, a lone hegemon is unlikely to look closely at these problems, because more pressing issues are happening elsewhere, in places where trade and technology are growing. By contrast, a world of several great powers is a more interest-rich environment in which nations must look in less obvious places to find new sources of advantage. In such a system, it's harder for troublemakers to spring up, because the cracks and seams of globalization are held together by stronger ties.

Axiom 3. Without a real chance to find useful allies to counter a superpower, opponents will try to neutralize power, by going underground, going nuclear, or going "bad."

Axiom 3 is a story about the preferred strategies of the weak. It's a basic insight of international relations that states try to balance power. They protect themselves by joining groups that can hold a hegemonic threat at bay. But what if there is no

viable group to join? In today's unipolar world, every nation from Venezuela to North Korea is looking for a way to constrain American power. But in the unipolar world, it's harder for states to join together to do that. So they turn to other means. They play a different game. Hamas, Iran, Somalia, North Korea, and Venezuela are not going to become allies anytime soon. Each is better off finding other ways to make life more difficult for Washington. Going nuclear is one way. Counterfeiting U.S. currency is another. Raising uncertainty about oil supplies is perhaps the most obvious method of all.

Here's the important downside of unipolar globalization. In a world with multiple great powers, many of these threats would be less troublesome. The relatively weak states would have a choice among potential partners with which to ally, enhancing their influence. Without that more attractive choice, facilitating the dark side of globalization becomes the most effective means of constraining American power.

Sharing Globalization's Burden

The world is paying a heavy price for the instability created by the combination of globalization and unipolarity, and the United States is bearing most of the burden. Consider the case of nuclear proliferation. There's effectively a market out there for proliferation, with its own supply (states willing to share nuclear technology) and demand (states that badly want a nuclear weapon). The overlap of unipolarity with globalization ratchets up both the supply and demand, to the detriment of U.S. national security.

It has become fashionable, in the wake of the Iraq war, to comment on the limits of conventional military force. But much of this analysis is overblown. The United States may not be able to stabilize and rebuild Iraq. But that doesn't matter much from the perspective of a government that thinks the Pentagon has it in its sights. In Tehran, Pyongyang, and many other capitals, including Beijing, the bottom line is simple: The U.S. military could, with conventional force, end those regimes tomorrow if it chose to do so. No country in the world can dream of challenging U.S. conventional military power. But they can certainly hope to deter America from using it. And the best deterrent yet invented is the threat of nuclear retaliation. Before 1989, states that felt threatened by the United States could turn to the Soviet Union's nuclear umbrella for protection. Now, they turn to people like A.Q. Khan. Having your own nuclear weapon used to be a luxury. Today, it is fast becoming a necessity.

North Korea is the clearest example. Few countries had it worse during the Cold War. North Korea was surrounded by feuding, nuclear-armed communist neighbors, it was officially at war with its southern neighbor, and it stared continuously at tens of thousands of U.S. troops on its border. But, for 40 years, North Korea didn't seek nuclear weapons. It didn't need to, because it had the Soviet nuclear umbrella. Within five years of the Soviet collapse, however, Pyongyang was pushing ahead full steam on plutonium reprocessing facilities. North Korea's founder, Kim Il Sung, barely flinched when former U.S. President Bill Clinton's administration readied war plans to strike his nuclear installations preemptively. That brinkmanship paid off. Today North Korea is likely a nuclear power, and

Kim's son rules the country with an iron fist. America's conventional military strength means a lot less to a nuclear North Korea. Saddam Hussein's great strategic blunder was that he took too long to get to the same place.

How would things be different in a multipolar world? For starters, great powers could split the job of policing proliferation, and even collaborate on some particularly hard cases. It's often forgotten now that, during the Cold War, the only state with a tougher nonproliferation policy than the United States was the Soviet Union. Not a single country that had a formal alliance with Moscow ever became a nuclear power. The Eastern bloc was full of countries with advanced technological capabilities in every area except one—nuclear weapons. Moscow simply wouldn't permit it. But today we see the uneven and inadequate level of effort that non-superpowers devote to stopping proliferation. The Europeans dangle carrots at Iran, but they are unwilling to consider serious sticks. The Chinese refuse to admit that there is a problem. And the Russians are aiding Iran's nuclear ambitions. When push comes to shove, nonproliferation today is almost entirely America's burden.

The same is true for global public health. Globalization is turning the world into an enormous petri dish for the incubation of infectious disease. Humans cannot outsmart disease, because it just evolves too quickly. Bacteria can reproduce a new generation in less than 30 minutes, while it takes us decades to come up with a new generation of antibiotics. Solutions are only possible when and where we get the upper hand. Poor countries where humans live in close proximity to farm animals are the best place to breed extremely dangerous zoonotic disease. These are often the same countries, perhaps not entirely coincidentally, that feel threatened by American power. Establishing an early warning system for these diseases—exactly what we lacked in the case of SARS a few years ago and exactly what we lack for avian flu today—will require a significant level of intervention into the very places that don't want it. That will be true as long as international intervention means American interference.

If there were rival great powers with different cultural and ideological leanings, globalization's darkest problem of all— terrorism—would look different.

The most likely sources of the next ebola or HIV-like pandemic are the countries that simply won't let U.S. or other Western agencies in, including the World Health Organization. Yet the threat is too arcane and not immediate enough for the West to force the issue. What's needed is another great power to take over a piece of the work, a power that has more immediate interests in the countries where diseases incubate and one that is seen as less of a threat. As long as the United States remains the world's lone superpower, we're not likely to get any help. Even after HIV, SARS, and several years of mounting hysteria about avian flu, the world is still not ready for a viral pandemic

in Southeast Asia or sub-Saharan Africa. America can't change that alone.

If there were rival great powers with different cultural and ideological leanings, globalization's darkest problem of all— terrorism—would also likely look quite different. The pundits are partly right: Today's international terrorism owes something to globalization. Al Qaeda uses the Internet to transmit messages, it uses credit cards and modern banking to move money, and it uses cell phones and laptops to plot attacks. But it's not globalization that turned Osama bin Laden from a small-time Saudi dissident into the symbolic head of a radical global movement. What created Osama bin Laden was the predominance of American power.

A terrorist organization needs a story to attract resources and recruits. Oftentimes, mere frustration over political, economic, or religious conditions is not enough. Al Qaeda understands that, and, for that reason, it weaves a narrative of global jihad against a "modernization," "Westernization," and a "Judeo-Christian" threat. There is really just one country that both spearheads and represents that threat: the United States. And so the most efficient way for a terrorist to gain a reputation is to attack the United States. The logic is the same for all monopolies. A few years ago, every computer hacker in the world wanted to bring down Microsoft, just as every aspiring terrorist wants to create a spectacle of destruction akin to the September 11 attacks inside the United States.

Al Qaeda cells have gone after alternate targets such as Britain, Egypt, and Spain. But these are not the acts that increase recruitment and fundraising, or mobilize the energy of otherwise disparate groups around the world. Nothing enhances the profile of a terrorist like killing an American, something Abu Musab al-Zarqawi understood well in Iraq. Even if al Qaeda's deepest aspirations lie with the demise of the Saudi regime, the predominance of U.S. power and its role supporting the house of Saud makes America the only enemy really worth fighting. A multipolar world would surely confuse this kind of clear framing that pits Islamism against the West. What would be al Qaeda's message if the Chinese were equally involved in propping up authoritarian regimes in the Islamic, oil-rich Gulf states? Does the al Qaeda story work if half its enemy is neither Western nor Christian?

Restoring the Balance

The consensus today in the U.S. foreign-policy community is that more American power is always better. Across the board. For both the United States and the rest of the globe. The National Security Strategy documents of 2002 and 2006 enshrine this consensus in phrases such as "a balance of power that favors freedom." The strategy explicitly defines the "balance" as a continued imbalance, as the United States continues "dissuading potential competitors . . . from challenging the United States, its allies, and its partners."

In no way is U.S. power inherently a bad thing. Nor is it true that no good comes from unipolarity. But there are significant downsides to the imbalance of power. That view is hardly revolutionary. It has a long pedigree in U.S. foreign-policy thought. It was the perspective, for instance, that George Kennan brought to the table in the late 1940s when he talked about the desirability of a European superpower to restrain the United States. Although the issues today are different than they were in Kennan's time, it's still the case that too much power may, as Kennan believed, lead to overreach. It may lead to arrogance. It may lead to insensitivity to the concerns of others. Though Kennan may have been prescient to voice these concerns, he couldn't have predicted the degree to which American unipolarity would lead to such an unstable overlap with modern-day globalization.

America has experienced this dangerous burden for 15 years, but it still refuses to see it for what it really is. Antiglobalization sentiment is coming today from both the right and the left. But by blaming globalization for what ails the world, the U.S. foreign-policy community is missing a very big part of what is undermining one of the most hopeful trends in modern history—the reconnection of societies, economies, and minds that political borders have kept apart for far too long.

America cannot indefinitely stave off the rise of another superpower. But, in today's networked and interdependent world, such an event is not entirely a cause for mourning. A shift in the global balance of power would, in fact, help the United States manage some of the most costly and dangerous consequences of globalization. As the international playing field levels, the scope of these problems and the threat they pose to America will only decrease. When that happens, the United States will find globalization is a far easier burden to bear.

Steven Weber is professor of political science and director of the Institute of International Studies at the University of California, Berkeley. **Naazneen Barma**, **Matthew Kroenig**, and **Ely Ratner** are PhD candidates at U.C., Berkeley, and research fellows at its New Era Foreign Policy Center.

Hegemony on the Cheap

Liberal Internationalism from Wilson to Bush

Colin Dueck

One of the conventional criticisms of the Bush administration's foreign policy is that it is excessively and even disastrously unilateralist in approach. According to the critics, the administration has turned its back on a longstanding and admirable American tradition of liberal internationalism in foreign affairs, and in doing so has provoked resentment worldwide.[1] But these criticisms misinterpret both the foreign policy of George W. Bush, as well as America's liberal internationalist tradition. In reality, Bush's foreign policy since 9/11 has been heavily influenced by traditional liberal internationalist assumptions—assumptions that all along have had a troubling impact on U.S. foreign policy behavior and fed into the current situation in Iraq.

The conduct of America's foreign relations has—for more than a hundred years, going back at least to the days of John Hay's "Open Door" Notes and McKinley's hand wringing over the annexation of the Philippines—been shaped, to a greater or lesser extent, by a set of beliefs that can only be called liberal. These assumptions specify that the United States should promote, wherever practical and possible, an international system characterized by democratic governments and open markets.[2] President Bush reiterated these classical liberal assumptions recently, in his speech last November to the National Endowment for Democracy, when he outlined what he called "a forward strategy of freedom in the Middle East." In that speech, Bush argued that "as long as the Middle East remains a place where freedom does not flourish, it will remain a place of stagnation, resentment, and violence ready for export." In this sense, he suggested, the United States has a vital strategic interest in the democratization of the region. But Bush also added that "the advance of freedom leads to peace," and that democracy is "the only path to national success and dignity," providing as it does certain "essential principles common to every successful society, in every culture."[3] These words could just as easily have been spoken by Woodrow Wilson, Franklin Roosevelt—or Bill Clinton. They are well within the mainstream American tradition of liberal internationalism. Of course, U.S. foreign policy officials have never promoted a liberal world order simply out of altruism. They have done so out of the belief that such a system would serve American interests, by making the United States more prosperous, influential, and secure. Americans have also frequently disagreed over how to best promote liberal goals overseas.[4] Nevertheless, it is fair to say that liberal goals and assumptions, broadly conceived, have had a powerful impact on American foreign policy, especially since the presidency of Woodrow Wilson.

The problem with the liberal or Wilsonian approach, however, has been that it tends to encourage very ambitious foreign policy goals and commitments, while assuming that these goals can be met without commensurate cost or expenditure on the part of the United States. Liberal internationalists, that is, tend to define American interests in broad, expansive, and idealistic terms, without always admitting the necessary costs and risks of such an expansive vision. The result is that sweeping and ambitious goals are announced, but then pursued by disproportionately limited means, thus creating an outright invitation to failure. Indeed, this disjuncture between ends and means has been so common in the history of American diplomacy over the past century that it seems to be a direct consequence of the nation's distinctly liberal approach to international relations.

The Bush administration's current difficulties in Iraq are therefore not an isolated event. Nor are they really the result of the president's supposed preference for unilateralism. On the contrary, the administration's difficulties in Iraq are actually the result of an excessive reliance on classically liberal or Wilsonian assumptions regarding foreign affairs. The administration has willed the end in Iraq—and a very ambitious end—but it has not fully willed the means. In this sense, the Bush administration is heir to a long liberal internationalist tradition that runs from Woodrow Wilson, through FDR and Harry Truman, to Bill Clinton. And Bush inherits not only the strengths of that tradition, but also its weaknesses and flaws.

The Lost Alliance

The liberal internationalist pattern of disjuncture between ends and means really begins in earnest with Woodrow Wilson. Wilson, of course, traveled to Europe at the end of 1918, in the wake of the First World War, intending to "make the world safe for democracy" while insisting that a universal League of Nations serve as the linchpin for a new international order. Wilson intended the League to function as a promoter of collective security arrangements, by guaranteeing the territorial integrity and political independence of all member states. But Wilson also intended the League to function, more broadly, as the embodiment of a nascent liberal international order where war would be outlawed and self-determination would remain supreme. The other great powers were to be asked to abandon their imperialistic spheres of influence, their protectionist tariff barriers, their secretive military alliances, and their swollen armories.[5]

Needless to say, in practice, such concessions were hard to extract. The actual outcome at the Paris Peace Conference, contrary to Wilson's desire, was a series of compromises: Japan maintained its sphere of influence in the Chinese province of Shantung; Britain maintained its great navy, as well as its colonial conquests from Germany and Turkey; many of the arrangements negotiated in secret by the Allied powers during the war were in fact observed, though running contrary to Wilson's own pronouncements (including the famous Fourteen Points); and in blatant disregard of Wilson's alleged aversion to "old diplomacy" horse trading, France and Britain had their way vis-à-vis the peace terms imposed on Germany at Versailles while obtaining an explicit security guarantee from the United States.[6] To be sure, Wilson did succeed in winning the assent of the other victorious powers toward common membership in a new League of Nations. Furthermore, it is clear that he took the League's collective security obligations quite seriously. He certainly hoped that future acts of territorial aggression could be prevented through such peaceful means as deterrence, arbitration, and the use of economic sanctions. But in the final analysis, he understood perfectly well that collective security would at times have to be enforced militarily, through the use of armed force on the part of member states. Indeed, Wilson said quite explicitly that the League was meant to function as "a single overwhelming, powerful group of nations who shall be the trustee of the peace of the world."[7] And the United States was to be the leading member of this group.

Still, at the same time that Wilson laid out this extremely ambitious vision, he refused to draw the logical implications for the United States. Obviously, under any sort of meaningful commitment to a worldwide collective security system, the United States would henceforth be obliged to help enforce the peace in areas outside its traditional sphere of influence as proclaimed in the Monroe Doctrine (and subsequent "corollaries")—that is to say, in Europe and Asia. This would necessarily require maintaining a large standing army. Yet Wilson refused to admit that any such requirement existed, just as he disingenuously maintained that the League's covenant would not impinge on America's sovereignty, by insisting that said article carried only a "moral" obligation. In fact, he argued that the League would render a large standing army unnecessary.

Some of Wilson's Republican critics, especially in Congress, far from being isolationist know-nothings, saw through the contradictions in the president's vision, and advocated a pragmatic alternative. Led by Sen. Henry Cabot Lodge, these conservative internationalists called for a straightforward security pact with France and Great Britain as the key to their and America's own postwar security. Lodge and his supporters were willing to enter into the new League of Nations, but not into any global collective security arrangement. These Republican internationalists favored clear but restricted U.S. strategic commitments within Western Europe as the best guarantee of future peace.[8]

Lodge's alternative of a limited, Western alliance actually made perfect sense, strategically speaking. It avoided the impossible implication that America would come to the aid of any state, worldwide, whose territory or integrity was threatened. At the same time, it specified that the United States would defend France from any future attack by Germany while encouraging Britain to do the same. In this way, America's strategic commitments would be based upon concrete, vital national interests, rather than upon vague universalities; and upon real military capabilities, rather than utopian aspirations. The one problem with this alternative vision is that it seems to have been incompatible with domestic liberal pieties. Even Lodge admitted in 1919—at the time of the battle in the Senate over the League—that the idea of a League of Nations was quite popular in America. As Wilson himself suggested, the only way to preserve America's sense of moral superiority, while at the same time bringing its weight to bear in favor of international stability, was through membership in a universal organization, rather than through any particular and

"entangling alliances."[9] Lodge and his supporters managed to defeat Wilson's League in the Senate, but they did not succeed in replacing it with a more realistic alternative.

Containment

During the Second World War, Franklin Roosevelt attempted to learn from Wilson's mistakes by carefully building domestic support for American membership in a postwar United Nations. Roosevelt was much more flexible in his approach than Wilson had been. But in terms of his substantive vision for the postwar order, Roosevelt was hardly any less idealistic than Wilson. Roosevelt's "grand design" was that the five major powers fighting the Axis would cooperate in policing the postwar system, each power (more or less) within its own regional sphere of influence. At the same time, however, each great power was to respect such liberal norms as nonaggression, democratic institutions, and free trade within its own sphere.[10] FDR was strikingly successful in nudging the American public toward a new internationalist consensus. His administration laid the groundwork for U.S. postwar leadership of a more liberal international political and economic order. The one great stumbling block to Roosevelt's plans was the Soviet Union. Roosevelt recognized that Moscow would end the war with disproportionate influence over Eastern Europe, but he insisted that such influence be exercised in a benign, democratic, and non-coercive fashion. Stalin, of course, would not accept such conditions, whatever his rhetorical commitments to the contrary. Once this basic clash of interests between Washington and Moscow became visible for all to see, by the end of 1945, American officials were faced with the inevitable dilemma of how to respond to Soviet behavior. To allow the Soviet Union to construct, with impunity, an autarchic, militarized sphere of influence within Eastern Europe—and beyond—would have flown in the face of America's wartime objectives. The United States, under Truman, therefore settled on a strategy of containment in order to curb Soviet power and at the same time preserve FDR's hope for a more liberal world order.

Containment was a pragmatic strategy, but it was also very much influenced by Wilsonian assumptions regarding the nature of international relations. The purpose of containment, after all, was not simply to check or balance the Soviet Union, but also to nurture the long-term vitality and interdependence of an American-led, liberal international order outside of the Communist bloc.[11] The strategists of containment refused to accept permanent Soviet control over Eastern Europe, or to negotiate in earnest with Moscow over the outlines of a general postwar settlement that did not accord with Wilsonian principles. Instead, they hoped to achieve an eventual geopolitical, economic, and ideological victory over the Soviet Union by using every means short of war.[12] The goal was not to learn to coexist with the enemy, but gradually to convert and/or help him destroy himself. It was precisely this ideological, uncompromising tone that gave containment its political viability at home.

During the late 1940s, under the strategy of containment, the United States embarked upon a series of dramatic and unprecedented commitments abroad. Military and economic aid was extended to friendly governments worldwide; anticommunist alliances were formed around the globe; and U.S. troops were deployed in large numbers to Europe and Asia. The Truman Doctrine, the Marshall Plan, and NATO all embodied this new commitment to a forward strategic presence overseas. The problem, however, was that the Truman administration hoped to implement this very ambitious strategy without sacrificing the traditional American preference for limited liability abroad. Defense expenditures, in particular, were at first kept at a level that was exceedingly low, given the diverse and worldwide military commitments the United States had actually undertaken. In effect, the administration gambled that the Soviet Union and its clients would not test America's willingness or ability to contain military aggression by conventional means.[13] With the outbreak of the Korean War in 1950, this gamble proved to be a failure. As a result, in the early 1950s, the United States finally raised defense expenditures to a level commensurate with its strategic commitments overseas. Inevitably, the Wilsonian preference for low-cost internationalism reasserted itself: high levels of defense spending turned out to be politically unsustainable at home, leading the Eisenhower administration to return to a potentially risky reliance on nuclear deterrence. Americans wanted to contain the Soviet Union—an ambitious and in many ways a remarkably idealistic strategy—but they did not necessarily want to bear the full costs of such a strategy. In this sense, even at the height of the Cold War, U.S. foreign policy operated very much within the Wilsonian tradition.

The implementation of containment continued to be characterized by a persistent gap between ambitious liberal ends, and somewhat limited capabilities. In the early 1960s, John F. Kennedy made a concerted effort to close this gap through a strategy of "flexible response," emphasizing conventional and counterinsurgent, as well as nuclear, capabilities. Yet at the same time, Kennedy escalated America's military involvement in Vietnam, without providing any clear idea of how that conflict could be won. The decision to stand by Saigon, on the part of both Kennedy and, later, Lyndon Johnson, was driven primarily by concerns over the credibility of America's worldwide alliance commitments. But this decision was also very much informed by the Wilsonian belief that developing countries such as Vietnam could be reformed, liberalized, and won over to America's side through a vigorous, U.S.-assisted program of nation building.[14] In the words of Walt Rostow, one of Kennedy's leading foreign policy advisors, "Modern societies must be built, and we are prepared to help build them."

In Vietnam, America's willingness to sustain serious costs on behalf of a liberal strategy of containment and nation building was tested to the breaking point. Within the United States, domestic political support for a protracted, expensive, and bloody engagement in Southeast Asia proved to have definite limits. The Johnson administration itself was unwilling to call for maximum effort on behalf of its goals in the region; instead, it tried to achieve them through a process of limited and gradual escalation. The Nixon administration, having inherited this immense commitment, attempted to square the circle through a policy of "Vietnamization." The United States would slowly withdraw its forces from the conflict, relying upon air power and increased military aid to bolster the regime in Saigon. But Nixon's approach was no more able to achieve its stated aims than Johnson's. If Communist forces in Vietnam could not be defeated by half a million American troops, a lower level of American engagement was not going to do the trick. In the end, the United States proved neither willing nor able to bear the costs of meeting its commitments to Saigon—commitments that had been deeply informed by liberal internationalist assumptions.

Even as they experimented with Vietnamization, the Nixon-Kissinger team attempted to place the United States in a more sustainable strategic position by toning down the Wilsonian rhetoric. The new emphasis was on great power relations, rather than on ideological crusades to liberalize or reform the internal politics of other states. As Henry Kissinger put it in 1969, "We will judge other countries, including Communist countries, on the basis of their actions and not on the basis of their domestic ideologies."[15] This more pragmatic approach bore considerable fruit through a relaxation of

tensions with the Soviet Union, as well as a dramatic improvement in relations with China. Despite these successes, Nixon and Kissinger were attacked from both left and right for abandoning America's Wilsonian mission overseas. Both Jimmy Carter, who took office in 1977, and Ronald Reagan, who succeeded him in 1981, criticized the policy of détente from a Wilsonian perspective. Both Carter and Reagan, despite their many differences, insisted that U.S. foreign relations should be rebuilt upon the premise that the United States had a vital practical as well as moral interest in the promotion of a liberal world order. The collapse of the Soviet Union in 1989 seemed to many to have vindicated the Wilsonian approach. But it was the combined economic and military power of the United States and its allies, not Wilsonian idealism, that finally brought the Soviet Union to its knees. In the euphoria over the collapse of communism, the fact that for over 40 years the United States had often pursued a sweeping and ambitious foreign policy with inadequate means was forgotten. The United States had been forced to pay for this strategic mismanagement in both Korea and Vietnam. In the end, the relative weakness of the Soviet Union gave U.S. policy makers considerable room for error. However, the upshot was that Americans misattributed their victory in the Cold War to the unique virtues of the Wilsonian tradition, which only led to a continuing gap between ends and means in the conduct of American foreign policy.

Democratic Enlargement

Following the end of the Cold War, the United States was faced with the choice of either expanding its military and political presence abroad, or retrenching strategically. The Clinton administration decided to do both. Thus it pursued a very ambitious strategy of "democratic enlargement," designed to promote the spread of market democracies worldwide. This included, notably, a new emphasis on humanitarian intervention in civil conflicts of seemingly peripheral interest to the United States. But it also tried to carry out this strategy at an extremely low cost in terms of blood and treasure. Defense expenditures, for example, were kept at a level that was unrealistically low, given the global range of America's military commitments. Just as significantly, Clinton also proved remarkably reluctant to use force in support of his Wilsonian agenda.

Clinton came into office having criticized the foreign policy of George H. W. Bush for being insufficiently true to America's democratic ideals. The new president promised to be more consistent than his immediate predecessor in promoting democracy and human rights in countries such as China, the former Yugoslavia, and Haiti. A leading test of the Clinton administration's rhetorical commitment to the liberal internationalist credo was on the question of humanitarian intervention. Clinton and his advisors repeatedly stated that the United States had a vital humanitarian interest in cases of civil war and disorder. The administration therefore placed a new emphasis on American-led peacekeeping, peacemaking, and nation-building operations.[16] More broadly, foreign policy officials articulated a doctrine of "enlargement," by which they meant that the United States would press for the expansion of free trade, open markets, democratic governments, and human rights worldwide.[17] Their assumption—building on the old Wilsonian gospel—was that such an expansion would encourage an upward cycle of global peace and prosperity, serving American interests and allowing the United States to deemphasize its own military strength.

Under the Clinton administration, the liberal internationalist assumptions of democratic enlargement informed U.S. policy in virtually every region of the globe. In Central Europe, three new members were brought into NATO. In Russia, democratic market reforms were the price demanded for improved bilateral relations with the United States. In China, U.S. diplomats pressed Beijing on human rights issues while working to bring the People's Republic into the international economic system. And in Bosnia, Haiti, Somalia, and Kosovo, Washington undertook to help create or recreate stable, democratic polities, through military intervention, amidst generally unfavorable conditions.[18]

Nevertheless, even as President Clinton laid out his extremely ambitious foreign policy goals, he proved unwilling to support them with the necessary means. In particular, he proved reluctant to support these initiatives with the requisite amount of military force. In one case after another of humanitarian intervention, a pattern emerged: the Clinton administration would stake out an assertive and idealistic public position, then refuse to act on its rhetoric in a meaningful way. Yet in every such case, whether in Somalia, Haiti, Bosnia, or Kosovo, the president was ultimately forced to act, if only to protect the credibility of the United States.[19] The result was a series of remarkably halfhearted, initially low-risk interventions, which only reinforced the impression that the United States was unwilling to suffer costs or casualties on behalf of its stated interests overseas.[20]

It might be argued that the nature of U.S. interventions during the Clinton years was a function of the low geopolitical stakes involved, rather than a reflection of the administration's naiveté. Certainly, the stakes were relatively low. But from a classical realist perspective, the answer would have been to avoid putting America's reputation on the line in the first place—to avoid defining American interests in such an expansive manner as to then call the nation's credibility into question. The fact is that the Clinton administration said, in each case, that the United States had a vital national interest in the pursuit of liberal or humanitarian goals. Then it refused to protect this stated interest with requisite seriousness until American credibility had already been undermined. This may have been partially the result of a presidency characterized by unusual fecklessness on matters of national security. But it was also a pattern of behavior very much in the liberal internationalist tradition: sweeping commitments, too often supported by inadequate means.

Wilson Redux

At first, the inauguration of George W. Bush seemed to indicate, if nothing else, that America's national security capabilities would be brought into line with the nation's strategic commitments. As a candidate for president, Governor Bush had called for significant increases in defense spending. At the same time, he criticized what he termed the "open-ended deployments and unclear military missions" of the Clinton era.[21] Bush was especially critical of employing armed force in nation-building operations overseas; indeed, he suggested that he would not have intervened in either Haiti or Somalia. As Bush phrased it during a debate with Al Gore in October 2000, while referring to the question of intervention, "I would be very guarded in my approach. I don't think we can be all things to all people in the world. I think we've got to be very careful when we commit our troops."[22]

To be sure, neoconservative visions of American primacy always had a certain influence on Bush's thinking, but for the most part, the dominant tone of Bush's foreign policy pre-9/11 was one of "realism." The new administration was determined to be more selective on questions of nation building and humanitarian intervention than its predecessor. American foreign policy was to be refocused on considerations of great power politics and more immediate national interests, and the United States was to play down its pretensions as an international social engineer. Key figures such as Colin Powell and Richard Haass in the State Department and Condoleezza Rice at the

National Security Council were well within the tradition of Republican pragmatism on foreign affairs, and hawks such as Vice President Dick Cheney and Secretary of Defense Donald Rumsfeld were either unwilling or unable to press for a comprehensive strategy of primacy across the board.[23] Above all, Bush seemed uninterested in any new, sweepingly ambitious—i.e., Wilsonian—foreign policy departures.

The terrorist attacks of September 11, 2001, changed all of that, coming as a severe shock to the president, his advisors, and the American public at large. These attacks stimulated the search for a new national security strategy. Key advocates of a different approach—at first within the administration, and then including the president himself—took advantage of the opportunity to build support for a new foreign policy agenda. This new national security strategy would be considerably more assertive than before and, in important ways, considerably more idealistic.[24]

Within days of the September 11 attacks, and over the following months, the Bush administration began to outline and articulate a remarkable departure in American foreign policy. The clearest and most elaborate explanation of the new approach came in the National Security Strategy of September 2002. In that document, best known for its embrace of preventive military action against rogue states, the administration began by pointing out that "the United States possesses unprecedented—and unequaled—strength and influence in the world." It renounced any purely realpolitik approach to foreign policy, arguing instead that "the great strength of this nation must be used to promote a balance of power that favors freedom." The promotion of free trade and democratic institutions was held up as a central American interest. Democracy and human rights were described as "nonnegotiable demands." And, interestingly, the possibility of traditional great power competition was played down. Instead, other powers were urged to join with the United States in affirming the global trend toward democracy and open markets.[25]

Of course, this broad affirmation of classical liberal assumptions was no doubt employed, in part, for reasons of domestic political consumption. Liberal arguments have historically been used to bolster strategic arguments of any kind. But the United States had been no less liberal—broadly speaking—in the year 2000, when the nascent Bush team was stressing the need for realism in foreign affairs. So the new rhetoric does seem to have reflected a real shift on the part of the administration toward a more aggressive and, at the same time, more Wilsonian approach.

The implications of this new Wilsonianism were most visible in the decision for war against Iraq. The argument made by the pro-war camp was that a defeated Iraq could be democratized and would subsequently act as a kind of trigger for democratic change throughout the Middle East. As Bush put it in an address last February to members of the American Enterprise Institute, "a new regime in Iraq would serve as a dramatic and inspiring example of freedom for other nations in the region. . . . Success in Iraq could also begin a new stage for Middle Eastern peace, and set in motion progress toward a truly democratic Palestinian state."[26] From the perspective of many leading officials inside the Bush administration, this argument was probably secondary to more basic geopolitical and security concerns. But it did seem to have an effect on the president. And again, 9/11 was the crucial catalyst, since it appeared to demonstrate that U.S. support for authoritarian regimes in the region had only encouraged Islamic fundamentalism, along with such terrorist organizations as al-Qaeda.[27]

Here was a remarkably bold vision for American foreign policy, combining the argument for preventive war with Wilsonian visions of a liberalized or Americanized international system. The goals outlined were so ambitious as to invite intense domestic as well as international criticism. The most common objections to the Bush

Doctrine, at least among foreign policy experts, were that the new national security strategy would lead America into "imperial over-stretch"; that it would trigger antagonism and hostility toward the United States abroad; that it would set a precedent for aggression on the part of other countries; and that it would undermine sympathy and support for the United States overseas. These were the most frequently articulated criticisms, but in fact an even more likely danger was the opposite one: that the Bush team would fail to make good on its promise of a serious commitment to achieving peace, stability, and democratization in Iraq, let alone in the Middle East as a whole.

Certainly the precedent in Afghanistan was not encouraging. There, the United States relied upon proxy forces, supported by air-strikes, special forces operations, and financial aid, in order to overthrow the Taliban. The failure to send in American ground troops early on meant that many members of al-Qaeda were able to escape and reconstitute their terrorist camps along the Afghan-Pakistani border. Worse yet, the Bush administration proved unwilling to contribute substantially to the postwar political, military, or economic reconstruction of Afghanistan, leaving its central government without effective control over the countryside outside Kabul.[28]

Iraq's postwar reconstruction was even less well considered than Afghanistan's. Certainly, the Bush foreign policy team understood that Saddam Hussein would not be overthrown without a major commitment of American ground troops. But in terms of planning for a post-Saddam Iraq, the administration seems to have based its initial actions upon the most optimistic assumptions: ordinary Iraqis would rise up in support of U.S. forces; these same forces would rapidly transfer authority toward a friendly interim government; the oil would flow, paying for reconstruction efforts; and the great majority of American troops would come home quickly. These were never very likely prospects, and with all of the warnings that it received, the administration should have known better. As Bush himself said during the 2000 presidential campaign, nation building is difficult and expensive. The administration's preference has been to avoid nation-building operations—an understandable predilection in itself. But once the administration made the decision to go to war against Saddam Hussein, it was also obliged to prepare for the foreseeable likelihood of major, postwar nation-building operations—not only for humanitarian reasons, but in order to secure the political objectives for which it had gone to war in the first place.

The Bush administration's early reluctance to plan for Iraq's post-war reconstruction has had serious and deadly consequences. Once Saddam's government was overthrown, a power vacuum was created, and the United States did not initially step in to fill the void. Wide-spread looting, disorder, and insecurity were the inevitable result. This set the tone for the immediate postwar era. Moreover, because of these insecure conditions, many of Saddam's former loyalists were given the opportunity to develop and pursue a dangerous, low-level insurgency against American forces. The subsequent learning curve within the Bush administration has been steep. By necessity, the president has come a considerable distance toward recognizing how expensive this particular process of nation building is going to be. The approval by Congress of $87 billion for continuing operations in Iraq and Afghanistan is clearly a step in the right direction. Bush has indicated repeatedly that the United States cannot cut and run from its commitments. At the same time, there are disconcerting signs, with American casualties mounting, and the president's reelection looming, that the White House may in fact decide to withdraw American forces from Iraq. Indeed, the administration's latest adjustment seems to be toward a version of Vietnamization: handing over authority to a transitional government in Baghdad, while encouraging Iraq's own police and security forces to take up the greater burden with respect to counterinsurgency operations. In itself, this approach has certain virtues, but if it indicates a comprehensive withdrawal of U.S. resources and personnel from Iraq, then the results will not be benign, either for the United States, or for the Iraqi people. Nation-building operations sometimes fail, even under favorable conditions. But without robust involvement on the part of outside powers, such operations simply cannot succeed. It is an illusion to think that a stable, secure, and democratic Iraq can arise without a significant long-term U.S. investment of both blood and treasure.[29]

The administration responded to the challenge of 9/11 by devising a more assertive, Wilsonian foreign policy. The stated goals of this policy have been not only to initiate "rogue state rollback" but to promote a more open and democratic world order. By all accounts, Bush and his advisors really do believe that 9/11 has offered the United States, in the words of Secretary of Defense Donald Rumsfeld, an "opportunity to refashion the world."[30] The problem is not that the president is departing from a long tradition of liberal internationalism; it is that he is continuing some of the worst features of that tradition. Specifically, in Iraq, he is continuing the tradition of articulating and pursuing a set of extremely ambitious and idealistic foreign policy goals, without providing the full or proportionate means to achieve those goals. In this sense, it must be said, George W. Bush is very much a Wilsonian.

Whatever the immediate outcome in Iraq, America's foreign policy elites are not likely to abandon their longstanding ambition to create a liberal world order. What is more likely, and also more dangerous, is that they will continue to oscillate between various forms of liberal internationalism, and to press for a more open and democratic international system, without willing the means to sustain it.

Under the circumstances, the choice between unilateralism and multilateralism, which currently characterizes public debate over U.S. foreign policy, is almost beside the point. Neither a unilateral nor a multilateral foreign policy will succeed if Americans are unwilling to incur the full costs and risks that are implied in either case. It is impossible to promote the kind of international system that America's foreign policy elites say that they want without paying a heavy price for it. Iraq is simply the latest case in point. Americans can either take up the burden of acting on their liberal international-ist rhetoric and convictions, or they can keep costs and risks to a minimum by abandoning this ambitious interventionist agenda. They cannot do both. They cannot have hegemony on the cheap.

Notes

1. For representative criticisms in this vein, see David C. Hendrickson, "Toward Universal Empire: The Dangerous Quest for Absolute Security," *World Policy Journal,* vol. 19 (fall 2002), pp. 1–10; G. John Ikenberry, "America's Imperial Ambition," *Foreign Affairs,* vol. 81 (September/October 2002), pp. 44–60; Robert S. Litwak, "The New Calculus of Preemption," *Survival,* vol. 44 (winter 2002), pp. 53–79; and Joseph S. Nye, Jr., *The Paradox of American Power: Why the World's Only Superpower Can't Go It Alone* (New York: Oxford University Press, 2002), pp. 15, 39, 141–63.

2. See Michael H. Hunt, *Ideology and US Foreign Policy* (New Haven: Yale University Press, 1988), pp. 17–18.

3. "Remarks by the President at the 20th Anniversary of the National Endowment for Democracy," Washington, D.C.,

November 6, 2003, available at www.whitehouse.gov/news/releases/2003/11/iraq/20031106-2.html.

4. For a discussion of various schools of thought in the American foreign policy tradition, see Henry R. Nau, *At Home Abroad: Identity and Power in American Foreign Policy* (Ithaca: Cornell University Press, 2002), pp. 43–59; and Walter Russell Mead, *Special Providence: American Foreign Policy and How It Changed the World* (New York: Knopf, 2001).

5. See Arthur S. Link, *Woodrow Wilson: Revolution, War and Peace* (Wheeling, Ill.: Harlan Davidson, 1979), pp. 72–103.

6. In the former Ottoman Empire, for example, Wilson's initial pronouncements in favor of self-determination had raised hopes for postwar national independence among Arabs, Armenians, Jews, and Turks. At Paris, Wilson even promised a U.S. protectorate over an independent Armenia. Yet the eventual settlement in the region, disguised through the creation of League "mandates," closely resembled a classic sphere-of-influence bargain among Europe's great powers. The one major exception was in Turkey itself, where Kemal Atatürk rallied nationalist forces and ejected foreign troops from the Anatolian heartland. In this way, American promises with regard to Armenia were rendered completely irrelevant, even before the Senate's rejection of the Versailles Treaty. For a lively discussion of the postwar settlement within the Middle East, see Margaret MacMillan, *Paris 1919: Six Months That Changed the World* (New York: Random House, 2002), pp. 347–455.

7. Ray Stannard Baker and William Dodd, eds., *Public Papers of Woodrow Wilson,* (New York: Harper and Brothers, 1925–1927), vol. 5, pp. 341–44.

8. William C. Widenor, *Henry Cabot Lodge and the Search for an American Foreign Policy* (Berkeley: University of California Press, 1980), pp. 298, 331.

9. Baker and Dodd, eds., *Public Papers of Woodrow Wilson,* vol. 5, pp. 352–56.

10. See Warren F. Kimball, *The Juggler: Franklin Roosevelt as Wartime Statesman* (Princeton: Princeton University Press, 1991), pp. 63–81, 107–57.

11. See Melvyn P. Leffler, *A Preponderance of Power: National Security, the Truman Administration, and the Cold War* (Stanford: Stanford University Press, 1992), pp. 8–9, 15–18.

12. As George Kennan put it, "Our first aim with respect to Russia in time of peace is to encourage and promote by means short of war the gradual retraction of undue Russian influence from the present satellite area." See George Kennan, NSC 20/1, "US Objectives with Respect to Russia," August 18, 1948, in Thomas H. Etzold and John Lewis Gaddis, eds., *Containment: Documents on American Policy and Strategy, 1945–1950* (New York: Columbia University Press, 1978), p. 184.

13. See Steven L. Rearden, *History of the Office of the Secretary of Defense: The Formative Years, 1947–1950* (Washington, D.C.: United States Government Printing Office, 1984), pp. 532–36.

14. See John Lewis Gaddis, *Strategies of Containment* (New York: Oxford University Press, 1982), pp. 202–03, 217–18, 223–25.

15. Ibid., p. 284.

16. Stephen John Stedman, "The New Interventionists," *Foreign Affairs,* vol. 72 (spring 1993), pp. 4–5.

17. Anthony Lake, Assistant to the President for National Security Affairs, at Johns Hopkins University, September 21, 1993, in *Vital Speeches of the Day, 1993,* vol. 60, p. 15.

18. See Karin von Hippel, *Democracy by Force: U.S. Military Intervention in the Post-Cold War World* (New York: Cambridge University Press, 2000).

19. See, for example, in the case of Bosnia, James Gow, *Triumph of the Lack of Will: International Diplomacy and the Yugoslav War* (New York: Columbia University Press, 1997), pp. 208, 218.

20. Daniel L. Byman and Matthew C. Waxman, *The Dynamics of Coercion: American Foreign Policy and the Limits of Military Might* (New York: Cambridge University Press, 2002), p. 143.

21. Governor George W. Bush, "A Period of Consequences," September 23, 1999, The Citadel, South Carolina, available at www.citadel.edu/pao/addresses/pres_bush.html.

22. Presidential debates, October 3, 2000, at Boston, Massachussetts, and October 11, 2000, at Winston-Salem, North Carolina, available at www.foreignpolicy2000.org/debate/candidate/candidate.html and www.foreignpolicy2000.org/debate/candidate/candidate2.html.

23. For a good exposition of the initially "realist" bent of one of Bush's leading foreign policy advisors, see Condoleezza Rice, "Campaign 2000: Promoting the National Interest," *Foreign Affairs,* vol. 79 (January/February 2000), pp. 45–62.

24. Nicholas Lemann, "Without a Doubt," *The New Yorker,* October 14 and 21, 2002, p. 177.

25. The National Security Strategy of the United States of America (Washington, D.C.: The White House, September 2002), pp. 1, 3–4, 26–28.

26. George W. Bush, "President Discusses the Future of Iraq," February 26, 2003, Washington Hilton Hotel, Washington, D.C., available at www.whitehouse.gov/news/releases/2003/02/iraq/20030226-11.html.

27. George Packer, "Dreaming of Democracy," *New York Times Magazine,* March 2, 2003, pp. 46–49.

28. Anja Manuel and Peter W. Singer, "A New Model Afghan Army," *Foreign Affairs,* vol. 81 (July/August 2002), pp. 44–59.

29. Frederick Kagan, "War and Aftermath," *Policy Review,* no. 120 (August/September 2003), pp. 3–27.

30. "Secretary Rumsfeld Interview," *New York Times,* October 12, 2001.

COLIN DUECK is assistant professor of political science at the University of Colorado, Boulder.

The Eagle Has Crash Landed

Pax Americana is over. Challenges from Vietnam and the Balkans to the Middle East and September 11 have revealed the limits of American supremacy. Will the United States learn to fade quietly, or will U.S. conservatives resist and thereby transform a gradual decline into a rapid and dangerous fall?

IMMANUEL WALLERSTEIN

The United States in decline? Few people today would believe this assertion. The only ones who do are the U.S. hawks, who argue vociferously for policies to reverse the decline. This belief that the end of U.S. hegemony has already begun does not follow from the vulnerability that became apparent to all on September 11, 2001. In fact, the United States has been fading as a global power since the 1970s, and the U.S. response to the terrorist attacks has merely accelerated this decline. To understand why the so-called Pax Americana is on the wane requires examining the geopolitics of the 20th century, particularly of the century's final three decades. This exercise uncovers a simple and inescapable conclusion: The economic, political, and military factors that contributed to U.S. hegemony are the same factors that will inexorably produce the coming U.S. decline.

Intro to Hegemony

The rise of the United States to global hegemony was a long process that began in earnest with the world recession of 1873. At that time, the United States and Germany began to acquire an increasing share of global markets, mainly at the expense of the steadily receding British economy. Both nations had recently acquired a stable political base—the United States by successfully terminating the Civil War and Germany by achieving unification and defeating France in the Franco-Prussian War. From 1873 to 1914, the United States and Germany became the principal producers in certain leading sectors: steel and later automobiles for the United States and industrial chemicals for Germany.

The history books record that World War I broke out in 1914 and ended in 1918 and that World War II lasted from 1939 to 1945. However, it makes more sense to consider the two as a single, continuous "30 years' war" between the United States and Germany, with truces and local conflicts scattered in between. The competition for hegemonic succession took an ideological turn in 1933, when the Nazis came to power in Germany and began their quest to transcend the global system altogether, seeking not hegemony within the current system but rather a form of global empire. Recall the Nazi slogan *ein tausendjähriges Reich* (a thousand-year empire). In turn, the United States assumed

the role of advocate of centrist world liberalism—recall former U.S. President Franklin D. Roosevelt's "four freedoms" (freedom of speech, of worship, from want, and from fear)—and entered into a strategic alliance with the Soviet Union, making possible the defeat of Germany and its allies.

World War II resulted in enormous destruction of infrastructure and populations throughout Eurasia, from the Atlantic to the Pacific oceans, with almost no country left unscathed. The only major industrial power in the world to emerge intact—and even greatly strengthened from an economic perspective—was the United States, which moved swiftly to consolidate its position.

But the aspiring hegemon faced some practical political obstacles. During the war, the Allied powers had agreed on the establishment of the United Nations, composed primarily of countries that had been in the coalition against the Axis powers. The organization's critical feature was the Security Council, the only structure that could authorize the use of force. Since the U.N. Charter gave the right of veto to five powers—including the United States and the Soviet Union—the council was rendered largely toothless in practice. So it was not the founding of the United Nations in April 1945 that determined the geopolitical constraints of the second half of the 20th century but rather the Yalta meeting between Roosevelt, British Prime Minister Winston Churchill, and Soviet leader Joseph Stalin two months earlier.

The formal accords at Yalta were less important than the informal, unspoken agreements, which one can only assess by observing the behavior of the United States and the Soviet Union in the years that followed. When the war ended in Europe on May 8, 1945, Soviet and Western (that is, U.S., British, and French) troops were located in particular places—essentially, along a line in the center of Europe that came to be called the Oder-Neisse Line. Aside from a few minor adjustments, they stayed there. In hindsight, Yalta signified the agreement of both sides that they could stay there and that neither side would use force to push the other out. This tacit accord applied to Asia as well, as evinced by U.S. occupation of Japan and the division of Korea. Politically, therefore, Yalta was an agreement on the status quo in which the Soviet Union controlled about one third of the world and the United States the rest.

Washington also faced more serious military challenges. The Soviet Union had the world's largest land forces, while the U.S. government was under domestic pressure to downsize its army, particularly by ending the draft. The United States therefore decided to assert its military strength not via land forces but through a monopoly of nuclear weapons (plus an air force capable of deploying them). This monopoly soon disappeared: By 1949, the Soviet Union had developed nuclear weapons as well. Ever since, the United States has been reduced to trying to prevent the acquisition of nuclear weapons (and chemical and biological weapons) by additional powers, an effort that, in the 21st century, does not seem terribly successful.

Until 1991, the United States and the Soviet Union coexisted in the "balance of terror" of the Cold War. This status quo was tested seriously only three times: the Berlin blockade of 1948–49, the Korean War in 1950–53, and the Cuban missile crisis of 1962. The result in each case was restoration of the status quo. Moreover, note how each time the Soviet Union faced a political crisis among its satellite regimes—East Germany in 1953, Hungary in 1956, Czechoslovakia in 1968, and Poland in 1981—the United States engaged in little more than propaganda exercises, allowing the Soviet Union to proceed largely as it deemed fit.

Of course, this passivity did not extend to the economic arena. The United States capitalized on the Cold War ambiance to launch massive economic reconstruction efforts, first in Western Europe and then in Japan (as well as in South Korea and Taiwan). The rationale was obvious: What was the point of having such overwhelming productive superiority if the rest of the world could not muster effective demand? Furthermore, economic reconstruction helped create clientelistic obligations on the part of the nations receiving U.S. aid; this sense of obligation fostered willingness to enter into military alliances and, even more important, into political subservience.

Finally, one should not underestimate the ideological and cultural component of U.S. hegemony. The immediate post-1945 period may have been the historical high point for the popularity of communist ideology. We easily forget today the large votes for Communist parties in free elections in countries such as Belgium, France, Italy, Czechoslovakia, and Finland, not to mention the support Communist parties gathered in Asia—in Vietnam, India, and Japan—and throughout Latin America. And that still leaves out areas such as China, Greece, and Iran, where free elections remained absent or constrained but where Communist parties enjoyed widespread appeal. In response, the United States sustained a massive anticommunist ideological offensive. In retrospect, this initiative appears largely successful: Washington brandished its role as the leader of the "free world" at least as effectively as the Soviet Union brandished its position as the leader of the "progressive" and "anti-imperialist" camp.

One, Two, Many Vietnams

The United States' success as a hegemonic power in the postwar period created the conditions of the nation's hegemonic demise. This process is captured in four symbols: the war in Vietnam, the revolutions of 1968, the fall of the Berlin Wall in 1989, and the terrorist attacks of September 2001. Each symbol built upon the

prior one, culminating in the situation in which the United States currently finds itself—a lone superpower that lacks true power, a world leader nobody follows and few respect, and a nation drifting dangerously amidst a global chaos it cannot control.

What was the Vietnam War? First and foremost, it was the effort of the Vietnamese people to end colonial rule and establish their own state. The Vietnamese fought the French, the Japanese, and the Americans, and in the end the Vietnamese won—quite an achievement, actually. Geopolitically, however, the war represented a rejection of the Yalta status quo by populations then labeled as Third World. Vietnam became such a powerful symbol because Washington was foolish enough to invest its full military might in the struggle, but the United States still lost. True, the United States didn't deploy nuclear weapons (a decision certain myopic groups on the right have long reproached), but such use would have shattered the Yalta accords and might have produced a nuclear holocaust—an outcome the United States simply could not risk.

But Vietnam was not merely a military defeat or a blight on U.S. prestige. The war dealt a major blow to the United States' ability to remain the world's dominant economic power. The conflict was extremely expensive and more or less used up the U.S. gold reserves that had been so plentiful since 1945. Moreover, the United States incurred these costs just as Western Europe and Japan experienced major economic upswings. These conditions ended U.S. preeminence in the global economy. Since the late 1960s, members of this triad have been nearly economic equals, each doing better than the others for certain periods but none moving far ahead.

When the revolutions of 1968 broke out around the world, support for the Vietnamese became a major rhetorical component. "One, two, many Vietnams" and "Ho, Ho, Ho Chi Minh" were chanted in many a street, not least in the United States. But the 1968ers did not merely condemn U.S. hegemony. They condemned Soviet collusion with the United States, they condemned Yalta, and they used or adapted the language of the Chinese cultural revolutionaries who divided the world into two camps—the two superpowers and the rest of the world.

The denunciation of Soviet collusion led logically to the denunciation of those national forces closely allied with the Soviet Union, which meant in most cases the traditional Communist parties. But the 1968 revolutionaries also lashed out against other components of the Old Left—national liberation movements in the Third World, social-democratic movements in Western Europe, and New Deal Democrats in the United States—accusing them, too, of collusion with what the revolutionaries generically termed "U.S. imperialism."

The attack on Soviet collusion with Washington plus the attack on the Old Left further weakened the legitimacy of the Yalta arrangements on which the United States had fashioned the world order. It also undermined the position of centrist liberalism as the lone, legitimate global ideology. The direct political consequences of the world revolutions of 1968 were minimal, but the geopolitical and intellectual repercussions were enormous and irrevocable. Centrist liberalism tumbled from the throne it had occupied since the European revolutions of 1848 and that had enabled it to co-opt conservatives and radicals alike. These ideologies returned and once again represented a real gamut of choices. Conservatives would again become conservatives, and radicals, radicals. The centrist liberals did not disappear, but they were cut down to size. And in the process, the official U.S. ideological position—antifascist, anticommunist, anticolonialist—seemed thin and unconvincing to a growing portion of the world's populations.

The Powerless Superpower

The onset of international economic stagnation in the 1970s had two important consequences for U.S. power. First, stagnation resulted in the collapse of "developmentalism"—the notion that every nation could catch up economically if the state took appropriate action—which was the principal ideological claim of the Old Left movements then in power. One after another, these regimes faced internal disorder, declining standards of living, increasing debt dependency on international financial institutions, and eroding credibility. What had seemed in the 1960s to be the successful navigation of Third World decolonization by the United States—minimizing disruption and maximizing the smooth transfer of power to regimes that were developmentalist but scarcely revolutionary—gave way to disintegrating order, simmering discontents, and unchanneled radical temperaments. When the United States tried to intervene, it failed. In 1983, U.S. President Ronald Reagan sent troops to Lebanon to restore order. The troops were in effect forced out. He compensated by invading Grenada, a country without troops. President George H.W. Bush invaded Panama, another country without troops. But after he intervened in Somalia to restore order, the United States was in effect forced out, somewhat ignominiously. Since there was little the U.S. government could actually do to reverse the trend of declining hegemony, it chose simply to ignore this trend—a policy that prevailed from the withdrawal from Vietnam until September 11, 2001.

Meanwhile, true conservatives began to assume control of key states and interstate institutions. The neoliberal offensive of the 1980s was marked by the Thatcher and Reagan regimes and the emergence of the International Monetary Fund (IMF) as a key actor on the world scene. Where once (for more than a century) conservative forces had attempted to portray themselves as wiser liberals, now centrist liberals were compelled to argue that they were more effective conservatives. The conservative programs were clear. Domestically, conservatives tried to enact policies that would reduce the cost of labor, minimize environmental Constraints on producers, and cut back on state welfare benefits. Actual successes were modest, so conservatives then moved vigorously into the international arena. The gatherings of the World Economic Forum in Davos provided a meeting ground for elites and the media. The IMF provided a club for finance ministers and central bankers. And the United States pushed for the creation of the World Trade Organization to enforce free commercial flows across the world's frontiers.

While the United States wasn't watching, the Soviet Union was collapsing. Yes, Ronald Reagan had dubbed the Soviet Union an "evil empire" and had used the rhetorical bombast of calling for the destruction of the Berlin Wall, but the United States didn't really mean it and certainly was not responsible for the Soviet Union's downfall. In truth, the Soviet Union and its East European imperial zone collapsed because of popular disillusionment with the Old Left in combination with Soviet leader Mikhail Gorbachev's efforts to save his regime by liquidating Yalta and instituting internal liberalization (perestroika plus glasnost). Gorbachev succeeded in liquidating Yalta but not in saving the Soviet Union (although he almost did, be it said).

The United States was stunned and puzzled by the sudden collapse, uncertain how to handle the consequences. The collapse of communism in effect signified the collapse of liberalism, removing the only ideological justification behind U.S. hegemony, a justification tacitly supported by liberalism's ostensible ideological opponent. This loss of legitimacy led directly to the Iraqi invasion of Kuwait, which Iraqi leader Saddam Hussein would never have dared had the Yalta arrangements remained in place. In retrospect, U.S. efforts in the Gulf War accomplished a truce at basically the same line of departure. But can a hegemonic power be satisfied with a tie in a war with a middling regional power? Saddam demonstrated that one could pick a fight with the United States and get away with it. Even more than the defeat in Vietnam, Saddam's brash challenge has eaten at the innards of the U.S. right, in particular those known as the hawks, which explains the fervor of their current desire to invade Iraq and destroy its regime.

Between the Gulf War and September 11, 2001, the two major arenas of world conflict were the Balkans and the Middle East. The United States has played a major diplomatic role in both regions. Looking back, how different would the results have been had the United States assumed a completely isolationist position? In the Balkans, an economically successful multinational state (Yugoslavia) broke down, essentially into its component parts. Over 10 years, most of the resulting states have engaged in a process of ethnification, experiencing fairly brutal violence, widespread human rights violations, and outright wars. Outside intervention—in which the United States figured most prominently—brought about a truce and ended the most egregious violence, but this intervention in no way reversed the ethnification, which is now consolidated and somewhat legitimated. Would these conflicts have ended differently without U.S. involvement? The violence might have continued longer, but the basic results would probably not have been too different. The picture is even grimmer in the Middle East, where, if anything, U.S. engagement has been deeper and its failures more spectacular. In the Balkans and the Middle East alike, the United States has failed to exert its hegemonic clout effectively, not for want of will or effort but for want of real power.

The Hawks Undone

Then came September 11—the shock and the reaction. Under fire from U.S. legislators, the Central Intelligence Agency (CIA) now claims it had warned the Bush administration of possible threats. But despite the CIA's focus on al Qaeda and the agency's intelligence expertise, it could not foresee (and therefore, prevent) the execution of the terrorist strikes. Or so would argue CIA Director George Tenet. This testimony can hardly comfort the U.S. government or the American people. Whatever else historians may decide, the attacks of September 11, 2001, posed a major challenge to U.S. power. The persons responsible did not represent a major military power. They were members of a nonstate force, with a high degree of determination, some money, a band of dedicated followers, and a strong base in one weak state. In short, militarily, they were nothing. Yet they succeeded in a bold attack on U.S. soil.

George W Bush came to power very critical of the Clinton administration's handling of world affairs. Bush and his advisors did not admit—but were undoubtedly aware—that Clinton's path had been the path of every U.S. president since Gerald Ford, including that of Ronald Reagan and George H.W. Bush. It had even been the path of the current Bush administration before September 11. One only needs to look at how Bush handled the downing of the U.S. plane off China in April 2001 to see that prudence had been the name of the game.

Following the terrorist attacks, Bush changed course, declaring war on terrorism, assuring the American people that "the outcome is certain" and informing the world that "you are either with us or against us." Long frustrated by even the most conservative U.S. administrations, the hawks finally came to dominate American policy. Their position is clear: The United States wields overwhelming military power, and even though countless foreign leaders consider it unwise for Washington to flex its military muscles, these same leaders cannot and will not do anything if the United States simply imposes its will on the rest. The hawks believe the United States should act as an imperial power for two reasons: First, the United States can get away with it. And second, if Washington doesn't exert its force, the United States will become increasingly marginalized.

Today, this hawkish position has three expressions: the military assault in Afghanistan, the de facto support for the Israeli attempt to liquidate the Palestinian Authority, and the invasion of Iraq, which is reportedly in the military preparation stage. Less than one year after the September 2001 terrorist attacks, it is perhaps too early to assess what such strategies will accomplish. Thus far, these schemes have led to the overthrow of the Taliban in Afghanistan (without the complete dismantling of al Qaeda or the capture of its top leadership); enormous destruction in Palestine (without rendering Palestinian leader Yasir Arafat "irrelevant," as Israeli Prime Minister Ariel Sharon said he is); and heavy opposition from U.S. allies in Europe and the Middle East to plans for an invasion of Iraq.

The hawks' reading of recent events emphasizes that opposition to U.S. actions, while serious, has remained largely verbal. Neither Western Europe nor Russia nor China nor Saudi Arabia has seemed ready to break ties in serious ways with the United States. In other words, hawks believe, Washington has indeed gotten away with it. The hawks assume a similar outcome will occur when the U.S. military actually invades Iraq and after that, when the United States exercises its authority elsewhere in the world, be it in Iran, North Korea, Colombia, or perhaps Indonesia. Ironically, the hawk reading has largely become the reading of the international left, which has been screaming about U.S. policies—mainly because they fear that the chances of U.S. success are high.

But hawk interpretations are wrong and will only contribute to the United States' decline, transforming a gradual descent into a much more rapid and turbulent fall. Specifically, hawk approaches will fail for military, economic, and ideological reasons.

Undoubtedly, the military remains the United States' strongest card; in fact, it is the only card. Today, the United States wields the most formidable military apparatus in the world. And if claims of new, unmatched military technologies are to be believed, the U.S. military edge over the rest of the world is considerably greater today than it was just a decade ago. But does that mean, then, that the United States can invade Iraq, conquer it rapidly, and install a friendly and stable regime? Unlikely. Bear in mind that of the three serious wars the U.S. military has fought since 1945 (Korea, Vietnam, and the Gulf War), one ended in defeat and two in draws—not exactly a glorious record.

Saddam Hussein's army is not that of the Taliban, and his internal military control is far more coherent. A U.S. invasion would necessarily involve a serious land force, one that would have to fight its way to Baghdad and would likely suffer significant casualties. Such a force would also need staging grounds, and Saudi Arabia has made clear that it will not serve in this capacity. Would Kuwait or Turkey help out? Perhaps, if Washington calls in all its chips. Meanwhile, Saddam can be expected to deploy all weapons at his disposal, and it is precisely the U.S. government that keeps fretting over how nasty those weapons might be. The United States may twist the arms of regimes in the region, but popular sentiment clearly views the whole affair as reflecting a deep anti-Arab bias in the United States. Can such a conflict be won? The British General Staff has apparently already informed Prime Minister Tony Blair that it does not believe so.

And there is always the matter of "second fronts." Following the Gulf War, U.S. armed forces sought to prepare for the possibility of two simultaneous regional wars. After a while, the Pentagon quietly abandoned the idea as impractical and costly. But who can be sure that no potential U.S. enemies would strike when the United States appears bogged down in Iraq?

Consider, too, the question of U.S. popular tolerance of nonvictories. Americans hover between a patriotic fervor that lends support to all wartime presidents and a deep isolationist urge. Since 1945, patriotism has hit a wall whenever the death toll has risen. Why should today's reaction differ? And even if the hawks (who are almost all civilians) feel impervious to public opinion, U.S. Army generals, burnt by Vietnam, do not.

And what about the economic front? In the 1980s, countless American analysts became hysterical over the Japanese economic miracle. They calmed down in the 1990s, given Japan's well-publicized financial difficulties. Yet after overstating how quickly Japan was moving forward, U.S. authorities now seem to be complacent, confident that Japan lags far behind. These days, Washington seems more inclined to lecture Japanese policymakers about what they are doing wrong.

Such triumphalism hardly appears warranted. Consider the following April 20, 2002, *New York Times* report: "A Japanese laboratory has built the world's fastest computer, a machine so powerful that it matches the raw processing power of the 20 fastest American computers combined and far outstrips the previous leader, an I.B.M.-built machine. The achievement. . . is evidence that a technology race that most American engineers thought they were winning handily is far from over." The analysis goes on to note that there are "contrasting scientific and technological priorities" in the two countries. The Japanese machine is built to analyze climatic change, but U.S. machines are designed to simulate weapons. This contrast embodies the oldest story in the history of hegemonic powers. The dominant power concentrates (to its detriment) on the military; the candidate for successor concentrates on the economy. The latter has always paid off, handsomely. It did for the United States. Why should it not pay off for Japan as well, perhaps in alliance with China?

Finally, there is the ideological sphere. Right now, the U.S. economy seems relatively weak, even more so considering the exorbitant military expenses associated with hawk strategies. Moreover, Washington remains politically isolated; virtually no one (save Israel) thinks the hawk position makes sense or is worth encouraging. Other nations are afraid or unwilling to stand up to Washington directly, but even their foot-dragging is hurting the United States.

Yet the U.S. response amounts to little more than arrogant arm-twisting. Arrogance has its own negatives. Calling in chips means leaving fewer chips for next time, and surly acquiescence breeds increasing resentment. Over the last 200 years, the United States acquired a considerable amount of ideological credit. But these days, the United States is running through this credit even faster than it ran through its gold surplus in the 1960s.

The United States faces two possibilities during the next 10 years: It can follow the hawks' path, with negative consequences for all but especially for itself. Or it can realize that the negatives are too great. Simon Tisdall of the *Guardian* recently argued that even disregarding international public opinion, "the U.S. is not able to fight a successful Iraqi war by itself without incurring immense damage, not least in terms of its economic interests and its energy supply. Mr. Bush is reduced to talking tough and looking ineffectual." And if the United States still invades Iraq and is then forced to withdraw it will look even more ineffectual.

President Bush's options appear extremely limited, and there is little doubt that the United States will continue to decline as a decisive force in world affairs over the next decade. The real question is not whether U.S. hegemony is waning but whether the United States can devise a way to descend gracefully, with minimum damage to the world, and to itself.

For links to relevant Web sites, access to the *FP* Archive, and a comprehensive index of related Foreign Policy articles, go to www.foreignpolicy.com.

IMMANUEL WALLERSTEIN is a senior research scholar at Yale University and author of, most recently, *The End of the World As We Know It: Social Science for the Twenty-First Century* (Minneapolis: University of Minnesota Press, 1999).

Grand Strategy for a Divided America

CHARLES A. KUPCHAN AND PETER L. TRUBOWITZ

Mind the Gap

The United States is in the midst of a polarized and bruising debate about the nature and scope of its engagement with the world. The current reassessment is only the latest of many; ever since the United States' rise as a global power, its leaders and citizens have regularly scrutinized the costs and benefits of foreign ambition. In 1943, Walter Lippmann offered a classic formulation of the issue. "In foreign relations," Lippmann wrote, "as in all other relations, a policy has been formed only when commitments and power have been brought into balance. . . . The nation must maintain its objectives and its power in equilibrium, its purposes within its means and its means equal to its purposes."

Although Lippmann was mindful of the economic costs of global engagement, his primary concern was the political "solvency" of U.S. foreign policy, not the adequacy of the United States' material resources. He lamented the divisive partisanship that had so often prevented the United States from finding "a settled and generally accepted foreign policy." "This is a danger to the Republic," he warned. "For when a people is divided within itself about the conduct of its foreign relations, it is unable to agree on the determination of its true interest. It is unable to prepare adequately for war or to safeguard successfully its peace. . . . The spectacle of this great nation which does not know its own mind is as humiliating as it is dangerous." Lippmann's worries would prove unfounded; in the face of World War II and the onset of the Cold War, the bitter partisanship of the past gave way to a broad consensus on foreign policy that was to last for the next five decades.

Today, however, Lippmann's concern with political solvency is more relevant than ever. After the demise of the Soviet Union, the shock of September 11, and the failures of the Iraq war, Republicans and Democrats share less common ground on the fundamental purposes of U.S. power than at any other time since World War II. A critical gap has opened up between the United States' global commitments and its political appetite for sustaining them. As made clear by the collision between President George W. Bush and the Democratic Congress over what to do in Iraq, the country's bipartisan consensus on foreign policy has collapsed. If left unattended, the political foundations of U.S. statecraft will continue to disintegrate, exposing the country to the dangers of an erratic and incoherent foreign policy.

The presidential candidate who understands the urgency and gravity of striking a new balance between the United States'

purposes and its political means is poised to reap a double reward. He or she would likely attract strong popular support; as in the 2006 midterm elections, in the 2008 election the war in Iraq and the conduct of U.S. foreign policy are set to be decisive issues. That candidate, if elected, would also enhance U.S. security by crafting a new grand strategy that is politically sustainable, thereby steadying a global community that continues to look to the United States for leadership.

Formulating a politically solvent strategy will require scaling back U.S. commitments, bringing them into line with diminishing means. At the same time, it will be necessary to stabilize the nation's foreign policy by shoring up public support for a new vision of the United States' global responsibilities. Solvency is the path to security; it is far better for the United States to arrive at a more discriminating grand strategy that enjoys domestic backing than to continue drifting toward an intractable polarization that would be as dangerous as it would be humiliating.

Finding the Water's Edge

For Americans who lived through the bipartisan consensus of the Cold War era, the current political warfare over foreign policy seems to be a dramatic aberration. To be sure, Bush has been a polarizing president, in no small part due to the controversial invasion of Iraq and the troubled occupation that has followed. But in fact, today's partisan wrangling over foreign policy is the historical norm; it is the bipartisanship of the Cold War that was the anomaly.

Soon after the republic's founding, political parties formed to help overcome the obstacles that federalism, the separation of powers, and sectionalism put in the way of effective statecraft. With them came partisanship. During the nation's early decades, the main line of partisan competition ran along the North-South divide, pitting the Hamiltonian Federalists of the Northeast against the Jeffersonian Republicans of the South. The two parties disagreed on matters of grand strategy—specifically whether the United States should lean toward Great Britain or France—as well as on matters of political economy.

The Federalists worried that the new republic might fail if it found itself in a conflict with the British; they therefore favored tilting toward Great Britain rather than extending the alliance with France that was struck during the American Revolution. On economic matters, the Federalists defended the interests of the North's aspiring entrepreneurs, arguing for tariffs to protect the region's infant industries. The Republicans, however, continued to lean toward France, hoping to balance Great Britain's power by supporting its main European rival. And as champions of the interests of the nation's farmers, the Republicans clamored for free trade and westward expansion. At George Washington's behest, the two parties found common ground on the need to avoid "entangling alliances," but they agreed on little else.

Partisan passions cooled with the end of the Napoleonic Wars in Europe, and an era of solvency in the conduct of the nation's foreign affairs ensued. The collapse of the Federalist Party and the revival of an economy no longer disrupted by war ushered in what one Boston newspaper called "an Era of Good Feelings." For the first time, the United States enjoyed a sustained period of political consensus. Meanwhile, the peace preserved by the Concert of Europe, coupled with the tentative rapprochement with London that followed the War of 1812, made it possible for the nation's elected officials, starting with James Monroe, to turn their energies to the demands of "internal improvement." Americans focused on the consolidation and westward expansion of the union, limiting the nation's reach to what was sustainable politically and militarily.

This consensus was upended in 1846, when James Polk took the country to war against Mexico in the name of "manifest destiny." The Democrats—the southern heirs to Jefferson's Republicans—championed seizing Mexican territory and saw the war as an opportunity to strengthen their hold on the levers of national power. Fearing exactly that, the northeastern Whigs—the forerunners to modern Republicans—waged a rear-guard battle, challenging the legitimacy of Polk's land grab and the rise of southern "slave power." Polk's war, the United States' first war of choice, unleashed a new round of partisan struggle, aggravating the sectional tensions that would ultimately result in the Civil War.

An uneasy domestic calm set in after the Civil War, but it was soon brought to an end by divisions over the United States' aspirations to great-power status. Over the course of the 1890s, the United States built a world-class battle fleet, acquired foreign lands, and secured foreign markets. Republican efforts to catapult the United States into the front ranks, however, reopened sectional wounds and invited strong Democratic resistance. The Republicans prevailed due to their monopoly on power, but their geopolitical ambitions soon proved politically unsustainable. Starting with the Spanish-American War, the United States engaged in what Lippmann called "deficit diplomacy": its international commitments exceeded the public's willingness to bear the requisite burdens.

After the turn of the century, U.S. foreign policy lurched incoherently between stark alternatives. Theodore Roosevelt's imperialist adventure in the Philippines quickly outstripped the country's appetite for foreign ambition. William Taft tried "dollar diplomacy," preferring to pursue Washington's objectives abroad through what he called "peaceful and economic" means. But he triggered the ire of Democrats who viewed his strategy as little more than capitulation to the interests of big business. Woodrow Wilson embraced "collective security" and the League of Nations, investing in institutionalized partnerships that would ease the costs of the United States' deepening engagement with the world. But the Senate, virtually paralyzed by partisan rancor, would have none of it. As Henry Cabot Lodge, one of the League of Nations' staunchest opponents in the Senate, quipped, "I never expected to hate anyone in politics with the hatred I feel towards Wilson." By the interwar period, political stalemate had set in. Americans shunned both the assertive use of U.S. power and institutionalized multilateralism, instead preferring the illusory safety of isolationism advocated by Warren Harding, Calvin Coolidge, and Herbert Hoover.

The collapse of bipartisanship and liberal internationalism did not start with George W. Bush.

One of Franklin Roosevelt's greatest achievements was overcoming this political divide and steering the United States toward a new era of bipartisanship. With World War II as a backdrop, he built a broad coalition of Democrats and Republicans behind liberal internationalism. The new course entailed a commitment to both power and partnership: the United States would project its military strength to preserve stability, but whenever possible it would exercise leadership through consensus and multilateral partnership rather than unilateral initiative. This domestic compact, although weakened by political struggles over the Vietnam War, lasted to the end of the Cold War.

The nature of the geopolitical threat facing the United States helped Roosevelt and his successors sustain this liberal internationalist compact. Washington needed allies to prevent the domination of Eurasia by a hostile power. The strategic exigencies of World War II and the Cold War also instilled discipline, encouraging Democrats and Republicans alike to unite around a common foreign policy. When partisan passions flared, as they did over the Korean War and the Vietnam War, they were contained by the imperatives of super-power rivalry.

The steadiness of bipartisan cooperation on foreign policy was the product not just of strategic necessity but also of changes in the nation's political landscape. Regional divides had moderated, with the North and the South forming a political alliance for the first time in U.S. history. Anticommunism made it politically treacherous to stray too far to the left, and the public's worries about nuclear Armageddon reined in the right. The post–World War II economic boom eased the socioeconomic divides of the New Deal era, closing the ideological distance between Democrats and Republicans and making it easier to fashion a consensus behind free trade. Prosperity and affluence helped nurture the United States' political center, which served as the foundation for the liberal internationalism that lasted a half century.

A Nation Redivided

Contrary to conventional wisdom, the collapse of bipartisanship and liberal internationalism did not start with George W. Bush. Bipartisanship dropped sharply following the end of the

Cold War, reaching a post–World War II low after the Republicans gained control of Congress in 1994. Repeated clashes over foreign policy between the Clinton administration and Congress marked the hollowing out of the bipartisan center that had been liberal internationalism's political base. The Bush administration then dismantled what remained of the moderate center, ensuring that today's partisan divide is every bit as wide as the interwar schism that haunted Lippmann. Democratic and Republican lawmakers now hold very different views on foreign policy. On the most basic questions of U.S. grand strategy—the sources and purposes of U.S. power, the use of force, the role of international institutions—representatives of the two parties are on different planets.

Most Republicans in Congress contend that U.S. power depends mainly on the possession and use of military might, and they view institutionalized cooperation primarily as an impediment. They staunchly back the Bush administration's ongoing effort to pacify Iraq. When the new Congress took its first votes on the Iraq war in the beginning of this year, only 17 of the 201 Republicans in the House crossed party lines to oppose the recent surge in U.S. troops. In the Senate, only two Republicans joined the Democrats to approve a resolution calling for a timetable for withdrawal. In contrast, most Democrats maintain that U.S. power depends more on persuasion than coercion and needs to be exercised multilaterally. They want out of Iraq: 95 percent of House and Senate Democrats have voted to withdraw U.S. troops in 2008. With the Republicans opting for the use of force and the Democrats for international cooperation, the bipartisan compact between power and partnership—the formula that brought liberal internationalism to life—has come undone.

To be sure, the Republican Party is still home to a few committed multilateralists, such as Senators Richard Lugar (of Indiana) and Chuck Hagel (of Nebraska). But they are isolated within their own ranks. And some Democrats, especially those eyeing the presidency, are keen to demonstrate their resolve on matters of national defense. But the party leaders are being pushed to the left by increasingly powerful party activists. The ideological overlap between the two parties is thus minimal, and the areas of concord are superficial at best. Most Republicans and Democrats still believe that the United States has global responsibilities, but there is little agreement on how to match means and ends. And on the central question of power versus partnership, the two parties are moving in opposite directions—with the growing gap evident among the public as well as political elites.

In a March 2007 Pew Research Center poll, over 70 percent of Republican voters maintained that "the best way to ensure peace is through military strength." Only 40 percent of Democratic voters shared that view. A similar poll conducted in 1999 revealed the same partisan split, making clear that the divide is not just about Bush's foreign policy but also about the broader purposes of U.S. power. The Iraq war has clearly widened and deepened ideological differences over the relative efficacy of force and diplomacy. One CNN poll recorded that after four years of occupying Iraq, only 24 percent of Republicans oppose the war, compared with more than 90 percent of Democrats. As for exporting American ideals, a June 2006 German Marshall

Fund study found that only 35 percent of Democrats believed the United States should "help establish democracy in other countries," compared with 64 percent of Republicans. Similarly, a December 2006 CBS News poll found that two-thirds of Democrats believed the United States should "mind its own business internationally," whereas only one-third of Republicans held that view.

Fueled by these ideological divides, partisanship has engulfed Washington. According to one widely used index (Voteview), Congress today is more politically fractious and polarized than at any time in the last hundred years. After Democrats gained a majority in Congress in the 2006 midterm elections, many observers predicted that having one party control the White House and the other Congress would foster cooperation, as it often has in the past. Instead, the political rancor has only intensified. The White House, despite its initial pledge to work with the opposition, has continued its strident ways, dismissing the Democrats' call for a timetable for withdrawal from Iraq as a "game of charades." Just after capturing the House and the Senate, the Democrats also promised to reach across the aisle. But as soon as the 110th Congress opened, they gave Republicans a taste of their own medicine by preventing the minority party from amending legislation during the initial flurry of lawmaking.

Partisan confrontation is a recipe for political stalemate at home and failed leadership abroad.

The sources of this return to partisan rancor are international as well as domestic. Abroad, the demise of the Soviet Union and the absence of a new peer competitor have loosened Cold War discipline, leaving the country's foreign policy more vulnerable to the vicissitudes of party politics. The threat posed by international terrorism has proved too elusive and sporadic to act as the new unifier. Meanwhile, the United States' deepening integration into the world economy is producing growing disparities in wealth among Americans, creating new socioeconomic cleavages and eroding support for free trade.

Within the United States, the political conditions that once encouraged centrism have weakened. Regional tensions are making a comeback; "red" America and "blue" America disagree about what the nature of the country's engagement in the world should be as well as about domestic issues such as abortion, gun control, and taxes. Moderates are in ever shorter supply, resulting in the thinning out of what Arthur Schlesinger, Jr., aptly labeled "the vital center." Congressional redistricting, the proliferation of highly partisan media outlets, and the growing power of the Internet as a source of campaign financing and partisan mobilization have all contributed to the erosion of the center. A generational change has taken its toll, too. Almost 85 percent of the House was first elected in 1988 or after. The "greatest generation" is fast retiring from political life, taking with it decades of civic-minded service.

With the presidential campaign now building up to full speed and the domestic landscape already deeply etched along regional and ideological lines, the partisan confrontation is poised to intensify—a recipe for political stalemate at home and failed leadership abroad.

Restoring Solvency

In the early twentieth century, deep partisan divisions produced unpredictable and dangerous swings in U.S. foreign policy and ultimately led to isolation from the world. A similar dynamic is unfolding at the beginning of the twenty-first century. The assertive unilateralism of the Bush administration is proving politically unsustainable. Eyeing the 2008 elections, the Democrats are readying ambitious plans to breathe new life into international institutions. But they, too, will find their preferred grand strategy politically unsustainable. The Republican Party, virtually bereft of its moderates after the 2006 elections, has little patience for cooperative multilateralism—and will gladly deploy its power in the Senate to block any programmatic effort to bind Washington to international agreements and institutions. Especially amid the domestic acrimony spawned by the war in Iraq, partisanship and stalemate at home could once again obstruct U.S. statecraft, perhaps even provoking an unsteady retreat from abroad.

The U.S. electorate already appears to be heading in that direction. According to the December 2006 CBS News poll, 52 percent of all Americans thought the United States "should mind its own business internationally." Even in the midst of impassioned opposition to the Vietnam War, only 36 percent of Americans held such a view. Inward-looking attitudes are especially pronounced among younger Americans: 72 percent of 18- to 24-year-olds do not believe that the United States should take the lead in solving global crises. If Washington continues to pursue a grand strategy that exceeds its political means, isolationist sentiment among Americans is sure to grow.

The United States needs to pursue a new grand strategy that is politically solvent. In today's polarized landscape, with Democrats wanting less power projection and Republicans fewer international partnerships, restoring solvency means bringing U.S. commitments back in line with political means. Finding a new domestic equilibrium that guarantees responsible U.S. leadership in the world requires a strategy that is as judicious and selective as it is purposeful.

First, a solvent strategy would entail sharing more burdens with other states. Great powers have regularly closed the gap between resources and commitments by devolving strategic ties to local actors. The United States should use its power and good offices to catalyze greater self-reliance in various regions, as it has done in Europe. Washington should build on existing regional bodies by, for example, encouraging the Gulf Cooperation Council to deepen defense cooperation on the Arabian Peninsula, helping the African Union expand its capabilities, and supporting the Association of Southeast Asian Nations' efforts to build an East Asian security forum. Washington should urge the European Union to forge a more collective approach to security policy and assume greater defense burdens. The United States also ought to deepen its ties to emerging regional powers, such as Brazil, China, India, and Nigeria. Washington would

then be able to better influence their behavior so that it complements rather than hinders U.S. objectives.

Second, where the war on terrorism is concerned, U.S. strategy should be to target terrorists rather than to call for regime change. This would mean focusing military efforts on destroying terrorist cells and networks while using political and economic tools to address the long-term sources of instability in the Middle East. Recognizing that reform in the Arab world will be slow in coming, Washington should pursue policies that patiently support economic development, respect for human rights, and religious and political pluralism. It should also fashion working partnerships with countries prepared to fight extremism. Pursuing regime change and radical visions of transforming the Middle East will only backfire and continue to overextend U.S. military power and political will.

Third, the United States must rebuild its hard power. To do so, Congress must allocate the funds necessary to redress the devastating effect of the Iraq war on the readiness, equipment, and morale of the U.S. armed forces. The Pentagon should also husband its resources by consolidating its 750 overseas bases. Although the United States must maintain the ability to project power on a global basis, it can reduce the drain on manpower by downsizing its forward presence and relying more heavily on prepositioned assets and personnel based in the United States.

Fourth, the United States should restrain adversaries through engagement, as many great powers in the past have frequently done. In the nineteenth century, Otto von Bismarck adeptly adjusted Germany's relations with Europe's major states to ensure that his country would not face a countervailing coalition. At the turn of the twentieth century, the United Kingdom successfully engaged the United States and Japan, dramatically reducing the costs of its overseas empire and enabling it to focus on dangers closer to home. In the early 1970s, Richard Nixon's opening to China substantially lightened the burden of Cold War competition. Washington should pursue similar strategies today, using shrewd diplomacy to dampen strategic competition with China, Iran, and other potential rivals. Should U.S. efforts be reciprocated, they promise to yield the substantial benefits that accompany rapprochement. If Washington is rebuffed, it can be sure to remain on guard and thereby avoid the risk of strategic exposure.

The fifth component of this grand strategy should be greater energy independence. The United States' oil addiction is dramatically constricting its geopolitical flexibility; playing guardian of the Persian Gulf entails onerous strategic commitments and awkward political alignments. Furthermore, high oil prices are encouraging producers such as Iran, Russia, and Venezuela to challenge U.S. interests. The United States must reduce its dependence on oil by investing in the development of alternative fuels and adopting a federally mandated effort to make cars more efficient.

Finally, the United States should favor pragmatic partnerships over the formalized international institutions of the Cold War era. To be sure, international collaboration continues to be in the United States' national interest. In some areas—fighting climate change, facilitating international development, liberalizing international trade—institutionalized cooperation is likely to endure, if not deepen. It is already clear, however, that congressional support for the fixed alliances and robust institutions that were created after World War II is quickly waning. Grand visions of a global alliance of democracies need to be tempered by political reality. Informal groupings, such as the "contact group" for the Balkans, the Quartet, the participants in the six-party talks on North Korea, and the EU-3/U.S. coalition working to rein in Iran's nuclear program, are rapidly becoming the most effective vehicles for diplomacy. In a polarized climate, less is more: pragmatic teamwork, flexible concerts, and task-specific coalitions must become the staples of a new brand of U.S. statecraft.

Far from being isolationist, this strategy of judicious retrenchment would guard against isolationist tendencies. In contrast, pursuing a foreign policy of excessive and unsustainable ambition would risk a political backlash that could produce precisely the turn inward that neither the United States nor the world can afford. The United States must find a stable middle ground between doing too much and doing too little.

Break on Through
to the Other Side

Former Secretary of State Dean Acheson once claimed that 80 percent of the job of foreign policy was "management of your domestic ability to have a policy." He may have exaggerated, but he expressed an enduring truth: good policy requires good politics. Bringing ends and means back into balance would help restore the confidence of the American public in the conduct of U.S. foreign policy. But implementing a strategic adjustment will require dampening polarization and building a stable consensus behind it. As Roosevelt demonstrated during World War II, sound leadership and tireless public diplomacy are prerequisites for fashioning bipartisan cooperation on foreign policy.

The next president will have to take advantage of the discrete areas in which Democrats and Republicans can find common purpose. Logrolling may be necessary to circumvent gridlock and facilitate agreement. Evangelicals on the right and social progressives on the left can close ranks on climate change, human rights, and international development. Democrats might support free trade if Republicans are willing to invest in worker retraining programs. The desire of big business to preserve access to low-wage labor may be consistent with the interests of pro-immigration constituencies; building a bridge between the two groups would reconcile corporate interests in the North with immigrant interests in the Southwest. Democrats who support multilateralism on principle can team up with Republicans who support institutions as vehicles for sharing global burdens. Although these and other political bargains will not restore the bipartisan consensus of the Cold War era, they will certainly help build political support for a new, albeit more modest, grand strategy.

So will more efforts to reach across the congressional aisle. Roosevelt overcame the Republicans' opposition to liberal internationalism by reaching out to them, appointing prominent Republicans to key international commissions and working closely with Wendell Willkie, the candidate he defeated in the 1940 election, to combat isolationism. The next administration should follow suit, appointing pragmatic members of the opposition to important foreign policy posts and establishing a high-level, bipartisan panel to provide regular and timely input into policy deliberations. Form will be as important as substance as U.S. leaders search for a grand strategy that not only meets the country's geopolitical needs but also restores political solvency at home.

CHARLES A. KUPCHAN is Professor of International Affairs at Georgetown University, a Senior Fellow at the Council on Foreign Relations, and Henry A. Kissinger Scholar at the Library of Congress. **PETER L. TRUBOWITZ** is Associate Professor of Government at the University of Texas, Austin, and a Senior Fellow at the Robert S. Strauss Center for International Security and Law.

The Palmerstonian Moment

Richard N. Haass

The 44th president of the United States will assume the job at a time when the country he (or she) leads will be stretched militarily, dependent on enormous daily inflows of oil and dollars, vulnerable to many of the darker manifestations of globalization and broadly unpopular. Few previous inhabitants of the Oval Office have started off with a situation of comparable difficulty.

But first, a rare piece of good news. Noticeably absent from the agenda will be great power conflict. This was the central dynamic of international relations for the past few centuries. But it no longer is and need not be for the 21st century. This will allow the next president to focus his energies on the signature challenges of this era, many of which are fostered by globalization. He can work not just with traditional friends like Europe, Japan and Australia, but also on occasion China, Russia, India, South Africa and Brazil—as partners rather than rivals.

The bad news for the United States is that support from its long-standing allies is far from assured. In the 21st century, formal alliances will increasingly count for less. Alliances require predictability: of threat, outlook, obligations. But it is precisely these characteristics that are likely to be in short supply in a world of shifting threats, differing perceptions, and societies with widely divergent readiness to maintain and use military force.

This is in no way an expression of unilateralist sentiment. But it is a recognition that many in Europe disagree with some U.S. objectives, how the United States goes about realizing them, or both. Such disagreements will prove more fundamental and enduring than the recent improvement in transatlantic relations resulting from the coming to power of more centrist and pro-American governments in Germany and France. As a result, the United States often will not be able to count on the support of its traditional allies. Also weakening Europe's centrality to U.S. foreign policy is that its capacity for global intervention is diminishing, especially in the military field, even on those occasions it does find itself inclined to act with or in support of the United States. Much the same holds true for Japan, although there the principal dynamic stems more from a lack of domestic political consensus to act globally than it does from an unwillingness to invest.

As a result, Americans will have to become comfortable with the notion of "selective cooperation." Not too long ago I told an audience at the Woodrow Wilson Center for International Scholars that "we are entering an era of American foreign policy and indeed international relations that is almost Palmerstonian in certain ways, where countries are not clear adversaries or allies with the automaticity or predictability of either. . . . They may be active partners on one issue and largely inactive observers on another." Or they may carry out alternative or even opposing policies.

The post–Cold War world, in many respects, is far more dynamic and fluid than the relatively stable and predictable bipolar arrangements of the Cold War. It thus demands a much greater degree of flexibility from policymakers. All of this is in keeping with Lord Palmerston's dictum that a nation has neither permanent friends nor permanent enemies—just permanent interests.

But there is a silver lining. Opposition from former adversaries is also not assured. Indeed, one-time opponents may become limited partners. Take, for example, the assistance given by China in pressuring North Korea to abandon its nuclear program. Beijing, in this case—not NATO—was and is the most important partner for Washington in its efforts to denuclearize North Korea. This does not, however, mean that China is on the verge of becoming a U.S. ally. This, too, is an example of a "Palmerstonian moment", one that served U.S. objectives.

Increasingly, policymakers will need to come to terms with the reality that the defining challenges of this era stem from globalization. Globalization has led to an increase in the flow of people, ideas and goods across borders—along with greenhouse gases, drugs, weapons and viruses, computer as well as the more familiar kind. Globalization is best understood as a reality, not a choice. In such a world, every country, no matter how powerful, is vulnerable to transnational threats. No country can shut itself off. (North Korea is something of an exception, but only at an enormous cost, and even then Pyongyang cannot fully insulate itself as much as it might try.) The United States, in particular, cannot embrace protectionism given its dependence on the inflow of dollars, oil and goods. Nor can it flirt with isolationism given its inability to insulate itself from various threats that may originate elsewhere, but have the ability to reach American soil or harm American interests.

Yet, there is a pronounced lag between the realities of globalization and the U.S. (and, in particular, congressional) response.

There is a discernible spike in protectionist sentiment—against trade, investment and people. None of these biases stands scrutiny. Most of the jobs that disappear do so because of technological innovation, not cheap imports or outsourcing. The proper response is doing more to make mid-career education and training available and affordable. Portable health care not tied to employment would also help. The next president needs to push for renewed Trade Promotion Authority and to push back against agricultural subsidies and anachronistic tariff and non-tariff barriers. If the price of achieving most or all of this is building an extensive safety net, it is worth paying given all the strategic and economic benefits to this country that would accrue from a successful conclusion to the Doha round.

The growth in investment protectionism—dramatically highlighted by the opposition to proposed acquisitions by the Dubai Ports Authority and the Chinese National Offshore Oil Company in the United States—also makes little sense. Absent clear and overriding national-security concerns tied to specific investments, the United States needs to remain open to dollar inflows. Such openness is good for the U.S. economy, gives others a stake in good and stable relations with the United States, and helps spread good business practices. The case in favor of remaining open to immigration is similarly strong. Immigration is one of the factors that has made this country what it is. Immigrants perform jobs that in many cases Americans are unable or unwilling to fill. Deporting the 13 million immigrants who are here without documentation is inconceivable. Some compromise that allows for earned citizenship but that also provides for enhanced security and larger legal flows of immigrants remains the only way to move forward.

Absent amidst all this protectionism is a concerted effort to take desirable and feasible domestic measures to reduce U.S. vulnerability to another dimension of globalization, namely, energy dependence. The new administration and Congress should take meaningful steps to reign in skyrocketing demand for energy—not simply to reduce the American contribution to climate change, but also to reduce the vulnerability of the American economy to supply interruptions and price increases and to slow the flow of dollars to governments that in many instances are pursuing policies inimical to U.S. national security. Energy policy is at the core of national security. Even climate change is assuming national-security dimensions. Some within the traditional security community do not see some of these issues as major threats on par with the challenges of the Cold War. It is true that countries are unlikely to go to war over levels of greenhouse gas emissions. But they may well go to war over the results of climate change, including water shortages and large-scale human migration.

Finally, no country can contend successfully with globalization on its own. This debate is largely settled—and in many ways it was a faux debate to begin with. The United States can achieve few if any of its foreign-policy objectives via unilateral action. It is not simply that there are limits to American power and resources; it is that the challenges themselves are not amenable to being met by anything less than a collective response. The next president of the United States will be forced to adopt a more multilateral approach to foreign policy.

Multilateralism as a response to globalization should not be equated with global or universal arrangements. As we are seeing in the trade realm, it is increasingly difficult to generate consensus when the number of participants swells. The result has been the proliferation of regional and bilateral accords. Something similar is possible or even likely when it comes to climate change. It will be extraordinarily difficult to negotiate a single successor to the Kyoto Protocol, one that includes all developed as well as developing countries and that addresses all of the principal dimensions of the challenge. Instead, what is likely to emerge—or, more accurately, evolve—is an amalgam of national policies, corporate programs, and regional and global arrangements limited in scope (say, devoted to one functional aspect of the challenge, such as encouraging forestation and discouraging deforestation) and participation. As a rule of thumb, global order is best served by effective and permanent institutions with broad membership, but in many instances coalitions of the willing and other such *ad hoc* arrangements are the best that can be achieved in the near or medium term. Again, it is important to note the Palmerstonian dimension of this approach—a successful coalition of states coping with one specific issue should not be expected to be transformed into a permanent alignment where there is agreement on all issues.

This is why it should also be stressed that not all standing bodies promise to be all that helpful. One suggestion that is not promising is the call for various assemblages of democracies to assume a more central role in U.S. foreign policy. Aside from questions of what would qualify as a democracy and how to get anything done with so many in the room, a democracy-based foreign policy makes no sense in a world in which the cooperation of non-democracies, above all China and Russia, is often essential if we are to prevent rogue states and the dark side of globalization from gaining the upper hand. A democracy-based foreign policy also makes little sense given how difficult it can be to promote successfully and how dangerous partial democracies can be in their behavior toward their neighbors and their own citizens.

Several years ago, in these pages, I discussed how a doctrine of "integration" might replace the Cold War vision of "containment" as the main organizing principle for U.S. foreign policy.[1] A policy of integration would aim to create a cooperative relationship among the world's mid-level and major powers, built on a common commitment to promoting certain principles and outcomes. It would seek to translate this commitment into effective and lasting arrangements and actions wherever and whenever possible. Nomenclature aside, and whether one speaks of "stakeholders" or a modern-day "concert", the idea of integration is gaining currency. Integration is the only way to tackle the challenges of a new era, especially those generated by globalization, such as protectionism, proliferation, terrorism and climate change.

But coming to terms with the foreign-policy choices demanded by a strategy of integration is not just for the United States. Other major powers will also be confronted with serious choices. Again, China is a good place to start. Traditionally, foreign policy has been approached by China's leaders through a domestic prism. The goal of foreign policy has been to create a secure environment in which domestic economic growth could occur. But Beijing is moving to an appreciation that it has a stake in the world, that what happens elsewhere affects China and that increasingly China will be held accountable for its actions. As work on a post-Kyoto framework intensifies, China will find itself on the defensive if it becomes the principal obstacle to new climate change arrangements. It is already on the defensive over the value of its currency and its failure to meet all of its trade-related obligations. Chinese officials and intellectuals are increasingly aware of China's integration into the global system—after all, any country whose economy is so dependent on imports and exports cannot help but be concerned with how the international system is organized. Questions remain, though, about the extent to which this awareness will translate into policy, and about how China's leaders will react if and when there is tension between the demands of domestic and foreign policy.

This is in contrast to more recent developments in Russia. Moscow, now flush with energy wealth, enjoys a degree of autarky on many issues and can choose more often than most to opt out of the global system. China does not have that luxury. As a result, it is less difficult to see China as an "integrated country" in the near future than Russia. Of course, Japan and many of the Europeans are already committed to the strategy of integration, since multilateral arrangements are at the core of their foreign policies, although in the Japanese case in particular there is a gap between this orientation and the narrower focus of its domestic politics, a focus that tends to limit what Japan is prepared to do in the world. India, for its part, is also increasingly integrated, but mostly in the economic realm.

This gap or lag between the realities and politics of globalization is widespread and holds for democracies (including the United States) and non-democracies alike. Lobbies and special interests continue to be less than willing to give up privileges, protected positions or preferred outcomes in the name of finding compromises with other countries. The truth is that, with all of the benefits globalization has wrought, it also brings risks and constraints. Even for superpowers like the United States, the international order brought into being by globalization limits the range of choices and options available to any one individual state to pursue its own course of action. But this is a necessary and, on balance, desirable trade-off if globalization is to be successfully managed.

In thinking about this agenda, however, we should not assume that we must wait until January 2009 and a new presidential administration. On the contrary, talk about President George W. Bush being a "lame duck" and therefore unable to achieve much is exaggerated. It ignores the Constitution's bias in favor of the executive when it comes to foreign policy, the potential for unexpected developments (to create opportunities or pressures to act) and the proclivities of Mr. Bush. For better or worse, he retains the ability to shape the world that will await his successor.

The Greater Middle East will continue to absorb the lion's share of the administration's attention and resources during its final year. (Iraq, ironically, may be the one matter that actually receives less attention.) We appear to be on the cusp of a consensus, a "reduction strategy", one that lies in between the surge (which appears to have improved the security situation but has not altered the underlying political dynamics of the country) and complete and sudden withdrawal (which could not only lead to chaos in Iraq but also cause the entire American position in the Middle East to be undermined). This involves a recasting of the U.S. mission toward a residual force that would aim to contain the violence, secure the borders and train Iraqi forces, in the process scaling back the U.S. combat role and relocating U.S. personnel away from Baghdad and other Iraqi population centers. This consensus may calm the debate in Washington, but it is unlikely to change the fundamentals in Baghdad and across much of central and southern Iraq, which will remain messy and violent and influenced more by militias and sects than by a national government, national forces or a national identity.

There is greater uncertainty when it comes to U.S. policy toward Iran. We may end up moving toward a situation where the United States would be faced with two choices, both highly unattractive—either having to tolerate Iran with a nuclear weapon (or the means to construct one in short order) or having to use military force to prevent or, more realistically, delay this from occurring. Either policy would run enormous risks and costs for U.S. interests in the region and beyond. The Bush Administration deserves some responsibility for this state of affairs, having allowed five years and various diplomatic openings to pass while it held out for the desirable but predictably unrealistic option of regime change. Beginning in 2005, though, Washington began to pursue a diplomatic option, but then only through the UN Security Council and contingent on a demand that Iran suspend all enrichment activity, a precondition Iran rejects. New multilateral sanctions, quite possibly without Security Council support, will be necessary to help sway the Iranian government. But so, too, is a new flexibility in Washington's stance on Tehran. The real question for the Bush Administration (or, more likely, for its successor) is whether the United States will drop its requirement that Iran first suspend its nuclear program and instead open direct talks with Tehran to negotiate verifiable limits to Iran's enrichment program, which would leave Iran well short of a nuclear-weapons capability (and outsiders the means to verify this judgment), in return for a reduction in Western economic sanctions and the provision of security guarantees. There is no guarantee Tehran would accept such a package, but it might if it faces broad international pressure and if the terms of a fair compromise are made public and resonate with the Iranian people. Regardless, this approach is worth exploring given the two costly policy paths otherwise available and the importance of demonstrating that all other options were fully explored before choosing either of them.

The administration (and Secretary of State Condoleezza Rice in particular) has decided to concentrate considerably more attention on the Israeli-Palestinian question than in the past. It is a surprising amount of activity—some might consider it to be a "Hail Mary" pass on the part of an administration that has had so many other setbacks in the Middle East—but it also rests on an assessment that Israelis and Palestinians both are desperate enough to take the steps needed to get the peace process back on track. The new emphasis also reflects a judgment that many of the Sunni regimes (including Egypt and Saudi Arabia) are sufficiently anxious about the reach of Iranian influence to play a helpful role. It is not clear, however, that Israelis and Palestinians are prepared to agree to terms the other side could accept—and even if they are, it is not clear they have the means to sell the number and scale of compromises that any accord would require to their respective domestic bases. Some "sorting out" will almost certainly be necessary from both sides before the situation moves closer to being ripe for resolution. This process could be facilitated by U.S. articulation of the basics of final status, something that would help moderate Palestinian leaders justify opting for negotiations over violence. And if a Palestinian leadership emerged that was both willing and able to compromise, the Israelis would likely follow suit. In the meantime, the United States would do well to reconsider its coolness to engaging Syria, where a leadership does exist that is strong enough to negotiate and that might be prepared to enter into a peace accord with Israel.

Even outside the Middle East, this administration continues to face a daunting array of challenges. North Korea is one. The administration has made progress, albeit belatedly, in what appears to be a successful strategy of conditional engagement, linking concessions to Pyongyang to verifiable proof that its nuclear program has ended. The challenge obviously lies in the extent to which this agreement is actually implemented. What is certain, though, is that the United States and others will have to contend with a closed North Korea that possesses nuclear weapons and at least intermediate-range missiles for years to come.

Pakistan is another. Or rather "Pakistan-Afghanistan." These are two countries increasingly joined more than divided by a long border. In both countries, the challenge is to promote economic growth and political reform amidst difficult security challenges stemming from the strength of the Taliban, Al-Qaeda and local extremists. The lack of adequate military and policing capabilities limits any progress either government can expect to realize. Growing nationalism and anti-Americanism also tend to limit what the United States can accomplish. The stakes could hardly be greater, though, given that this area is now a sanctuary for the world's most dangerous terrorists and, in the case of Pakistan, home to dozens of nuclear weapons. Pakistan's political crisis, by dividing and distracting the country, will only make it more difficult for the government to confront its real enemies. On these and a host of other trouble spots, like Venezuela, Cuba, Darfur, Zimbabwe, Nigeria and Kosovo, to name a few, it is clear that the Bush Administration is going to hand off unfinished business to its successor.

This puts a tremendous premium on statecraft. It means that future administrations will have to become much more comfortable and adept at meaningful consultations and building coalitions with other states. The biggest danger is that the United States and other countries will not be able to find ways to cooperate together where they can and should because of the spillover from where they disagree. It makes for a challenge that Lord Palmerston could readily appreciate. Navigating this reality will be anything but easy given the geopolitical setting we are living in. But it will be essential if integration is to come about and if globalization is to be managed on terms we desire.

Note

1. See Richard N. Haass, "The Case for 'Integration'", *The National Interest,* No. 81 (Fall 2005).

RICHARD N. HAASS is the president of the Council on Foreign Relations. His most recent book is *The Opportunity: America's Moment to Alter History's Course* (PublicAffairs, 2005).

Strategic Fatigue

GRAHAM E. FULLER

In the words of George W. Bush, conducting foreign policy is "hard work." As the immensely ambitious strategic vision of the Bush Administration enters its fifth year, numerous indications of strategic fatigue are in evidence. There is talk of troop withdrawals from Iraq and Afghanistan, even though the insurgencies are not subsiding in either country. The vigor for prosecuting the Global War on Terror is slowing, and, more importantly, the zeal for instigating regime change in other countries—North Korea, Iran, Syria and perhaps Venezuela— has visibly waned. The much scorned, traditional diplomatic processes shepherded by the State Department have returned. Congress is slightly less supine. Changes are evident in both substance and style as Condoleezza Rice demonstrates a newfound preference not to get out too far in front of the creaky wheels of multinational institutions that were the bane of administration activists. The administration's bark is minimized, and much of the bite seems gone.

Has superpower fatigue set in? Clearly so, to judge by the administration's own dwindling energy and its sober acknowledgment that changing the face of the world is a lot tougher than it had hoped. Of course, some degree of wear and tear is normal five years into any administration, regardless of policies. But fatigue emerges in direct proportion to the ambitiousness of the undertaking. From its early days, this administration adopted a strategic vision and peremptory posture whose implementation would prove exhausting under the best of circumstances. Administration documents and statements have regularly indicated that "we are at the beginning" of "a long war" fought globally in well over one hundred countries, probably "lasting for decades", until "victory over terrorism" is achieved. Even more, this all ties in with "the ultimate goal of ending tyranny in our world." The task is Sisyphean, the enemy generalized, the goals unclear, the scope open-ended.

The taxing character of U.S. foreign policy betrays signs of morphing into "imperial overreach." And there should be no doubt that we are talking about empire here, albeit in a new form. Neo-conservatives embrace the term openly, while the ultra-nationalists, headed by Dick Cheney and Donald Rumsfeld, do not disavow the concept. The extent of U.S. global reach— the overseas military installations and complex base-rights agreements that often dominate our relations with small nations, the peripatetic military-command representatives who over-

shadow ambassadors, a broad variety of active military presences, a worldwide intelligence and strike capability—is well documented. The U.S. global "footprint"—a revealing word regularly employed by the Pentagon without irony—is massive and backed by the world's most powerful military machine in history. While different in structure and intent than the British, French or even Roman imperial presence, current U.S. ambition for projection of power is sweeping. And pursuit of this goal generates ever newer challenges that quickly contribute to strategic fatigue.

Most empires ultimately founder on economic grounds. But the short-term economic cost of the administration's policies, while high, has not yet become unbearable. Still, there are a number of longer-term indicators that do raise worries about American economic capacities on into this century: massive domestic debt, an ever greater trade imbalance, the extraordinary and broadening gap in domestic wealth between rich and poor that has no parallel in other industrial nations, the growing outsourcing of jobs, and the rise of economic competitors who are hungry for a place in the sun. But it is the immediate political cost of the expansion of empire that is fatiguing, even before the economic cost fully bites in.

"Superpowerdom" imposes the psychological burden of being on the firing line all the time, everywhere—and almost alone. The unprecedented unilateral character of U.S. exercise of global power was of course a conscious choice, reflecting a strong desire to liberate Washington from wearying, nit-picking and encumbering consultations with other world players. It bespeaks a desire to simplify the decision-making process and to clear the decks for action. *Ad hoc* allies were to serve primarily as diplomatic window-dressing and hopefully to pick up some of the bills. But the broader backlash to U.S. unilateralism and its resultant isolation and loneliness it has imposed on Washington were not entirely anticipated.

The administration's foreign policy has been conducted on at least three levels, all of which had an impact on its global reception: strategic, tactical and stylistic. The strategic level could be summed up by the Pentagon's use of the term "full spectrum dominance." Although it specifically refers to desired military capabilities, the choice of words leaves little doubt about its political implications as well. The United States is the globally pre-eminent power, resolved to prevent the emergence of any peer. The task is the indefinite extension and projection of U.S. power to shape the world with little resistance. Entirely predictably, ambitious regional great-power centers—the European Union, China, Russia, India and Brazil to name a few—instinctively objected to this open bid for American hegemony. And their distaste at the strategic level complicates policy acceptance at the *tactical* level, since U.S. tactics, however well conceived in any given situation, nonetheless contribute directly to an unwanted American strategic project. Thus the removal of Saddam Hussein, or even the Taliban, whatever the merits of each case, could not be viewed in isolation but only as key building blocks in a grand U.S. strategic agenda. Similarly, as distasteful and worrying as Tehran's regional and nuclear ambitions might be, neither Russia nor China (nor even Europe) are entirely willing to see Washington crush Iran's independent global posture in a way that leaves the United States entirely free to do its bidding in the Gulf.

Finally, at the level of style, the American dispensation with diplomatic finesse in the lead-up to Iraq and the Global War on Terror alienated many allies in nearly all continents. Washington was willing to make occasional nods to formal multilateralism as long as events closely followed the American script, as with the "coalition" in Iraq. But in the end the gratuitous alienation of many U.S. allies has exacted a measurable and ongoing political cost on U.S. capabilities, now dramatically acknowledged with Condoleezza Rice's new look at the State Department.

But as unpalatable as the uncompromising manner was to so many, it was surpassed by a much more distressing phenomenon: the emergence of a *unipolar world*. The world is quite unaccustomed to the phenomenon of unipolarity and is still trying to cope with its many implications: in politics, economics, energy, war and the fate of international institutions. And, more importantly, the world is now busily engaged in the process of chipping away at that unipolarity wherever it can.

The reality is that no serious player on the international scene can embrace a unipolar world. All states value options. It may well be that if there has to be any sole superpower, most might prefer it to be the United States—at least that appeared to be the case up to five years ago. But what matters is that few accept the status quo. There is genuine global concern with the overwhelming character of American power, against which, it is implied, serious resistance is futile. Major states prefer the more complicated, traditional balances among powers that limit the exercise of excessive power by any state. A multipolar world multiplies the power of smaller states, enabling them to form *ad hoc* coalitions capable of deterring the actions of the dominant power when need be.

There would have been diminished temptation for the Bush Administration to embrace unilateralism as a policy except that the emergence of a unipolar world made unilateralism an option. Our unrivalled power beginning in 1991 was heady brew, liberating the ideological forces of neoconservatism that could, for

the first time, credibly speak of imposing an American agenda on the world order.

Yet it is an old political science cliché that a unipolar system over time invariably engenders its own counterweight. Nature abhors a sole superpower; other powers eventually bandwagon against it. So our present strategic fatigue may stem less from the immediate commitments in which we are embroiled and rather more from an unceasing necessity to maintain that sole superpower status against all comers—because that is what the very nature of unipolarity requires.

This exhaustion is perhaps most sapping at the domestic level: Americans are dying in meaningful numbers abroad; there is a lurking fear that the world is not safer, and maybe more dangerous, because of Iraq; Americans prefer to be liked abroad and are uncomfortable with their isolation; U.S. international business is unhappy; and the budget is soaring out of sight, even if its costs haven't yet touched the private pocketbook.

The intensified nationalist and neoconservative agenda within the administration, with its dramatic policy consequences, has greatly divided the nation. While the shock of 9/11 helped create a certain national "can-do" spirit of solidarity against foreign terrorists, that sentiment was rapidly depleted by Bush's broader response to 9/11. The resultant ongoing bitter domestic divisions require the administration's foreign policy architects to drag along a large and hostile domestic minority even before dealing with an unsympathetic world as well.

Abroad, the administration now faces widespread international resistance. The honeymoon of the early post-9/11 days gave way to international reconsideration of the full implications of the Global War on Terror, particularly American doctrines of unilateralism and strategic pre-emption. In the last few years, diverse countries have deployed a multiplicity of strategies and tactics designed to weaken, divert, alter, complicate, limit, delay or block the Bush agenda through a death by a thousand cuts. That opposition acts out of diverse motives, and sometimes narrowly parochial interests, but its unifying theme—usually unspoken—is resistance to nearly anything that serves to buttress a unipolar world.

Regrettably, that kind of resistance now seems nearly indiscriminate. For example, most reasonable people might have agreed that, whatever the merits of the invasion may have been, the overthrow of Saddam is now a *fait accompli* and that further deterioration of the Iraqi scene is in no one's interest. Nonetheless, most of the world has in fact preferred, sometimes almost petulantly, to watch the United States twist in the wind in Iraq, rather than to coordinate an international effort to stabilize a dangerously drifting situation. While the early, gratuitously abrasive American diplomacy contributed to European distancing from Iraq, the unspoken European goal has been to lessen the superpower's freedom of action and to work towards a more multipolar world. This global trend will stamp the character of global politics for a decade or more.

While Europe is more circumspect, other major powers, most notably Russia, China and even India, are more explicitly committed to ending a unipolar world. To be sure, they lack the power—economic, political, military, cultural—to create an alternative power polarity of their own, but they have acted subtly, or even not so subtly, to complicate or block many of Washington's major initiatives. They have worked with European powers to this same end on an *ad hoc* basis. Thus Moscow and Beijing have in one sense or another helped strengthen the ability of Iran, North Korea, Syria, Palestine's Hamas and even Venezuela deflect the broadsides of American power and impose a process-driven, compromising and consultative approach that frustrates American resolve—precisely the nightmare of the Bush unilateralists from the outset.

While no state—not even China—wishes to explicitly declare itself at odds with the United States, the common agenda, almost in principle, remains the ability to stymie Washington's will. As self-defeating, negative and unrealistic as these anti-unipolar tactics may appear to Washington, they happen to drive much of the rest of the world. Furthermore, we witness a growing body of foreign policy observers inside the United States who share that rising doubt: Is a unipolar world truly desirable, even for American interests?

Among the many risks emerging from such unfettered national power has been the growth of an unprecedented American arrogance in its diplomacy—widely discussed by most foreign states. Washington itself is still fiercely driven by the awareness that no alternative forces exist capable of offering an alternative global agenda, much less the capability to implement it. The expectation is that other countries should simply acknowledge the reality of the new world order and get on with it. This creeping arrogance of expectation contributes at a minimum to a kind of "passive aggressive" backlash across the globe.

Finally, the greatest casualty of all is the credibility of American ideology itself. For America as sole superpower, it takes only a short step to conflate our own interests with "universal" interests. Our goals—because of their global reach—seem to take on universal validity. It becomes harder, at least in our eyes, to differentiate between our national interests and the interests of the globe. By one more step of logic, perpetuation of the American imperium becomes openly justifiable in the name of universal values. But what happens when those values then become compromised on the ground?

We may perceive democracy as a universal good—and in principle it may well be. But the ideal now becomes transformed into an *instrument* of U.S. policies. And as a policy tool, the call for democratization in fact has become an instrument to intimidate, pressure or even overthrow regimes that resist the global American project. Yet for Americans, any resistance to democratization becomes an affront to the very principle itself, an irrational, petty act of resistance against the "forces of history." Democratization just might gain some international credence if truly applied across the board as the central principle of U.S. foreign policy. But to date, democratization has largely been a punishment visited upon our enemies, never a gift bestowed upon friends. Selectivity of application heavily undermines Washington's protestations of support for universal principle; in the eyes of others it merely becomes another superpower tool opportunistically employed for its own transient ends. And now even Washington is dismayed and hesitant as democratization fails to produce new governments ready to embrace the American project. This is especially true in the Muslim world, but also in a growing wave across Latin America as well. The administration's extremely spotty and inconsistent record on democratization has heavily damaged our case for democracy. Indeed, is democracy in fact the global ideology most conducive to a superpower's continuing maintenance of its own hegemony? The democratic process more often than not tends to empower nationalist-minded publics who resent and resist foreign hegemony. Here, the pliable dictators so valued in Washington in the Cold War may soon be on their way back as Washington's most useful instruments for running a U.S.-dominated globe.

Globalization as a "universal" value presents similar problems. History demonstrates that globalization is almost invariably the favored political value of dominant world states—and why not, for which but those states are best poised to benefit from globalization? Economists debate the upsides and downsides of globalization, and each position has its own ideological camp and true believers, but for better or for worse, globalization is now increasingly perceived as a particular American agenda designed to serve American interests. It is therefore held in suspicion by many.

The upshot is that the message, whatever its virtue, becomes fatally tainted by the messenger. George Bush could today proclaim his support for the restoration of the Islamic caliphate and he would be hooted down in Cairo, Riyadh and Islamabad because of deep suspicions now of *any* position adopted by the sole superpower. Such a situation over time saps our best intentions and our wisest steps taken in pursuit of foreign policy, as the audience becomes more obsessed with the messenger than the message.

Many states therefore resist the processes of democratization or globalization simply out of concern that they represent mere instruments in America's tool-kit for promoting the American agenda. Our inevitably selective record of implementation strengthens the perception of American double standards. These international reactions discourage and even embitter an American public and their policymakers who fail to understand how other peoples, except out of sheer perversity, would resist such patently commendable values.

This problem transcends the Bush Administration. The ultimate lesson is perhaps that no sole superpower can promote its "universal values" without tainting them. While not the first U.S. administration to operate in a unipolar world, this administration was the first to drive the logic of such unchecked power to its ultimate unilateral policy conclusions, thereby validating early global fears about a unipolar world.

The setbacks and disappointments for the United States—both in policy failures and their international backlash—are of course intense. Yet our national debate still revolves around only the tactical or the specific—Afghanistan, Iraq, Iran, the Global

War on Terror, the Patriot Act, even unilateralism—but there has been no serious discussion at all about the implications of a unipolar world in itself—except to celebrate it.

But by now there is not much celebration left. We are indeed confronted by strategic fatigue. We did not create all of the conditions that led to the emergence of a unipolar world; obviously the collapse of the USSR had much to do with it. But our strategic exhaustion will likely grow as more and more Lilliputians arise to tie new knots in the web of nets that hold down the superpower whose military power is ill suited to changing the existing political situation.

Of course, the United States cannot simply decide to cease being the sole global superpower. But it may have to reconsider the uncertain blessings that emerge from a unipolar world to avoid the costly and growing hostility that hinders American freedom of action as never before, especially at the hands of former friends. Indeed, our revealing national penchant for early and dogged identification of potential "threats" on the horizon that might challenge American hegemony has a strong tendency to create self-fulfilling prophecies. And maybe the emergence of additional great-power centers—dare I say some elements of "balance of power" politics?—might not be quite the disaster it appears, despite Rice's brush-off that we've been there and done that and it doesn't work. It's not as if the world is likely to rally around any of those new contenders, either—except perhaps right now, in an urgent quest for a more multipolar world.

GRAHAM E. FULLER is a former vice-chair of the National Intelligence Council at CIA. His latest book is *The Future of Political Islam* (2004).

UNIT 2

The United States and the World: Regional and Bilateral Relations

Unit Selections

8. **Exploiting Rivalries: Putin's Foreign Policy,** Mark N. Katz
9. **Russia and the West: Mutually Assured Distrust,** Marshall I. Goldman
10. **America's Asia-Pacific Strategy Is out of Kilter,** William T. Tow
11. **China's Challenge to U.S. Hegemony,** Christopher Layne
12. **North Korea's Nuclear Neurosis,** Jacques E. C. Hymans
13. **Requiem for the Monroe Doctrine,** Daniel P. Erikson
14. **Mirror-Imaging the Mullahs,** Reuel Marc Gerecht
15. **U.S. Africa Command,** Sean McFate

Key Points to Consider

- Construct a list of the top five regional or bilateral problems facing the United States. Justify your selections. How does this list compare to one that you might have composed 5 or 10 years ago?

- What is the most underappreciated regional or bilateral foreign policy problem facing the United States? How should the United States address it?

- How much weight should the United States give to the concerns of other states in making foreign policy decisions? Should we listen to some states more than others? If so, whom should we listen to?

- What should the United States expect from other states in making foreign policy decisions?

- Five years from now, what do you expect will be the most important regional or bilateral issue facing the United States?

- What is the major complaint other states have about U.S. foreign policy today? How should the United States respond to this complaint?

Student Web Site

www.mhcls.com/online

Internet References

Inter-American Dialogue (IAD)
> http://www.iadialog.org

Political Science Resources
> http://www.psr.keele.ac.uk/psr.htm

Russian and East European Network Information Center
> http://reenic.utexas.edu/reenic/index.html

World Wide Web Virtual Library: International Affairs Resources
> http://www.etown.edu/vl/

Possession of a clear strategic vision of world politics is only one requirement for a successful foreign policy. Another is the ability to translate that vision into coherent bilateral and regional foreign policies. What looks clear-cut and simple from the perspective of grand strategy, however, begins to take on various shades of gray, as policymakers grapple with the domestic and international realities of formulating specific foreign policy. This will be particularly true in seeking the support of others in pursuing one's foreign policy goals. Cooperation will often come at a price. That price may be as simple as increased access to U.S. officials or it may carry very real military and economic price tags. It may take the form of demands for American acquiescence to the foreign or domestic policies of others.

No single formula exists to guide presidents in constructing a successful foreign policy for dealing with other states and organizations. Still, it is possible to identify three questions that should be asked while formulating a foreign policy. First, what are the primary problems that the United States needs to be aware of in constructing its foreign policy toward a given country or region? Second, what does the United States want from this relationship? That is, what priorities should guide the formulation of that policy? Third, what type of "architecture" should be set up to deal with these problems and realize these goals? Should the United States act unilaterally, with selected allies, or by joining a regional organization?

Each succeeding question is more difficult to answer than the previous one. Problems are easily cataloged. The challenge is to distinguish between real and imagined ones. Prioritizing goals is more difficult because it forces us to examine critically what we want to achieve with our foreign policy and what price we are willing to pay. Constructing an architecture is even more difficult because of the range of choices available and the inherent uncertainty of whether the chosen plan will work.

The readings in this section direct our attention to some of the most pressing bilateral and regional problem areas in American foreign policy today. During the Cold War, relations with Europe and the Soviet Union always dominated this list. Today, in spite of disagreements with its European allies over the conduct of the Iraq War and its aftermath, the bilateral and regional relations with Europe are relatively calm. Relations with Russia remain more contested. More and more it is relations with Asia that are garnering high level attention in Washington. Relations with the South continue to occupy a low priority except in periods of crisis.

The first readings in this unit examine U.S. relations with Russia. "Exploiting Rivalries: Putin's Foreign Policy," asserts that the core element of Russia's foreign policy toward other countries is that of playing rivals off against one another, in order to maximize Russian influence. The next essay, "Russia and the West: Mutually Assured Distrust," argues that a central problem in U.S.-Russia relations is the way the two sides view domestic

Defense Dept. photo by U.S. Navy Petty Officer 1st Class Chad J. McNeeley

developments in Russia. While the United States and the west are highly critical of movement away from democratic and free market reforms, Russians see them as necessary corrections of past efforts for reform. The result is increasing mistrust between the two sides.

The next section examines U.S. foreign policy toward Asia. The first two essays in this section look at U.S.-China relations. "America's Asia-Pacific Strategy is out of Kilter" cites problems in U.S. foreign policy with China, Japan and North Korea. It argues that if not corrected, the United States risks becoming locked into an unstable multi-polar struggle that might go on for decades and drain American resources. "China's Challenge to U.S. Hegemony" sees the relationship between the two states as potentially being destabilizing for the region and the world. It argues that this is not inevitable and the crucial factor in determining the future will be U.S. foreign policy. The final essay on Asia examines North Korea's pursuit of nuclear weapons. "North Korea's Nuclear Neurosis" places Korea's pursuit of nuclear weapons in a historical context and argues over a central and overlooked factor: the presence of "oppositional nationalist" thought on the part of North Korean leaders.

The final set of readings examines the complex issues of dealing with the South. "Requiem for the Monroe Doctrine," deals with U.S. foreign policy toward Latin America and warns against attempts to resurrect the Monroe Doctrine in an era of globalization. "Mirror-Imaging the Mullahs" is critical of U.S. foreign policy for its failure to appreciate the role that religion plays in the decision making calculus used by leaders in the Middle East. It argues that the days of pro-American secular elites are long gone and will not return. The last essay, "U.S. Africa Command," explains why the United States has established a new military command in Africa at this time and argues that a close and underappreciated relationship exists between security and development.

Exploiting Rivalries: Putin's Foreign Policy

"Russian foreign policy-makers seem convinced that playing both sides against the middle with other nations is a clever way to advance Moscow's interests. It may take many more foreign policy setbacks before they are persuaded otherwise."

MARK N. KATZ

Like previous Russian leaders—whether czarist, Soviet, or post-Soviet—President Vladimir Putin is determined to see Russia acknowledged as a great power. Indeed, many Russians across the country's political spectrum share this goal. There is, however, a serious obstacle in the path to achieving it: Russia's diminished military and economic strength. That strength underlay czarist and Soviet Russia's ability to act and be acknowledged as a great power. Today, Russia's ability to credibly threaten the use of force abroad has been undermined by its inability to defeat Chechen rebels within its own borders.

Of course, the fact that Russia no longer is regarded as a threat by most nations (except some of its neighbors) raises the possibility that Moscow can get what it wants through persuasion and cooperation. Moscow's post-Soviet experience, however, has taught it that good relations with Russia are not sufficiently important to most other states that they will alter their policies to accommodate Russian interests. Neither feared as a threat nor valued as a friend, Russia has often found itself simply ignored—much to the chagrin of both the Putin administration and the Russian public generally.

Putin appears to have found a solution to this problem. He has strived to exploit situations in which Moscow, despite its diminished circumstances, can affect the balance between opposing sides on a given issue, thus providing one side or even both an incentive to court Russia. Securing such a position can deliver not just tangible economic benefits for Moscow, but also the gratification that comes with being courted, as well as the self-image of Russia as a great power that this feeds. Of course, Russia is not the only country, nor is Putin the only Russian leader to attempt to exploit rivalries between other states. Putin, however, has made this strategy the centerpiece of Russian foreign policy.

But how successful has the Russian leader been in pursuing this diplomacy? And what has Moscow actually gained by attempting to exploit rivalries between others? A look at the various areas in which Russia has tried this approach shows it has yielded far less than Moscow anticipated.

The Iraqi Oil Game

Well before Putin came to power, Moscow saw Iraqi-American hostility as a golden opportunity for Russia to exploit. With the cooperation of Soviet President Mikhail Gorbachev, stiff international economic sanctions were imposed on Iraq after its 1990 invasion of Kuwait. Although Iraqi President Saddam Hussein was undoubtedly displeased that Moscow, a once-staunch ally, had cooperated with Washington against him in the UN Security Council, his regime soon after the war over Kuwait began negotiating with several Russian firms lucrative oil development contracts that would come into effect once sanctions were lifted. Baghdad thereby provided Moscow with an incentive to seek repeal of the Security Council's sanctions while Saddam was still in power. Moscow, in fact, did repeatedly call for the lifting of the sanctions regime, albeit without success because the United States and Britain used their veto power in the Security Council to block the move. Even under sanctions, Baghdad managed to favor Russian firms when it came to signing oil development agreements under the Security Council imposed "oil for food" program that allowed Iraq to use oil sale revenues only for domestic "humanitarian" purposes.

This practice continued after Putin became president at the end of 1999. Beginning in late summer 2002, however, it became increasingly difficult for Moscow to exploit Iraqi-American hostility after the Bush administration made clear that it sought Saddam's ouster. At this point, the question that concerned Moscow was whether the oil development contracts Russian firms had signed (or initialed, negotiated, or just discussed) with Saddam's regime would be honored after his downfall. Moscow sought assurances both from Washington and American backed Iraqi opposition groups on this score, but they said that only a future Iraqi government could decide this. Further, Saddam became angry about Moscow's making these overtures. So he canceled the one major contract that a Russian oil firm—Lukoil—had actually signed to pump oil from Iraq's West Qurna field, which is believed to contain 15 billion barrels of oil.

Lukoil has insisted that Saddam's regime did not have a legitimate reason to cancel its contract, and that it remains valid. But neither the United States nor the Iraqi government has confirmed this. Lukoil, for its part, has threatened to sue any other company awarded a production contract for West Qurna. On March 9, 2004, the Iraqi oil ministry signed a contract allowing Lukoil to explore West Qurna, but not to extract oil from it. At the end of June 2004—when a new Iraqi interim government came into being—Lukoil's president said that his company would start producing oil in Iraq in 2005, but it is unclear whether the Iraqi government has reached an agreement to allow this to happen.

What Moscow had sought both from Saddam's regime and from Washington was certainty that Lukoil would retain the West Qurna contract even if regime change took place in Iraq. Having received no such certainty, it now faces the very task it had wanted to avoid: obtaining the new regime's permission for Lukoil to exploit West Qurna. Lukoil may yet succeed in operating the field, if only because neither the new Iraqi government nor other oil companies want to deal with the legal hassle Lukoil has threatened to create. But if Lukoil does get its way, Iraqi resentment over Lukoil's and Moscow's behavior in this matter may limit Baghdad's willingness to let Lukoil or other Russian firms develop Iraq's other proven but undeveloped oil fields.

Gaming the Iraq War

Russia was not alone in opposing a U.S.-led intervention in Iraq. France, Germany, and many other countries did as well. French and German opposition offered Putin an opportunity to align Moscow with the impeccably democratic governments of two of the three most important West European states. However, while France opposed an American-led intervention against Iraq unless UN inspectors found incontrovertible evidence of an Iraqi weapons of mass destruction program, and Germany opposed war even if they did, Russia's opposition was far less categorical. Beginning about six months prior to the intervention, Moscow signaled Washington that it would drop its opposition to a Security Council resolution authorizing the use of force against Iraq—for a price.

Accounts of what Moscow demanded included recognition of Russia's economic interests in Iraq (especially oil contracts and debt repayment). Some reports also said Moscow wanted Washington to drop its objections to Russian aid to the Iranian nuclear energy program and to grant Moscow a free hand to intervene in Georgia's Pankisi Gorge (a region where Moscow claimed many Chechen rebels had found refuge). At the same time, Moscow hoped that its alignment with France and Germany would lead those two countries to make certain concessions to Russia, including a halt to their criticism of Russian human rights violations in Chechnya and acceptance of visa-free travel for Russian citizens between Russia and its Kaliningrad exclave after Lithuania joined the European Union (and adopted its immigration policies regarding non-EU citizens). Some Russian commentators also hoped that the schism between Washington and "Old Europe" (as U.S. Defense Secretary Donald Rumsfeld dubbed France and Germany) had become so deep that both sides would need Moscow to mediate between them.

> **Moscow has long recognized Iranian-American hostility as an opportunity for Russia to sell atomic energy technology and weaponry to Tehran.**

In the end Putin did not obtain any of the concessions he had hoped to gain, either from the United States or from France and Germany. Washington intervened in Iraq without conceding to any of Moscow's demands. And France and Germany declined to compensate Russia for siding with them against the United States. The EU and France have continued to criticize Russian policy in Chechnya. And the only concession made on the Kaliningrad issue was to call the papers that Russians must obtain an "expedited travel document" instead of a visa. Neither the Bush administration nor the governments of "Old Europe" called on Moscow to act as a mediator.

Aiding Iran's Nuclear Program

Another conflict that Putin has sought to exploit is between Iran and the United States. Moscow has long recognized Iranian-American hostility as an opportunity for Russia to sell atomic energy technology and weaponry to Tehran. During a more cooperative period of U.S.-Russian relations in 1995, Washington and Moscow reached a secret agreement (signed by Vice President Al Gore and Prime Minister Viktor Chernomyrdin) whereby Russia agreed to limit its military and nuclear cooperation with Iran in exchange for U.S. support for the Russian space program. But in late 2000, at a more acrimonious time in U.S.-Russian relations, Putin renounced the Gore-Chernomyrdin agreement. Partly to assert Russia's independence from the United States and partly to earn money from Iran, the Putin administration indicated it would hasten the completion of the atomic energy reactor it was building for Iran, and expressed a willingness to sell additional reactors as well.

In response to Washington's concern that Tehran might divert spent fuel from its Russian-built nuclear reactors to fabricate nuclear weapons, Moscow publicly parroted Tehran's claims that the Iranian nuclear energy program was for peaceful purposes only and was in full compliance with International Atomic Energy Agency (IAEA) safeguards. Privately, the Putin administration indicated that it was willing to make a deal: Russia would end its assistance to the Iranian nuclear program in return for compensation.

Washington thought it had made just such a deal with the 1995 Gore-Chernomyrdin agreement, whereby the removal of U.S. government obstacles to Russia's launch of communications satellites using American technology was seen as compensation to Russia for limiting its sales of nuclear and military technologies to Iran. Putin's abrogation of the Gore-Chernomyrdin agreement raised doubts that Moscow would honor any other compensation arrangement. Moreover, Putin seemed unwilling or unable to curb the ambitions of Russia's atomic energy agency to sell nuclear reactors to Iran—something the agency saw as vital to its very survival given the dearth of other customers for these products. Finally, as Iran appeared to be inching closer and closer toward being able to build a nuclear weapon, even an end to Russian atomic energy assistance to Iran seemed unlikely to prevent this from happening. Compensating Moscow to halt its nuclear assistance to Tehran appeared increasingly pointless to Washington.

While some Russian commentators have expressed concern about Iran's acquiring nuclear weapons, Putin administration officials insist that Iran cannot do this. Some have even claimed that Washington is not worried about this either, but wants Russia to stop selling nuclear reactors to Iran so that American firms can.

And yet, despite Iran's seeming dependence on Russia for the sale of nuclear reactors and conventional weaponry, Putin's government has been unable to get much of what it wants from Tehran. In an ongoing dispute over the delimitation of the oil-rich Caspian Sea, for example, Tehran has not accepted the "modified median line" proposed by Russia, Azerbaijan, and Kazakhstan that would give Iran 13 percent of the Caspian. Iran has insisted on a 20 percent share—even though it had only 11 percent of the Caspian Sea during the Soviet era.

In addition, as of mid-2004, Tehran had not signed an agreement to return spent fuel to Russia that Moscow says must occur if it is going to provide the uranium to operate the nuclear reactor it is building. Press reports indicate that such an agreement might be signed this fall. Although Russia hopes to build up to five more reactors in Iran, Tehran insists that it will not sign contracts for further construction until the first reactor is completed (there have been numerous delays).

Instead of being able to exploit Tehran's dependence on Moscow to extract concessions from Iran, the Putin administration appears fearful that pressuring Iran on issues of concern to Moscow (not to mention Washington) could result in the Russian atomic energy industry's failure to secure contracts for the additional nuclear reactors it hopes to build for Iran.

Kyoto in the Balance

Putin also has sought international advantage in negotiations over the Kyoto climate treaty. The decision by the Bush administration and the Republican-controlled Senate not to ratify the agreement has provided Russia with extraordinary leverage over the treaty's fate. The Kyoto treaty will take effect only if the industrial nations that were responsible for 55 percent of greenhouse gas emissions in 1990 have ratified it by 2008. So far, the treaty has been ratified by nations—including Japan, Canada, and members of the EU—that produced 44 percent of the 1990 emissions levels. (The United States produced 21 percent.) Because Russia has an emissions share of 17 percent, its ratification alone could bring the treaty into effect. Aware of this, the Putin administration has sought to exploit Russia's position as the country that determines Kyoto's fate.

The treaty requires that the ratifying industrial nations reduce output of certain emissions to below the levels they were producing in 1990. But it allows states producing over their quota to purchase emissions credits from states producing under theirs. In addition, countries (or companies) producing over their quotas can invest in projects that cut greenhouse gases elsewhere, with the resulting reductions positively affecting the quota of the investing country. Because Russian greenhouse gas emissions have dropped by nearly a third since 1990 (as a result of economic decline—not greater environmental cleanup efforts), Russia would have a massive amount of spare emissions credits to sell and could be an attractive

destination for foreign investors seeking credit from projects that cut Russian emissions.

The Putin administration was not satisfied with the potential for making money that ratifying the Kyoto treaty offered. Instead, it wanted guarantees from the EU, Japan, and Canada that they would purchase credits from—or make investments in—Russia in the amount of $3 billion annually. The three refused. Indeed, the EU in particular made clear that it was displeased by this form of bargaining. Putin, after first indicating that Russia would ratify the Kyoto treaty, now raised the possibility in September 2003 that Russia might not do so.

If these tactics were a ploy to pressure the Europeans into meeting Moscow's demands for fear of the treaty's not otherwise coming into effect, they backfired. Instead of giving in to Moscow's demands, the EU made its approval for Russian admission into the World Trade Organization conditional on a pledge that Russia would ratify the Kyoto treaty. Putin himself delivered the pledge at the EU-Russian summit in May 2004. The Russian Duma (the legislative body that must actually ratify the treaty) has not yet acted on it, and Moscow may still attempt to extract "guarantees" from the EU. But in this case it appears the EU has more leverage over Russia than vice versa. For if Moscow does not ratify the treaty by 2008 (when it will lapse if it has not yet gone into effect), the emissions credits and incentives to invest in the Russian energy sector created by Kyoto will not materialize.

Oil Pipeline Politics

Russia's oil riches have created an opportunity to play off China and Japan against each other. Both China and Japan seek to reduce their dependence on oil imports from the volatile Middle East by purchasing oil from Siberia. Because Siberia does not appear to have enough oil to satisfy both China and Japan, a competition between them has emerged over which Siberian oil pipeline route Russia will build. Putin administration machinations and a dispute between two Russian oil companies have complicated the competition. Although there are numerous Russian oil companies, many of which have been privatized, the state-owned (and often slow and inefficient) Transneft exercises monopoly control over the construction and operation of oil pipelines in Russia. Privately owned Yukos, Russia's largest oil company, sought to break this monopoly by building a pipeline that would carry oil from fields it owned in eastern Siberia to Daqing, a city in China's northeastern interior.

While the cost of playing games with Beijing over Siberian oil export routes is not yet clear, it is certain that an annoyed China will impose some cost on Russia.

As this deal was being finalized, the Japanese government proposed that Russia build a pipeline from eastern Siberia to Nakhodka on Russia's Pacific coast. This route would be twice as long (and two to four times more expensive) than Yukos's proposed pipeline to Daqing. But the Japanese argued that the Nakhodka route would benefit Russia more because oil piped there could be exported by sea to many different countries (including both Japan and China), whereas the Daqing route would make purchases of oil through that pipeline dependent on China alone.

Although Tokyo offered to buy all the oil from the Nakhodka route and to provide low-interest loans to cover the cost of its construction, Russian Prime Minister Mikhail Kasyanov indicated in April 2003 that it was the Daqing route that would be built. The following month, Yukos signed an agreement to sell oil to China from the Daqing route, which it expected to complete in 2005. But as the Putin administration turned against Yukos (both in retaliation for the political challenge that its chief, Mikhail Khodorkovsky, posed to the president and possibly as a means for Putin supporters to seize Yukos's assets for themselves), completion of the Daqing route looked less and less likely.

In September 2003, the Russian Ministry of Natural Resources indicated that it would issue a negative assessment of the Daqing pipeline route on environmental grounds (it also had environmental objections to the Nakhodka pipeline route). On a visit to Beijing later that month, Prime Minister Kasyanov informed his Chinese hosts that construction of the Daqing pipeline would be "postponed." Shortly thereafter, Japan offered a beefed up package for the Nakhodka route, including $5 billion in financing to support pipeline construction and $2 billion for Siberian oil field development. Since then, press coverage indicates that Transneft will build the Nakhodka pipeline route, although Moscow will not make a final decision until the end of 2004.

A desire to exploit Sino-Japanese rivalry over export routes has not been the sole factor in the Putin administration's decision making on this issue; Transneft's interest in retaining its pipeline monopoly and Putin's vendetta against Yukos chairman Khodorkovsky also have played a role. Still, the existence of Sino-Japanese competition for Siberian oil certainly pushed Tokyo to provide very generous financial incentives in an attempt to induce Moscow to build the Nakhodka route.

On the other hand, the Putin administration irritated Beijing by derailing the deal for the Daqing pipeline route after it had been agreed to. And Beijing is in a position to impose some costs on Russia. China's decision in January 2004 to impose anti-dumping tariffs on Russian steel (announced as the Russian foreign minister was arriving in Beijing) was seen as clear retaliation for Moscow's backtracking on the Daqing pipeline deal. Beijing has also revived its efforts to have an oil pipeline built from Kazakhstan to China's western Xinjiang region. Whatever oil China buys from Kazakhstan would represent lost sales for Russia.

The Scorecard

How well has Putin's policy of attempting to exploit rivalries between others worked? There have been some positive results. In Iraq Russia gained the promise of oil deals in the summer of

2002 just as the Iraqi-American crisis was heating up. Its international image may have been burnished as Germany and France and America and Britain courted Russia in the lead-up to the U.S.-led invasion of Iraq. Moscow also appears to have prompted Japan to up the financial ante in the rivalry over where a Siberian oil pipeline should be built.

Often, however, Putin's attempts to exploit rivalries have produced negative results for Russia. Saddam canceled the Lukoil contract for the West Qurna field because Moscow was seeking commitments from Washington and the Iraqi opposition to honor the contract if Saddam was overthrown. The U.S.-led Coalition Provisional Authority did not agree to restore it, nor has the Iraqi interim government done so yet. Despite Iran's dependence on Russia for completion of a nuclear reactor, Tehran has made no concessions to Moscow on the division of the Caspian Sea, and has not yet signed contracts for additional reactors or for the return to Russia of spent fuel from the one reactor Moscow is building. Not only did Moscow fail in its attempts to elicit guarantees that it would receive $3 billion annually from the EU in return for ratifying the Kyoto treaty, but the EU made its approval for Russian admission into the World Trade Organization conditional on a pledge from Putin that Russia would ratify Kyoto. And while the cost of playing games with Beijing over Siberian oil export routes is not yet clear, it is certain that an annoyed China will impose some cost on Russia.

A more general problem associated with attempting to exploit rivalries between other countries is that the other countries resent this approach. They may make some concessions to Moscow to get it to change its behavior. But if the Putin administration continues to play both sides off against each other, other governments may conclude that making concessions to Moscow does not buy them anything—hence concessions are not worth making. When one or both sides to an exploited rivalry decides there is nothing to be gained from acceding to Russia's wishes, then the Putin administration looks weak for setting forth demands that are rejected or ignored. And when this happens, Putin's ultimate goal of having Russia acknowledged by others as a great power becomes increasingly elusive.

Putin's efforts to seek advantage in international rivalries appear to have produced more losses than gains for Russian foreign policy. Yet it is doubtful that his administration will abandon this approach. Even though it has resulted in important setbacks, Russian foreign policy-makers seem convinced that playing both sides against the middle with other nations is a clever way to advance Moscow's interests. It may take many more foreign policy setbacks before they are persuaded otherwise.

MARK N. KATZ is a professor of government and politics at George Mason University.

From *Current History,* October 2004, pp. 337–341. Copyright © 2004 by Current History, Inc. Reprinted by permission.

Russia and the West: Mutually Assured Distrust

"In their determination to validate their recovery and return to world leadership, the Russians sometimes overreact, even if in the process this means straining relations with the West."

Marshall I. Goldman

A story is told that goes something like this. Before President Vladimir Putin's July 2007 visit to former President George H. W. Bush's home in Kennebunkport, Maine, a television reporter sought to interview a White House aide for a brief comment on Russian relations with the West, particularly the United States. But the reporter's producer cautioned him that, because of time constraints, all he could record was a one-word answer. Meeting with a member of the White House staff, the reporter asked for a one-word characterization of US-Russian relations. "Good," the official replied.

Just then the program's producer realized that he had a bit more time and so he told the reporter he could actually have a two-word answer. The question was asked again. "How in two words would you describe Russian relations with the West?" "Not good."

The Responsible Power

Paradoxically, this joke does seem to characterize the current diplomatic climate between Russia and the West. On the good side, Russia has not only been admitted to the Group of Seven (making it the G-8), but in 2006 Putin chaired the group's May meeting—convening it in St. Petersburg, his hometown. In an unusually warm gesture, this year Putin was invited to meet with President George W. Bush at the home of the president's father in Kennebunkport, the first foreign leader to have been invited there by the current president.

This unusual welcome was in part a reflection of the close bond the two men have established. In part it also reflected recognition of Russia's cooperation in preventing the trafficking of nuclear and radioactive materials and, even more important, Moscow's sharing with Western countries intelligence about Islamist terrorist activities in Afghanistan and the Middle East. Indeed, to help facilitate the United States' response to the 9-11 attacks, Russia erected no obstacles when Washington sought to establish military bases in Kyrgyzstan and Uzbekistan in support of operations in Afghanistan.

Following the meeting in Maine, Putin flew on to Guatemala, where he appealed in English and French to the International Olympic Committee to select Sochi, Russia, as the site of the 2014 Winter Olympics. Putin's appearance in person (he was the only world leader to attend) and his promise to provide necessary financing impressed the committee so much that, against almost all predictions, Russia won and Sochi was selected. The Olympic Committee apparently accepted Putin's guarantee that Russia would be able to absorb the costs, handle the logistics and scheduling, and meet other international responsibilities that come with hosting the Olympics. The committee made its decision even though, at the time of the decision, no facilities in Sochi were in place. Russia's backers were right to claim this represented a vote of confidence in Russia and its international standing as a responsible country.

That the West has accepted Russia is proven further by the rush of Western businesses and banks seeking to set up operations there. Whereas during the 1990s, capital flight from Russia averaged $1 billion a month, in 2006 an estimated $41 billion flowed *into* Russia—that is more than $3 billion a month. Thirty-one billion dollars of that total came in foreign direct investment, meaning that foreign companies were confident enough of the business and political climate to set up mining, manufacturing, and service operations in Russia. For its part, Russia has committed itself to the West as a major energy supplier. Its natural gas and petroleum pipelines now provide on average 25 percent of the gas that Western Europe imports and about the same percentage of oil.

Rising Tensions

Winning the right to hold the Olympics, plugging into the world's gas and oil network, attracting large sums of foreign direct investment, joining the G-8—these are all reflections of Russia's good standing in the world community. But not everything is so positive. Indeed, signs of mutual tension, distrust, and even hostility are serious and seem to be growing. In response to Moscow's refusal to extradite the prime suspect in the murder of Alexander Litvinenko, a Putin critic and former KGB agent who had been living in London, Great Britain in July expelled four Russian diplomats, alleged to be spies. Russia subsequently expelled four British diplomats from Moscow, while Russian bombers threatened to overfly British airspace. And this is hardly the only evidence of worsening relations between Russia and the West.

Although something even more dramatic than the mutual expulsion of suspected spies could happen tomorrow, perhaps the most threatening sign of the growing tension was Putin's announcement on July 14, 2007, that Russia intended to withdraw within five months from the 1999 Conventional Forces in Europe treaty. This treaty committed signatories, both Russia and members of the NATO alliance, to limit the number of tanks and combat aircraft deployed in Europe. Officially, Russia explained that it was renouncing the treaty because, while it had ratified an amended version of the treaty, too many NATO countries had not.

This was but one of Russia's grievances. Russian officials were also upset that, not only had the United States itself announced in 2002 that it was withdrawing from the Anti-Ballistic Missile (ABM) treaty that was intended to mark the end of the cold war, but in 2007 the Americans sought to install a radar unit in the Czech Republic and an actual battery of antiballistic missiles in Poland. The Russians brushed aside official US insistence that this ABM system was intended to protect the West from Iran and North Korea or that the system had not been successfully tested. Given NATO's past broken promises—that former members of the Warsaw Pact would not be recruited into NATO, nor would NATO station offensive military forces in Eastern Europe (as it then did in Bulgaria and Romania)—the Russians suspect that the purportedly anti-Iranian, anti–North Korean system would in fact turn out to be an anti-Russian system.

It was in order to provoke opposition in the West to both the withdrawal from the ABM treaty and the plan to install antiballistic missiles in Eastern Europe that Putin threatened to withdraw from the Conventional Forces in Europe treaty. Sergei Ivanov, his former minister of defense, also warned that if the United States were to install its ABM system in Eastern Europe, Russia would respond by again targeting its missiles on Western Europe, just as it did during the cold war. If each side carries out its plans, this would amount to a scary replay of the mutual-destruction nightmare that characterized the cold war.

While the West may disapprove of Putin's policies, clearly most Russians do not.

Western Grievances

Such disputes reflect the growing contempt with which each side views the other side's behavior and political and social mores. For its part, the West has become more and more critical of what it sees as the continual undoing of market reforms and democratic reforms that were introduced after the col-

lapse of the communist system. The Russians see the situation differently. They regard Putin's changes as an effort to correct reforms that were too far-reaching. As they see it, during Boris Yeltsin's years as president their country fell into chaos, which the people abhorred.

One priority for Russians, then, was to reexamine the results of privatization. Whatever the official purpose of the privatization program of the 1990s, most Russians now view the transfer of state-owned entities to private owners as something just short of highway robbery. Not surprisingly, while the West views Putin's renationalization of many of these assets, especially the valuable energy companies, as a step backward, to the Russians it represents a rectification of serious errors.

This explains why, within Russia, there is today widespread approval of the fact that the share of crude oil produced by state-controlled companies has increased from under 20 percent at the peak of privatization in 2000 to approximately 50 percent in 2007. Moreover, under Putin, even companies in which the state has no or only a minority share again act as if they were agents of the state—or national champions, as Putin calls them. What observers in the West see is a form of state capitalism.

There is also widespread criticism outside Russia of the way Putin's government has been in effect nationalizing property theoretically owned by Western companies. When the state forced the Russian oil company Yukos into bankruptcy, broke it up, and renationalized most of it as a subsidiary of state-owned Rosneft, that could in part be rationalized as an internal matter. Yukos and its owners were accused of all manner of illegal acts, from tax evasion to buying votes in the Duma to murder. It was clear that Russian courts, in finding guilty the chief owner of Yukos, Mikhail Khodorkovsky, were merely doing the Kremlin's bidding. But at the same time, Yukos and Khodorkovsky were not innocent victims.

The state's treatment of foreign oil companies is another matter. Shell Oil, for example, has been charged with polluting a work site and as a consequence has been forced to surrender majority ownership of its multibillion-dollar exploration effort on the island of Sakhalin to Gazprom, the state-owned gas monopoly. It is not that there was no pollution, but in comparison with the way most Russian companies ignore pollution regulations, Shell was far from the most serious offender. This is simply a case where the Russian government wanted to reclaim oil and gas fields that it had leased to foreign companies in the 1990s when no Russian firm had the wherewithal to operate in such challenging conditions. Nor is Shell the only Western company to see its original concessions and contracts nullified. Virtually every foreign energy business operating in Russia in difficult and hostile geological conditions has been forced to sell out or accept Gazprom as a partner. Those affected include BP of the United Kingdom, Exxon-Mobil of the United States, and Total of France.

Kremlin officials who justify this renationalization argue that the original agreements were made when Russia was under undue duress and that Western companies at the time took unfair advantage. Now that Russia is stronger and better able to protect its interests, it has the right to restore the proper balance. Besides, the Western companies had indeed created pollution. And in the case of Shell, the company without warning suddenly claimed that its total cost of operation in Sakhalin had soared from $10 billion to $20 billion. Since Shell was operating under a production-sharing agreement that allowed the company to recoup all of its expenses before it had to share revenues with Russia, this increase in costs was viewed as a scheme by Shell to prevent Russia from sharing the profits of the operation for years to come.

The state's takeover of Russia's major television networks has worked much the same way, with the owners claiming theft and the government asserting that too much was given away too readily and cheaply in the 1990s. In particular, Putin justified the return of media outlets to state control by pointing out that the oligarchs who came to own these assets were using them not to provide fair and unbiased coverage of the news, but instead to carry out their own private vendettas and corporate battles.

The leaders who have recently come to power in Europe appear initially to be much more critical of Russia and especially Putin.

Nor have many Russians opposed what observers in the West view as a step backward in democratization: the abolition of direct elections for governor. Most Russians accept Putin's argument that the whole process had become a farce and that the wealthy were using their money to buy up voters and corrupt the elections. Putin insists that, as president, he is in a much better position to weed out the corrupt and appoint more capable and honest officials. Of course, the democratic process in the United States also has room for improvement. (Some still say that corruption in Chicago in the 1960 presidential election swung Illinois from Richard Nixon to John Kennedy. Others still question the 2000 vote count in Florida, the state that put George W. Bush over the top against Al Gore. Putin has often cited the latter election to demonstrate that the United States has nothing to brag about.) Still, the American system appears more in tune than the Putin version with what the West generally considers to be democracy. As Putin has begun to act arbitrarily in more and more circumstances, he has replaced the rule of law with what seems to be the law of the ruler.

Despite all this, it is the assassination of the former KGB agent Litvinenko that seems to have drawn the most concern from the public in the West, especially in Great Britain. Many were particularly troubled that the killer used polonium 210, a radioactive isotope, to commit the murder. That seemed an unusually nasty thing to do, more so than a run-of-the-mill gunshot killing. As the newly installed British Foreign Minister David Miliband pointed out, Litvinenko's "murder put hundreds of others, residents and visitors, at the risk of radioactive contamination."

Radioactive poisoning triggers a whole new set of concerns and makes the person who committed the crime (British authorities allege it is a former KGB agent, Andrei Lugovoi) appear to be particularly reckless and diabolical. It certainly did nothing for Russia's image that Litvinenko's death came as a series of political and media figures who had been critical of Putin and Kremlin policies were murdered. Some murders are just ordinary crimes, but others clearly carry a political connotation and seem more ominous, especially in the West.

The Pride of Russia

It is not that the Russians take pride in these assassinations. But what is galling to them is that, ever since the 1980s, they have been continually harangued about this and other so-called shortcomings by Western officials, moralists, and former Sovietologists. This hectoring has had a devastating impact on their national ego. It was bad enough that they had ceased to be a military and economic superpower. Beginning in the 1990s, nobody seemed to seek their input or care about them. At the time, one could only guess how humiliating all this was to the public psyche. Now as the country has regained its footing, at least in the economic sphere, we are finding out just how deeply felt was Russia's temporary fall from prominence and influence.

There are an embarrassing number of illustrations. For example, in response to the British demand that the Russian government extradite Lugovoi, Konstantin Kosachyov, the chairman of the Duma's Foreign Affairs Committee and an otherwise reasonable legislator, complained about British arrogance. "You can act this way toward a banana republic, but Russia is not a banana republic," he said. Valentina Matviyenko, the governor of St. Petersburg, has expressed a similar view, arguing that Russia will no longer tolerate being treated as an inferior. In a July 2007 interview in the weekly newspaper *Argumenty I Fakty,* she boasted that "Russia has now regained a sense of self-respect. We spent so many years feeling there was something wrong with us—others lecturing us on how we should live and where we should go. But we have overcome our inferiority complex."

If only it were so. Based on recent behavior, it seems as if Putin and other Russian officials are still seeking to prove themselves. Putin has been particularly outspoken. In a June 2007 speech in St. Petersburg, he went so far as to challenge the way the World Trade Organization, the International Monetary Fund, and the World Bank are run. He called them "archaic, undemocratic, and awkward," largely because they are too dependent on the European Union, the United States, and Japan—and by implication, not Russia. This, he insisted, disadvantaged developing countries. Even more pointedly, Putin suggested that the world should have more than two reserve currencies, implying that the dollar and the euro are not enough. As he sees it, now that oil exports have made Russia so prosperous, the ruble should fill the same role.

In an even more revealing initiative, Putin earlier this year announced his support for a new textbook for Russian schools. It is time to reassert the correctness of Russia's behavior in the past, he declared. Putin attacked the West for suggesting that Russia should be ashamed of such things as the Stalinist purges, collectivization, and the subjugation of national groups in the former Soviet Union and Eastern Europe. If anything, he argued, it is the West that should be ashamed.

As an example, Putin agreed with the new textbook that Stalin's "Great Terror" of 1937, in which at least 700,000 people were executed, was not as bad as the Americans' use of atomic bombs in Japan, not to mention the use of chemical weapons (napalm) against civilians in Vietnam. Putin has accused the United States of using its campaign to spread democracy to create a global empire under American control. In a May 2007 speech, he seemed to compare the United States with Nazi Germany, though he later denied it. Putin's speech described a "global threat in which, as in the time of the Nazi Third Reich, we saw the same contempt for human life, the same claims to world exclusivity and diktat."

A Nation That Matters

In their determination to validate their recovery and return to world leadership, the Russians sometimes overreact, even if in the process this means straining relations with the West. A good example is the way the Russians reacted this spring to Estonia when it relocated a statue dedicated to Soviet military heroism against German troops in World War II. The Moscow police, disregarding international protocol, stood by while members of a Russian youth group demonstrated outside the Estonian embassy and harassed Estonian diplomats. Protesters also attacked the Swedish ambassador's car. (On another occasion, after he attended a meeting of dissidents, the British ambassador to Russia was similarly harassed.) In addition, the government suspended the flow of petroleum to Estonia and stood by while Russian hackers assaulted Estonian computers and web-sites in an effort to disrupt communications to and from the country and within it.

The Russians seemed to be acting as if Estonia were still a subservient republic of the Soviet Union and not a sovereign independent nation. Moscow assumed that it had license to treat Estonia as it pleased and ignore not only Estonian protests but also complaints from Estonia's fellow members in the European Union and NATO. To some extent, Russians even seem to welcome such criticism, taking it as a sign that the outside world has begun to take notice of their country again and that what Russia thinks and does matters, even if it is to be condemned.

Moscow has also taken to harassing Lithuania, Estonia's close Baltic neighbor. Russian authorities suspended pipeline shipments of petroleum to Lithuania's Mazeikiai refinery after Russian companies were unable to buy the refinery. (Lithuania wanted to sell it to a Polish group of buyers because they were not Russian and, in addition, they offered a higher price.) Again, there was the implication that Lithuania had no choice but to keep this refinery, which was built in the Soviet era, within what used to be the Soviet family.

Some Russian actions are reflexive responses expressing historic Russian positions that date back to the czarist era. One example is how Russia has opposed Kosovo's independence from Serbia. Russia traditionally has viewed itself as the protector of the Serbs and their Christian Orthodoxy against encroachments from the Muslim world. This is not something new—Russia reacted that way in the nineteenth century when it sought to protect Serbia from the Ottoman Empire. It is trying to do the same in the twenty-first century by protecting Serbs in Kosovo from the Muslim Albanians there who make up the vast majority of the population.

Not everything that upsets present-day Russia is an overreaction. It is easy to see that Putin, sitting in the Kremlin,

would be upset by the behavior of some nongovernmental organizations—particularly NGOs financed by groups and governments outside Russia, ones that seek to build up political parties that are independent of the state. Kremlin officials see this as interference in the internal affairs of another country. They point to political upheaval in Georgia and Ukraine that was sparked by various NGOs, some financed by the US government and private foundations that have openly announced that their next target will be Russia. Arguably, it would have been irresponsible for Putin to have ignored such a possibility.

It is the assassination of the former KGB agent Litvinenko that seems to have drawn the most concern from the public in the West.

This explains to a substantial degree Putin's support for a youth group like Nashi (Ours), which backs the president and his political party and is willing to risk confrontation with anti-Putin protesters. The group's loyalty is to Putin more than to the party, and its actions are often patterned more after the Komsomol (the Soviet-era Young Communist League) or even the Hitler Youth than after the Girl or Boy Scouts. In the same way, the government's heavy-handed use of riot police to suppress only opposition demonstrations—especially when the protests are as disorganized and inconsequential as they have been—comes across as antidemocratic.

Hectoring Hypocrites

While there have indeed been instances of antidemocratic actions in Russia, the Russians regard the United States as hypocritical when it demands good behavior from Russia while disregarding America's own shortcomings. What gives the United States the right to preach to Russia about corporate governance and the way Gazprom behaves, the Russians ask, when some US corporations seem equally if not more in need of lessons in proper governance? Are the senior executives at MMM or SBS-Agro (companies whose executives have had to face charges of illegal behavior) any more in need of corporate ethics lessons, or more deserving of jail sentences, than their American counterparts such as Kenneth Lay of Enron or Bernard Ebbers of WorldCom?

Russians extend the same criticism to US attacks on the inadequacy of Russian law, human rights, and individual safeguards. What gives the United States and Western Europe the right to criticize Russia when Western countries ban demonstrations or their police fire rubber bullets to suppress rioters, as happened outside Paris in the fall of 2005? How do those who call for human rights accept the jailing of British bombing suspects even though no formal charges have been lodged against them? As for the United States, how can it reconcile detention without trial of Islamic terror suspects for months, even years, at its Guantánamo prison facility? Whatever happened to habeas corpus? US federal courts have decreed that certain government practices violate the American constitution, yet they seem to continue.

Of course, not all such criticisms of the United States and its behavior are unique to Russia. Many Europeans, not to mention Arabs, oppose what they see as America's unilateral behavior, be it in Iraq or in Eastern Europe, where the United States seeks to install the missiles referred to previously. Others worry that NATO expansion to the east and to Russia's borders, even if it is important for Eastern European and Baltic states as a sign that they are no longer part of the Soviet empire, is unduly provocative. Many Europeans can understand, along with the Russians, why the Kremlin would regard as a hostile act any effort to extend NATO further into Georgia and Ukraine.

The Challenge Ahead

Prediction is always hazardous—particularly, as Yogi Berra noted, when it deals with the future. Yet it has to be said that prospects for relations between Russia and the West are not especially promising. The leaders who have recently come to power in Europe—Angela Merkel in Germany, Nicolas Sarkozy in France, and Gordon Brown in Britain—appear initially to be much more critical of Russia and especially Putin than were their predecessors. Certainly there is not yet the personal warmth or bond between Putin and this group that all three of their predecessors had with him.

Given the criticisms Democrats have leveled at President Bush's policies, and the likelihood that a Democrat will succeed Bush in the White House, it is to be expected that there will also be less tolerance in the United States for Russian behavior after the 2008 presidential election than there has been in the seven years corresponding with the Bush and Putin administrations. For that matter, Putin himself is due to leave office in March 2008. There is a strong probability he will be succeeded by someone even more determined to restore Russia's place in the world as an independent force and as a check on America's role as a unilateral actor.

Regardless of whether leaders from the East and West bond personally, there is likely to be greater concern within the European Union over what some will see as a return to cold war antagonisms. Many aspects of the old communist-versus-capitalist class struggle may no longer be relevant. Yet it is a bit of a surprise to see how some of the issues dividing East and West today so resemble the dividing philosophies of the cold war. The Kremlin under Putin, as it did in the Soviet era, has effectively eliminated meaningful democracy and has come close to eliminating criticism in the media, especially on television. As the power of the state has grown, the rights of individuals have been sharply constrained. While there is still private business, state controls are considerably more intrusive than they were in the mid-1990s.

To be clear, these increased state powers fall far short of what the Soviet state had. Yet the trend in Russia today is not encouraging for those who support a restricted role for the state and reasonably expansive rights for the individual. A return to something closer to authoritarianism, stripped of the ideology of the cold war, may reflect widespread nostalgia among Russians for their country's long czarist history and the czar's strong hand—particularly after what many saw as a laissez-faire attitude during Yeltsin's 1990s.

With over 70 percent of polled Russians approving of his administration, Putin seems to be doing something right. While the West may disapprove of Putin's policies, clearly most Russians do not. Many of them do not accept the notion that Putin is backing away from democracy. And if he is, they do not seem to care. For that matter, Putin himself asserts over and over again that what the West calls democracy is flawed, and that what he is fashioning comes closer to true democracy. His response to a German reporter in a June 1, 2007, press conference is typical. When asked if he considered himself a pure democrat, Putin laughed and said:

> Am I a pure democrat? Of course I am, absolutely. But do you know what the problem is? Not even a problem but a real tragedy? The problem is that I am all alone, the only one of my kind in the whole wide world. Just look at what's happening in North America. It's simply awful: torture, homeless people, Guantánamo, people detained without a trial and investigation. Just look at what's happening in Europe: harsh treatment of demonstrators, rubber bullets and tear gas. . . . There is no one to talk to since Mahatma Gandhi died.

All of this was said with a straight face. In a follow-up question, the same reporter sought confirmation. "And your country is not moving at all back toward a totalitarian regime?" Putin replied: "There is no truth in that. Do not believe what you hear."

Relations between the East and West are not hot or cold, but neither are they warm. At a time when Russia and the West have such different interpretations of democracy, it will take great effort to reduce tensions. Without great skill, even simple matters that would pose no problem between members of the EU or NATO are likely to lead to misunderstandings and hostility between Russia and the West. As Russia continues to prosper with its oil exports and the United States remains entangled in Iraq and Afghanistan, no matter who the new presidents of the United States and Russia turn out to be, keeping a civil tone in US-Russian as well as Russian-EU relations is likely to be a continuing challenge, more than it has been in the past two decades.

MARSHALL I. GOLDMAN, a senior scholar at Harvard University's Davis Center for Russian and Eurasian Studies, is a professor emeritus at Wellesley College and author of the forthcoming *Petroleum, Putin, and Power* (Oxford University Press, 2008).

America's Asia-Pacific Strategy Is Out of Kilter

"If Washington is effective in linking its Asia-Pacific and global security postures, it can maintain its status as a preeminent power in the region. If it fails, it may find itself involved in a dangerous and unstable multipolar rivalry. . . ."

WILLIAM T. TOW

It would be understandable in a post–9-11 world if American policy makers, at the expense of other regions, became fixated on international terrorism and related Middle East challenges. Such an approach to security policy, however, would be misguided and ill-fated. Ultimately, the United States' geopolitical destiny is likely to be shaped by pursuing the same goals on which U.S. foreign policy has been focused since the founding of the republic: preventing hegemonic powers from controlling American global strategy; ensuring U.S. access to key international markets; and promoting liberal democratic values abroad. Much of this agenda, albeit not all, is conducted at the traditional "state-centric" level of international relations, the rise of non-state actors notwithstanding.

In this context, the Asia-Pacific region is shaping up as the most important in the world for the United States' evolving strategic interests and force postures. The U.S.-China relationship has developed into the world's most critical bilateral relationship. Taiwan and North Korea remain volatile flashpoints capable of involving the United States in conflicts that could be far more lethal than Iraq. And Asian economies, generating around 34 percent of the world's total gross national product, are among the most dynamic and fastest-growing in the world.

As Americans prepare to elect a new president next year, their country is approaching a historic juncture in its strategic relations with the expansive "region" encompassing a vast area that stretches from the eastern Indian Ocean to Southeast Asia to littoral East Asia to Oceania and the South Pacific. If Washington is effective in linking its Asia-Pacific and global security postures, it can maintain its status as a preeminent power in the region. If it fails, it may find itself involved in a dangerous and unstable multipolar rivalry with China, Russia, and other major powers that would consume America's energy and sap its resources for decades to come.

U.S. Power Challenged

The specter of China growing strong—whether through a "peaceful rise," as Beijing insists is occurring, or as a hegemonic threat to U.S. global primacy, as many of China's critics see it—is for U.S. policy planners the most substantial Asia-Pacific challenge today. Resolving the Taiwan question is directly related to the future course of Sino-American relations; permanently defusing the nuclear crisis on the Korean peninsula also depends increasingly on the ability of China and the United States to comanage that process.

There is no shortage, however, of other regional security challenges that could test Washington's future ability to help underwrite regional stability. These include sustained historical tensions between China and Japan, the United States' most important Asia-Pacific ally; tensions between China and India as the region's two most rapidly growing economic and strategic powers; and protracted religious and territorial disputes between India and Pakistan that could potentially spill over to affect stability throughout much of Central and Southeast Asia. Russia looms just over the horizon with continued territorial grievances against Japan and nationalist-based apprehensions about China. Observers concerned with the issue of good governance question the legitimacy of various Southeast Asian governments (Burma, Thailand, and the Indochinese states) and worry that nascent democracies (such as Indonesia and the Philippines) remain vulnerable to protracted ethnic, religious, or ideological pressures. Finally, an array of so-called "transregional security" and "human security" challenges have recently emerged in the Asia-Pacific region that have obvious global ramifications. These include nuclear nonproliferation, climate change (with China and India projected to become the world's largest energy consumers within a decade or so), energy security, pandemics, and food and water security.

The United States, as a global trading and maritime power that depends greatly on continued access to the region's markets and sea-lanes of communication, has a major interest in promoting conflict avoidance. It wants Asia-Pacific rivalries and vulnerabilities not to escalate into open confrontation, and wants to prevent the development of an extremist, anti-Western bloc in the region. Neither does it wish an intensification of nuclear or conventional arms races in the region.

Asia-Pacific security challenges that affect U.S. interests in the region and in the wider world also include the proliferation of weapons of mass destruction, the spread of terrorism, and the intensification of trade protectionism. The administration of George W. Bush has insisted, in national security strategy documents, that a key objective is to sustain U.S. regional engagement by preserving robust security partnerships with allies such as Japan, South Korea, Singapore, and Australia that support a credible American forward defense posture.

Yet it is critical in this context to strike an appropriate balance between cooperative and competitive American security behavior in the region. Unfortunately, current U.S. strategy puts excessive emphasis on competition. The U.S. Department of Defense 2006 Quadrennial Defense Review represented U.S. engagement strategy as a policy instrument to hedge against the ascendancy of China as a military competitor to the United States, demarcating U.S. regional allies as deterrence assets. In April 2006, U.S. National Security Adviser Steven Hadley described the following items as the three pillars of U.S. Asia-Pacific strategy: promoting democracy and freedom with allied support; building networks of cooperative regional security with those allies and other regional states; and finding the right combination of engagement and balancing to project toward an increasingly powerful China. What appeared to be missing from Hadley's list was an acknowledgement that all three processes would require investment of considerable time and effort, that they would have to be adjusted according to the region's political and cultural sensitivities, and that regional actors must claim joint ownership of future regional security architectures.

Rivalry with China

How successful Washington's strategy will be rests largely on the future of Sino-American relations. China's gross domestic product is now larger than that of Britain and France; if its current rate of growth is sustained, China is projected to become the world's biggest economy by 2030. The economies of China and the United States are increasingly interdependent, with two-way trade increasing from $33 billion in 1992 to $263 billion in 2006. At the same time, China's authoritarian political system and human rights practices clash with an American tendency to export democratic values as universal commodities. Sino-American military and diplomatic competition is also increasing. Many U.S. analysts, for example, view the recent intensification of China's multilateral security diplomacy with the Association of Southeast Asian Nations (ASEAN) as nothing more than a divide-and-rule strategy designed to marginalize U.S. strategic influence in the region.

American diplomacy, too, has been criticized as polarizing the region. Washington's recent efforts to strengthen alliance relations in the Asia-Pacific, including so-called alliance transformation initiatives with Japan and the formalization of the Australia-Japan-U.S. Trilateral Strategic Dialogue, are illustrative. Chinese leaders perceive such efforts as an American-led containment strategy directed against their own country. Beijing and Washington both fear the other will pursue "zero-sum" policies at its own expense. This tendency must eventually be tempered if greater stability is to be realized in the Asia-Pacific region.

War avoidance in the Taiwan Strait and on the Korean peninsula constitutes the most immediate benchmark for how successfully these fears will be overcome. Crisis intensity varies in both regional flashpoints as China and the United States intermittently vie with each other to demonstrate their continuing loyalty to old Cold War allies, or collaborate to curtail steps toward independence by Taiwan and the policy excesses of the North Korean regime.

Beijing's leadership insists it has the right to assimilate Taiwan by force if the current or a future Taiwanese government crosses the "red line" established in China's March 2005 anti-secession law and declares independence from China. Any Chinese use of force against Taiwan would violate the Taiwan Relations Act that suggests the United States might intervene on that island polity's behalf if such a contingency were to transpire. In Beijing and Washington, memories of the two countries' near-clash in 1996 are still raw. At that time, when the People's Liberation Army carried out military exercises and missile tests adjacent to Taiwan's shores in an effort to influence Taiwan's presidential election, China underestimated U.S. resolve to intervene against hard-line Chinese actions.

The United States successfully faced down the Chinese leadership to end that crisis, but thereafter the Clinton and Bush administrations showed little inclination to confront China on the Taiwan issue. They instead adopted a harder line against Taiwanese President Chen Shui-bian's often-strident independence tendencies. To be sure, Beijing still complains about U.S. "interference in internal affairs" concerning Taiwan. China is also tailoring its military buildup to help it prevail in any future confrontation with the United States over Taiwan. Its deployment of hundreds of short-range ballistic missiles in Fujian province, which is adjacent to the Taiwan Strait, and its recent antisatellite test, presumably carried out with U.S. command and control networks in mind, exemplify this trend. Such Chinese efforts, however, have hardly overshadowed an inclination by both China and the United States since 1996 to avoid direct confrontation over Taiwan.

Achieving balance depends on the United States transforming itself from a hierarchical player in the Asia-Pacific region into one more comfortable with sharing power and negotiating compromises.

Troubles with Allies

Although it is not necessarily linked to the United States' harder line toward Taiwanese independence, China has recently adopted a tough position against its longstanding communist ally, North Korea. The Chinese, with Washington's blessing, have assumed a pivotal role in multilateral talks, pressuring North Korea's "Dear Leader," Kim Jong Il to take tangible steps toward nuclear disarmament in return for U.S. economic and diplomatic concessions. Of course, China is concerned about what might happen if the communist regime were suddenly to implode. The ramifications for China's own border security, the probable influx of North Korean refugees into Jilin and Liaoning provinces, and the removal of an ideological bedfellow (albeit an eccentric and often cantankerous one) adjacent to its own territory would be less than acceptable for China's leadership.

Denuclearization of the Korean peninsula, however, is critical to Chinese security, if for no other reason than that it gives China and the United States, as "nuclear have" powers under the terms of the nuclear Non-Proliferation Treaty (NPT), a better chance to stem the tide of state-centric nuclear proliferation in Northeast Asia and beyond. For China it would be a geopolitical nightmare to face a Japan that had developed a nuclear force in response to unbridled North Korean development of nuclear weapons capabilities. With this in mind, China has been relentless in pressuring the North Koreans to participate in successive formal rounds of six-party talks and to join numerous working groups to prepare for the more formal negotiating sessions. It has also threatened the North Koreans with extensive sanctions in the export of food and fuel if Pyongyang becomes too recalcitrant. (China provides 80 to 90 percent of North Korea's fuel supplies and about one-third of its food supplies.)

China and the United States have demonstrated a willingness and capacity to work with each other to restrict the ability of minor regional powers to disrupt the Asia-Pacific region's central strategic balance. But this does not mean they are necessarily becoming more compatible in managing the broader Asia-Pacific geopolitical landscape. Serious and potentially divisive differences persist in their strategic objectives and diplomatic style. The United States is feeling increasingly comfortable, for example, with Japan's resurgence as a "normal power." This may prove a barrier to sustaining any implicit Sino-American strategic bargain on comanaging the Taiwanese and North Korean flashpoints.

Strengthening the U.S.-Japan alliance is a core feature of Washington's emerging grand strategy to encourage the rise of "friendly powers" such as Japan, Australia, and India to contain Chinese ambitions and capabilities and to preserve its own position of decisive strategic influence. Key officials in the Bush administration also see the U.S.-Japan alliance as a burgeoning instrument of international security politics that could be applied to the global war on terror, preventing nuclear proliferation, and safeguarding vital sea-lanes of communication.

Japanese political leaders are increasingly considering revisions to their country's postwar "peace constitution." And U.S.-Japan collaboration in such defense technology areas as theater missile defense is now ingrained within the alliance. Japanese weapons procurement designed to integrate such technologies into its military infrastructure is resulting in Japan's deploying what is de facto an increasingly offense-oriented defense force. All of these trends only intensify China's threat perceptions of the U.S.-Japan alliance as a challenge to its core geopolitical interests.

Another source of tension relates to China's ambitions for regional dominance. Beijing promotes variations of a "New Security Concept" as the most appropriate road to achieving greater regional stability. China has become an enthusiastic supporter of ASEAN's "comprehensive security" formula for confidence-building measures and for other collective security approaches in the Asia-Pacific region. It has directly contrasted this approach to the U.S. insistence on maintaining its "hierarchical" or "hegemonic" bilateral security alliances in the region. American critics of China's diplomatic behavior insist that Beijing is using multilateralism in a way its traditional advocates never intended—to drive a wedge between the United States and its regional allies by forcing them to choose between emerging regional security organizations (with the idea that this will increasingly lead them to accept Chinese dominance).

For China it would be a geopolitical nightmare to face a Japan that had developed a nuclear force in response to unbridled North Korean development of nuclear weapons capabilities.

Forward, but Flexible

America's military preoccupation with Iraq and Afghanistan has led to a widespread perception that U.S. military power is declining as the "long war" against international terrorism intensifies. An April 2007 Congressional Budget Office report, for example, noted that only between three and eleven U.S. Army brigades would be available if a crisis in another part of the world were to require American military intervention. U.S. plans to defend South Korea have previously envisioned deploying up to 20 or 21 brigades. Former Secretary of Defense Donald Rumsfeld's vision of defense transformation, in which forward basing would be reduced, seems irrelevant at a time when the United States is increasingly dependent on coalition partners to help carry out critical military missions.

A steady, qualitative improvement in China's defense industries, supplemented by a thriving Russian-Chinese arms sales relationship, promises to bring China into equality with the United States in areas of military technology where equality was until recently unimaginable. China's increased ability to disrupt U.S. information networks, its development of special operations forces to strike at U.S. regional basing operations, and its broadening of ballistic, cruise, and other missile systems threaten to neutralize traditional U.S. strategic superiority in the Asia-Pacific maritime theater of operations. North Korea's military capabilities also remain formidable, in the event a war breaks out on the Korean peninsula. And there is no guarantee that a strategically resurgent Russia would stay neutral in any future East Asian conflict if it believed its security interests were directly threatened by the United States. Russia maintains a significant security relationship with China via the Shanghai Cooperation Organization and still honors a low-key defense accord with Pyongyang.

To contend with these realities, recent U.S. doctrinal planning has focused on increasing the flexibility of American forces deployed in the Asia-Pacific region. The numerical strength of ground forces will shrink in South Korea (a 2004 agreement calls for the reduction of U.S. forces from 37,500 to 25,000 by next year) and in Okinawa (where 8,000 Marines will be transferred to the U.S. territory of Guam), as domestic politics in both South Korea and Japan now favors national security strategies less dependent on a permanent U.S. force presence. Both countries, however, have agreed to continue hosting major operating bases from which U.S. forces could maneuver in future regional contingencies. The U.S.-Japan Defense Policy Review Initiative and the U.S.-South Korea Future of the Alliance Talks have mapped out a de facto triangle of U.S. force positioning affording Washington maximum flexibility to apply its military power. Guam is particularly important in this equation, as the home for substantial levels of U.S. air and naval forward strike capabilities. This strategy at least partially compensates for the present lack of mass in U.S. force structure.

Both South Korean and Japanese forces are planning to achieve greater interoperability with U.S. units even as they mature toward assuming more responsibility for their own national defense. The U.S.-South Korea Combined Forces Command will soon give way to the South Korean government's assumption of control over its own country's forces during wartime. Japan will increasingly develop missile defense technology, provide training for Southeast Asian antipiracy and related maritime capabilities, and act as an important coalition partner in U.S.-initiated global security operations such as the Proliferation Security Initiative and international counterterrorism efforts.

Achieving the United States' strategic interests in Southeast Asia requires that U.S. policy makers think about this region in wide strategic terms, and not merely as a theater for counterterrorism. Although a very substantial terrorist threat, the suppression of which is crucial to the United States' regional and global security objectives, has emerged in Indonesia, the Philippines, and other parts of the subregion, the Asian financial crisis illustrated that Southeast Asian leaders fundamentally believe that economics *is* security. This largely explains China's growing geopolitical appeal among the ASEAN states, notwithstanding their lingering suspicions about China's ultimate strategic intentions. It also highlights a perception held by many Southeast Asians that the United States is increasingly indifferent to their area of the world, except for counterterrorism.

A Broader Security Paradigm

During the Bush administration's second term in office, the United States has attempted to respond to ASEAN's embrace of a broader security paradigm. In November 2005, the United States signed the ASEAN-U.S. Enhanced Partnership agreement, which was intended to increase collaboration on security, economic, and cultural issues by treating these categories as interdependent. The same month, Washington lifted its longstanding ban on arms exports to Indonesia, having realized that the burgeoning Indonesian democracy's efforts to promote security could never entirely satisfy the U.S. Congress's unbending expectation that Indonesia adhere to U.S.-style human rights standards and behavior. The December 2004 tsunami underscored the relevance of disaster relief as a key nonmilitary component in ASEAN's security agenda. The SARS pandemic's physical and psychological impact on the populations of Singapore and Vietnam drove home the point that Washington's contemporary security approaches to Southeast Asia need to be innovative and multifaceted.

Even the military dimensions of Southeast Asian geopolitics are changing rapidly. Traditional cold war alliances emphasizing containment and deterrence have given way to relationships defined by how an external power can assist smaller states in preserving domestic political stability. The United States has designated both the Philippines and Thailand as major non-NATO allies, yet both countries are mired in conflicts with domestic insurgency groups, including jihadists, and both have recently confronted extra-constitutional challenges to their fragile democratic institutions.

Unlike their Northeast Asian counterparts and Australia, therefore, the Philippines and Thailand, along with most other ASEAN states, have been unable to devote the resources needed to modernize their military infrastructures so that they can be integrated easily into U.S. strategic operations. Thailand—though it continues to host the annual Cobra Gold military exercise for the United States, Singapore, and allied nations—has declined several recent requests by Washington for permission to preposition U.S. military supplies for use in the Persian Gulf. The extent to which Thailand is now contributing viably to a U.S. regional "footprint" is in doubt. The Philippines withdrew its small contingent of military personnel from Iraq in July 2004 in response to a civilian Filipino truck driver being taken hostage and threatened with beheading. Given this behavior by the United States' Southeast Asian treaty allies, cynical observers of U.S. policy can feel justified in treating the phrase "coalition of the willing" with at least some derision.

U.S. defense officials respond to such skepticism by noting that Thailand, the Philippines, and other ASEAN countries can contribute to regional security by pursuing the niche areas of defense most relevant to their own regional security environments. Examples would include countries' procuring precision-guided munitions and advanced combat aircraft to defend their 200-mile exclusive economic zones and maritime approaches from external state-centric predators or from substate threats such as piracy. However, a more conventional ASEAN multi-lateral defense—especially one in which the United States plays a key supporting role—appears to be only a distant prospect. Indonesia and Malaysia's rejection in mid-2004 of a proposal floated by the United States Pacific Command for a Regional Security Maritime Initiative illustrates the difficulty facing the United States in reversing Southeast Asian governments' historical preference for the "ASEAN Way," with its emphasis on noninterference in internal affairs and its general aversion to great-power domination. ASEAN will balance and hedge against both American and Chinese power as long as neither becomes dominant.

Making and Keeping Friends

The Bush administration has enjoyed more tangible success in its efforts to upgrade strategic relations with India. Official policy statements have designated India as a rising democratic power ready to undertake global security responsibilities in partnership with the United States. Recent signs of closer strategic collaboration support this view: the issuing of a joint statement on strategic partnership by President Bush and Prime Minister Manmohan Singh; the Indian Navy escorting U.S. freighters through the Malacca Straits in April 2004 to support the U.S. war effort in Afghanistan; the acceleration of joint naval exercises between 2005 and 2007; and, in March 2006, the U.S.-India Civil Nuclear Cooperation Initiative.

American critics insist that China is using multilateralism to drive a wedge between the United States and its regional allies.

The latter development was significant in bringing India at least partially into the NPT regime. Although criticism of the Bush administration for recognizing a non-NPT state as a "legitimate nuclear power" has persisted in the U.S. Congress, that body in December 2006 passed legislation supporting U.S.-India civilian nuclear cooperation. The overall momentum for deepening U.S.-India ties is unmistakably strong. In early 2007, Vice President Dick Cheney proposed that India join Australia, Japan, and the United States in forming a quadrilateral mechanism for security consultation and collaboration (an informal coalition of democratic states, rather than a formal alliance) to pursue mutual security interests in the Asia-Pacific region.

It is unlikely India will abandon its traditional stance of neutrality to such an extent. But it is clear that New Delhi is pursuing balancing strategies of its own, positioning itself as a significant power whose views and interests must be taken into greater account by Washington, Beijing, and other regional security actors. These efforts are likely to succeed if China persists in building its military power to levels that increase American apprehensions about Beijing's intentions and drive Washington

to expand its defense relations with other regional powers. India's status in America's eyes as a potential strategic counterweight will also be enhanced if Pakistan—India's nuclear rival and another U.S. "major non-NATO ally"—continues to lose stability internally to the point that its utility as a partner in counterterrorist operations becomes questionable.

If Japan has remained the United States' most important Asia-Pacific ally, Australia has continued as Washington's most steadfast regional security partner. In the past decade Australia, under John Howard's conservative government, has joined the United States and Britain as a key contributor to military operations in Afghanistan and Iraq, as a guarantor of stability in the arc of instability stretching from eastern Indonesia and East Timor into the wider South Pacific, and as a peripheral but increasingly polished interlocutor in multilateral regional security politics. The extent of Australia's intelligence collaboration with (and access to) U.S. counterparts is remarkable for a middle power. Washington places a high value on Australia's propensity to cooperate with the United States in missile defense research and development, and to contribute unique defense capabilities in niche areas of asymmetrical warfare.

How strongly Australian-American security collaboration persists beyond the Howard years—the Australian prime minister faces a strong electoral challenge from Mandarin-speaking Kevin Rudd before the end of 2007—will invariably be affected by future developments in Sino-American relations. China has recently moved past Japan to become Australia's largest trading partner. For Australia, the prospect of having to choose between supporting the United States in a Taiwan conflict and remaining neutral, with all the risks that would entail for Canberra's security relationship with Washington, constitutes a policy nightmare.

Reshaping Strategy

How can the United States most effectively relate its security interests in the Asia-Pacific region to its ongoing global strategic posture in the post–9-11 era? Three broad approaches might be considered: treating the Asia-Pacific region as a critical element within an increasingly interrelated international security environment; integrating Asia-Pacific policy makers' concerns about nontraditional security problems more fully into future U.S. strategic planning; and assigning greater priority to regional multilateral security initiatives.

Successive post–cold war U.S. administrations have chosen, as their primary strategies for realizing U.S. global interests, the promotion of American-style democracy and the linking of international security with trading policies and practices. This policy orientation, while appealing to the American public, has often been viewed by Asian policy makers as excessively unilateral and hegemonic, and has precipitated a defense of "Asian values" to neutralize what many Asians see as excessive American intrusion on their own cultural identities. Future U.S. policy will need to focus on long-term U.S. interests that Asia-Pacific and other international actors can understand and negotiate without fearing that they will only gain U.S. support by adopting what the Americans would regard as good governance. Over time, globalization and capitalism will provide far more incentives for liberalization in developing societies than will any quest for social engineering emanating from Washington.

At the same time, it is justifiable and urgent for the United States to pursue interregional geopolitical alignments that are beneficial for all parties involved. Such a pursuit must entail the establishment and perpetuation of stable Asia-Pacific and global power balances, the preservation of sufficient U.S. military and economic assets for Washington to strongly influence how those power equilibriums will be shaped, and the incorporation of Asia-Pacific partners in regional security initiatives. Such initiatives should address minimizing the proliferation of weapons of mass destruction, neutralizing terrorism, and securing access to markets and energy by guaranteeing the safety of maritime commerce and the sustained development and distribution of global energy supplies.

The December 2004 Asian tsunami was seminal in sensitizing U.S. policy makers and the American public to the intersection of traditional and non-traditional security dynamics. The policy management of future pandemics, global warming, food and water resources, and forced people movements—all important issues in many Asia-Pacific citizens' daily existence—needs to be integrated into future U.S. strategic planning for the region. To its immense credit, the U.S. Pacific Command has already demonstrated a keen awareness of this imperative, spearheading joint training and development programs with regional counterparts for responding to future human security contingencies. The challenge inherent in such programs, however, is how to win the hearts and minds of the programs' intended beneficiaries without simultaneously appearing to establish dominance over their cultural and sociopolitical identities and values. This problem becomes all the more difficult for strategic thinkers in a world where asymmetrical conflicts and resource deprivation are increasingly common. Striking a judicious and acceptable balance between intervention and the politics of assistance is a key requirement for successfully integrating regional and global security politics.

Ultimately achieving this balance depends on the United States transforming itself from a hierarchical player in the Asia-Pacific region and within global institutions into one more comfortable with sharing power and negotiating compromises. The days of hub-and-spoke alliances in America's network of Asian bilateral security relationships are clearly numbered, yet no alternative form of regional security governance has emerged to take their place.

A New Security Architecture?

American neoconservatives have recently envisioned the creation of new institutional entities organized around common democratic values or, more crudely, a China containment rationale. China, Russia, and others critical of this approach point to an expanded NATO (which now embraces consultations with "Pacific partners" such as Japan and Australia) as a destabilizing force in southeastern Europe and Central Asia. They have created new mechanisms such as the Shanghai Cooperation Organization to neutralize what they regard as NATO's unwarranted evolution into a global alliance. This trend correlates with China's application of its New Security Concept to Asian institution-building. It illustrates the difficulties facing the United States in achieving strategic consensus among both its traditional rivals and its prospective security partners, a consensus that must be achieved if the region is to avoid slipping into a highly dangerous condition of multipolarity.

Avoiding this outcome fundamentally depends on finding a common basis for translating the interests and concerns of both the United States and Asia-Pacific countries into a new, more effective regional security architecture. The United States, although it remains a truly global strategic actor, has yet to demonstrate the will and capacity to interact with Asia-Pacific states in ways that allow it to be widely viewed as a valued and engaged security partner in an institutional context. Overcoming America's image as indifferent is mandatory if the United States is to play an integral role in shaping future Asia-Pacific security politics and simultaneously to achieve its global security objectives.

WILLIAM T. TOW a professor at the Australian National University, is author of *Asia-Pacific Strategic Relations: Seeking Convergent Security* (Cambridge University Press, 2001).

China's Challenge to U.S. Hegemony

"If the United States tries to maintain its current dominance in East Asia, Sino-American conflict is virtually certain. . . ."

CHRISTOPHER LAYNE

The Soviet Union's collapse transformed the bipolar cold war international system into a "unipolar" system dominated by the United States. During the 1990s, the U.S. foreign policy community engaged in lively debate about whether America's post–cold war hegemony could be sustained over the long haul or was merely a "unipolar moment." More than 15 years after the cold war's end, it is obvious that American hegemony has been more than momentary. Indeed, the prevailing view among policy makers and foreign policy scholars today is that America's economic, military, and technological advantages are so great that it will be a long time before U.S. dominance can be challenged.

There is mounting evidence, however, that this view is mistaken, and that, in fact, the era of American hegemony is drawing to a close right before our eyes. The rise of China is the biggest reason for this. Notwithstanding Washington's current preoccupation with the Middle East, in the coming decades China's great power emergence will be the paramount issue of grand strategy facing the United States.

Whether China will undergo a "peaceful rise"—as Beijing claims—is doubtful. Historically, the emergence of new poles of power in the international system has been geopolitically destabilizing. For example, the rise of Germany, the United States, and Japan at the end of the nineteenth century contributed to the international political frictions that culminated in two world wars. There is no reason to believe that China's rise will be an exception.

However, while it is certainly true that China's rise will cause geopolitical turmoil, a Sino-American war is not inevitable. Whether such a conflict occurs will hinge more on Washington's strategic choices than on Beijing's.

Rise of a Great Power

From the mid-1980s through the late 1990s China's economy grew at a rate of approximately 10 percent a year. From the late 1990s until 2005 its economy grew at 8 percent to 9 percent annually. In 2006 China's annual growth rate was above 11 percent, as it is projected to be for 2007. China's phenomenal economic growth is driving its emergence as a great power—and

this is a familiar pattern in international politics. The economic power of states grows at different rates, which means that some states are always gaining power and some are losing power relative to others. As Paul Kennedy demonstrated in his 1987 book *The Rise and Fall of the Great Powers,* time and again these relative economic shifts have "heralded the rise of new great powers which one day would have a decisive impact on the military/territorial order."

The leadership in Beijing understands the link between economic strength and geopolitical weight. It realizes that, if China can continue to sustain near–double digit growth rates in the early decades of this century, it will surpass the United States as the world's largest economy (measured by gross domestic product). Because of this astonishing economic growth, China is, as journalist James Kynge has put it (with a nod to Napoleon), truly shaking the world both economically *and* geopolitically. Studies by the U.S. Central Intelligence Agency and others have projected that China will be a first-rate military power and will rival America in global power by 2020.

Engage or Contain?

In fact, China's rise has been on the radar screens of U.S. foreign policy experts since the early 1990s. Broadly speaking, the debate about how the United States should respond to China's emergence as a great power has focused on two policy alternatives: engagement and containment.

Engagement assumes that, as China's contacts with the outside world multiply, its exposure to Western (that is, mostly American) political and cultural values will result in evolutionary political change within China. The proponents of engagement believe that the forces of domestic political liberalization and economic globalization will temper Beijing's foreign policy ambitions and lead to a peaceful Sino-American relationship.

On the economic side, the logic of engagement is that, as China becomes increasingly tied to the international economy, its interdependence with others will constrain it from taking political actions that could disrupt its vital access both to foreign markets and capital and to high-technology imports from the

United States, Japan, and Western Europe. This was the claim made in the 1990s by the Clinton administration and its supporters during a debate about whether the United States should extend permanent normal trade relations to China and support Beijing's accession to the World Trade Organization.

Proponents of engagement have also argued that the United States can help foster political liberalization in China by integrating the country into the international economy and embedding it in the complex web of international institutional arrangements. A China so engaged, it is said, will have strong interests in cooperation and will not be inclined to pursue security competition with America or with its Asian neighbors.

Engagement is a problematic strategy, however, because it rests on a shaky foundation. The conventional wisdom notwithstanding, there is little support in the historical record for the idea that economic interdependence leads to peace. After all, Europe never was more interdependent (not only economically but also, among the ruling elites, intellectually and culturally) than before World War I. It was famously predicted, on the eve of World War I, that the economic ties among Europe's great powers had ushered in an era in which war among them was unthinkable. Yet, as we know, the prospect of forgoing the economic gains of trade did not stop Europe's great powers from fighting a prolonged and devastating war.

Beijing's actual foreign policy furnishes a concrete reason to be skeptical of the argument that interdependence leads to peace. China's behavior in the 1996 crisis with Taiwan (during which it conducted missile tests in waters surrounding the island in the run-up to Taiwan's presidential election) suggested it was not constrained by fears that its muscular foreign policy would adversely affect its overseas trade.

Of course, during the past decade, China has been mindful of its stake in international trade and investment. But this does not vindicate the U.S. strategy of engagement. China's current policy reflects the fact that, for now, Beijing recognizes its strategic interest in preserving peace in East Asia. Stability in the region, and in Sino-American relations, allows China to become richer and to catch up to the United States in relative power. For a state in China's position vis-à-vis the United States, this is the optimal realpolitik strategy: buying time for its economy to grow so that the nation can openly balance against the United States militarily and establish its own regional hegemony in East Asia. Beijing is pursuing a peaceful policy today in order to strengthen itself to confront the United States tomorrow.

The era of American hegemony is drawing to a close right before our eyes.

The belief that a democratic—or more liberal—China would be pacific and collaborative in its external policies is similarly dubious. This view rests on the so-called "democratic peace theory" which is near and dear to many U.S. foreign policy experts. In fact, the democratic peace theory is another one of those bits of foreign policy conventional wisdom that is based on flimsy evidence. The historical record demonstrates that when vital national interests have been at risk, democratic states have routinely practiced big-stick diplomacy against other democracies (including threats to use force). In other words, when the stakes are high enough, great powers act like great powers even in their relations with other democracies. Thus, even if China does undergo political liberalization in the future, there is no reason to believe that its foreign policy behavior would be fundamentally affected.

A U.S. containment strategy for China differs from engagement in that it relies mostly on the traditional "hard power" tools of military might and alliance diplomacy to thwart China's great power emergence. Containment calls for the United States to emulate its anti-Soviet cold war strategy by assembling a powerful coalition of states sharing a common interest in curbing rising Chinese power—particularly by tightening the U.S. security relationship with Japan while simultaneously investing that alliance with an overtly anti-Chinese mission. Containment would require the United States to pledge explicitly to defend Taiwan while bolstering Taiwanese military capabilities. Some containment advocates also argue that the United States should engage in covert operations to destabilize China, especially by fomenting unrest among China's ethnic minorities.

To contain China, the United States would maintain both its nuclear and conventional military superiority over China, and would develop a credible first strike option based on a combination of robust offensive nuclear capabilities and effective ballistic missile defenses. Advocates of containment hope that the various measures encompassed by this strategy could halt China's rise and preserve American dominance in East Asia. However, as argued for example by Missouri State University's Bradley A. Thayer, if these steps failed to stop China's great power emergence, the United States would have to consider "harsher measures." In other words, the United States should be prepared to engage in a preventive war against China. Containment, therefore, is a strategy that at best would result in an intense Sino-American security competition. At worst, it could lead to war.

The Actual Strategy

Engagement and containment are "ideal type" grand strategies toward China. In the real world, Washington's actual approach fashions elements of both engagement and containment into a hard-edged grand strategy that requires China to accept U.S. geopolitical and ideological hegemony—or else. In this respect, American policy toward China is the specific manifestation of overall U.S. grand strategy, which rests on both strategic and idealistic pillars.

Strategically, the goal of post–cold war U.S. strategy has been to prevent the emergence of new great powers (or, as the Pentagon calls them, "peer competitors"). This strategy was first articulated in March 1992 in the initial draft of the Pentagon's *Defense Planning Guidance* document for fiscal years 1994–1999. It stated that the goal of U.S. grand strategy henceforth would be to maintain America's preponderance by preventing new great powers from emerging. The United States, it declared, "must maintain the mechanisms for deterring potential competitors from even aspiring to a larger regional or global role."

The Clinton administration similarly was committed to the perpetuation of U.S. preponderance. And the administration of George W. Bush has embraced the hegemonic strategy of its two immediate predecessors. The 2002 *National Security Strategy of the United States* promises that America will act to prevent any other state from building up military capabilities in the hope of "surpassing, or even equaling, the power of the United States."

Ideologically, U.S. grand strategy amounts to "real-politik-plus," to borrow Brandeis University professor Robert Art's phrase. As such, national interests are defined in terms of both hard power and the promotion of American ideals. As the *National Security Strategy* puts it, U.S. grand strategy is "based on a distinctly American internationalism that reflects the union of our values and our national interests."

Some observers have described this formula as "liberal realism," "national security liberalism," or (as neoconservative pundit Charles Krauthammer puts it) "democratic realism." This sort of liberalism is more muscular and offensive than idealistic. The spread of democracy and economic openness are imbedded in American grand strategic thought because policy makers believe that U.S. power, influence, and security are enhanced in a world comprised of "free market democracies."

America's post–cold war strategy is based firmly on these twin pillars of military superiority and liberal internationalist ideology. And because domestic ideology is the fundamental driver of U.S. grand strategy, America's geopolitical aims transcend those traditionally associated with power politics. Not only does the emergence of a powerful challenger in general threaten America's ability to control its environment, but China in particular is seen as a threat because its politico-economic system challenges America's need for a world compatible with—and safe for—its own liberal ideology. China's rise threatens to close East Asia to U.S. economic and ideological penetration.

Liberalize—Or Else

Because of ideology, engagement has a role in U.S. strategy, but it is engagement with (bared) teeth. The United States is willing to give China the opportunity to integrate itself into the U.S.-led international order—on Washington's terms. Thus, as a Pentagon document has put it, the United States wants China to become a "responsible member of the international community." Responsibility, however, is defined as Beijing's willingness to accept Washington's vision of a stable international order. As President Bush declared in a November 2005 speech in Kyoto, responsibility also requires China to achieve political liberalization and develop as a free market economy firmly anchored to the international economy.

Indeed, U.S. policy makers believe that, over the long term, peaceful relations are possible with Beijing *only* if China undergoes domestic political and economic liberalization. As a result, the United States aims to promote China's internal transformation. As the Bush administration's *National Security Strategy* declares: "America will encourage the advancement of democracy and economic openness" in China, "because these are the best foundations for domestic stability and international order."

As then-Deputy Secretary of State Robert Zoellick said in 2005, "Closed politics cannot be a permanent feature of Chinese society."

U.S. officials believe that nations such as China that do not adopt American-style political and economic systems, and that do not play by the rules of the American-led international order, are *ipso facto* threats to U.S. interests—threats to which America must be prepared to respond aggressively.

Here is where America's willingness to employ the hard fist of military power against China comes into play. The Bush administration has said it "welcomes a confident, peaceful, and prosperous China that appreciates that its growth and development depend on constructive connections with the rest of the world." At the same time, however, Washington has made crystal clear that it will not countenance a China that emerges as a great power rival and challenges American primacy. The 2002 *National Security Strategy* enjoins Beijing from challenging the United States militarily and warns that, "In pursuing advanced military capabilities that can threaten its neighbors in the Asia-Pacific region, China is following an outdated path that, in the end, will hamper its own pursuit of national greatness. In time, China will find that social and political freedom is the only source of that greatness."

As Washington sees it, China has no justifiable grounds for regarding the U.S. military presence in East Asia as threatening to its interests. Then–Defense Secretary Donald Rumsfeld made this point in 2005 when he stated that any moves by China to enhance its military capabilities necessarily are signals of aggressive Chinese intent. According to Rumsfeld, China's military modernization cannot possibly be defensive because "no nation threatens China." Rumsfeld's view was echoed in the administration's 2005 report on *The Military Power of the People's Republic of China,* which stated that "China's military modernization remains ambitious," and warned that in coming years "China's leaders may be tempted to resort to force or coercion more quickly to press diplomatic advantage, advance security interests, or resolve disputes."

Similarly, at an October 2007 conference on Sino-American relations Admiral Timothy Keating, the commander in chief of the U.S. Pacific Command, made three points with respect to America's China strategy. First, the United States will seek to maintain its present military dominance over China. Second, America will, through arms sales, ensure there is a cross-Strait military balance between Taiwan and China. Third, the United States will not allow China to change the status quo in Taiwan by force. In short, the United States is determined both to make sure that China does not emerge as a peer competitor and to impose itself as an obstacle to China's overriding national goal of reunification with Taiwan.

Strangling the Baby

China's rise affects the United States because of what international relations scholars call the "power transition" effect: Throughout the history of the modern international state system, ascending powers have always challenged the position of the dominant (hegemonic) power in the international system—and these challenges have usually culminated in war. Notwithstanding Beijing's talk about a "peaceful rise," an ascending China inevitably will challenge the geopolitical equilibrium in East Asia. The doctrine of peaceful rise thus is a reassurance strategy employed by Beijing in an attempt to allay others' fears of growing Chinese power and to forestall the United States from acting preventively during the dangerous transition period when China is catching up to the United States.

Does this mean that the United States and China are on a collision course that will lead to a war in the next decade or two? Not necessarily. What happens in Sino-American relations largely depends on what strategy Washington chooses to adopt toward China. If the United States tries to maintain its current dominance in East Asia, Sino-American conflict is virtually certain, because U.S. grand strategy has incorporated the logic of anticipatory violence as an instrument for maintaining American primacy. For a declining hegemon, "strangling the baby in the crib" by attacking a rising challenger preventively—that is, while the hegemon still holds the upper hand militarily—has always been a tempting strategic option.

An Alternative Plan

Washington, however, faces perhaps a last chance to adopt a grand strategy that will serve its interests in ensuring that Chinese power is contained in East Asia but without running the risk of an armed clash with Beijing. This strategy is "offshore balancing," a concept that is finding increasing favor with a group of influential American scholars in the field of security studies. According to this strategy, the United States should deploy military power abroad only in the face of direct threats to vital American interests. The strategy recognizes that Washington need not (and in fact cannot) directly control vast parts of the globe, that it is better off setting priorities based on clear national interests and relying on local actors to uphold regional balances of power. The idea of offshore balancing is to husband national power for maximum effectiveness while minimizing perceptions that this power represents a threat.

By adopting an offshore balancing strategy, the United States could better preserve its relative power and strategic influence.

As an offshore balancer in East Asia, the United States would embrace a new set of policies regarding Sino-American economic relations, political liberalization in China, the defense of Taiwan, and America's strategic posture in the region.

An offshore balancing strategy would require the United States to approach economic relations with China based on a policy of strategic trade rather than free trade. A strategic trade policy would seek to curtail the flow of high technology and direct investment from the United States to China. It also would require a shift in current U.S. trade policy to drastically reduce the bilateral trade deficit, which is a de facto American subsidy of the very economic growth that is fueling China's great power emergence.

Second, the United States would abandon its efforts to effectuate political liberalization in China. This policy is a form of gratuitous eye-poking. Because the United States lacks sufficient leverage to transform China domestically, the primary effect of trying to force liberalization on China is to inflame Sino-American relations.

An offshore balancing strategy also would require a new U.S. stance on Taiwan, a powder-keg issue because China is committed to national reunification and would regard a Taiwanese declaration of independence as a *casus belli*. If U.S. policy fails to prevent a showdown between China and Taiwan, the odds are that America will be drawn into the conflict because of its current East Asia strategy. There would be strong domestic political pressure in favor of U.S. intervention. Beyond the arguments that Chinese military action against Taiwan would constitute aggression and undermine U.S. interests in a stable world order, powerful incentives for intervention would also arise from ideological antipathy toward China, concerns for maintaining U.S. "credibility," and support for a democratic Taiwan in a conflict with authoritarian China.

Notwithstanding these arguments, which are underpinned by a national security discourse that favors American hegemony, the issues at stake in a possible showdown between China and Taiwan simply would not justify the risks and costs of U.S. intervention. Regardless of the rationale invoked, the contention that the United States should go to war to prevent Beijing from using force to achieve reunification with Taiwan (or in response to a unilateral declaration of independence by Taipei) amounts to nothing more than a veiled argument for fighting a "preventive" war against a rising China.

Sharing the Burden

The final element of a U.S. offshore balancing strategy would be the devolution from the United States to the major powers in Asia of the responsibility for containing China. An offshore balancing strategy would rely on the balance-of-power dynamics of a twenty-first century multipolar global order to prevent China from dominating East Asia. The other major powers in Asia—Japan, Russia, and India—have a much more immediate interest in stopping a rising China in their midst than does the United States.

In a multipolar system, the question is not whether balancing will occur, but which state or states will do the heavy lifting. Because the United States is geographically distant from China—and protected both by the expanse of the Pacific Ocean and by its own formidable military (including nuclear) capabilities—the United States has the option of staying out of East Asian security rivalries (at least initially) and forcing Beijing's neighbors to assume the risks and costs of stopping China from attaining regional hegemony. Because its air and naval power is based on long-range strike capabilities, the United States can keep its forces in an over-the-horizon posture with respect to East Asia and limit itself to a backstopping role in the unlikely event that the regional balance of power falters.

It is hardly surprising—indeed, it parallels in many ways America's own emergence as a great power—that China, the largest and potentially most powerful state in Asia, is seeking a more assertive political, military, and economic role in the region, and even challenging America's present dominance in East Asia. However, this poses no direct threat to U.S. security. Japan, India, and Russia, on the other hand, are worried about the implications of China's rapid ascendance for *their* security. They should bear the responsibility of balancing against Chinese power.

An incipient drift toward multipolarity—which is the prerequisite for the United States to adopt an offshore balancing strategy—is already apparent in East Asia. Driven by fears of U.S. abandonment in a future East Asian crisis, Japan has embarked on a buildup of its military capabilities and has even hinted that it is thinking about acquiring nuclear weapons. Moreover, the past several years have seen a significant escalation in tensions between China and Japan, fueled both by nationalism and by disputes over control of the South China and East China seas (which may contain large energy deposits).

Great powers that seek hegemony are always opposed—and defeated—by the counterbalancing efforts of other states.

From the standpoint of offshore balancing, Japan's military buildup in response to its fear of China is a good thing if it leads to Japan's reemergence as an independent geopolitical actor. However, Japan's military resurgence is not so good (for the United States) if it takes place under the aegis of the U.S.-Japan security alliance, and if the United States remains in the front lines of the forces containing China. Under those conditions, the United States could find itself ensnared in an Asian conflict; its alliance with Japan risks dragging it into a war with China in which American strategic interests would not be engaged. The idea of an offshore balancing strategy is to get the United States out of China's crosshairs, not to allow it to remain a target because of its present security commitments to allies in the region.

The wisdom of risking war with China to maintain U.S. hegemony in East Asia is all the more doubtful because America's predominance in the region is ebbing in any event. One indication of this is that U.S. economic supremacy in East Asia is waning as China rises. China is emerging as the motor of the region's economic growth.

While the United States has been preoccupied with Iraq, Iran, and the so-called war on terrorism, China has used its burgeoning economic power to extend its political influence throughout East and Southeast Asia. Indeed, most of the smaller states in Southeast Asia are gradually slipping into Beijing's political orbit because their own prosperity is ever more closely tied to their relations with China.

America's strategy of trying to uphold the geopolitical status quo in East Asia clashes with the ambitions of a rising China, which has its own ideas about how East Asia's political and security order should be organized. If the United States puts itself in the forefront of those trying to contain China, the potential for future tension—or worse—in Sino-American relations can only increase. By pulling back from its hegemonic role in East Asia and adopting an offshore balancing strategy, the United States could better preserve its relative power and strategic influence. It could stand on the sidelines while that region's great powers enervate themselves by engaging in security competitions.

The Temptation of Power

If American strategy were determined by the traditional metrics that have governed the grand strategies of great powers—the distribution of power in the international system, geographic proximity of rivals, and military capabilities—China would not be considered much of a threat to the United States. The wellspring of U.S. grand strategy lies elsewhere, however: in Wilsonian ideology. This is why the United States remains wedded to a strategy of upholding its predominance in East Asia, as well as in Europe and the Middle East.

One of the few ironclad lessons of history is that great powers that seek hegemony are always opposed—and defeated—by the counterbalancing efforts of other states. Yet the prevailing belief among the American foreign policy community is that the United States is exempt from the fate of hegemons. This belief, really a form of American exceptionalism, is wrong. If Washington gives in to the temptation of hegemonic power, dangerous times lie ahead.

CHRISTOPHER LAYNE is a professor at Texas A&M University's George H. W. Bush School of Government and Public Service. He is author of *The Peace of Illusions: American Grand Strategy from 1940 to the Present* (Cornell University Press, 2006), and (with Bradley A. Thayer) *American Empire: A Debate* (Routledge, 2007).

From *Current History,* January 2008, pp. 13–18. Copyright © 2008 by Current History, Inc. Reprinted by permission.

North Korea's Nuclear Neurosis

**Building the Bomb is a form of national self-expression—
and that's especially the case for Kim Jong Il.**

JACQUES E. C. HYMANS

North Korea's nuclear test of October 9, 2006 shook the world—or at least lightly jostled it. The moribund six-party talks awoke from their slumber. On February 13, North Korea and its five negotiating partners (South Korea, China, Russia, Japan, and the United States) reached an agreement that foresees a modest transfer of heavy fuel oil to the poverty-stricken country within 60 days, in exchange for an initially provisional freeze on plutonium production and reprocessing at its Yongbyon nuclear facility. The deal also sketches the broad outlines for a more comprehensive arrangement to be hammered out in the future.[1]

Though the fate of the February 13 agreement was unknown at the time of this writing, it was nevertheless clear that the deal would not be the end of the North Korean nuclear saga. Indeed, few observers are confident that it even represents the beginning of the end; the debate over how to handle the newest declared nuclear weapon state is far from over. As Secretary of State Condoleezza Rice stated, "This is still the first quarter."[2]

In the United States, the debate has long been stuck between two broad camps. On one side stand the proponents of engagement who say "let's make a deal"; on the other stand the proponents of confrontation who say "let's make 'em squeal." Neither side is particularly enthralled with the six-party talks framework.

According to the let's-make-a-deal proponents, the October nuclear test was yet another indication that North Korea longs for respect—which it measures in hard currency. Distasteful though Pyongyang's behavior may be, given the great dangers posed by its nuclear program we simply have no choice but to enter into intensive bilateral negotiations that set the price for peace. As the Nautilus Institute's Peter Hayes wrote after the North announced its forthcoming test, "Koreans have a saying: 'Sword to sword: rice cake to rice cake.' It is time to throw away the sword and hold up the ricecake."[3] And in a comment offering thin praise for the February agreement, Hayes chided the parties for the "measly" good-faith down payment they offered the North. In his view, the rice cake will need to be at least $4 billion–$5 billion.[4]

The let's-make-'em-squeal proponents agree that North Korea is using its nuclear development in a bid for aid and respect, but they argue that giving Kim Jong Il what he is asking

for now will merely increase his appetite for more later. From this vantage point, the February agreement is a step in the wrong direction, a cave-in to the North's aggressive posturing. The only way to rein in Kim's nuclear ambitions, in the words of Aaron Friedberg, Vice President Dick Cheney's former national security adviser, is to make him "an offer he cannot refuse": Either dismantle the nuclear program verifiably, "or face a steadily rising risk of overthrow and untimely death."[5]

Despite the heated arguments between the proponents of these two points of view, they actually start from the same basic assumptions: Pyongyang can be viewed as a unitary, rational actor; it knows how to build the Bomb; and its nuclear weapons drive is a function of the external incentive structure it faces. The major difference between the two camps simply concerns the relative sizes of the carrots and sticks they think will convince Kim Jong Il to throw in the towel on his nuclear adventure. But what if their shared basic assumptions were wrong?

It's not that Washington has missed the point about North Korea per se. Indeed, the idea that North Korea is uniquely incorrigible—a rogue regime led by a "malignant narcissist" who allegedly killed his brother as a young boy—is another old warhorse of the policy debate.[6] The particularities of Kim Jong Il's personality should certainly be taken seriously, but the main source of U.S. diplomatic frustration lies in the failure to understand the *general* issue of nuclear proliferation, *wherever* it occurs. (After all, as 130,000 soldiers stationed in Iraq today will tell you, Korea is hardly the only place where the U.S. analysis and response to proliferation threats have proven flawed.) And the first step toward understanding the general issue of nuclear proliferation is to recognize that leaders decide to go nuclear more with their hearts than with their heads.

National Identity, Emotions, and the Bomb

The list of leaders who have sought to thrust their nations into the nuclear club includes the powerful and the weak, the democratic and the dictatorial, the religious and the secular, the

Western and the Eastern, the Northern and the Southern. These leaders share little in common, with the crucial exception of similar basic conceptions of their nations' identities.[7]

Most leaders' national identity conceptions do not pull them toward a definitive decision for the Bomb, because that is a revolutionary act with unpredictable consequences both externally and internally. Indeed, clear nuclear weapons ambitions have historically been much less common than is often assumed. For instance, the United States totally misinterpreted Argentina's nuclear efforts of the 1970s and 1980s. Archival research has revealed that the Argentine military junta, distasteful though it was in many respects, not only made no Bomb drive but did not even contain a significant Bomb lobby. The usual suspects for such a lobby—military strategists and geopolitical thinkers—concluded that the country's tense relations with the United States, Britain, and neighboring Brazil reflected a limited conflict of interests, not an existential one. As such, they believed that launching a nuclear arms race would be a "strategic absurdity."[8]

But whereas most leaders prefer to sidestep the question of going nuclear, such is not the case for leaders who are "oppositional nationalists"—individuals who possess intense fear of an external enemy combined with an equally intense pride in their nation's natural capacity to face down the enemy. The effect of these identity-driven emotions of fear and pride is to replace the typical hesitations with an unshakable determination to get the Bomb at any cost, no matter what the consequences. Indeed, oppositional nationalists want the Bomb not just as a means to an end, but as an end in itself—as a matter of national self-expression.

Consider, for instance, the French decision to go nuclear. Prime Minister Pierre Mendès-France was no "malignant narcissist." He agonized over the choice to endanger the world by bringing another nuclear weapon state into being. Yet confronted with the (strictly conventional) rearmament of Germany, he launched his nation's drive for the Bomb on December 26, 1954. This hasty decision came years before France was technically ready to implement it and left many loose ends—including the crucial question of strategic delivery systems. Mendès-France's controversial choice was the product of his twin emotions of oppositional fear of Germany and nationalist pride in France. Years later, Bertrand Goldschmidt, a former Manhattan Project scientist who became a key player in France's nuclear program, tried to convey the deep sources of the pro-nuclear sentiments of the day: "We had just been occupied by Germany. . . . It was a kind of revenge, if you want, from this humiliating occupation. We had to have . . . differentiation."[9]

There are strong parallels between the French decision of 1954 and the Indian decision of 1998. Indian Prime Minister Atal Bihari Vajpayee was the author of a moving poem about the tragedy of Hiroshima. Yet he took less than a month after arriving in power before deciding to conduct the tests that marked India's definitive, explosive entry into the nuclear weapons club. Again, oppositional nationalism—in this case Vajpayee's controversial Hindu nationalist antagonism toward Muslim Pakistan—lay at the root of his nuclear leap of faith. Indeed, so certain was Vajpayee in the rightness of his choice

that he told anxious aides during the run-up to the tests, "There is no need for much thought. We just have to do it."[10] Naturally, it turned out that more thought was needed, as the South Asian region entered a period of great instability marked by a series of tense nuclear standoffs.

Rooted in oppositional fear and nationalistic pride, definite nuclear ambitions harden quickly in leaders' minds and are very hard to dislodge.

But for Vajpayee, these mundane concerns were essentially beside the point: "The greatest meaning of these tests," he told *India Today* in their immediate aftermath, "is that they have given India *shakti,* they have given India strength, and they have given India self-confidence."[11]

Rooted as they are in oppositional fear and nationalist pride, definite nuclear ambitions harden quickly in leaders' minds and are subsequently very hard to dislodge, whether via threats or inducements. Moreover, once the order comes from on high, dedicated nuclear weapons efforts tend to put down deep institutional and psychological roots within the state and are thus typically revocable only at times of severe regime disillusionment, if not complete dissolution. The case of North Korea needs to be seen in light of these general proliferation patterns.

Fear and Pride, North Korea–Style

North Korea's leaders, first the father Kim Il Sung and now his son Kim Jong Il, have always been dyed-in-the-wool oppositional nationalists. This national identity conception probably solidified over the course of the Korean War. As historian Kathryn Weathersby has put it, "The experience of having survived sustained bombing by U.S. planes for nearly three years created the dangerous, if paradoxical, combination of a profound sense of threat and a faith in the country's ability to prevail in a future military conflict."[12]

Oppositional nationalists want the Bomb, and the oppositional nationalists of Pyongyang are no exception. As the archives of former Communist states make clear, North Korea's nuclear intention was there very early on. It is simply historically inaccurate to view Pyongyang's nuclear weapon desires as a recent development, however many diplomatic blunders the Bush administration may have made. For instance, consider the recently unearthed 1962 statement of North Korean Foreign Minister Pak Song Chol to the Soviet ambassador in Pyongyang: "Who can impose such a [nonproliferation] treaty on countries that do not have nuclear weapons, but are perhaps successfully working in that direction?"[13] Pyongyang eventually did consent to join the Nuclear Non-Proliferation Treaty in 1985 but without abandoning its drive for the Bomb—an indication of its capacity for great tactical flexibility in pursuit of fixed strategic ends.

Pak's outburst to his Soviet "comrade" is revealing in another important way. Pyongyang's oppositional nationalism is not directed solely against the United States. Rather, the North Korean regime sees history as ceaseless combat by the Korean nation against existential threats that have come from every direction—from the United States and Japan, of course, but also from Russia and China. The regime has even made a great point of embracing (and embroidering) the legacy of the "Korean" Goguryeo Kingdom that long waged war against Imperial China until finally succumbing in 668 A.D. One can also discern this racial, Korea-versus-the-world attitude in the country's nuclear diplomacy, and not least in Kim Il Sung's secret 1972 offer to South Korea to jointly develop the Bomb.[14]

There is a lesson for policy makers here: If North Korea's leadership is oppositional nationalist *in general,* then its nuclear program is likely also directed more broadly than just at the U.S. imperialists—and therefore even a bona fide reconciliation with the United States would probably not be enough to shake it from its ultimate nuclear objective.

Why Now?

A fear of enemies on all sides coupled with intense national pride was on display for all to see in Pyongyang's official statement on its test, which vaunted this "great leap forward in the building of a great, prosperous, powerful socialist nation," dubiously claimed that the test was the result of "indigenous wisdom and technology, 100 percent," and pointedly warned that this "powerful self-reliant defense capability" would "contribute to defending the peace and stability on the Korean Peninsula and in the area around it."[15] But why did Kim end up testing the Bomb when he did?

Many analysts have attempted to discern the "message" that Pyongyang meant to send this past October. Some speculated that it was in response to the U.S. crackdown on North Korea's international bank accounts. Others saw it as a strategy to hurt President George W. Bush in the midterm elections. Still others saw it as a desperate attempt to regain the spotlight at a time when Washington had suddenly become more interested in the nuclear crisis with Iran. Some of these hypotheses may have merit. But they all share a common, yet debatable assumption that North Korea was simply waiting to test until it felt it was necessary to make some political point.

That assumption would be more credible if the test had been a technical success, but it can hardly be counted as such.[16] Kim wanted a loud bang but ended up with a fizzle: perhaps 10 percent of the 4-kiloton yield he was apparently expecting. True, the test's yield was far bigger than even the largest conventional bombs, but it does not spell Hiroshima. Moreover, it is well to remember that Kim's previous strategic weapons foray had been a long-range missile test in July 2006 that failed less than a minute after launch. North Korea thus ended the year with greatly reduced deterrence credibility compared to when it was simply leaving things up to the outside world's imagination.

In light of the nuclear test fizzle, rather than asking why North Korea finally tested, perhaps we should ask instead, why did it jump the gun? What led it to test a device that was so unbelievably bad that people started speculating it might be some kind of fraud?

Again, consider the impact of Kim's oppositional nationalism. Oppositional nationalists are not satisfied with "latent" or "opaque" nuclear arsenals. Their fear and pride drive them to covet the real thing. So, far from waiting for just the right moment to test, Kim may well have been actively pushing his weapons program officials for months or even years to throw caution to the wind and get the device ready to test. Such behavior would also fit the larger pattern of North Korean industrial development efforts. To increase productivity, the regime relies heavily on "speed battles" reminiscent of Chinese leader Mao Zedong's "great leap forward." The cumulative effect of decades of speed battles is an economy that cannot even get the lights on at night. The sorry result of Kim's speed battle for strategic weapons in 2006 was a missile that exploded spectacularly and a Bomb that hardly exploded at all.

History suggests that, despite its technical difficulties and acceptance of the February 13 agreement, North Korea's motivation to build and maintain a working nuclear arsenal remains high. Even vocal critics of the Bush administration's previous confrontational posture toward Pyongyang have expressed concern that Kim may be using the six-party talks simply to play for time "until the international community is accustomed to its being a declared nuclear state."[17] But although North Korea is indeed a "declared" nuclear state, saying it does not make it so.

The Mouse That Squeaked

The paltry recent test results indicate a level of technical incompetence in North Korea's strategic weapons programs that few analysts would have dared to suggest in years past. Just as we need to question the mainstream assumption that Pyongyang's desire for the Bomb stems from a rational strategic calculation, we also need to question the assumption that the regime is capable of rationally organizing itself to achieve its nuclear ends.

North Korea is a prototypical "sultanistic" regime, wherein authority is concentrated entirely in the hands of a single individual whose legitimacy claims rest heavily on a cult of personality.[18] These regimes tend to be terrible at running nuclear development programs. This is because building the Bomb is not just about money or access to high technology. It is also about the ability to instill an ethic of scientific professionalism and a long-term planning perspective. Such an undertaking is nearly impossible for sultanistic regimes, hampered as they are by arbitrary decision making, palace intrigues and sycophancy, and above all, a generalized and radical level of personal insecurity.

The historical contrast between the nuclear programs of sultanistic and other types of regimes is striking. Consider that, in the era of the slide rule, the first Soviet, British, and French nuclear tests each came after merely six years of dedicated effort—and the United States did it in three. By contrast,

Saddam Hussein's Iraq spent an entire decade and more than $1 billion without succeeding in producing any weapon-grade highly enriched uranium by the time of the first Gulf War.[19] And Iraq was, relatively speaking, a near miss. Despite three decades of effort and a mountain of equipment supplied by A. Q. Khan, Libya's program was in an utter state of shambles when Muammar Qaddafi finally gave it up in late 2003.[20]

Then there's the experience of Communist Romania, probably the closest historical parallel to North Korea in terms of its basic nature—a Stalinist state run like a family business. The tyrant Nicolae Ceausescu's nuclear dreams failed to come true despite the great willingness of the West at the time to provide him with financial credits and advanced nuclear technology.

What went wrong? As with other major industrial development projects that the regime initiated, the basic problem was managerial. At the top of the country's science policy ladder stood Ceausescu's wife Elena, who doggedly replaced professional scientists with political hacks who were willing to promote her candidacy for the Nobel Prize in chemistry. At the bottom of the ladder, the construction of a planned series of Canadian-designed CANDU nuclear plants relied on masses of forced laborers—a strategy that the on-site Canadian engineer later suggested would have been more appropriate to a potato harvest than to high-technology construction. And in the middle, the hapless project managers made great efforts to hide the growing mess from their political masters with tactics that would have made Potemkin blush.[21]

When seen in the context of the basic similarities between its regime type and that of Communist Romania, North Korea's spectacular technical failures of 2006 start to seem more than a mere hiccup. They instead suggest that Kim's Bomb effort may well suffer from many of the same systemic ills that plagued Ceausescu's program. The Romanian analogy casts doubt on the widespread claim that if we do not do something drastic, then the North will start turning out nuclear weapons like sausages. Indeed, it isn't even good at turning out sausages.

The paltry recent test results indicate a level of technical incompetence in North Korea's strategic weapons programs that few analysts would have dared to suggest in years past.

For much the same reason, we should be more than a little skeptical about the notion of North Korea becoming the world's nuclear Wal-Mart. However much it would like to peddle its wares in exchange for hard currency, Pyongyang's first objective for its nuclear program is undoubtedly to deter its adversaries. And recall the basics of deterrence theory: Acquisition of a mere handful of bombs is not a deterrent; it is a provocation. To achieve deterrence, North Korea needs to be able to boast a credible second-strike capability—against no less an opponent than the United States. If Kim does not understand that yet, he surely soon will. Yet North Korea's plutonium production has

been achingly slow.[22] As a result, Kim is highly unlikely to part with any of his precious plutonium at this time. He probably also will try to wiggle out of his pledge to negotiate the "abandonment" of Yongbyon. Indeed, if I were in charge of U.S. intelligence, I would be as much on the lookout for North Korean attempts to *import* as to export fissile material in the coming years.[23]

Getting the Big Things Right

However incomplete or puny it may be, the developing North Korean nuclear arsenal is a matter of grave concern. So, what's to be done?

Even if negotiations stall, the United States should exclude the option of a "preemptive" military strike both in private and in public. This irresponsible idea somehow continues to attract people who really should know better. The (non-nuclear) North Korean response to such a strike could easily claim 100,000 casualties—among them U.S. forces—in Seoul and its environs within just a few days.[24] And such a strike would undoubtedly create a lasting and dangerous rift between the United States and China.

Direct, broad-ranging bilateral negotiations between the United States and North Korea that leave the other four parties far in the background are also highly unlikely to produce the definitive disarmament breakthrough that engagement advocates expect. As noted earlier, Pyongyang's behavior is not driven by the tense relationship with Washington alone, but by its us-against-the-world mentality.

That leaves the option of staying the course—engaging in the complicated, slow-going six-party talks for as long as there is a regime in North Korea to engage with. Proponents of engagement and confrontation alike have maligned this approach as lacking a proper degree of urgency; they advocate either immediately dangling more carrots or wielding a bigger stick. But the most likely result of infusing ourselves with such urgency is frustration. Furthermore, by virtue of its poverty and managerial incompetence, North Korea cannot muster a full-scale nuclear breakout. So, in fact, tomorrow likely will not be much worse than today.

Meanwhile, the six-party talks are yielding tangible benefits by serving as a forum for all the states to better appreciate each other's interests and threat perceptions. After all, the greatest threat Pyongyang poses to East Asian peace and security lies not in what it itself might do. Rather, the greatest threat lies in the potential of this crisis to play the role that the Balkan crises played in Europe in the run-up to 1914—exacerbating preexisting regional rivalries and ultimately fomenting a great power war.

The six-party talks framework can help avert that potential disastrous outcome. Indeed, North Korea's off-the-charts obstreperousness presents not just a challenge but also an opportunity for the region to develop a sense of common interest that so far has been sorely lacking. The October nuclear test actually was perfectly timed to help Japanese Prime Minister Shinzo Abe and Chinese President Hu Jintao place their two countries' relations on a more productive path. Washington should do everything it can to support the continuation of this positive trend in the relations among the region's heavyweights.

Ultimately, North Korea's behavior will be largely driven by internal factors. We cannot expect simply to bend it to our will. However, by continually promoting regional and global cohesion—not only on proliferation, but also on the other critical security problems of our time—we can maximize the chances that Pyongyang's actions will never truly shake the world, but only lightly jostle it.

Notes

1. "Joint Statement: Six-Party Talks on N. Korea Disarmament," *Washington Post,* February 13, 2007.

2. "Nuclear Bargaining," *Washington Post,* February 14, 2007, p. A18.

3. Peter Hayes, "The Stalker State: North Korean Proliferation and the End of American Nuclear Hegemony," Nautilus Institute Policy Forum Online 06-82A, October 4, 2006, available at www.nautilus.org/fora/security/0682Hayes.html.

4. Peter Hayes, "The Beijing Deal is Not the Agreed Framework," Nautilus Institute Policy Forum Online 07-014A, February 14, 2007, available at www.nautilus.org/fora/security/07014Hayes.html.

5. Aaron Friedberg, "An Offer Kim Can't Refuse," *Washington Post,* October 16, 2006, p. A21.

6. See Jerrold M. Post, *Leaders and Followers in a Dangerous World: The Psychology of Political Behavior* (Ithaca: Cornell University Press, 2004), chap. 12.

7. For a more detailed discussion, see my book *The Psychology of Nuclear Proliferation: Identity, Emotions, and Foreign Policy* (New York: Cambridge University Press, 2006).

8. Fernando A. Milia, "Armamento Nuclear en el Cono Sur: Un Dislate Estratégico" ("Nuclear Arms in the Southern Cone: A Strategic Absurdity"), *Boletín del Centro Naval,* vol. 113, no. 777, January/March 1995, pp. 87–92.

9. Transcript of Bertrand Goldschmidt interview for WGBH Boston television series *The Nuclear Age,* accessed at Liddell Hart archives, King's College, London.

10. Quoted in Raj Chengappa, *Weapons of Peace: The Secret Story of India's Quest to be a Nuclear Power* (New Delhi: HarperCollins, 2000), p. 49.

11. Atal Bihari Vajpayee, interview with *India Today,* May 25, 1998.

12. Kathryn Weathersby, "The Enigma of the North Korean Regime: Back to the Future?" in James M. Lister, ed., *Challenges Posed by the DPRK for the Alliance and the Region* (Washington: Korea Economic Institute, 2005), p. 46.

13. Balazs Szalontai and Sergey Radchenko, "North Korea's Efforts to Acquire Nuclear Technology and Nuclear Weapons: Evidence from Russian and Hungarian Archives," Cold War International History Project Working Paper #53 (Washington: Woodrow Wilson International Center for Scholars, August 2006), p. 33.

14. Ibid., p. 7

15. "Text of North Korea Announcement," *New York Times,* October 9, 2006, p. 6.

16. Richard L. Garwin and Frank N. Von Hippel, "A Technical Analysis of North Korea's October 9 Nuclear Test," *Arms Control Today,* November 2006, p. 14.

17. Comment by former State Department Korea desk chief David Straub, cited in Peter Ford, "Tenuous Deal for North Korea," *Christian Science Monitor,* February 14, 2007, p. 1.

18. See Houchang E. Chehabi and Juan J. Linz, *Sultanistic Regimes* (Baltimore: Johns Hopkins University Press, 1998). Note that Chehabi and Linz specifically exclude Stalinist Russia and Maoist China from the sultanistic category.

19. David Albright, "Iraq's Programs to Make Highly Enriched Uranium and Plutonium Prior to the Gulf War," Institute for Science and International Security, October 2002, available at www.isis-online.org/publications/iraq/iraqs_fm_history.html.

20. The Commission on the Intelligence Capabilities of the United States Regarding Weapons of Mass Destruction, *Report to the President of the United States,* March 31, 2005, p. 259. See also John Prados, "How Qaddafi Came Clean," *Bulletin of the Atomic Scientists,* November/December 2005, pp. 26–33.

21. "A CANDU Fiasco in Romania," Canadian Broadcasting Corporation, January 16, 1990, available at archives.cbc.ca/IDC-1-75-104-907/science_technology/candu/clip9.

22. David Albright and Paul Brannan, "The North Korean Plutonium Stock, February 2007," Institute for Science and International Security, February 20, 2007, available at www.isis-online.org/publications/dprk/DPRKplutoniumFEB.pdf.

23. Note that the country's supposed uranium enrichment capacity is a wild card here, but analysts now doubt the extent of such a program. See Carol Giacomo, "N. Korean Uranium Enrichment Program Fades as Issue," *Reuters,* February 10, 2007.

24. Scott Stossel, "North Korea: The War Game," *Atlantic Monthly,* July/August 2005, pp. 96–108.

JACQUES E. C. HYMANS is assistant professor of government at Smith College. He is the author of *The Psychology of Nuclear Proliferation: Identity, Emotions, and Foreign Policy* (2006).

From *Bulletin of the Atomic Scientists,* May/June 2007, pp. 45–49, 74. Copyright © 2007 by Bulletin of the Atomic Scientists. Reprinted by permission.

Requiem for the Monroe Doctrine

"The era when the United States could treat Latin America and the Caribbean as its backyard . . . is receding ever faster into history."

Daniel P. Erikson

The United States has long been suspicious of foreign powers that meddled in the Western Hemisphere. In recent years, Latin America's increasingly diverse international relations have stoked such fears anew, as the region has drawn closer to Washington's global rivals at a moment when US influence is facing unprecedented challenges. The alliance forged between Venezuela's Hugo Chávez and Iranian President Mahmoud Ahmadinejad is only the most dramatic example of a new trend that has seen Latin America and the Caribbean seek greater independence from the United States while deepening ties with emerging powers outside the hemisphere such as China, India, and Russia.

Many US policy makers understand intellectually that this increasingly complex mosaic of international relationships is the product of a more globalized world. Still, there is an underlying current of unease that American primacy in the Western Hemisphere is being threatened in subtle but important ways.

Of course, a precept of US foreign policy has long existed to address precisely this problem. It is called the Monroe Doctrine, after its creator President James Monroe, and it constitutes the iconic assertion of the United States' right to oppose foreign powers in the Western Hemisphere. Like a cat with nine lives, the Monroe Doctrine has died many times since its first articulation in 1823, only to reemerge in slightly different forms at different historical moments. Most recently, the Monroe Doctrine was buried with full honors at the end of the cold war in the early 1990s, when the collapse of the Soviet Union left the United States without an enemy to fight in Latin America.

But today the ghost of President Monroe, once a secretary of state himself, continues to stalk the halls of Foggy Bottom, and suspicions of foreign encroachment in the hemisphere are growing. The realities that formed the basis for the Monroe Doctrine have fundamentally changed, yet the United States has been slow to adjust its attitudes accordingly. If Washington wishes to be effective in Latin America, it must resist the temptation to revive the Monroe Doctrine and instead work to restore trust in inter-American relations as the region adapts to an increasingly globalized era.

What Bush Owes Monroe

If President George W. Bush were given the opportunity to go back in time and meet any historical figure, it is a safe bet that Monroe would not top his list. At first blush, the fifth and forty-third presidents appear to have little in common. Elected in 1816, Monroe was by most accounts a detail-oriented pragmatist whose nonpartisan approach to politics ushered in the "Era of Good Feelings." Bush, by contrast, preferred after his election in 2000 to focus on the big picture while leaving the details to others, and his early promises to be a "uniter not a divider" have fallen prey to rancorous partisanship and an era of unease.

Monroe did, however, lay claim to a "big picture" achievement that Bush could surely envy: creating a doctrine, bearing his name, that guided American foreign policy for well over a century. December 2, 2008, will mark the 185th anniversary of the Monroe Doctrine, the declaration by President Monroe that the United States would no longer tolerate the meddling of European powers in Latin America. Speaking in his seventh State of the Union address to Congress, Monroe declared that "the American continents, by the free and independent condition which they have assumed and maintain, are henceforth not to be considered as subjects for future colonization by any European powers. . . . We should consider any attempt on their part to extend their system to any portion of this hemisphere as dangerous to our peace and safety."

Monroe's words outlived the parochial concerns of that era to provide the philosophical underpinning for US foreign policy for decades to come. During the cold war, the doctrine was reinterpreted to support American efforts to contain the expansion of Soviet influence into the hemisphere. In 1962, for example,

President John F. Kennedy defended US actions against Cuba by saying that "the Monroe Doctrine means what it has meant since President Monroe and John Quincy Adams enunciated it, and that is that we would oppose a foreign power extending its power to the Western Hemisphere." Ronald Reagan was perhaps the last US president whose policies toward Latin America so clearly reflected the Monroe Doctrine's core principles, demonstrated especially by his administration's support for the rebels fighting against the Sandinistas—and, by proxy, the Soviets—in Nicaragua.

The Monroe Doctrine has become the phantom limb of America's posture in the hemisphere.

Presidents George H. W. Bush and Bill Clinton worried less about containing foreign powers in Latin America, instead emphasizing democratic consolidation, the war on drugs, and economic integration as the cornerstones of US policy in the region. The elder Bush presided over the last unilateral US military action in the hemisphere: the 1989 invasion of Panama to arrest the military dictator Manuel A. Noriega, an American ally turned embarrassing drug trafficker. Five years later, when Clinton staked US credibility on a well-intentioned but ultimately ill-fated effort to restore democracy to Haiti, he first asked the United Nations for permission. The Monroe Doctrine remained an animating idea in the national security consciousness, but with the end of the cold war it no longer provided a serious source of foreign policy guidance.

When George W. Bush arrived at the White House, he found a hemisphere that was increasingly democratic and market-friendly, and the specter of rival powers competing in the Americas seemed a thing of the past. On September 11, 2001, when the United States was struck by terrorist attacks, Secretary of State Colin Powell was in Lima, Peru, signing the Inter-American Democratic Charter along with representatives of 33 other democratic countries in the hemisphere.

Within a year, President Bush had made a series of major foreign policy pronouncements that came to be known collectively as the Bush Doctrine. It essentially asserted an American right to exercise unilateral military power to respond preemptively to threats from wherever they might emanate. The administration's ex post facto justifications for the Iraq War expanded the Bush Doctrine to incorporate sweeping calls to liberate the world from tyranny. In Latin America and the Caribbean, this all sounded hauntingly familiar.

It was not only the United States' southern neighbors who perceived links between the Monroe Doctrine and the Bush Doctrine. When Washington unveiled its strategy for preemptive war in 2002, a number of analysts heard echoes of the earlier doctrine. A Canadian commentator, Paul Knox, wrote in the *Toronto Globe and Mail* that "One way to read the National Security Strategy that Mr. Bush unveiled last week is as a Monroe Doctrine for the entire planet. It proposes explicitly to maintain overwhelming military supremacy around the globe."

The foreign affairs editor of London's *The Observer* argued that the Bush Doctrine recalled the Monroe Doctrine, except that "in the following 180 years, America has moved from local to regional and then to global superpower. . . . The country that once challenged those renewing their imperial ambitions in its orbit is now declaring in this document the 'manifest destiny' of Americans to exercise good across the world."

The comparisons of the two doctrines continued into Bush's second term. Reflecting on the president's second inaugural speech in January 2005, the author Tom Wolfe wrote an essay in *The New York Times* entitled "The Doctrine That Never Died." Recalling how Theodore Roosevelt dragged the Monroe Doctrine into the twentieth century by proclaiming that the United States had a right to reshape hemispheric nations guilty of "chronic wrongdoing," Wolfe argued that Bush had issued a new corollary to the Monroe Doctrine. "The notion of a sanctified Western Hemisphere depended upon its separation from the rest of the world by two vast oceans, making intrusions of any sort obvious," he wrote. "By Mr. Bush's Inauguration Day, the Hemi in Hemisphere had long since vanished, leaving the Monroe Doctrine with—what?—nothing but a single sphere . . . which is to say, the entire world." Bush, in short, wanted to update the Monroe Doctrine for the twenty-first century by extending its messianic mission around the globe.

Alas, it was not to be. The flame of the Bush Doctrine burned brightly for a few years, but its failures have extinguished much of its light. The US military experience in Iraq will likely dampen any enthusiasm for future preemptive wars, and the prospects for the United States' provoking another global wave of democratization look increasingly dim. Despite its sweeping rhetoric against tyranny, the Bush administration has failed to advance liberty in countries like Myanmar, Belarus, Pakistan, and Russia.

Meanwhile, if the Bush Doctrine was intended to raise the Monroe Doctrine to a higher plane, the result has been to crush the original doctrine's foundations. In Latin America and the Caribbean, the practical effects of the Bush Doctrine, far from revitalizing US sway in the region, have instead distracted the United States from hemispheric affairs, alienated its closest neighbors, and left Washington ill-equipped to prevent rivals from gaining a foothold in its sphere of influence. And this has occurred at a moment when Latin America is more independent and self-assured, and when the heavyweights of the developing world are seeking to cultivate alliances with countries in the region.

In recent years, China has charged into South American commodity markets to snap up goods including oil.

The New Assertiveness

The 9-11 attacks and their aftermath caused the Bush administration largely to neglect Latin America, but Washington's absence did not make the region's heart grow fonder. Instead, during the past six years virtually every country in Latin America and the

Caribbean has responded by forging its own path, showing ever less regard for US preferences. The new geopolitical environment in fact accelerated what had been a gradual trend under way in the region. This movement toward greater political independence has occurred quickly in many of the nations of South America, and more slowly in Mexico, Central America, and the Caribbean, but all countries in the region have come to grips with the post–9-11 reality.

Of course, the United States remains the dominant economic partner and an important political reference for all of Latin America and the Caribbean. Trade between the United States and the region totaled more than $550 billion in 2006, and the more than 20 million Latino immigrants who live in the United States send back another $45 billion in remittances annually. This process of integration makes it all the more ironic that Washington's views now carry far less weight in the region than at any other point in recent memory.

The decline of US influence in Latin America is driven by a confluence of positive and negative trends. The most favorable change is that the Western Hemisphere has arrived at a consensus on democratic norms, a consensus ratified by the Inter-American Democratic Charter. Setting aside the troubling case of Cuba, the spread of democracy has increased the political legitimacy of governments throughout the hemisphere—including those that dislike the United States. Washington's foes, such as Venezuela's Chávez and Nicaragua's Daniel Ortega, now have a level of democratic legitimacy that did not exist during the region's long periods of military dictatorship. The United States helped democracy take root in Latin America and the Caribbean in the 1990s, but this has created new limits on Washington's ability to intervene in these countries to pursue its own interests.

Since his election in 1998, Chávez has been the leader who poses the most severe test for US power in the region. Chávez rejects the United States' historical leadership role (which he terms "imperialism") and has strived to create a network of alliances and institutions independent of US influence. He wants to replace the International Monetary Fund and the World Bank in the region with the Latin America–dominated Banco del Sur, and exchange the Free Trade Area of the Americas for a social trade pact known as the Bolivarian Alternative for Latin America. He has funded a new Spanish-language news station, Telesur, as an alternative to American media sources. Chávez has won a limited following for these ideas in the region, and despite his recent defeat in a constitutional referendum, he still benefits from high oil prices and has five years left in his presidential term.

In an interview with *Time* magazine shortly after he called President Bush "the devil" in a speech before the United Nations in 2006, Chávez described his "Bolivarian Revolution" in the following way: "For two centuries in this hemisphere we've experienced a confrontation between two theses: America's Monroe Doctrine, which says the US should exercise hegemony over all the other republics, and the doctrine of Simón Bolívar, which envisioned a great South American republic as a counterbalance. Bush has spread the Monroe thesis globally, to make the US the police of the world—if you're not with us, he says, you're against us. We're simply doing the same now with the Bolívar thesis, a doctrine of more equality and autonomy among nations, more equilibrium of power."

Brazil, with the world's fifth-largest population and tenth-largest economy, is similarly interested in a realignment of global power that recognizes its own political and economic heft. Unlike Venezuela, however, Brazil has sought to avoid conflict and instead strengthen its global influence in tandem with its ties to the United States. Indeed, Brazilian President Luiz Inácio Lula da Silva enjoys one of the warmest relationships with President Bush of any Latin American leader, and their two nations have agreed to cooperate on a new ethanol initiative.

Still, Brazilian opposition to the Free Trade Area of the Americas helped cause its demise in 2005. And the country, as a leader of the G-20 group of developing countries, which also includes China, India, and South Africa, has clashed with the United States in world trade talks. Brazil's aggressive bid to win a permanent seat on the UN Security Council has led Lula on an international tour to drum up support for his country's global aspirations. Such diplomacy has included special outreach to the Middle East: Brazil hosted the first-ever summit between South American and Arab countries in 2005—and pointedly left Washington off the invitation list.

This independent streak is increasingly apparent throughout South America. Leaders in Ecuador, Bolivia, and Argentina have all taken steps to distance themselves from the United States. Chile and Peru have signed free trade agreements with the United States but are increasingly focused on building trade relationships in the Asia-Pacific region. Colombia remains reliant on US military aid but its stalled free trade deal in Washington has clearly soured relations with the government of Alvaro Uribe. In Mexico, Central America, and the Caribbean, economic interconnectedness with the United States remains the dominant fact of politics in the region. Mexican President Felipe Calderón has pledged to work closely with the United States to solve the problem of drug-related insecurity along the border, and El Salvador maintains troops in Iraq. Still, all Latin American countries are experiencing a diversification of political relationships, and the Caribbean is looking increasingly to China and Venezuela as key partners.

The result is that the United States can no longer dictate decisions that were once considered solely in its purview. In the 2005 election for the secretary general of the Organization of American States, the region rebuffed Washington's preferred candidates from El Salvador and Mexico, forcing it to accept Chilean socialist José Miguel Insulza as the consensus candidate. In 2006, US officials disapproved of awarding a first-round election victory to presidential candidate René Préval in Haiti when his vote tally fell just short of the 50 percent margin required for outright victory. But the Bush administration's reluctance to join the UN mission in Haiti left Latin American nations like Brazil, Argentina, and Chile in the driver's seat, and they brushed aside US concerns to deliver a quick victory to Préval. Even in Cuba, the United States vowed to block Fidel Castro's succession strategy, only to watch from the sidelines as Raúl Castro consolidated his power and renewed the island's relations with Europe, Latin America, and Asia. The power dynamic in the Western Hemisphere has tilted away from the United States, but Washington has been reluctant to adapt its playbook accordingly.

Expanding Horizons

Latin America and the Caribbean in recent years have sought to capitalize on booming commodity prices in global markets to diversify their trade ties beyond the United States, especially with Europe and Asia. In 2006, total trade between the European Union and Latin America reached a record $177 billion. Although this equals only one-third of US–Latin American trade, the EU's share is growing at a fast pace, led by Germany, Spain, Italy, and the Netherlands. Currently, the EU's top trading partners in the region are Brazil, Mexico, Chile, Argentina, and Venezuela. The union is also negotiating a trade agreement with the Central American countries, and is in preliminary discussions with the Andean Community and the South American Common Market (Mercosur). In December, Mercosur signed a free trade agreement with Israel, its first with any country outside the Western Hemisphere, and Brazil's foreign minister declared that the trade bloc "is open to the world."

In Asia, Japan remains one of Latin America's biggest investors and trading partners. Japanese officials, worried that trade growth is languishing, are focusing on reactivating the economic relationship with the region. China is already having a big impact on Latin American economies. India, also scouring the region for investments in the oil sector, is the next giant on the horizon.

Even Russia is renewing ties with Latin America that had been virtually dormant since the collapse of the Soviet Union. In June 2004, Vladimir Putin made the first-ever visit to Mexico by a Russian president for talks focusing on military sales. Later that year he attended the Asia-Pacific Economic Cooperation summit in Chile, and then visited Brazil to initiate cooperation in satellite technology and oil exploration. In 2007, the Russian leader attended an international Olympics meeting in Guatemala and then promised to cooperate with that country on electricity production, prompting then-President Oscar Berger to describe Putin as "one of the brightest leaders in today's world."

As a network of ties emerges between Iran and Latin America, Chávez is vowing to "unite the Persian Gulf and the Caribbean."

Russian arms sales to the region amounted to only $300 million for the period from 1998 to 2001, but they have since escalated dramatically. In 2006, Russia's military sales to Venezuela alone totaled $3 billion (including 100,000 Kalishnikov assault rifles), and hundreds of millions more in weapons were sold to other Latin American countries. If the pace of military trade continues, Russia's arms sales to Latin America will soon surpass the records set by the Soviet Union.

But perhaps no country has flummoxed US policy makers as much as the People's Republic of China, which has established itself as the new power to be reckoned with in the Western Hemisphere.

China's Inroads

China's emerging role in Latin America and the Caribbean perfectly encapsulates the new challenge facing US policy makers in the hemisphere as they wrestle with the legacy of the Monroe Doctrine. On one hand, China is viewed as a growing rival that is seeking to achieve economic and military parity with the United States and must therefore be treated with caution. On the other hand, the United States and China have deep economic ties, including one of the largest trade relationships in the world, and the two countries cooperate on a wide range of issues.

In recent years, China has charged into South American commodity markets to snap up goods including oil, agricultural products, and heavy metals, and has used promises of trade and aid to win over most of Taiwan's remaining allies in the region. Just a decade ago, China was viewed as a peripheral actor in the Western Hemisphere. Today, though far from being a dominant player, China is a top-five trading partner of most Latin American countries, and has become a relevant actor in hemispheric affairs.

In 2001, Chinese President Jiang Zemin's landmark visit to the region was followed by a wave of exchanges among Chinese and Latin American senior officials and business leaders to discuss political, economic, and military concerns. Jiang's successor, Hu Jintao, traveled to Argentina, Brazil, Chile, and Cuba in 2004 and visited Mexico in 2005. The presidents of all of these countries (and several others) have subsequently paid reciprocal visits to China. Growing political engagement has accompanied the skyrocketing volume of trade between China and the region, which totaled an estimated $80 billion in 2007. China has also become a strong competitor with the United States in sales of manufactured goods, making deep inroads into markets in Mexico and Central America and, more recently, in Brazil and Argentina.

Rising Chinese influence in Latin America has prompted some US officials and members of Congress to view China as the most serious challenge to US economic and security interests in the region since the end of the cold war. American policy makers cite concerns about stable access to the Panama Canal, the deployment of Chinese peace-keepers in Haiti, China's support for Castro, and Beijing's growing claims to Venezuelan oil. In 2004, when President Hu's three-week tour through Latin America sparked feverish speculation about how this new relationship would affect US interests, a rash of publications warned of the "China threat" on America's southern flank.

There is little question that Chinese competition for Latin America's energy resources has created a new and uncertain dynamic for US policy makers. Even the most benign interpretation of Chinese penetration into Latin American markets—that China is growing and needs resources, while the region is searching for new customers—implies a potential loss for US business interests. Some analysts in 2004 ominously warned of an emerging anti-American alliance, led by China and Venezuela, that might include other energy-exporting nations in Latin America and elsewhere. Others argued that China's new role could benefit both Latin America and the United States by fueling the region's economic growth.

Seeking to defuse the growing wariness about Chinese intentions in Latin America, the United States has shifted course to engage China from a more cooperative stance. In 2004, China became an observer at the Organization of American States, and discussions are ongoing about bringing the country into the Inter-American Development Bank. In the spring of 2006, US Assistant Secretary of State Thomas Shannon traveled to Beijing for a first round of dialogue with Chinese officials on Latin American affairs, and follow-up talks were held in Washington in November 2007. The United States even persuaded China to back a one-year extension of the UN peacekeeping mission in Haiti (which includes 125 Chinese riot police), despite the fact that Haiti's recognition of Taiwan remains a sore spot for Beijing.

Only time will tell if the State Department's vision of converting China from a potential threat into a responsible stakeholder in Latin America will be achieved. Still, the new emphasis on diplomacy offers a novel strategy for dealing with rival powers in the US sphere of influence, replacing containment with mechanisms for cooperation. Whether this would leave Monroe nodding his approval or spinning in his grave is anyone's guess.

Mullahs in the Backyard

Washington's China fever had barely dissipated when a new and more ominous specter raised its head in Latin America—in the form of the Islamic Republic of Iran. In September 2007, the Bush administration's efforts to curtail Iran's nuclear ambitions had brought the two countries to the brink of confrontation at the United Nations. By that time, Iran had already succeeded in cultivating a range of new allies in Latin America, most prominently Chávez. President Ahmadinejad encountered a hostile reception in New York during his September trip to speak at the UN, but afterwards he flew directly to Caracas, where Chávez warmly greeted him.

The Venezuelan president praised Ahmadinejad's Columbia University speech, which had followed a harshly critical introduction by the university's president. "An imperial spokesman tried to disrespect you, calling you a cruel little tyrant," Chávez told him. "You responded with the greatness of a revolutionary." From Venezuela, Ahmadinejad traveled to Bolivia. That country's president, Evo Morales, had just days earlier appeared on "The Daily Show with Jon Stewart," during which he said, "Please don't consider me part of the 'axis of evil.'" But back in Bolivia, Morales met with Ahmadinejad for five hours, established diplomatic relations between the two countries, and signed an economic cooperation agreement worth $1 billion over five years.

Ahmadinejad's most recent trip to Latin America highlighted the Iranian government's ambitious diplomatic efforts to create new allies in the traditional US sphere of influence. Chávez has emerged as the godfather and relationship manager, striving to draw in other allies such as Bolivia, Ecuador, and Nicaragua. Iran's courtship is moving quickly. In September 2006, Ahmadinejad attended the Non-Aligned Movement summit in Havana and met with Chávez in Caracas. In January 2007, the Iranian president was treated as an honored guest in Venezuela, Nicaragua, and Ecuador. Chávez called him a "hero of the struggle against American imperialism." Nicaraguan President Daniel Ortega met with him to discuss "common interests, common enemies, and common goals." Ecuadorian President Rafael Correa exchanged warm words with Ahmadinejad as well.

Chávez and Ahmadinejad see political benefits to their alliance, and they also claim economic benefits. The two countries have signed 180 agreements since 2001, in areas such as gas and oil exploration and petrochemical and agricultural production. Officials claim the agreements are worth $20 billion, though bilateral trade has been less than $20 million annually. Chávez recently granted Iran observer status in the Bolivarian Alternative for the Americas, his leftist trade-pact group. Iran and Venezuela have also announced a $2 billion development fund for "anti-imperialist" countries, though the money has been predictably slow to materialize. And Tehran has promised to finance a $350 million deep-water port and build 10,000 houses in poverty-stricken Nicaragua, whose president has defended Iran's nuclear program at the UN.

To be sure, Ahmadinejad remains an unwelcome figure in other parts of Latin America—including Argentina, where Iran was allegedly involved in the 1994 bombing of a Jewish community center in Buenos Aires; and in Brazil, where Lula has repeatedly rebuffed meeting requests. Even so, the United States has been at a loss about how to counter Iran's growing influence in the region, or even how to fully calculate its impact on US interests.

Clearly, Iran is neither a benign force in world affairs nor a major power capable of posing a threat on par with the Soviet Union during the cold war. Iran's interest in Latin America could just be an example of normal state-to-state diplomacy or an attempt to lay the foundation for more sinister plans. But the fact that it is occurring at all unearths latent fears associated with the Monroe Doctrine. It also underlines that the United States has limited options in its efforts to counteract foreign powers in the Western Hemisphere, with intelligence collection and diplomacy taking precedence over unilateral military action. Meanwhile, as a network of ties emerges between Iran and Latin America, Chávez is vowing to "unite the Persian Gulf and the Caribbean."

Is There a Doctrine in the House?

President Bush entered office vowing to strengthen and intensify US relations with Latin America. His administration instead has presided over an era that paradoxically has seen expanded economic ties between the United States and Latin America while leaving Washington's political influence in the hemisphere greatly reduced. Still, the United States has much to be happy about in Latin America. To some degree, US policy has been a victim of its own success in ensuring that democratic norms have taken hold throughout the region. Moreover, Latin American peoples have largely elected leaders whose respect for democracy and commitment to market economics are in sync with the United States.

Frictions on trade policy and immigration continue to plague US relations with the two largest countries in the region—Brazil and Mexico—but this has not prevented constructive ties on a wide range of issues. US relations with the Caribbean and much of Central and South America remain positive on balance. Venezuela's Chávez will continue to be a thorn in the side of the United States for the foreseeable future, but his "Bolivarian Revolution" shows signs of reaching its natural limits.

Latin America's increasing connectedness with the rest of the world does not inherently undermine US interests, but Washington will continue to find these links disturbing in certain cases. Despite the current calm, China's role in the Western Hemisphere will become increasingly controversial as that country evolves into a major world power in the coming decades. Iran is a new factor to contend with, and broader links between Latin America and the Middle East are certain to grow. Putin's Russia is selling billions of dollars' worth of weapons in the region, and other nontraditional actors likely will emerge in the years to come. Even the "hermit kingdom" of North Korea has opened talks with the Dominican Republic and Guatemala.

What does all this mean for President Monroe's doctrine? The Bush Doctrine may share an intellectual heritage with the Monroe Doctrine, but the practical implementation of Bush's foreign policy has created a climate that has eviscerated what was left of the Monroe Doctrine's relevance in Latin America. The United States has been distracted at a time when rivals like China, Iran, and Russia are newly emboldened to seek alliances in the region. Economic globalization in any event has assured Latin America's increasing connectivity to nations across the oceans, essentially rendering obsolete Monroe's vision of a hemisphere under US tutelage. In 2008, the Monroe Doctrine has become the phantom limb of America's posture in the hemisphere: US policy makers still occasionally feel its tingle, but no weight can be put on it.

The major candidates for the American presidency have all vowed, with varying degrees of enthusiasm and specificity, to reverse the perception of US neglect and reenergize relationships with Latin America and the Caribbean. The change in presidential administrations will undoubtedly introduce fresh thinking that will be helpful to US-Latin American relations, whoever wins the White House. President Bush's successor, however, will find a region that has changed dramatically since the 1990s, in ways both good and bad, and that is increasingly reluctant to resume its dependence on US leadership.

Given all the pressing challenges elsewhere in the world that will confront the next administration, prospects for developing a major new doctrine to replace the Monroe Doctrine as a guide for US policy in the hemisphere seem remote at best. With serious engagement and intelligent policy choices, the next US president will still have the opportunity to help guide the hemispheric community of nations. But the era that began 185 years ago with the declaration of the Monroe Doctrine—the era when the United States could treat Latin America and the Caribbean as its backyard—is receding ever faster into history.

DANIEL P. ERIKSON is a senior associate for US policy and director of Caribbean programs at Inter-American Dialogue.

Mirror-Imaging the Mullahs
Our Islamic Interlocutors

Reuel Marc Gerecht

In 1993, Bernard Hourcade, a geographer, sociologist, and Persianist who was the head of Iranian studies at the Centre National de la Recherche Scientifique, got a bit of a shock. After completing lengthy negotiations on the first cultural and scientific exchange between France and the Islamic Republic, the Iranian delegation demanded the agreement open with the words: *Bismillah ar-Rahman ar-Rahim* ("In the Name of God, the Compassionate and the Merciful"). The negotiations were supposed to be a friendly *arrangement,* something less formal than an *accord.* So the French were aghast that the Iranians, whom Hourcade and the other French scholars and diplomats had known for years, would demand the Koranic invocation. The Iranians understood well the secular ethos of France. Ali Akbar Hashemi-Rafsanjani, then the president of the Islamic Republic, was even then making a determined pitch for more French investment and trade.

Exasperated and operating independently from the French foreign ministry, Hourcade responded that Tehran would either withdraw this stipulation or Paris would begin booting Iranian scholars and scientists from France. Within twenty-four hours, the Iranians informed Hourcade that the Islamic Republic would not object to the removal of the Koran's most famous lines.

The episode, like the contretemps provoked by President Mohammad Khatami when he visited France in 1999 and Spain in 2002, and insisted that wine not be served at official banquets (the French and the Spanish cancelled the dinners rather than forego the wine), conveys a truth not so easy for Westerners to accept. Even on *minor* issues, religion—and in particular, the devout version of Islam that governments like Iran's embrace—can intrude, distort, and paralyze. The Koran says nothing about banning wine for non-believers, let alone non-believers living in their own lands, or that wine by its mere presence compromises the faithful. Ayatollah Ruhollah Khomeini, who spent most of his life explicating and defending the Holy Law, upheld the religious right of Iranian Christians in Iran to produce and drink wine in their homes and in their churches. Yet here we were seventeen years later listening to a reformist cleric, who had loudly promoted a "dialogue of civilizations," demand that Frenchmen abstain from their national drink.

There is a lesson here: God may be kaput in most of the West, but he has hardly been reduced to the status of personal philosophy in Islamic lands. And, yet, our God-diminishing, mirror-imaging impulse keeps blinding us to Islam's place at the center of the political realm. The tendency to view Muslims through secular eyes, or to recast them and their faith into a version of Christianity ("Islam is a religion of peace"), is perhaps the greatest impediment to rational American policy. Whether it be clerical Iran's nuclear program, Pakistan on the brink, the Israeli-Palestinian imbroglio, Saudi Arabia and its Wahhabis, or Egypt's ice-cold relations with Israel, religion offers the one indispensable prism through which to peer into the region. For if we cannot see the Middle East first and foremost on its own terms, which means, among other things, never forgetting that Muslim states define themselves as exactly that, then we will surely find ourselves caught in binds worse than Iraq.

In March 2003, the State Department and the Central Intelligence Agency—the two institutions that enjoyed the most contact with Iraqis under Saddam Hussein—viewed Iraq as the most secular nation in the Arab world. Influential Iraqi expatriates, among them Ayad Allawi, Ahmed Chalabi, Adnan Pachachi, and Kanan Makiya, bolstered this view, suggesting further that a free Iraq could and should be led by Westernized Iraqis not known for their religious beliefs. In truth, Iraq under Saddam Hussein had become a profoundly religious place for Sunnis and Shiites alike. That no one seemed to realize this owes something to the fact that Iraqi intellectuals, usually smitten with some variation of Arab nationalism, socialism, or Communism, were not inclined to linger on antiquated topics such as religion. Western scholars, usually possessed of the same progressive mindset, avoided probing too deeply. Regional experts, for example, considered Hanna Batatu's magisterial work, *The Old Social Classes and New Revolutionary Movements of Iraq,* published in 1978, to be the bible of contemporary Iraq studies. It is also a wasteland. We can read that enormous work and come away thinking that modern Iraq, one of the central lands of Islamic history, and key to the development of Shiite identity, is a country of irreversibly fading faith. If the Bush administration, for one, had understood that the opposite was true, it would have also understood that election plans that ignored Grand Ayatollah Ali Sistani, the country's preeminent Shiite jurisprudent, were doomed; it would have recognized at the outset how rich Sunni soil was for al-Qaeda and other Islamic extremists; it would have gleaned the depth of the Sunni-Shiite divide; and it would have sent more troops.

Then again, we always make the same mistakes. In the nine years (1985–1994) that I spent in the Central Intelligence Agency working on Middle Eastern issues, especially on the "Iranian target," I cannot recall a single serious conversation about Islam as a faith, and about why a glimpse of the divine inspired an entire generation of young Iranian men to draw closer to God through war and death. In part this was because the organization veered toward "hard-fact" reporting. Intelligence services need to know about the size, disposition, and quality of soldiers and their material, about potentially lethal imports and exports, and about technical progress in the drive for weapons of mass destruction. Needless to say, few Iranians with a passionate commitment to the Almighty associated with the CIA. Serving Allah and serving Langley was a difficult philosophical proposition.

The CIA, like the State Department, is a secular institution where officers typically do not discuss their faith (or, more to the point, lack thereof) or the faith of others. Friends at Langley tell me that even today there remains little sustained attention to the question of how believing Muslims, country by country, view the outside world, or how Saudi-supported militant Salafi teachings have gobbled up mosques and religious schools throughout the once virulently anti-Wahhabi lands of the eastern Mediterranean. For spooks, such "hearts and minds" reporting belongs in the arena of covert action, not "foreign intelligence" collection, where proper case officers ply their trade. And covert action, never a large-scale enterprise in the Middle East as it was in Cold War Europe, is dead as a doornail at Langley.

More broadly, educated Westerners tend to assume that, like themselves, well-educated Middle Eastern Muslims possess too much common sense for religion to determine their political behavior. People naturally associate with their own kind. Secularists attract secularists. Westerners usually don't seek out devout Muslims, at least not for long. The effect of all this on our image of the Muslim Middle East has been substantial. The American-educated Iranian political scientist, Mohammad Hadi Semati, who until recently worked at the Woodrow Wilson Center, had a significant impact on Washington's Iran analysts. A delightful fellow who socialized easily with Americans, Semati, who has since returned to the University of Tehran, offered up a treasure trove of information about the Westernized Iranians who hover around the clerical elite's "pragmatists" and reformers. For Washington's Iran-lookers, who rarely if ever travel to the Islamic Republic because the regime won't issue them visas (or because it will imprison them), Semati provided what Western journalists rarely do: detailed, colorful, and delicious gossip about the players in Tehran.

Yet, Semati and his fellow Iranian progressives, precisely because they think and dream more or less as we do, have also been among the most errant analysts of their homeland. Iran's liberal intellectual elite, whose members flourished briefly under Mohammad Khatami's presidency, and who have become devotees of former president Ali Akbar Hashemi Rafsanjani, labor mightily to depict an Iran that is beyond a Thermidorian Reaction. Real innovative religious discussions—the kind of anti-clerical philosophical commentary that one used to hear from the lay (and now downtrodden) Islamist Abd al-Karim Soroush—don't figure in this progressive crowd simply because the religious dimension has too much salience. Thus, Semati didn't anticipate Mahmoud Ahmadinejad being a serious contender in Iran's 2005 presidential election. Instead, he predicted another victory by Rafsanjani, the ultimate pragmatist. "All of my friends thought Rafsanjani was going to win," Semati remarked to me after Ahmadinejad crushed the *gorbeh* (the cat), Iran's most politically adept and probably most despised cleric. In the progressive telling, Ahmadinejad was just too religious, too coarse to prevail in "post-revolutionary" Iran, which, the progressives assured us, was more prepared to make peace with America than America was prepared to make peace with it.

Not surprisingly, then, their American friends assumed no differently. When I was an advisor to the Iraq Study Group, the overwhelming majority of my colleagues thought that America under George W. Bush, not Iran under Ali Khamenei, deserved more blame for delaying the restoration of "normalcy" between the two states. In its deliberations and its final recommendations, the ISG barely acknowledged Islam. Read a stack of essays and op-eds about the Middle East by Bush père's former national security advisor, Brent Scowcroft, one of America's preeminent realists, and the words "Islam" and "Muslim" seldom appear, much less any discussion of how Islam as understood and practiced by Iran's rulers could affect American diplomacy—which, in Scowcroft's eyes, really ought to be able "to assuage Iran's security concerns and temper its urge to acquire a nuclear capability." (Realists have a way of making devout Muslims sound as if they mostly require a sympathetic and reassuring psychotherapist.) For his part, Zbigniew Brzezinski prefers to see contemporary "Islamism" as a movement "led by secular intellectuals," which combines "militant populism with a religious gloss."

Islamism, however, comes much closer to being an authentic expression of Islam than Brzezinski realizes. Devout Muslims probably constitute a majority in every Muslim country in the Middle East. Iran may—just may—be the exception, twenty-eight years of theocracy having dampened the average Iranian's attachment to his faith and its clerical custodians. Who, then, qualifies as devout? Someone who believes the Koran embodies the literal word of God and that the Holy Law, the *Sharia,* ought to be revered and obeyed. Devout Muslims can pick and choose to an extent, allowing local customs, man-made legislation, and human weaknesses to intrude into their everyday lives. But the Sacred Law remains the beloved ideal.

A devout Muslim also loves history. He may do so selectively, ignoring the complexity and diverse strains of medieval and modern Islam in favor of the imagined clarity of early Islam under the Prophet Mohammad. The glories of Islam, foremost among them the faith's unrivaled military conquests, endure vividly for the believer. So, too, memories of the Christian counterattack in the Levant and Andalusia (memories revived, ironically, by Western Orientalists; Saladin has a special place in contemporary Muslim literature not least because Christians recall, seldom accurately, Richard the Lionheart, not because Muslims have always revered Saladin). Memories notwithstanding, devout Muslims can certainly be sincere and devoted friends of Americans. They can, in the right circumstances, even be America's friends.

But it is neither a natural nor easy friendship. In the congressionally sponsored 2003 report on Public Diplomacy for the Arab and Muslim World, "Changing Minds Winning Peace," former ambassador Edward Djerejian, the chairman of the advisory group, avers that "Our adversaries' success in the struggle of ideas is all the more stunning because American values are so widely shared. As one of our Iranian interlocutors put it, 'Who has anything against life, liberty, and the pursuit of happiness?'" Odds are extraordinarily good that this Iranian is highly Westernized, doesn't pray often or at all, and would be hard-pressed to discuss the Koran in detail. For a devout Muslim, "happiness" derives exclusively from the believer's faithfulness to God's commandments and hence his odds of going up, not down, in the afterlife. The idea of "fun" is something difficult for him to digest fully.

If the urge to pursue "happiness" is not a self-evident truth, as Djerejian implies, neither is the Western concept of liberty—that is, the rights that the individual can claim against government, and the corollary freedom to follow one's curiosity and dreams so long as they do not impinge on the autonomy of others. Having banished religion from their conversation, American and European elites are supremely confident—devout Muslims would say mistakenly so—that their enlightened ideas and values have universal resonance. Yet, it is preposterous to suggest, as some in the West do, that only Taliban-like Muslims oppose what we label as basic human or "universal" rights. Hard-core fundamentalists aren't the only Muslims who understand that the Koranic injunction, "commanding the right and forbidding the wrong," probably the defining ethical commandment in the Muslim Holy Book, is inherently incompatible with modern Western sentiment and law.

In the Islamic world, moreover, the personal really is political. Although Muslim governments often have awful relations with each other, and friendlier relations with Washington, this isn't a reality they advertise with pride. The contemporary Muslim ideal, as expressed in the Organization of the Islamic Conference, tends to be highly traditional on this count: Muslims ought to have closer relations with one another than they have with nonbelievers. Sayyid Qutb, one of the primary theoreticians behind today's Islamic revival, was hardly alone among Muslims in reacting to America's pulsating culture with both fascination and horror. As Osama bin Laden knows well, Saudis, among the most repressed Muslims on the planet, constantly bounce between this yin and yang. Believing Muslims who have no intention whatsoever of becoming holy warriors frequently react to American permissiveness and consumerism with the same mixture of curiosity and revulsion.

To be sure, exposure to the West has colored the dreams, professional expectations, and worldly knowledge of Muslims. The Islamic World has always been highly syncretistic—up to a point. When the Mongols nearly buried Islam in the thirteenth century, the Mameluks, the resolutely devout slave soldiers of Egypt who stopped the Mongol advance in 1260 at Ayn Jalut, acquired many of the trappings of Mongol culture. Since the eighteenth century, the Islamic World has absorbed Western language, thought, manners, architecture, food, furniture, and clothes. But that does not mean Muslims became any less Muslim. It does mean that today's devout Muslims comprehend Western concepts—and Western challenges—better than their forefathers. Ayatollah Mohammad Taqi Mesbah Yazdi, the so-called spiritual advisor to Ahmadinejad, who can expatiate endlessly on the poisonous nature of the West, can easily give the Karl Popper–obsessed Mohammad Khatami a run for his money in his appreciation of Plato, Aristotle, and the philosophical foundations of Western thought. Men of unquestionable faith can be "populists" or calm, black-eyed lawyers who connect in solitary ways with God; they can be pacifists and warriors. As much as Saint Augustine or Saint Thomas Aquinas, the Algerian Islamist leaders Abbassi Madani and Ali Belhadj, or Iran's Mohammad Khatami and Mesbah-Yazdi, view themselves as God's men trying to keep the faithful on the "straight path." Their brand of Islam has no less authenticity than a spinning Sufi dervish whose spiritual roots lie in pagan and Christian neo-Platonism.

Members of the U.S. foreign policy bureaucracy tend to see these members of the ruling Iranian elite as bearded versions of themselves—men who do not believe that morality and other "abstract" ideas have much of a role in foreign affairs. They have the hardest time seeing the obvious: When Khamenei, a man of principle and integrity, calls the United States the "enemy of God," he means it.

The Islamic Republic, itself based on the idea that Iran exists to further the cause of Islam, has always taken substantial risks in the name of its mission. It seized American hostages and kept them for a year; it aided and abetted the killing of 241 American servicemen in Lebanon; it sent or supported assassination teams around the globe during the 1990s to murder Jews and dissidents in the very same countries where it was trying to promote trade ties; in 1996, it murdered nineteen American airmen in Saudi Arabia three weeks before making its formal application to the World Trade Organization; and it granted, according to the 9/11 Commission Report, free passage to members of al-Qaeda after the 1998 bombing of the U.S. embassies in Africa.

American and European realists tend to ignore this last episode since it unravels the conceit that the Islamic Republic has become, for all its theological eccentricities and deplorable behavior at home, a country you can do business with. Or, if absolutely necessary, contain. Regardless of what one thinks of the latest National Intelligence Estimate, those prone to substituting Communism for Iran's militant faith and suggesting that, like the Soviet Union or Red China before it, Iran's clerical regime can be deterred from reckless conduct abroad and overwhelmed by its own internal contradictions, ought to recall that the Soviet Union as a going philosophical proposition lasted fewer than seven decades. The jihadist impulse in Islam has lasted almost 1400 years. Communism was a post-Christian, Western materialist dream: it did not aim to save men's souls. It promised to improve their mundane lives—and could be graded accordingly. Is it really necessary to point out that Islam, by contrast, is not about economics? When Iran's rulers refer to the United States as the "enemy of God," they aren't taking their cues from the dialectic.

To Iran's clerics, the obstacle to closer relations is fairly straightforward: America epitomizes the anti-Islamic. For Rafsanjani, Khomeini and Ahmadinejad, who view Iran, like their beloved teacher Khomeini, as the sword and shield of God's will on earth, mutually beneficial relations between the United States and the Islamic Republic do not fall within the realm of theological possibility. Short-term compromises can be found only on issues that do not raise existential questions. For example, Tehran encouraged the Sunni Dari-speaking Afghan Tajiks to cooperate with the non-Taliban, American-backed Pashtuns in establishing a government in Kabul. (Primary benefit to the clerical regime: One million–plus much-disliked Sunni Afghan refugees could go home.) But the occasional compromise does not mean that Iran has forsaken its faith and will to expend blood and treasure—to the outsider's eye, often with irrational zeal—to advance its causes. Saudi Arabia and Iran have spent billions of dollars—at times when neither country was flush with funds—to advance their respective visions of Islam. The issues that animate the Islamic Republic's *mission civilisatrice*—support to Hizbollah, Hamas and Islamic Jihad, or the radicalization of the Iraqi Shia, which counts, with the possible exception of the quest for nuclear weaponry, as the most important foreign policy goal of the clerical regime—are not up for negotiation.

Viewing the Middle East through an Islamic lens leaves us uneasy, though not in complete despair. The Islamic revival, which has been vigorously underway since the 1960s, shows no signs of diminishing; there exists scant evidence that the dictatorships and kingdoms, which have done so much to encourage the trend, can reverse it now. Unlike Christianity, Islam dominates the public square, and until Muslims begin to battle openly about the proper scope of public discourse, reforming the theory and practice of Islamic law and governance seems extremely unlikely.

Even if Iraq stabilizes and democracy in the country gains depth, anti-Americanism will still be a staple of the Iraqi street. However, anti-American excuses and conspiracy theories can only go so far in electoral politics. In the end, democracy in Iraq ought to be a significant check at least on the holy-warrior virus. Elsewhere, as the Islamic identity grows stronger in the Arab heartland, a lasting Israeli-Palestinian accommodation will recede further into the future. A more self-consciously Islamic Egypt, the great intellectual engine of anti-Americanism in the Arab world, will continue to pump out hatred of America and the West, and behind the scenes, for both religious and selfish reasons, do what it can to sabotage Israeli–Palestinian negotiations. And Pakistan, perhaps the most dynamic Islamist stronghold, where first-rate minds with first-rate educations espouse ever-harsher ideologies, could radicalize even further under an impossible burden: To be a nation-state defined exclusively by Islamic identity when only Islamists really have any firm idea of what this means. (One thing it certainly means is that the United States can expect to be fighting in neighboring Afghanistan for a *very* long time.)

On the upside of the ledger, modernity, especially the female side of it, continues to rearrange the ethics of Muslim homes and communities. The Westernization of Muslim women appears to be unstoppable, although it's not so clear how this will play out. Highly Westernized Muslim women in Europe and the Middle East are, like their brothers, rediscovering their Islamic identities and re-segregating themselves from men. But modernization could eventually modify this arrangement, and one has to suspect that the fundamentalist critics of Western rights for women have it right: they will reorder Islamic societies as they exist today.

Also on the personal scale, the Islamic conception of each believer as a deputy of God—the certainty that every Muslim can discern the beauty and superiority of his faith—contains within it the seeds of religious reformation and possibly even democratic growth. Grand Ayatollah Sistani's call to Muslims to exercise their God-given right to vote amounts to a variation of this theme. In particular, modern Sunni Islam's profound egalitarianism—the insistence that God and His law treat all men equally and a distaste for state-controlled religious authority—seems tailor-made for a system of representative government. Restored democracy in Pakistan—the protesting lawyers in Pakistan today should give us hope—could break and reverse the country's radicalization, as Muslims of all stripes debate the relationship between Man, God, and parliamentary legislation.

For the most part, this is not a liberal debate, as we witnessed with the Islamic Salvation Front in Algeria. It is simply a debate about how believing Muslims can encourage legitimate governance. The dialogue in the Arab Middle East is, if anything, part of the region's growing religiosity. Unintentionally, the Islamic Republic of Iran has accelerated the trend by making everything public have a religious dimension. What would be everyday civic criticism in the West assumes religious overtones in Iran. In fact, many clerical dissidents see political pluralism as a means of salvaging the faith. The clerical regime still boasts many hard-core adherents who define happiness as wounding America. But the live-to-die drive, which al-Qaeda has in spades, seems attenuated among most Iranians, if not their rulers.

Alas, Islamic terrorism of the 9/11 variety remains an omnipresent possibility, at least until the Islamist wave recedes among Sunnis and from the halls of power in Tehran. Until things do calm down, it would be good to recall what Bernard Hourcade knew in 1993: the West can intimidate and deter Islamic militants if the West responds to them with sufficient force, and soon enough—before they conclude, as they often have, that the West won't do anything at all. We should not deceive ourselves into believing that Muslim societies express themselves hypocritically: if Wahhabis or Khomeinists dominate political culture at home, they will dominate foreign policy abroad. The secular, "pro-American" autocratic political cultures that have defined much of the Middle East since World War II are dying, if not dead. The United States would do well not to pretend otherwise.

REUEL MARC GERECHT is a resident fellow at the American Enterprise Institute. He is the author of *Know Thine Enemy: A Spy's Journey into Revolutionary Iran* and *The Islamic Paradox: Shiite Clerics, Sunni Fundamentalists, and the Coming of Arab Democracy.*

From *World Affairs Journal,* Winter 2008, pp. 91–100. Copyright © 2008 by World Affairs Journal. Reprinted by permission.

U.S. Africa Command
A New Strategic Paradigm?

SEAN McFATE

This new command will strengthen our security cooperation with Africa and help to create new opportunities to bolster the capabilities of our partners in Africa. Africa Command will enhance our efforts to help bring peace and security to the people of Africa and promote our common goals of development, health, education, democracy, and economic growth in Africa.[1]

—President George W. Bush

On 6 February 2007, the president announced the establishment of a tenth unified combatant command called Africa Command, or "AFRICOM." Its area of responsibility will cover Africa, and it will have an unprecedented number of interagency civilians in leadership roles (including a civilian deputy commander). This new command's objective will be to enhance Department of Defense (DOD) efforts to assist African partners in achieving a more stable environment through security cooperation.

Yet questions abound. AFRICOM's vision, as outlined by the president on the day of its public unveiling, is anomalous among unified commands. Words like "development, health, education, democracy, and economic growth" are atypical of military missions, which traditionally center on fighting and winning wars. In many ways, AFRICOM is a post-Cold War experiment that radically rethinks security in the early 21st century based on peacebuilding lessons learned since the fall of the Berlin Wall. Will it work? This article explores possibilities by analyzing AFRICOM's origins, timing, strategy, and composition as well as the early challenges that will confront the nascent command.

Why AFRICOM?

AFRICOM originated as an internal administrative change within DOD that remedies "an outdated arrangement left over from the Cold War," in the words of Secretary of Defense Robert Gates.[2] Or, in the words of Ambassador Robert Loftis, the former senior State Department member of the AFRICOM transition team, it was created because "Africa is more important to us strategically and deserves to be viewed through its own lens."[3] That lens is the new unified command.

Unified commands, or combatant commands, were instituted during the Cold War to better manage military forces for possible armed confrontation with the Soviet Union and its proxies. Today, they are prisms through which the Pentagon views the world. Each command is responsible for coordinating, integrating, and managing all Defense assets and operations in its designated area of responsibility, per the Unified Command Plan. This plan is regularly reviewed, modified as required, and approved by the president.

The unified command design has proven problematic for DOD's involvement in Africa, a continent not viewed as strategically significant during the Cold War. That DOD never designated a unified command for Africa evinces the want of concern for one of the largest and most conflict-prone continents on the planet. Instead, DOD divided African coverage between three unified commands: European Command (EUCOM), Central Command (CENTCOM), and Pacific Command (PACOM). This lack of focus had several deleterious effects.

The first effect is that Africa was never a number-one priority for any unified command. Each viewed its strategic imperative as being elsewhere, leaving Africa as a secondary or even tertiary concern. For example, EUCOM's strategic center of gravity has always been Europe, with the overwhelming majority of its forces, staff, and resources dedicated to that continent, even after the fall of the Berlin Wall.

Second, the three-part division of responsibility violates the principle of unity of command, increasing the likelihood of an uncoordinated DOD effort in Africa. This disunity can occur especially at the "seams" between unified commands; for instance, a hypothetical U.S. military response to the crisis in the Darfur region might be complicated because the area of interest straddles the EUCOM and CENTCOM boundary, causing coordination challenges.[4]

Third, owing to historical disinterest, DOD never developed a sizable cadre of dedicated African experts. Only within the past decade has DOD invested in the Africa Center for Strategic Studies (a think tank akin to the George C. Marshall European Center for Security Studies in Germany) to support the development of U.S. strategic policy towards Africa.

Lastly, Africa has never benefited from the advocacy of a four-star commander whose undiluted mandate includes helping policymakers understand the perspectives of African countries and formulate effective African security policy.

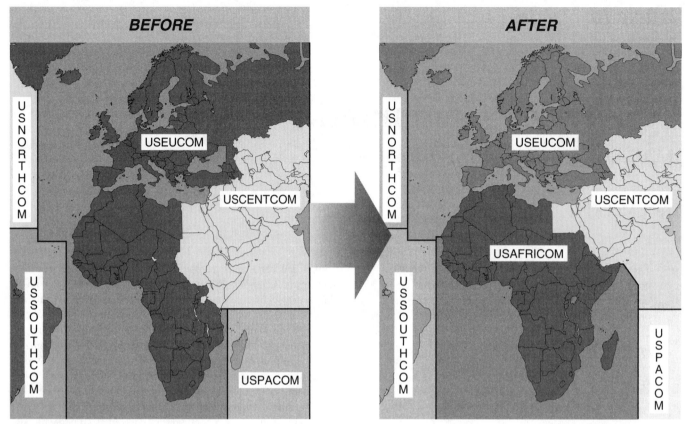

Figure 1 AFRICOM (right) will take over responsibility for all of Africa (except Egypt) from EUCOM, CENTCOM, and PACOM (left) in October 2008.

Taken together, these four deficiencies resulted in a disjointed and hindered approach towards Africa that lacked primacy within the Pentagon and, by extension, U.S. interagency networks.

Partly in response to this unwarranted lack of attention, DOD decided to redraw the unified command landscape by creating AFRICOM (see Figure 1). As Secretary Gates testified before the Senate, creating AFRICOM "will enable us to have a more effective and integrated approach than the current arrangement of dividing Africa between [different unified commands]."[5] AFRICOM combines under a single unified command all but one of the countries conventionally considered "African." (Egypt is the exception, owing to its relationship with the Middle East in general and Israel in particular. It remains covered by CENTCOM).

AFRICOM will be a distinct unified command with the sole responsibility of Africa.[6] A four-star general will command it and its approximately 400–700 staff members. It will be temporarily located in Stuttgart, Germany, as a sub-unified command, but is scheduled to move to Africa (place to be determined) and be operational by 1 October 2008.[7] Its four-star commander will be able to enhance policy decisions regarding Africa by advocating for African security issues on Capitol Hill and raising the military's strategic awareness of the continent.

DOD intends AFRICOM's presence to be innocuously transparent to African countries. Ryan Henry, the principal deputy under secretary of defense for policy, continually reiterates: "The goal is for AFRICOM not to be [sic] a U.S. leadership role on the continent but rather to be supporting the indigenous leadership efforts that are currently going on."[8] The theme of partnership is ubiquitous in DOD's dealings with AFRICOM and Africa. The department has, for example, conducted high-level delegations to African countries to discuss the creation of the command. As Theresa Whelan, deputy assistant secretary of defense of African affairs, explains, "If we take partnership seriously, then we must go out in a way never done before and consult with the nations affected. This manner of approaching partnership was not done with EUCOM, PACOM, or CENTCOM."[9]

Why Now?

AFRICOM is more than just an administrative change within DOD; it responds to Africa's increased geopolitical importance to U.S. interests. As Deputy Under Secretary Henry has stated, "Africa . . . is emerging on the world scene as a strategic player, and we need to deal with it as a continent."[10] U.S. strategic interests in Africa are many, including the needs to counter terrorism, secure natural resources, contain armed conflict and humanitarian crisis, retard the spread of HIV/AIDS, reduce international crime, and respond to growing Chinese influence.

Counterterrorism dominates much of U.S. security policy as the U.S. prosecutes its War on Terrorism. In a stark reversal of Cold War thinking, the 2002 *National Security Strategy* asserts that "America is now threatened less by conquering states than . . . by failing ones."[11] From the U.S. perspective, the inability or unwillingness of some fragile states to govern territory within their borders can lead to the creation of safe-havens for terrorist organizations. Government recalcitrance was indeed the case with Afghanistan in the late

1990s, when the Taliban permitted Al-Qaeda to operate unfettered within its boundaries, leading to the events of 11 September 2001. Africa contains the preponderance of fragile states in the world today, placing it squarely in the crosshairs of the War on Terrorism. AFRICOM will oversee current U.S. counterterrorism programs in Africa, such as Operation Enduring Freedom: Combined Joint Task Force-Horn of Africa (CJTF-HOA), and the Trans Sahara Counter-terrorism Initiative (TSCTI).[12]

America is also interested in Africa's natural resources, especially in terms of energy security. As instability in the Middle East grows and international demand for energy soars, the world—and the United States in particular—will become increasingly beholden to Africa's ability to produce oil, an inelastic commodity. Central Intelligence Agency estimates suggest Africa may supply as much as 25 percent of imports to America by 2015.[13] Already by 2006, sub-Saharan African oil constituted approximately 18 percent of all U.S. imports (about 1.8 million barrels per day). By comparison, Persian Gulf imports were at 21 percent (2.2 million barrels per day).[14]

At present, Nigeria is Africa's largest supplier of oil and the fifth largest global supplier of oil to the United States.[15] However, instability in the Niger Delta region has reduced output periodically by as much as 25 percent, escalating world oil prices. For instance, the price of oil jumped more than $3 per barrel in April 2007 after Nigeria's national elections were disputed, and it spiked again in May after attacks on pipelines in the delta. To help control this volatility, AFRICOM may become increasingly involved in the maritime security of the Gulf of Guinea, where the potential for deep-water drilling is high. "You look at West Africa and the Gulf of Guinea, it becomes more focused because of the energy situation," General Bantz Craddock, EUCOM Commander, told reporters in Washington. Safeguarding energy "obviously is out in front."[16]

Stemming armed conflict and mitigating humanitarian catastrophe also remain important U.S. objectives. Africa has long endured political conflict, armed struggle, and natural disasters, all of which have exacted a grave toll on Africans and compromised international development efforts. The direct and indirect costs of instability are high in terms of human suffering and economic, social, and political retardation. Although Africa is afflicted by fewer serious armed conflicts today than it was a decade ago, it hosts a majority of the United Nations peacekeeping operations.[17]

African militaries make up a sizable contingent of the African peacekeeping operations conducted by the UN and such regional organizations as the African Union and the Economic Community of West African States (ECOWAS). Despite a willingness to participate in these operations, many African militaries lack the command, training, equipment, logistics, and institutional infrastructure required for complex peacekeeping, leaving the onus of support on the international community. This burden has prompted some donor countries to help build the capacity of African militaries, thereby enhancing their ability to participate in peacekeeping operations. In 2004 the G-8 introduced its Global Peace Operations Initiative (GPOI), a multilateral program that plans to create a self-sustaining peacekeeping force of 75,000 troops, a majority of them African, by 2010. The U.S. Department of State manages GPOI, as it does the Africa Contingency Operations Training Assistance (ACOTA) program, which also trains peacekeepers.[18] According to Chip Beck, who heads ACOTA, "Our job is to help African countries enhance their capabilities to effectively take part in peacekeeping operations."[19] Although AFRICOM will not manage GPOI

or ACOTA, it should offer technical assistance to such programs and partner with African states in security sector reform (SSR).

HIV/AIDS is the leading cause of death on the continent, and controlling its global spread remains a critical concern for the U.S. In 2004, then-Secretary of State Colin Powell described HIV/AIDS as "the greatest threat of mankind today."[20] According to the UN, nearly 25 million Africans were HIV-positive in 2006, representing 63 percent of infected persons worldwide.[21] The rate of infection in some African security forces is believed to be high (between 40 and 60 percent in the case of the Democratic Republic of the Congo), raising concerns that those forces may be unable to deploy when needed and may even be vectors of the disease's spread.[22]

International crime in Africa is also a U.S. interest, especially the narcotics trade. West Africa has become the newest center for trafficking drugs. In the past year Nigeria, West Africa's economic hub, has made 234 drug-trafficking arrests at the Lagos airport, which is just grazing the surface, according to government officials.[23] Guinea-Bissau, another West African country, is quickly developing into a narco-state. Its soldiers have been caught facilitating the transfer of narcotics to mostly European markets.[24] To suggest the scale of this emerging problem, there were two seizures of over 600 kilos of cocaine, worth over $30 million each, during the past year. In Guinea-Bissau, narcotics trafficking accounts for almost 20 percent of GDP.[25] African trade in contraband such as narcotics, small arms, and human beings is a continuing global concern.

The People's Republic of China's (PRC) expanding influence in Africa is also a continuing worry for the United States. The continent is quickly emerging as a competitive battlefield in what some U.S. defense intellectuals are describing as a proxy economic cold war with China, especially in the quest for resources.[26] China's insatiable appetite for oil and other natural resources is the product of its own success. The PRC's economy has maintained an incredible average of 9 percent growth per annum over the last two decades, nearly tripling the country's GDP during that time. African oil fuels this growth. Until 1993, China was a net exporter of oil; now it is the world's second-largest energy consumer, obtaining 30 percent of its oil from African sources, especially Sudan, Angola, and Congo (Brazzaville).[27] Competition for natural resources, and oil in particular, is a strategic concern for the United States.

China is also seeking new markets for its goods. As its policy paper on Africa bluntly asserts: "The Chinese Government encourages and supports Chinese enterprises' investment and business in Africa, and will continue to provide preferential loans and buyer credits to this end."[28] Currently, over 700 Chinese state companies conduct business in Africa, making China the continent's third largest trading partner, behind the United States and France, but ahead of Britain. A series of diplomatic initiatives buttress these commercial ventures, aimed initially not only at isolating Taiwan but also at broader policy objectives. The PRE has diplomatic relations with 47 of Africa's states and offers limited, but not inconsiderable, development assistance in exchange for diplomatic support. China also engages in multilateral efforts to build strategic partnerships in Africa. In 1999, then-president Jiang Zemin petitioned the Organization of African Unity (now the African Union) to create a Forum on China-Africa Cooperation. A year later the first ministerial conference took place in Beijing with 44 African states participating. In 1995, two-way trade between Africa and China hovered at less than U.S. $1 billion. By the end of 2006, it exceeded U.S. $50 billion.

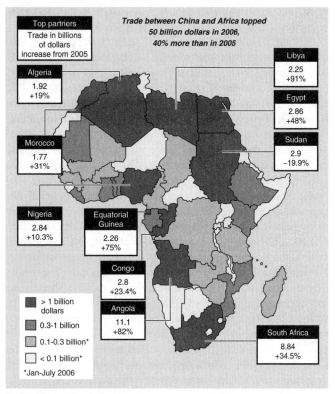

China Africa trade.

Source: China Ministry of Commerce

At the core of China's rapid push into African markets is its drive to forge strategic alliances. African countries constitute the largest single regional grouping of states within any international organization, accentuating their importance to Chinese diplomacy. Furthermore, in multilateral settings such as the UN, African countries tend to engage in bloc-voting, an effective tactic for influencing rules formulation, multilateral negotiations, and other international processes. China has relied on African support in the past to overcome staunch international criticism. For example, African votes were crucial to blocking UN Commission on Human Rights resolutions that condemned Chinese human rights abuses.[29] In the words of Premier Wen Jiabao: "China is ready to coordinate its positions with African countries in the process of international economic rules formulation and multilateral trade negotiations."[30] Strategic relationships with Africa will give China, at relatively low cost, the means to secure its position in the World Trade Organization and other multilateral venues.

This clout rankles the United States, which has admonished the PRC not to support "resource-rich countries without regard to the misrule at home or misbehavior abroad of those regimes."[31] Nevertheless, Beijing has secured many African alliances, public and private, through direct aid and concessionary loans with "no political strings" attached. As Premier Wen told African delegates at the 2003 China-Africa Cooperation summit at Addis Ababa, "We do offer our assistance with the deepest sincerity and without any political conditions."[32]

Perhaps the best-known beneficiary of China's "don't ask, don't tell" policy is Sudan. China is both the largest direct foreign investor in, and the largest customer of, Sudan's petroleum production. The PRC owns 13 of the 15 largest companies working in Sudan

and purchases more than 50 percent of Sudan's crude oil.[33] In return, China is arming the Sudanese regime: according to recent Amnesty International reports, it is violating the UN arms embargo by illegally exporting weapons—including fighter jets—to Khartoum at the height of the Darfur conflict. By Amnesty's estimation, the PRC has exported $24 million worth of arms and ammunition, nearly $57 million worth of parts and military equipment, and $2 million worth of helicopters and airplanes to Sudan.[34] If this estimate is correct, then China's implicit willingness to abet genocide puts it squarely at odds with multiple U.S. positions, especially in terms of national security policy. As a permanent member of the UN Security Council, China must realize that its actions contravene the council's own mandatory arms embargo.

In sum, U.S. security interests in Africa are considerable, and Africa's position in the U.S. strategic spectrum has moved from peripheral to central. In 2006, EUCOM's then-commanding general James Jones said that his staff was spending more than half its time on African issues, compared to almost none three years prior.[35] The current EUCOM commander, General Craddock, was unequivocal in his written testimony for Congress: "The increasing strategic significance of Africa will continue to pose the greatest security stability challenge in the EUCOM AOR [Area of Responsibility]. The large ungoverned area in Africa, HIV/AIDS epidemic, corruption, weak governance, and poverty that exist throughout the continent are challenges that are key factors in the security stability issues that affect every country in Africa."[36]

This relatively new interest in Africa is not confined to EUCOM, which currently covers the majority of the continent for the military. The president, for one, has mandated increased interest in Africa. The March 2006 U.S. *National Security Strategy* affirms that "Africa holds growing geo-strategic importance and is a high priority of this Administration," and that "the United States recognizes that our security depends upon partnering with Africans to strengthen fragile and failing states and bring ungoverned areas under the control of effective democracies."[37] AFRICOM is a product of this broad policy. More than a mere map change, it represents a response to the early 21st century's new security environment.

A New Strategic Paradigm

How should AFRICOM help secure Africa, a continent in crisis? It must begin by adopting a new security paradigm, one that regards security and development as inextricably linked and mutually reinforcing. This linkage is the nucleus of the security-development nexus, the strategic paradigm most likely to produce more durable security in Africa.

Since the Cold War's end, development donors have come to realize that if the security sector operates autonomously—with scant regard for the rule of law, democratic principles, and sound management practices—then sustainable, poverty-reducing development is nearly impossible to achieve. Africa has been the recipient of several Marshall Plans worth of foreign aid since World War II's end, yet it remains arguably as impoverished today as it was in 1946. This situation partly stems from the World Bank, U.S. Agency for International Development (USAID), and other organs of development traditionally eschewing security-related development, allowing the cycle of violence in Africa's fragile states to continue.

As U.S. problems in Iraq have shown, if there is a single lesson to be learned from recent nation-building experiences, it is that security is a precondition of development.[38] This axiom should play a central role in formulating a new security strategy for Africa, the most underdeveloped continent on Earth. Sadly, however, U.S. security and development institutions have long been divorced from one another in terms of perspective, operations, and outcomes. USAID is prohibited by law from supporting defense-oriented reform, resulting in a strained toleration of corrupt police forces and abusive militaries that tend to spoil the fruits of development. DOD traditionally shuns noncombat missions, limiting its involvement to narrow venues such as the Joint Combined Exchange Training and Foreign Military Financing programs, which are necessary but insufficient for wholesale security sector transformation. Over time, the schism between these two communities has ossified into interagency intransigence, lack of interoperability, and absence of strategic coordination, all of which have contributed to Africa's failure to develop despite decades of dedicated resources.

AFRICOM's mission should not be development, but the failures of development may drive AFRICOM. This paradoxical relation stems from the principal threats to African security, which are not interstate but intrastate in nature. For example, the largest threat to Liberian security is not a Sierra Leonean blitzkrieg across its border, but internal: guerilla warfare, insurgency, *coup d'etat,* or terrorism. Full-scale invasions of one country by another are uncommon in African military history. African conflicts have sprung mostly from domestic armed opposition groups. Such groups find it easier to change governments through violence rather than through the legitimate means of democracy, given the political exclusion many regimes practice, the paltry rule of law, easy access to small arms, and expanses of ungoverned territory in which to find sanctuary.

Domestic armed groups do have a weakness: they must rely upon local popular support to hide, survive, and thrive within the borders of a country. To attain this support, they must gain public sympathy by exploiting public grievances—real or perceived—that often can be attributed to failures of development. Common grievances include disproportionate distribution of wealth, lack of social justice, political exclusion of some groups, ubiquitous economic hardship, ethnic violence, inadequate public security, and failure of democracy.

To deny the sanctuary in which armed groups incubate and thereby stave off internal conflict, governments must address the root causes of public grievances. These grievances are development based; therefore, the security solution must be development based. The best weapons against intrastate threats often do not fire bullets; in fact, large, idle security forces can incite violence as much as check it. As Jacques Paul Klein, the former special representative of the secretary general for the United Nations mission in Liberia, has quipped, not entirely tongue-in-cheek, many African armies "sit around playing cards and plotting coups."[39]

Only by addressing the challenges of development can security be achieved and maintained. This is the core of the security-development nexus. Failure to heed this linkage results in a "security-development gap," where the lack of security prevents development from taking root, thus perpetuating conflict and compromising development in a vicious cycle. AFRICOM's strategic mandate must be to narrow the security-development gap.

Securing Development

Narrowing the security-development gap does not mean militarizing development. Nor does it mean transforming DOD into an aid agency. Narrowing the gap means shifting military strategic priorities from combat to noncombat operations; it means focusing on conflict prevention rather than conflict reaction. For some, the idea of a military command without a combat orientation is heretical. To others, AFRICOM represents an experiment in early 21st-century security, and potentially serves as a prototype for post-Cold War unified commands. As Deputy Assistant Secretary of Defense Whelan explains, "Ultimately we [were] simply reorganizing the way we do business in DOD. But then we saw an opportunity to do new things, to capture lessons observed since the fall of the Berlin Wall, to create an organization designed for the future and not the past."[40] In many ways, AFRICOM is an opportunity to institutionalize and operationalize peace-building lessons captured over the past 15 years.[41]

The first lesson is that strategic priority should be given to conflict prevention rather than reaction. Owing to the size and complexity of Africa, concentrating on fragile states before they fail or devolve into conflict represents an economy of force. Intervening only after a crisis festers into conflict, as in Somalia in 1993, is costly in terms of American blood, treasure, and international standing. Moreover, such military interventions rarely achieve durable peace because they fail to address the root causes of conflict.

By focusing on pre-conflict operations, AFRICOM will help "prevent problems from becoming crises and crises from becoming conflicts," as the 2006 *Quadrennial Defense Review* advocates.[42] Military campaigns are conventionally understood to proceed in four stages: phase I-"deter/engage," phase II-"seize initiative," phase III-"decisive operations," and phase IV-"transition/stability operations." Recently, military thinkers have introduced an additional phase, "phase zero," which encompasses all activities prior to the beginning of phase I. In other words, phase zero is purely preventative in nature, focusing on everything that can be done to avert conflicts from developing in the first place.[43] In a shift of traditional unified command strategy, AFRICOM should adopt conflict prevention as its primary mission, as Ryan Henry makes clear: "The purpose of the command is . . . what we refer to as anticipatory measures, and those are taking actions that will prevent problems from becoming crises, and crises from becoming conflicts. So the mission of the command is to be able to prevent that."[44]

The second lesson informing AFRICOM is that phase IV, transition/stability operations, may eclipse combat operations when it comes to determining "victory." The situations in Iraq and Afghanistan have made it patently evident that lethal force alone is no longer the decisive variable in military campaigns. To this end, in 2005 the White House issued "National Security Presidential Directive 44," which recognizes the primacy of reconstruction and stabilization operations.[45] Although a rudimentary document, it forms the foundation for interagency coordination of all stability and reconstruction programs. Additionally, that same year the Pentagon issued *DOD Directive 3000.05,* which defines stability operations as a "core U.S. military mission" that "shall be given priority comparable to combat operations."[46] This definition marks a revolution in military strategy for a military that has traditionally focused on fighting and winning wars. Moreover, these new policies are influencing DOD,

State, USAID, and others' funding and program development for 2008 and beyond. This new focus represents a seismic shift in military thought, as it prioritizes noncombat functions above traditional warfighting missions in the pursuit of durable security.

A Civilian-Heavy Military Command

The shift of strategic focus from combat to noncombat missions will require a commensurate shift in how unified commands function. If AFRICOM is expected to supervise an array of missions that are a hybrid of security and development, then it must forge interagency modalities, fusing the capabilities of DOD with State, USAID, and other civilian organizations. This coordination will prove difficult. As Ambassador Loftis puts the challenge, "How do you create a structure that is both a military Unified Command but needs to incorporate enough civilian inputs yet does not appear to take over these agencies and authorities?"[47] Issues concerning organizational structure, institutional culture, lines of authority, funding sources, best practices, and perspectives will mire efforts to create synthesis. Moreover, there are fears—both inside and outside the U.S. Government—that AFRICOM signals the militarization of U.S. foreign aid. Pentagon officials object to this perception, stressing that DOD will not be crossing into "other people's lanes" but simply wants to work more effectively with other agencies, recognizing the symbiotic relationship between it and the interagency in peace-building missions.[48] Only time will tell.

Forging particular interagency modalities will be a gradual process with few shortcuts. The effort was initiated by a decision to staff AFRICOM heavily with interagency civilians, many of them in key decision-making positions and not just traditional liaison roles. In fact, AFRICOM will be the most civilian-heavy unified command in history. In an unprecedented break from tradition, one of two deputy commanders will be a civilian, most likely an ambassador.[49] That DOD sees AFRICOM as becoming a "combatant command plus," with the plus being the exceptionally high number of civilians from other agencies, indicates the department's commitment to addressing security challenges on the continent in a thoroughly interagency manner.[50] But again, this process will take time. As Theresa Whelan confirms, "The command will continue to evolve over time, and will ultimately be an iterative process. It will not become a static organization in October 2008, but will continue to be a dynamic organization, as circumstances merit."[51]

Security Sector Reform

Moving beyond a strategy of conflict prevention and post-conflict transition, the best tactic for narrowing the African security-development gap is SSR. Security sector reform is the essence of "security cooperation," as it builds indigenous capacity and professionalizes the security sector so that African governments can effect development for themselves. As a senior USAID official and member of the AFRICOM transition team with extensive experience in Africa explains, "Security sector reform could contribute to a security architecture that ensures that citizens are provided with effective, legitimate, and democratically accountable external and internal security. What is needed is security sector reform that professionalizes forces for the protection of civilians and enables development. This would be a significant contribution."[52]

SSR is the complex task of transforming organizations and institutions that deal directly with security threats to the state and its citizens. SSR's ultimate objective is to create a security sector that is effective, legitimate, and accountable to the citizens it is sworn to protect. This objective is the essence of "cooperative security," as it can only be achieved in partnership with the host nation, civil society, and other indigenous stakeholders. SSR programs can range from building the capacity of a single military unit, such as a joint-combined exchange training mission, to the total reconstitution of a country's armed forces and ministry of defense, as in the Joint U.S.-Liberia Security Sector Reform Program. SSR is crosscutting transformation, requiring a multidisciplinary, "whole-of-government" approach by the U.S. Government.

DOD's role in SSR is essential but not all-inclusive. Building security-sector capacity and professionalizing actors requires many kinds of expertise, which fundamentally dictates an interagency effort. For example, DOD is not the best agency to train border control forces or set up criminal courts, two parts of the security sector. Rather, the Department of Homeland Security is best suited to train customs and immigration agencies, while the Department of Justice can assist with criminal justice reform. DOD's strong suit is transforming the military sector, which goes far beyond current train-and-equip programs and may entail a comprehensive, soup-to-nuts approach, especially in failed states.

Lastly, institutional transformation is key to SSR, since all institutions must rise together. DOD, for instance, cannot begin to train indigenous soldiers until the ministry of finance has the capacity to pay their salaries, which may be dependent on training from the U.S. Treasury Department. Failure to synchronize development may cause a relapse into conflict, as unpaid soldiers and police forces are a precipitant to violence. AFRICOM will be dependent on other agencies to implement SSR, hence its civilian-heavy nature.[53]

African Perceptions of AFRICOM

Despite DOD's exceptional campaign of consultations on the continent, American efforts to headquarter AFRICOM in Africa have met with resistance. A sampling of headlines from African newspapers is revealing: "Stop AFRICOM;" "New U.S. Command Will Militarise Ties with Africa;" "Wrong for Liberia, Disastrous for Africa;" "Why U.S.'s AFRICOM Will Hurt Africa;" "AFRICOM—the Invasion of Africa?" "Southern Africa says 'No' to U.S. Military Bases In Region;" and "We're Misunderstood, Says U.S."[54] Regional superpowers Nigeria and South Africa have refused to give the U.S. permission to establish AFRICOM on their soil, and they have warned their neighbors to do the same. Morocco, Algeria, and Libya, too, have reportedly refused U.S. requests to base AFRICOM forces in their countries. Member states of such regional organizations as the 14-country Southern African Development Community (SADC) have also agreed not to host AFRICOM, and there is discussion within the 16-country ECOWAS to do the same.[55] South African Defense Minister Mosiuoa Lekota summarizes the sentiment of many countries: "If there was to be an influx of armed forces into one or other of the African countries, that might affect the relations between the sister countries and not encourage an atmosphere and a sense of security." He warns that it would be better for the United States not "to come and make a presence and create uncertainty here."[56]

There are other reasons behind the suspicion and refusals. To name a few, AFRICOM has been equated with CENTCOM, which is fighting wars in Iraq and Afghanistan; the U.S. interest in African oil is well known and perceived to be predatory; and Africa's colonial past has ingrained distrust in its leaders.

Some of the opposition may also be in response to AFRICOM's inability, despite its consultative approach, to articulate its message to Africans. Rwandan General Frank Rusagara, former secretary general of the Rwandan Defense Ministry and top policymaker for Rwanda's military development, expresses a frustration common among military officers on the continent: "The lack of information [about AFRICOM] has resulted in people not knowing what it is and how it will relate to Africa." This statement is especially worrisome because Rusagara is no stranger to U.S. military operations and doctrine: he attended military courses at the U.S. Naval Post-Graduate School in Monterey, California, and the Africa Center for Strategic Studies in Washington, DC. Rusagara thinks that if AFRICOM wants to contribute to African security, it must do three things. First, it must embrace new strategic thinkers and innovative concepts of security, such as "human security," for peace-building in Africa. Second, U.S. officers must explain AFRICOM to their African peers—the command cannot simply rely on senior DOD officials to brief senior African government officials. Third, AFRICOM must enhance African capacity for peacekeeping operations.[57]

Not all African countries have turned their backs on AFRICOM, however. Some, such as Liberia, see it as a boon to the continent. Having just emerged from a brutal 14-year civil war, Liberia has a significant perspective on African security. Liberian Minister of Defense Brownie Samukai explains that AFRICOM has the potential to "build partnerships, lead to the convergence of strategic interest, prevent conflict, and conduct operations other than war." He also believes that professionalizing African militaries through SSR will promote good governance, buttress development, and enhance peacekeeping operations. Samukai adds that supporting AFRICOM does not indicate naiveté about U.S. interests in Africa, but rather shows a willingness to find synergies of interest between the U.S. and African countries. Owing to this understanding, he says, "ECOWAS stands to benefit most in terms of cooperation, interest and intervention, if necessary."[58] Liberia not only supports AFRICOM, but has also offered to host it.

Working with External Organizations

Another major challenge is courting nontraditional military partners early, such as non-government organizations (NGOs) and private voluntary organizations (PVOs).[59] These organizations often know the African lay of the land better than DOD, have decades' worth of operational know-how, are development experts, and have access to places that may be denied to the U.S. military. Moreover, NGOs (both developmental and humanitarian) and DOD have complementary interests in terms of securing development and providing support for complex humanitarian crisis response. Their responses to the 2004 tsunami in Indonesia and the 2005 earthquake in Pakistan demonstrate their convergence.

However, there are several challenges facing this partnership, each of which deserves examination. First, many NGOs are uneasy about working with the U.S. military, believing it puts their people at risk of violent reprisals from groups targeted by U.S. combat operations. As Jim Bishop of InterAction, a large umbrella organization for many NGOs, explains: "Humanitarian organizations

may want to keep some distance between themselves and the U.S. military, especially in environments with potential for violent opposition to the U.S."[60] Second, some NGOs believe that aligning themselves with the military impugns their neutrality or impartiality, sometimes their only guarantee of safety in conflict-prone areas. Similarly, working with neutral or impartial NGOs may prove incompatible for AFRICOM, since "neutral" NGOs do not take sides and "impartial" NGOs give assistance where needed most, even if that conflicts with U.S. interests. Third, Defense's understanding of the complexly diverse NGO community remains limited, and it risks viewing that community as a monolithic whole, which would have adverse consequences. Fourth, AFRICOM might find it difficult to partner with NGOs since they often receive money (and mandates) from multiple countries and sources, do not operate like contractors, and typically demand relative autonomy over program management and outcomes.

Still, there is reason to be hopeful. Currently, both DOD and elements of the NGO community are working to bridge the military-NGO divide. Defense is sensitive to NGO concerns regarding neutrality, as Theresa Whelan acknowledges: "We recognize that their [NGOs'] safety depends upon their neutrality, and we are looking for mechanisms that allow all of us to work together without undermining their mission."[61] Mechanisms under consideration include the African Center for Strategic Studies and the U.S. Institute of Peace (USIP), either of which could function as a "neutral space" for the government and NGOs to jointly explore opportunities for partnership.

Another alternative is working through NGO umbrella organizations like Global Impact or InterAction, which could act as credible interlocutors. Global Impact represents more than 50 U.S.-based international charities (e.g., the overseas Combined Federal Campaign), has worked with DOD in the past, and has even participated in AFRICOM planning cells. InterAction is a coalition of approximately 150 humanitarian organizations that provide disaster relief, refugee assistance, and sustainable development programs worldwide. On 8 March 2005, representatives from DOD, State, USAID, and InterAction met at USIP to launch a discussion of U.S. armed forces and NGO relations in hostile or potentially hostile environments. The meeting yielded pragmatic guidelines that could serve as a foundational model for AFRICOM.[62]

Lastly and perhaps most importantly, AFRICOM should draw on USAID's considerable experience and expertise working with NGOs. USAID staff can help translate perspectives, objectives, and best practices for both NGOs and AFRICOM, thereby deconflicting efforts on the ground and mitigating misunderstanding. As a senior USAID member of the AFRICOM transition team explains, "Effective and agreed upon mechanisms for dialogue could help keep each other informed about each other's efforts and [help everyone] . . . coordinate differing approaches as appropriate. Such dialogue could also provide an opportunity for NGOs to discuss pressing concerns or issues."[63] Although many challenges persist to forging a functional NGO-AFRICOM relationship, there are also many avenues for potential cooperation.

Conclusion: Will It Work?

Skeptics consider achieving durable security in Africa a sisyphusian task, and it probably is, if dependent upon the dominant security paradigm. Therefore AFRICOM must eschew this paradigm and adopt a new strategic focus that links security with development and regards them as inextricably linked and mutually reinforcing—the core of the security-development nexus. In Africa, most armed threats are intrastate in nature and reliant upon the support of the local population to hide, survive, and thrive within the borders of a country. To attain this, they exploit public grievances, real or perceived, that result from the failures of development. However, by "securing development" and narrowing the security-development gap, AFRICOM will deny armed groups their sanctuary, thus fostering durable security on the continent.

Strategically, AFRICOM will narrow this gap by prioritizing conflict prevention and post-conflict transition over traditional "fighting and winning wars." This represents a major shift in military strategy, and it requires a holistic interagency approach to security, hence AFRICOM's extraordinary civilian-heavy structure and unprecedented civilian deputy commander. Tactically, AFRICOM will narrow the gap through security sector reform and other programs that professionalize forces, promote good governance, and help Africans improve their own security. Security sector reform is at the center of AFRICOM's conflict prevention and security cooperation mandate.

Will it work? Clearly it is too early to tell, with major challenges ahead, including instituting interagency best practices, addressing African concerns, and attracting NGO/PVO partners. These challenges may not be resolved by October 2008, but that does not mean AFRICOM will ultimately fail in its bid to stabilize the continent. The strategy it will employ is a promising one, suggesting that there is sufficient reason to be hopeful.

Notes

1. The White House Office of the Press Secretary, "President Bush Creates a Department of Defense Unified Combatant Command for Africa," 6 February 2007.

2. Robert Gates, secretary of defense, in testimony before the Senate Armed Services Committee, 6 February 2007.

3. Robert G. Loftis, ambassador in the State Department's Bureau of Political and Military Affairs and a member of the Africa Command transition team, personal interview, 27 June 2007.

4. It should also be noted that the issue of "seams" is not unique to DOD. The Department of State also divides Africa between sub-Saharan Africa and northern Africa/Middle East, rather than treat the continent as an organic whole. The Bureau of African Affairs is responsible for sub-Saharan Africa and the Bureau of Near Eastern Affairs is responsible for northern Africa and the Middle East.

5. Gates testimony.

6. AFRICOM Public Brief, United States Department of Defense, 2 February 2007.

7. Lauren Ploch, "Africa Command: U.S. Strategic Interests and the Role of the U.S. Military in Africa," *CRS Report for Congress,* 16 May 2007, 9.

8. Ryan Henry, Principal Deputy Under Secretary of Defense, Office of the Secretary of Defense, DOD News press briefing, 23 April 2007.

9. Theresa M. Whelan, Deputy Assistant Secretary of Defense of African Affairs, Office of the Secretary of Defense, personal interview, 9 July 2007.

10. Henry press briefing.

11. *The National Security Strategy United States of America* (September 2002), 1.

12. For more information, see Peter Pham, "Next Front? Evolving United States–African Strategic Relations in the 'War on Terrorism' and Beyond," *Comparative Strategy* 26 (2007): 39–54.

13. Central Intelligence Agency, *Global Trends 2015: A Dialogue About the Future With Non-government Experts,* December 2000.

14. Edward Harris, "Oil Boom, Politics Shape Africa's Future," *Associated Press,* 29 June 2007.

15. Ploch, CRS Report, 12.

16. Tony Capaccio, "Securing African Oil a Major Role for New Command (Update1)," *Bloomberg.com,* 18 May 2007.

17. "Progress Report of the Secretary-General: Causes of Conflict and the Promotion of Durable Peace and Sustainable Development in Africa," *UN Report A/59/285,* 20 August 2004.

18. For more information about GPOI/ACOTA and U.S. interest, see Nina M. Serafino, "The Global Peace Operations Initiative: Background and Issues for Congress," *CRS Report* RL32773, 11 June 2007.

19. Jim Fisher-Thompson, "US Military Training Program Benefits African Peacekeepers," *U.S.INFO,* 20 March 2007, <http://usinfo.state.gov> (14 July 2007).

20. Colin L. Powell, Secretary of State, speech at the Gheskio Clinic, Port-au-Prince, Haiti, 5 April 2004.

21. UNAIDS, AIDS Epidemic Update, December 2006.

22. Kevin A. O'Brien, "Headlines Over the Horizon: AIDS and African Armies," *Atlantic Monthly* 292, no. 1, July/August 2003.

23. "That's all they needed," *The Economist,* 8 December 2007.

24. "Guinea-Bissau: Pushers' Paradise," *The Economist,* 7 June 2007.

25. *CIA World Factbook,* Guinea-Bissau, <https://www.cia.gov/library/publications/the-world-factbook/geos/pu.html> (13 July 2007).

26. Donovan C. Chau, "Political Warfare in Sub-Saharan Africa: U.S. Capabilities and Chinese Operations in Ethiopia, Kenya, Nigeria, and South Africa" (monograph, Strategic Studies Institute, 26 March 2007).

27. Capaccio.

28. See <http://news.xinhuanet.com/english/2006-01/12/content_4042521_3.htm> (14 July 2007).

29. Chris Alden, "Emerging countries as new ODA players in LDCs: The case of China and Africa," *Institut du développement durable et des relations internationales,* 01/2007.

30. *BBC Monitoring Asia,* 15 December 2003.

31. *National Security Strategy,* 42.

32. *Peoples Daily,* 16 December 2003, <www.englishpeopledaily.com.cn>.

33. Peter Pham, "China Goes on Safari," *World Defense Review,* 24 August 2006.

34. *Amnesty International Report,* AI Index: AFR 54/019/2007, May 2007, *Amnesty International Report,* AI Index: ASA 17/030/2006, June 2006.

35. Greg Mills, "World's Biggest Military Comes to Town," *Business Day,* 9 February 2007.

36. Bantz J. Craddock, General, Commander U.S. Southern Command, Testimony to the Senate Armed Services Committee, 19 September 2006.

37. *National Security Strategy.*

38. For more information on the preconditions of nation-building see James Dobbins, Seth G. Jones, Keith Crane, Beth Cole, "The Beginner's Guide to Nation-Building," *RAND Corporation Monograph MG-557,* 2007.

39. Jacques Paul Klein, Special Representative of the Secretary General, UN Mission in Liberia, statement made 5 November 2003.

40. Whelan interview.

41. In some ways, Southern Command (SOUTHCOM) is a model for AFRICOM, as it has incorporated some of the security-development lessons learned since the end of the Cold War. However, AFRICOM is envisaged to expand this model significantly.

42. *Quadrennial Defense Review,* 6 February 2006, 17.

43. General Charles Wald, "The Phase Zero Campaign," *Joint Force Quarterly* 43 (4th Quarter 2006).

44. Henry, press briefing. See also, *Quadrennial Defense Review,* 17.

45. President, "National Security Presidential Directive 44: Management of Interagency Efforts Concerning Reconstruction and Stabilization," 7 December 2005.

46. *DOD Directive 3000.05: Military Support for Stability, Security, Transition, and Reconstruction (SSTR) Operations,* 28 November 2005.

47. Loftis interview.

48. Whelan interview.

49. Henry press briefing.

50. "Pentagon: AFRICOM Won't Boost U.S. Troop Presence on the Continent," *Inside the Army,* 12 February 2007.

51. Whelan interview.

52. USAID senior conflict mitigation advisor and member of the AFRICOM Transition Team, personal interview, 16 August 2007.

53. Currently, the U.S. Institute of Peace is working with DOD and other U.S. agencies to develop a "whole of government" approach to SSR.

54. Editorial, "Stop AFRICOM," *Leadership* (Abuja), 28 September 2007, Salim Lone, "New U.S. Command Will Militarise Ties with Africa," *Daily Nation,* 9 February 2007; Ezekiel Pajibo and Emira Woods, "AFRICOM: Wrong for Liberia, Disastrous for Africa," *Foreign Policy in Focus,* 26 July 2007; Michele Ruiters, "Why U.S.'s AFRICOM Will Hurt Africa," *Business Day* (Johannesburg), 14 February 2007; Obi Nwakanma, "AFRICOM—the Invasion of Africa?" *Vanguard* (Lagos), 18 November 2007; Isdore Guvamombe, "Southern Africa says 'No' to U.S. Military Bases In Region," *The Guardian,* 26 September 2007; Oyedele Abuja, "'We're Misunderstood,' Says U.S.," *This Day* (Lagos), 30 November 2007.

55. Guvamombe.

56. Shaun Benton, "Africa opposed to U.S. command base," *BuaNews,* 29 August 2007.

57. General Frank Rusagara, Rwanda Defence Forces, personal interview, 1 December 2007.

58. Brownie Samukai, Liberian Minister of Defense, personal interview, 30 November 2007.

59. For the purposes of this discussion, NGOs and PVOs will be treated as the same.

60. Jim Bishop, Vice President for Humanitarian Policy and Practice InterAction, personal interview, 29 June 2007.

61. Whelan interview.

62. *Guidelines for Relations Between U.S. Armed Forces And Non-Governmental Humanitarian Agencies,* <http: www.usip .org/pubs.guidelines_pamphlet.pdf> (21 August 2007).

63. USAID senior conflict mitigation advisor interview.

SEAN MCFATE is an expert in African security policy. He was a principal architect of U.S. peace-building efforts in Liberia, Burundi, and Sudan, including the Liberian Security Sector Reform Program. Previously, he served as an officer in the U.S. Army's 82nd Airborne Division. Mr. McFate holds a master of public policy from Harvard University's Kennedy School of Government and dual bachelor's degrees from Brown University.

From *Military Review,* January/February 2008, pp. 10–21.

UNIT 3

The Domestic Side of American Foreign Policy

Unit Selections

16. **Foggy Bloggom,** David Frum
17. **The War We Deserve,** Alasdair Roberts
18. **The Tipping Points,** Daniel Yankelovich
19. **Trade Talk,** Daniel Drezner

Key Points to Consider

- Should policymakers listen to the U.S. public in making foreign policy decisions? Defend your answer.

- What types of foreign policy issues are the American public most informed about?

- Conduct a public opinion poll to measure the relative support for internationalism and isolationism among students. What did you expect to find? Were your expectations correct?

- In what ways is U.S. foreign policy true to traditional American values?

- What is the most effective way for Americans to express their views on foreign policy to policymakers?

- What foreign policy issues do you want to see debated by the candidates for elected office? Why?

- Does global involvement threaten to destroy American national values? If so, what steps might be taken to prevent this from happening?

- Where do you draw the line between the public's right to know about foreign policy matters and the government's desire to keep information secret?

Student Web Site

www.mhcls.com/online

Internet References

American Diplomacy
http://www.unc.edu/depts/diplomat/
Carnegie Endowment for International Peace (CEIP)
http://www.ceip.org
RAND
http://www.rand.org

Conventional political wisdom holds that foreign policy and domestic policy are two very different policy arenas. Not only are the origins and gravity of the problems different, but the political rules for seeking solutions are dissimilar. Where partisan politics, lobbying, and the weight of public opinion are held to play legitimate roles in the formulation of health, education, or welfare policy, they are seen as corrupting influences in the making of foreign policy. An effective foreign policy demands a quiescent public, one that gives knowledgeable professionals the needed leeway to bring their expertise to bear on the problem. It demands a Congress that unites behind presidential foreign policy doctrines rather than one that investigates failures or pursues its own agenda. In brief, if American foreign policy is to succeed, politics must stop "at the water's edge."

This conventional wisdom has never been shared by all who write on American foreign policy. Two very different groups of scholars have dissented from this inclination to neglect the importance of domestic influences on American foreign policy. One group holds that the essence of democracy lies in the ability of the public to hold policymakers accountable for their decisions, and therefore, elections, interest group lobbying, and other forms of political expression are just as central to the study of foreign policy as they are to the study of domestic policy. A second group of scholars sees domestic forces as important because they feel that the fundamental nature of a society determines a country's foreign policy. These scholars direct their attention to studying the influence of forces such as capitalism, American national style, and the structure of elite values.

The terrorist attack of September 11, 2001, altered the domestic politics of American foreign policy at least for the short run. Unity replaced division in the aftermath of the attacks as the public rallied behind President Bush. This unity began to fray somewhat as the Bush administration made its case for war with Iraq but overall it remained in place. Domestic political forces began to reassert themselves after President Bush declared that major fighting had ended. Now issues such as the cost of the war, the length of time American forces would remain in Iraq, the constant attacks on American occupying forces, and the handling of pre-war intelligence came under close scrutiny. By June 2004, for the first time, public opinion polls showed a majority of Americans (54.6%) saying sending troops to Iraq was a mistake and that the war had made the United States less safe from terrorism.

As George W. Bush's second term got underway the influence of domestic politics on the conduct of American foreign policy had become more visible and has remained so. His nomination of John Bolton to be ambassador to the United Nations produced a lengthy and highly charged debate in the Senate that focused as much on Bush's foreign policy as it did on Bolton's qualifications. The rising tide of imports from China brought forward complaints from domestic producers and workers and led the administration to file complaints against it with the World Trade Organization for illegal trade practices. Allegations of the mistreatment of prisoners and the Koran at Guantanamo Bay brought forward vigorous defenses and condemnations of American foreign policy and the role of the media. Revelations of spying on American's in the name of the war on terrorism brought forward protests and the question of how to deal with illegal immigration

Defense Dept. photo by Sebastian J. Sciotti Jr.

became a thorny political issue that divided the Republican Party. And finally, the 2008 presidential primary and election campaigns place sharp limits on the political feasibility of undertaking any new American foreign policy initiatives.

The readings in this section provide us with an overview of the ways in which U.S. domestic politics and foreign policy interact. The first reading in this unit focuses on the growing influence that the new media has on American foreign policy. "Foggy Bloggom" examines the tone and content of foreign policy blogs. The author finds them to be heavily liberal and democratic in tone yet it raises many of the same issues championed by neo-conservatives a few years back. The second essay, "The War We Deserve," takes a critical look at how Americans view the government and argues that the problems encountered in Iraq exemplify the tendency of Americans to expect much of their government while at the same time being unwilling to sacrifice. It asserts that under these conditions a global war on terrorism cannot succeed. In the third reading, "The Tipping Points," pollster Daniel Yankelovich provides us with recent evidence of how Americans think about specific foreign policy issues. He is most concerned with identifying those at or near the tipping point: issues which most Americans hold important and which they feel the government is not responding to in an appropriate fashion. The final essay, "Trade Talk" contends that presidents can no longer make trade policy in a political vacuum. The author presents three iron laws of trade politics that help to explain the current political debate over American trade policy. Much confusion exists on this point and the author provides a valuable roadmap for navigating through the rhetoric, and constructing a more sophisticated view of how different denominations tend to see the world, and America's place in it.

Foggy Bloggom

DAVID FRUM

My name is David Frum, and I am a blogger. Every day I post some hundreds of words of commentary at the *National Review* website—often (to fulfill the cliché) while still wearing my pajamas. But I am also a proud, suit-wearing member of the foreign-policy community, with my very own office in a think tank to prove it.

There is no avoiding the sad truth that my two communities despise each other.

The foreign-policy community (henceforward, "FPC") values moderation of views and modulation of tone. It insists upon formal credentials, either academic or bureaucratic (ideally both). It respects seniority, defers to office, mistrusts overt self-promotion and is easily offended by discourtesy.

As for the bloggers—well, they're pretty much the opposite, aren't they?

Here, for example, is the popular left-of-center blogger known as Arrios complaining that:

[Presidential] candidates are judged by the rather arbitrary rules of the "foreign policy community" which demand they engage in these absurd rhetorical dances so they can fit themselves into the Grand Foreign Policy Community Consensus. Anyone who just tells them to shove it is doing the right thing.[1]

And here's another left-of-center blogger, Matthew Yglesias, quoting a third, Steve Clemons:

"People like me," [Clemons] says, "were being fed quite a bit of inside information from people who were every bit as horrified" [about Iraq] but very few people said anything. And it's true—alongside the famously pro-war elements of the establishment, there's a shockingly large number of people at places like Brookings, csis, the cfr, etc. where if you try to look up what they said about Iraq it turns out that they said . . . nothing at all.

His perspective, he says, is that Washington is "a corrupt town." From that perspective, he says that "the political-intellectual arena is essentially a cartel"—a cartel that's become extremely timid and risk-averse in the face of a neoconservative onslaught—and "blogs allow smart people to break the cartel." That all seems very true to me, and I'm not sure what I have to add.[2]

Finally, Here is Glenn Greenwald at Salon.com:

The Foreign Policy Community . . . is not some apolitical pool of dispassionate experts examining objective evidence and engaging in academic debates. Rather, it is a highly ideological and politicized establishment, and its dominant bipartisan ideology is defined by extreme hawkishness, the casual use of military force as a foreign policy tool, the belief that war is justified not only in self-defense but for any "good result," and most of all, the view that the U.S. is inherently good and therefore ought to rule the world through superior military force.[3]

Such criticisms—so personal, so rude and so imperfectly grammatical—elicit only countervailing scorn from their targets.

In the summer of 2007, *The Economist* invited Gideon Rose to guest host their blog, Democracy in America. Rose is the managing editor of *Foreign Affairs,* and thus *ex officio* a member in highest standing of the FPC, or at any rate, its recording secretary.

He responded at considerable length to accusations like those of Atrios, Yglesias, Clemons and Greenwald. Here's just a bit:

The lefty blogosphere . . . has gotten itself all in a tizzy over the failings of the "foreign policy community." The funny thing is . . . hell, I'll just come out and say it: the netroots' attitude toward professionals isn't that different from the neocons', both being convinced that the very concept of a foreign-policy clerisy is unjustified, anti-democratic and pernicious, and that the remedy is much tighter and more direct control by the principals over their supposed professional agents.

The charges the bloggers are making now are very similar to those that the neocons made a few years ago: mainstream foreign-policy experts are politicised careerists, biased hacks, and hide-bound traditionalists who have gotten everything wrong in the past and don't deserve to be listened to in the future. . . . Back then, the neocons directed their fire primarily at the national security bureaucracies—freedom-hating mediocrities at the cia, pin-striped wussies at the State Department, cowardly soldiers at the Pentagon. Now the bloggers' attacks are generally aimed at the think-tank world.[4]

Because the "neocons" are regarded as public-enemy number one by *both* lefty bloggers *and* most of the FPC, Rose's words put the cat among the pigeons. For all their ferocity, the bloggers as a group are intensely sensitive to criticism. They crave the very thing for which they vilify the FPC: respectability. Nothing infuriates them more than its withholding. With shrewd intuition, then, members of the FPC go out of their way to make clear their lack of regard—that is, on those rare occasions when they deign to take notice of the bloggers at all.

Here, for example, is a marvelous demonstration of the mutual torment practiced upon each other by the bloggers and the FPC.

On August 14, 2007, Brookings Institution scholar Michael O'Hanlon was asked on a radio show about Glenn Greenwald's lengthy and highly personal attacks upon him. He replied,

> Well, I don't have high regard for the kind of journalism that Mr. Greenwald has carried out here. I'm not going to spend a whole lot of time rebutting Mr. Greenwald because he's had frankly more time and more readership than he deserves.

This put-down was featured on the left-leaning website CrooksandLiars.com and provoked 71 responses, including this one:

> Dear Michael O'Hacklon, Armstrong Williams wants his job back, the one that you are currently occupying. . . . Anyway, there never seems to be a shortage of your special brand of treasonous frauds running around. Enjoy the ride while it lasts.

And this one:

> Oh my goodness Mr. O'Hanlon, so sorry the caviar was not up to your supreme standards. We'll have the beluga beaten immediately.

And this one:

> two words for you o'hanlon: f—you (sorry for the language C&L)
>
> glenn greenwald is a true patriot, working to ensure the continued viability of our ever-so fragile democracy, and, ohanlon? nothing but a blowhard caught in inaccuracies and, like armstrong williams and gannon/guckert, a tool of the administration, the question i have for o'hanlon is just how much money it took for you to sacrifice your integrity.
>
> good job mikey, you have done serious damage to the brookings institute, from now on any 'finding' or opinion stemming from this now-compromised "think" tank will be followed by an asterisk, saying: beware, some brookings fellows spew govt propaganda and try to pass it off as independent conclusions. . . .[5]

Bitter! And also strange. Michael O'Hanlon, as readers of *The National Interest* will know, is the editor of the *Iraq Index*,

a source relied upon by people of almost all points of view. He served in the Congressional Budget Office during the last Democratic majority and has strongly criticized the Bush Administration almost from Inauguration Day. What makes him such a detested target?

To find the answer, revert for a minute to a key point in Gideon Rose's above-quoted paragraphs: *The bloggers' attacks are generally aimed at the think-tank world.* Which is to say: at members of the FPC who are currently out of power. Which is to say: at Democrats. Especially at moderate Democrats, internationalist-minded Democrats, Democrats who in 2002–2003 expressed support for the Iraq War. The bloggers hurling the invective are Democrats too, usually more liberal Democrats.

The blogosphere of 2007 is a predominantly liberal and Democratic place. This was not always the case: As recently as 2005, former Vice President Al Gore castigated "digital brown-shirts" who bullied and intimidated critics of George Bush. He would have no such complaint today. Today, it is the critics of George Bush who do the brown-shirting.

Thus, the generally liberal journalist Joe Klein complained in June 2007 of the

> fierce, bullying, often witless tone of intolerance that has overtaken the leftwing sector of the blogosphere. Anyone who doesn't move in lockstep with the most extreme voices is savaged and ridiculed—especially people like me who often agree with the liberal position but sometimes disagree and are therefore considered traitorously unreliable.[6]

While online readership surveys are notoriously unreliable, such data as exists suggests that the liberal site Daily Kos out-draws Rush Limbaugh's website. Traffic on participatory conservative sites like Free Republic and Red State has plunged, and as this election cycle opens, one senses greater energy and sees more comments on big liberal blogsites like TalkingPoints Memo.com and the WashingtonMonthly.com than on their conservative counterparts. Technologically, liberal sites like the HuffingtonPost and MediaMatters seem a generation ahead of counterparts like Drudge and the Media Research Project.

So when we talk about the antagonism that has arisen between bloggers and the FPC, we are really talking about liberal bloggers and the Democratic half of the FPC. This is a family feud, one that bears more than a passing resemblance to the great Democratic schism over Vietnam.

Back then, it was the party's intellectuals who revolted against its regulars; J. K. Galbraith, Richard Goodwin and Arthur Schlesinger against George Meany and Richard Daley. This time, it is the regulars who are rebelling against the intellectuals.

Then as now, the incumbents belittled the influence of the insurgents. John Roche, serving in the Lyndon Johnson White House, dismissed critics of the Vietnam War as a "bunch of Upper West Side Jacobins." (The journalist to whom he issued the dismissal, Jimmy Breslin, unfamiliar with French history, transcribed the word as "jackal bins." The next day, the story goes, half the Upper West Side found itself wondering, "What the hell is a jackal bin?")

Now as then, however, the insurgents are slowly shifting the incumbents. Just as the post-1968 Democratic Party came to look more like Eugene McCarthy's movement than Hubert Humphrey's coalition, so today's liberal FPC is gradually adopting not only many of the actual views, but much of the tone, style and manner of the left blogosphere.

Few Presidential candidates have drawn more support from the liberal FPC than Barack Obama. Obama has been endorsed by former National Security Advisor Zbigniew Brzezinski and advised by Harvard professor Samantha Power, Clinton counter-terrorism czar Richard Clarke and even George W. Bush's former NSC Senior Director for the Middle East, Bruce Riedel. Compared to Obama's, Hillary Clinton's foreign-policy team looks a little like a gala performance in Branson, Missouri: all the names you remember from decades ago. ("Madeleine Albright is still *fabulous!*")

And yet as Obama has struggled to come from behind in Iowa and New Hampshire, this once-irenic candidate now hurls accusations with the brio of a blogger on the Daily Kos.

Here is Obama on the Senate's Kyl-Lieberman amendment, a non-binding "sense of the Senate" resolution urging the administration to designate Iran's Revolutionary Guards as a terrorist organization, a resolution that won the votes of a majority of Senate Democrats:

> Why is this amendment so dangerous? Because George Bush and Dick Cheney could use this language to justify keeping our troops in Iraq as long as they can point to a threat from Iran. And because they could use this language to justify an attack on Iran as a part of the ongoing war in Iraq.

Three years ago, Barack Obama was willing to contemplate outright war against Iran. Running for Senate in 2004, he told interviewers that he regarded an Iranian nuclear bomb as a "worse" outcome than air strikes against Iran. Now, though, he has been pushed toward the blogger view that war is not to be contemplated, period. And he has adopted the blogger habit of attributing deceit and bad faith to anyone who disagrees with him—or even to anyone who agrees today with the positions he used to hold yesterday.

The Blogosphere exerts its influence in two ways—one as hard as cash, the other as whispery as a mirage.

In two consecutive presidential election cycles, the Internet has proven itself the most effective fundraising technology since the advent of direct mail. The last cycle's Internet darling, Howard Dean, raised money at the fastest pace ever seen: a million dollars a week, almost all of it in very small gifts, in the second two quarters of 2003. In the first quarter of 2007, Barack Obama matched Hillary Clinton's astonishing fundraising totals by tapping almost twice as many donors: 100,000 against her 50,000. On November 5, 2007, Ron Paul used the Internet to raise the largest one-day total in the history of political fundraising, $4.5 million.

Any medium that lucrative is bound to hold the attention of politicians. And bloggers look very much like the custodians of the political Internet.

The more whispery power comes from the strange echo-chamber effect of the Internet. The blogosphere links people all over the planet. It can generate volumes of comments and email that feel like a tidal wave to those accustomed to the milder responsiveness of the print medium. When I worked on the opinion page of *The Wall Street Journal*, then the largest circulation newspaper in America, a very provocative article might have elicited as many as a hundred letters to the editor. Today, an exciting post on a major blog can generate thousands of posted comments and emails. Few people possess the internal fortitude to stand up to a seeming barrage like this. (Joe Klein, whom I cited above as a special target of the left blogosphere, has retreated under pressure into something very like the party-line liberalism he once disdained.)

For those who participate in it, the blogosphere takes on the scale and reality of an alternative world—a world whose controversies and feuds are so absorbing, whose alliances and enmities burn with so much passion, that only the most level-headed of the participants ever seem to remember that somewhere between 97 and 98 percent of American voters have never looked at a blog in their lives.

The Virtual-Reality quality of the blogosphere accounts for one of the most puzzling traits of the left-wing bloggers: their ability to believe simultaneously in a) the supreme importance of winning elections for Democrats and b) the supreme importance of moving the Democratic Party to the left—"Running as a progressive will lead to victory", predicts Matt Stoller, one of the left blogosphere's leading voices—in flat contradiction of four decades of post-1968 experience that running as a progressive leads Democrats only to disaster.

But if everyday progressives sustain themselves in a hothouse atmosphere of positive feedback—if any murmur of doubt or skepticism is met with a barrage of abuse—if all the human instincts toward tribe and clan are harnessed to a partisan cause, then such things as historical experience or cautionary opinion polls can easily be shrugged aside.

Or anyway, shrugged aside up to the point where reality becomes undeniable.

And perhaps it is the power of undeniably adverse reality that prevents the right blogosphere from using the kind of force and power on foreign policy that its left counterpart exerts.

Any Republican attuned in any way to current events knows that the party faces grave difficulties and dangers going into 2008. Republicans cannot afford to indulge the illusions with which progressives can entertain themselves this cycle. (I should say: most Republicans. There is the countervailing example of the Ron Paul fanatics, who have convinced themselves that their man can sweep to victory on a platform that last won a presidential election in 1836.) For this reason, the Republican field is led by two men, who each in their way offer a new centrism.

The conservative blogosphere scored its last great triumph in 2005, when it led the rebellion that forced the withdrawal of the Supreme Court nomination of Harriet Miers. Its next great cause—exposing the pervasive faking of images in the 2006 Israeli-Hizballah war and the probable forgery of the video purporting to show the shooting of Muhammad al-Dura—has not achieved anything like such success. One Reuters photographer was caught in the act and forced to resign, but the creation of doctored images, like the al-Dura video, continues to command wide acceptance even in the West.

The Blogosphere is a place of anger and enthusiasm. In 2007, Republicans are less angry and enthusiastic than Democrats, and so their share of the territory is both smaller and less energetic. That will not always remain true. If Democrats do less well in 2008 than they now anticipate, some in the party will blame the blogosphere for pushing the party too far to the anti-war extreme. Alternatively, if Democrats capture the White House, the left blogosphere may well lose the energy of opposition, as conservative talk radio did after Bill Clinton left office.

Yet there is reason to think that the gravitational effect exerted on the liberal FPC by the left blogosphere will extend across party lines—and beyond the current political cycle.

Through the twentieth century, the management of American foreign policy has time and again been snatched away from the mandarins who regard themselves as its proper custodians. A populist eruption thwarted the hopes of the liberals around Woodrow Wilson in 1919–20. After the defeat of the Versailles Treaty, public interest waned—and Republican presidents were left free to conduct "dollar diplomacy." Another populist moment deterred Franklin Roosevelt from responding to the rise of Hitler in the 1930s, until Pearl Harbor put the experts back in control again. There they stayed until Korea and Joe McCarthy dethroned them—and back onto the throne they scrambled again during the "thinking the unthinkable" years from 1955 to 1965. And so it has continued into our own time. The frustrations over Iraq have triggered a reaction very similar to that generated by the stalemate in Korea, creating an audience for similar kinds of explanations—with "neocons" this time taking the part once assigned to the "striped-pants boys" in the State Department, and the high-toned Professors Stephen M. Walt and John J. Mearsheimer reinterpreting the role formerly played by William Knowland and Senator McCarthy.

Yet on each round of the cycle, the spread of education and the improvement of communications have raised the level of debate. The populist protesters of 2007 are far more informed and far more sophisticated than their predecessors of 1973, who were in turn a major improvement over those of 1950, 1935 and 1920. And the foreign-policy community that guided U.S.

foreign affairs in the 1990s was a much larger and more diverse group than the corresponding elites that wielded power in the quiet days of the 1950s, who were in turn a less cloistered club than that of the 1920s.

It is, as was famously predicted by Yeats, a widening gyre. And it can safely be predicted that when today's controversies simmer down, and the blogging energy turns to health care or climate change or issues as yet unforeseen, the "foreign-policy community" that reassumes its former ascendancy will likewise be an expanded and enlarged community. The expertise and sophistication of the FPC at its best will always be needed by a country whose natural tendencies are inward-looking and isolationist. And that expertise and sophistication can only be enhanced when today's FPC is reinforced, as surely it will be, by young people who gained their first introduction to foreign affairs when they were inspired by 9/11 to join the military or enter academia or learn a foreign language . . . or (why not?) start a blog.

Notes

1. http://atrios.blogspot.com/2007_07_29_archive
   .html#3650175445070888364

2. http://matthewyglesias.theatlantic.com/archives/2007/08/
   community_standards.php

3. http://www.salon.com/opinion/greenwald/2007/08/20/rose/index.html

4. http://www.economist.com/blogs/democracyinamerica/2007/08/
   how_the_netroots_are_like_the.cfm

   In the interest of fair disclosure, I should add here that Gideon Rose's piece includes some indirect criticism of me personally. I did not notice this criticism until after I had finished work on the above article. The criticism did not influence my thinking, and I did not alter the text after reading it.

   That said, I might add here that the criticism was tendentious. Rose complained that unnamed persons "expelled" Iraq War dissenters from the conservative movement. He then linked to an article by me in *National Review* that explicitly welcomed debate over the Iraq War—but that criticized those conservatives whose radical alienation from their country had led them to oppose the entire War on Terror from its very inception after 9/11. One suspects he had not actually read the piece to which he linked—a very bad blogging practice!

5. http://www.crooksandliars.com/2007/08/14/michael-ohanlon-
   responds-to-the-unserious-glenn-green-wald/

6. http://www.time.com/time/nation/article/O,8599,1630004,00.html

DAVID FRUM is a resident fellow at the American Enterprise Institute and writes a daily column for *National Review Online*.

The War We Deserve

It's easy to blame the violence in Iraq and the pitfalls of the war on terror on a small cabal of neocons, a bumbling president, and an overstretched military. But real fault lies with the American people as well. Americans now ask more of their government but sacrifice less than ever before. It's an unrealistic, even deadly, way to fight a global war. And, unfortunately, that's just how the American people want it.

There's an uncomplicated tale many Americans like to tell themselves about recent U.S. foreign policy. As the story has it, the nation was led astray by a powerful clique of political appointees and their fellow travelers in Washington think tanks, who were determined even before the 9/11 attacks to effect a radical shift in America's role in the world. The members of this cabal were known as neoconservatives. They believed the world was a dangerous place, that American power should be applied firmly to protect American interests, and that, for too long, U.S. policy had consisted of diplomatic excess and mincing half measures. After 9/11, this group gave us the ill-conceived Global War on Terror and its bloody centerpiece, the war in Iraq.

This narrative is disturbing. It implies that a small cadre of officials, holding allegiance to ideas alien to mainstream political life, succeeded in hijacking the foreign-policy apparatus of the entire U.S. government and managed to skirt the checks and balances of the U.S. Constitution. Perversely, though, this interpretation of events is also comforting. It offers the possibility of correcting course. If the fault simply lies in the predispositions of a few key players in the policy game, then those players can eventually be replaced, and policies repaired.

Unfortunately, though, this convenient story is fiction, and it's peddling a dangerously misguided view of history. The American public at large is more deeply implicated in the design and execution of the war on terror than it is comfortable to admit. In the six years of the war, through an invasion of Afghanistan, a wave of anthrax attacks, and an occupation of Iraq, Americans have remained largely unshaken in their commitment to a political philosophy that demands much from its government but asks little of its citizens. And there is no reason to believe that the weight of that responsibility will shift after the next attack.

The Path of Least Resistance

Since at least the election of Ronald Reagan in 1980, a political philosophy known as neoliberalism has dominated the American political landscape. Defined by a commitment to tax reduction, discipline in fiscal and monetary policy, light regulation of the private sector, and free trade, it has risen above party politics. Leading Democrats have advocated the neoliberal creed, even if they did not use the phrase. It was former President Bill Clinton, after all, who promised the American people in 1996 that "the era of big government [was] over"; that the federal bureaucracy would shrink; and that the federal government would adhere to a program of fiscal balance, regulatory restraint, and trade liberalization.

This neoliberal philosophy is built on a bedrock of skepticism about the role of central government and the effectiveness of grand governmental projects. As a consequence, politics got small. Political leaders learned to shy away from policies that threatened to disrupt the status quo and make great demands of the American polity. A hallmark of the Clinton administration in its later years, after the Democrats' drubbing in the 1994 midterm elections, was its enthusiasm for "micropolicies"—initiatives that could be linked to great themes but did not incur great costs.

The rejection of sacrifice on a national scale contributed to the bungled war the United States finds itself in today.

This rejection of sacrifice on a national scale contributed to the bungled war the United States finds itself in today. The war on terror is not simply a neoconservative project. It is as much a neoliberal project, shaped by views about the role of government that enjoy broad public support.

It may seem extraordinary, given the experience of the past six years, to suggest that President George W. Bush's administration pursued a Clinton-style strategy of accommodation to neoliberal realities. After all, key Bush advisors flaunted their determination to throw off the constraints that bound the executive branch. And the Bush administration's policies have had cataclysmic consequences—in Iraq alone, there are tens of thousands dead and more than a million people displaced. How can we call this "small politics"?

However, we must first recognize the critical distinction between what the Bush administration intended to do, and what actually transpired. The material point about the planned invasion of Iraq was that it appeared to its proponents to be feasible with a very small commitment of resources. It would be a cakewalk, influential Pentagon advisor Kenneth Adelman predicted in February 2002. The cost of postwar reconstruction would be negligible. Former Deputy Secretary of Defense Paul Wolfowitz suggested that it might even be financed by revenues from the Iraqi oil industry.

Of course, there were critics inside and outside the U.S. government who warned that these forecasts were unduly optimistic. But the administration's view was hardly idiosyncratic. There were many Americans who believed, based on the experience of the previous decade—including the first Gulf War, subsequent strikes on Iraq, and other interventions such as Kosovo—that the U.S. military had acquired the capacity to project force with devastating efficiency. Consequently, it wasn't hard to imagine that the invasion and occupation of a nation of 27 million, more than 6,000 miles away, could be accomplished without significant disruption to American daily life.

Even the larger war on terror remains a relatively small affair, asking for little from its masters. Although U.S. defense expenditures have grown substantially during the Bush administration—by roughly 40 percent in inflation-adjusted terms between 2001 and 2006—it is growth from a historically low base. In the five years after 9/11, average defense expenditure as a share of gross domestic product (3.8 percent) was little more than half of what it was during the preceding 50 years (6.8 percent). The proportion of the U.S. adult population employed in the active-duty military (roughly 0.6 percent) remained at a low not seen since before the attack on Pearl Harbor.

This determination to execute policy without disrupting daily life was maintained even as it became clear that the war on terror was faltering. The U.S. "surge" of troops in Iraq beginning in January 2007, designed to wrest control of the country from insurgents, was advertised as a substantial increase in U.S. commitments in Iraq. In August, the *New York Times* called it a "massive buildup." But by historical standards, it has been negligible. The United States had more boots on the ground in Japan 10 years after its surrender in 1945 and in Germany at the end of the Cold War. It deployed twice as many troops in South Korea and three times as many in Vietnam.

In 2003, the conflict in Iraq might reasonably have been described as George W. Bush's war. In 2007, however, it has become a bipartisan war—that is, a conflict whose course is shaped by the actions of a Republican president and by Democratic majorities in Congress. The stakes are substantial: Continued failure in Iraq is bound to have tremendous human and diplomatic costs. Yet the range of policy options is still arbitrarily limited to a token "surge" or various forms of "phased withdrawal." No major political actor, Democrat or Republican, dares to contemplate a genuine surge that would raise the U.S. commitment in Iraq to the level said to be essential by several military leaders before the invasion. Similarly, there has been no serious consideration of a return to the draft, despite strains on the U.S. military. This, the *New York Times* said—echoing the argument made by Milton Friedman during Vietnam—would be inconsistent with the "free-choice values of America's market society."

Follow the Money

It isn't just in Iraq where this preference for small-scale politics has shaped the war on terror. Vice President Dick Cheney claimed in 2005 that the Bush administration had been "very aggressive . . . using the tools at our disposal" to defend the U.S. home-land against terrorism. But the administration has not been aggressive in imposing regulatory burdens on the private sector, which owns many of the United States' most vulnerable targets. In 2002, for example, it declined to assert that the Clean Air Act gave it authority to impose safety requirements on U.S. chemical facilities. Instead, it encouraged voluntary corporate efforts to improve security in this and other sectors of the economy.

First and foremost, the aim was to keep the economy humming. "One of the great goals of this nation's war," President Bush said immediately after 9/11, "is to restore confidence in the airline industry." His administration quickly launched a "pro-consumption publicity blitz" (in the words of the *Boston Globe*) on behalf of the U.S. travel industry. The president starred in a campaign by the Travel Industry Association of America, designed, as one industry executive put it, to "link travel to patriotic duty." Many Americans interpreted the campaign as a call to spend more money to boost the economy. "The important thing, war or no war, is for the economy to grow," then White House Press Secretary Ari Fleischer said in 2003.

The extension of such pro-growth policies in a declared time of war has created jarring rhetorical inconsistencies. Historically, war has been regarded—by definition—as a grand project, requiring deep societal shifts and the subordination of other priorities. Traditionally, presidents had the responsibility to remind citizens of this fact. They called on Americans to "make the sacrifices that the emergency demands," as President Franklin D. Roosevelt did less than a year before Pearl Harbor.

President Bush feigns continuing this tradition when he tells Americans that "a time of war is a time of sacrifice." But this attempt to link the war on terror and earlier campaigns fails, precisely because today the state is not able to demand comparable sacrifices from its constituents. Asking for real sacrifices and tax hikes doesn't go over well at the ballot box. And so, when President Bush was asked in 2001 precisely how Americans should contribute to fighting the war on terror, he replied: "Well,

I think the average American must not be afraid to travel. . . . They ought to take their kids on vacations. They ought to go to ball games. . . . Americans ought to go about their business."

Another sad attempt at analogy was made by the new Transportation Security Administration (TSA), which launched a research-and-development program to achieve "revolutionary" improvements in methods for screening airline passengers and baggage. Part of this program was coined the "Manhattan II Project"—an homage to the crash program that produced a nuclear bomb in the Second World War. But the original Manhattan Project was a vast and expensive enterprise. It consumed 1 percent of GDP (in contemporary terms, one quarter of the annual defense budget); employed 130,000 people; enlisted scientists and engineers from leading universities and private industry; and continued until an atomic weapon had been successfully detonated. Manhattan II, by contrast, expended $6 million in its first two years—or less than one ten-thousandth of 1 percent of U.S. GDP.

The TSA's research-and-development program eventually fell prey to "competing priorities in a tight budget environment." In 2003, the agency cut its R&D budget by half to meet shortfalls elsewhere in the agency. R&D was just one of many areas in which investments in homeland security clashed fatally with fiscal constraints. "From Day One," said Clark Kent Ervin, the former inspector general of the Department of Homeland Security (DHS), attempts to improve domestic security were compromised by a "lack of money."

Conservatives often countered that one consequence of the war on terror has been a complete loss of budgetary discipline in Washington. It is a gross exaggeration. On the contrary, a remarkable feature of post-9/11 budgeting is the extent to which federal expenditures continued long-standing patterns, even as policymakers profess commitment to a "total war" on terrorism. Federal spending rose from 18.5 percent of GDP in 2001 to 20.3 percent of GDP in 2006, but it was not an extraordinary shift: The average for the 40 years ending in 2006 was 20.6 percent of GDP. Spending on non-entitlement domestic programs, including DHS programs, remains well within historical parameters. Indeed, the largest increase in annual federal outlays between 2000 and 2006 was not on non-defense discretionary spending (a change of $177 billion) or even on defense ($225 billion), but on Social Security, Medicare, Medicaid, and other forms of mandatory spending ($461 billion).

Broadly speaking, three familiar forces have shaped federal budgets since 9/11. The first is the continuing weight of the doctrine of fiscal discipline, which discredits the idea of borrowing to fund security needs. The second is the continued difficulty of entitlement reform, evidenced by the Bush administration's failed attempt to reform Social Security in 2005, and thus the inability to control growth in mandatory spending.

The third consideration is a resistance to taxation. As a share of GDP, federal taxes increased to their highest level in modern history during the later Clinton years, and popular resentment about federal taxes grew right alongside them. As a consequence, the popularity of the Bush administration's tax cuts endured after 9/11. One month after the attacks, three quarters of respondents told a Gallup poll that they wanted the first round of tax cuts, introduced in June 2001, to take effect immediately. More than 60 percent favored additional cuts.

Bush's tax reforms reduced the overall tax burden to the historical average. The result, however, has been another stark discontinuity between the rhetoric of the war of terror and the realities on the ground. President Bush claimed that the United States had undertaken a "historic mission" after 9/11. But this was a highly unusual security crisis—one in which the tax burden imposed by the federal government *declined*. The president even defended the tax cuts as a critical component of protecting the home front in the war on terror, designed to safeguard an economy targeted by al Qaeda. Tax cuts, said Bush, would "make sure that the consumer has got money to spend in the short term." The effects of this pro-consumption policy have sometimes been perverse. For example, containerized maritime imports rose by 64 percent after 9/11, even as policymakers wrung their hands about weaknesses in container and port security.

Liberty for Some

So, if taxes have declined, a draft has been avoided, and regulatory burdens have been minimized, were there any other ways in which the broad mass of the American public might have carried a heavier load after 9/11?

Civil libertarians certainly think Americans have paid a large if intangible price in the rollback of their civil liberties. Here, critics also reach for analogies between the war on terror and earlier conflicts. They accuse the Bush administration of trampling on civil liberties in the name of national security, just as the government had during the First and Second World Wars, the Cold War, and the domestic turmoil of the late 1960s and early 1970s. The steps taken after 9/11 were "chillingly familiar," reported the *San Francisco Chronicle*. The historian Alan Brinkley said the government's treatment of civil liberties was a "familiar story." In 2002 *The Progressive* said, "We've been here before."

But we haven't been here before. Infringement of Americans' rights after 9/11—that is, actual rather than anticipated infringements—were different in type and severity than those suffered in earlier crises. Citizens were not imprisoned for treason, as they were during the First World War. Thousands of citizens were not detained indefinitely, as they were during the Second World War. Citizens were not deported, or denied passports, or blacklisted, as they were during the Red scares.

Were there serious issues about the denial of citizens' rights after 9/11? Undoubtedly. But those violations often had a distinctly postmillennial character. New surveillance programs were launched in secrecy and designed so that their footprint could not be easily detected. In effect, government was adapting to political realities, searching for techniques of maintaining domestic security that did not involve obvious disruptions of everyday life.

Foreigners, in contrast, had a much rougher time. The second distinguishing feature of the war on terror, insofar as basic rights are concerned, is the extent to which the heaviest burdens were sent abroad. The most obvious and grievous harms—kidnapping, secret detention, abusive interrogation, denial of habeas corpus—have been deliberately perpetrated against foreigners rather than citizens.

Indeed, the spirit of sacrifice doesn't even permeate the Bush administration itself. The president's first choice as head of the Federal Emergency Management Agency resigned 15 months after 9/11 to head a consulting business that would "take advantage of business opportunities in the Middle East following the conclusion of the U.S.-led war in Iraq." By 2006, two thirds of the Department of Homeland Security's senior executives had departed, often taking more lucrative positions as lobbyists for DHS contractors. A 2007 report for the Home-land Security Advisory Council worried about a "Homeland Security 'meltdown'" because of turnover in DHS leadership.

Some have borne serious costs in this war on terror, though, beginning of course on Day One. And as of today, more than 4,000 U.S. soldiers have been killed in Iraq and Afghanistan, and more than 13,000 have been injured so severely that they could not return to duty. At least 70,000 Iraqis have died since March 2003. Immigrant communities within the United States complain of surveillance and the abusive application of immigration laws. These pains are substantial but concentrated, often on politically marginal constituencies.

In fact, some of these costs are aggravated precisely because the Bush administration wants to avoid policies that incur more broadly distributed burdens. "We're fighting the enemy abroad," the Bush White House said in 2005, "so that we don't have to fight them here." This course of action has been presented as a matter of national security—a sensible form of forward defense. However, it's also good domestic politics. "Fighting them here" would mean higher taxes, bigger bureaucracies, tighter regulation, clearer challenges to civil liberties, and more impediments to trade. The Bush administration did not want that, because it understood correctly that most Americans did not want it, either.

But the consequences of this basic policy decision have been profoundly harmful to U.S. interests. The United States has failed to take steps domestically that would enhance security. It has stumbled into overseas conflicts marred by poor planning and vague objectives. Its standing as a champion of human rights has been badly damaged. It has left itself open to charges of hypocrisy—using the language of sacrifice to cloak a policy of business as usual.

Meanwhile, Americans are still as committed to the principles of fiscal discipline, low taxes, light regulation, and free trade as they were on Sept. 10, 2001. They remain deeply skeptical of "big government" and federal bureaucracy. Indeed, a 2006 Gallup poll found that a large majority of Americans, Republicans and Democrats alike, believed that "big government" posed the biggest threat to the country in the future, ahead of both "big business" and "big labor."

Was the war on terror devised and promoted by a small cadre of neoconservatives? Perhaps. But it was also a response to crisis that recognized and largely respected the well-defined boundaries of acceptable political action in the United States today. In important ways, the war on terror is not their war but our war. The desires and preferences of the American people have shaped the war on terror just as profoundly as any neoconservative doctrine on the conduct of U.S. foreign policy.

So Americans can keep reciting their favorite myth—even as the broad currents of U.S. politics remain unchanged. But the next time the war suffers a setback or a terror attack hits home, we shouldn't expect the country's response to differ much from the war the Bush administration launched six years ago. Americans might try to pin their problems on a few powerful neocons. In truth, though, they must shoulder some of the blame.

ALASDAIR ROBERTS is professor of public administration at the Maxwell School of Citizenship and Public Affairs at Syracuse University and author of the forthcoming book *The Collapse of Fortress Bush: The Crisis of Authority in American Government* (New York: New York University Press, 2008).

From *Foreign Policy*, November/December 2007. Copyright © 2007 by the Carnegie Endowment for International Peace. Reprinted with permission. www.foreignpolicy.com

The Tipping Points

Daniel Yankelovich

From Bad to Worse

Terrorism and the war in Iraq are not the only sources of the American public's anxiety about U.S. foreign policy. Americans are also concerned about their country's dependence on foreign energy supplies, U.S. jobs moving overseas, Washington's seeming inability to stop illegal immigration, and a wide range of other issues. The public's support for promoting democracy abroad has also seriously eroded.

These are a few of the highlights from the second in a continuing series of surveys monitoring Americans' confidence in U.S. foreign policy conducted by the nonprofit research organization Public Agenda (with support from the Ford Foundation), of which I am chair. The first survey, conducted in June of last year, found that only the war in Iraq had reached the "tipping point"—the moment at which a large portion of the public begins to demand that the government address its concerns. According to this follow-on survey, conducted among a representative sample of 1,000 American adults in mid-January 2006, a second issue has reached that status. The U.S. public has grown impatient with U.S. dependence on foreign countries for oil, and its impatience could soon translate into a powerful demand that Washington change its policies.

Overall, the public's confidence in U.S. foreign policy has drifted downward since the first survey. On no issue did the government's policy receive an improved rating from the public in January's survey, and on a few the ratings changed for the worse. The public has become less confident in Washington's ability to achieve its goals in Iraq and Afghanistan, hunt down terrorists, protect U.S. borders, and safeguard U.S. jobs. Fifty-nine percent of those surveyed said they think that U.S. relations with the rest of the world are on the wrong track (compared to 37 percent who think the opposite), and 51 percent said they are disappointed by the country's relations with other countries (compared to 42 percent who are proud of them).

As for the goal of spreading democracy to other countries, only 20 percent of respondents identified it as "very important"—the lowest support noted for any goal asked about in the survey. Even among Republicans, only three out of ten favored pursuing it strongly. In fact, most of the erosion in confidence in the policy of spreading democracy abroad has occurred among Republicans, especially the more religious wing of the party. People who frequently attend religious services have been among the most ardent supporters of the government's policies, but one of the recent survey's most striking findings is that although these people continue to maintain a high level of trust in the president and his administration, their support for the government's Iraq policy and for the policy of exporting democracy has cooled.

What Matters, and Why

A question always hovers in the background whenever public attitudes on foreign policy are reported: What influence do shifts in such attitudes have on the actual day-to-day conduct of foreign policy? Unlike for domestic policy, where it is clear that public opinion is always relevant, for foreign policy it is often difficult to understand whether changes in public opinion lead to changes on the ground.

The reason for this murkiness is that the public grants the president and Congress far more authority for decision-making on foreign policy than on domestic affairs. Americans assume that the president and his advisers have special information about international relations to which they are not privy. Some Americans may also lack confidence in their ability to judge the wisdom of particular foreign policies. All of this translates into a good deal of leeway for policymakers. Still, the public puts limits on this freedom and sometimes takes it away abruptly. Under certain conditions, public opinion can have a decisive influence. The trick is understanding what those conditions are.

In mid-2005, we found that in addition to the war in Iraq, three other issues were moving toward the tipping point, where public opinion would become strong enough to influence policy. These issues were the outsourcing of jobs to other countries, illegal immigration, and the United States' deteriorating relations with the Muslim world. Based on the January survey, concern over outsourcing and illegal immigration has grown a bit more intense, and the worry about the growing hatred of the United States in Muslim countries has modestly receded. On the other hand, U.S. dependence on foreign energy sources, which was not an urgent issue in mid-2005, has leapt to the forefront of the public's consciousness.

In studies that track attitudes, there are always more views that do not change than views that do. This survey is no exception. It is a striking—and encouraging—illustration of the public's thoughtfulness and consistency. Respondents still awarded the government high marks (an A or a B) on its performance in achieving foreign policy goals such as helping other nations when natural disasters strike and making sure the United States has a strong and well-supplied military. Respondents continued to believe that the government deserves intermediate ratings on its efforts to make peace between the Israelis and the Palestinians and help improve the lives of people in the developing world. And respondents still gave the government failing grades on issues such as stopping the importation of illegal drugs. This context of overall stability makes any changes in opinion that the survey did find all the more striking and significant.

The war in Iraq, already at the tipping point in mid-2005, remains the primary foreign policy issue on which public pressure continues to mount. Although illegal immigration and outsourcing moved closer to the tipping point in the January 2006 poll, neither has actually reached it. In contrast, the public's concern over U.S. relations with the Muslim world moved slightly away from the tipping point. And the issue of energy dependence, which had ranked far down the list, leapfrogged ahead to move into tipping-point territory.

No change is more striking than that relating to the public's opinion of U.S. dependence on foreign oil. Americans have grown much more worried that problems abroad may affect the price of oil. The proportion of those who said they "worry a lot" about this occurring has increased from 42 percent to 55 percent. Nearly nine out of ten Americans asked were worried about the problem—putting oil dependence at the top of our 18-issue "worry scale." Virtually all Americans surveyed (90 percent) said they see the United States' lack of energy independence as jeopardizing the country's security, 88 percent said they believe that problems abroad could endanger the United States' supply of oil and so raise prices for U.S. consumers, and 85 percent said they believe the U.S. government would be capable of doing something about the problem if it tried. This last belief may be the reason that only 20 percent of those surveyed gave the government an A or a B on this issue; three-quarters assigned the government's performance a C, a D, or an F.

The oil-dependency issue now meets all the criteria for having reached the tipping point: an overwhelming majority expresses concern about the issue, the intensity of the public's unease has reached significant levels, and the public believes the government is capable of addressing the issue far more effectively than it has until now. Should the price of gasoline drop over the coming months, this issue may temporarily lose some of its political weight. But with supplies of oil tight and geopolitical tensions high, public pressure is likely to grow.

The only other issue that has reached the tipping point is the war in Iraq. It continues to be the foreign policy issue foremost in the public's mind, and respondents consistently deem the war (along with the threat of terrorism) to be the most important problem facing the United States in its dealings with the rest of the world. Concern about mounting U.S. casualties in Iraq is particularly widespread—82 percent of respondents to the June 2005 survey said they cared deeply about the issue; in January 2006, 83 percent said they did. Although the level and intensity of concern about Iraq has remained fairly stable, the public's appraisal of how well the United States is meeting its objectives there has eroded slightly. Last summer, 39 percent of respondents gave the government high marks on this issue; 33 percent

did in January. The erosion, moreover, comes almost entirely from Republicans: 61 percent gave the government an A or a B on Iraq in the first survey, but only 53 percent did in the second. Confidence in U.S. policy on Iraq is also down significantly among those who regularly attend religious services, who also show rising levels of concern about casualties.

One reason for the downward trend is skepticism about how truthful Washington has been about the reasons for invading Iraq. Fifty percent of respondents said they feel that they were misled—the highest level of mistrust measured in the survey. Another source of skepticism may be more troublesome for the government: only 22 percent of Americans surveyed said they feel that their government has the ability to create a democracy in Iraq.

What's on Deck

Three other issues are approaching the tipping point but have not yet reached it: the outsourcing of jobs, illegal immigration, and U.S. relations with the rest of the world, and especially Muslim countries.

An impressive 87 percent of respondents expressed some degree of concern about outsourcing, 52 percent said they "worry a lot" about it, and 81 percent of respondents gave the government poor grades (a C, a D, or an F) on its handling of the issue. Thus, outsourcing now meets two of the three criteria for reaching the tipping point. But it falls short on the third criterion, the ability of the government to take effective action on the issue. Most Americans surveyed (74 percent) felt that it was unlikely that U.S. companies would keep jobs in the country when labor is cheaper elsewhere. And 52 percent of respondents believed it was unrealistic to think that the government could do anything to stop corporations from sending jobs abroad. On the other hand, a large plurality (44 percent) said they believe the U.S. government could do a lot to prevent jobs from moving overseas if it really tried. Should this plurality become a majority—which we suspect will happen during 2006—outsourcing will have reached the tipping point.

Concern about illegal immigration has also grown. Two out of five Americans surveyed (41 percent) said they "worry a lot" about this issue, and half (50 percent) said they believe that tighter controls on immigration would greatly enhance U.S. security. Almost half (48 percent) also said they believe the government could do a lot to slow illegal immigration, and respondents gave Washington even lower grades on protecting U.S. borders in the most recent survey than they did in mid-2005.

Interestingly, the public's feelings on a third issue have moved in the opposite direction. This issue is the intangible but important question of U.S. relations with the rest of the world, and specifically with Muslim countries. During the period between the two surveys, the U.S. public grew marginally less worried about anti- Americanism in the Muslim world and elsewhere. The number of respondents who said they "worry a lot" about growing hatred of the United States in the Muslim world decreased from 40 percent to 34 percent, and the share of those who were deeply concerned about losing the trust of people in other countries declined from 40 percent to 29 percent, one of the larger changes in the survey. The reasons for these changes are not self-evident. The sense of shame about the treatment of prisoners at Abu Ghraib, so strong in 2005, seems to have receded with the passage of time.

Only about a third of Americans surveyed (35 percent) said they think the U.S. government could do a lot to establish good relations with moderate Muslims—but almost two-thirds (64 percent) nevertheless gave the government poor marks because of its failure to do so. We expect opinions on this issue to be volatile in the future. Nearly a third of respondents said they "worry a lot" about the rise of Islamic extremism around the world (31 percent) and the possibility that U.S. actions in the Middle East have aided the recruitment of terrorists (33 percent). Almost half (45 percent) said they believe that Islam encourages violence, and survey respondents estimated that about half or more of all Muslims in the world are anti-American. But a clear majority (56 percent) continued to have confidence that improved communications with the Muslim world would reduce hatred of the United States.

Americans may also be getting used to the once-shocking notion that they are not well loved abroad. A majority of respondents (65 percent) have realized that the rest of the world sees the United States in a negative light. When Americans are asked to describe the image of the United States in other countries, the results show a great deal of ambivalence and confusion. Even though a majority said they believe the United States is seen negatively, large majorities ascribed positive elements to the country's image abroad. Four out of five respondents said they think the United States is seen as "a free and democratic country" (81 percent) and "a country of opportunity for everyone" (80 percent). Nearly as many said they believe the United States is seen as generous to other countries (72 percent) and as a strong leader (69 percent). But equal numbers said the United States is seen as "arrogant" (74 percent), "pampered and spoiled" (73 percent), "a bully" (63 percent), and a "country to be feared" (63 percent).

Unity and Division

The U.S. public holds a strikingly clear view of what Washington's foreign policy priorities should be. The goals the public highlights range widely. Those that receive the most public support are helping other nations when they are struck by natural disasters (71 percent), cooperating with other countries on problems such as the environment and disease control (70 percent), and supporting UN peacekeeping (69 percent). A surprisingly high level of support shows up for goals that represent the United States' humanitarian (as distinct from its political) ideals, such as improving the treatment of women in other countries (57 percent), helping people in poor countries get an education (51 percent), and helping countries move out of poverty (40 percent). Receiving less support are goals such as encouraging U.S. businesses to invest in poor countries (22 percent). And receiving the least support is "actively creating democracies in other countries" (20 percent).

Not surprisingly, there are partisan differences over what the United States' goals should be. The largest gap between

Republicans and Democrats relates to "initiating military force only when we have the support of our allies." Almost two-thirds of Democrats surveyed (64 percent) endorsed this multilateralist principle, in contrast to slightly more than a third of Republicans (36 percent). There are no significant differences between Republicans and Democrats on humanitarian ideals. The parties do differ, however, on the desirability of promoting democracy in other countries (30 percent of Republicans surveyed supported this goal, compared to only 16 percent of Democrats). But even a majority of Republicans have little stomach for this priority of the Bush administration.

This last point merits some elaboration. A majority of the U.S. public supports the ideal of spreading democracy (53 percent of respondents said they believe that "when more countries become democratic there will be less conflict"), but Americans are skeptical that an activist U.S. policy can contribute much to this outcome. A majority of those surveyed (58 percent) said they feel that "democracy is something that countries only come to on their own." As such skepticism grows, support for trying to create democracies abroad declines. In the 2005 survey, 50 percent of respondents thought that the United States was doing well at that task; in the more recent survey, the number fell to 46 percent, and only 22 percent said they believe that Washington can do a lot to build a democratic Iraq.

The 2005 survey described the huge gap that divided Republicans and Democrats on most aspects of foreign policy. The most recent survey found that partisan differences remain pronounced. The gap between the parties is at its widest with regard to how the United States is doing in its foreign policy and how much the Bush administration can be trusted. The most striking difference is in the expression of pride in the nation's foreign policy, with a whopping 58-point spread between the percentage of Republicans and the percentage of Democrats who believe that there is "plenty to be proud of" in U.S. dealings with the world. Essentially, Republicans think the country is doing well in foreign policy, whereas Democrats think it is failing miserably.

But digging into the numbers reveals that although Republicans generally endorse the country's current foreign policy, they share with Democrats a critical appraisal on a number of specific issues. Both groups are reluctant to give an A or a B to the government for its efforts to stop illegal immigration, achieve energy independence, block drugs from entering the country, limit the extent of foreign debt, or negotiate beneficial trade agreements.

Back to the Fold?

The first survey showed a remarkable parallel between the views of Republican respondents and the views of those respondents who said they frequently attend religious services. (By "religious services," we mean services of any kind—in churches, synagogues, mosques, or elsewhere.) The second survey showed reduced enthusiasm for some of the administration's policies among devoted service attendees, especially regarding the war in Iraq. In fact, most of the erosion in confidence in the government's foreign policy in the seven months between

Reduced Polarization of Opinion Between Americans Who Frequently Attend Religious Services and the U.S. Population at Large

Statement	Respondents who agreed		Respondents who frequently attend religious services who agreed		Opinion gap	
	2005	2006	2005	2006	2005	2006
"Worry a lot" that the war in Iraq is leading to too many casualties	56%	56%	45%	52%	11	4
"Worry a lot" that the war in Iraq is requiring too much money and attention	44%	43%	32%	40%	12	3
The U.S. is "generally doing the right thing, with plenty to be proud of," in its relations with the rest of the world	40%	39%	52%	46%	12	7
The U.S. can help other countries become democracies	38%	36%	48%	37%	10	1

the two surveys came from this source. Although there are still striking differences between the views of Americans who do not attend religious services frequently and the views of those who do, the gap has started to narrow, suggesting reduced polarization on the basis of religion.

In the first survey, a minority of frequent attendees at religious services (45 percent) expressed serious worry about casualties in Iraq, compared to 56 percent of the total sample. Now that number has increased to 52 percent, closer to the proportion of the population as a whole, which has remained at 56 percent. Although people who frequently attend religious services are still the respondents most supportive of U.S. policy in Iraq, fewer of them (41 percent of those surveyed) gave a high grade to the government on meeting U.S. objectives there than did seven months earlier (46 percent). In the first survey, 32 percent of those who frequently attend religious services said they worried a lot that the war in Iraq was taking up too much money and attention; in January, 40 percent did. Almost half of those surveyed in June 2005 (48 percent) said they believed that the United States could help other countries become democracies; in January, that number had dropped to 37 percent, in line with the 36 percent of the general population. And in the more recent surveys only 46 percent agreed that the United States was "generally doing the right thing" in its relations with the rest of the world, down from 52 percent in the earlier survey.

These are not big changes, but they follow a consistent pattern, suggesting that the most actively religious Americans are starting to react more like the rest of the public. This conclusion is supported by the results of the broad overview question asking whether U.S. foreign policy is going in the right or the wrong direction: 57 percent of those who frequently attend religious services said the latter in January, matching the 58 percent of the rest of the population who said this. Still, despite the mounting reservations of actively religious Americans about some policies, a majority (54 percent) continue to trust the government to tell them the truth about the country's relations with others, in contrast to the 37 percent of respondents who do not frequently attend religious services.

A recent survey of public opinion in Arab countries, conducted in late 2005 by Zogby International and University of Maryland Professor Shibley Telhami, showed results that are dismaying from the United States' point of view, with large majorities believing that the war with Iraq will make Iraqis worse off and the region less peaceful, breed more terrorism, and worsen the prospects for settling the Arab-Israeli dispute. Comparably large majorities said they consider U.S. foreign policies to be driven not by a desire to spread democracy, but by oil, a quest to dominate the Middle East, the goal of protecting Israel, or a desire to weaken the Muslim world.

Nevertheless, one ray of light shines through. Asked what the primary motivation for Bush's Middle East policy is, only 13 percent of those Arabs surveyed in the Zogby/Telhami poll cited "the need to spread . . . Christian religious convictions"; most (61 percent) chose instead "the pursuit of [the United States'] national interest." Why does this offer grounds for hope? Because our most recent survey showed that the religious divide over U.S. foreign policy seems to be narrowing, and the Zogby/Telhami survey revealed a similar finding: that the Arab world sees secular, rather than religious, motivations as crucial to U.S. foreign policy. However difficult differences rooted in interests might be to solve, and however long it might take to solve them, clashes rooted in identity and religion are even more problematic and take far longer to surmount.

DANIEL YANKELOVICH is Chair and Co-founder of the organizations Public Agenda, DYG, and Viewpoint Learning.

Trade Talk

DANIEL DREZNER

American perceptions about international trade have changed dramatically in the past two decades. Presidents can no longer craft positions on foreign economic policy in a vacuum. Trade now intersects with other highly politicized issues, ranging from the war on terror to environmental protection to bilateral relations with China. Old issues such as the trade deficit and new issues such as offshore outsourcing have made a liberal trade policy one of the most difficult political sells inside the Beltway.

Indeed, shifts in domestic attitudes have created the least hospitable environment for trade liberalization in recent memory. Unfortunately, this inhospitable environment has arisen at a time when trade is more vital to the U.S. economy than ever. The challenge for this President and for those who succeed him will be to reinvigorate U.S. trade policies despite the current public mood. In short, it is the challenge to lead.

The first thing any president must do to lead effectively on economic issues is to persuade the country that trade matters. This should not be that hard, for trade manifestly does matter. In 1970 the sum of imports and exports accounted for less than 12 percent of U.S. GDP; by 2004 that figure had doubled to 24 percent. Approximately one out of every five factory jobs in the United States depends directly on trade. U.S. exports accounted for approximately 25 percent of economic growth during the 1990s, supporting an estimated 12 million jobs. U.S. farmers export the yield of one out of every three acres of their crops. In 2003 the United States exported $180 billion in high-tech goods and more than $280 billion in commercial services. From agriculture to manufacturing to technology to services, the U.S. economy needs international trade to thrive.

Researchers at the Institute for International Economics recently attempted to measure the cumulative payoff from trade liberalization since the end of World War II. Scott Bradford, Paul Grieco and Gary Hufbauer conservatively estimated that free trade generates economic benefits ranging from $800 billion to $1.45 trillion dollars per year in added output. This translates into an added per capita benefit of between $2,800 and $5,000—or, more concretely, an addition of between $7,100 and $12,900 per American household. The gains from future trade expansion have been estimated to range between $450 billion and $1.3 trillion per year in additional national income, which would increase per capita annual income between $1,500 and $2,000. There are few tools in the U.S. government's policy arsenal that consistently yield rewards of this magnitude.

Trade expansion brings several benefits to the U.S. economy. It allows the United States to specialize in making the goods and services in which it is most productive. The bigger the market created by trade liberalization, the greater the benefits from specialization. Trade also increases competition within economic sectors. Over the past decades economists have repeatedly shown that industries exposed to trade are more productive than sectors in which cross-border exchange is limited or impossible. As available markets expand, the rate of return for technological and organizational innovations increases. With freer trade, firms and entrepreneurs have a greater incentive to take risks and to invest in new inventions and innovations.

These benefits also make it easier for the Federal Reserve to run a bullish monetary policy. An open market is a significant reason why the United States has been able in recent years to sustain robust economic growth, dramatic increases in labor productivity, low unemployment, modest inflation and historically low interest rates. The combination of these effects boosts the trajectory of feasible economic growth without triggering inflation, which in turn has allowed the Fed to pursue more expansionary monetary policies than would otherwise have been possible.

Trade is equally vital to American foreign policy. The regions of the world that have embraced trade liberalization—North America, Europe and East Asia—contain politically stable regimes and, despite some problems with radical Islamist minorities, make our best partners in the war on terror. The regions of the world with the most tenuous connection to global markets—the Middle East and Africa—are plagued by unstable regimes and remain hotbeds of terrorist and criminal activity. Trade is not a silver bullet for U.S. foreign policy; many other factors affect the rise of terrorism and political instability. Nevertheless, trade is a handmaiden to hope. It provides significant opportunity to individuals in poor countries, offering a chance for a better life for them and their children. Creating hope among people is a powerful long-term weapon in the war on terror.

Multiple economic analyses demonstrate that trade promotes economic freedom and economic development. Trade will be essential to advancing the Millennium Development Goals of halving global poverty by 2015. Exposure to the global economy correlates strongly with the spread of democracy, the rule of law and the reduction of violence.

Over the long term, trade liberalization is a win-win proposition among countries and therefore serves a useful purpose in promoting American interests and values. Most of the time, trade helps to reduce frictions between countries and serves as one of the most powerful tools of soft power at America's disposal. Bilateral relations have improved with every country that has signed a free-trade agreement (FTA) with the United States. If countries perceive that the rules of the global economic game benefit all participants—and not merely the United States—these countries will be more favorably disposed toward the United States on other foreign policy dimensions.

Over the very long term, U.S.-led trade expansion can cement favorable perceptions of the United States among rising powers. Both the CIA and private sector analysts project that China and India will have larger economies than most G-7 members by 2050. Decades from now, it would serve American interests if these countries looked upon the United States as a country that aided rather than impeded their economic ascent. Trade liberalization undertaken now serves as a down payment for good relations with rising great powers in the future.

Our Ambivalent Public

Despite these significant economic and diplomatic benefits, the American public is increasingly hostile to freer trade. Between 1999 and 2004, public support for free trade dropped off a precipice. The most dramatic shift in opinion came from Americans making more than $100,000 a year: Support for promoting trade dropped from 57 percent to 28 percent in this group. According to a July 2004 poll jointly conducted by the Pew Research Center and the Council on Foreign Relations, 84 percent of Americans thought that protecting the jobs of American workers should be a top priority of American foreign policy. The same month, a poll conducted by the German Marshall Fund of the United States concluded that only 4 percent of Americans still supported NAFTA. Americans are also less enthusiastic about further international trade deals than are Europeans: 82 percent of the French and 83 percent of the British want more international trade agreements, compared to just 54 percent of Americans.

Hostile attitudes toward trade liberalization are even more concentrated when the focus turns to newer forms of trade, such as outsourcing. In 2004 at least ten different surveys asked Americans how they felt about the growing number of jobs being outsourced overseas. The results were consistently and strongly negative. Depending on the poll, between 61 and 85 percent of respondents agreed with the statement that outsourcing is bad for the American economy. Between 51 and 72 percent of Americans were even in favor of the government penalizing U.S. firms that engage in outsourcing. In a Harris poll taken in May and June of 2004, 53 percent of Americans said U.S. companies engaging in outsourcing were "unpatriotic." This hostility remains consistent regardless of how respondents are categorized. A 2004 *CFO Magazine* survey of chief financial officers revealed that 61 percent of them believed outsourcing was bad for the economy, while an April 2004 Gallup poll showed 66 percent of investors believed outsourcing was hurting the investment climate in the United States.

Free traders assert that greater liberalization will always benefit the economy. The polling data reveal that most Americans do not buy the "always", and instead believe in "fair trade." They believe that the expansion of trade leads to an increase in economic insecurity that outweighs any increase in national income. A fair-trade doctrine recommends the use of safeguards, escape clauses and other legal protections to slow down the economic and social effects of import competition. Such views have become dominant in the United States over the past two decades. But why?

The Iron Laws of Trade Politics

Three political facts of life have caused many Americans to shift their support from free trade to fair trade. First, during economic downturns or periods of slack job growth, public suspicion of free-trade policies explodes into hostility. Inevitably, foreign countries become the scapegoat for business cycle fluctuations that have little to do with trade. When presented with economic theories and statistical data on the one hand showing that trade is good for the economy, and

anecdotes of job losses due to import competition on the other, most Americans are swayed by the anecdotes. There may be no discernible economic correlation between trade and overall employment, but many Americans believe there is one—a belief that policymakers ignore at their peril.

Combine this with a massive trade deficit and the perception problem becomes even more acute. Most Americans think a large trade deficit is bad for the economy, even though such deficits correlate *positively* with strong economic growth. Indeed, the growth in the trade deficit since 1998 has been accompanied by strong GDP growth and excellent productivity gains. Nevertheless, the U.S. trade deficit is projected to top $670 billion this year—in absolute dollar terms, the largest trade deficit in world economic history. In an uncertain economy, that number will lead to greater public skepticism about the merits of freer trade. To be sure, there are valid reasons to be concerned about the size of the current account deficit, but even those economists who voice such concerns do not recommend higher tariffs as the answer.

The second reason American support for free trade has dropped is that it is particularly difficult to make the case for trade expansion during election cycles. Trade generates large, diffuse benefits but concentrated—if smaller—costs. Those who bear the costs are more likely to vote on the issue—and make campaign contributions based on it—than those who reap the benefits. In this situation, politicians will always be tempted to engage in protectionist rhetoric. The latest example of this came when politicians on both sides of the aisle demanded government action to halt outsourcing. As election cycles continue to lengthen, this political temptation will only get stronger.

The third iron law of trade politics is that both advocates and opponents talk about trade in ways that simultaneously inflate its importance and frame the issue as a zero-sum proposition. Trade is both blamed and praised for America's various economic strengths and ills, even though domestic factors such as macroeconomic policy, stock market fluctuations and the pace of innovation are far more significant determinants of America's overall economic performance. Politicians routinely address trade issues by discussing how changes in policy will affect the trade deficit. The implicit understanding in their arguments is that it is better to run a trade surplus than a deficit, even though there is no economic data to support that view. Debates about trade inevitably revolve around the question of jobs, even though trade has a minimal effect on aggregate employment levels.

We should be used to this by now. A decade ago, the political debate over NAFTA was framed in terms of job creation and job destruction, despite the fact that every sober policy analysis concluded that NAFTA would not significantly affect the employment picture in the United States one way or the other. As a result, even politicians who advocate trade liberalization do so by focusing on increasing American exports and downplaying imports. If politicians talk about trade in a mercantilist, zero-sum way, Americans will be led to think about the issue this way as well.

New Constraints on Trade Politics

The next presidential election is three years away. The economy has created a net gain of nearly 2 million new jobs in the past year, so the public should be more receptive to a discussion of free trade now than it was a year ago. Public opinion polls, however, say otherwise. Part of the reason is that, in a world of high oil prices and frequent natural disasters, many Americans remain nervous about the state of the American economy. A bigger part of the problem, however, is that new trade-related issues have made talking about trade policy more difficult than before. Even as the economy continues to add jobs, there are sound reasons to believe that public antipathy toward trade liberalization will not abate. If anything, it will increase.

One new problem is that the percentage of the American economy exposed to international competition is on the rise. Over the next decade, technological innovation will convert what have been thought to be nontradable sectors into tradable ones. Trade will start to affect professions that have not changed their practices all that much for decades—fields such as accounting, medicine, education and law. This will increase the number of Americans who perceive themselves to be vulnerable to international competition and economic insecurity. This insecurity is the driving force behind the growing hostility to free trade among the upper income brackets.

Another relatively new issue is the rise of China. Twenty years ago, there was a great deal of American hand-wringing at the prospect of Japan "overtaking" the U.S. economy. For *realpolitik* reasons, the current fear of China's economic rise will be worse. At least Japan was a stable democratic ally of the United States. China is neither democratic nor an ally, and the jury is still out with respect to its long-term stability.

Beijing has brought some of this enmity on itself. China's central bank has increasingly intervened in foreign exchange markets to maintain the dollar's strength against the yuan, even though China's currency has risen in value compared to other major currencies. In July 2005, China's central bank announced a slight devaluation against the dollar, with an intention to move to a managed float. However, Beijing has continued to purchase dollars at an extraordinary rate, ensuring that the yuan will not appreciate significantly anytime soon. China's interventions have exacerbated the U.S.-China trade deficit: In 2004 the bilateral deficit was a record $162 billion.

These practices—combined with China's high growth rate, the media firestorm over outsourcing and a recent flurry of Chinese corporate takeover efforts directed at U.S. firms—have created intense domestic pressures for some kind of retaliatory policy. In April 2005, a bill was introduced in the U.S. Senate that threatens a 27.5 percent tariff on Chinese goods unless Beijing revalues its currency; the bill garnered a veto-proof majority. In May, the House of Representatives proposed a different piece of legislation to widen the definition of exchange-rate manipulation to include China as an offender. Many congressmen reacted negatively to the proposed takeover of Unocal by the China National Offshore Oil Corporation, with the House passing a measure urging the President to block the purchase on national security grounds. This congressional hostility helped to scotch the proposed takeover.

China's energy diplomacy has led to ambitious deals with authoritarian regimes.

China's economic growth and aggressive trade diplomacy also pose significant challenges to the United States from a security perspective. In 2004 China accounted for 31 percent of global growth in the demand for oil. China's energy diplomacy has led to ambitious deals with authoritarian regimes in Myanmar, Iran and Sudan, and has placed China's diplomacy in all three cases at loggerheads with that of the United States. China's growing interest in commercial relations with other Pacific Rim countries contrasts with U.S.

regional policy, which prioritizes the war on terror. At a fundamental level, even if the United States benefits from the bilateral trading relationship, China appears to benefit more—and that could clash with the stated *National Security Strategy* objective of "dissuad[ing] potential adversaries from pursuing a military buildup in hopes of surpassing, or equaling, the power of the United States."

The content of current trade negotiations has also made trade a tougher sell. World Trade Organization negotiations have shifted much of their focus away from tariff reduction to ensuring that disparities in national regulations do not interfere with international trade. In large part this is due to the WTO's success at reducing border-level trade restrictions. For most areas of merchandise trade (agricultural, textile and clothing products excepted), tariffs and quotas have been at nominal levels since completion of the Uruguay Round in 1994. As for agriculture and textiles, liberalization of either sector will not be an easy sell. The end of the Multi-Fibre Agreement in January 2005 has led to "bra wars" between the developed world and China, with the Bush Administration using every tool at its disposal to staunch the flow of textile imports. As for agriculture, the lack of progress in those negotiations now threatens to derail the upcoming WTO's Ministerial Conference in Hong Kong.

Increasingly, trade negotiations inside and outside the WTO have revolved around the residual non-tariff barriers to trade—social and business regulations. The most obvious examples include labor standards, environmental protection, consumer health and safety, antitrust, intellectual property rights and immigration controls. Because most regulatory policies were originally devised as domestic policies, they are more politically difficult to change than tariffs or quotas.

Some of these new trade negotiations will touch third rails of American politics. For example, developing countries are pushing in the WTO for greater liberalization in the trade of "Mode 4" services, in which the person performing the service crosses a border to do his or her job. The benefits of such liberalization for the United States economy would be significant; Microsoft chairman Bill Gates warned early this year that visa restrictions were limiting U.S. access to highly trained computer engineers from other countries, undercutting America's ability to innovate. Despite the economic advantages, however, such a move raises politically sensitive questions. One obvious concern would be the effect this kind of liberalization would have on homeland security. Another prominent concern would be the effect on U.S. immigration policies: Opponents would claim that the liberalization of trade in services was back-door immigration.

The American public's growing hostility to freer trade has made congressional passage of trade agreements more difficult, and this in turn has worsened the public image of trade. The victory margins in congressional votes for trade legislation have narrowed over the years. In December 2001, the Bush Administration secured Trade Promotion Authority by a single vote in the House of Representatives. (Trade Promotion Authority—which used to be called "fast track"—allows the president to submit trade deals for congressional approval via a simple up-or-down vote, preventing any poison-pill amendments.) In July 2005, the Central American Free Trade Agreement passed by only two votes, and that was after significant White House lobbying of wavering representatives. The smaller the margin of victory, the more leverage wavering representatives have to extract district-specific spending or trade-distorting measures that undercut the original purpose of the trade deal. As a result, congressional negotiations over trade agreements have begun to give off the same whiff of pork that comes with transportation and agricultural bills.

What Can Be Done?

Can the public's turn against free trade perhaps be ignored? Political analysts and trade experts alike argue that the political significance of this attitudinal shift remains an open question. Americans are skeptical about the benefits of trade, but they are not particularly passionate about it. Polling data, purchasing behavior and experimental evidence all suggest that American consumers talk like mercantilists but purchase goods like free traders. It is difficult to point to specific members of Congress who have lost their seats because they adopted an unpopular position on trade policy.

That said, international trade is viewed as increasingly salient by many Americans. Now is not the time for a policy of trade expansion to lose political legitimacy. This is particularly true given the Bush Administration's full plate of trade issues for the next several years. At the top of the list is the Doha Round of WTO talks. Thorny negotiations remain on the liberalization of trade in services and the reduction of internal price supports and market restrictions for agricultural producers. The nominal deadline for these negotiations is the Hong Kong Ministerial Conference scheduled for December 2005. That deadline will not be met, but it cannot be extended indefinitely, since other countries will want to see the Doha Round completed well before the expiration of U.S. Trade Promotion Authority in 2007.

At the regional level, efforts to advance the Free Trade Area of the Americas and the Middle Eastern Free Trade Area Initiative are continuing, albeit at less than breakneck speed. At the bilateral level, the Administration has stepped up its use of freetrade agreements with favored allies. In the first term, FTAs were ratified with Singapore, Australia, Morocco and Chile. FTAs have been negotiated and signed with Bahrain and Oman. Negotiations with Panama, Peru, Ecuador, Colombia, Thailand and the United Arab Emirates are ongoing.

Can public attitudes be changed? The primary impediment to boosting public support for trade liberalization is not one of economics but of psychology. People *feel* that their jobs and wages are threatened. Even if the probability of losing one's job from import competition or outsourcing is small, the percentage of workers who know someone who has lost his or her job because of trade is much larger. In this sense, public perceptions about trade are akin to perceptions about crime: Knowing a victim of crime often makes the problem appear to be greater than it actually is. While these fears may be exaggerated, they are nonetheless real.

Psychology, not economics, holds down public support for freer trade.

If the Bush Administration decides to follow through on its ambitious trade agenda, it will need new strategies to counteract shifts in public opinion. The good news is that while the current political environment is challenging, it is not hopeless. Polling strongly suggests that a healthy majority of Americans—including skeptics of freer trade—supports policies that pair liberalization with policies that reduce the disruptions to groups that are negatively affected. These policies can take the form of expanded insurance opportunities, greater public investment in research and development, and retraining programs. The 2002 expansion of the Trade Adjustment Assistance program is a good first step, but more steps are needed: a wider use of wage insurance schemes, increased portability of health care coverage and including service-sector workers in assistance programs.

Another useful tactic would be to link trade to larger foreign policy priorities. One reason the United States was able to advance trade liberalization during the Cold War was the bipartisan consensus that a liberal trading system aided the cause of containment. Trade expansion can and should be presented as a critical element of the long-term grand strategy of the United States to spread democracy and defeat terrorism. Security arguments resonate with a broad majority of the American public. According to new polls, a large majority of Americans support promoting international trade with poor, democratic governments—a message consistent with President Bush's second Inaugural Address. As with the Cold War, a communications strategy that markets economic diplomacy as "America's first line of offense" would blunt the arguments of protectionists while promoting the virtues of trade liberalization. Greater presidential involvement in shifting public attitudes—including aggressive use of the bully pulpit—will be needed.

The alternative to blunting the shift in public opinion is to go with the flow. While politically expedient, adopting a more protectionist foreign economic policy will hurt the U.S. economy and ultimately undermine global stability. If barriers are placed on trade, the effect would be to preserve jobs in less competitive sectors of the economy and destroy current and future jobs in more competitive sectors. Trade protectionism would therefore lead to higher consumer prices, lower rates of return for investors and reduced incentives for innovation in the United States. The International Monetary Fund recently warned that trade protectionism in the United States would also magnify the negative effects of any global economic shock.

Ignoring public attitudes about trade is dangerous in the long run, and following the public mood on trade would be an unfortunate abdication of leadership by the Bush Administration in the short run. If the first step to recovery is recognizing that there is a problem, then responsible policymakers in Washington need to appreciate the extent to which the political terrain has shifted. The next step will be changing the American public's mind—a difficult but achievable task, if there is true leadership in the White House.

DANIEL DREZNER is assistant professor of political science at the University of Chicago and author of *U.S. Trade Strategy: Choices and Consequences,* published by the Council on Foreign Relations in December 2005. This article is adapted from a chapter of the book.

UNIT 4

The Institutional Context of American Foreign Policy

Unit Selections

Key Points to Consider

• How relevant is the Constitution to the conduct of American foreign policy? Do courts have a legitimate role to play in determining the content of U.S. foreign policy?

• To what extent should the United States adjust its foreign policy and laws according to the decisions made by international bodies such as the World Trade Organization or the International Criminal Court?

• What is the proper role of Congress in making foreign policy?

• How much power should the president be given in making foreign policy?

• Which of the foreign affairs bureaucracies discussed in this unit is most important? Which one is most in need of reform? Which is most incapable of being reformed?

Student Web Site

www.mhcls.com/online

Internet References

Central Intelligence Agency (CIA)
   http://www.cia.gov
The NATO Integrated Data Service (NIDS)
   http://www.nato.int/structur/nids/nids.htm
U.S. Department of State
   http://www.state.gov/index.html
United States Institute of Peace (USIP)
   http://www.usip.org
U.S. White House
   http://www.whitehouse.gov

Central to any study of American foreign policy are the institutions responsible for its content and conduct. The relationship between these institutions is often filled with conflict, competition, and controversy. The reasons for this are fundamental. Edwin Corwin put it best: The Constitution is an "invitation to the president and Congress to struggle over the privilege of directing U.S. foreign policy." Today, this struggle is not limited to these two institutions. At the national level, the courts have emerged as a potentially important force in the making of American foreign policy. State and local governments have also become highly visible players in world politics.

The power relationships that exist between the institutions that make American foreign policy are important for at least two reasons. First, different institutions represent different constituencies and thus advance different sets of values regarding the proper direction of American foreign policy. Second, decision makers in these institutions have different time frames when making judgments about what to do. The correct policy on conducting a war against terrorism looks different to someone coming up for election in a year or two than it does to a professional diplomat.

This close linkage between institutions and policies suggests that if American foreign policy is to successfully conduct a war against terrorism, policy-making institutions must also change their ways. Many commentators are not confident of their ability to respond to the challenges of the post-September 11 foreign policy agenda. Budgetary power bases and political predispositions that are rooted in the cold war are seen as unlikely to provide any more of a hospitable environment for a war against terrorism than they were for promoting human rights or engaging in peacekeeping operations. The creation of the Department of Homeland Security was a first institutional response to the terrorist attacks of September 11. The appointment of a Director of National Intelligence, a post advocated by investigative reports of why 9/11 happened and how intelligence was handled in the lead up to the Iraq War, was a second.

We can organize the institutions that make American foreign policy into three broad categories. The first composes of elected officials and their staffs: the Presidency and Congress. One topic of enduring interest is the relationship between these bodies. Considerable variation has existed over time with such phrases as the "imperial presidency," "bipartisanship," and "divided government" being used to describe it. A more contemporary issue that has raised considerable concern is the ability of elected officials to manage and organize their appointed staffs effectively, so as to retain control over, and responsibility for, making decisions.

Bureaucratic organizations constitute a second set of institutions that need to be studied when examining American foreign policy. The major foreign policy bureaucracies are the State Department, Defense Department, and the Central Intelligence Agency. Often agencies with more domestic focus such as the

Library of Congress

Commerce Department and Treasury Departments also play important foreign policy roles in highly specialized areas. The Department of Homeland Security might be described as the first foreign policy bureaucracy to have a domestic mandate. Bureaucracies play influential roles in making foreign policy by supplying policy-makers with information, defining problems, and implementing the selected policies. The current international environment presents these bureaucracies with a special challenge. Old threats and enemies have declined in importance or disappeared entirely and new ones have arisen. To remain effective these institutions must adjust their organizational structures and ways of thinking, or risk being seen by policy-makers as irrelevant anachronisms.

The final institutional actor of importance in making American foreign policy are the courts. Their involvement tends to be sporadic and highly focused. Courts serve as arbitrators in the previously noted struggle for dominance between the president and Congress. A key issue today is one that involves determining the jurisdictional boundary of the American legal system and international bodies such as an International Criminal Court and the World Trade Organization. Another is one, which involves determining the boundary of legitimate national security concerns and Constitutional rights and protections of those accused or suspected of engaging in terrorist activities.

The essays in this section survey recent developments and controversies surrounding the key institutions that make American foreign policy. The first essay, "The Return of the Imperial Presidency?" looks at the relationship between Congress and the president. The author cautions against becoming overly enamored with the concept of an imperial presidency and urges that presidential power be examined in the context of congressional power and the influence of the public. In the next essay, "The Truman Standard," the authors examine the oft made comparison between George W. Bush and Harry Truman. This is an analogy favored by the Bush administration but the authors caution that it may highlight its weaknesses more than its strengths.

The next series of essays look at the bureaucracy. "Extraordinary Rendition and the Wages of Hypocrisy" looks at the CIA's policy of transferring individuals without legal process to another country. The author concludes that there are significant diplomatic and strategic costs to this policy. The next essay, "The Homeland Security Hash," takes a critical look at the operation of the Department of Homeland Security and recommends ways to improve its performance. Richard Kohn, "Coming Soon," directs our attention to the growing rift between civilians and professional military officers. He argues four areas that stand out in need of attention: ending the Iraq War, reorganizing for 21st century military operations, overcoming budget problems, and dealing with social issues such as gays in the military. The final bureaucracy essay is by Paul Pillar, a retired CIA official. In "The Right Stuff," he reviews three intelligence estimates on Iraq that the CIA and the intelligence community got right but that the Bush administration ignored. The final essay in this section looks at Congress. "When Congress Stops Wars" presents the argument that Congress is not powerless in dealing with presidents but that it tends only to challenge presidential war powers when there exists a partisan divide between the party that controls the White House and the party that controls the Congress.

The Return of the Imperial Presidency?

One lesson of American politics since September 11 is that some tensions between presidents and Congress spring from a deeper source than the partisan passions of the moment.

DONALD R. WOLFENSBERGER

Moments after President George W. Bush finished his stirring antiterrorism speech before Congress last September, presidential historian Michael Beschloss enthusiastically declared on national television that "the imperial presidency is back. We just saw it."

As someone who began his career as a Republican congressional staff aide during the turbulence of Vietnam and Watergate in the late 1960s and early 1970s, I was startled by the buoyant tone of Beschloss's pronouncement. To me, "imperial presidency" carries a pejorative connotation closely tied to those twin nightmares. Indeed, *Webster's Unabridged Dictionary* bluntly defines *imperial presidency* as "a U.S. presidency that is characterized by greater power than the Constitution allows."

Was Beschloss suggesting that President Bush was already operating outside the Constitution in prosecuting the war against terrorism, or did he have a more benign definition in mind? Apparently it was the latter. As Beschloss went on to explain, during World War II and the Cold War, Congress deferred to presidents, not just on questions of foreign policy and defense, but on domestic issues as well. Whether it was President Dwight D. Eisenhower asking for an interstate highway system or President John F. Kennedy pledging to land a man on the moon, Congress said, "If you ask us, we will." Without such a galvanizing crisis, the president would not be able to define the national interest so completely. "Now," continued Beschloss, "George Bush is at the center of the American solar system; that was not true 10 days ago." In fact, just nine months earlier Beschloss had described Bush as "the first post-imperial president" because, for the first time since the Great Depression, "we were not electing a president under the shadow of an international emergency like the Cold War or World War II or an economic crisis." Then came September 11.

Still, it's hard to join in such a warm welcome for the return of an idea that was heavily burdened just a generation ago with negative associations and cautionary experiences. Presidential scholars understandably become admirers of strong presidents and their presidencies. But a focus on executive power can become so narrow as to cause one to lose sight of the larger governmental system, with its checks and balances. To invest the idea of the imperial presidency with an aura of legitimacy and approbation would be a serious blow to America's constitutional design and the intent of the Framers.

It was historian Arthur M. Schlesinger, Jr., who popularized the term *imperial presidency* in his 1973 book by that title. Schlesinger, who had earlier chronicled the strong presidencies of Andrew Jackson and Franklin D. Roosevelt in admiring terms, admits in *The Imperial Presidency* his own culpability in perpetuating over the years "an exalted conception of presidential power":

> American historians and political scientists, this writer among them, labored to give the expansive theory of the Presidency historical sanction. Overgeneralizing from the [pre-World War II] contrast between a President who was right and a Congress which was wrong, scholars developed an uncritical cult of the activist Presidency.

The view of the presidency as "the great engine of democracy" and the "American people's one authentic trumpet," writes Schlesinger, passed into the textbooks and helped shape the national outlook after 1945. This faith of the American people in the presidency, coupled with their doubts about the ability of democracy to respond adequately to the totalitarian challenge abroad, are what gave the postwar presidency its pretensions and powers.

Uniforms redolent of imperial pomp briefly appeared on White House guards in the Nixon administration, only to vanish after a public outcry.

"By the early 1970s," Schlesinger writes, "the American President had become on issues of war and peace the most absolute monarch (with the possible exception of Mao Tse Tung of

China) among the great powers of the world." Moreover, "the claims of unilateral authority in foreign policy soon began to pervade and embolden the domestic presidency."

The growth of the imperial presidency was gradual, and occurred "usually under the demand or pretext of an emergency," Schlesinger observes. Further, "it was as much a matter of congressional abdication as of presidential usurpation." The seeds of the imperial presidency were sown early. Schlesinger cites as examples Abraham Lincoln's 1861 imposition of martial law and his suspension of habeas corpus, and William McKinley's decision to send 5,000 American troops to China to help suppress the Boxer Rebellion of 1900. It is a measure of how much things have changed that Theodore Roosevelt's 1907 decision to dispatch America's Great White Fleet on a tour around the world was controversial because he failed to seek congressional approval. Then came Woodrow Wilson's forays into revolutionary Mexico, FDR's unilateral declaration of an "unlimited national emergency" six months before Pearl Harbor, and Harry Truman's commitment of U.S. troops to the Korean War in 1950, without congressional authorization, and his 1952 seizure of strike-threatened steel mills.

In 1973, the year *The Imperial Presidency* was published, Congress moved to reassert its war-making prerogatives during non-declared wars by enacting the War Powers Resolution over President Nixon's veto. The following year, prior to Nixon's resignation under the imminent threat of impeachment, Congress enacted two more laws aimed at clipping the wings of the imperial presidency and restoring the balance of power between the two branches. The Congressional Budget and Impoundment Control Act of 1974 was designed to enable Congress to set its own spending priorities and prohibit the president from impounding funds it had appropriated. The Federal Election Campaign Act of 1974 was supposed to eliminate the taint of big money from presidential politics. Subsequent years witnessed a spate of other statutes designed to right the balance between the branches. The National Emergencies Act (1976) abolished scores of existing presidential emergency powers. The Ethics in Government Act (1978) authorized, among other things, the appointment of special prosecutors to investigate high-ranking executive branch officials. The Senate, in 1976, and the House, in 1977, established intelligence committees in the wake of hearings in 1975 revealing widespread abuses; and in 1980 the Intelligence Oversight Act increased Congress's monitoring demands on intelligence agencies and their covert operations.

Since those Watergate-era enactments, presidential scholars have decried the way Congress has emasculated the presidency. As recently as January of last year, political scientist Richard E. Neustadt, author of the classic *Presidential Power* (1964), lamented that "the U.S. presidency has been progressively weakened over the past three decades to the point where it is probably weaker today than at almost any time in the preceding century." Neustadt cited congressional actions as one of several causes of the decline.

As one who worked in the House of Representatives from 1969 to 1997, I have long been puzzled by such complaints.

They have never rung true. What I witnessed during those years was the continuing decline of the legislative branch, not its ascendancy. Even Congress's post-Watergate efforts to reassert its authority look rather feeble in the harsh light of reality. The War Powers Resolution has been all but ignored by every president since Nixon as unconstitutional. They have abided by its reporting requirements, but presidential military forays abroad without explicit congressional authority continue unabated. Bosnia, Kosovo, Haiti, Somalia, and Serbia come readily to mind.

The congressional budget act has been used by every president since Ronald Reagan to leverage the administration's priorities by using budget summits with Congress to negotiate the terms of massive reconciliation bills on taxes and entitlements. The independent counsel act has been allowed to expire twice—though, in light of the unbridled power it gives counsels and the potential for abuse, this may have been wise. Federal funding of presidential campaigns has not stopped campaign finance abuses. And congressional oversight of perceived executive abuses has met with mixed results at best.

In the meantime, presidents have been relying more heavily than before on executive agreements to avoid the treaty ratification process, and on executive orders (or memorandums) of dubious statutory grounding in other areas. Administrations have defied Congress's requests for information with increasing frequency, dismissing the requests as politically motivated. And they have often invoked executive privilege in areas not previously sanctioned by judicial judgments.

The most recent example is Vice President Richard Cheney's refusal, on grounds of executive privilege, to turn over to the General Accounting Office (GAO), an arm of Congress, information about meetings between the president's energy task force and energy executives. The controversy took on added interest with the collapse of Enron, one of the energy companies that provided advice to the task force. Vice President Cheney, who served as President Gerald R. Ford's White House chief of staff, said his action was aimed at reversing "an erosion of the powers" of the presidency over the last 30 to 35 years resulting from "unwise compromises" made by past Administrations. President Bush backed Cheney's claim of executive privilege, citing the need to maintain confidentiality in the advice given to a president.

It is revealing in this case that the congressional requests for information came not through formal committee action or subpoenas but more indirectly from the GAO, at the prompting of two ranking minority committee Democrats in the House, even though their Senate party counterparts are committee chairmen with authority to force a vote on subpoenas. The committee system, which should be the bulwark of congressional policymaking and oversight of the executive branch, has been in steady decline since the mid-1970s. Not the least of the causes is the weakening of committee prerogatives and powers by Congress itself, as a response to members' demands for a more participatory policy process than the traditional committee system allowed. Party leaders eventually replaced committee leaders as the locus of power in the House, a shift that was not altered by the change in party control of Congress in 1995.

Another contributing factor has been the shift in the Republican Party's base of power to the South and West, which has given a more populist and propresidential cast to the GOP membership on Capitol Hill.

Even with recent promises by Speaker of the House Dennis Hastert (R-Ill.) and Senate Majority Leader Tom Daschle (D-S.D.) to "return to the regular order" by giving committees greater flexibility and discretion in agenda setting and bill drafting, Congress is hamstrung by self-inflicted staff cuts and three-day legislative workweeks that make deliberative lawmaking and careful oversight nearly impossible. The "permanent campaign" has spilled over into governing, diminishing the value members see in committee work and encouraging partisan position taking and posturing. (It also makes members eager to get back to their districts for the serious work of campaigning, which explains the three-day work week in Washington.) It is easier to take a popular campaign stand on an unresolved issue than make a painful policy choice and explain it to the voters.

Bill Clinton had the common touch—and an imperial taste for sending U.S. troops abroad without congressional approval.

Is it any wonder that even before the current emergency the executive was in a stronger position than Congress? Such power alone is not necessarily a sign of an imperial presidency. But testing the limits of power seems to be an inborn trait of political man, and presidents are no exception. Even presidential power proponent Richard Neustadt, who sees the presidency at the beginning of this 21st century as the weakest it's been in three decades, concedes that none of the formal limits on presidential powers by Congress or the courts have managed to eliminate those powers of greatest consequence, including the "plentitude of prerogative power" (a Lockean concept of acting outside the constitutional box to save the nation) that Lincoln assumed during the Civil War.

Both presidents George H. W. Bush and George W. Bush, to their credit, sought authorization from Congress for the use of force against Iraq and international terrorists, respectively, before committing troops to combat. Yet both also claimed they bad inherent powers as president to do so to protect the national interest. (The younger Bush was on firmer ground since even the Framers explicitly agreed that the president has authority to repel foreign invasions and respond to direct attacks on the United States.)

The presidency is at its strongest at the outset of a national crisis or war. Just as President Franklin D. Roosevelt was encountering public and congressional wariness over his depression-era policies in the late 1930s, along came World War II and a whole new lease on the throne. Presidential power tends to increase at the expense of Congress. Alexander Hamilton put it succinctly in *The Federalist* 8: "It is of the nature of war to increase the executive at the expense of the legislative authority."

One way to gauge this balance of power is to look at the extent to which Congress deliberates over policy matters and the extent to which it gives the president most of what he requests with minimal resistance. Two weeks after Congress passed a $40 billion emergency spending bill and a resolution authorizing the president to use force against those behind the World Trade Center attacks, Senator Robert S. Byrd (D-W.Va.) rose in a nearly empty Senate chamber to remind his colleagues of their deliberative responsibilities. "In the heat of the moment, in the crush of recent events," Byrd observed, "I fear we may be losing sight of the larger obligations of the Senate."

> Our responsibility as Senators is to carefully consider and fully debate major policy matters, to air all sides of a given issue, and to act after full deliberation. Yes, we want to respond quickly to urgent needs, but a speedy response should not be used as an excuse to trample full and free debate.

Byrd was concerned in part about the way in which language relating to the controversy over adhering to the 1972 antiballistic missile treaty had been jettisoned from a pending defense authorization bill in the interest of "unity" after the terrorist attacks. But he was also disturbed by the haste with which the Senate had approved the use-of-force resolution "to avoid the specter of acrimonious debate at a time of national crisis." Byrd added that he was not advocating unlimited debate, but why, he asked, "do we have to put a zipper on our lips and have no debate at all?" Because of the "paucity of debate" in both houses, Byrd added, there was no discussion laying a foundation for the resolution, and in the future "it would be difficult to glean from the record the specific intent of Congress."

A review of the *Congressional Record* supports Byrd's complaint. Only Majority Leader Daschle and Minority Leader Trent Lott (R-Miss.) spoke briefly before the Senate passed the emergency spending bill and the use-of-force resolution. The discussion was truncated chiefly because buses were waiting to take senators and House members to a memorial service at the National Cathedral.

The House, to its credit, did return after the service for five hours of debate on the resolution, which it passed 420 to 1. Some 200 members spoke for about a minute each—hardly the stuff of a great debate. At no time did any member raise a question about the breadth, scope, or duration of the authority granted by the resolution. The closest some came were passing references to the way in which President Lyndon B. Johnson had used the language of the 1964 Gulf of Tonkin Resolution as authority to broaden U.S. involvement in Vietnam.

To the credit of Congress, a small, bipartisan leadership group had earlier negotiated a compromise with the White House to confine the resolution's scope to "those nations, organizations or persons" implicated in the September 11 attacks. The original White House proposal was much broader, extending the president's authority "to deter and pre-empt any future acts of terrorism or aggression against the United States." The language change is significant. If President Bush cannot demonstrate that Iraq was somehow involved in the September 11 attacks but decides to take military action against it, he will have to decide whether to seek additional authority from Congress or act without it, as President Bill Clinton did before him.

In times of war or national emergency, presidents have always acted in what they thought to be the national interest. That is not to say that Congress simply becomes a presidential lap dog. While it tends to defer to the commander in chief on military matters once troops have been committed to combat, it continues to exercise oversight and independence on matters not directly affecting the war's outcome. For example, President Bush was forced to make drastic alterations in his economic stimulus package by Senate Democrats who disagreed with his tax relief and spending priorities. And even in the midst of the war on terrorism, the House and Senate intelligence committees launched a joint inquiry into why our intelligence services were not able to detect or thwart the September 11 terrorist plot. In the coming months, moreover, Congress is sure to have its own ideas on how the federal budget can best be allocated to meet the competing demands for defense, homeland security, and domestic social-welfare programs.

I s the imperial presidency back? While at this writing the White House has not overtly exercised any extraconstitutional powers, the imperial presidency has been with us since World War II, and it is most likely to be re-energized during times of national crisis. Every president tends to test the limits of his power during such periods in order to do what he deems necessary to protect national security. To the extent that Congress does not push back and the public does not protest, the armor of the imperial presidency is further fortified by precedent and popular support against future attacks.

What is the danger in a set of powers that have, after all, evolved over several decades into a widely recognized reality without calamitous consequences for the Republic? As James Madison put in *The Federalist* 51, "The separate and distinct exercise of the different powers of government . . . is admitted on all hands to be essential to the preservation of liberty." The "great security against a gradual concentration of power in the same department," he went on, is to provide each department with the "necessary constitutional means and personal motives to resist. . . . Ambition must be made to counteract ambition."

The Constitution's system of separated powers and checks and balances is not a self-regulating machine. Arthur M. Schlesinger, Jr., observed in *The Imperial Presidency,* that what kept a strong presidency constitutional, in addition to the president's own appreciation of the Framers' wisdom, was the vigilance of the nation. "If the people had come to an unconscious acceptance of the imperial presidency," he wrote, "the Constitution could not hold the nation to ideals it was determined to betray." The only deterrent to the imperial presidency is for the great institutions of our society—Congress, the courts, the press, public opinion, the universities, "to reclaim their own dignity and meet their own responsibilities."

DONALD R. WOLFENSBERGER is director of the Congress Project at the Wilson Center and the author of *Congress and the People: Deliberative Democracy on Trial (2000).* He retired as chief of staff of the House Rules Committee in 1997 after a 28-year career on the staff of the U.S. House of Representatives.

The Truman Standard

DEREK CHOLLET AND JAMES M. GOLDGEIER

"Soon after arriving at the State Department," Secretary of State Condoleezza Rice wrote in December 2005, "I hung a portrait of Dean Acheson in my office." The reason for choosing the visage of Harry Truman's second Secretary of State to gaze down upon her? "Like Acheson and his contemporaries, we live in an extraordinary time—one in which the terrain of international politics is shifting beneath our feet and the pace of historical change outstrips even the most vivid imagination."[1]

In and of itself, this is nothing new. Since the end of the Cold War, it has become customary for American secretaries of state to compare the challenges before them to those confronted by Truman and his two distinguished top diplomats, Acheson and his predecessor, General George C. Marshall. But the second term Bush team has taken this comparison to a new level. Particularly at the State Department, the Truman-Acheson reference has become a mantra, part of the standard, bedrock rhetoric of the Secretary both in her prepared and extemporaneous remarks. Secretary Rice and President Bush clearly want this comparison to be accepted and made by others. But in some important ways the analogy, if thought through, highlights more of the Administration's shortcomings than its strengths. What, then, is the Truman Standard, and how does the Bush Administration really measure up to it?

Analogies, Intended and Not

It's easy to see why Secretary Rice, President Bush and others in the Administration invoke Truman and Acheson when explaining their own circumstances and choices. Like Truman, Bush takes pride in being plainspoken and enjoys needling Washington's political and policy elite. The Truman Administration, facing novel and unexpected challenges, rose to the occasion with sharp analysis, bold policy change and courageous leadership in the face of much hidebound skepticism and fear. The principals of the Bush Administration fancy themselves as having done the same thing.

In a way, this has been inevitable. After all, the Cold War story of danger, struggle, determination and victory is the happy-ending story they know best. Rice often mentions that when she was watching the USSR break apart as the White House Soviet specialist during 1989–1991, she "was only harvesting the good decisions that had been taken in 1947, in 1948, and in 1949." A half century from now serious historians may conclude that the British success at defeating the Indian Rebellion of 1857—which sparked broad unrest against British rule on the subcontinent—is a better analogy to the American "war on terror", but no one should expect American leaders to draw from that or any other similarly distant historical event.

Besides, there are arguable parallels between the late 1940s and the early years of this century. Then, some sixty years ago, the Soviet Union had occupied half of Europe and exploded an atomic bomb, and with communism sprouting up in Asia, Africa and elsewhere, Truman and his team feared a new existential threat to the United States just a few short years after the defeat of fascism. Now, the challenges posed by the nexus of al-Qaeda and the perils of WMD proliferation seem similarly to pose an existential threat, and again a threat rising unexpectedly just after a great victory. So as the Truman Administration recognized the scope of the threat and responded to scale, the Bush Administration strives to do the same. Just as freedom and democracy were the guiding inner lights of Truman's vision, so they are for George W. Bush. And just as building democratic allies in Germany and Japan were the key arenas for the success of containment, so the Bush team views the creation of a democratic Iraq and Afghanistan as similar in importance to the success of its long-term strategy. None of this is far-fetched.

No less important a Truman parallel is the belief that George W. Bush will be vindicated by history, despite his increasing unpopularity among the American people today—not to speak of how unpopular he may be when he leaves office in January 2009. In this way, the Truman comparisons offer a kind of psychological comfort for the beleaguered Bush team. As Secretary of Defense Rumsfeld said at a press briefing late last year, Truman, who is:

> now remembered as a fine president, [left] office in 1953 with an approval rating of about 25 percent, one of the lowest recorded ratings since folks started measuring those things. . . . Back then, a great many people questioned whether young Americans should face death and injury in Korea, thousands of miles from home, for a result that seemed uncertain at best. And today the answer is the Korean peninsula.[2]

Former *New York Times* columnist William Safire predicted for 2006 that, "As Bush's approval rises, historians will begin to equate his era with that of Truman."[3]

It is true that Harry Truman is held in far higher esteem today than when he left office. He is now considered one of America's greatest presidents, much admired for his humble style and his decisive, gutsy leadership. Yet what such comparisons overlook is that the Truman Administration not only helped build up two major new democracies and established the strategy of containment, but developed the tools to implement its policy over the long haul. That Administration created the United Nations, the Marshall Plan, NATO, the General Agreement on Tariffs and Trade, the IMF and the World Bank, institutions that have underpinned American leadership in world politics for more than half a century.

There is yet another Truman parallel that, unsurprisingly, the Bush team does not go out of its way to emphasize. In the 1952 election, with an unpopular president mired in war in Korea, both Democratic candidate Adlai Stevenson and Republican candidate Dwight Eisenhower ran against the Truman legacy. The year 2008 will witness the first presidential election since 1952 in which, presumably, neither the sitting president nor the vice president is running. If George W. Bush cannot turn things around in Iraq—which appears depressingly likely—candidates from both parties may well run against his record, and not just in foreign policy. The skyrocketing budget deficit, lagging health care reform, the prescription drugs-for-seniors mess, and the continuing ethics scandals that often plague second-term administrations are available as campaign grist, as well. The Republicans are already heading into a difficult mid-term election in November (in the 1950 midterm elections, Truman's Democrats were trounced, losing 5 Senate seats and 28 in the House). So at least in the short run, Bush might prove to be a lot like Truman, leaving office with little popularity and a legacy that politicians from both parties treat as a liability.

But will Bush win big in his long-term gamble—that, as with Truman, future historians will esteem him as a visionary leader? That is not clear on account of the biggest difference between the Truman of 1950 and the Bush of 2006. Truman not only created international institutions, but he also built his foreign policy with bipartisan support, so that his successors—Republican and Democratic alike—were destined to operate within the framework he created. So far, President Bush has done nothing of that scale and scope. Not only has he largely disdained formal institutions, he has also spurned bipartisanship. There is thus no lasting institutional or political legacy to ensure that his successors will adopt his general approach to world affairs.

Work to Do

What would President Bush have to accomplish in the final three years of his presidency to make his Truman show—and Rice's supporting act to compare herself to Acheson—less a theatrical slogan than an achievement historians and the public will truly come to appreciate?

The Truman Administration faced five unprecedented challenges: turning vanquished adversaries into democratic allies; defending the free states of Europe from possible Soviet aggression; developing a new architecture for managing the global economy; creating international legitimacy for American actions abroad; and deterring the Soviet nuclear threat. As President Bush and Secretary Rice have asserted, today's challenges are somewhat comparable. It is in America's interest to spread freedom in the broader Middle East, not just in Afghanistan and Iraq, but in the Palestinian Authority, Iran and Syria. Strong alliances continue to be important for that and other purposes. The global economy is under significant strain. America needs to ensure that its foreign policy actions are perceived as legitimate. And the United States faces a range of foreign policy threats, including nuclear programs in North Korea and Iran, the continued threat posed by al-Qaeda, the uncertain future of a growing China, and the reassertion of Russian power, this time not least in tightening global energy markets.

The Administration has a long way to go to meet the Truman Standard, and its most serious impediment is the Iraq problem.

In the 1950s, America ensured that Germany and Japan became pro-American allies because they had been occupied after the war with sufficient numbers of American troops and protracted American oversight. In Iraq, the United States bungled badly the postwar occupation. And if Iraqi democracy—or chaos and collapse—leads to greater Iranian dominance of the region, the effort will hardly be compared to postwar American leadership in Europe and Asia.

There are some areas where the Bush team is showing promising course corrections. For example, the Administration did not necessarily need to create new alliances because it inherited those created during the Cold War. But having initially decided not to work through NATO in Afghanistan and then splitting the alliance over Iraq, the Administration recognized early in its second term a need to repair the damage it had done. Deciding that the first overseas trip of his second term would be to Europe, the President stirred hopes for better relations by visiting not only NATO but the European Union in Brussels. And with an increasing NATO role in Afghanistan, Iraq and Darfur, it appeared in 2005 and early this year that Bush might yet infuse the alliance with new shared purpose. Unfortunately, the disputes over treatment of terrorist suspects on European territory and U.S. policies of preventive detention have complicated efforts to forge that renewed sense of purpose.

On trade, the Administration decided early in its tenure to pursue bilateral deals and the relatively small Central American Free Trade Agreement rather than to reach for more ambitious multilateral accords. This left tough issues of the Doha Round on the back burner until it was too late to forge a comprehensive agreement at the WTO's December meeting in Hong Kong. There is no question that concluding the Doha Round would be a real challenge for any administration given the range of demands from Europe and some of the leading developing countries, but rising to that challenge would go a long way toward defining Bush as Trumanesque.

Having soured relations with the United Nations, and alienated much of the world by the way it has handled its policies toward terrorist detainees and interrogations, the Administration seems unable to decide where to turn to rebuild American legitimacy in global affairs. The September deal with North Korea appears insubstantial; negotiations with Iran have faltered; bin Laden and Zarqawi remain at large, China has begun to dominate Asian affairs, and a more authoritarian Russia has been working to counter American democratization efforts along its borders. The Administration has made clear that it does not trust formal institutions and does not want to create new bureaucracies to develop global governance. It has preferred to work through less formal structures like the G-8, the loose frame-work Bush used to promote his Broader Middle East and North Africa Initiative, and the Six Party Talks for solving the North Korean nuclear problem. Some of these informal structures have been useful, but they are hardly firstorder institutions. And they often exclude countries whose cooperation is essential to solving global problems. It seems unlikely, for example, that the G-8 can really handle major transnational issues like proliferation, terrorism and global health when countries like China, India and Brazil stand on the sidelines.

There is also the question of how lasting Bush's grand strategy, defined by preemption and democracy promotion, will really be. Will preemption get enshrined in the first half of the 21st century as containment did in the second half of the 20th? Perhaps. After all, any president faced with imminent threats of the kind that struck the United States on September 11, 2001 will want to preempt them.

Yet the first test of the new strategy, Iraq, was sold as preemption in the face of an imminent weapons of mass destruction threat. Since we now know that there was no such imminent threat, the American public and the Congress might be much less compliant in future crises. A debacle in Iraq could well be the undoing of the Bush team's efforts to develop an enduring grand strategy for the post-9/11 era.

The future of the other strategic pillar of the Bush policy, democracy promotion, is also uncertain. Secretary Rice speaks often of "transformational diplomacy", which is underpinned by the idea (if not the practice) of promoting freedom everywhere. She has made some sensible reforms in the way professional diplomats are trained and where they are stationed. What's missing from this notion, however, is a coherent strategy for pursuing not only democratization but other American interests as well. Few would argue against the idea that a freer and more democratic world is in America's interests. This idea is not new; "transformational diplomacy" is little different from the doctrine of "democratic enlargement" enunciated by Bill Clinton's first National Security Advisor, Anthony Lake, in 1993. Yet what the idea lacked in 1993, and still lacks today, is a way to apply it globally in a meaningful way. In the Cold War we knew what we wanted to contain, and where we wanted to contain it. Clinton and Bush have stated a desire to enlarge the community of democracies, but there is no consensus domestically on where, how or when to do so.

So, what can President Bush do? Like Truman, he has already shuffled some key personnel. But as even sympathetic observers have suggested, he could do a lot more in this regard and make an honest stab at bipartisanship. It might go against his every instinct and anger his base, which, with the exception of the immigration issue, he has been unwilling to do so far. But he has to do it if he is to meet the Truman Standard. To gain support for the Marshall Plan, Truman reached out to Republican senator Arthur Vandenberg and chose Republican businessman Paul Hoffman to head the agency that would oversee disbursement of the funds. Would George Bush work in partnership with the Vandenbergs of today, like Delaware Senator Joseph Biden? Would he choose a Democrat with experience in foreign aid to head his Millennium Challenge Corporation? If he did, it would be a sign that he was not simply talking about Truman but actually taking a page from the Truman playbook.

The President could also do some second-term institution building. New domestic and international institutions were critical to the Cold War strategic framework. Truman engineered the National Security Act of 1947 and the institutional architecture of America's modern foreign policy and military establishment. Bush has taken major steps to reform intelligence and homeland security, but he still has a long way to go to reform how we go about promoting democratization and development. Without fundamental changes to the ways we use our so-called soft power—or what Pentagon planners call the tools to win the "long war"—the U.S. approach will continue to be piecemeal, lack focus, and ultimately fall short.

International institutions embedded American ideals and habits of cooperation into the structure of global politics, and they helped lend legitimacy to American actions. This has hardly worked perfectly, as the deep flaws of institutions like the United Nations make clear. Yet despite the boldness of his rhetoric, President Bush's efforts to create new avenues for American legitimacy—through institutions or otherwise—have been underwhelming. The Administration's most successful new international programs—the Proliferation Security Initiative and the Millennium Challenge Account—hardly compare with the creation of NATO or the World Bank. To meet the Truman Standard, Bush will have to develop new ways to build American legitimacy to act internationally. Perhaps transforming the Community of Democracies from an ineffectual and occasional talk-fest into a real, working alliance, with a permanent secretariat and a real budget, would be one way to do this. But the Administration has consistently opposed any such idea—at least up to now.

Finally, there is the political reality of the Bush legacy. Unless the President can find a way to turn the Iraq situation around and get American troops out gracefully, and without leaving behind a civil war, by 2008, the next presidential election will be defined by which candidates can better distinguish (and distance) themselves from the current Administration. And to leave something lasting behind, the Administration will need to reinvigorate NATO and elevate U.S. cooperation with the EU; find the key to success in the Doha Round; gain consensus with Europe, China and Russia on containing the threats posed by North Korea and Iran; capture or kill bin Laden and Zarqawi; and counter Russian and Chinese diplomacy in places like Ukraine, the Caucasus, Central Asia and Southeast Asia while finding ways to engage those two countries on matters of common strategic interest.

If Bush fails to do any of this, he will likely leave office politically hobbled, with his opponents emboldened and a country deeply disillusioned about his policies around the world. He will be remembered as a leader who tried to do big things and articulate a new vision for America, but because of his stubbornness and insularity failed to garner the support to sustain his policies beyond his term in office. The result might be an America more withdrawn from the world and reluctant to take on significant challenges. And instead of evoking comparisons to Harry Truman, President Bush will leave a more mixed legacy closer to another of his predecessors—Woodrow Wilson.

Notes

1. Condoleezza Rice, "The Promise of Democratic Peace", *Washington Post,* December 11, 2005.

2. Rumsfeld quoted in Al Kamen, "Bush and Turman Don't Match Up", *Washington Post,* November 7, 2005.

3. Safire, "The Office Pool, 2006", *New York Times,* December 30, 2005.

DEREK CHOLLET is a fellow at the Center for Strategic and International Studies and a non-resident fellow at the Brookings Institution. **JAMES M. GOLDGEIER** is a professor of political science at George Washington University and an adjunct senior fellow at the Council on Foreign Relations.

From *The American Interest,* Summer 2006, pp. 107–112. Copyright © 2006 by American Interest. Reprinted by permission.

Extraordinary Rendition and the Wages of Hypocrisy

Aziz Z. Huq

"Extraordinary rendition" is the governmental transfer without legal process of a person to another country where it is more likely than not he will be tortured. The case of the Syrian-born Canadian Maher Arar illustrates the gap between extraordinary rendition and the mundane legal process of extradition. Detained in September 2002, at John F. Kennedy Airport while returning home from vacation, Arar was held in solitary confinement without access to legal counsel in a Brooklyn detention center on suspicion of being a member of al-Qaeda. He was first shipped off to Jordan against his will and subsequently transferred to a Syrian prison, where he was detained for nearly a year without charge or legal process. The 35-year-old software engineer recounts being beaten repeatedly with two-inch thick cables and threatened with electrocution while being questioned about al-Qaeda. After his release, the Syrian ambassador to the United States, Imad Moustapha, declared that Syria had found no evidence of Arar's complicity in terrorism.[1] Arar's case is not unusual. There is substantial anecdotal evidence that the United States routinely and knowingly "outsources" the application of torture by transferring terrorist suspects to countries that violate international human rights norms.

Extraordinary rendition evolved out of pre-9/11 practices intended to facilitate the judicial process, and only after 9/11 became a purposive way to evade U.S. legal prohibitions against torture. Since the 1800s, the United States has "rendered" criminal suspects from overseas to be tried in the United States, and the U.S. Supreme Court twice endorsed criminal prosecutions after such "renditions to justice."[2] In the 1980s, however, the United States began rendering suspects not only to the United States but also to third countries, such as Egypt, in expanding counterterrorism operations. In 1995, Pakistani intelligence arrested Ramzi Yousef, instigator of the 1993 World Trade Center bombing, in Islamabad, and handed him over for transport and trial in the federal court for the Southern District of New York.[3] That same year, the Central Intelligence Agency (CIA) captured Talaat Fouad Qassem, a key leader and spokesman of al-Gamaa al-Islamiya, an Egyptian armed Islamist group, in Croatia. Later, Qassem disappeared into Egyptian custody.[4]

On September 17, 2001, America's rendition policy changed in scale and purpose. That day, President George W. Bush signed a secret presidential finding that authorized the CIA to kill, capture, or detain members of al-Qaeda anywhere in the world. Despite the magnitude of the powers granted in this order, the Bush administration has resisted efforts to secure its public disclosure. The order also authorized secret offshore prisons known as "black sites" where the CIA could send suspects for coercive interrogation of the sort that is illegal in the United States. The presidential finding did not require the CIA, in detaining and transferring suspects, to seek case-by-case approval from the White House, the State Department, or the Justice Department.[5]

The administration's avowed aim was to allow the transfer of suspects to jurisdictions with laxer constraints on coercive interrogation. Former director of central intelligence George Tenet candidly told Congress, "It might be better sometimes for . . . suspects to remain in the hands of foreign authorities, who might be able to use more aggressive interrogation techniques."[6] Torture thus became a primary goal, not merely a collateral consequence, of rendition to third countries. In this respect, the post-9/11 extraordinary rendition system is qualitatively different from the renditions program that preceded it.

The practice of extraordinary rendition jars discordantly with the American commitment to government limited by law and due process. Disappearances and torture cannot be justified. Moreover, they do grave harm to U.S. strategic interests. The Bush administration's efforts to suppress public inquiry into these practices, and the hypocritical nature of its public statements with respect to them, have hindered cooperative international counterterrorism efforts.

Hollow Assurances

Before leaving on a whistle-stop European trip in December 2005 to secure European cooperation in U.S. counterterrorism efforts, Secretary of State Condoleezza Rice gave a speech on the tarmac at Andrews Air Force Base seeking to allay mounting European concerns about extraordinary rendition. Rice claimed that rendition, as practiced by the United States, was permitted under both U.S. and international law. Her statement was unapologetic and unequivocal. "The United States does not permit, tolerate, or condone torture under any circumstances," she said. It was the "policy" of the administration, moreover, that "the United States does not transport, and has not transported, detainees from one country to another for the purpose of interrogation using torture. . . . The United States has not transported anyone, and will not transport anyone, to a country when we believe he will be tortured." She added, "Where appropriate, the United States seeks assurances that transferred persons will not be tortured."[7]

Rice's comments echoed previous statements by Attorney General Alberto Gonzales and President Bush. Nine months earlier, in March 2005, President Bush explained that the goal of extraordinary rendition was "to arrest people and send them back to their country of origin with the promise that they won't be tortured. That's the promise we receive." Attorney General Gonzalez said that it was U.S. policy not to send suspects "to countries where we believe or we know that they're going to be tortured." But Gonzalez cautioned that the United States "can't fully control" what happens to a suspect sent elsewhere.[8]

America's European allies responded skeptically, even contemptuously, to these justifications and rationalizations. The administration's use of phrases like "believe or know" revealed an underlying hypocrisy. An administration marketed in terms of plainspoken truthfulness was now resorting to anodyne and hypertechnical legalisms to evade admitting to a policy condoning torture. Both Rice and Gonzalez spoke of "policy" and carefully avoided talking of "law." A policy is a nonbinding preference that may be overridden.[9] The term trades on a loophole embedded in federal statutes. When the United States ratified the Convention against Torture and Other Cruel, Inhuman or Degrading Treatment or Punishment in 1994, it also adopted a swarm of "declarations," "reservations," and "understandings" that limit American duties under the convention. One of these caveats stated that ratification alone did not endow the convention's primary rules of conduct with legal force under U.S. law (i.e., the rules were non-self-executing). Laws would need to be enacted by Congress and signed by the president for legal consequences to flow.

One of the laws enacted to implement the convention addresses *overseas* transfers and renditions. The act, however, speaks of "policy," not binding law. The 1998 Foreign Affairs Reform and Restructuring Act states: "It shall be the policy of the United States not to expel, extradite, or otherwise effect the involuntary return of any person to a country in which there are substantial grounds for believing the person would be in danger of being subjected to torture, regardless of whether the person is physically present in the United States." In asserting that the United States was following the law with respect to rendition, Rice's and Gonzalez's statements failed to acknowledge the act's nonbinding character. The resulting divergence between public impressions and underlying legal realities hardly prompted confidence in the integrity of the administration's position.[10]

Rice's reference to diplomatic "assurances," or formal representations from one government to another concerning a specific suspect's treatment after transfer, were even more troubling. The form such assurances take is unclear. Nor is it clear which government agency is responsible for obtaining them. According to the *Washington Post,* the CIA's general counsel demands a "verbal assurance from each nation that detainees will be treated humanely,"[11] although written assurances also exist. In Maher Arar's case, the State Department apparently sought and received "appropriate assurances from Syrian officials" prior to his transfer.[12]

Such diplomatic assurances are intended to provide political figures with "plausible deniability"—the ability to dissociate themselves from an action or the clear and predictable consequences of that action. Except with extraordinary rendition, diplomatic assurances are not plausible. On the contrary, they underscore the hypocritical divergence between statements of American values on the one hand and U.S. practices on the other.

When Maher Arar was sent to Syria, it was no secret that torture was employed in Syrian prisons. A recent State Department human rights report takes Syria to task for "continuing serious abuses including the use of torture in detention, which at times, results in death; poor prison conditions; arbitrary arrest and detention; [and] prolonged detention without trial."[13] When the CIA delivered Talaat Fouad Qassem to the Egyptian authorities, it was certainly aware of how he would be treated. A 2004 State Department report on Egypt paints a grim picture of "a systematic pattern of torture by the security forces" that included "stripping and blindfolding victims; suspending victims from a ceiling or doorframe with feet just touching the floor; beating victims with fists, whips, metal rods, or other objects; using electric shocks; and dousing victims with cold water."[14]

In light of such reports, let alone other evidence of the pervasive employment of torture by states that collaborate in extraordinary rendition, there is no reason to credit diplomatic assurances that rendered prisoners are not being tortured. Countries that routinely violate their own laws against torture and ignore their obligations under international conventions to which they are signatories are being asked by the U.S. government to "promise" not to treat rendered prisoners as they are known to treat their own prisoners. These assurances are simply not credible.

Such diplomatic assurances are sought as a cover for the administration's assertion that the United States is not violating its obligations under the Convention against Torture. This treaty, which the United States has signed and ratified, bars a signatory state from expelling, returning, or extraditing a person to another state "where there are substantial grounds for believing he would be in danger of being subjected to torture." These terms are not satisfied by empty formalities. The treaty directs signatories to "take into account all relevant considerations including, where applicable, the existence in the State concerned of a consistent pattern of gross, flagrant, or mass violations of human rights." Thus the convention demands that the actual risk to a person be considered before transferring him to the custody of authorities in another country. It does not suffice to say that a country has anti-torture laws or that it has given assurances that a person will not be tortured. Indeed, as the Yale scholar Oona Hathaway has noted, "Treaty ratification is not infrequently associated with worse human rights ratings than otherwise expected." Whatever laws against torture may bind Syrian intelligence officers, they have little relevance to the question how a Maher Arar will be treated.[15]

Nor is there reason to believe that assurances given by the Syrian authorities were believed by the United States. As Human Rights Watch has noted, there is no known instance "where assurances have been sought from a county in which torture and ill-treatment were not acknowledged human rights problems."[16] Every country to which the United States has rendered a terrorism suspect since 9/11 has been a persistent and egregious violator of human rights, and has been recognized as such by the State Department. The Bush administration, in seeking diplomatic assurances from these states that they will not torture rendered prisoners, is asking the American public and people elsewhere to believe a transparently absurd fiction.

Unsurprisingly, there is no evidence to suggest that the United States has ever protested to Syria, Egypt, or any other of its extraordinary rendition partners about torture after transfer. In February 2005, the new director of central intelligence, Porter Goss, told Congress that the CIA had an "accountability program" to monitor post-transfer conduct, but that once a prisoner was out of the CIA's control "there's only so much we can do."[17] Indeed, why would the United States do anything if another country applied the "advanced interrogation techniques" the CIA had sought permission to use itself? Diplomatic assurances, in sum, are a convenient "check the box" means of evading the international prohibition against returns to torture.

International Outrage

A diplomatic strategy based on the assumption that others are fools is bound to fail. Disclosures of Maher Arar's removal to Syria, as well as of extraordinary renditions from Italy and Sweden to Egypt, combined with the Bush administration's refusal to acknowledge the hypocrisy of diplomatic assurances with respect to torture, triggered widespread revulsion at American conduct.

European audiences greeted Secretary of State Rice's defense of extraordinary rendition with skepticism. European politicians and journalists roundly condemned the practice. A British Conservative MP described Rice's comments as "surgically precise language to obfuscate and distract" that had been "drafted by lawyers with the intention of misleading an audience." Journalists in Britain and elsewhere seized on the ambiguities in Rice's speech surrounding the term "policy" and the reliance on diplomatic assurances as evidence of overt hypocrisy on the part of the Bush administration.[18] The weakness of the legal argument with respect to diplomatic assurances, moreover, unavoidably conveyed the impression that Rice believed her audience to be idiots or toadies.

The public uproar that followed revelations of the practice of extraordinary rendition led Canada, Sweden, Italy, Germany, and the European Union, to initiate judicial or parliamentary investigations of specific cases concerning their citizens or the use of their territory. During Rice's visit to Europe, German officials pressed her to clarify the American position. Rice's evasive responses only added fuel to the fire. "No one believes these [diplomatic] assurances," concluded the conservative German newspaper *Die Welt.* With less restraint, Berlin's *Die Tageszeitung* ran a fake CIA recruiting advertisement: "Torturers Wanted: U.S. Citizens May Not Apply." Rice's visit, rather than answering European concerns, served to crystallize the view, held across the European political spectrum, that the American government was engaged in morally reprehensible policies with which European states should have no truck.[19]

Rice's attempts to justify U.S. policy also prompted a sharply worded judicial rebuke. In December 2005, Britain's House of Lords, the nation's highest court, issued an opinion holding that evidence gained by torture could not be introduced in U.K. immigration proceedings. Uniformly praised across the political spectrum in Britain, the Lords' judgment goes out of its way to condemn the extraordinary rendition system in no uncertain terms. "The use of torture is dishonorable," wrote Lord Goff, who adjudicated the case. "It corrupts and degrades the state which uses it and the legal system which accepts it. . . . In our own century, many people in the United States, heirs to the common-law tradition, have felt their country dishonored by its use of torture outside the jurisdiction and its practice of extra-legal 'rendition,' of suspects to countries where they would be tortured." The reference to contemporary events, hardly essential to disposition of the case, flags a deep-seated unease with American counterterrorism tactics.[20]

To many scholars of international relations, the violation of international legal norms and the widespread popular and judicial

opprobrium engendered by extraordinary renditions are of little strategic consequence in the pragmatic world of international relations. The realist John Mearsheimer has written that states should be understood as "billiard balls"—i.e., discrete units whose internal politics are irrelevant to their foreign policy positions—acting in service of a clearly defined, rational "national interest." International legal norms, he contends, "have minimal influence on state behavior and thus hold little promise for promoting stability in the post-Cold War world."[21] According to the Mearsheimer thesis, we should not worry about moral indignation over extraordinary rendition because it has scant relevance to the decisions of foreign governments respecting national security.

Mearsheimer's analysis may well be true in regard to relations between states. But in the context of counterterrorism operations against nonstate actors, domestic political pressure matters. Popular discontent and official investigations of U.S. misconduct on foreign soil have led to diplomatic pressure on Washington, and foreign governments have restricted intelligence and police cooperation with U.S. agencies. A further concern is that extraordinary rendition takes advantage of lawless elements in state intelligence and security services in receiving countries, as well as the gaps between different legal systems in which the legal protection of rights is unclear. As former CIA agent Reuel Marc Gerecht observes, by lending legitimacy to these holdouts against the rule of law, extraordinary rendition "works against the growth of democracy in the Middle East," which is "the only sure way of breaking bin Ladenism."[22]

The Harm Done

Consider first the diplomatic consequences of extraordinary rendition. In the "world of stark and harsh competition" depicted by Mearsheimer, states red in tooth and claw do not have time to pause and ruminate on the morality of counterterrorism cooperation, let alone sanction their allies for overreaching: "All states are forced to seek the same goal: maximum relative power."[23] But disputes over extraordinary rendition have resulted in tangible setbacks for the United States. For example, in 2005, Foreign Minister Ben Bot suggested that the Dutch contribution to NATO deployments in Afghanistan would be jeopardized if American officials "continue[d] to beat around the bush" on the matter of black sites. In 2003, Turkish prime minister Recep Tayyip Erdogan refused to allow U.S. troops to be stationed on its border with Iraq out of a fear of public backlash against what was seen in Turkey as an illegal war. To be sure, the Turkish reaction did not concern extraordinary rendition and black sites, but it reflected the view of the Turkish public that the United States does not play by the same international rules as everyone else. (A popular recent Turkish motion picture casts Americans as villains for the unlawful invasion of Iraq and the torture of detainees there.) In Germany, too, a groundswell of public opinion opposed to Iraq invasion as illegal nearly stymied efforts by former chancellor Gerhard Schröder to accord the United States overfly rights.[24]

Notwithstanding a shared vulnerability to al-Qaeda and its sympathizers, European governments have seen the advantage in yielding to public protests over extraordinary rendition. Their objections to extraordinary rendition are a way of seizing moral high ground, a valuable position as European governments try to foster good relations with their substantial Muslim communities, a task complicated by the recent dispute over cartoons first published in the Danish newspaper *Jyllands-Posten* that incited widespread unrest in the Middle East and Asia. Reflecting on growing European resistance to American counterterrorism positions, the writer Robert Kagan has observed that "ideals and self-interest frequently collide, and Europe's assaults on the legitimacy of U.S. dominance may also become an effective way of constraining and controlling the superpower." European positions on extraordinary rendition, in short, reflect a confluence of domestic electoral self-interest and international advantage. Even if Mearsheimer is correct that states act only out of narrowly conceived "national security" motives, institutions and laws may be seen as the best way of furthering that end. Deterioration in the tenor and amicability of alliances may be incremental. But each small setback directly harms American counterterrorism efforts. Given America's diminished reputation, other countries become less likely to accede to Washington's requests for aid. Resistance from allies furthermore undercuts Washington's ability to set the international agenda by establishing shared goals and values.[25]

Extraordinary rendition has also made cooperation between U.S. and European police and intelligence agencies more difficult. Faced with public pressure over news reports that European intelligence services were collaborating with U.S. agents in extraordinary renditions, European police and judiciaries have limited the scope of counterterrorism cooperation. For example, when Swedish television reported that Swedish police had handed over to the CIA two Egyptian asylum seekers who were sent back to Egypt (where one of the men was later allegedly tortured and tried and sentenced to 25 years in prison by a military tribunal), the resulting public outcry forced the Swedish police to issue regulations requiring that any prisoner transfer be conducted by Swedish officials.[26]

Resistance to intelligence and law enforcement cooperation with the United States comes from institutional sources too. As noted, the British House of Lords in December 2005 prohibited the use of possibly coerced evidence in political asylum and deportation matters, rejecting the claim, made by Eliza Manningham-Buller, head of Britain's security intelligence service MI5, that such tainted evidence was a vital source of intelligence. Manningham-Buller argued that eliminating use of this evidence would cut off one avenue for the apprehension and transfer of suspected terrorists.[27]

German prosecutors have faced serious difficulties prosecuting alleged co-conspirators in the 9/11 plot due to American refusals to share exculpatory evidence from captured senior al-Qaeda leaders held at black sites. Mounir el-Motassadeq's 2003 conviction as an accessory to the murder of the 9/11 victims was overturned on appeal because the U.S. government had declined to produce captured senior al-Qaeda members to testify at his trial. In his 2005 retrial, however, the United States provided some evidence from its interrogations at black sites, enough at least for Motassadeq to be convicted of a lesser charge of belonging to al-Qaeda. He was acquitted of the original conspiracy charge, however. Another German resident, Abdelghani Mzoudi, was acquitted of complicity in the 9/11 plot in 2004 due to American refusals to pass on evidence from interrogations at black sites.[28]

In another case, public prosecutors in Milan initiated an investigation into the actions of CIA agents who in February 2003 snatched an Egyptian cleric, Osama Moustafa Hassan Nasr, from the streets of Milan in broad daylight. As a university student, Nasr had joined Jamaat al-Islamiya, a loose coalition of Islamists who had hewed to violence even as Egypt's Muslim Brotherhood turned to political participation in the mid-1980s. When the state cracked down on Jamaat al-Islamiya, Nasr fled first to Albania, then to Germany, and finally to Italy, settling in Milan. After his kidnapping, Nasr's wife and two children had no word of him until April 2005, when they received a letter from him, mailed from Alexandria in Egypt. The kidnapping—"the inspiration of the CIA station chief in Rome, who wanted to play a more active role in taking suspected terrorists off the street"—was undertaken without full Italian cooperation.[29]

In June 2005, Milan prosecutor Armando Spataro issued arrest warrants charging 22 alleged CIA operatives with the kidnapping. Because these warrants are valid throughout Europe under EU rules, the persons named in them are subject to arrest if they enter any European country. Spataro explained that Nasr had been the subject of an ongoing Italian investigation, and that his kidnapping by the CIA had "seriously damaged counterterrorism efforts in Italy and Europe. . . . In fact, if [Nasr] had not been kidnapped, he would now be in prison, subject to a regular trial, and we would have probably identified his other accomplices." To make matters worse, a month after the kidnapping, the CIA had misleadingly reported to its Italian counterpart that Nasr had fled to the Balkans on his own volition. Revelations that the CIA operatives involved in the kidnapping had stayed in luxury hotels in Milan, Florence, and Venice before and after the kidnapping, racking up more than $100,000 in bills, added to the impression that the operation had been conceived in a reckless and foolish manner.[30]

There is yet another harm that results from extraordinary rendition, which is perhaps less dramatically evident than the harm done to ongoing investigations of terrorism suspects but no less damaging in the long run. When formal legal channels are circumvented, international judicial and prosecutorial cooperation is also weakened. By exploiting the fragility of the rule of law in countries such as Egypt and Syria, the extraordinary rendition system deepens that vulnerability. In the context of a long-term counterterrorism strategy that depends on eliminating lawless pockets in which al-Qaeda and other terrorist groups can thrive and on strengthening democratic governance in countries where terrorist groups seeks recruits, a tactic that retards the development of the rule of law is pernicious.

Extraordinary rendition strengthens intelligence services in nondemocratic states against forces seeking democratic reform. Since the overthrow of the Egyptian monarchy in 1952, Egypt has labored under "total executive domination," in which democratic and parliamentary resistance is subdued though a host of constitutional and extralegal methods. The parliamentary elections of 2005 were accompanied by violent repression by security forces. In December 2005, an Egyptian court sentenced Ayman Nour, the leading opposition figure, to five years of hard labor for election-related fraud in a case widely seen as retribution for his having run against the long-ruling Hosni Mubarek. The Egyptian prime minister has admitted that by mid-2005 Egypt had received "60 to 70" terrorist suspects through rendition or by extradition since 9/11. In the same period, Egypt received approximately $50 billion annually in U.S. aid, with a significant amount doubtless flowing to the security agencies that work with the CIA. Egyptian-American cooperation in extraordinary rendition strengthens the least law-abiding elements of the Egyptian state, its internal security forces, and thus corrodes the prospects for full Egyptian democracy.[31]

President Mubarek has declared that U.S. policy with respect to extraordinary rendition and black sites proves "that we were right from the beginning in using all means, including military tribunals, to combat terrorism." Sudan and Zimbabwe have justified "disappearances" of political foes to the ruling regimes on the ground that the United States also "disappears" people. American efforts to reform the United Nations Human Rights Commission have been stymied in part because the United States is no longer viewed as a credible human rights advocate. The Zimbabwean representative to that body swatted away American criticisms of abuses by his government, proclaiming that "those who live in glass houses should not throw stones." America, he said, had "a lot of dirt on its hands."[32]

The harm to the rule of law from extraordinary rendition and the condoning of torture is no abstract concern. Perceptive scholars of the Islamist threat say that political reform in the core Arab states such as Saudi Arabia and Egypt is pivotal in the effort to thin al-Qaeda's ranks. "Al Qaeda draws many of it[s] recruits from closed societies that are intolerant of dissent," observes the writer Peter Bergen. "For this reason it is no coincidence that Saudis and Egyptians play such a key role in the group." Bergen was echoing an insight stated by the 9/11 Commission, which underscored the need for the United States to "offer an example of moral leadership in the world, committed to treat people humanely, abide by the rule of law, and be generous and caring to our neighbors," and to choose its allies carefully: "When Muslim governments, even those who are friends, do not respect these principles, the United States must stand for a better future." Extraordinary rendition, of course, is antithetical to these goals. "One of the lessons of the long Cold War," the commission noted, "was that short-term gains in cooperating with the most repressive and brutal governments were too often outweighed by long-term setbacks for America's stature and interests."[33]

Supporting the rule of law in the countries from which al-Qaeda and other terrorist organizations draw their recruits and the general task of moral leadership are intertwined. Undermining al-Qaeda's growth demands the strengthening of liberal democracy and political pluralism across the Middle East. The damage to the rule of law inflicted by extraordinary rendition retard this labor. In practical terms, extraordinary rendition empowers local factions who are opposed to democratic development. And to millions of Arabs and Muslims, stories of extraordinary rendition and secret offshore prisons speak louder than words about American values. They suggest that America is unwilling to accord foreigners the same basic human dignity enjoyed by its own citizens, that American ethics are purely instrumental. Extraordinary rendition has given al-Qaeda a potent recruiting tool. In the end, the battle of ideas that al-Qaeda has sought to precipitate may be the only war that really counts. In ceding the high moral ground, the United States is letting a precious advantage slip from its grasp.

Notes

The author gratefully acknowledges the substantial input and edits of Frederick A. O. Schwarz, Jr. in the preparation of this article.

1. The details of Arar's case are from Jane Mayer, "Outsourcing Torture," *New Yorker,* February 14, 2005, p. 106; Canadian Broadcasting Company, "Missing Ottawa Engineer Turns Up in Syria," October 22, 2002, available at http://www.cbc .ca/stories/2002/10/21/arar_021021; Thomas Walkom, "Arar's Troubles Rooted in the Cold War," *Toronto Star,* September 17, 2005; Complaint and Demand for Jury Trial in *Arar v. Ashcroft,* January 20, 2005, available at http://www.ccr-ny.org/v2/legal/ september_11th/docs/ArarComplaint.pdf.

2. See *United States v. Alvarez-Machain,* 504 U.S. 655 (1992); *Ker v. People,* 110 Ill. 627 (1884), aff'd 119 U.S. 436 (1886).

3. Steve Coll, *Ghost Wars: The Secret History of the CIA, Afghanistan and Bin Laden, from the Soviet Invasion to September 10, 2001* (London: Penguin, 2004), pp. 272–75.

4. See Anthony Shadid, "America Prepares the War on Terror," *Boston Globe,* October 7, 2001; "Wife of Egyptian Prominent Fundamentalist Asks Croatia to Reveal His Destiny," *Arabic News,* available at http://www.arabicnews.com/ansub/Daily/ Day/000915/2000091502.html; Kareem Fahim, "The Invisible Men," *Village Voice,* April 6, 2004, p. 37.

5. Dana Priest, "Foreign Network at Front of CIA's Terror Fights," *Washington Post,* November 18, 2005; idem, "CIA Holds Terror Suspects in Secret Prisons: Debate Is Growing over Legality and Morality of Overseas System Set Up After 9/11," *Washington Post,* November 2, 2005; Douglas Jehl and David Johnston, "Rule Change Lets C.I.A. Freely Send Suspects Abroad," *New York Times,* March 6, 2005; Shaun Waterman, "CIA 'Too Cautious' in Killing Terrorists," UPI Wire Service, February 27, 2005.

6. John Barry, Michael Hirsch, and Michael Isikoff, "The Roots of Torture," *Newsweek,* May 24, 2004, p. 16.

7. Remarks of Secretary of State Condoleezza Rice upon Her Departure for Europe, December 5, 2005, Andrews Air Force Base.

8. Dana Priest, "CIA's Assurances on Transferred Suspects Doubted," *Washington Post,* March 17, 2005; R. Jeffrey Smith, "Gonzalez Defends Transfer of Detainees," *Washington Post,* March 8, 2005.

9. Responses of Alberto R. Gonzalez, Nominee to be Attorney General of the United States to Written Questions of Senator Richard J. Durbin, response 1(b).

10. See Committee on International Human Rights of the Association of the Bar of the City of New York and the Center for Human Rights and Global Justice, New York University School of Law, "Torture by Proxy," 2004, p. 3, n. 5; Foreign Affairs Reform and Restructuring Act of 1998, Pub. L. No. 105-277, div. G. Title XXII, S 1242(a).

11. Priest, "CIA's Assurances on Transferred Suspects Doubted."

12. Ibid.

13. U.S. Department of State, "Syria: Country Reports on Human Rights Practices, 2004."

14. U.S. Department of State, "Egypt: Country Reports on Human Rights Practices, 2004."

15. See Convention against Torture, art. 3(1) and (2). The U.S. interpretation is less stringent than the generally accepted international view. See "Torture by Proxy," pp. 37–38. For the gap between treaty signature and compliance, see Oona Hathaway, "Do Human Rights Treaties Make a Difference?" *Yale Law Journal,* vol. 111 (2002), p. 1935.

16. See Human Rights Watch, "Still at Risk: Diplomatic Assurances No Safeguard Against Torture," April 2005, p. 7, available at http://www.hrw.org.

17. For Goss's statement see, Tracy Wilkinson and Bob Drogin, "Missing Imam's Trail Said to Lead From Italy to CIA," *Los Angeles Times,* March 3, 2005. See also Human Rights Watch, "Still at Risk"; Priest, "CIA's Assurances on Transferred Suspects Doubted."

18. Richard Bernstein, "Skepticism Seems to Erode Europeans' Faith in Rice," *New York Times,* December 7, 2005; Bronwen Maddox, "Tough Words from Rice Leave Loopholes," *The Times* (London), December 6, 2005. For a perceptive and pithy

rejection of Secretary Rice's position, see editorial, "A Weak Defense," *Washington Post,* December 6, 2005.

19. For national reactions, see editorial, "Tortured Logic," *Miami Herald,* December 11, 2005; David Crossland, "Europe Skeptical of U.S. Assurances," *Newsday,* December 9, 2005; Anne Gearan, "U.S. Admits Botched Detention, Merkel Says," *WashingtonPost.com,* December 6, 2005; David Rose, "MI6 and CIA 'Sent Student to Morocco to Be Tortured,'" *Observer* (U.K.), December 11, 2005. For the EU's reaction, see Glenn Kessler, "E.U. Seeks Details on Secret CIA Jails," *Washington Post,* December 1, 2005.

20. According to the *New York Times,* "It would be hard to imagine a more sudden and thorough tarnishing of the Bush administration's credibility than the one taking place [in Europe]" (Richard Bernstein, "Skepticism Seems to Erode Europeans' Faith in Rice," *New York Times,* December 7, 2005); editorial, "A Weak Defense," *Washington Post,* December 6, 2005; Luke Hardin, "CIA's Secret Jails Open Up New Transatlantic Rift," *Guardian,* December 5, 2005 (detailing tensions with Germany); Tracy Wilkinson and Bob Drogin, "Missing Imam's Trail Said to Lead from Italy to CIA," *Los Angeles Times,* March 3, 2005. For the House of Lords judgment, see A (FC) v. *Secretary of State,* 2005 UKHL 71, ¶ 83. On the UK press reaction, see editorial, "Tortured Logic," *The Times* (London), December 9, 2005.

21. John J. Mearsheimer, "The False Promise of International Institutions," *International Security,* vol. 19 (winter 1994–95), pp. 5–7; J. Martin Rochester, "The Paradigm Debate in International Relations and Its Implications for Foreign Policy Making: Toward a Redefinition of the 'National Interest,'" *Western Political Quarterly,* vol. 31 (March 1978), p. 48.

22. Reuel Marc Gerecht, "Against Rendition," *Weekly Standard,* May 16, 2005.

23. Mearsheimer, "False Promise of International Institutions," p. 48.

24. For reports of diplomatic friction, see Kessler, "E.U. Seeks Details on Secret CIA Jails"; Ian Fisher, "Reports of Secret U.S. Prisons in Europe Draw Ire and Otherwise Red Faces," *New York Times,* December 1, 2005; Steven R. Weisman and Ian Fisher, "U.S. to Respond to Inquiries over Detentions in Europe," *New York Times,* November 30, 2005. For the Turkish debate see Deborah Sontag, "The Erdogan Experiment," *New York Times Magazine,* May 11, 2003, p. 43. For the German debate, see "Germany Guarantees U.S. Air Rights" CNN, March 19, 2003.

25. For Europe's attitudes, see Olivier Roy. *Les illusions du 11 septembre: Le débat stratégique face au terrorisme* (Paris: Editions de Seuil: 2002), pp. 22–25. For Kagan, see Robert Kagan, "America's Crisis of Legitimacy," *Foreign Affairs,* vol. 83 (March/April 2004), pp. 65, 72. For a canonical explanation of the importance of nonmilitary modes of power, see Joseph S. Nye Jr., *The Paradox of American Power: Why the World's Only Superpower Can't Go It Alone* (New York: Oxford University Press, 2002), pp. 8–9.

26. "Torture by Proxy," pp. 9–10; Victor L. Simpson, "U.S. Allies Resist Secret Deportations," *WashingtonPost.com,* June 19, 2005; *Agiza v, Sweden,* Committee Against Torture, Communication No. 233/2003, U.N. Doc. CAT/C/34/ D/233/2003.

27. A (FC) v. *Secretary of State,* 2005 UKHL 71; Statement of Eliza Manningham-Buller to the House of Lords in A (FC) v. *Secretary of State,* ¶ 6.

28. Richard Bernstein, "German Court Convicts Man of Qaeda Ties," *New York Times,* August 20, 2005; Mark Landler, "German 9/11 Trial Gets Exculpatory Evidence from U.S.," *New York Times,* August 12, 2005; Richard Bernstein, "Germans Free Moroccan Convicted of a 9/11 Role," *New York Times,* April 8, 2004.

29. Craig Whitlock, "CIA Ruse Is Said to Have Damaged Probe in Milan," *Washington Post,* December 6, 2005; Tom Hundley and John Crewdson, "Wife Was Left Behind with the Children," *Chicago Tribune,* July 3, 2005.

30. Whitlock, "CIA Ruse Is Said to Have Damaged Probe in Milan"; Hundley and Crewdson, "Wife Was Left Behind with the Children." For the Munich case, see Dominik Cziesche et al., "CIA Operations in Germany: Cooperation and Concern from Berlin," *Der Spiegel,* December 12, 2005. On the hotel bills, see Craig Whitlock and Dafna Linzer, "Italy Seeks Arrest of 13 in Alleged CIA Action," *Washington Post,* June 25, 2005.

31. For details of Egypt's nonfunctioning democratic framework, see Nathan J. Brown, *Constitutions in a Nonconstitutional World: Arab Basic Laws and the Prospects for Accountable Government* (Albany: State University of New York Press, 2002), pp. 122–29; Milton Viorst, *In the Shadow of the Prophet: The Struggle for the Soul of Islam* (Boulder, CO: Westview, 2001), pp. 331–77. For the 2005 elections and Nour's case, see Michael Slackman, "Testing Egypt, Mubarak Rival Is Sent to Jail," *New York Times,* December 25, 2005; "Not Yet a Democracy," *Economist,* December 10, 2005, p. 54; Michael Slackman, "Egypt Holds a Multiple-Choice Vote, But the Answer Is Mubarak," *New York Times,* September 8, 2005.

32. For Egypt, see Lawyers Committee for Human Rights, "Assessing the New Normal: Liberty and Security for the Post-September 11 United States," 2003, p. 77. For Sudan and Zimbabwe, see Human Rights Watch, "The United States' 'Disappeared': The CIA's Long-Term 'Ghost Detainees,'" October 2004. For the U.N. Human Rights Commission see Warren Hoge, "Zimbabwe's Role in U.N. Human Rights Panel Angers U.S.," *New York Times,* April 28, 2005.

33. Peter Bergen, "A Discussion of Some of the Underlying Causes of Al Qaeda Terrorism," in *Working Group Papers Prepared for the National Policy Forum on Terrorism, Security and America's Purpose* (Washington, DC: New America Foundation, September 2005), pp. 10–11; *The 9/11 Commission Report: Final Report of the National Commission on Terrorist Attacks Upon the United States* (New York: Norton, 2004), p. 376.

AZIZ Z. HUQ is associate counsel at the Brennan Center for Justice at the New York University School of Law.

This excerpt is adapted from the forthcoming book *Unchecked and Unbalanced: Presidential Power in a Time of Terror* by Aziz Huq and Frederick A. O. Schwarz to be published by The New Press in March 2007.

The Homeland Security Hash

The Department of Homeland Security gets little credit for the fact that terrorists have not staged an attack on American soil since 2001, and it is an open question whether it deserves much. Conceived in haste and crippled by its design, the newest addition to the cabinet desperately needs an overhaul.

PAUL C. LIGHT

Four years after it opened its doors, the Department of Homeland Security is by general agreement one of the most troubled cabinet-level agencies in the federal government. Hardly a day goes by without some fresh report on a contract gone bad, a new technology that does not work, a new Coast Guard cutter that is not seaworthy, or more cargo that slips through port without inspection. Year after year, virtually every assessment, including those by Congress, the 9/11 Commission, and the department's own inspector general, has given the department the same mediocre grades. "While the terrorists are learning and adapting, our government is still moving at a crawl," said 9/11 Commission chairman Thomas Kean in December 2005.

Homeland Security's personnel agree. According to the federal government's latest survey of its own employees, the department is the worst place to work in the government. It received the lowest ratings of 36 federal agencies for job satisfaction, management, and leadership. It is plagued by high turnover, internal bureaucratic struggles, and a variety of structural handicaps stemming from its creation in the aftermath of the 9/11 attacks.

As a result, the department is far behind in achieving many goals. It still needs funding to inspect more cargo shipments; the authority to regulate and protect chemical plants and railroad cars; a clear strategy for protecting bridges, roads, trains, subways, and other critical infrastructure; more personnel to reduce the backlog of immigration cases; an effective screening program for airport employees; better technology for detecting hidden explosives; an accurate watch list of potential terrorists; and perhaps most important, improved intelligence capabilities.

If destiny is largely determined by birth, this is a federal bureaucracy destined to stumble, and perhaps to fail. The product of the largest and most complex governmental merger since the creation of the Department of Defense in 1949, it was cobbled together by White House aides in just a few frenzied weeks.

With 180,000 employees and a $43 billion budget, the department is a collage of 22 distinct government agencies drawn from different corners of the federal organization chart and glued together into a single, largely dysfunctional unit. Even as they continue doing all the unrelated tasks they brought with them—from screening airline passengers for weapons and explosives to administering the national flood insurance program and rescuing boaters in distress—its component agencies have been directed to make defending the nation against terrorism their top priority. It is as if a group of widget makers were brought together in a private-sector merger and told they must now start producing software.

Homeland Security is a collage of 22 distinct government agencies glued together into a single, largely dysfunctional unit.

Homeland Security is still striving simply to win the hearts and minds of its own employees. Many of them do not doubt that defending against terrorism is an important mission, but they do not necessarily see it as the primary job of their particular unit. It is no wonder they think this way. Only 65 percent of the department's budget is spent on programs properly defined as homeland security. That points toward the fundamental problem. The Department of Homeland Security includes bureaucratic pieces that do not belong in an organization designed to protect the nation from terrorism. It may have a mission statement, but it lacks a unified mission.

Secretary Michael Chertoff recently reminded Congress that it took 40 years for the Department of Defense to finally come together—and that was after the first secretary committed suicide. But the nation does not have four decades to wait for the Department of Homeland Security to succeed. There are important steps that can be taken now.

Homeland Security was born in the wake of 9/11 in a climate of fear and shared determination to prevent fresh terrorist attacks, but political considerations were never far from the forefront. Congress and President George W. Bush agreed on the need to coordinate the agencies that would caulk the borders and track those the president had labeled the "evil-doers" Yet the administration hoped to deflect calls for what Vice President Dick Cheney dismissed as a "big government" approach by recruiting former Pennsylvania governor Tom Ridge in October 2001 to head a tiny White House Homeland Security Council.

Ridge himself soon concluded that his office was not strong enough to do the job and began pushing for a merger of the Border Patrol, the Customs Service, and the Immigration and Naturalization Service (INS). As Ridge later told *The Washington Post,* "The only person at the time that thought it was a good idea was yours truly."

The Democrat-controlled Senate was already well ahead of Ridge. The Senate Governmental Affairs Committee held its first hearings on the need for reorganization the day after the 9/11 attacks, and in the spring of 2002 recommended the creation of a cabinet-level department. The proposal focused primarily on border security, with elements of the Border Patrol, the Coast Guard, the Customs Service, the Federal Emergency Management Agency (FEMA), and the INS at its core.

Much as it opposed a new department, the Bush administration felt it could not let the Senate Democrats take the lead on homeland security, especially not with the congressional elections looming in November. By early spring, the White House had decided to design its own merger.

It could not be just any merger, however. According to a 2005 retrospective by *Washington Post* reporters Susan B. Glasser and Michael Grunwald and a study last year by four researchers at the Naval Postgraduate School's Center for Defense Management Reform (*Legislating Civil Service Reform: The Homeland Security Act of 2002*), the White House concluded that if it wanted to take back the homeland security issue, nothing but the biggest merger in modern history would do. Ignoring warnings of bureaucratic train wrecks and a clash of cultures, the administration put five White House aides to work on designing a maximum merger.

Selected for their loyalty more than their collective knowledge of government reorganization, the Gang of Five—or the G-5, as its members liked to call themselves—included a future Internal Revenue Service commissioner, a National Guard major general, and three other mid-level aides. But experienced or not, the G-5 was given firm instructions to think big. "The overriding guidance" G-5 member Bruce M. Lawlor later told the *Post,* "was that everything was on the table for consideration"

The members of the G-5 took their mandate seriously, and began searching the federal organization manual for merger targets. Although the G-5 used the Senate proposal as a foundation and certainly knew enough to get started, the planners soon strayed far from the notion that the new department should be built around agencies with similar missions. What about adding the Federal Bureau of Investigation (FBI)? The Secret Service?

The National Guard? The Drug Enforcement Administration? The Federal Aviation Administration?

The choices seemed endless. The G-5 even considered detaching the Lawrence Livermore nuclear research laboratory from the Department of Energy and slipping it into Homeland Security. Richard Falkenrath, a G-5 member, simply called up a friend and asked which laboratory might fit: "He goes, 'Livermore.' And I'm like, 'All right. See you later.' Click."

It was all part of the maximum-merger zeitgeist. More agencies equaled a better reorganization.

The secrecy came at a price. As the G-5 proposal took shape in the White House basement, it was shielded from what could have been useful scrutiny.

Even Cheney offered suggestions. According to Lawlor, the G-5 started out with the eight agencies already in the Senate bill. "Then the vice president came along and said, 'You've got to do something more about bioterrorism.' " Other White House aides also weighed in, later leading one anonymous insider to criticize the merger as the work of "people who didn't know a whole lot about the boxes they were moving around."

Throughout the process, the G-5 operated in secrecy. That provided what one G-5 member called "freedom of deliberation" and protected the group from attack, especially by the affected agencies. "Everybody realized the agencies were not going to look at mission first; they were going to look at turf first," Lawlor recalled.

The secrecy came at a price. As the G-5 blueprint took shape in the White House basement, it was shielded from what could have been useful scrutiny. As Falkenrath remembered, there were dozens of questions during his first encounters with congressional staff after weeks of hush-hush tinkering. "Every one of these staffers had some little angle on something that we hadn't thought of. I was like, 'We better go figure out what we've missed here.' "

The secrecy also showed in the holes in the department's organization chart, notably in the failure to provide for a high-level policy planning unit of the kind normally found in a cabinet department. Policy planning staffs typically look at department-wide issues and take a longer-term perspective than bureaucrats charged with day-to-day responsibilities. When they work well, they can serve as the strategic brain trust of a department. Lacking such a unit, which was not created until a Chertoff-sponsored reorganization in 2005, the new department would be able to implement strategic plans, but not make them.

The G-5 also forgot to create the post of chief intelligence officer. Without a top official to provide leadership, the department's tiny intelligence unit drifted for its first three years. That post, too, was finally created in 2005, but a second handicap remains. The department is not authorized to collect intelligence on its own but must rely on the FBI, the Central Intelligence Agency, and a host of other sources in order to create a picture of potential threats to the homeland and plan its next moves.

June 6, 2002, was a very important day for the White House. Not only was it the date chosen to announce the creation of the new department, but it was also to be the moment when FBI agent Coleen Rowley would testify before the Senate Judiciary Committee about her office's aborted efforts to investigate Zacarias Moussaoui, who had paid cash to train on a Boeing 747 flight simulator in Minnesota less than a month before 9/11. Rowley had been rebuffed by her supervisors when she asked for permission to seek a warrant to search Moussaoui's laptop computer.

It was precisely the kind of testimony that would dominate the front pages. But the story was easily eclipsed by the White House proposal. Under the Bush administration's rollout strategy, Ridge released the proposal the morning of the 6th, an assortment of White House aides and enthusiastic members of Congress made the rounds of the major television outlets in the afternoon, and Bush made a nationally televised speech at 8 PM. By the next morning, the president was back in charge of the homeland security issue. He signed the White House bill into law on November 25.

When the new Department of Homeland Security formally opened for business in March 2003, the facts of geography revealed an unhappy truth about its position in the Washington power matrix. At his new headquarters in an old Navy annex building tucked away in the northwest corner of Washington, Secretary Tom Ridge was miles away from the White House, the Capitol, and the headquarters of other federal departments, not to mention the nearly two dozen separate organizations that were now part of his new department.

Even Ridge came to wonder about the scope of the reorganization. "The notion that everyone was going to join hands and sing 'Kumbaya,'" he later told *The Washington Post*, "I don't think anybody in our leadership expected that to happen. And it didn't." It still hasn't. Turf wars over budgets and staffing rage inside the department, especially among the remnants of the Customs Service and the INS, which have similar missions. On Capitol Hill, congressional committees and subcommittees refused to reshape their jurisdictions to match all the organizational shifts that occurred when agencies were wrenched out of their old homes. Last year, as a result, department officials were required to testify before 70 different congressional units. And in the federal budget process, top administrators have been forced to fight for every spending increase.

There is nothing quite like the Homeland Security merger in the history of the federal government. The creation of the Defense Department after World War II involved more people, but the Homeland Security merger involved many more agencies, split and recombined many of their component parts, and, astoundingly, demanded that they focus on a mission almost none of them had ever dealt with before: combatting terrorism.

Moreover, Congress wanted the new department to operate without any budget or personnel increases. Savings were supposed to come from the elimination of duplication and

A Big Agenda

Weapons of Mass Destruction

This is "the gravest danger facing America," according to the Department of Homeland Security. Plans include a ring of radiation detectors 50 miles from Manhattan. Technology is a limitation: Today's detectors can be triggered by banana peels and often miss nuclear materials. The multibillion-dollar Project BioShield effort to create defenses against viruses, toxins, and chemicals has produced few results.

Aviation

DHS screens 730 million people traveling on commercial airlines each year—and all 700 million pieces of their checked luggage. But federal investigators with bomb-making materials successfully passed security at all 21 airports tested last year.

Critical Infrastructure

This year, DHS will award $445 million in grants to protect everything from ports to commuter rail lines against threats such as bombs and biological weapons.

Border Protection

Though the spotlight shines on the Mexican border, terrorists have sought to enter the United States from the north. Each day, 18,000 trucks cross the Canada-U.S. border. No passport is necessary until 2009.

Pandemic Outbreak

Avian flu is a top concern. In February a Food and Drug Administration panel endorsed the first vaccine, though it had been successful in less than half of the clinical trials.

Cyber Security

Viruses and other forms of attack on computer networks cost some $50 billion worldwide each year. The National Cyber Security Division of DHS leads collaboration between the public and private sectors to combat technological infiltration.

Natural and Manmade Disasters

Nine of the 10 most costly presidentially declared disasters have been natural—either hurricanes or earthquakes. September 11, number two on the list after Hurricane Katrina, is the sole exception.

overlap. The department's different agencies were expected to incorporate the war on terrorism into their existing missions, and somehow find enough dollars and employees to add it to their already complicated mandates.

The merger combined some of the best and worst agencies in the federal government. Indeed, some of the pieces of the Homeland Security collage were thrown in chiefly to ensure that the department was not composed only of sub-par performers. In its "Government Performance Project" series, which concluded just before the merger, *Government Executive* magazine rated the Coast Guard one of Washington's most successful agencies, applauding its planning, esprit de corps, and ability to do more with less. It also rated FEMA near the top of the class. But the magazine's reporters rated the Customs Service as average at best, citing its antiquated information technology and problems collecting and accounting for duties, taxes, and fees. And they reserved their harshest assessment for the INS, noting among other things its long history of mismanagement, top-heavy bureaucracy, and decaying detention facilities. The Transportation Security Administration (TSA), with its 43,000 airport security screeners and other personnel, was too new to be rated.

Homeland Security's leaders have less access to information than many state and local security offices.

Adding to the turmoil, Homeland Security has experienced extraordinary personnel turnover. In its first four years, the department has gone through two secretaries (Ridge resigned late in 2004), three deputy secretaries, eight under secretaries, three FEMA administrators, four TSA administrators, a dozen assistant secretaries, hundreds of senior executives, and nearly 100,000 civil servants, many of whom left the baggage and screener lines in search of higher pay.

It is surprising that a department built around this uneven inventory of assets and liabilities was able to design a logo and seal, let alone create a sense of common identity across its agencies. It is even more surprising given the 22 personnel offices, 19 financial systems, 13 contracting units, and eight payroll processes that its agencies brought with them, along with every uniform color in the spectrum, from Coast Guard blue to Border Patrol green.

Many of Homeland Security's problems came to the fore in the summer of 2005, during Hurricane Katrina, when virtually everything that could go wrong did. FEMA was late in responding to the catastrophe, and the White House ignored the obvious need for action. It is well known that FEMA was led by a group of inexperienced political appointees headed by Michael Brown, fresh from an unsuccessful stint as commissioner of the International Arabian Horse Association. But there were other factors involved. FEMA's natural disaster budget was in shreds after three years of cutbacks designed to free money for antiterrorism efforts. It had lost dozens of experienced senior executives. Buried deep in the new department's organization chart, FEMA lacked the direct access to the White House it had once enjoyed. Moreover, the agency had been stripped of its responsibility for preparing the nation for natural and terrorist disasters only weeks before Katrina as part of Chertoff's reorganization, so its executives lacked the key connections with state and local officials that might have accelerated its response.

Although Congress recently restored at least part of FEMA's independence, including its direct line to the president and its

preparedness duties, terrorism still consumes three-quarters of its budget, leaving few resources for the next Katrina.

It is still too early to declare the Homeland Security merger a failure. While we do not know how much credit the department can claim, the United States has not suffered another terrorist attack on its soil. The department has produced notable gains in border security. Most U.S. seaports will have radiation detectors within three years, airplane cockpit doors are impenetrable, and the Border Patrol is still catching illegal immigrants. The department has regained at least some of the productivity its components lost at the start of the merger, and it has built some of the missing parts the G-5 neglected to create.

It is also making progress in its partnerships with state and local governments, particularly through the "fusion" centers that blend information from state and local law enforcement with intelligence from federal sources. Secretary Chertoff's reorganization in 2005 finally gave the department two essentials, a policy planning staff and an intelligence chief, as well as a much greater sense of shared purpose.

Yet Homeland Security still falls short. In coping with the great uncertainty involved in defending against terrorism, four characteristics are vital: alertness, agility, adaptability, and alignment around a core mission. Alertness depends on access to information, and the department is still fighting for that. It has been forced to rely on the cooperation of strangers in the intelligence community to find out what it needs to know, a disadvantage that has been compounded by the fact that the community's own reorganization under the national director of intelligence has been highly contentious. The department is often the last to know, and its leaders have less access to information than many state and local security offices (which, ironically, are funded by the department itself).

Despite the TSA's quick reaction to last summer's terrorist plot to bomb U.S.-bound airplanes with liquid explosives, the department as a whole has a well-deserved reputation for poor agility and missed deadlines. The long-promised "virtual border" composed of drones, pole-mounted cameras, satellite monitors, and 700 miles of two-layered fence at selected points along the U.S.-Mexico border is years away from implementation; new technology for inspecting seaborne cargo containers is proving much more expensive than expected; and a promised "bioshield" for protecting the nation from biological attacks and pandemics is still an expensive dream. And none of these projects will necessarily prove effective.

In its lagging effort to improve adaptability, the department is still looking for a reasonable rate of return on the billions it has spent seeking new technologies to further its mission, including radiation detectors for the borders, information technology for tracking foreign tourists and students as they enter and exit the country, and cameras that can detect illegal immigrants as they cross the border. Homeland Security's research directorate, with a limited staff and an inadequate $800 million budget, is still struggling to integrate the eight research programs that were merged under its authority.

Finally, the department has yet to resolve the tensions among the competing missions its agencies brought into the merger. Just visit the Coast Guard's homepage (www.uscg.mil) on any given day and read its news summary, which reports such things as emergency rescues, ice-breaking work, and environmental protection efforts, but rarely anything about terrorism. To be a truly unified department, Homeland Security will need to create a department-wide identity around one all-encompassing mission.

The department's creation followed standard Washington procedure in moments of national crisis. New missions demand new bureaucracy, and the bigger the mission, the bigger the bureaucracy. The conventional wisdom also holds that a seat at the president's cabinet table provides a fulcrum to leverage greater coordination while creating the high visibility that is needed to get big jobs done.

Sometimes a new bureaucracy *is* essential to success. Every one of the federal government's greatest achievements of the past half-century involved at least some new bureaucracy—the National Aeronautics and Space Administration helped the United States win the space race in the 1960s, the Environmental Protection Agency opened a new era in clean air and water in the 1970s, and dozens of other agencies such as the Centers for Disease Control and Prevention and the National Institutes of Health have produced stunning gains in Americans' lifespan. But sometimes a new bureaucracy can turn out badly. Thirty years after its launch, the Energy Department is still in disarray, and still searching for a coherent policy to end the nation's addiction to foreign oil.

The Coast Guard's modernization efforts have produced an undue number of horror stories about delays, cost overruns, and bad management.

Congress and the president now face a simple choice. They can either hope the merger will eventually work out or undertake an ambitious new reorganization. The chief goal would be to tighten the department's focus on a single core mission of preventing terrorism, with the related task of dealing with natural and terrorist disasters. There are three ways to do it:

Give some agencies back to their original owners. Although all Homeland Security agencies share at least part of the same mission, many share so little common ground that they should go.

There is no reason that the Secret Service should stay in Homeland Security, for example. In addition to protecting the president and other top officials, it guards against counterfeiting and financial fraud. It was perfectly comfortable as a quasi-independent agency housed in the Treasury Department, as was the Federal Protective Service, which guards federal office buildings, as part of the General Services Administration, the

Federal Law Enforcement Training Center, as part of Treasury, and elements of the Animal and Plant Health Inspection Service as part of Agriculture.

All could easily move home, thereby reducing the span of the department to a more manageable number of agencies and offices.

Reduce the number of agencies through internal mergers. Assuming that it rebuilds quickly, FEMA could easily absorb the department's entire preparedness bureaucracy, including the Fire Administration, which helps local fire departments buy new equipment and educate the public on fire prevention, as well as the $3 billion state and local grants program, which provides the dollars for preparedness for both natural disasters and terrorist attacks.

The department could also merge two of its other bureaus, Customs and Border Protection and Immigration and Customs Enforcement. Both share law enforcement responsibilities, focus on the same entry points, and undergo similar training. Although such an internal merger would introduce its own costs in lost productivity in the short term, the longer-term benefits for border security would outweigh the costs. The two agencies have been squabbling for the past four years about budgets and responsibilities, in part because they overlap so much.

Set some agencies free. Alter more than 200 years of operating first within the Treasury Department and later within the Transportation Department without a break in performance, the Coast Guard has earned its independence. It not only has one of the broadest missions in government, it also has some of the most pressing needs for modernization. Its efforts so far have produced an undue number of horror stories about delays, cost overruns, and bad management by the Coast Guard and the rest of the Department of Homeland Security. Given its freedom, the Coast Guard could pursue modernization without constant worries about the antiterrorism agenda.

The more one looks at the Department of Homeland Security, the more one admires the parsimony of Tom Ridge's original proposal for an agency with a highly focused border security agenda. Instead of taking on a host of unrelated missions, such an organization could spend its time and resources on a much more sharply defined mission. Ridge may have been the only one who thought it made sense, but it looks more and more like the kind of department that could work.

Homeland Security can still become one of the federal government's success stories. This organization born in a fever of necessity and politics can be repaired if common sense is allowed to prevail. The price of failure is too high for the country to shoulder.

PAUL C. LIGHT, the Paulette Goddard Professor of Public Service at New York University's Robert F. Wagner School of Public Service, has frequently testified before Congress on the Homeland Security merger. He is the author of *The Four Pillars of High Performance* (2005).

Coming Soon
A Crisis in Civil-Military Relations

RICHARD H. KOHN

When Bill Clinton won the presidency in November 1992, few could have anticipated that his first crisis would be a full-blown clash with the armed forces, unhinging his administration even before it took office. His, after all, was to be a domestic presidency. Clinton inherited a military rebuilt from its Vietnam nadir, led by generals and admirals jubilant from success in the Persian Gulf and cheered on by an admiring public. When Clinton pushed for the right of homosexuals to serve in uniform, the brass revolted, culminating in the spectacle of a president forced to surrender to his own generals.

Fast forward to 2008. The president elected in November will inherit a stinking mess, one that contains the seeds of a civil-military conflict as dangerous as the crisis that nearly sank the Clinton team in 1993. Whether the new president is a Republican or Democrat makes only a marginal difference. The issues in military affairs confronting the next administration are so complex and so intractable that conflict is all but inevitable.

When a new president takes office in early 2009, military leaders and politicians will approach one another with considerable suspicion. Dislike of the Democrats in general and Bill Clinton in particular, and disgust for Donald Rumsfeld, has rendered *all* politicians suspect in the imaginations of generals and admirals. The indictments make for a long list: a beleaguered military at war while the American public shops at the mall; the absence of elites in military ranks; the bungling of the Iraq occupation; the politicization of General David Petraeus by the White House and Congress; an army and Marine Corps exhausted and overstretched, their people dying, their commitments never-ending. Nearly six years of Donald Rumsfeld's intimidation and abuse have encouraged in the officer corps a conviction that military leaders ought to—are obliged to—push back against their civilian masters. Egged on by Democrats in Congress—and well-meaning but profoundly mistaken associates who believe the military must hold political leaders accountable for their mistakes—some flag officers now opine publicly and seemingly without hesitation. Though divided about Iraq strategy, the four-stars unite in their contempt for today's political class and vow not to be saddled with blame for mistakes not of their own making.

For its part, the new administration will enter office mindful and jealous of the military's iconic status in the public mind, even if, ironically, the rhetoric of politicians does much to inflate that prestige. In truth, increasing politicization of the armed forces has generated considerable cynicism and distrust among elected officials of every stripe, kept private only out of fear of appearing not to support the troops. The new administration, like its predecessors, will wonder to what extent it can exercise civilian "control." If the historical pattern holds, the administration will do something clumsy or overreact, provoking even more distrust simply in the process of establishing its own authority.

In the background, as always, will be the legacy of civil-military tensions going back to the beginning of the Republic, but magnified whenever a new administration comes to office. One four-star general put it this way in 2001 at the outset of the Bush presidency: "It's like waking up in the morning, looking across the bed, and discovering you've got a new wife. You've never met her, you don't know what she wants or what she's thinking, and you have no idea what will happen when she wakes up." He added, "we on this side of the river don't have to take it, either."

The problem here is not the ordinary friction between the military and its political bosses. That is understandable and, to a degree, typical and functional; the two sides come from different worlds, with different perspectives and different requirements. No decision in war, no military policy proposed to or considered by the Congress, no military operation—nothing in the military realm—occurs that does not derive in some way from the relationship between civilians, to whom the U.S. Constitution assigns responsibility for national defense, and the military leadership, which manages, administers, and leads the armed forces.

When the relationship works—when there is candor, argument, and mutual respect—the result aligns national interest and political purpose with military strategy, operations, and tactics. The collaboration between Franklin Roosevelt, his secretaries of war and navy, and the heads of the two armed services is considered the model in this regard. Each side kept the other mostly informed; the military were present at all the major allied conferences; Army Chief of Staff George C. Marshall spoke candidly with the president and consulted daily with Secretary of War Henry Stimson. When the relationship does not work—when the two sides don't confer, don't listen, don't compromise—the decisions and policies that follow serve neither the national interest nor conform to the bitter realities of war. The distrust, manipulation, and absence of candor that colored relations between President Lyndon Johnson, Defense Secretary Robert McNamara, and his senior military advisors offers a case in point; to this day Robert Strange McNamara arouses hatred and contempt among military officers who were not even born when he ruled the Pentagon.

While civil-military relations at the beginning of the Republic involved real fears of a coup, for the last two centuries the concern has revolved around relative influence: can the politicians (often divided among themselves) really "control" the military? Can the generals and admirals secure the necessary resources and autonomy to accomplish the government's purposes with minimal loss of blood and treasure? Until World War II, the influence of the regular military even in its own world was limited. After the war, the integration of foreign and military policies, the creation of the intelligence community, new weapons systems, and other elements of the Cold War national security establishment decidedly enhanced the military's say in policy deliberations. The end of the Cold War and an operational *tour de force* in the first Persian Gulf War cemented the military's position as the public's most trusted and esteemed institution. During the Clinton administration, the military leadership had a virtual veto over military policy, particularly the terms and conditions of interventions overseas. The power of the military has waxed and waned since the 1940s, but not a single secretary of defense has entered office trusting the armed forces to comply faithfully with his priorities rather than their own.

Four problems, in particular, will intensify the normal friction: the endgame in Iraq, unsustainable military budgets, the mismatch between twenty-first century threats and a Cold War military establishment, and social issues, gays in the military being the most incendiary.

As to the first of these, Iraq confounds the brightest and most knowledgeable thinkers in the United States. George W. Bush has made it clear that he will not disengage from Iraq or even substantially diminish the American military presence there until the country can govern, sustain, and defend itself. How to attain or even measure such an accomplishment baffles the administration and war critics alike. That is precisely why a majority of the American people supports withdrawing.

It follows that no candidate will be elected without promising some sort of disengagement. An American withdrawal would probably unleash the all-out civil war that our presence has kept to the level of neighborhood cleansing and gangland murder. Sooner or later that violence will burn itself out. But a viable nation-state that resembles democracy as we know it is far off, with the possibility that al-Qaeda will survive in Iraq, requiring American combat forces in some form for years to come.

In the civil-military arena, the consequences of even a slowly unraveling debacle in Iraq could be quite ugly. Already, politicians and generals have been pointing fingers at one another; the Democrats and some officers excoriating the administration for incompetence, while the administration and a parade of generals fire back at the press and anti-war Democrats. The truly embittered, like retired Army Lieutenant General Ricardo Sanchez, who commanded in Iraq in 2003–04, blame everyone and everything: Bush and his underlings, the civilian bureaucracy, Congress, partisanship, the press, allies, even the American people. Last November, Sanchez went so far as to deliver the Democrats' weekly radio address—and, with it, more bile and invective. Thomas Ricks, chief military correspondent of the *Washington Post,* detects a "stab in the back narrative . . . now emerging in the U.S. military in Iraq. . . . [T]he U.S. military did everything it was supposed to do in Iraq, the rest of the U.S. government didn't show up, the Congress betrayed us, the media undercut us, and the American public lacked the stomach, the nerve, and the will to see it through." Ricks thinks this "account is wrong in every respect; nonetheless, I am seeing more and more adherents of it in the military."

If the United States withdraws and Iraq comes apart at the seams, many officers and Republicans will insist that the war was winnable, indeed was all but won under General David Petraeus. The new administration will be scorned not only for cowardice and surrender, but for treachery—for rendering meaningless the deaths, maiming, and sacrifice of tens of thousands of Americans in uniform. The betrayed legions will revive all of the Vietnam-era charges, accusing the Democrats of loathing the military and America and of wishing defeat. The resentments will sink deep into the ranks, at least in the army and the Marines, much as the Praetorian myths about Vietnam still hold sway today in the Pentagon. The response—namely, that the war was a strategic miscalculation bungled horribly by the Bush administration—will have no traction. There will only be a fog of anger, bitterness, betrayal, and recrimination.

The second source of civil-military conflict will revolve around the Pentagon budget. The administration's request for the coming year, nearly $650 billion, is plainly unsustainable, although it accounts for only 20 percent of the federal budget and less than 4.5 percent of the gross domestic product. The figure understates true costs by excluding veterans affairs, homeland security, and other national security expenditures, which could boost the total upward of $850 billion, more than the rest of world combined spends on defense and larger than any military budget since World War II. This will be a red flag to a Democratic Congress, and certainly to a Democratic White House. However eager they may be to deflect charges of being weak on national defense, the Democrats will have no choice but to cut, and over time, cut deeply.

That is because the dilemma is substantially worse than even these figures suggest. The bill does not include the wearing out of military equipment, from overworked transport jets to tanks and trucks, or the expansion of ground forces. Then, too, there is the need for additional spending on homeland security, which several presidential candidates have vowed to do. Port defense, transportation, border integrity, the stockpiling of vaccines—the ability of the United States to respond to and recover from a successful nuclear or biological attack remains rudimentary, and by consensus underfunded. Finally, the Pentagon budget will have to compete with domestic spending priorities: for roads, water systems, and other infrastructure; for the FBI, the air traffic control system, the IRS, and other national agencies; for Social Security and Medicare to support the flood of retiring baby boomers; and for expanding and reforming health care. Claims on the national treasury could arise suddenly, like the hundred billion–plus dollars promised to New Orleans. A Republican administration could press for further tax cuts. (Some years ago, before 9/11, I asked Newt Gingrich whether Republicans, if they had to choose, favored tax reduction or a stronger national defense. He answered: tax cuts.) Expanding deficits could relentlessly drive up interest costs. A recession in turn would diminish tax receipts and raise the deficit even higher, setting in motion a downward spiral that would challenge any Congress, administration, or Federal Reserve chairman.

When presented with these fiscal challenges, military leaders are likely to cede nothing. They are at war around the world. They are charged not only with national defense, but with the stewardship of institutions rooted in past glory and expected to triumph over any and all foes. Officers recognize their historic role and they embrace it. Every year when budgets arise in discussion at war colleges, student officers—the up-and-comers in each service, many destined for flag rank—demand more money. In September, the air force asked for an additional $20 billion for aircraft. The Joint Chiefs and the combatant commanders understand the squeeze. New weapons systems must be funded and the cost of recruiting and retention bonuses has jumped to more than one billion dollars a year for the army alone. One petty officer recently told me that the navy paid him $80,000 to re-enlist, something he intended to do anyway. Some specialties command $150,000 in douceurs. And even these fees do not suffice. "I have in the last several years arrived at a point," Chairman of the Joint Chiefs of Staff Admiral Mike Mullen said recently, "where I think as a country we're just going to have to devote more resources to national security in the world that we're living in right now." Needless to say, Mullen was hardly speaking for himself alone.

The ways out of this jam all invite some sort of conflict. Least controversial would be to tackle that old bugbear, Pentagon waste. Several of the presidential candidates have vowed to do exactly this. But the gold-plated weapons systems always survive. And, clichés notwithstanding, the actual savings would be minimal in any case. Another perennial favorite is centralization or consolidation, an impulse that led to the creation of the Defense Department in 1947 and something attempted regularly ever since. Certainly, there are more opportunities here. Are six war colleges really still necessary? Does each service really need its own weather, chaplain, medical, and legal corps? Do both the navy and Marine Corps need their own air forces, since they fly many of the same aircraft, all

of them integrated on aircraft carriers? Are military academies a necessity? A larger percentage of ROTC graduates than of West Pointers stay in the army past the ten-year mark.

Yet imagine the outcry any one of these proposals would provoke, and the resistance it would generate from the services, agencies, and congressional committees whose ox was being gored. The delegation or defense company about to lose a base or a weapons contract would certainly howl—and mobilize. Organizational change in any bureaucracy provokes enormous and almost always successful resistance. In the Pentagon, the battles have been epic.

The world has a say in all this, too. The next administration will take office nearly twenty years after the fall of the Berlin Wall. Yet the American military establishment is essentially the same one created in the 1940s and 1950s to deter the Soviet Union. The United States today boasts four independent armed services with the same weapons, upgraded and more capable to be sure, as those known to George Marshall, Dwight Eisenhower, Chester Nimitz, and Curtis LeMay. Not only are the ships, planes, tanks, vehicles, and guns similar, but they are organized similarly, performing virtually the same roles and missions assigned them in the late 1940s.

The United States after 1989 did not demobilize. It "downsized." Successive administrations cut the budget by ten percent and the size of the force by about 25 percent, while the Pentagon substituted regional threats for the Soviet menace in its planning. Even in the midst of a "Global War on Terrorism," neither the generals nor their bosses in the White House and Congress have been able to rethink the purpose, organization, command and control, or even operation of the armed forces. Two decades is a long time. The decades between 1895 and 1915, 1935 and 1955, and 1975 and 1995 all involved paradigm shifts in America's role in the world and in its national security requirements. Today's security situation differs no less radically from the Cold War for which today's military establishment was devised. Are these the armed forces we really need?

Bitter fights over strategy, budgets, weapons, and roles and missions dating back sixty-plus years suggest the question may not be answerable in any practical sense. To understand fully just how difficult it will be to raise fundamental concerns about defense policies, consider the recent confusion over what exactly the role and purpose of the National Guard and reserves ought to be. A week before 9/11, I participated in a roundtable discussion of the subject for the Reserve Forces Policy Board. There was general agreement that reserve forces should concentrate more on homeland defense and less on backstopping active duty forces on the battlefield. Yet the former head of the National Guard Bureau insisted, without evidence and in the face of great skepticism, that the Guard and reserves could do both. The past five years have proved him wrong; reserve forces are underequipped and stretched thinner than the active duty army and Marine Corps.

Today, a congressionally chartered commission on the National Guard and reserves still struggles with how to shape and organize the reserves (particularly the National Guard, which reports to each state governor unless summoned for federal service). Admittedly, the National Guard and reserves possess unusual political power and since 1789 have been more resistant to rational military policy than any other part of the national security community. Robert McNamara, who transformed American defense more than any other Pentagon leader, failed utterly to budge the Guard and reserve. None of his successors possessed the nerve even to try. But the problem cannot be avoided. As the commission wrote in bureaucratic understatement, in March 2007, "the current posture and utilization of the National Guard and Reserve as an 'operational reserve' is not sustainable over time, and if not corrected with significant changes to law and policy, the reserve component's ability to serve our nation will diminish."

All the more so because Iraq and Afghanistan compose the first substantial, extended military conflicts the United States has fought with a volunteer force in more than a century. Today's typical combat tour of fifteen months is the longest since World War II. Expensive procurement programs are underway, but sooner or later they will be robbed to pay for other costs, such as war operations, the expansion of ground forces, or medical and veterans costs. Already, the Project on Defense Alternatives has proposed cutting two Air Force wings, two Navy wings, and two aircraft carriers for a total savings of more than $60 billion over the next five years. Eventually, the bill comes due, either in blood, defeat, or political crisis. As the old Fram oil filter advertisement put it, "Pay me now, or pay me later."

L ast on the list of issues certain to provoke civil-military tension is social concerns, two of which will surely arise in a Democratic administration and also may be unavoidable in a Republican one.

At a time when the Pentagon spends huge sums of money annually to recruit and retain soldiers, it makes no sense to eject hundreds of fully trained, dutifully serving volunteers, many of whom—the several dozen Arab linguists forced out in the last few years come to mind—possess skills in short supply in the military. The old arguments about gays undermining unit cohesion or threatening discipline have lost credibility; foreign militaries allow homosexuals to serve at all levels, including in command and at flag rank, without detrimental effect. Young people today, even from the more conservative demographics likely to enlist, express little concern about serving alongside gays. But for many older men in uniform, it's a different story, as recently-retired Chairman of the Joint Chiefs of Staff Marine General Peter Pace made clear when he labeled homosexuality immoral. All the Democratic presidential candidates support lifting the ban; sooner rather than later Democrats in Congress are likely to try to change the law. Both sides will drag in the armed services, reviving the emotional debate of the early 1990s, escalating tensions within the military's leadership and between it, Congress, and the administration. Not all of this will make the newspapers, but within the Pentagon the disagreements will provoke tension, anger, mistrust, and perhaps open dissent.

Another issue bound to cause friction involves the right of evangelical chaplains to pray at public events in the name of Jesus Christ, and of evangelical officers to proselytize according to the principles of their faith. The issue pits freedom of religion against the duty of chaplains to minister to a diverse military in an ecumenical fashion, for their units comprise people of many faiths (and sometimes none), with varying degrees of commitment. The historian of religion Ann Loveland, now retired from the history department at Louisiana State University, has documented the evangelical mission to the military first undertaken in World War II. Believing that military service could debauch American youth, the Christian evangelical movement sought to spread the gospel inside the services by encouraging its clergy to become chaplains, founding and supporting organizations to support and spread evangelical faith, and working to boost the number of evangelicals in the military leadership. In the early 1980s these efforts began to generate anxiety in the officer corps. Commanders who held prayer breakfasts and Bible readings for their officers were sometimes suspected of favoring their fellow worshippers in the yearly evaluations so critical to promotion and assignment. Early in this decade, a scandal erupted at the U.S. Air Force Academy when it was discovered that the football coach, commandant of cadets, and faculty and chaplains were subtly pressing cadets to join the faith, and disparaging others who did not. Just last year, four generals were recommended for reprimand for participating in uniform in a video used by an evangelical organization to proselytize.

Now, it could be argued that none of these four great problems will trigger a crisis. Republicans, for example, might not risk a break with the evangelical community by strictly enforcing policies against proselytizing. And they would be only too happy to continue lavishing funds on the Pentagon. But how will they reconcile tax cuts, balanced budgets, and robust defense spending? Iraq, for which Republican presidential candidates have offered no solution beyond more of the same, makes the election of a Republican administration unlikely in any case. Yet, if elected, it too would have to disengage, lest the army and Marines become so exhausted and alienated that their leaders go public with their resentments.

The Democrats would surely prefer to finesse these dilemmas and, with them, charges of weakness on national defense. Hillary Clinton has labored assiduously to gain the trust of the military, mindful of how it nearly crippled her husband's administration. Yet escape will be impossible, particularly when it comes to Iraq and the budget. Significantly, Clinton has made no promises to the military, not even a ritualistic pledge to maintain a strong national defense. Civil-military relations under Democratic administrations, from Truman to Kennedy to Johnson to Carter to Clinton, became more toxic with each. The leading Democratic contenders today have no military experience or feel for military culture. All would find themselves under extraordinary pressure from their constituencies to exit Iraq, cut the budget, allow gays to serve without prejudice, and apply the separation of church and state with rigor. None would wish to expend political capital on less sexy, but more consequential, questions related to the proper roles, missions, scope, and resources of the military establishment. Nor would the Congressional Democrats. Yet if they don't set the terms of the debate, the military will do it for them.

However it begins, a clash between the next administration and the armed forces need not metastasize into a full-blown crisis. Military leaders should start to consider how they will react to civilian demands, and which of their traditions they will choose. Will they acquiesce after due advice and consultation, as the Constitution and our tradition of civilian control suggests? Or will they resist, employing techniques borne of decades of inside-the-beltway maneuvering? Will they confine dissent to the appropriate channels? Or will they go public, enlisting their allies in Congress, industry, and veterans groups? Will they collaborate with their new civilian superiors? Or will they work to thwart every recommendation harmful to their service? Much will depend on the capacity of military leaders to establish a workable relationship with their civilian superiors and to embrace their own tradition of professionalism.

Civilians have equal obligations. Will they tackle thorny defense issues in a serious, nonpartisan way, or will they succumb to their own posturing? Will they box themselves in with their campaign promises? Will they apply Band-Aids to the Pentagon budget, or will they address the more fundamental problem of reorganizing a Cold-War military for an age of asymmetric threats? Will they consider seriously, if not always heed, the counsel of military expertise?

A crucial intermediary here will be the next secretary of defense. Someone in the mold of Melvin Laird or James Schlesinger or William Perry will be indispensable—that is, someone knowledgeable and politically skilled who can gain and keep the confidence of the military, Congress, and the president. Whoever wins the job must wear his or her authority without bluster or arrogance, and lead firmly while holding the military to account. Above all, the secretary must act with courtesy, fairness, and decisiveness. A new administration might even ask Robert Gates to stay on; he has presided over the Pentagon with a calming, steady hand after Rumsfeld's departure.

Staffing decisions at less senior levels will be nearly as important. Neither party can afford to populate the Defense Department with politicians on the make, congressional staffers beholden to special interests, or young know-nothings looking to plus-up their résumés. These positions require knowledgeable people from the business community, the federal bureaucracy, and other professions who understand and respect the military but will not be awed by medals and campaign ribbons. The service secretaries have the closest relationship with the military leadership and have a critical say in picking senior leaders for advancement into the key commands and the Joint Chiefs. Finding the right individuals for these slots will be essential. The new secretary of defense would do well to assemble his deputy, under secretaries, and service secretaries into a cohesive executive committee that would formulate an agenda, rethink policy, and oversee its implementation.

The next administration should also act quickly to insulate the military leadership from partisan politics. The first act will be, after due consideration, the reappointment of Admiral Mullen as chairman. Then there should be a concerted search within the services for loyal but independent thinkers who understand the American system of civilian control but also know how to be dead honest in their advice. The recent appointment of General James Mattis of the Marines to head Joint Forces Command sends exactly the right message. Whoever comes into office in January 2009, in turn, needs to make clear up front that he or she will not hide behind the military, that he or she will not compromise the military's professional ethos by delivering partisan speeches in front of uniformed audiences or trotting out the brass to market administration policies.

Last of all, the new president ought to reach out to the armed forces in their own communities: visiting bases, praising the military with genuine sincerity, addressing veteran's care, making certain that as troops are withdrawn from Iraq, no blame falls unfairly on them for what follows. The political leadership will have to consult widely about changes, cuts, consolidations, and other modifications to the defense establishment. The next administration will need to establish a precedent for strict civilian control from the outset, all the while spending political capital on national defense and boosting the morale of what will likely be an anxious force. Consistent and vocal praise for military (and public) service would go a long way—easy for a Republican who abandons the demonization of government, difficult for a Democrat accustomed to ignoring or criticizing the military.

Soldiers and civilians alike will have momentous decisions to make. Politicians will have to choose whether to lead or to hide, whether in the name of maintaining or establishing their bona fides as "supporters of the military" they will put off decisions that upend the current and unsustainable order of things. Military leaders face their most important choice in more than half a century: whether to cooperate and assist in this effort, or to resist past the point of advice and discussion, to the detriment of their service, national defense, and indeed their professional souls.

Richard H. Kohn is Professor of History and Peace, War, and Defense at the University of North Carolina at Chapel Hill. He was Chief of Air Force History for the USAF, 1981–1991. Last year, he was the Omar N. Bradley Professor of Strategic Leadership at Dickinson College and the U.S. Army War College.

The Right Stuff

PAUL R. PILLAR

W hat comes to mind when someone mentions intelligence and the Iraq War? Why, of course, the intelligence estimate on Iraqi unconventional weapons programs—excoriated in a 500-page report that the Senate Select Committee on Intelligence issued with much fanfare in July 2004, further torn apart in another 500-page report by a White House–appointed commission, and scorned and vilified ever since.

But the estimate on weapons was one of only three classified, community-coordinated assessments about Iraq that the intelligence community produced in the months prior to the war. Don't feel bad if you missed the other two, which addressed the principal challenges that Iraq would present during the first several years after Saddam's removal and the likely repercussions of regime change in Iraq on the surrounding region. After being kept under wraps (except for a few leaks) for over four years, the Senate committee quietly released redacted versions of those assessments on its website on a Friday as Americans were beginning their Memorial Day weekend.

The Bush Administration had not requested any of the three assessments. Democrats on the Senate Intelligence Committee asked for the weapons estimate, which was rushed to completion before Congress voted on the resolution endorsing the war. I initiated the other two assessments and also supervised their drafting and coordination. My responsibilities at the time as the National Intelligence Officer for the Near East and South Asia concerned analysis of political, economic and social issues in those regions. Although the first duty of any intelligence officer is to respond to policymakers' requests, the duties also include anticipating policymakers' future needs. With the administration's determination to go to war already painfully clear in 2002, I undertook these assessments to help policymakers, and those charged with executing their decisions, make sense of what they would be getting into after Saddam was gone.

The origin of these assessments was not advertised in the documents themselves. Although self-initiated analysis is an important and major part of the intelligence community's work, responsiveness to policymakers' requests tends to be seen as a more respectable measure of the community's relevance and worth. Fulfilling a request also helps to avoid mischievous accusations that intelligence officers are going out of their way to poke sticks in policymakers' eyes. So a common practice with self-initiated assessments—certainly for those of us on the National Intelligence Council (NIC)—was to solicit the interest of a policy office and its agreement to be listed on the document as the customer of record. For the assessments on Iraq, the State Department's Policy Planning Staff agreed to fill this role.

We worked on the assessments with no delusions. Our analysis was unlikely to derail the policy train. Even when we began our work, the administration was rushing headlong into war. Our more modest hopes were to provide useful insights to those in Baghdad and Washington who would face the extremely difficult task of managing the ensuing mess. Ultimately, the assessments received broad distribution at both senior and working levels, and there was no good reason they could not or should not have influenced the basic decision to go to war.

What We Knew

Anyone who paid any attention to the assessments should have had grave doubts about that decision. The first "key judgment" of the assessment on challenges in post-Saddam Iraq was that the greatest difficulty would be building a stable and representative political system—a process that would be "long, difficult, and probably turbulent", amid an authoritarian political culture that does not foster liberalism or democracy. The next judgment was that any post-Saddam authority would face a "deeply divided society with significant chance that domestic groups would engage in violent conflict with each other unless an occupying force prevented them from doing so." This prospect was based on the incompatible goals of Sunni Arabs facing the loss of their long-standing privileged position, Shi'a seeking power commensurate with their majority status and Kurds intent on securing control over oil resources in northern Iraq.

The third judgment was that notwithstanding Iraq's oil, the country's economic options would be "few and narrow", with economic reconstruction requiring measures akin to a Marshall Plan. The fourth judgment spoke of the major outside assistance that would be required to meet humanitarian needs, with a refugee problem and civil strife combining to strain Iraq's already inadequate public services. And in direct contradiction to U.S. goals, the final judgment, which addressed foreign and security policies over the horizon, noted that Iraq's threat perceptions and self-image as a regional power would, without the right security guarantees, revive its interest in WMD. Making matters worse, the more immediate security challenge would be Al-Qaeda or other terrorist groups operating from Iraqi territory if Baghdad were unable to exert control over the countryside.

These were not selected pieces of bad news. They were the main points, expressed in a summary section of less than two pages (at the front of a 38-page assessment), that intelligence community analysts believed would be most descriptive of post-Saddam Iraq.

The larger assessment did not venture a prediction on how Iraqis would regard coalition forces when they first invaded, but it did assess what would shape Iraqi attitudes after the first few weeks or months. Those attitudes would depend above all on the coalition's performance in providing security, stability and basic public services. Insofar as it failed to provide them—which unfortunately has been the case—Iraqis' traditional antipathy toward foreign occupation would manifest itself in hostility toward the latest invaders.

The assessment about regional repercussions concluded that the war would give a region-wide boost to political Islam, including its extremist variants. Any violence in Iraq would serve as a magnet for extremists elsewhere in the region. Al-Qaeda would exploit the conflict. The regional assessment also noted that even if the experiment in politically reconstructing Iraq were successful, there would not be (with the possible exception of Iran) the hoped-for "democratic domino" effect; political and economic reform in other regional countries would continue to face significant obstacles and would be influenced chiefly by conditions within those countries.

The overall implication of these assessments for the advisability of launching the expedition was summed up by one of my colleagues on the NIC as the papers were undergoing final review. As he said, no one who accepted and reflected upon the assessments' conclusions could possibly think the war was a good idea. Quite so, and that would be true even if one accepted the judgments in the weapons estimate.

Used and Abused

The judgments of the two assessments did not influence policy on Iraq because the war-makers consistently and assiduously tuned out all types of expert and professional input (except when it suited their purposes). That same deaf ear also ignored the State Department's comprehensive study addressing many of the same post-Saddam Iraq issues. It was exhibited as well in the slapping down of the Army Chief of Staff, General Eric Shinseki, when he offered a military judgment before the war about the number of troops needed to pacify Iraq—Shinseki estimated "several hundred thousand"; the recent surge has brought U.S. troop strength to just over 160,000.

A related pattern was the absence of any identifiable process for making the decision to go to war—at least no process visible at the time, or even now, despite the work of able investigative journalists. There was no meeting, no policy-options paper, no showdown in the Situation Room when the wisdom of going to war was debated or the decision to do so made. And this meant scant opportunity to inject judgments, invited or uninvited, that should have been central to the decision.

The military solicited important input from the intelligence community in its war-planning. But at the policy level, the administration excluded the intelligence community from playing the traditional, proper, accepted role of intelligence, which is to provide reporting and analysis to inform policy decisions yet to be made.

On Iraq, the Bush Administration instead used the intelligence community to provide material to sell the public a foregone conclusion. Lost amid all the brouhaha over the weapons-related intelligence has been any appreciation of how fundamentally different this function is from the traditional and proper one. Lost as well has been any sense of the relative importance of different issues underlying the decision. The weapons estimate has received enormous attention, but the issues addressed in the other assessments—which spoke directly to the instability, conflict, and black hole for blood and treasure that for the past four years we have come to know as Iraq—turned out to be far more important, and should have been at least as important all along.

The estimate on Iraqi weapons programs did not drive the administration's decision to launch the expedition. Not only had the administration never requested it, as the White House later admitted, neither the president nor the national security advisor even read it (nor did most members of Congress). The administration had firmly established its public line about Iraqi weapons programs—with the vice president in particular going beyond what the intelligence community ever said in any of its products—before the estimate was even initiated. The estimate, flawed though it was, assessed that Iraq probably was still years away from any nuclear-weapons capability. Most important, the presumption of active Iraqi unconventional weapons programs simply did not equate with a need to go to war, despite the administration's tremendous rhetorical effort intoning frightening visions of mushroom clouds and dictators passing weapons to terrorists. The administration's *not* launching wars against the other members of its "axis of evil", despite broad agreement that they had more advanced nuclear programs than Iraq did, is one indication of the war's less-than-pressing nature. Another is the fact that many thoughtful people, both at home and abroad, who shared the misperceptions about active Iraqi weapons programs nonetheless opposed the war, some vociferously so, in favor of other ways of dealing with Saddam.

The estimate contained judgments about the Iraqi leader's likely use of any WMD he did have, judgments that were directly opposed to the administration's rhetoric. The intelligence community assessed that Saddam probably would not use such weapons against U.S. interests unless the United States attempted to destroy his regime (as through a military invasion). It further judged that only at this extreme would Saddam even consider passing such weapons to terrorist groups. These determinations were so starkly at odds with this aspect of the administration's campaign to sell the war that Senate Democrats insisted they be made public. Of course, we will never know if those judgments were sound, but they clearly did not support the decision to invade.

The other main issue the administration used in its sales campaign was the supposed "alliance" between Saddam's regime and Al-Qaeda. The intelligence community believed—as expressed in several CIA papers—that the few past contacts between the Iraqi regime and Al-Qaeda were no more than two organizations keeping tabs on each other and perhaps looking for opportunities to exploit—there was no alliance or operational partnership. Given everything known today, this judgment was accurate. But for the administration, the judgment also was very inconvenient, directly undercutting its effort to parlay the national trauma suffered on September 11 into support for a war on Iraq. The pressure exerted on the intelligence agencies on this one issue was substantial, including endless sparring with the office of the vice president over scraps of reporting that conceivably could be construed as indicating more of a relationship and calls by that office to change a draft assessment on the topic.

The intelligence agencies bent—somewhat—under this pressure, serving the administration's fixation with enormous time and attention otherwise better spent. And though they bent, they did not break, maintaining there was no alliance. Their position, however, did not stop the administration from continuing to push this theme in its campaign. A unit in the Pentagon reporting to Undersecretary Douglas Feith labored to weave the threads into an alternative story, and advised others in the administration to "ignore" the judgments of the intelligence community. The rhetoric was a success—leading a majority of Americans to believe that Saddam Hussein not only was allied with Al-Qaeda but also was involved in the September 11 attack.

Lessons Learned

The failure to pay more attention to the considered judgments of the intelligence community on issues central to the expedition on which the administration would embark—particularly given how conspicuously those judgments disagreed with the administration's assumptions—is crucial. It needs to be a major part of histories written about this tragic episode in American foreign policy. Yet it is not the imperviousness of the administration's war hawks to expert advice and their particular disdain for the intelligence community that should be highlighted—after all, that is already well-known.

A more timely lesson concerns the current debate over what to do about the Iraqi quagmire and what there is to learn from the intelligence community's judgments. The assessments support the proposition that the Iraq War always was a fool's errand—rather than a good idea spoiled by poor execution—implying that a continued search for a winning strategy is likely fruitless. That in turn argues for policies that emphasize cutting losses and that aim to draw down the U.S. military presence sooner and faster. Though some support for the poor-execution hypothesis can be found in the assessments—such as the observation that Iraq's regular army could make an important contribution in providing security (thus implicitly questioning in advance the wisdom of ever disbanding the army)—the analysts had no reason to assume poor execution, and their prognosis was dire nonetheless. It was dire for reasons intrinsic to Iraq's history, culture and ethnic geography and to the limits of what any foreign occupation, however wisely led, could accomplish.

Moreover, amid the stultifying policy environment that prevailed when the assessments were prepared—in which it was evident that the administration was going to war and that analysis supporting that decision was welcome and contrary analysis

was not—it is all the more remarkable that the analysts would produce such a gloomy view. If there was any bias in their work, it was in the direction of trying to find places to sugarcoat what was an unavoidably distinctly negative message.

A second lesson concerns the severely truncated and deficient nature of what passed for a national debate on the war prior to March 2003. This deficiency involved not just the administration but also Congress, the press and the public. A thorough debate would have considered all the objectives that a war might have pursued—including the administration's true objectives of refashioning the politics of the Middle East and enhancing U.S. influence there, not just its selling points—and critically examined how a war would or would not be likely to achieve those ends. It would have assiduously examined all the options for dealing with Iraq, and all the pros and cons of each alternative. Above all, it would have considered in detail what the United States was getting into by invading Iraq, including all the ramifications of trying to pacify, reconstruct and politically transform that country. These were exactly the ramifications that the intelligence community addressed in the two long-suppressed assessments.

The chairman of the Senate Intelligence Committee at the time, Bob Graham (D-FL)—who did consider seriously some of these other issues, and who voted against the war resolution—expressed understandable astonishment when he discovered in the fall of 2002 that the administration had never requested an intelligence-community estimate on the purported Iraqi weapons program, even though it had played such a large part in their rhetoric. (Once the estimate was produced, Graham was one of the few members of Congress who bothered to read it.) Members should have been equally astonished that the administration also never requested anything like the other two assessments.

That the complicated and messy postwar issues were difficult to weigh when evaluating the idea of going to war was not an excuse for failing even to try to weigh them. Four members of the Republican minority on the Senate Intelligence Committee, in a comment attempting to downplay the importance of the assessments about postwar repercussions, noted that "collected intelligence reporting" did not play a significant role in the assessments. Of course it didn't: Fortune-tellers are not recruited as intelligence agents, and intelligence reporting about the future is awfully hard to come by. On behalf of all of the analysts who were involved, I accept the minority's comment as a compliment on how prescient the analysis nonetheless proved to be. Given the challenge not only of projecting into the future, but into a future heavily influenced by the actions of the United States (at a time when the Coalition Provisional Authority was not even a gleam in anyone's eye), it perhaps is remarkable that the intelligence community came as close to the mark as it did.

The minority comment also quoted an observation I had made in earlier testimony to the committee: that the committee members themselves, "who know from first-hand experience what it takes to make our democracy work, probably have at least as much basis for trusting their own judgment on such things [as building a stable democracy] as those of us who are intelligence analysts have for trusting ours." My remark certainly was not intended as advice to disregard the assessments the intelligence would offer on this subject; otherwise, why bother writing them? Instead, it was an invitation—and a challenge—to the members to apply their own considerable political acumen to the proposition that the administration was about to put to test: That the values and habits of liberal democracy could, at acceptable cost and risk, be injected into Iraq through the barrel of a gun.

In anticipating this test, the war-makers held an optimistic expectation that was casually constructed, ideologically inspired, largely implicit rather than openly expressed and not subjected to criticism and review. The far more pessimistic assessment of the intelligence community reflected not only all the available expertise inside the community but also (as made clear in the assessments' prefaces) consultation with outside experts. It was the product of about three months (not three weeks, as with the weapons estimate) of rigorous review and coordination. And the final assessments received the unanimous concurrence of all the intelligence agencies (unlike the weapons estimate, in which the uncertainties were reflected in dissents so prominent that, in the words of one Senate Foreign Relations Committee staffer, they "leaped out . . . almost like flashing light"). It may have been surprising that anyone could have come as close to the mark about postwar Iraq as the intelligence community did; it should not have been surprising that the intelligence community would come much closer than the hawks in the administration.

Most members of Congress—and most of the press, and the public that follows the lead of both—did not rise to the challenge I posed. It is a tribute to the agenda-setting power of the White House that debate on the war was mostly reduced to the administration's chosen selling point of WMD (and to a lesser extent, Iraq's chimerical "alliance" with Al-Qaeda) and that the nation swallowed the unjustified proposition that a presumption of Iraqi unconventional weapons programs implied a need to use military force to eliminate the programs. The lesson is that this kind of dangerous reductionism must not be allowed to afflict future debates on important national-security issues.

The issue of the Iranian nuclear program certainly comes to mind. Judgments about the status of that program should be only the starting point of any consideration given to use of military force against Iran. Questions involving the efficacy of a military strike, likely Iranian responses, the long-term impact on U.S.-Iranian relations, and the many secondary and tertiary effects on America's standing in the region and the world are at least as important. Similarly, comprehensive analysis should be applied before any other contemplated exercise of U.S. power, regardless of how frightening or condemnable the target of that exercise may be.

A third lesson—bearing in mind how long it took for these assessments to be made public—is that evaluation of the intelligence community's performance tends to be heavily politicized, with much criticism having more to do with agendas and interests of the critics than with the intelligence community's actions. The two assessments about postwar issues, which contained very little sensitive reporting, should have been far easier to declassify than the Top Secret estimate on weapons. Yet it has taken almost three more years, and a change in party control in Congress, to release them or any report based on them. (But give the Senate committee credit for even belatedly doing something that neither its House counterpart nor the executive branch did.)

The Republican interest in protecting the administration, and in so doing shifting blame for the Iraq disaster to the intelligence community, clearly is a large part of this. But the scapegoating has a bipartisan element as well. For all members of Congress who supported the war, the assessments about postwar consequences are an inconvenient reminder of how they bought into the administration's false equation of a presumed weapons program with the need to invade, and how in trying to protect themselves against charges of being soft on national security they failed to consider all of the factors that should have influenced their votes.

Spinning the intelligence community's performance through selective attention has consequences that go far beyond institutional pride or historical record. One consequence is to divert attention from the real reasons for ill-informed or ill-directed foreign policy. The more attention that is consumed by aluminum tubes or other minutiae of weapons-related intelligence, the less attention is available to direct to the far more fundamental decision-making pathology that led to the Iraq War. Another consequence is disruption of the work of the intelligence community itself in the name of "fixing" it. The enactment in late 2004 of an intelligence reorganization of doubtful effectiveness depended in large part on the public perception—incomplete and incorrect—that intelligence on Iraq had been all wrong.

A final observation concerns how the intelligence community really did perform on Iraq. It offered judgments on the issues that turned out to be most important in the war, even though those judgments conspicuously contradicted the administration's rosy vision for Iraq. And for the most part, the judgments were correct. Missed opportunities all the way down.

PAUL R. PILLAR is on the faculty of the Security Studies Program at Georgetown University.

From *The National Interest,* September/October 2007. Copyright © 2007 by National Interest. Reprinted by permission.

When Congress Stops Wars
Partisan Politics and Presidential Power

WILLIAM G. HOWELL AND JON C. PEVEHOUSE

For most of George W. Bush's tenure, political observers have lambasted Congress for failing to fulfill its basic foreign policy obligations. Typical was the recent Foreign Affairs article by Norman Ornstein and Thomas Mann, "When Congress Checks Out," which offered a sweeping indictment of Congress' failure to monitor the president's execution of foreign wars and antiterrorist initiatives. Over the past six years, they concluded, Congressional oversight of the White House's foreign and national security policy "has virtually collapsed." Ornstein and Mann's characterization is hardly unique. Numerous constitutional-law scholars, political scientists, bureaucrats, and even members of Congress have, over the years, lamented the lack of legislative constraints on presidential war powers. But the dearth of Congressional oversight between 2000 and 2006 is nothing new. Contrary to what many critics believe, terrorist threats, an overly aggressive White House, and an impotent Democratic Party are not the sole explanations for Congressional inactivity over the past six years. Good old-fashioned partisan politics has been, and continues to be, at play.

It is often assumed that everyday politics *stops* at the water's edge and that legislators abandon their partisan identities during times of war in order to become faithful stewards of their constitutional obligations. But this received wisdom is almost always wrong. The illusion of Congressional wartime unity misconstrues the nature of legislative oversight and fails to capture the particular conditions under which members of Congress are likely to emerge as meaningful critics of any particular military venture.

The partisan composition of Congress has historically been the decisive factor in determining whether lawmakers will oppose or acquiesce in presidential calls for war. From Harry Truman to Bill Clinton, nearly every U.S. president has learned that members of Congress, and members of the opposition party in particular, are fully capable of interjecting their opinions about proposed and ongoing military ventures. When the opposition party holds a large number of seats or controls one or both chambers of Congress, members routinely challenge the president and step up oversight of foreign conflicts; when the legislative branch is dominated by the president's party, it generally goes along with the White House. Partisan unity, not institutional laziness, explains why the Bush administration's Iraq policy received such a favorable hearing in Congress from 2000 to 2006.

The dramatic increase in Congressional oversight following the 2006 midterm elections is a case in point. Immediately after assuming control of Congress, House Democrats passed a resolution condemning a proposed "surge" of U.S. troops in Iraq and Senate Democrats debated a series of resolutions expressing varying degrees of outrage against the war in Iraq. The spring 2007 supplemental appropriations debate resulted in a House bill calling for a phased withdrawal (the president vetoed that bill, and the Senate then passed a bill accepting more war funding without withdrawal provisions). Democratic heads of committees in both chambers continue to launch hearings and investigations into the various mishaps, scandals, and tactical errors that have plagued the Iraq war. By all indications, if the government in Baghdad has not met certain benchmarks by September, the Democrats will push for binding legislation that further restricts the president's ability to sustain military operations in Iraq.

Neither Congress' prior languor nor its recent awakening should come as much of a surprise. When they choose to do so, members of Congress can exert a great deal of influence over the conduct of war. They can enact laws that dictate how long military campaigns may last, control the purse strings that determine how well they are funded, and dictate how appropriations may be spent. Moreover, they can call hearings and issue public pronouncements on foreign policy matters. These powers allow members to cut funding for ill-advised military ventures, set timetables for the withdrawal of troops, foreclose opportunities to expand a conflict into new regions, and establish reporting requirements. Through legislation, appropriations, hearings, and public appeals, members of Congress can substantially increase the political costs of military action—sometimes forcing presidents to withdraw sooner than they would like or even preventing any kind of military action whatsoever.

The Partisan Imperative

Critics have made a habit of equating legislative inactivity with Congress' abdication of its foreign policy obligations. Too often, the infrequency with which Congress enacts restrictive statutes is seen as prima facie evidence of the institution's failings. Sometimes it is. But one cannot gauge the health of the U.S. system of governance strictly on the basis of what Congress does—or does not do—in the immediate aftermath of presidential initiatives.

After all, when presidents anticipate Congressional resistance they will not be able to overcome, they often abandon the sword as their primary tool of diplomacy. More generally, when the White House knows that Congress will strike down key provisions of a policy initiative, it usually backs off. President Bush himself has relented, to varying degrees, during the struggle to create the Department of Homeland Security and during conflicts over the design of military tribunals and the prosecution of U.S. citizens as enemy combatants. Indeed, by most accounts, the administration recently forced the resignation of the chairman of the Joint Chiefs of Staff, General Peter Pace, so as to avoid a clash with Congress over his reappointment.

To assess the extent of Congressional influence on presidential war powers, it is not sufficient to count how many war authorizations are enacted or how often members deem it necessary to start the "war powers clock"—based on the War Powers Act requirement that the president obtain legislative approval within 60 days after any military deployment. Rather, one must examine the underlying partisan alignments across the branches of government and presidential efforts to anticipate and preempt Congressional recriminations.

During the past half century, partisan divisions have fundamentally defined the domestic politics of war. A variety of factors help explain why partisanship has so prominently defined the contours of interbranch struggles over foreign military deployments. To begin with, some members of Congress have electoral incentives to increase their oversight of wars when the opposing party controls the White House. If presidential approval ratings increase due to a "rally around the flag" effect in times of war, and if those high ratings only benefit the president's party in Congress, then the opposition party has an incentive to highlight any failures, missteps, or scandals that might arise in the course of a military venture.

After all, the making of U.S. foreign policy hinges on how U.S. national interests are defined and the means chosen to achieve them. This process is deeply, and unavoidably, political. Therefore, only in very particular circumstances—a direct attack on U.S. soil or on Americans abroad—have political parties temporarily united for the sake of protecting the national interest. Even then, partisan politics has flared as the toll of war has become evident. Issues of trust and access to information further fuel these partisan fires. In environments in which information is sparse, individuals with shared ideological or partisan affiliations find it easier to communicate with one another. The president possesses unparalleled intelligence about threats to national interests, and he is far more likely to share that information with members of his own political party than with political opponents. Whereas the commander in chief has an entire set of executive-branch agencies at his beck and call, Congress has relatively few sources of reliable classified information. Consequently, when a president claims that a foreign crisis warrants military intervention, members of his own party tend to trust him more often than not, whereas members of the opposition party are predisposed to doubt and challenge such claims. In this regard, Congressional Democrats' constant interrogations of Bush administration officials represent just the latest round in an ongoing interparty struggle to control the machinery of war.

Congressional Influence and Its Limits

Historically, presidents emerging from midterm election defeats have been less likely to respond to foreign policy crises aggressively, and when they have ordered the use of force, they have taken much longer to do so. Our research shows that the White House's propensity to exercise military force steadily declines as members

of the opposition party pick up seats in Congress. In fact, it is not even necessary for the control of Congress to switch parties; the loss of even a handful of seats can materially affect the probability that the nation will go to war.

The partisan composition of Congress also influences its willingness to launch formal oversight hearings. While criticizing members for their inactivity during the Bush administration, Ornstein and Mann make much of the well-established long-term decline in the number of hearings held on Capitol Hill. This steady decline, however, has not muted traditional partisan politics. According to Linda Fowler, of Dartmouth College, the presence or absence of unified government largely determines the frequency of Congressional hearings. Contrary to Ornstein and Mann's argument that "vigorous oversight was the norm until the end of the twentieth century," Fowler demonstrates that during the post-World War II era, when the same party controlled both Congress and the presidency, the number of hearings about military policy decreased, but when the opposition party controlled at least one chamber of Congress, hearings occurred with greater frequency. Likewise, Boston University's Douglas Kriner has shown that Congressional authorizations of war as well as legislative initiatives that establish timetables for the withdrawal of troops, cut funds, or otherwise curtail military operations critically depend on the partisan balance of power on Capitol Hill.

Still, it is important not to overstate the extent of Congressional influence. Even when Congress is most aggressive, the executive branch retains a tremendous amount of power when it comes to military matters. Modern presidents enjoy extraordinary advantages in times of war, not least of which the ability to act unilaterally on military matters and thereby place on Congress (and everyone else) the onus of coordinating a response. Once troops enter a region, members of Congress face the difficult choice of either cutting funds and then facing the charge of undermining the troops or keeping the public coffers open and thereby aiding a potentially ill-advised military operation.

On this score, Ornstein and Mann effectively illustrate Bush's efforts to expand his influence over the war in Iraq and the war on terrorism by refusing to disclose classified information, regularly circumventing the legislative process, and resisting even modest efforts at oversight. Similarly, they note that Republican Congressional majorities failed to take full advantage of their institution's formal powers to monitor and influence either the formulation or the implementation of foreign policy during the first six years of Bush's presidency. Ornstein and Mann, however, mistakenly attribute such lapses in Congressional oversight to a loss of an "institutional identity" that was ostensibly forged during a bygone era when "tough oversight of the executive was common, whether or not different parties controlled the White House and Congress" and when members' willingness to challenge presidents had less to do with partisan allegiances and more to do with a shared sense of institutional responsibility. In the modern era, foreign-policy making has rarely worked this way. On the contrary, partisan competition has contributed to nearly every foreign policy clash between Capitol Hill and the White House for the past six decades.

Divided We Stand

Shortly after World War II—the beginning of a period often mischaracterized as one of "Cold War consensus"—partisan wrangling over the direction of U.S. foreign policy returned to Washington, ending a brief period of wartime unity. By defining U.S. military involvement in Korea as a police action rather than a war, President Truman effectively freed himself from the constitutional requirements regarding war and established a precedent for all subsequent presidents to circumvent Congress when sending the military abroad. Although Truman's party narrowly controlled both chambers, Congress hounded him throughout the Korean War, driving his approval ratings down into the 20s and paving the way for a Republican electoral victory in 1952. Railing off a litany of complaints about the president's firing of General Douglas MacArthur and his meager progress toward ending the war, Senator Robert Taft, then a Republican presidential candidate, declared that "the greatest failure of foreign policy is an unnecessary war, and we have been involved in such a war now for more than a year. . . . As a matter of fact, every purpose of the war has now failed. We are exactly where we were three years ago, and where we could have stayed."

On the heels of the Korean War came yet another opportunity to use force in Asia, but facing a divided Congress, President Dwight Eisenhower was hesitant to get involved. French requests for assistance in Indochina initially fell on sympathetic ears in the Eisenhower administration, which listed Indochina as an area of strategic importance in its "new look" defense policy. However, in January 1954, when the French asked for a commitment of U.S. troops, Eisenhower balked. The president stated that he "could conceive of no greater tragedy than for the United States to become involved in an all-out war in Indochina." His reluctance derived in part from the anticipated fight with Congress that he knew would arise over such a war. Even after his decision to provide modest technical assistance to France, in the form of B-26 bombers and air force technicians, Congressional leaders demanded a personal meeting with the president to voice their disapproval. Soon afterward, Eisenhower promised to withdraw the air force personnel, replacing them with civilian contractors.

Eventually, the United States did become involved in a ground war in Asia, and it was that war that brought Congressional opposition to the presidential use of force to a fever pitch. As the Vietnam War dragged on and casualties mounted, Congress and the public grew increasingly wary of the conflict and of the power delegated to the president in the 1964 Gulf of Tonkin resolution. In 1970, with upward of 350,000 U.S. troops in the field and the war spilling over into Cambodia, Congress formally repealed that resolution. And over the next several years, legislators enacted a series of appropriations bills intended to restrict the war's scope and duration. Then, in June 1973, after the Paris peace accords had been signed, Congress enacted a supplemental appropriations act that cut off all funding for additional military involvement in Southeast Asia, including in Cambodia, Laos, North Vietnam, and South Vietnam. Finally, when South Vietnam fell in 1975, Congress took the extraordinary step of formally forbidding U.S. troops from enforcing the Paris peace accords, despite the opposition of President Gerald Ford and Secretary of State Henry Kissinger.

Three years later, a Democratic Congress forbade the use of funds for a military action that was supported by the president—this time, the supply of covert aid to anticommunist forces in Angola. At the insistence of Senator Dick Clark (D-Iowa), the 1976 Defense Department appropriations act stipulated that no monies would be used "for any activities involving Angola other than intelligence gathering." Facing such staunch Congressional opposition,

President Ford suspended military assistance to Angola, unhappily noting that the Democratic-controlled Congress had "lost its guts" with regard to foreign policy.

In just one instance, the case of Lebanon in 1983, did Congress formally start the 60-day clock of the 1973 War Powers Act. Most scholars who call Congress to task for failing to fulfill its constitutional responsibilities make much of the fact that in this case it ended up authorizing the use of force for a full 18 months, far longer than the 60 days automatically allowed under the act. However, critics often overlook the fact that Congress simultaneously forbade the president from unilaterally altering the scope, target, or mission of the U.S. troops participating in the multinational peacekeeping force. Furthermore, Congress asserted its right to terminate the venture at any time with a one-chamber majority vote or a joint resolution and established firm reporting requirements as the U.S. presence in Lebanon continued.

During the 1980s, no foreign policy issue dominated Congressional discussions more than aid to the contras in Nicaragua, rebel forces who sought to topple the leftist Sandinista regime. In 1984, a Democratic-controlled House enacted an appropriations bill that forbade President Ronald Reagan from supporting the contras. Reagan appeared undeterred. Rather than abandon the project, the administration instead diverted funds from Iranian arms sales to support the contras, establishing the basis for the most serious presidential scandal since Watergate. Absent Congressional opposition on this issue, Reagan may well have intervened directly, or at least directed greater, more transparent aid to the rebels fighting the Nicaraguan government.

Regardless of which party holds a majority of the seats in Congress, it is almost always the opposition party that creates the most trouble for a president intent on waging war. When, in the early 1990s, a UN humanitarian operation in Somalia devolved into urban warfare, filling nightly newscasts with scenes from Mogadishu, Congress swung into action. Despite previous declarations of public support for the president's actions, Congressional Republicans and some Democrats passed a Department of Defense appropriations act in November 1993 that simultaneously authorized the use of force to protect UN units and required that U.S. forces be withdrawn by March 31, 1994.

A few years later, a Republican-controlled Congress took similar steps to restrict the use of funds for a humanitarian crisis occurring in Kosovo. One month after the March 1999 NATO air strikes against Serbia, the House passed a bill forbidding the use of Defense Department funds to introduce U.S. ground troops into the conflict without Congressional authorization. When President Clinton requested funding for operations in the Balkans, Republicans in Congress (and some hawkish Democrats) seized on the opportunity to attach additional monies for unrelated defense programs, military personnel policies, aid to farmers, and hurricane relief and passed a supplemental appropriations bill that was considerably larger than the amount requested by the president. The mixed messages sent by the Republicans caught the attention of Clinton's Democratic allies. As House member Martin Frost (D-Tex.) noted, "I am at a loss to explain how the Republican Party can, on one hand, be so irresponsible as to abandon our troops in the midst of a military action to demonstrate its visceral hostility toward the commander in chief, and then, on the other, turn around and double his request for money for what they call 'Clinton's war.'" The 1999 debate is remarkably similar to the current wrangling over spending on Iraq.

Legislating Opinion

The voice of Congress (or lack thereof) has had a profound impact on the media coverage of the current war in Iraq, just as it has colored public perceptions of U.S. foreign policy in the past. Indeed, Congress' ability to influence executive-branch decision-making extends far beyond its legislative and budgetary powers. Cutting funds, starting the war powers clock, or forcing troop withdrawals are the most extreme options available to them. More frequently, members of Congress make appeals designed to influence both media coverage and public opinion of a president's war. For example, Congress' vehement criticism of Reagan's decision to reflag Kuwaiti tankers during the Iran-Iraq War led to reporting requirements for the administration. Similarly, the Clinton administration's threats to invade Haiti in 1994 were met with resistance by Republicans and a handful of skeptical Democrats in Congress, who took to the airwaves to force Clinton to continually justify placing U.S. troops in harm's way.

Such appeals resonate widely. Many studies have shown that the media regularly follow official debates about war in Washington, adjusting their coverage to the scope of the discussion among the nation's political elite. And among the elite, members of Congress—through their own independent initiatives and through journalists' propensity to follow them—stand out as the single most potent source of dissent against the president. The sheer number of press releases and direct feeds that members of Congress produce is nothing short of breathtaking. And through carefully staged hearings, debates, and investigations, members deliberately shape the volume and content of the media's war coverage. The public posturing, turns of praise and condemnation, rapid-fire questioning, long-winded exhortations, pithy Shakespearean references, graphs, timelines, and pie charts that fill these highly scripted affairs are intended to focus media attention and thereby sway the national conversation surrounding questions of war and peace. Whether the media scrutinize every aspect of a proposed military venture or assume a more relaxed posture depends in part on Congress' willingness to take on the president.

Indeed, in the weeks preceding the October 2002 war authorization vote, the media paid a tremendous amount of attention to debates about Iraq inside the Beltway. Following the vote, however, coverage of Iraq dropped precipitously, despite continued domestic controversies, debates at the United Nations, continued efforts by the administration to rally public support, and grass-roots opposition to the war that featured large public protests. Congress helped set the agenda for public discussion, influencing both the volume and the tone of the coverage granted to an impending war, and Congress' silence after the authorization was paralleled by that of the press.

Crucially, Congressional influence over the media extended to public opinion as well. An analysis of local television broadcast data and national public-opinion surveys from the period reveals a strong relationship between the type of media coverage and public opinion regarding the war. Even when accounting for factors such as the ideological tendencies of a media market (since liberal markets tend to have liberal voters and liberal media, while conservative districts have the opposite), we found that the airing of more critical viewpoints led to greater public disapproval of the proposed war, and more positive viewpoints buoyed support for the war. As Congress speaks, it would seem, the media report, and the public listens.

As these cases illustrate, the United States has a Congress with considerably more agenda-setting power than most analysts presume and a less independent press corps than many would like. As the National Journal columnist William Powers observed during the fall of 2006, "Journalists like to think they are reporting just the facts, straight and unaffected by circumstance." On the contrary, he recognized, news is a product of the contemporary political environment, and the way stories are framed and spun has little to do with the facts. In Washington, the party that controls Congress also determines the volume and the tone of the coverage given to a president's war. Anticipating a Democratic Congressional sweep in November 2006, Powers correctly predicted that "if Bush suffers a major political setback, the media will feel freed up to tear into this war as they have never done before."

With the nation standing at the precipice of new wars, it is vital that the American public understand the nature and extent of Congress' war powers and its members' partisan motivations for exercising or forsaking them. President Bush retains extraordinary institutional advantages over Congress, but with the Democrats now in control of both houses, the political costs of pursuing new wars (whether against Iran, North Korea, or any other country) and prosecuting ongoing ones have increased significantly.

Congress will continue to challenge the president's interpretation of the national interest. Justifications for future deployments will encounter more scrutiny and require more evidence. Questions of appropriate strategy and implementation will surface more quickly with threats of Congressional hearings and investigations looming. Oversight hearings will proceed at a furious pace. Concerning Iraq, the Democrats will press the administration on a withdrawal timetable, hoping to use their agenda-setting power with the media to persuade enough Senate Republicans to defect and thereby secure the votes they need to close floor debate on the issue.

This fall, the Democrats will likely attempt to build even more momentum to end the war in Iraq, further limiting the president's menu of choices. This is not the first instance of heavy Congressional involvement in foreign affairs and war, nor will it be the last. This fact has been lost on too many political commentators convinced that some combination of an eroding political identity, 9/11, failures of leadership, and dwindling political will have made Congress irrelevant to deliberations about foreign policy.

On the contrary, the new Democratic-controlled Congress is conforming to a tried-and-true pattern of partisan competition between the executive and legislative branches that has characterized Washington politics for the last half century and shows no signs of abating. Reports of Congress' death have been greatly exaggerated.

WILLIAM G. HOWELL and **JON C. PEVEHOUSE** are Associate Professors at the Harris School of Public Policy at the University of Chicago and the authors of *While Dangers Gather: Congressional Checks on Presidential War Powers*.

UNIT 5

The Foreign Policy Making Process

Unit Selections

Key Points to Consider

- Construct an ideal foreign policy making process. How close does the United States come to this ideal? Is it possible for the United States to act in the ideal manner? If not, is the failing due to the individuals who make foreign policy or the institutions in which they work? Explain.

- What is the single largest failure of the foreign policy making process? How can it be corrected? What is the single largest strength of the foreign policy making process?

- What changes, if any, are necessary in the U.S. foreign policy making process for the United States to act effectively with other countries in multilateral efforts?

- What advice would you give to the president who is considering undertaking military action?

- How would you run a meeting organized to respond to a terrorist act? Whom would you invite? What would you expect of those you invite? How much dissent would you permit?

Student Web Site

www.mhcls.com/online

Internet References

Belfer Center for Science and International Affairs (BCSIA)
http://belfercenter.ksg.harvard.edu/
The Heritage Foundation
http://www.heritage.org
National Archives and Records Administration (NARA)
http://www.archives.gov/index.html
U.S. Department of State: The Network of Terrorism
http://usinfo.state.gov/products/pubs/

We easily slip into the habit of assuming that an underlying rationality is at work in the conduct of foreign policy. A situation is identified as unacceptable or needing change. Goals are established, policy options are listed, the implications of competing courses of action are assessed, a conscious choice is made as to which policy to adopt, and then the policy is implemented correctly. This assumption is comforting because it implies that policymakers are in control of events and that solutions do exist. Moreover, it allows us to assign responsibility for policy decisions and hold policymakers accountable for the success or failure of their actions.

As comforting as this assumption is, it is also false. Driven by domestic, international, and institutional forces, as well as by chance and accident, perfect rationality is an elusive quality. This is true regardless of whether the decision is made in a small group setting or by large bureaucracies. Small groups are created when the scope of the foreign policy problem appears to lie beyond the expertise of any single individual. This is frequently the case in crisis situations. The essence of the decision making problem here lies in the overriding desire of group members to get along with each other. Determined to be a productive member of the team and not rock the boat, individual group members suppress personal doubts about the wisdom of what is being considered and become less critical of the information before them, than they would be, if they alone were responsible for the decision. They may stereotype the enemy, assume that the policy cannot fail, or believe that all members of the group are in agreement on what must be done.

The absence of rationality in decision making by large bureaucracies stems from their dual nature. On the one hand, bureaucracies are politically neutral institutions that exist to serve the president and other senior officials by providing them with information and implementing their policies. On the other hand, they have goals and interests of their own that may not only conflict with the positions taken by other bureaucracies but may be inconsistent with the official position taken by policymakers. Because not every bureaucracy sees a foreign policy problem in the same way, policies must be negotiated into existence, and implementation becomes anything but automatic. Although it is essential for building a foreign policy consensus, this exercise in bureaucratic politics robs the policy process of much of the rationality that we look for in government decision making.

The problem of trying to organize the policy process to conduct a war against terrorism is an especially daunting task. In part, this is because the enormity of the terrorist attacks and the language of war embraced by the Bush administration lead to expectations of an equally stunning countermove. Rationality is also strained by the offsetting pressures for secrecy and the need for a speedy response on the one hand, and the need to harmonize large numbers of competing interests on the other. Finally, no matter how many resources are directed at the war against terrorism, there will continue to be the need to balance resources and goals. Priorities will need to be established and trade-offs

The McGraw-Hill Companies, Inc./Jill Braaten, photographer

accepted as is evidenced by the debate over the legality and value of domestic spying programs in support of the war on terrorism. There is no neutral equation or formula by which this can be accomplished. It will be made through a political process of bargaining and consensus building, in which political rationality rather than any type of substantive rationality will triumph.

The readings in this unit provide insight into the process by which foreign policy decisions are made by highlighting the activities involved at different points in the policy making process. The first essay, "Law, Liberty, and War," presents a debate between Anne-Marie Slaughter and Jeremy Rabkin over the proper constitutional balance between Congress and the president in conducting foreign policy in the war against terrorism and the Iraq War. The second essay, "Words vs. Deeds," looks at the central place the public opinion polling now holds in foreign policy decision making. The next essay, "Neo-Conservatives, Liberal Hawks, and the War on Terror," speaks of the importance of the ideas that shape American foreign policy. It is critical of both neo-conservatives and liberal hawks for holding utopian visions of what goals American foreign policy might pursue and unrealistic ideas about the potential uses of American power. The final essay by John Prados, "The Pros from Dover," casts a critical eye on decision-making processes and structures put into place by the Bush administration. He asserts that either the system did not work or it worked keeping terrorism off the foreign policy agenda in its first months in office.

Law, Liberty and War
Originalist Sin

Has the Bush Administration run roughshod over American civil liberties and distorted Constitutional balances during the Global War on Terror? *You bet it has,* argues Anne-Marie Slaughter. *No way,* says Jeremy Rabkin.

ANNE-MARIE SLAUGHTER

How historical periods are defined depends on the purposes of the definer. Geologists look to rock structure, demarking eras such as the Cretaceous, Jurassic, Triassic, Mesozoic and Paleozoic. Economists look to the primary source of wealth: the Iron Age, the Bronze Age, the Industrial Age and now the Information Age. Chroniclers of foreign affairs look to catastrophes: While their business is war *and* peace, their timelines are chiefly defined by wars. Consider how we talk and write about the 20th century: World War I, the interwar period, World War II, the Cold War. After the Cold War came the post-Cold War period, until 9/11, which marked the beginning of the War on Terror. The military is currently planning for "The Long War" against terrorism—and, if there is such a long war, it is a good bet that decades hence historians and political analysts will still be defining time in the cadences of war.

But why not focus instead on naming periods of peace? John Lewis Gaddis has written about "the long peace", describing how United States and the Soviet Union managed to get through over four decades of the Cold War without fighting one another directly. Yet proclaiming peace has not caught on, notwithstanding occasional references to Pax Americana, Pax Britannia and Pax Romana. The reason is not hard to find: Telling citizens that they live in wartime is good for boosting defense budgets. It is also good for expanding presidential power. "War makes the state", wrote celebrated sociologist Charles Tilly, "and the state makes war."

Such ruminations make a worthy backdrop for reading and assessing John Yoo's provocative book, *Powers of War and Peace: The Constitution and Foreign Affairs After 9/11.* Yoo writes to rectify an awkward legal contradiction for political conservatives. Ardent advocates of originalism—a school of Constitutional interpretation that prizes the intent of the Framers and literal reading of the text of our founding document—have heretofore found themselves arguing against the seemingly clear Constitutional text granting Congress the power to declare war. And they must explain away contemporaneous accounts in the *Federalist Papers* making clear that the Framers wanted to give the Executive authority to make war, but only once Congress had decided to go to war in the first place. As Thomas Jefferson put it, "We have . . . given . . . one effectual check to the Dog of war by transferring the power of letting him loose from the Executive to the Legislative body, from those who are to spend to those who are to pay." In foreign affairs debates, therefore, liberal constitutionalists like Louis Henkin and Harold Koh have been able to claim the originalist high ground, while conservatives have instead made sweeping claims about how the evolving nature of war and new threats to American national security require that the Constitution be interpreted in light of two centuries of practice—the very argument anathema to them in, say, constitutional debates over abortion or the death penalty.

No longer. Yoo offers an originalist understanding of a vast Executive foreign affairs power, checked not by the Constitution itself but only by Congress' ability to push back. The Framers, according to Yoo, designed "a flexible system for making foreign policy in which the political branches could opt to cooperate or compete." In this system, the roles of Congress and the courts are narrowly confined to the specific powers granted them in Articles I and III, respectively. Article II, on the other hand, which defines the Executive's powers, "effectively grants to the president any unenumerated foreign affairs powers not given elsewhere to the other branches."

Yoo's book reads as a long footnote to a Supreme Court brief.

The Powers of War and Peace offers the theoretical grounding for this expansive view of Executive power based on evidence from practice in early U.S. history, the intent of the Framers, and the text and structure of the Constitution. The book reads as a long footnote to a Supreme Court brief upholding the Bush Administration's controversial claims to lawfully detain U.S. citizens as enemy combatants or disregard treaties that have become inconvenient. With Yoo in hand, the Bush Administration need not argue to the courts that it must push out the boundaries of our Constitution in this national emergency. Giving such enormous power to the president in foreign affairs was what the Framers intended in the first place: Congress could fend for itself, Yoo writes, "[s]imply by refusing to do anything, by not affirmatively acting to vote funds or to enact legislation. . . . [T]he appropriations power and the power to raise the military gives Congress a sufficient check on presidential warmaking."

The key point, of course, is that the Framers wrote in a time of no standing armies, no established political parties and relatively little difficulty in demarcating the line between foreign and domestic affairs. Without standing armies, the Congressional power of the purse was necessary to put soldiers in the field, a very real check on executive war-mongering. But with 1.4 million men and women on active duty in the military today and another 860,000 in the reserves, the Executive branch tends to shoot first and ask Congress to fund later, when our young men and women in uniform are already on the front lines. The political calculus, as any modern president well knows, overwhelmingly favors lining up behind the troops once they are in the field—a decision, according to Yoo, that is entirely up to the president.

Without entrenched partisan politics, it was possible to imagine members of Congress serving as a genuine voice of the people in opposition to the Executive. But with the most partisan system the nation has seen in a century, the President's party votes with him, and it is the opposition alone that must face accusations of starving the troops in the field.

Without shrinking oceans, instant communications and a global economy it was at least possible to limit even a broad Executive foreign affairs power to distinctively and definably "foreign" affairs. But in an age of terrorism practiced by non-state groups both within the territory of the United States and without, by aliens and citizens alike, through a complex system of financing and support that travels through a tangled trail of domestic and foreign transactions, what a president can do abroad—wiretapping, for instance—he can also presume to do at home.

Yoo's history is, to say the least, highly selective. Despite his central claim that the Framers clearly intended a unified executive, Yoo's historical chapter about the writing of the Constitution opens with an admission of the Framers' "silence" about the separation of powers in foreign affairs. Manfully, Yoo tries to explain away messy historical facts—such as the Constitutional Convention's rejection of amendments that would have added to the Constitution explicit language setting out Yoo's own unconventional understanding of the treaty and war powers.

(Though these amendments failed, Yoo take pains to note that at least some of the Framers agreed with him.)

But by filling pages with every shred of evidence from the Founding period that might support a unified executive in foreign affairs, Yoo misses the real story. The Framers' animating purpose in abandoning the loose Articles of Confederation for our Constitution was not to resurrect the British monarchy's tradition of a dominant executive. Rather, the Framers were far more concerned about creating a strong central government to harmonize the dissonant foreign policies of the states, which had left the infant United States vulnerable in the 18th-century world of marauding mercantilist great powers. To the extent that the Framers sought what Alexander Hamilton called "energy in the executive", as Stanford's Pulitzer Prize-winning historian Jack Rakove writes in "Making Foreign Policy: The View from 1787", the constitutional provisions "that laid the strongest foundation for a major executive role in foreign policy are more safely explained as a cautious reaction against the defects of exclusive senatorial control of foreign relations than as a bold attempt to convert the noble office of a republican presidency into a vigorous national leader in world affairs."

In light of George Washington's difficulties with a war run by committee during the Revolution, the Framers explicitly chose not to give Congress the power to "make war", that is, to actually conduct it. But they equally explicitly gave Congress the power to "declare war", that is, to start it. Indeed, at the Constitutional Convention, when Pierce Butler of South Carolina formally proposed giving the president the power on his own to start war, Elbridge Gerry of Massachusetts said he "never expected to hear in a republic a motion to empower the executive to declare war." The Constitutional Convention quickly rejected Butler's motion.

Yoo's version of the Constitution is both disingenuous and dangerous.

Moreover, the practice of early presidents confirms this understanding. In 1801, facing depredations by the Barbary pirates, President Jefferson took certain defensive actions but went before the Congress to explain himself. He told the Congress that anything beyond defensive action was for them to authorize. Four years later, during a dispute with Spain, Jefferson put the matter as plainly as possible: "Congress alone is constitutionally vested with the power of changing our situation from peace to war."

By contrast, Yoo's version of the Constitution is both disingenuous and dangerous. Take the striking inconsistency between Yoo's understanding of "flexibility" in the Constitution's treatment of the War Powers and Treaty powers. Yoo argues that "[t]he Constitution did not intend to institute a fixed, legalistic process" in foreign affairs, and goes to great lengths to explain why Articles I and II do not actually restrict the president's war powers in the way historians and legal scholars have long understood. But, flexibility for Yoo does not extend to the treaty power, even though treaties are clearly instruments of foreign affairs. Instead, Yoo insists that treaties must not only satisfy the requirements of Article II, but that they also be subject to additional rigid legal requirements to have the force of law. Yoo infers such "fixed, legalistic process" for implementing treaties in the United States even though no specific language in the Constitution sets out such requirements. This conveniently allows the president to dispose of a host of inconvenient treaties that might restrain his power if their terms had the force of domestic law. And despite Yoo's own history describing the Framers' concern with the states ignoring treaties, he even questions how much the Federal government today can require the states to follow U.S. treaty obligations. Such conclusions leave the reader wondering how much of this book is pure Constitutional interpretation, and how much a manual for the Bush Administration's vision of American unilateralism.

Yoo's most sweeping and dangerous claim is hidden as a legal technicality.

Given Yoo's recent service in an intensely ideological administration, his partisanship here is hardly surprising and easy to spot. Yoo's most sweeping—and most dangerous—claim is hidden as a legal technicality. "Article II", he writes, "effectively grants to the president any unenumerated foreign affairs powers not given elsewhere to the other branches." In other words, whatever is not explicitly granted ("enumerated") to Congress or the courts belongs to the Executive. All that is necessary is to identify a particular power as a "foreign affairs power."

The danger of this view is that the president can claim any new threat to American national security—and those appear all the time—as one he alone is empowered to address. Take the war on terror. The Bush Administration has claimed that the president has the power to declare any American citizen an "enemy combatant", to keep such combatants in jail indefinitely without bringing criminal charges, and to try them through a separate court system without the core protections of the Bill of Rights. Even judges in President Bush's conservative camp are unwilling to trust a president that much. In 2003 the Supreme Court—in an opinion joined by Antonin Scalia—rejected Bush's claim that the president's war powers meant that enemy combatants could not challenge their detention in court. And this past December, a conservative appellate judge once on Bush's Supreme Court short-list (Michael Luttig of the Fourth Circuit) wrote a biting opinion holding that the Bush Administration could not move a U.S. citizen in and out of the protections of the criminal justice system simply by invoking the shibboleth of terrorism and national security.

Yoo's position not only threatens our civil liberties; it is equally dangerous to our national security. He is right about the profound changes America faces in the world and the resulting need for a flexible framework governing foreign affairs powers—a push and pull between the Executive and Congress, with periodic intervention by the courts. But rather than

expanding Executive power while pretending that Congress can cut funding to stop U.S. troops already deployed on foreign soil, the solution is to draw clear Constitutional boundaries around the Executive's power, enforceable by the courts if necessary, and to find ways to force, commit or lure Congress to do the job it is supposed to do.

Leslie Gelb and I recently suggested ("Declare War", *The Atlantic Monthly,* November 2005) one approach to this: a new law that would restore the Framers' intent by restoring the declaration of war, and requiring Congress actually to declare war in advance of any commitment of troops that promises sustained combat. The president would be required to present Congress with critical information about war aims and plans; and Congress would in turn hold hearings to scrutinize for itself the intelligence justifying the recourse to war, the costs of fighting, and the administration's plans for the war's aftermath. A full floor debate and vote would follow. The lack of a Congressional declaration would automatically deny funds to that military operation. In Jefferson's words, "Congress must be called on to take it, the right of reprisal being expressly lodged with them by the Constitution, and not with the Executive." Congress must be called on, or must precommit itself, to take the same responsibility with respect to how we treat enemy prisoners and fight other critical fronts in the War on Terror.

Congressional participation in foreign affairs, however, is not an end in itself. The Framers' genius was to recognize the practical benefits of American democracy in conducting foreign affairs. In a world of shadowy and immeasurable threats, the real danger of getting war powers wrong is not simply the abuse of power by any one branch of government, but also the use of power without sufficient information, deliberation and imagination to succeed. As any global business recognizes, success today requires managing change and risk under conditions of uncertainty. So too with government. In this effort, many minds are better than one—to sift through and assess the quality of our information, to question and improve our strategies, and to brainstorm and troubleshoot so that tactics too narrowly conceived will not lead us astray.

The intelligence failures that enabled the attacks on September 11 and the rush to war in Iraq (leaving aside the accuracy of the limited intelligence presented to Congress) underscore the danger of leaving critical questions of war solely in the hands of the Executive. Congress' job is not simply to fund or not to fund. It is to question, to probe, to deliberate and to decide, together with the President, on behalf of the people whose sons and daughters will be sent to war and whose tax dollars will be spent. That is the originalist understanding of the Constitution, and the ensuing centuries have only strengthened the case for this interpretation of its text.

ANNE-MARIE SLAUGHTER is dean of the Woodrow Wilson School of Public and International Affairs and the Bert G. Kerstetter University Professor of Politics and International Affairs at Princeton University.

War Stories

JEREMY RABKIN

In the immediate aftermath of 9/11, most Americans wanted to fight the terrorists and the regimes that aided them. Even before that year ended, however, some voices warned that the impulsive, reckless policies of the Bush Administration would ultimately pose more of a danger to Americans and their way of life than the terrorists and their allies: We were, according to such critics, falling into the trap that clever terrorists always set, conspiring unwittingly in our own undoing. That opinion has gained ground as the shock of the initial terror attacks has receded. It is an opinion that owes far less to actual incursions on domestic liberties, however, than to insinuations and second thoughts about whether we need to be "at war" at all.

It is certainly possible to endorse a war while criticizing its conduct abroad and its policy repercussions at home. Such distinctions are not inherently illogical. But almost invariably, the loudest protests against wartime abuses come from those who reject the war in the first place. The fiercest critics of President Lincoln's war measures were the Copperheads, who opposed from the outset the effort to coerce the South by force of arms. The most outspoken critics of Cold War measures were those who dismissed the notion that communists or communism could threaten American security. And so it is with the War on Terror.

The current war has stimulated some measures that might be questioned in peacetime. They look altogether intolerable to those who reject the need for war. On the other hand, those who accept a "war" policy in current circumstances often hesitate to criticize particular security measures lest such criticism undermine general support for the war. It is hard in this setting to sort out competing claims about domestic security measures of the Bush Administration. The debate almost immediately shifts from actual experience to generalized claims about the Administration's posture in the world. After years of debate about the supposed excesses of the Patriot Act, for example, critics in Congress acquiesced earlier this year to its re-enactment with only minor changes. The Patriot Act seems to have been not so much a source of dispute in itself as a symbol of some wider, more amorphous complaint.

Several points about this larger debate do seem reasonably clear, however. The first is that, compared with our experience in past wars, the current war has been quite mild in its impact on domestic civil liberties. In World War II, the Federal government incarcerated more than 120,000 Japanese-Americans, including women, children and old people—all of them long-standing residents and most of them either citizens or immediate relatives of citizens. These unfortunates were held behind barbed wire in excess of two years, and the Supreme Court endorsed the practice essentially on the say-so of the President.

After 9/11 fewer than five thousand people were rounded up. All of them were aliens, almost all recent arrivals and unmarried males of suitable age for combat or terror operations. They were all released within a few weeks. Today's true legal counterpart of *Korematsu,* the 1943 case endorsing the mass detention of Japanese-Americans without any sort of due process, is the case of José Padilla—one person, who is now to be tried before an ordinary civilian court (though admittedly after years of military detention without trial or formal charges).

The same pattern holds regarding freedom of speech. In the Civil War, President Lincoln authorized military trials for antiwar agitators. He deployed the army to shut down an antiwar newspaper in New York and to suppress anti-conscription riots there. There was comprehensive official censorship during World War I and a Federal program to coach state universities on proper wartime curricula. The Cold War saw American Communist Party leaders prosecuted for conspiring to incite unspecified acts of disloyalty in unspecified future circumstances. The House Un-American Activities Committees hounded left-wing screenwriters. Some were ultimately sentenced to prison terms for refusing to testify about possible decades-old communist affiliations of associates in the movie industry. Yet the angriest charge against the Bush Administration is that it has used rhetoric that puts its critics on the defensive, as by ostensibly improper allusions to the 9/11 victims.

Today's legal counterpart to *Korematsu* is the case of Jos Padilla—*one person.*

So, too, with surveillance. There was a great uproar when it was revealed at the end of 2005 that the Bush Administration had, without proper judicial warrants, monitored phone calls between al-Qaeda suspects overseas and individuals in the United States. Yet President Roosevelt invoked national security to authorize wiretaps on domestic phone calls of suspicious individuals more than a year before the United States entered World War II. The practice continued during the Cold War. It was not until the late 1970s, amid revelations of abusive FBI surveillance activities, that Congress even attempted to regulate such practice with the Foreign Intelligence Surveillance Act.

In the recent dispute about when FISA procedures apply, a second point stands out: Even though the government is acting with greater restraint than in past wars, the clamor about threats to civil liberties is louder today because we now hold the government to higher standards. What critics now regard as outrageous was once regarded as more or less standard practice.

There are often good reasons for moving the goal posts in such ways. Past abuses prompt greater cautions in succeeding generations. No one wants to repeat Cold War abuses. J. Edgar Hoover himself cautioned during World War II against repeating the excesses committed by the Wilson Administration in World War I. Sometimes new technology raises new issues, as with the NSA surveillance systems that today allow immensely powerful computers to monitor vast volumes of telephone and Internet communication without direct human "listening."

Still, in an era in which so much constitutional debate proceeds on the basis of evolving standards, this particular debate has become disorienting. Those most indignant about threats to the Constitution tend to appeal not to traditional standards but to those that are recent or even heretofore unheard of. Over the past few years, for example, some of America's most distinguished law faculties have endorsed the claim that law schools have a First Amendment right to exclude military recruiters from their job fairs without forfeiting Federal funds, as current law requires. When the Supreme Court rejected this argument earlier this year, not a single justice offered so much as a sympathetic nod to this strange new constitutional theory. The harshest critics of constitutional abuses tend to be those who, in other contexts, champion the theory of a "living Constitution", one whose provisions are never quite settled. It is hard *not* to violate a "constitution" that keeps expanding in this way.

A third point follows from the second: Debates about civil liberties in wartime have now expanded to embrace standards regarded as global in scope, supposedly binding on America because they are "international law." Thus has a vast amount of debate centered on the treatment of captured terrorists at Guantánamo: Are they treated in accord with the Geneva Convention? Are they being interrogated in ways prohibited by the UN Convention Against Torture? Is the Bush Administration's disdain for these accepted international standards a threat to America's global leadership? Does the Administration's stance threaten Americans at home who rely on the protections of law?

and domestic critics that even overseas the U.S. military will follow what judges can certify as proper legal standards.

One can certainly argue that extreme brutality, even toward foreign prisoners in wartime, has a corrosive effect on military discipline, and that it may ultimately have poisonous moral consequences for any society that sponsors or tolerates such practices. But surely a lot depends on context. Stephen Ambrose's book about a company of paratroopers in World War II, *Band of Brothers,* reports that patrols were sent out behind enemy lines to capture low-ranking German soldiers whom American interrogators would then shoot or threaten to shoot to make others reveal information about enemy positions. It did not occur to Ambrose, author of many works on American military history, to denounce this tactic or to depict it as aberrant. Nor did the producers of the HBO mini-series based on the book feel obliged to suppress this unpleasant fact of history. Neither Ambrose nor his Hollywood adaptors even bothered to incorporate an acknowledgement that such tactics were in violation of the Hague Conventions and the applicable Geneva Convention at the time.

If one takes the idea of war seriously enough, one risks excusing almost anything in the interest of victory. That is the charge hurled most insistently at John Yoo, a professor of law at Berkeley who served as a top advisor in the Department of Justice in George W. Bush's first term. Yoo's internal memos, subsequently leaked by an Administration once thought to be strongly averse to leaks, have been denounced as authorizing torture and encouraging disregard of law.

No U.S. court has ever before presumed to judge military compliance with the Geneva standards.

The last question, though insistently posed by many critics, has scarcely anything to do with the others. The five hundred or so detainees in Guantánamo were taken to that naval base in the Caribbean precisely because it is not, technically, American soil. No American court had ever presumed to question U.S. military actions outside the United States. The Supreme Court had specifically repudiated such interference in a 1950 case about war prisoners held by the U.S. military in occupied Germany. The Court's exceedingly narrow, divided ruling in *Rasul v. Bush* in 2004 has left most questions about the status of Guantánamo detainees open, but assures that domestic courts will now, for the first time, have some role in monitoring external military actions. Some justices have indicated both in concurring opinions and in off-the-bench speeches that U.S. courts should indeed consider whether international standards have been properly applied in these settings. That would be another great novelty: No U.S. court has ever before presumed to judge military compliance with the Geneva standards. But many legal advocates now insist that the Court reassure foreign skeptics

Most past presidents have tacitly agreed with Yoo's constitutional constructions.

Now Yoo has published an academic study, *Powers of War and Peace: The Constitution and Foreign Affairs Since 9/11.* The book, however, says almost nothing about the convention against torture or the detentions at Guantánamo, and even less about domestic civil liberties. Instead, Yoo pursues seemingly legalistic questions about the separation of powers: Who decides when and whether the United States is at war? Who decides when and whether the United States is still bound by international treaties? Yoo argues that the Founders saw decisions about the resort to war just as they saw decisions about repudiating treaties as inherently an Executive branch prerogative. The power given to Congress to "declare" war simply entails the authority to announce a formality rather than control the strategic decision. Congress retains ultimate authority because it can finally deny funds to any presidential initiative, but the president retains broad powers of initiative in foreign affairs.

Conventional legal scholarship has run strongly in the other direction since the Vietnam War. But Yoo makes a very strong case for his interpretations based on the British practice familiar to the Framers, on what defenders of the Constitution said in ratification debates, and on what their opponents did not say. An honest reading of American history suggests that most past presidents have tacitly assumed the correctness of Yoo's constitutional constructions.

Still, the ultimate point at issue is not historical but philosophical. If one thinks that Congress is supposed to have the first word about the resort to war as well as the last, then one thinks that war must be, generally speaking, a legislative decision that we can adopt or reject like a tax cut. To think that, one must suppose that the world is fundamentally peaceful or at least that the United States is fundamentally at peace with the world, with conflict a rare and discretionary exception. Such a supposition makes it easy to embrace the notion of an international legal system that covers even the conduct of war in its smallest details. One can then suppose that such standards have great authority, even if some of the combatants in a conflict ignore them altogether, because the world remains in some way governed by a fine mesh of legal standards. Many advocates certainly want to live in a world of this kind. It happens, however, not to be the world in which we actually live.

Legal standards have value to the extent that they can be sustained. It does not promote law to ground it on merely wishful or fanciful premises. A proposal for law on such premises is offered in *Before the Next Attack: Preserving Civil Liberties in an Age of Terrorism,* a recent book by Yale law professor Bruce Ackerman. Ackerman acknowledges that terror attacks may indeed require emergency measures. He thinks, however, the responses of the Bush Administration were "disasters" for law and civil liberties because they have not been checked by adequate constraints. So Ackerman advocates a new scheme under which Congress could authorize suspensions of civil liberties for brief periods after an attack, but could only renew such emergency provisions contingent on successively higher majorities within Congress. Nothing in the Constitution warrants requiring Congress to abide by supermajority requirements in this way, but Ackerman argues that the courts could

nonetheless enforce something of the kind if Congress accepted the basic scheme.

Those who are familiar with Ackerman's work will not be surprised by this suggestion. He is best known for arguing that the Constitution can be amended not only by the formal process set out in Article V, but also by an informal political "process": When a contested new approach to the Constitution is defended by a political party or administration and the voters return them to office, that provides endorsement for the new approach. Ackerman's favorite example is, of course, the New Deal. He may now expect that his own constitutional doctrines will be ratified by voters in future elections. Ackerman is the quintessential cheerleader for a "living Constitution", stimulated by growth hormones slipped to it by attentive law professors.

Several times in *Before the Next Attack* Ackerman insists that we do not now face an "existential threat" comparable to that posed by Germany and Japan in the 1940s, and so we cannot now justify such significant abridgement of civil liberties in response. But was Germany really going to land an army in New England, or the Japanese in California? Was a German victory parade in Washington ever more likely than a mass-casualty terror attack today on an American city? No matter: If one wants to advance uniquely high standards of protectiveness toward supposed threats to civil liberties, it is easier to pretend that World War II was a unique exception and that the current war is more like the Cold War, when law professors could insist that the enemy was a figment of the imagination of McCarthyite demagogues.

I concede that war is always a potential threat to civil liberties. But so is defeat in war. Forced to choose between the risk of domestic abuses and the risk of defeat in war, most Americans will not harp on domestic legal standards. It is reasonable to worry about government excesses. It is escapist to pretend, at a time when terrorists plot new assaults on American cities, that our own government is the greatest threat to our security.

JEREMY RABKIN is a professor of government at Cornell University and serves on the board of directors of the Center for Individual Rights.

Words vs. Deeds
President George W. Bush and Polling

Kathryn Dunn Tenpas

President George W. Bush pledged repeatedly throughout his presidential campaign that his administration would have no use for polls and focus groups: "I really don't care what polls and focus groups say. What I care about is doing what I think is right." Shackled by that promise, President Bush and his staff have shrouded his polling apparatus, minimizing the relevance of polls and denying their impact. But public records available from the Federal Election Commission, documents from presidential libraries, and interviews with key players paint a fairly clear picture of the Bush polling operation. The picture, which turns out to be a familiar one, calls into question the administration's purported "anti-polling" ethos and shows an administration closely in keeping with historical precedent.

President Bush in Historical Context

Every president since Richard Nixon has hired professional pollsters to take, periodically, the pulse of the electorate. Earlier presidents clearly had relationships with pollsters, who obligingly tacked questions onto their existing polls for the benefit of the administration. But polling was not under White House control. Nixon's use of pollsters marked a turning point in the history of presidential polling because it signaled the birth of White House-commissioned polls. No longer tethered to the timetables and agendas of pollsters like Lou Harris and George Gallup, presidents began to direct both the timing and the substance of their polls. Nor were polls limited to the campaign season; presidents and their staff could test the popularity of various programs and policy initiatives on their own schedule. Scholars, noting that the transfer of campaign tactics to governing was blurring the distinction between the two, began describing the result as the "permanent campaign."

Rapid advances in technology played a big part in the new ways presidents used polling. By the time Nixon took office, computers, though costly, had become sophisticated enough to process vast quantities of data. Not only were telephones ubiquitous enough to make their use in polling methodologically feasible, but the advent of random digit dialing increased the efficiency and validity of telephone polling. In short, the "science" of polling became more mature, enabling presidents not only to learn about their past performance but to gain "prospective" intelligence. Today, testing key phrases in a speech or catchphrases designed to sell a policy or program has become so commonplace that presidential speeches and public pronouncements endure many rounds of focus group testing before being judged ready for primetime. Innovative techniques like the mall intercept (interviewing shoppers at a mall storefront), tracking polls, overnight polling, dial meters, and focus groups are part of any professional pollster's repertoire. And new Internet focus groups are being used, by the Bush pollsters among others, as a more timely, less expensive way to conduct focus groups. Though still in its nascent stages, Internet polling is thought to be the next generation of survey research, significantly lowering costs while increasing the speed with which polls can be conducted.

The names of many past presidential pollsters are familiar, if not exactly household names. Robert Teeter did polling for Presidents Nixon, Ford, and George H.W. Bush; Patrick Caddell for President Carter; Richard Wirthlin for President Reagan; and Stanley Greenberg (1993-94) and Mark Penn (1995-2000) for President Clinton. Most began as pollsters for the campaign and were "promoted" to presidential pollsters, taking on a higher profile in the process. Indeed, the unprecedented visibility and perceived influence of Clinton's pollsters created much advance interest in President George W. Bush's prospective pollsters. But Bush's determination to be the "anti-Clinton" and his repeated campaign promises to give polls and focus groups no role in his administration led him to relegate his pollsters to near anonymity. Still, their low profile, particularly compared with that of Clinton's pollsters, has not kept them from performing essential polling for the White House.

By the Numbers

The Republican and Democratic National Committees subsidize presidential political expenses such as polling and political travel and routinely report those expenses to the Federal Election Commission. Table 1 sets out polling expenditures only for designated presidential pollsters during the first two years of the Reagan, Bush I, Clinton, and Bush II administrations. The pollsters for the second Bush administration come in well behind those of Presidents Reagan and Clinton and only slightly ahead of the first Bush administration. Though the parties spent extraordinary amounts on both Reagan and Clinton, Reagan's administration was popularly perceived as being driven by deeply rooted philosophical principles while Clinton's was seen as merely pandering—suggesting that polling does not always taint a president's reputation.

When the party of the president is in power, the national committee becomes a veritable White House annex staffed with loyalists eager to secure the president's reelection. Toward that end, no amount of polling is too much, particularly when the polling can also inform broader party strategy and statewide campaigns. A look at Republican National Committee spending on polling more generally (not just designated presidential pollsters) reveals that it spent roughly $3.1 million during the first two years of the current Bush administration. And even that figure understates the polling available to the White House because it does not include polling conducted on behalf of the National Republican Senatorial Committee and the National Republican Congressional Committee, which totals some $6.5 million—more than double what the RNC spent on polling. Though neither of those organizations is responsible for subsidizing White House polling, Bush's presidential pollsters, Jan van Lohuizen (Voter/Consumer Research) and Fred Steeper (Market Strategies), have done work for these committees totaling more than $800,000—a sum that if added to presidential polling would bump up the Bush total to $2.5 million, more than $1 million more than Bush I. And Karl Rove's extraordinary sway makes it unlikely that any request by him for statewide polls that might be of interest to the president would be denied either by the president's pollsters or by any pollsters doing work for the RNC. In addition, the RNC spent $2.7 million on "political consulting." And although the FEC reports do not detail the various projects, the reports include work by former White House adviser Karen Hughes and a broad range of Republican consulting firms.

As interesting as the total amount of RNC spending on polling is its timing (figure 1). Rather than being more or less consistent monthly, spending peaks in ways that seem hard to explain. Though noteworthy events—the September 11 attacks and the midterm elections—may account for two of the peaks, Matthew Dowd, senior adviser at the RNC, has indicated that events do not necessarily drive polling. And while pollsters may be interested in gauging the impact of unexpected events or new developments, their billing is not systematic in a way that could support the event-driven explanation. Nevertheless, a statistical regression analysis reveals a general trend upward, roughly an average increase of $4,000 a month, suggesting that, over time, there are forces driving the RNC to spend more money on polling. Short of obtaining White House-commissioned polls, it is impossible to define the precise role that events play in polling. Regardless, the variation in spending reflects the idiosyncratic usage of polling within the Bush administration.

National Party Presidential Polling Expenditures (In 2002 dollars)

Administration	First Year	Second Year	Total
Reagan— Richard Wirthlin	1,635,000	2,531,000	4.1 million
Bush I— Robert Teeter	831,683	470,811	1.3 million
Clinton— Stanley Greenberg	2,433,000	2,415,000	4.8 million
Bush II— Jan van Lohuizen and Fred Steeper	715,771	947,422	1.7 million

*Data for the current administration obtained on-line from fec.gov with the assistance of Elizabeth Redman and Larissa Davis of the Brookings Institution, April 2003. All other data obtained by author from the Federal Election Commission.

Why Poll?

Presidential documents and interviews with White House staff and pollsters from past administrations suggest that presidents use polling for two primary reasons. The first is tactical. Given the limited resources available to them, new presidents must determine the best way to sell their agenda, minimizing costs and maximizing their influence. Campaign professionals, armed with state-of-the-art public opinion technology and an "outside the Beltway" perspective on pressing issues and problems, provide a service that the modern White House is unequipped to offer. The second reason, rooted in democratic theory, is a president's desire to represent his constituents by acting in consonance with a majority of the public. Although the Bush administration is willing to admit it uses polls to help package and sell its policies to the public, it regards as heresy any suggestion that it follows the polls (even the Clinton administration denied that it used polls for this purpose).

Regardless, presidential pollsters from all administrations since Nixon's have been known to poll on foreign and domestic issues alike. Nixon polled about Vietnam and about admitting China to the United Nations. Carter surveyed American attitudes toward Israel and the Iran hostage crisis. Reagan tracked polls on the Iran-Contra affair and the Marine barracks bombing in Lebanon. During President George H.W. Bush's administration, pollsters Robert Teeter and Fred Steeper conducted polls and focus groups both before and during the Gulf War. Examples of polling on domestic policy—busing, agriculture, government regulation, bilingual education, health care policy, energy, and the budget—abound. Presidential pollsters provide additional data before midterm elections and become pivotal during the president's reelection campaign. Typically, the fourth year of the president's term generates the highest spending on polling. Speech content is another area where pollsters can provide useful advice. Finally, all presidential pollsters need to collect national tracking polls on a regular basis to provide an internal baseline to compare against other polls. In short, presidential polling is a staple of the modern presidency.

Consumer of Polls: The Bush Political Machine

The way one political insider explained President Bush's attitude toward polling reinforced the president's campaign mantra: "One of the worst arguments a White House adviser can make to the president is to say that 'the polls show X.' " But despite the president's disdain for public opinion polls, he has created a formidable White House political operation that focuses closely on them. The Office of Strategic Initiatives monitors and analyzes the results of numerous public surveys by major networks and news organizations as well as the findings of privately commissioned polls. And access to state surveys and other polls conducted by GOP pollsters informs their analyses. Why does the nature of the White House political operation matter? Because no amount of polling is worthwhile unless it is properly analyzed and incorporated into White House policy and political discussions.

President Bush's chief political confidant, Karl Rove, is considered by Republicans and Democrats alike to be an extraordinarily shrewd presidential adviser. On entering the White House in 2001, Bush established the first White House Office of Strategic Initiatives and appointed Rove its director—giving him a perch from which to survey the political landscape with the aim of expanding

Republican National Committee Polling Costs, 2001–2002

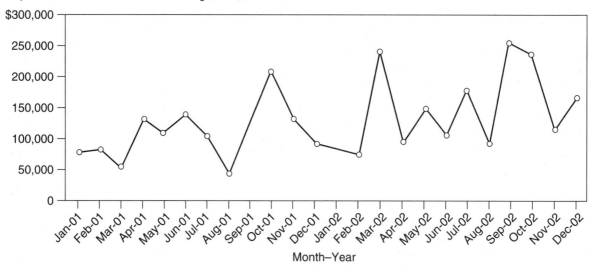

*Data obtained from fec.gov with the assistance of Larissa Davis and Elizabeth Redman of the Brookings Institution, April 2003.

the president's electoral coalition in 2004. Unlike Bush's father, who placed his chief political adviser, Lee Atwater, at the helm of the RNC, George W. Bush understands the importance of proximity. Though the president deliberately distances himself from pollster Jan van Lohuizen (political insiders claim the two rarely meet), his close relationship with Rove virtually ensures a key role for polling in presidential policymaking.

Assisting Rove as chief political adviser is Matthew Dowd, the RNC senior adviser who coordinates the pollsters and analyzes the political pulse with the help of van Lohuizen, who conducts focus groups as well as national surveys. And Fred Steeper, 1992 campaign pollster for Bush's father, is assigned a variety of special projects that address specific research questions, some of which involve focus groups. Combining the less "scientific" focus groups with polling enables the political shop to determine what people are thinking and then test those attitudes rigorously through national surveys. Unlike survey research, the focus group allows researchers to present text from a speech or a segment of a television ad and gauge the intensity of emotions, observe body language, and probe more deeply on key issues. The focus group alone may not be especially helpful, but combined with survey research, it can create a more refined questionnaire that zeroes in on previously tested issues and preferences. Similarly, the focus group technique can be applied after a national survey to probe specific questions and issues. The Steeper-van Lohuizen team clearly enhances the value of survey research while the Rove–Dowd–van Lohuizen/Steeper chain of command ensures that the pollsters stay well outside the political circle—and away from the eyes of the White House press corps.

The final part of this well-oiled political machine is the White House Office of Political Affairs director and recipient of polling data, Ken Mehlman. Since the Reagan administration, this office has become a standard component of all White House political operations, but its influence depends largely on the president and his chief aides. The first President Bush downplayed the office, and it experienced high turnover during the first term of the Clinton

administration. But in today's White House, Ken Mehlman's job is deemed an important one—though unlike Karl Rove's macropolitical strategy, Mehlman tends to the care and feeding of state and local partisans in hopes of paving the way for victory in 2004.

White House Polling in Perspective: Perception is Everything

President Bush's use of polling is by no means pathbreaking, nor is the amount of polling particularly astounding. What is unusual about the Bush team's polling operation is the chasm between its words and actions. Never before has a White House engaged in such anti-polling rhetoric or built up such a buffer between the pollsters and the president. The placement of longtime Bush loyalist Dowd at the RNC to coordinate the polling means that the pollsters do not have contact with the White House. Such unusual behavior reflects a broader tension between a determined attempt to avoid the mistakes of Bush the elder—especially the failure after the Persian Gulf War to consider the implications of a stagnant economy for the 1992 reelection campaign—and a continuous effort to shed the vestiges of the Clinton administration. The Bush team fully understands the value of polling, but the perceived overuse of polling within the Clinton administration has led to serious overcompensation, which in turn has bred secrecy and denial. All presidents are subjected to the pressures of the "permanent campaign." Information is integral to any successful presidency. Polling is part of a broader game of politics and policymaking. No one can dictate how presidents use polls, but denying the role of polls in the policy process is fruitless.

Kathryn Dunn Tenpas, a guest scholar in the Brookings Governance Studies program, is associate director of the University of Pennsylvania's Washington Semester Program.

Neo-Conservatives, Liberal Hawks, and the War on Terror

Lessons from the Cold War

ANATOL LIEVEN AND JOHN C. HULSMAN

Since 9/11, determined attempts have been made to resurrect the memory of the Cold War as an inspiration and model for the War on Terror. Proponents of this approach include neo-conservatives and others on the Right, and so-called "liberal hawks" in the Democratic camp. At a deeper, less evident level, the Cold War was also bound to have a profound impact on how America waged the War on Terror simply because the military, intelligence, bureaucratic, academic, ideological, and military-industrial institutions that have shaped U.S. strategy since 9/11 were created by the Cold War. They remained generally unreformed in the decade between the collapse of the Soviet Union and 2001.

Tragically, however, the Bush administration and dominant parts of the bipartisan U.S. establishment have, with almost deliberate perversity, ignored precisely those lessons of the Cold War that would have been most valuable. They have chosen instead to follow approaches that were rejected decades ago by the wisest American leaders and thinkers of the time.[1] The failure to heed the right lessons was demonstrated afresh by the response of the administration and the Democratic Party leadership to the war in Lebanon. Whatever Hezbollah's provocations, the Israeli response, and the way it was framed by most of the mainstream establishment, reflected historical amnesia.

This amnesia concerned the unwise and unethical character of preventive war except when truly and manifestly unavoidable; the extreme difficulty of suppressing guerrilla movements by military force, especially in a short campaign relying chiefly on bombardment; the fact that if guerrillas are joined to political parties with deep roots in a given society, they may well prove practically undefeatable; the critical role of local nationalism in empowering anti-American movements; and the central need to divide, rather than unite, hostile forces.

Perhaps most important, while paying lip service to the notion that the present struggle, like the Cold War, will inevitably be a "long war," far too many planners and analysts have in practice been focused on quick fixes (like "getting rid of Saddam Hussein") or unattainable ends (like "eliminating Hezbollah"). This has been combined with a shamefully short attention span when it comes to critically important long-term issues such as strengthening the fragile post-Taliban state in Afghanistan and supporting the Pakistan economy as a bulwark against Islamist extremism.

The Real Lessons

The Cold War leaders and thinkers who, in the late 1940s and early 1950s, authored a tough but restrained strategy of "containing" Soviet expansionism have been vindicated by events. They urged undermining communism through the force of the West's democratic and free-market example, and by massive economic support for key anticommunist states. This took longer than most of them hoped—but since the West triumphed completely, a few decades of mostly peaceful struggle were surely preferable to nuclear cataclysm.

By contrast, the "preventive war" and "rollback" schools of thought during the Cold War were proved wrong on just about everything. And a rolling river of wrongness has flowed down from them to their neo-conservative descendants, many of whose ideas derive directly from those of hardliners in the 1940s and 1950s.

In particular, the Bush administration and too many Democrats have not absorbed two critical Cold War lessons. The first, known to all the wisest Cold Warriors of the Truman and Eisenhower administrations, was that in the struggle between free-market democracy and communism, it was not enough to preach the virtues of democracy and freedom. Across the world, people looking to America had to see the real advantages in economic growth, jobs, services, education, and basic security. That was clearly perceived by everyone from former socialists like the theologian Reinhold Niebuhr to President Eisenhower himself. It has been too often ignored since 9/11.

Secondly, in much of the world, the struggle between American-backed, free-market democracy and Soviet-backed communism was only partly about their respective inherent virtues. It also mattered which side could appeal most successfully to local nationalism. Where America addressed the impassioned wish to escape Soviet domination, America ultimately won. Where communists were able to portray America as imperialist, and champion the continuing anti-colonial struggle for national independence, the communists won—at least for a while. The most intelligent advocates of containment, like George F. Kennan, and its most intelligent intellectual supporters, like Niebuhr and Hans Morgenthau, understood this from the start. Others in the U.S. establishment learned this lesson through America's ordeal in Vietnam.

The Bush administration's greatest mistake was to neglect the struggle with al Qaeda and instead pursue its irrelevant vendetta against Saddam Hussein. As of 2006, it risks repeating the same mistake even more disastrously by threatening conflict with Iran.

American foreign policy currently resembles a looking-glass version of policies pursued in Truman and Eisenhower's day, with a touch of Alice in Wonderland thrown in. Now, as then, after a season of bitter partisan strife over foreign policy, mainstream Republicans and Democrats have come to support what is basically the same program, though they themselves might fiercely deny this. Now, as then, those presenting real alternatives have been consigned to the fringes. The difference is that today the two parties have joined behind a somewhat moderated version of strategies put forward by the neo-conservatives in the Republican Party, and liberal hawks among the Democrats.

Today, exponents of utopian visions and over-ambitious uses of American power have moved center stage, and true centrists—the moderate, pragmatic descendants of Truman and Eisenhower—have been banished to the wings. Hence, it is vital to recall the values and positions for which Truman, Eisenhower, and their key advisors really stood.

Rollback Reborn

So completely has history vindicated containment that its opponents, the rollback and preventive war schools, have been not so much discredited as demolished. Just as nobody today seriously claims that Stalinism was basically benign and non-aggressive, so nobody seriously claims that it would have been right to launch a preventive nuclear war to destroy a Soviet Union that was always much weaker than it seemed and eventually crumbled of its own accord, as Kennan and Truman had predicted.

By the time Ronald Reagan assumed office, a generation after containment took root, the strategy had done its work: the communist economic, political, and ethical models were widely perceived as failures relative to the West. The credibility of communist ideology had ebbed throughout the Soviet bloc.

President Reagan sensed the inner rot in the Soviet bloc and increased U.S. pressure on Moscow. In doing so, he was also able to rally support from a majority of Americans of both parties. Although the most important factor in the Soviet collapse was internal decay, Reagan's policies certainly gave it an extra push.

But we should also remember that Reagan was heir not only of containment's results, but also of its philosophy. In his first term, Reagan adopted a tough posture that gave him the political cover in his second term to pursue an approach that was actually close to Kennan's philosophy of a mixture of containment and dialogue. He cooperated closely with Mikhail Gorbachev and Eduard Shevardnadze on international issues, implemented radical arms control measures, and conducted a peaceful wind-down of the Cold War. For doing this, he was attacked by some neo-conservatives.

By contrast, as historian Daniel Kelly said gently of one of the key intellectual works of the preventive war school, published by James Burnham in 1947, "the most obvious weakness of *The Struggle for the World* lay in the contrast between what it predicted and what actually happened."[2] (An example: Burnham's categorical statement that "if the communists succeed in consolidating what they have *already* conquered, then their complete world victory is certain. . . . We are lost if our opponent so much as holds his own."[3])

A question wisely raised by President Eisenhower in opposing preventive war: If the United States had destroyed Russia, or China, at low cost to itself, what would be the result? Instead of the troublesome but rational Russian and Chinese states of today, America would face hundreds of millions of ordinary people permanently possessed of a searing hatred of the United States and an implacable desire for vengeance.

We need to remember this when thinking about Iran. If we wait Iran out, then given the demographic reality of a youthful majority, there seems a good chance that in a generation we will have an Iran that is once again a basically pro-Western member of the international community (though we should never expect that this will make Iranians obedient followers of American strategy). To attack Iran, which is all too likely to lead to a major war with widespread destruction and civilian casualties, will gain us an implacable enemy for decades to come.

Yet the preventive war school remains alive and well in America among neo-conservatives, and even among leading Democrats. After 9/11, it enjoyed a rebirth; even under the false name of "preemption" it has been a central element of the Bush administration's National Security Strategies of both 2002 and 2006—with no acknowledgment that this approach had been proposed and carefully analyzed previously, and found hopelessly wanting.

The need to preempt a future Iraqi threat was the central justification for the attack on Iraq in 2003. The same rationale is being used today for an attack on Iran. But let us be clear: this is not "preemption" at all. The right of states to strike *preemptively* in the face of imminent attack by enemy states or coalitions—as Israel struck in 1967—has always been asserted as the right by all states, America included. A claim to the right of *preventive* war against a state that might possibly attack in the future is something altogether different. It represents a revolution in international affairs and a dismaying precedent for the behavior of others.

The supporters of preventive war today claim to be descendants of the containment school and, like Norman Podhoretz, in terms of personal lineage they sometimes are. But in terms of mentality, spirit, rhetoric, and understanding of the world, neo-conservatives like Podhoretz of *Commentary* magazine are the true descendants of James Burnham.

This can be seen in the tendency to grossly exaggerate the power both of America's enemies abroad and of real or alleged traitors at home. Burnham and Podhoretz both portrayed the Soviet Union as so strong, and American democracy as so pathetically weak, that unless America went to war quickly, doom beckoned. This recalls the old saying about the Austrian Empire's disastrous decision to go to war in 1914: "Out of fear of dying, we committed suicide." Burnham may have had some small cause for what he wrote in the late 1940s,[4] but Podhoretz was still repeating the same line in the early 1980s, a few years before the Soviet collapse.[5] Among neo-conservatives, an almost Teutonic obsession with power and will colors despair over America's "Athenian" democratic softness and respect for our enemies' "Spartan" authoritarian discipline. Burnham wrote that in the struggle with communism, "For us, international law can only be what it was at Nuremberg (and what it would have been at Moscow and Washington if the other side had conquered): a cover for the will of the more powerful."[6] A leading contemporary neo-conservative, Charles Krauthammer, writes:

America is no mere international citizen. It is the dominant power in the world, more dominant than any since Rome. Accordingly, America is in a position to reshape norms, alter expectations and create new realities. How? By unapologetic and implacable demonstrations of will.[7]

This obsession with will has had tragic effects on American policy. In its decision to escalate troop levels in Vietnam, the Johnson administration was heavily influenced by the belief that if it failed to do so, "it might as well give up everywhere else—pull out of Berlin, Japan, South America," as Johnson himself put it; a fantasy that helped cost the lives of 60,000 Americans and innumerable Vietnamese.[8]

Advocates of preventive war tend to portray pragmatists as Chicken Littles, but in fact it is they who forever warn that the sky is falling. For Burnham, a small mutiny of the Greek navy was "the beginning of World War III," and an Italian-Yugoslav squabble over the city of Trieste after World War II was the hinge on which hung the survival of the West.[9] For neo-conservatives throughout the 1990s, every petty ethnic clash in the ruins of the former Soviet Union heralded the restoration of that state as a mortal threat. Weak, isolated, and despised regional states with a tiny fraction of American power have been elevated into new equivalents of the Soviet superpower.

Burnham wrote that the idea of a Cold War persisting for decades was intolerable, because Western civilization could not stand the constant irritation. Yet constant itching is an inevitability in the international jungle—even during such comparatively peaceful times as the 1890s or the 1990s. In this sense, neo-conservatives, liberal hawks, and their ancestors are as utopian as communists used to be. They too believe in the possibility of what is in fact an impossibly stable world, a kind of global democratic nirvana under American hegemony.

Most dangerous of all has been this tradition's refusal to study individual nations and local conditions. Its exponents prefer instead to treat these realities with an ideological cookie-cutter, throwing away bits that don't fit. During the Cold War, all nations had to be neatly pro-Soviet or pro-American. Today they must be either pro-terrorist or pro-American. This near-racist contempt for the values, interests, identities, and politics of different nations—especially non-Western ones—led Burnham and others to predict in 1947 that, since the Indians were obviously incapable of governing themselves, once the British left, the country would fall into chaos and communism. He therefore urged Washington to assume quasi-imperial power over India, as an essential outpost of an American world if communism were to be resisted.[10]

Mercifully, America never attempted to rule India, and most of Burnham's wild prescriptions were rejected. But Burnham did contribute to an error which is being repeated in a new and disastrous form today: that all communist movements and states were an indissolubly unified threat to the West—a belief which survived Burnham once having dismissed Marshall Tito of Yugoslavia as being simply an agent of Stalin.

Kennan once wrote, "There seems to be a curious American tendency to search, at all times, for a single external center of evil, to which all our troubles can be attributed, rather than to recognize that there might be multiple sources of resistance to our purposes and undertakings, and that these sources might be relatively independent of each other."[11] This tendency stemmed, like so many others, from a desire to divide the world into black and white, good and evil. It has led above all to a determined refusal to study or understand the power of local nationalism, whether reflected in communism, Islamism, or whatever. This mistake led directly to America's tragic involvement in Vietnam, which was justified by fears of a united Sino-Soviet-North Vietnamese move to dominate Asia. In fact, even before the first Marine regiment set foot in Vietnam, the Sino-Soviet alliance had irretrievably broken up. Nevertheless, blinded by the vision of a united communism, many policy-makers declined to see the evidence before them. In a familiar pattern, lower level analysts in the State Department and the CIA who did see what was happening were forced to suppress or modify their views to suit the dominant consensus.[12]

Three years later, in 1968–69, while thousands of Americans were dying in Vietnam to resist a united communist threat, the two communist great powers were fighting in eastern Siberia, and coming close to a nuclear clash. Later, Vietnam and China fought their own border war. These clashes meant that America had no need to fight in Vietnam at all—it could, and eventually did, contain the spread of communism in the region by simply playing communist states against each other. Today, we see the equally absurd and potentially tragic risk of pursuing a policy of implacable hostility towards Muslim states like Iran and Syria that are among the fiercest enemies of the Sunni extremist camp from which Al Qaeda springs.

Kennan predicted national divisions within the communist camp from the start. So did Reinhold Niebuhr, who drew a distinction between Soviet communism and the various communist movements of Asia, including the Chinese and Vietnamese. He saw Soviet Russia as an imperial power, dominating other nations by force and terror. In Europe, the West could justly represent itself as a force for liberation. In Asia, because of the legacy of European colonialism, circumstances were more complicated. Communist movements there, however ruthless, could present themselves as forces for national liberation from Western domination. This inspired mass support of a kind that did not exist in the Soviet empire, outside Russia itself.

Niebuhr, Kennan, and others understood the importance of nationalism and foresaw that communist states would sooner or later fall out among themselves. As Niebuhr wrote in 1948, "A Communist China is not as immediate a strategic threat as imagined by some. The Communism of Asia is primarily an expression of nationalism of subject peoples and impoverished nations. . . . It may take a long time to prove that we are better friends of China than Russia is. But if Russia should prove as heavy-handed in dealing with China as she has with the Eastern European nations, it may not take as long as it now seems."[13]

This prediction proved entirely accurate. It must be added that this did not require miraculous powers of prophecy. Even before the Korean War, the split between Tito's Yugoslavia and Stalin's empire had shown that this was likely to be a future pattern. Later, Niebuhr, Kennan, and other founders of the containment school opposed the U.S. involvement in Vietnam on the strength of their convictions of the power of anticolonial nationalism and of the differences between communist movements.[14]

Forces of Political Religion

Recently, neo-conservatives and liberal hawks have come together in a disastrous repetition of this self-evident reality. During the Cold War, Podhoretz continually referred to "the Communists" as if they were all the same. Today, he refers to "radical Islamism and the states breeding, sheltering, or financing its terrorist armory"—as wildly varied a bunch as one could well imagine—as "the enemy."[15] This is like a Briton in former times talking about "The Hun" and "Johnny Chinaman."

Neo-conservatives have been joined in this regard since 9/11 by leading intellectual representatives of the liberal hawk tendency in the Democratic Party. The confluence of the two streams is noticeable in a widely shared term, namely "Islamic totalitarianism" (also called Islamofascism), frequently reiterated by President Bush. In *Terror and Liberalism,* the leading liberal hawk Paul Berman argues that secular radical Arab nationalism and Islamic fundamentalism are essentially the same phenomenon, since both are supposedly expressions of an antiliberal, totalitarian, international ethos and tradition stemming originally from European fascism and communism. "The

Baathists and the Islamists were two branches of a single impulse, which was Muslim totalitarianism—the Muslim variation on the European idea," he writes. The "global war on terror" is therefore a continuation of America's past struggle against Nazism and communism, a parallel taken up by President Bush. In Berman's view:

> The totalitarian wave began to swell some 25 years ago and by now has swept across a growing swath of the Muslim world. The wave is not a single thing. It consists of several movements or currents, which are entirely recognizable. These movements draw on four tenets: a belief in a paranoid conspiracy theory, in which cosmically evil Jews, Masons, Crusaders and Westerners are plotting to annihilate Islam or subjugate the Arab people; a belief in the need to wage apocalyptic war against the cosmic conspiracy; an expectation that post-apocalypse, the Islamic caliphate of ancient times will reemerge as a utopian new society; and a belief that meanwhile, death is good, and should be loved and revered.[16]

Seeing Arab Baathism, Iranian Shiism, and Pan-Islamic Sunni extremism as part of the same movement, and the "political culture" of different Muslim countries as identical, enables Berman to portray the invasion of Iraq approvingly as part of the struggle against al Qaeda and the transformation not just of the Arab polity but of the entire Muslim world:

> The American strategists noticed that terrorism had begun to flourish across a wide swath of the Arab and Muslim world. And they argued that something had to be done about the political culture across the whole of that wide swath. The American strategists saw in Saddam's Iraq a main center of that political culture, yet also a place where the political culture could be redressed and transformed.[17]

With the exception of a common hostility to Israel, this is surreal. The ideological and theological roots of radical Islamism were laid down more than a thousand years before fascism was conceived. To suggest that Salafism, Shiism, and Baathism form part of the same basic "movement" is the equivalent of suggesting that in Europe past, communism, Catholic conservatism, fascism, and Russian czarism were all basically part of the same movement because they were all hostile to liberal democracy. The "Islamic totalitarianism" argument applied to all the current strains of radicalism in the Muslim world is no less historically illiterate.

In adopting this line, liberal hawks and neo-conservatives have had less excuse than American analysts during the Cold War. For whereas the different Communist parties did at least officially subscribe to the same Marxist-Leninist dogmas, the chief forces in the Muslim world are fundamentally opposed in their basic doctrines and view of history.

In the case of Sunnis, like al Qaeda and its allies, on the one hand, and the Shia on the other, this has been true for 1,300 years. Radical secular Arab nationalism, as represented at its most extreme by the Baath parties in Iraq and Syria, did indeed draw on roots in European fascism. But the roots of both Sunni and Shia religious radicalism are infinitely older—dating back to the first decades of Islam's existence. Even the religious culture of al Qaeda and its allies, Salafism, derives from ancient roots in Sunni Islam; and al Qaeda's specific theology, Wahabism, originated more than two centuries ago in eighteenth-century Arabia.

Baathism has always been deeply and often violently opposed to both Sunni and Shia fundamentalism, just as secular nationalist parties in Europe used to detest the Catholic Church. Baathist Arab nationalism is deeply opposed to any attempt to restore the "Islamic caliphate of ancient times"—as envisioned by al Qaeda and its Sunni radical allies—because this would embrace all Muslims, and the Baath want to create a united Arab secular state under their own fascistic rule.

In any case, the ideological founder of the Baath, Michel Affleq, was a Christian Arab, as were some of Saddam Hussein's leading minions. As modernizing nationalists, much like their former European equivalents, Baathists regard Sunni fundamentalists as dangerous opponents of Arab progress. As to the Shia, the Baath see them as not only culturally alien and retrograde, but as Iranian agents. In this, the Baath have followed the original Italian fascist model that so influenced Afleq.

The fascists had their roots in bitterly anticlerical Italian radical nationalism. When in power, Italian fascists made pragmatic deals with the Catholic Church; but in Italy and Germany, fascism was never influenced by or close to the Christian religion. This does not, of course, make Saddam's Baathists or the fascists more likable. It does define their difference with the forces of political religion.

By refusing to grasp the basic distinction between Arab nationalists and Islamists, Berman demonstrates the same ignorance that led the Bush administration into Iraq in the belief that overthrowing the Baathists would also strike a mortal blow at Islamist terrorism. Worse, Berman and others fail to make the critical distinction between Shiite and Sunni Islam, and between the national agendas of Iran and various Arab states.

In strategic terms, the liberal hawks' and neo-conservatives' line is equivalent to an argument that the United States and its allies should have fought Nazism and Soviet communism not sequentially, but simultaneously. This strategy was indeed weighed by Churchill in the winter of 1939–40. If it had been followed, it would have insured Britain's defeat and a dark age for the world. Similarly, the most dangerous aspect of the Bush administration's approach to the War on Terror is the desire to lump together radically different elements in the Muslim world into a homogeneous enemy camp.

Shades of Hawkishness

Since 9/11, some liberal hawks have tried to appropriate the memory and teachings of Reinhold Niebuhr in a way that radically misinterprets his real views on strategy and the greater part of his philosophy. To bolster this appropriation, some point to the Americans for Democratic Action (ADA), a movement which Niebuhr helped create in 1947. The ADA played a critical role in the late 1940s in rallying American liberals to support the Truman administration, oppose Soviet communism, and support its containment by firm American action. Among its founders were Eleanor Roosevelt, John Kenneth Galbraith, Arthur Schlesinger, and Hans Morgenthau.[18]

Many of ADA's founders had taken part in the earlier struggle to persuade Americans to abandon isolation and join in the fight against Nazi and Japanese aggression. They recognized earlier than most the essentially new and especially dangerous character of the mid-twentieth century totalitarianisms. As Schlesinger wrote, the ADA helped to "fundamentally reshape" American liberalism, dropping its former tendencies towards pacifism and isolationism and committing it to an international struggle against totalitarian and aggression.[19]

Reviving the spirit of the ADA in the contemporary Democratic Party was the main theme of an essay by Peter Beinart, then editor of the *New Republic,* in December 2004, entitled "A Fighting Faith: An Argument for a New Liberalism." A book based on this essay was published in 2006.[20] Beinart and other liberal hawks have called on American liberals and Democratic Party supporters to fight a "world-wide crusade for democracy" against "totalitarian Islam," just as the ADA fought against totalitarian communism.[21]

Beinart supported the Iraq War, like Paul Berman, Leon Wieseltier, Thomas Friedman, Christopher Hitchens, and other leading Democratic intellectuals. Influential in their own right, these hawks are closely tied to the Democratic Leadership Council, and to the Democratic Party's foreign policy leadership, notably Senators Hillary Clinton and Joseph Biden, former secretary of state Madeleine Albright, and Ambassador Richard Holbrooke.[22]

In his new book, Beinart puts some new distance between himself and more hardline liberal hawks: he still uses the term "Islamist totalitarianism," but now makes clear that by this he means only the Salafi tradition from which al Qaeda is sprung. He no longer—in this book at least—attempts to extend this term to cover the Shia or radical Arab nationalists. In certain respects such distinctions are welcome, and form part of a desirable process of bridging an outdated, irrelevant, and damaging political divide over foreign policy. For the same reason, the recent more realist views of Francis Fukuyama, a semi-penitent from the neo-conservative camp, are also welcome. In an ideal world, these positions would gradually converge in a consensus that might provide real help in the struggle against al Qaeda and its allies.[23]

In the real world, however, Beinart—and even the more moderate and sensible liberal hawks—still have a long way to go. Commendably, Beinart now admits he was wrong to support the war in Iraq. This mistake he ascribes mainly to what the *American Observer* has rightly called "the incompetence dodge"—the argument that liberal hawks could not possibly have predicted the extent of the Bush administration's incompetence.[24] Beinart's new approach is also linked to a new and belated recognition of part of Niebuhr's message: the inherent limits on all human power and wisdom; and the particular need for America, although generally in the right, to recognize that it is also capable of great wrong, and to observe limits on its behavior accordingly. The problem is that when it comes to the recognition of limits, such liberal hawks are too representative of the U.S. establishment, in general. As a result of the Iraqi debacle, they have become more cautious, but not necessarily much wiser. Beinart writes of limits, but then, like the Bush administration's National Security Strategy of 2006, repeats his belief in America's mission to democratize the world.

This, however, is now to be done, according to Beinart, not by Washington acting unilaterally, but through an "alliance of democracies," which in real circumstances can only mean European democracies—with the possible addition of Turkey, Israel, and India. Here, Beinart reveals the central problem of the liberal hawk school when it comes to the War on Terror: an indifference verging on autism towards the views of the Muslim world in general, and the Arab world in particular.[25]

From the point of view of most Arabs, this "alliance of democracies" would simply mean replacing "American imperialism" with "Western imperialism." The addition of India and Israel would suggest to Muslims a global anti-Islamic alliance. And even the presence of Turkey would be problematic, given bitter Arab memories of Turkey's role as the former imperial power in the region. It is a strategy that completely ignores the role of nationalism in the countries concerned. As our analysis of the "Islamic totalitarianism" line

suggests, much of the liberal hawk and neo-conservative view of the Middle East—and, alas, of American perceptions in general—is overwhelmingly self-referential. Although ostensibly about backing Muslim liberals and extremists, it is not linked to real debates within the Muslim world.

In this too, the proponents of a Cold War—style struggle against Islamic totalitarianism, along the lines of the ADA's struggle against Soviet-backed communism, have been responsible for the creation, with bipartisan support, of the U.S. Arabic-language propaganda stations Al-Hurra Television (the "Free One") and Sawa Radio. These were founded on the explicit model of Cold War propaganda stations like Radio Liberty and Radio Free Europe—a model that is completely irrelevant to the Arab world.[26]

The early years of the Cold War were not only a struggle against Soviet expansionism; they were also an ideological civil war within Western Europe, and to a lesser extent within America. Let us not forget that Karl Marx was a German. Although communism triumphed spontaneously only within Russia and Yugoslavia, it came close to doing so at various times in Hungary, Germany, Spain, France, Italy, and Greece. For long periods, Communist parties had genuine mass appeal, and still more to the intelligentsia—especially when they were fighting against fascism. Even more dangerously, the communists often showed immense skill at forming "popular fronts" with Social Democratic and even Liberal parties—where communists used a democratic facade as cover for plans to seize power for themselves.

The ADA was founded precisely to counter moves towards such a "popular front" in America and to reach out to democratic forces in Western Europe to help them to resist communist blandishments. Instead of lumping all socialist movements together as enemies, the ADA appealed in particular to the non-communist European Left; this became the official strategy of the Truman administration, with the covert aid of the CIA.[27] In the 1940s and 1950s, the struggle for the soul of the progressive Western intelligentsia was critical to resisting communism.

The struggle with Sunni Islamist radicalism is very different. Beyond a few individual converts, Islam in general, and its extreme Salafi and Wahabi forms in particular, have little appeal to ordinary Westerners or the intelligentsia. Islamist extremism does have a threatening presence in the West, especially in Europe—but this stems from support for extremists among Muslim immigrants. Disaffection among these minorities is a serious problem, but unlike the communists, it does not pose a threat of revolution and the seizure of the state.

The ideological struggle against al Qaeda and Islamist radicalism is therefore one that can best be conducted by Muslims themselves. Unlike the leaders of the ADA in the Cold War, the liberal hawk intellectuals are irrelevant to this struggle—or even worse, insofar as they display arrogance and ignorance towards the Muslim world, and support U.S. and Israeli policies that even liberal Muslims generally find abhorrent. Thus, Washington's aid to Iranian liberal groups, far from helping them, is undermining their credibility in the eyes of most Iranians.

We must not allow the preaching of democracy, as advocated by neo-conservatives and liberal hawks alike and as embodied in the National Security Strategy of 2006, to become a substitute for tough but informed and enlightened diplomacy. We need the spirit that animates the philosophy of ethical realism, developed by Niebuhr, Morgenthau, and Kennan, as the philosophical basis for a radically new U.S. global strategy.

Notes

1. See, for example, Anatol Lieven, "Fighting Terrorism: Lessons from the Cold War," Carnegie Endowment for International Peace policy brief, no. 7, October 2001.

2. Daniel Kelly, *James Burnham and the Struggle for the World: A Life* (Wilmington, DE: ISI Books, 2002), p. 129. For a more sympathetic portrayal of Burnham's thought, see Samuel Francis, *Thinkers of Our Time: James Burnham* (London: Claridge Press, 1999).

3. James Burnham, *Containment or Liberation? An Inquiry Into the Aims of US Foreign Policy,* (New York: The John Day Co., 1952), pp. 251–54.

4. Kelly, p. 129.

5. Norman Podhoretz, *The Present Danger: Do We Have the Will To Reverse The Decline of American Power?* (New York: Simon and Schuster, 1980).

6. James Burnham, *The Struggle for the World* (New York: The John Day Co., 1947), p. 148.

7. Charles Krauthammer, "The Bush Doctrine," *Time,* March 5, 2001, vol. 157, iss. 9.

8. "Meeting on Vietnam," July 21, 1965, National Security File (LBJL), Country File, Vietnam; quoted in Steven M. Gillon, *Politics and Vision: The ADA and American Liberalism* (New York: Oxford University Press, 1987), p. 178.

9. Burnham, *The Struggle for the World,* pp. 1, 164.

10. Ibid, pp. 194-96; Kelly, pp. 168–70.

11. Kennan, *American Diplomacy,* p. 164.

12. See, for example, *Tracking the Dragon: National Intelligence Estimates on China During the Era of Mao, 1948–1976,* (Washington, DC: National Intelligence Council, 2004), pp. 215–48, in which the National Intelligence Estimate of August 9, 1960, on Sino-Soviet relations presents evidence of a deep and growing split but then concludes, strangely, that this will not amount to anything serious in the years to come.

13. *Chicago Sun-Times,* November 11, 1948, quoted in Alonzo L. Hamby, *Beyond the New Deal: Harry S. Truman and American Liberalism* (New York: Columbia University Press, 1973), p. 367. For similar views by other members of the ADA, see John K. Fairbank, "China: Three Lessons," in *ADA World,* September 22, 1949; ADA Board statement on Asia, *ADA World,* October 1950; David C. Williams, "Chinese Fanaticism Like Yugoslavs Prior to Break with Stalin," *ADA World,* November 1950.

14. David Halberstam, *The Best and the Brightest* (New York: Ballantine Books, 1992), p. 339.

15. Norman Podhoretz, "World War IV: How It Started, What It Means, and Why We Have to Win," *Commentary,* September 2004.

16. Paul Berman, *Terror and Liberalism* (New York: W. W. Norton, 2003).

17. Paul Berman, *Power and the Idealists: Or, The Passion of Joschka Fischer and Its Aftermath* (Brooklyn, NY: Soft Skull Press, 2005), quoted in Stephen Holmes, "The War of the Liberals," *The Nation,* November 14, 2005.

18. For the foundation of the ADA, see Gillon, *Politics and Vision,* pp. 16–24; Mark L. Kleinman, *A World of Hope, A World of Fear: Henry A. Wallace, Reinhold Niebuhr and American Liberalism* (Columbus, OH: Ohio State University Press, 1994), pp. 227–32; Kevin Mattson, *When America Was Great: The Fighting Faith of Postwar Liberalism* (New York: Routledge, 2004) pp. 45–46; Hamby, pp. 161–64.

19. Arthur Schlesinger, *The Vital Center: The Politics of Freedom* (first published 1949; republished Piscataway, NJ: Transaction Publishers, 1997).

20. Peter Beinart, "A Fighting Faith: An Argument for a New Liberalism," *New Republic,* December 13, 2004; Peter Beinart, *The Good Fight: How Liberals—And Only Liberals—Can Win the War on Terror and Make America Great Again* (New York: Harper Collins, 2006).

21. Peter Beinart, "Tough Liberalism," *Blueprint,* Progressive Policy Institute, October 21, 2005.

22. Ari Berman, "The Strategic Class," *The Nation,* August 29, 2005.

23. Anatol Lieven, "We Do Not Deserve These People," *London Review of Books,* vol. 27, no. 20 (October 20, 2005).

24. Sam Rosenfeld and Matthew Iglesias, "The Incompetence Dodge," *The American Prospect,* November 10, 2005.

25. Beinart, *The Good Fight,* p. 286.

26. Anatol Lieven and David Chambers, "The Limits of Propaganda," *Los Angeles Times,* February 13, 2006; Neil MacFarquhar, "Washington's Arabic TV Effort Gets Mixed Reviews," *New York Times,* February 19, 2004; Faye Bowers, "Al Hurra Joins Battle for Hearts and Minds," *Christian Science Monitor,* February 24, 2004; "US Voice in Arabia: Washington's Arabic Satellite TV Station Has Run Into Trouble," *Financial Times,* November 9, 2005; Anne Marie Baylouny, "Alhurra, the Free One: Assessing U.S. Satellite Television in the Middle East," *Strategic Insights,* vol. 4, no. 11 (November 2005).

27. See Schlesinger, p. 167, for an analysis of the "Non-Communist Left" strategy.

ANATOL LIEVEN is a senior research fellow at the New America Foundation covering American strategy and international relations. Formerly a journalist in South Asia and the former Soviet Union, his most recent book is *America Right or Wrong: An Anatomy of American Nationalism* (Oxford University Press, 2004). **JOHN C. HULSMAN** is the von Oppenheimer scholar in residence at the German Council on Foreign Relations in Berlin and a contributing editor to *The National Interest.* He was formerly a senior research fellow in international relations at the Heritage Foundation and has taught European security studies at the Johns Hopkins School of Advanced International Studies, and world politics and U.S. foreign policy at the University of St. Andrews, Scotland.

This essay is adapted from the authors' book, *Ethical Realism: A Vision for America's Role in the World,* published in September 2006 by Pantheon, New York.

The Pros from Dover

President Bush surrounded himself with what should have been a crack team of national security experts. So what went wrong? Did their system just not work, or did they have the wrong agenda?

JOHN PRADOS

There is a hilarious scene in the movie *M*A*S*H* where two young doctors from a field hospital at the front in the Korean War travel to Japan and proceed to have their way with local commanders and the military bureaucracy. Arriving to carry out the heart operation for which they have been summoned, the doctors call themselves the "pros from Dover."

In the way life has of imitating art, the national security process of the Bush administration has been the province of its own fresh set of professionals. The result has not been hilarity but something else. With the Bush people having gotten the United States enmeshed in situations of grave concern throughout the globe, it is important to ask whether the American government is up to handling the job, not in terms of capabilities but of policy process.

In the American system of government, the top executive authority, the president, is assisted in areas of foreign affairs and military matters by the National Security Council (NSC). The council consists of the president, vice president, secretary of state, and defense secretary. The national security adviser to the president does not have a statutory role but is typically made a senior member of the council. The director of central intelligence and chairman of the Joint Chiefs of Staff sit as advisers to the group. The president is the king of policy hill, of course, and may arrange the NSC and its work at his whim, organizing and reorganizing whenever it suits him. NSC staff members under the national security adviser directly serve the president by coordinating the issues and providing the chief executive with their understanding of the options, pros, and cons.

Three years into the Bush administration, in spite of a host of developments in the national security realm, there has yet to be any serious inquiry into its methods of policymaking and their impact on American security. That inquiry is overdue.

The Players

George W. Bush has certainly benefited from a dream team of senior advisers on his National Security Council. Bush chose carefully among people of conservative cast of mind to match his own, and while one may deplore the ideology of the crew, the president's right to be served by the officials he wants is unquestioned. Ideology notwithstanding, the Bush people have the right stuff—the credentials to actually be the pros from Dover—from the top people

on the NSC to the second tier at the agencies and staff. On January 21, 2001, an observer could have said this administration was primed for success.

In terms of organization of the policy process, the Bush administration also started out on familiar ground. Presidents create their own policy machinery, and different presidents have approached the national security process in a variety of ways.[1]

The Carter administration designed a two-committee structure that has become almost the standard NSC organization for subsequent presidencies, including that of George W. Bush. In the current scheme, the president meeting with his senior advisers constitutes the National Security Council. Without the president, the rump NSC meets as the Principals Committee, chaired by the vice president or national security adviser. These groups focus on decisions. Below them is the Deputies Committee, a group chaired by the deputy national security adviser, which concentrates on implementing the president's decisions. Staff assistants attend as required. Teleconferencing and secure video links between various U.S. government centers have enabled greater flexibility in participation, but the essence of the system remains the same.

The most remarkable aspect of Bush's national security organization is the role of the vice president. Historically, vice presidents have had a relatively minor impact on national security decision making. Walter Mondale and Al Gore were more active under presidents Carter and Clinton, and Bush's father, George H. W. Bush, had an enhanced role under Ronald Reagan. In the current administration, however, Dick Cheney is of critical importance in virtually all aspects of national security policy. From the first moments of George W. Bush's presidency, Cheney functioned as the power behind the throne, privately advocating policies, then coming out in public with discourse designed to build constituencies for those same policies. He also became the official whom Bush tapped for the tough jobs—and the president's hatchet man. Cheney emerged as an assistant with an agenda more ample than that of his master. His role encouraging Bush to make war on Iraq has been so widely remarked it has virtually eclipsed his work early in the administration heading a presidential commission on energy policy, his views on military transformation, and the task force on federal-local antiterrorism cooperation that Bush appointed him to chair four months before the 9/11 attacks.

To match his policy role, the vice president has crafted a sort of mini-NSC staff among his White House retinue. Where Al Gore as vice president employed Leon Fuerth as his national security adviser (plus a couple of staff aides), and Bush's father, as vice president under Reagan, had a security staff of two professionals (plus aides), Cheney employs a national security staff of 15. The importance Cheney gives that staff is indicated by the fact that his own overall chief of staff, I. Lewis ("Scooter") Libby, serves simultaneously as the vice president's national security adviser. Early last year, at a key moment in the run-up to the Iraq war, Cheney's deputy national security adviser Eric Edelman was appointed U.S. ambassador to Turkey, another indication of the standing of the Cheney national security staff. Edelman was succeeded by Aaron Friedberg, a China expert and former director of policy planning on the Cheney staff. That the staff even had a policy-planning component demonstrates the quantum advance of the Cheney operation over the staff resources available to previous vice presidents.

Cheney himself is no stranger to national security issues, or to government for that matter. In his current incarnation he is mostly known for his role as chief executive of the Halliburton Corporation during the 1990s, but less noted is the extent to which Halliburton worked with and for the U.S. military. More to the point, Cheney was defense secretary—the job Donald Rumsfeld now has—during the first Bush administration, including the first Gulf War. Before that, Cheney served as White House chief of staff to President Gerald R. Ford from 1975 to early 1977 and deputy chief of staff 1974–1975. At the time, he was deputy to Donald Rumsfeld, whom President Ford subsequently sent to the Pentagon. In the Ford White House, Cheney worked on a number of national security issues, most notably advising Ford on how to handle the intelligence scandals of 1975. Cheney was an architect of the presidential commission on intelligence (the Rockefeller Commission) created by Ford in an effort to head off what became the Church and Pike Committee investigations. While the attempt proved unsuccessful, Cheney gained experience he put to work later as a member of Congress and then in his own Pentagon job.

Next to the vice president, the person closest to the Oval Office is the national security adviser. For George Bush this is Condoleezza Rice. Like Cheney—like a number of the pros from Dover—Rice is no stranger to the issues, or even to the national security staff. Retired Air Force Gen. Brent Scowcroft (who held the post of national security adviser for Gerald Ford, alongside Cheney and Rumsfeld) discovered Rice during the 1980s at the Aspen Institute. She was then a recently minted academic with a doctorate in international relations from the University of Denver. Her dissertation was on Soviet political control of the Czechoslovak armed forces. She taught at Stanford University. When Scowcroft did a second tour as national security adviser in the administration of President George H. W. Bush, he brought in "Condi," as she is familiarly known, as director for Soviet affairs. Rice was active on the NSC staff during the passing of the Cold War, when the Soviet Union collapsed, Germany reunified, and the old Yugoslavia disintegrated, leaving in its wake the Bosnian civil war.

Among the stories told about Rice that show her willingness to do whatever was necessary is one from the beginning of the first Gulf War, when the NSC staff person responsible for the Iraq-Kuwait region was Richard Haass. When the first President Bush needed a set of talking points for his initial public comment on the Iraqi invasion of Kuwait, Haass could not respond quickly enough

because, unfamiliar with computers, he had to hunt and peck at the keyboard. Rice took over and typed out the paper even though Middle East matters were far from her own bailiwick. In 1991 Rice returned to Stanford as a teacher—but not for long. A month after receiving tenure in 1993 she was appointed provost of the university and held that key management position during difficult years. She quickly rallied to the presidential campaign of George W. Bush, however, and was its foreign policy director from early 1999. Rice not only coordinated Bush's issues papers but kept in line the "Vulcans"—the brain trust of national security experts who periodically assembled to give Bush the benefit of their accumulated wisdom. All the Vulcans (Richard Armitage, Robert Blackwill, Stephen J. Hadley, Richard Perle, Paul Wolfowitz, Dov Zakheim, Robert Zoellick) went on to important jobs or advisory posts in the Bush administration, and it was hardly surprising that Rice landed as national security adviser.

Stephen J. Hadley became Rice's deputy. The only other of the Vulcans to make the leap to work directly within the president's official family, Hadley regarded himself as a detail man. He too had a national security past, having served as assistant secretary of defense for policy under Dick Cheney in the first Bush administration. For those who worried about the influence of Cheney in the White House, Hadley's presence suggested that the vice president, in addition to having his own mini-NSC staff, simultaneously had a front man who was deputy director of the Rice staff itself.

As for the seniors, the members of the actual council of the NSC, they were pros from Dover, too. Donald Rumsfeld has already been mentioned. He is the only person to serve twice as defense secretary—in two different administrations, separated by more than two decades. Colin Powell, retired four-star army general, had been chairman of the Joint Chiefs of Staff during the first Gulf War, a deputy national security adviser to Ronald Reagan, and military assistant to Defense Secretary Caspar Weinberger. CIA Director George Tenet was held over from the Clinton administration and had worked on the Hill, at the White House, or at the CIA since the late 1980s. Their seconds, people like Wolfowitz and Armitage, had similar credentials.

The System

President George W. Bush enhanced the role of his national security adviser by endowing her with cabinet rank. But formal organization of the system remained in limbo until mid-February 2001, when Bush issued his National Security Presidential Directive (NSPD) 1. That document ended speculation as to Vice President Cheney's role—a number of observers had anticipated that Cheney's deep interest in these matters would be reflected by his being made chairman of the Principals Committee.[2] This did not happen. Instead Rice, as national security adviser, would chair the group. What did happen was more significant: By avoiding the chairmanship of the Principals Committee, Cheney left himself free to be an advocate at national security meetings rather than having any responsibility to ensure that all views be aired.

The other significant thing about NSPD 1 was its lateness in the cycle. Most new administrations enter office determined to hit the ground running and typically put out their directives on NSC machinery their first day in office. Bush did not get around to this business for almost a month. By then there had already been two meetings of the Principals Committee. Even the appointments of

Condi Rice and the top NSC staffers date from January 22, not the day after the inauguration. The implication is that, at least at the outset, Bush did not consider the national security agenda his top priority.

In terms of size and depth, the Rice NSC staff diminished from the standard under the Clinton administration, but this had more to do with notions of streamlining than with some idea of reducing the importance of national security. Rice cut the staff as a whole by about a third while reducing the number of professional staff from 70 to about 60. She eliminated the legislative affairs and communications offices, limited the staff to a single speechwriter and press spokesperson, and recast some functions. Most importantly, the Russian office merged into a single new desk that included all of Europe, the Balkans, and the former Soviet republics. The Asian affairs office reabsorbed Southeast Asia, which had been assigned to another regional unit in the Clinton White House. North Africa and the Middle East were combined as well. Africa and the Western Hemisphere completed the list of regional offices on the NSC staff. There were also functional specializations, including offices for defense policy and arms control and for intelligence.

Clinton had had an NSC staff unit to supervise nonproliferation and export controls. Under Rice this was reconceptualized as "Nonproliferation Strategy, Counterproliferation, and Homeland Defense." This is instructive for it served as a device to take the ballistic missile defense issue out of the defense policy basket and put it in the much more ideological framework of "homeland defense." That in turn became awkward after the September 11, 2001, attacks, when an Office of Homeland Defense was created at the White House as a parallel to the NSC staff, but in which "homeland defense" held a very different meaning.

The Clinton NSC staff also had a unit covering "transnational threats" and put terrorism at the top of that list. Clinton appointed Richard Clarke, a hard-headed advocate for proactive measures against those threats, to head the unit. Clarke stayed over into the Bush presidency even though, as a press account put it several weeks into the new era, what to do with the transnational threats office was "still up in the air."[3] It is here that the real story begins.

Bush and Terrorism

Bill Clinton's last national security adviser, Samuel ("Sandy") Berger, held a number of briefings for Condoleezza Rice and the incoming national security staff as part of the transition from the Clinton to Bush presidencies. Every NSC staff office had been directed to compile a report and present its view of America's strengths and weaknesses to the new crowd. According to an account that has been disputed, the only one of these sessions Sandy Berger personally attended was that which concerned terrorism (Rice has said through a spokesperson that she recalls no briefing at which Berger was present).[4] Berger had left by the time Richard Clarke made the main presentation, but there can be no doubt that the briefing highlighted the need to act on terrorism.

Berger clearly had terrorism on his plate. The question is, did Rice? Berger would tell the joint House-Senate committee investigating the September 11, 2001, attacks that he had convened the Principals Committee every day for a month in an effort to stave off terrorist attacks timed around the millennium celebrations.[5] He quoted himself as telling Rice, "You're going to spend more time during your four years on terrorism generally and Al Qaeda specifically than any [other] issue."[6] For her part, Rice had numerous questions for Clarke, who was asked to prepare a paper on steps against Al Qaeda. Clarke not only had the paper on Stephen J. Hadley's desk within days of the inauguration, he saw the opportunity to get the new president to sign on to an action plan against terrorism, and his paper amounted to an outline. So far, so good. But Clarke's plan then sat gathering dust for weeks.

In speeches, articles, and conversations during the 2000 campaign, Rice had written and spoken of the need in national security to separate the marginal issues from what was truly important.

What Rice and the Bush team made centrally important in the weeks and months after entering office was not terrorism but changing the U.S.-European relationship. The troubles with "Old Europe" that seem so intractable in the wake of the Iraqi war did not just happen coincidentally in 2002-2003. They were prefigured in the very stuff of the NSC staff reorganization, when the Russian and Western European offices were consolidated. Publicly the Bush administration sought to end any notion of a special relationship with Russia, the former Soviet Union, cutting back funding for special cooperative programs designed to help secure Russian nuclear weapons and expertise, abrogating the Anti-Ballistic Missile (ABM) Treaty, and in a variety of other ways. The move on the ABM Treaty also came as a shock to Old Europe, as did Bush's rejection of the Kyoto protocols on environmental action, and the equally sudden U.S. coyness on formation of an international criminal court. When President Bush made his first visit to Europe in June 2001, these issues were the main stuff of American diplomacy.

On the overarching front of defense policy, the maneuver on the ABM Treaty is itself indicative of the Bush administration's goals. Defense Secretary Rumsfeld used the word "transformation" so many times that it became enshrined as the descriptive term for Bush defense policy. Ballistic missile defenses were a key component, and indeed President Bush chose to deploy a technically immature defense system just to ensure that the United States had committed itself to this program. Rumsfeld's talk about space platforms, his predilection for air force programs, and his fight with the army over its future were the stuff of the transformation.

While circumstances dictated that an action plan on terrorism needed to move to the top of policy hill, the government was preoccupied with anything but that issue. It was only after Bush intervened that anything happened at all. One spring morning, following the departure of CIA briefers who had just given him news in the President's Daily Brief (PDB) of a manhunt for one particular terrorist, Bush complained to Rice: "I'm tired of swatting at flies. . . . I want to play offense, I want to take the fight to the terrorists," Bush said.[7] Rice took the implication that President Bush wanted a plan to attack the terrorists. When she asked the NSC staff how they could put something together, Richard Clarke had his original plan ready.

By late April 2001 the NSC was ready for a policy review on terrorism. After, we are told, six weeks of preliminary sessions, the Deputies Committee met on April 30 to consider an outline plan that Clarke presented. Stephen J. Hadley chaired the meeting, which included Scooter Libby (for Cheney), Richard Armitage (for Powell), Paul Wolfowitz (for Rumsfeld), and John McLaughlin (for Tenet). Here was a case in which the State Department favored going ahead but the CIA proved more cautious. Rather than initiating action, the Deputies Committee called for not one but three policy reviews, one on Al Qaeda, a second on Pakistani internal politics, and a third on the India-Pakistan problem.[8] According to Deputy National Security Adviser Hadley, "the goal was to move beyond the policy of containment, criminal prosecution, and limited retaliation for specific attacks, toward attempting to 'roll back' Al Qaeda."[9] The device of adding extra policy reviews inevitably slowed action, however. As Hadley noted in his response to 9/11 congressional investigators quoted above, between May and July there would be four successive meetings of the NSC Deputies Committee "directly related to the regional issues that had to be resolved in order to adopt a more aggressive strategy."[10] The last one of these sessions discussed the text of a draft presidential directive on July 16.

Meanwhile, on May 8 President Bush created a new unit to focus on terrorism within the Federal Emergency Management Agency, and a new interagency board to consider terrorism issues. He put Cheney in charge of that operation. This was the only actual action President Bush took before September 11, 2001, and it was not about rollback. Cheney's mandate was merely to study preparedness for homeland defense and make recommendations by October.

A second group, the Counterterrorism Security Group (CSG), part of the NSC interagency machinery, was chaired by Richard Clarke. It would be the CSG, not the vice president, that acted, or more properly, reacted. Beginning in March, U.S. intelligence and military sources received a series of reports indicating possible terrorist attacks. First came a report that Al Qaeda operatives in Canada might attack the United States in April.

In April, one source made a rather suggestive speculation that Osama bin Laden was interested in commercial aircraft pilots as terrorists for "spectacular and traumatic" attacks. In May came a report that Al Qaeda supporters were planning to enter the United States to carry out some operation using high explosives. There was also a Pentagon report that seven key suspected terrorists had begun moving toward Canada, the United States, and Britain. Between May and July, the National Security Agency intercepted no fewer than 33 communications suggesting an attack, including one evaluated at the time as an order to execute the plan. In June, the CIA Counterterrorism Center received information that key operatives were disappearing from view. At the end of June, Clarke convened the CSG, and by July 5 there were sufficient alarms to warrant a meeting among Rice, Clarke, and presidential chief of staff Andrew Card.

By then the intelligence scene had shifted and threats seemed centered on the American embassies in Rome, Paris, or Ankara. The CSG met again on July 6, and from then through the end of August, Clarke kept up meetings two or three times a week.[11]

In short, numerous disturbing intelligence reports came in over a period of months *after* President Bush had declared he wanted to go after terrorists, a period of time during which nothing happened with the U.S. government's planning for a rollback of Al Qaeda. Such Bush administration actions that occurred consisted entirely of putting certain selected military forces on precautionary (and defensive) alerts, or issuing warnings to the airlines.

Bush left for Crawford, Texas, and summer vacation on August 4. Two days later, he was given a fresh intelligence report—the PDB again mentioned terrorist attack. As characterized by national security adviser Rice, this PDB "was an analytic report that talked about [Osama bin Laden's] methods of operation, talked about what he

had done historically in 1997, in 1998. It mentioned hijacking, but hijacking in the traditional sense, and in a sense said that the most important and most likely thing was that he would take over an airliner holding passengers [and then make demands]."[12]

Much has been speculated about what Bush knew about the Al Qaeda terrorist threat, especially after the leak of the existence of the August 6, 2001 PDB and the report that it had mentioned aircraft hijacking. But the most important thing about the intelligence reports is something we already know: Neither the August 6 PDB, any of the other reports, nor the daily flurry of NSC staff activity on terrorist warnings moved Bush to demand the action plan he had supposedly called for in the spring, to ask that its preparation be accelerated, or to take any other action whatsoever. There is also no indication that Rice, whose job it was to be aware of these alarming reports, made any move to remind the president of his interest in the matter.

Absent presidential initiative, in fact, the plan to roll back Al Qaeda sat dormant six full weeks after mid-July 2001. The draft National Security Presidential Directive was finally considered by the NSC Principals Committee on September 4, and the group recommended that President Bush approve it. When Rice, or others, claim that an approved directive was on Bush's desk on 9/11, they exaggerate. The president had approved nothing. He had received a recommendation to sign a directive that had finally worked its way up through the bureaucracy.

The response of the Bush administration after 9/11 was rather different. When investigators raised questions regarding what Bush had done about intelligence he had received before the attacks, Vice President Cheney mounted a frontal assault on the 9/11 investigators, alleging they were responsible for the appearance in the press of reports of National Security Agency intercepts regarding the attacks, intercepts that White House spokesmen had themselves mentioned in press briefings in the days immediately after 9/11. Cheney demanded and got an FBI investigation of the investigators.

Ever since the 9/11 attacks the Bush White House has taken pains to avoid the revelation of any of the intelligence material provided to the president. The White House denied this material to the joint congressional committee investigating 9/11. It has also stonewalled the national commission inquiring into the attacks. The official rationale has been that no one should ever see the reports provided to a president.

That is not a legitimate declassification policy. A number of PDBs have been declassified and are in the public domain, including ones sent to President John F. Kennedy during the Cuban Missile Crisis and to President Lyndon Johnson during the Vietnam war. Excerpts of PDBs have been leaked on other occasions, not only the one to Bush for August 6, 2001, but one to his father before the Gulf War of 1990–1991. Our democracy has not been shaken by these revelations. And declassification is an ultimate step; the issue here is whether official inquiries operating under full security safeguards are entitled to view documents that are material to their investigations. The real reason to shield them is political: They would reveal the extent of warnings to George W. Bush in the face of which he stood immobile.

The November 2003 Bush compromise with the National Commission on Terrorist Attacks Upon the United States is designed to protect the president while appearing to cooperate. Under the arrangement, the White House will provide edited texts of some

PDBs to a team of four (out of ten) commissioners, who will be permitted to take notes that can then be edited by the White House. Two commissioners will be permitted to review all the PDBs and ask that the White House make available additional ones. This formula will be cumbersome in practice and will not ensure public confidence in the 9/11 investigation.

Fast Forward

The truth about 9/11 is one of two things. Either Rice's NSC machinery did not work, or else it worked perfectly to ensure that what Bush and his cohorts considered a marginal issue like terrorism did not clutter up the schedule of a president intent on another agenda—transforming America's relationships with traditional allies and former enemies. Either of these conclusions is disturbing. Once the Iraq war is factored into the equation the outlook is even more troubling. Again the NSC machinery operated in a fashion to prevent important objections or alternative policies from coming to the fore. U.S. policy going into the Iraq war was indifferent to alliance politics, to failures to attain needed U.N. approval, to U.S. military objections that the war plan was inadequate, to intelligence warnings that war would be succeeded by guerrilla resistance, to global public opinion, to international disarmament monitors who failed to turn up evidence supporting the Bush rationale for war, and more.[13] Dick Cheney served as an important driver of the policy that would be implemented. Condoleezza Rice became one of its most prominent public advocates; indeed Rice has served far more frequently as a public proponent than any of her national security adviser predecessors. Even Stephen J. Hadley, in the infamous manipulation of speech texts now encapsulated as the "Sixteen Words" controversy, made key contributions to a course of action that became an international and domestic political disaster.

The gang who produced all this were pros from Dover, using a tried and tested organizational structure for national security machinery. How could it be? Hubris, wishful thinking, incorrect assessment of the major issue facing the United States, wrongheaded notions of imposing change on the world—each played a role. Yet no heads have rolled. President George W. Bush promised to bring a new standard of accountability to Washington. In *that* he has succeeded. The picture is not a pretty one.

Notes

1. An overview of presidents' practices is in John Prados, *Keepers of the Keys: A History of the National Security Council from Truman to Bush* (New York: William Morrow, 1991). The Bush in the title is, however, George H. W. Bush, the current president's father. There is no good study of the NSC during the Clinton years.

2. Jane Perlez, "Directive Says Rice, Bush Aide, Won't Be Upstaged by Cheney," *New York Times*, Feb. 16, 2001, p. A10.

3. Karen DeYoung and Steven Mufson, "A Leaner and Less Visible NSC," *Washington Post*, Feb. 10, 2001, p. A6.

4. Massimo Calabresi et al., "They Had a Plan: Special Report: The Secret History," *Time*, August 12, 2002, p. 30. Clinton-era NSC staffer Daniel Benjamin, who worked with Richard Clarke in the transnational threats office, confirms both the briefing session itself and the presence of Berger. See Daniel Benjamin and Steven Simon, *The Age of Sacred Terror* (New York: Random House, 2002), p. 328.

5. Samuel R. Berger, "Joint Intelligence Committee Testimony," prepared text (copy in author's possession), September 19, 2002, pp. 4–5.

6. Daniel Benjamin and Steven Simon, *The Age of Sacred Terror*, p. 328.

7. Barton Gellman, "A Strategy's Cautious Evolution: Before September 11 the Bush Anti-Terror Effort Was Mostly Ambition," *Washington Post*, Jan. 20, 2002, p. A1.

8. The main sources for this account are the Barton Gellman story cited in note 7 and the study by a large team of *Time* correspondents cited in note 4.

9. United States Congress (107th Congress, 2nd Session). Senate Select Committee on Intelligence and House Permanent Select Committee on Intelligence, *Report: Joint Inquiry Into Intelligence Community Activities Before and After the Terrorist Attacks of September 11, 2001*, hereafter cited as 9/11 Congressional Report (Washington: Government Printing Office, 2003), p. 235. White House sources deny that Richard Clarke's original January memorandum had featured an actual "plan," Calabresi et al. (cited in footnote 4) note that Slide 14 of Clarke's presidential transition briefing on dealing with Al Qaeda included the words "rollback" and "breakup." Although dated December 2002, disputes with the Bush White House over secrecy of material on some of the very subjects under discussion here delayed the actual appearance of this report for many months, into the fall of 2003.

10. Ibid.

11. The data on intelligence indications is from the 9/11 Congressional Report, pp. 201–205; the material on Counterterrorism Security Group activities is from Condoleezza Rice at her news conference of May 16, 2002 as cited in "Excerpt From National Security Adviser's Statement," *New York Times*, May 17, 2002, p. A22.

12. Rice news conference, May 16, 2002.

13. This subject cannot be treated at length here, but see John Prados, *Hoodwinked* (forthcoming).

JOHN PRADOS is an analyst with the National Security Archive in Washington, D.C. His current books are *Hoodwinked* (forthcoming), on America headed into the Iraq war, and *White House Tapes* (2003), a selection of recordings that show American presidents at work on key issues of their times.

From *Bulletin of the Atomic Scientists*, January/February 2004, pp. 44–51. Copyright © 2004 by Bulletin of the Atomic Scientists. Reprinted by permission.

UNIT 6

U.S. International Economic Strategy

Unit Selections

Key Points to Consider

- Which type of international system: global free trade or regional trading blocs is in America's national interest? Explain.

- Which country or region is more important as a trading partner for the United States—Japan, China, Europe, or Mexico? Defend your answer.

- Select a country in need of debt relief or foreign aid. What type of foreign aid strategy should the United States pursue toward that country? How does this compare with current U.S. debt relief or foreign aid programs?

- Design an economic strategy for ensuring that the United States has an adequate supply of oil and other natural resources in the future.

- Put together an eight-person delegation to the next round of WTO trade talks. Defend your selections. What negotiating instructions would you give them?

- What measures would you use to rank of how powerful a country's economy is? How high would the United States rank?

Student Web Site

www.mhcls.com/online

Internet References

International Monetary Fund (IMF)
http://www.imf.org

United States Agency for International Development
http://www.usaid.gov/

United States Trade Representative
http://www.ustr.gov

World Bank
http://www.worldbank.org

As in so many areas of American foreign policy, the selection of U.S. international economic strategies during the Cold War seems to have been a rather straightforward process and the accompanying policy debates fairly minor compared to the situation that exists today. At the most fundamental level, it was taken for granted that the American economy would best be served by the existence of a global free trade system. To that end, international organizations were set up whose collective task was to oversee the operation of the postwar international economic order. Foremost among them were the General Agreement on Tariffs and Trade (GATT), the International Monetary Fund (IMF), and the International Bank for Reconstruction and Development (the World Bank). It was also widely accepted that many states would not be able to resist pressure from the Soviet Union or from domestic communist parties, due to the weak state of their economies and military establishments. Thus, containing communism would require foreign aid programs designed to transfer American economic and military expertise, goods and services, and financial resources to key states.

Events of the 1960s and 1970s shook the international economic system at its political and economic foundations. There followed a period of more than 20 years, in which, the international economic system was managed through a series of ad hoc responses to crises and the continued inability of foreign aid programs to produce real growth in the less developed world. U.S. international economic policy during this period was often characterized as one of "benign neglect."

The adequacy of this response is questioned today. Policy makers and citizens today see the international economic order as highly volatile and perhaps even threatening. The focal point of their concern is with the process of globalization. The IMF defines globalization as the growing economic interdependence of countries through the increasing volume and variety of border transactions in goods, services, and capital flows. Most fundamentally, globalization is change-inducing because of its ability to link activities around the world. From a policy perspective, the most significant aspect of globalization is that the international economic activity has become so large, rapid, and dense that it has outstripped the ability of governments and international organizations to manage it. Susan Strange described the situation as one of "casino capitalism" because, just as in a casino, a

U.S. Marine Corps photo by Cpl. Eric D. Arndt

large element of luck determines the success or failure of international economic policies.

It is against this changed backdrop of globalization that American international economic policy is now made and carried out. We can identify at least three major dimensions to American international economic foreign policy. They are trade, monetary policy, and foreign aid. Subsumed within them are a host of challenging issues and trade-offs such as economic growth, worker's rights, environmental protection, and global equity. The articles in this section highlight important issues that encompass questions in these areas.

The first reading, "America's Sticky Power," identifies economic power as a unique instrument of foreign policy having advantages that neither soft power nor military power possess. It attracts others to the United States voluntarily and then entraps them in a web of relations from which they cannot escape easily or without great cost. "The New Axis of Oil" examines how structural changes in the international oil market will impact on American economic prosperity and national security. The two key players in this new marketplace of buyers and sellers are Russia and China. The final reading in this section looks at the growing problem in American financial markets and what it ultimately means for United States foreign policy. "The Coming Financial Pandemic" argues that the financial crisis in the United States will become global in scope before it ends. Key areas that will be affected by it are trade, the value of the dollar and commodity prices.

America's Sticky Power

U.S. military force and cultural appeal have kept the United States at the top of the global order. But the hegemon cannot live on guns and Hollywood alone. U.S. economic policies and institutions act as "sticky power," attracting other countries to the U.S. system and then trapping them in it. Sticky power can help stabilize Iraq, bring rule of law to Russia, and prevent armed conflict between the United States and China.

WALTER RUSSELL MEAD

Since its earliest years, the United States has behaved as a global power. Not always capable of dispatching great fleets and mighty armies to every corner of the planet, the United States has nonetheless invariably kept one eye on the evolution of the global system, and the U.S. military has long served internationally. The United States has not always boasted the world's largest or most influential economy, but the country has always regarded trade in global terms, generally nudging the world toward economic integration. U.S. ideological impulses have also been global. The poet Ralph Waldo Emerson wrote of the first shot fired in the American Revolution as "the shot heard 'round the world," and Americans have always thought that their religious and political values should prevail around the globe.

Historically, security threats and trade interests compelled Americans to think globally. The British sailed across the Atlantic to burn Washington, D.C.; the Japanese flew from carriers in the Pacific to bomb Pearl Harbor. Trade with Asia and Europe, as well as within the Western Hemisphere, has always been vital to U.S. prosperity. U.S. President Thomas Jefferson sent the Navy to the Mediterranean to fight against the Barbary pirates to safeguard U.S. trade in 1801. Commodore Matthew Perry opened up Japan in the 1850s partly to assure decent treatment for survivors of sunken U.S. whaling ships that washed up on Japanese shores. And the last shots in the U.S. Civil War were fired from a Confederate commerce raider attacking Union shipping in the remote waters of the Arctic Ocean.

The rise of the United States to superpower status followed from this global outlook. In the 20th century, as the British system of empire and commerce weakened and fell, U.S. foreign-policymakers faced three possible choices: prop up the British Empire, ignore the problem and let the rest of the world go about its business, or replace Britain and take on the dirty job of enforcing a world order. Between the onset of World War I and the beginning of the Cold War, the United States tried all three, ultimately taking Britain's place as the gyroscope of world order.

However, the Americans were replacing the British at a moment when the rules of the game were changing forever. The United States could not become just another empire or great power playing the old games of dominance with rivals and allies. Such competition led to war, and war between great powers was no longer an acceptable part of the international system. No, the United States was going to have to attempt something that no other nation had ever accomplished, something that many theorists of international relations would swear was impossible. The United States needed to build a system that could end thousands of years of great power conflicts, constructing a framework of power that would bring enduring peace to the whole world—repeating globally what ancient Egypt, China, and Rome had each accomplished on a regional basis.

To complicate the task a bit more, the new hegemon would not be able to use some of the methods available to the Romans and others. Reducing the world's countries and civilizations to tributary provinces was beyond any military power the United States could or would bring to bear. The United States would have to develop a new way for sovereign states to coexist in a world of weapons of mass destruction and of prickly rivalries among religions, races, cultures, and states.

In his 2002 book, *The Paradox of American Power: Why the World's Only Superpower Can't Go It Alone,* Harvard University political scientist Joseph S. Nye Jr. discusses the varieties of power that the United States can deploy as it builds its world order. Nye focuses on two types of power: hard and soft. In his analysis, hard power is military or economic force that coerces others to follow a particular course of action. By contrast, soft power—cultural power, the power of example, the power of ideas and ideals—works more subtly; it makes others want what you want. Soft power upholds the U.S. world order because it influences others to like the U.S. system and support it of their own free will [see sidebar: A Sticky History Lesson].

Nye's insights on soft power have attracted significant attention and will continue to have an important role in U.S. policy debates. But the distinction Nye suggests between two types of hard power—military and economic power—has received less consideration than it deserves. Traditional military power can usefully be called sharp power; those resisting it will feel bayonets pushing and prodding them in the direction they must go. This power is the foundation of the U.S. system. Economic power can be thought of as sticky power, which comprises a set of economic institutions and policies that attracts others toward U.S. influence and then traps them in it. Together with soft power (the values, ideas, habits, and politics inherent in the system), sharp and sticky power sustain U.S. hegemony and make something as artificial and historically arbitrary as the U.S.-led global system appear desirable, inevitable, and permanent.

Sharp Power

Sharp power is a very practical and unsentimental thing. U.S. military policy follows rules that would have been understandable to the Hittites or the Roman Empire. Indeed, the U.S. military is the institution whose command structure is most like that of Old World monarchies—the president, after consultation with the Joint Chiefs, issues orders, which the military, in turn, obeys.

Like Samson in the temple of the Philistines, a collapsing U.S. economy would inflict enormous, unacceptable damage on the rest of the world.

Of course, security starts at home, and since the 1823 proclamation of the Monroe Doctrine, the cardinal principle of U.S. security policy has been to keep European and Asian powers out of the Western Hemisphere. There would be no intriguing great powers, no intercontinental alliances, and, as the United States became stronger, no European or Asian military bases from Point Barrow, Alaska, to the tip of Cape Horn, Chile.

The makers of U.S. security policy also have focused on the world's sea and air lanes. During peacetime, such lanes are vital to the prosperity of the United States and its allies; in wartime, the United States must control the sea and air lanes to support U.S. allies and supply military forces on other continents. Britain was almost defeated by Germany's U-boats in World War I and II; in today's world of integrated markets, any interruption of trade flows through such lanes would be catastrophic.

Finally (and fatefully), the United States considers the Middle East an area of vital concern. From a U.S. perspective, two potential dangers lurk in the Middle East. First, some outside power, such as the Soviet Union during the Cold War, can try to control Middle Eastern oil or at least interfere with secure supplies for the United States and its allies. Second, one country in the Middle East could take over the region and try to do the same thing. Egypt, Iran, and, most recently, Iraq have all tried and thanks largely to U.S. policy—have all failed. For all its novel dangers, today's efforts by al Qaeda leader Osama bin Laden and his followers to create a theocratic power in the region that could control oil resources and extend dictatorial power throughout the Islamic world resembles other threats that the United States has faced in this region during the last 60 years.

As part of its sharp-power strategy to address these priorities, the United States maintains a system of alliances and bases intended to promote stability in Asia, Europe, and the Middle East. Overall, as of the end of September 2003, the United States had just over 250,000 uniformed military members stationed outside its frontiers (not counting those involved in Operation Iraqi Freedom); around 43 percent were stationed on NATO territory and approximately 32 percent in Japan and South Korea. Additionally, the United States has the ability to transport significant forces to these theaters and to the Middle East should tensions rise, and it preserves the ability to control the sea lanes and air corridors necessary to the security of its forward bases. Moreover, the United States maintains the world's largest intelligence and electronic surveillance organizations. Estimated to exceed $30 billion in 2003, the U.S. intelligence budget is larger than the individual military budgets of Saudi Arabia, Syria, and North Korea.

Over time, U.S. strategic thinking has shifted toward overwhelming military superiority as the surest foundation for national security. That is partly for the obvious reasons of greater security, but it is partly also because supremacy can be an important deterrent. Establishing an overwhelming military supremacy might not only deter potential enemies from military attack; it might also discourage other powers from trying to match the U.S. buildup. In the long run, advocates maintain, this strategy could be cheaper and safer than staying just a nose in front of the pack.

Sticky Power

Economic, or sticky, power is different from both sharp and soft power—it is based neither on military compulsion nor on simple coincidence of wills. Consider the carnivorous sundew plant, which attracts its prey with a kind of soft power, a pleasing scent that lures insects toward its sap. But once the victim has touched the sap, it is stuck; it can't get away. That is sticky power; that is how economic power works.

Sticky power has a long history. Both Britain and the United States built global economic systems that attracted other countries. Britain attracted the United States into participating in the British system of trade and investment during the 19th century. The London financial markets provided investment capital that enabled U.S. industries to grow, while Americans benefited from trading freely throughout the British Empire. Yet, U.S. global trade was in some sense hostage to the British Navy—the United States could trade with the world as long as it had Britain's friendship, but an interruption in that friendship would mean financial collapse. Therefore, a strong lobby against war with Britain always existed in the United States. Trade-dependent New England almost seceded from the United States during the War of 1812, and at every crisis in Anglo-American relations for the next century, England could count on a strong lobby of merchants and bankers who would be ruined by war between the two English-speaking powers.

A Sticky History Lesson

Germany's experience in World War I shows how "sticky power"—the power of one nation's economic institutions and policies—can act as a weapon. During the long years of peace before the war, Germany was drawn into the British-led world trading system, and its economy became more and more trade-dependent. Local industries depended on imported raw materials. German manufacturers depended on foreign markets. Germany imported wheat and beef from the Americas, where the vast and fertile plains of the United States and the pampas of South America produced food much more cheaply than German agriculture could do at home. By 1910, such economic interdependence was so great that many, including Norman Angell, author of *The Great Illusion,* thought that wars had become so ruinously expensive that the age of warfare was over.

Not quite. Sticky power failed to keep World War I from breaking out, but it was vital to Britain's victory. Once the war started, Britain cut off the world trade Germany had grown to depend upon, while, thanks to Britain's Royal Navy, the British and their allies continued to enjoy access to the rest of the world's goods. Shortages of basic materials and foods dogged Germany all during the war. By the winter of 1916-17, the Germans were seriously hungry. Meanwhile, hoping to even the odds, Germany tried to cut the Allies off from world markets with the U-boat campaigns in the North Atlantic. That move brought the United States into the war at a time when nothing else could have saved the Allied cause.

Finally, in the fall of 1918, morale in the German armed forces and among civilians collapsed, fueled in part by the shortages. These conditions, not military defeat, forced the German leadership to ask for an armistice. Sticky power was Britain's greatest weapon in World War I. It may very well be the United States' greatest weapon in the 21st century.

—W.R.M.

The world economy that the United States set out to lead after World War II had fallen far from the peak of integration reached under British leadership. The two world wars and the Depression ripped the delicate webs that had sustained the earlier system. In the Cold War years, as it struggled to rebuild and improve upon the Old World system, the United States had to change both the monetary base and the legal and political framework of the world's economic system.

The United States built its sticky power on two foundations: an international monetary system and free trade. The Bretton Woods agreements of 1944 made the U.S. dollar the world's central currency, and while the dollar was still linked to gold at least in theory for another generation, the U.S. Federal Reserve could increase the supply of dollars in response to economic needs. The result for almost 30 years was the magic combination of an expanding monetary base with price stability. These conditions helped produce the economic miracle that transformed living standards in the advanced West and in Japan. The collapse

of the Bretton Woods system in 1973 ushered in a global economic crisis, but, by the 1980s, the system was functioning almost as well as ever with a new regime of floating exchange rates in which the U.S. dollar remained critical.

The progress toward free trade and economic integration represents one of the great unheralded triumphs of U.S. foreign policy in the 20th century. Legal and economic experts, largely from the United States or educated in U.S. universities, helped poor countries build the institutions that could reassure foreign investors, even as developing countries increasingly relied on state-directed planning and investment to jump-start their economies. Instead of gunboats, international financial institutions sent bankers and consultants around the world.

Behind all this activity was the United States' willingness to open its markets—even on a nonreciprocal basis—to exports from Europe, Japan, and poor nations. This policy, part of the overall strategy of containing communism, helped consolidate support around the world for the U.S. system. The role of the dollar as a global reserve currency, along with the expansionary bias of U.S. fiscal and monetary authorities, facilitated what became known as the "locomotive of the global economy" and the "consumer of last resort." U.S. trade deficits stimulated production and consumption in the rest of the world, increasing the prosperity of other countries and their willingness to participate in the U.S.-led global economy.

Opening domestic markets to foreign competitors remained (and remains) one of the most controversial elements in U.S. foreign policy during the Cold War. U.S. workers and industries facing foreign competition bitterly opposed such openings. Others worried about the long-term consequences of the trade deficits that transformed the United States into a net international debtor during the 1980s. Since the Eisenhower administration, predictions of imminent crises (in the value of the dollar, domestic interest rates, or both) have surfaced whenever U.S. reliance on foreign lending has grown, but those negative consequences have yet to materialize. The result has been more like a repetition on a global scale of the conversion of financial debt to political strength pioneered by the founders of the Bank of England in 1694 and repeated a century later when the United States assumed the debt of the 13 colonies.

In both of those cases, the stock of debt was purchased by the rich and the powerful, who then acquired an interest in the stability of the government that guaranteed the value of the debt. Wealthy Englishmen opposed the restoration of the Stuarts to the throne because they feared it would undermine the value of their holdings in the Bank of England. Likewise, the propertied elites of the 13 colonies came to support the stability and strength of the new U.S. Constitution because the value of their bonds rose and fell with the strength of the national government.

Similarly, in the last 60 years, as foreigners have acquired a greater value in the United States—government and private bonds, direct and portfolio private investments—more and more of them have acquired an interest in maintaining the strength of the U.S.-led system. A collapse of the U.S. economy and the ruin of the dollar would do more than dent the prosperity of the United States. Without their best customer, countries including China and Japan would fall into depressions. The financial strength of every country would be severely shaken should the United States collapse. Under those circumstances, debt becomes a strength, not a weakness, and other countries fear to break with the United States because they need its market and own its securities. Of course, pressed too far, a large national debt can turn from a source of strength to a crippling liability, and the United States must continue to justify other countries' faith by maintaining its long-term record of meeting its financial obligations. But, like Samson in the temple of the Philistines, a collapsing U.S. economy would inflict enormous, unacceptable damage on the rest of the world. That is sticky power with a vengeance.

The Sum of All Powers?

The United States' global economic might is therefore not simply, to use Nye's formulations, hard power that compels others or soft power that attracts the rest of the world. Certainly, the U.S. economic system provides the United States with the prosperity needed to underwrite its security strategy, but it also encourages other countries to accept U.S. leadership. U.S. economic might is sticky power.

How will sticky power help the United States address today's challenges? One pressing need is to ensure that Iraq's economic reconstruction integrates the nation more firmly in the global economy. Countries with open economies develop powerful trade-oriented businesses; the leaders of these businesses can promote economic policies that respect property rights, democracy, and the rule of law. Such leaders also lobby governments to avoid the isolation that characterized Iraq and Libya under economic sanctions. And looking beyond Iraq, the allure of access to Western capital and global markets is one of the few forces protecting the rule of law from even further erosion in Russia.

China's rise to global prominence will offer a key test case for sticky power. As China develops economically, it should gain wealth that could support a military rivaling that of the United States; China is also gaining political influence in the world.

Some analysts in both China and the United States believe that the laws of history mean that Chinese power will someday clash with the reigning U.S. power.

Sticky power offers a way out. China benefits from participating in the U.S. economic system and integrating itself into the global economy. Between 1970 and 2003, China's gross domestic product grew from an estimated $106 billion to more than $1.3 trillion. By 2003, an estimated $450 billion of foreign money had flowed into the Chinese economy. Moreover, China is becoming increasingly dependent on both imports and exports to keep its economy (and its military machine) going. Hostilities between the United States and China would cripple China's industry, and cut off supplies of oil and other key commodities.

Sticky power works both ways, though. If China cannot afford war with the United States, the United States will have an increasingly hard time breaking off commercial relations with China. In an era of weapons of mass destruction, this mutual dependence is probably good for both sides. Sticky power did not prevent World War I, but economic interdependence runs deeper now; as a result, the "inevitable" U.S.-Chinese conflict is less likely to occur.

Sticky power, then, is important to U.S. hegemony for two reasons: It helps prevent war, and, if war comes, it helps the United States win. But to exercise power in the real world, the pieces must go back together. Sharp, sticky, and soft power work together to sustain U.S. hegemony. Today, even as the United States' sharp and sticky power reach unprecedented levels, the rise of anti-Americanism reflects a crisis in U.S. soft power that challenges fundamental assumptions and relationships in the U.S. system. Resolving the tension so that the different forms of power reinforce one another is one of the principal challenges facing U.S. foreign policy in 2004 and beyond.

WALTER RUSSELL MEAD is the Henry A. Kissinger senior fellow in U.S. foreign policy at the Council on Foreign Relations. This essay is adapted from his forthcoming book, *Power, Terror, Peace, and War: America's Grand Strategy in a World at Risk* (New York: Knopf, 2004).

The New Axis of Oil

FLYNT LEVERETT AND PIERRE NOËL

While Washington is preoccupied with curbing the proliferation of weapons of mass destruction, avoiding policy failure in Iraq and cheering the "forward march of freedom", the political consequences of recent structural shifts in global energy markets are posing the most profound challenge to American hegemony since the end of the Cold War. The increasing control that state-owned companies exercise over the world's reserves of crude oil and natural gas is, under current market conditions, enabling some energy exporters to act with escalating boldness against U.S. interests and policies. Perhaps the most immediate example is Venezuela's efforts to undermine U.S. influence in Latin America. The most strategically significant manifestation, though, is Russia's willingness to use its newfound external leverage to counteract what Moscow considers an unacceptable level of U.S. infringement on its interests. At the same time, rising Asian states, especially China, are seeking to address their perceived energy vulnerability through state-orchestrated strategies to "secure" access to hydrocarbon resources around the world. In the Chinese case, a statist approach to managing external energy relationships is increasingly pitting China against the United States in a competition for influence in the Middle East, Central Asia and oil-producing parts of Africa.

We describe these political consequences of recent structural shifts in global energy markets by the shorthand "petropolitics." While each of these developments is challenging to U.S. interests, the various threads of petropolitics are now coming together in an emerging "axis of oil" that is acting as a counterweight to American hegemony on a widening range of issues.[1] At the center of this undeclared but increasingly assertive axis is a growing geopolitical partnership between Russia (a major energy producer) and China (the paradigmatic rising consumer) against what both perceive as excessive U.S. unilateralism. The impact of this axis on U.S. interests has already been felt in the largely successful Sino–Russian effort to rollback U.S. influence in Central Asia. But the real significance is being seen in the ongoing frustration of U.S. objectives on the Iranian nuclear issue. This will likely be a milestone in redefining the post-Cold War international order—not merely because Iran is likely to end up with at least a nuclear-weapons option, but because of what that will imply about the efficacy of America's global leadership.

Structural Changes

The age of oil has clearly entered a new chapter, as strong demand and a shortage of productive capacity have generated a significantly higher trading range for crude oil than the world has experienced during the last twenty years. The dramatic rise in demand has been fed by high economic growth in emerging markets (where the increments of energy demand associated with specific increments of economic growth are usually greater than in OECD countries), particularly China and India. Overall, surging demand for crude oil from emerging economies has been the most immediate factor exerting upward pressure on prices.

A second element defining the recent structural shift in the international oil market is shrinking surplus productive capacity all along the supply chain. (Global oil supply has increased in recent years, but not as much as demand.) The degree that oil producers around the world expand their productive capacity is likely to be the most important factor affecting oil prices in the future. Not surprisingly, one finds a range of views about the possibilities for relieving the current supply "crunch."

There is significant evidence that there is, in fact, more oil to be discovered and produced, or recovered from already-producing fields, around the world—at the right price and with appropriate levels in investment. Thus, we do not share the unrelieved pessimism of those who argue we have reached the peak point of global oil supplies. However, we are also not inclined to accept the unrestrained optimism of some economists, who argue that high prices will, as they have in the past, necessarily attract the investment required to expand production relative to demand growth. Our skepticism flows primarily from the reality that the upstream oil sector—the exploration and production of crude oil—is far from an open and competitive environment. After 25 years of massive investment by multinational oil companies in exploration and development in oil-producing areas outside of OPEC and the former Soviet Union, the cost of replacing reserves in this "competitive fringe" of the oil industry, where the upstream sector has been relatively open, is now rising rapidly. Meanwhile, a high proportion of the remaining areas suitable for comparatively low-cost renewal of reserves, mostly in the Middle East and former Soviet Union, are off-limits to the international oil industry.

The next quarter-century of the oil age will therefore look quite different from the previous quarter-century: The rise in demand and the decline of several non-OPEC countries' production will have to be met by increased supplies of conventional oil from the Middle East and the former Soviet Union, as well as by unconventional oil (oil shale, tar sands and extra-heavy oil) and synthetic liquids (gas-to-liquids, coal-to-liquids and bio-fuels). Prices will likely be much higher on average and more unstable than in the past, with demand continuing to bump up against productive capacity.

There is an explicitly political dimension to these developments. As the "competitive fringe" of the upstream oil sector has been exploited by the multinational oil industry, the percentage of the world's oil reserves held by publicly traded international oil companies (IOCs) has declined, while the percentage held by state-owned national oil companies (NOCs) has increased. Currently, 72 percent of the world's proven oil reserves are held by NOCs. The ten-largest upstream companies in the world, measured by booked reserves (not market capitalization or production), are all NOCs. ExxonMobil—the largest publicly traded IOC in the world and the iconic symbol of "big oil"—is only the twelfth-largest upstream company in the world in terms of booked reserves. This means that NOCs and their parent governments, not IOCs and their shareholders, ultimately control the pace of development of upstream oil and gas resources.

Under current conditions of rising demand and tight supply, this is giving energy-exporting countries a more subtle but also more durable basis for enhancing their influence and generating new strategic options for themselves than that displayed by OPEC during and immediately after the 1973–74 oil embargo. Only now is the world seeing the full extent of the "OPEC revolution" of the early 1970s: Beyond an explicit cartel of oil producers, there is today an implicit cartel of resource-owning governments that control a large share of the world's known reserves of oil and natural gas. The power of this implicit cartel has been dormant for three decades; its actualization is an event of major economic and political significance that is generating critical challenges to America's regional interests and global standing.

Markets and the Russian Agenda

Russia stands as perhaps the leading exemplar of supply-side trends. After several years of uncertainty and contestation, President Vladimir Putin has successfully reasserted a definitive measure of state control over Russia's upstream oil and gas sectors, with NOCs like Gazprom and Rosneft playing increasingly important roles, the country's pipeline network firmly in government hands, Russian private-sector companies operating within parameters established by Moscow, and formidable barriers in place to large-scale foreign investment.

Suggestions just a few years ago that Russia could supplant Saudi Arabia as a swing producer for the global oil market were misplaced. There is no evidence that Putin or other senior leaders aspire to such a status, or that the Russian oil industry could muster what it would take to play such a role. Nevertheless, under Putin's presidency the internal conditions have been established for Russia to derive a significant measure of external leverage from its status as an important energy producer. In this regard, Putin wants to use Russia's presidency of the G-8 this year to transform Russia's international status from that of a mere (albeit major) energy supplier to that of a global supplier of energy security.

Moscow is using its market power to push back against the United States in arenas where it perceives U.S. infringement on its interests. Since the collapse of the Soviet Union, the list of accumulated Russian grievances over U.S. initiatives has grown ever longer: NATO enlargement, abrogation of the Anti-Ballistic Missile Treaty, basing of U.S. forces in Central Asia, the Iraq War and support for the "color revolutions" in states neighboring Russia. Through the late 1990s, Russia's ability to respond to these provocations was negligible. The Russian military was bogged down in Chechnya, and low oil and gas prices

contributed to economic weakness—epitomized by Russia's 1998 currency crisis—making Russia dependent on the United States and other international players for assistance. In recent years, however, Russia's autonomy has been reinforced by high energy prices, and Putin and his advisors have decided they can use this market power to "push back" against the United States.

Russia's unfolding strategy for bolstering its influence in the "near abroad" exemplifies this approach. In some cases, as in the recent controversy over Russian gas shipments through Ukraine, the Kremlin's initiatives seem heavy-handed and not particularly productive. But its approach has been quite effective in establishing a new sphere of influence in the Eurasian south.

Much Western commentary on Russian policy in Central Asia has focused on Moscow's recent successes in establishing military bases in Kyrgyzstan and Tajikistan and encouraging Uzbekistan to evict U.S. military personnel from the Karshi-Kanabad air base. The real story, however, is rooted in energy and Russia's rising market power. Since 2003, Moscow has worked assiduously to establish a new sphere of influence in Central Asia, using regional autocrats' interest in resisting U.S. pressure to democratize, and China's interest in avoiding "encirclement" by U.S. forces, to maximize pressure on America. Russia's status as a major energy producer has given it important tools for pursuing Putin's regional strategy: investment capital with which to assume a leading role in the development and marketing of Central Asian energy resources (with NOCs like Gazprom acting as effective agents of Kremlin policy) and control over access to Russia's state-owned pipeline system, which is essential for moving Central Asian oil and gas to markets in Europe.

Less directly, the oil boom of the last few years has fueled much higher rates of growth in the Russian economy, helping to turn the Russian service sector into a provider of jobs for Central Asian expatriates. Remittances from the expatriate workers constitute an increasingly important source of income for several Central Asian states—perhaps as much as 30 percent of GDP in Tajikistan, for example—which gives Moscow another lever of influence over these states.[2]

Russia has also used its energy-based market power to bolster its political influence in other strategically vital regions in ways that could potentially weaken America's international position. Perhaps most notably, Moscow has taken advantage of its market power to reinforce and enhance its otherwise sagging strategic position in East Asia. Although geopolitical legacies and existing transportation infrastructure orient Russian energy exports toward Europe, Moscow has used the prospect of substantial energy exports from eastern Siberia and the Russian Far East to markets in East Asia to make itself a major factor in the foreign policies of both China and Japan, playing on the interests of Beijing and Tokyo in balancing traditional sources of hydrocarbons from the Middle East in their energy profiles.

The Asian Challenge

Of course, the market power of energy suppliers like Russia is an outgrowth of escalating demand-side pressures. As noted earlier, increased demand, especially from emerging Asia, has been one of the most important factors exerting upward pressure on oil prices since 2003: According to the U.S. Department of Energy, 40 percent of oil-demand growth worldwide since 2001 has come from China alone. Despite a slowdown in China's oil-demand growth in 2005, many market forecasts show demand growth in Asia continuing at impressive rates for years to come.

In the current climate, the political impact of these demand-side pressures is exacerbated by consumer countries' increasing reliance on statist strategies to secure access to hydrocarbon resources on privileged bases, rather than relying solely on international markets to meet their energy needs. The best example of this approach is China's. In 2002, around the time that Hu Jintao became general secretary of the Communist Party, China formally adopted a "going out" (*zou chu qu*) policy of encouraging its three major NOCs—the China National Petroleum Corporation (CNPC), the China National Petrochemical Corporation (Sinopec), and the China National Offshore Oil Corporation (CNOOC)—to purchase equity shares in overseas exploration and production projects around the world, and to build pipelines, particularly to Siberia and Central Asia. The goal of the "going out" strategy is to secure effective ownership of energy resources and transportation infrastructure, measures that China perceives as essential to improving the country's energy security. The adoption of the policy was effectively a codification of long-standing practice, as Chinese energy companies had already engaged in these activities since the 1990s.

China has pursued the "going out" strategy in a wide range of oil-producing regions, including the Caucasus, Central Asia, East and South Asia, Africa and Latin America. In the Middle East, China has employed the strategy in various ways with a number of oil-producing states, including Algeria, Egypt, Iran, Libya, Oman, Saudi Arabia, Syria, Sudan and Yemen. Beijing supports the efforts of Chinese energy companies to win deals with regular high-level visits to and from regions in which the companies are seeking access. China also follows up its network of energy deals by increasing exports of manufactured goods and capital to countries where its NOCs are operating. In some cases, the Chinese appear willing to put expensive packages of side investments on the table in order to secure energy deals, as was recently the case in Angola and Nigeria. Chinese and other Asian NOCs participating in bidding rounds in a number of countries have shown a willingness to pay high prices in order to secure exploration and production contracts, sometimes overbidding IOCs.

However, while increased demand from Asian economies has a very direct effect on global oil prices, the impact of China's statist strategy on the market is probably not as dramatic as some assessments would suggest. It seems doubtful that Chinese NOCs' fledgling efforts to lock up petroleum resources will succeed in keeping a critical mass of oil reserves off an increasingly integrated and fluid global oil market. There is also no reason to anticipate that China's willingness to pay market premiums for privileged access to oil resources in various parts of the world will bolster upward pressure on prices generated naturally by rising demand. The opposite is more likely: The flow of "cheap" Chinese capital into global exploration and production is increasing competition among oil companies to access reserves and forcing IOCs to increase spending and take more risks. Other things being equal, this should bring *more* oil, not less, to market.

Arguably, the Chinese strategy of competing for access to hydrocarbon resources challenges the rules-based international order for trade and investment in energy that the United States has long championed. At a minimum, statist initiatives to secure effective ownership over hydrocarbon resources in foreign countries—with an attendant willingness toward corruption, offering soft loans, and making investments in unrelated sectors and infrastructure projects as part of these initiatives—undercut OECD standards for export financing and other good-governance criteria. And there is a risk that the Chinese approach will be taken as a model by others. This is already happening to some extent with India's Oil & Natural Gas Corporation (ONGC), which is pursuing equity oil deals in many of the same places as the Chinese NOCs—in some cases, as in Iran and Sudan, in consortium with them. Last year, for example, China and India announced an "agreement" aimed at preventing competition over hydrocarbon assets between Chinese NOCs and ONGC from driving up the prices of those assets, as happened in the contest to buy Canada-based PetroKazakhstan. There is also a resurgent debate in Japan as to whether it should take a more statist approach to external energy policy to meet the Chinese challenge. But we are still far from a turning point of massive defections from the market by major consumers and suppliers.

Nevertheless, while the market impact of statist strategies like China's may be minimal, Beijng's "going out" strategy is rapidly becoming a source of geopolitical tensions between China and the United States, with potentially significant implications for the development of the world's most important bilateral relationship during the first quarter of the 21st century. China's search for oil is making it a new competitor to the United States for influence, especially in the Middle East, Central Asia and Africa. China's energy-driven engagement in the Middle East is creating new foreign policy as well as commercial options for energy exporting states, including those at odds with U.S. foreign policy goals, like Iran, Sudan and Syria. (With regard to Sudan, Beijing went so far as to use its status as a permanent member of the Security Council to block the imposition of sanctions on Khartoum over the Darfur genocide.)

In Central Asia, China's interest in diversifying its external sources of energy to mitigate its reliance on the Persian Gulf has motivated Beijing's leading role in the Shanghai Cooperation Organization's campaign to undercut U.S. influence in Central Asia. In oil-producing African countries, Chinese and other Asian NOCs make available to host governments a supply of exploration and production capital that is free from any good-governance and transparency conditions. This, combined with high oil prices, is weakening the leverage that Western governments and international financial institutions can use to improve management of the oil sector and reduce corruption in these countries.

Additionally, Beijing's statist approach to energy security is raising geopolitical tensions with Japan, with prospectively a negative impact on the development of a regional political framework to anchor growing trade and financial interdependence in the world's most dynamic economic zone. Competition between Beijing and Tokyo for specific energy deals in a variety of settings, a bilateral dispute about sovereignty over possible natural gas reserves in the East China Sea, and jockeying over the ultimate destination of a projected Russian eastern oil pipeline have all contributed to the ongoing deterioration of Sino–Japanese relations. Unless these tensions can be ameliorated, it will be increasingly difficult for the United States to manage China's rise on the East Asian scene in a way that ensures long-term regional stability.

Over time, Russian oil and gas could be a major factor buttressing closer Sino–Russian strategic collaboration. Putin's recent meeting with Hu in Beijing, during which the two leaders concluded an agreement for Russia to begin exporting natural gas to China by 2012, was the fifth such meeting in the last year. In theory, a successful commercially grounded oil and gas relationship between Russia and China could be positive for at least some U.S. interests by mitigating China's sense of energy insecurity through reduced dependence on the Middle East (and U.S.-secured Asian maritime routes for their transport). But Moscow is clearly playing on Beijing's sense of energy insecurity to foster a closer geopolitical partnership.

The Axis of Oil and Iran

The implications of the new petropolitics and an emerging axis of oil for America's international influence are illustrated by the way these forces are frustrating U.S. objectives on the Iranian nuclear issue. The policies of key players on this issue are conditioned far more by calculations about the economics and geopolitics of energy than was the case during the run-up to the Iraq War. As the Western powers consider what sort of action against Iran they might collectively support, it is clear that their options in the Security Council are severely limited by Russian and Chinese resistance to the imposition of sanctions or other strongly punitive measures.

With growing market power increasing Russia's capacity for strategic initiative, its calculus of interests regarding the Iranian nuclear issue has become more complex than most Western analysts and policymakers understand. Moscow's policy agenda toward Iran has expanded significantly. Russia continues to have important economic interests in Iran. Moscow anticipates a substantial increase in high-technology exports (for example, civil nuclear technology) to Iran over the next decade. The Iranian market is also potentially lucrative for Russian exporters of conventional weaponry, one of Russia's main sources of foreign-exchange earnings alongside hydrocarbon exports. But over the last three years, Russia has also come to see Iran as an important geopolitical partner in its efforts to rollback U.S. influence, not only in Central Asia but in the Caucasus as well. Moscow's recent proposal to resolve the impasse between the Islamic Republic and the West over Iran's nuclear activities by establishing Iranian–Russian joint-venture entities for uranium enrichment was calculated to serve all of these interests. Such a scheme would allow Moscow to maintain and even expand an Iranian market for its nuclear technology, while also nurturing its developing strategic partnership with Tehran.

It is also increasingly evident that the current leadership in Moscow views the Iranian nuclear issue as an opportunity to frustrate the Bush Administration's unilateralist inclinations. Russian Foreign Minister Sergei Lavrov—formerly Russia's permanent representative to the UN for ten years and a master of Security Council politics and procedure—and his colleagues anticipate that, in the end, the United States may take unilateral military action against Iran, including the Russian-built reactor at Bushehr. They do not expect to be able to block such action anymore than they could block the invasion of Iraq, but they are working prospectively to impose serious costs on the United States for

a military strike against Iran by ensuring that Washington lacks international legitimacy for its actions.

For its part, China's approach to the Iranian nuclear issue is directly linked to its assessment of its requirements for energy security. Beijing has already put down a marker, in the form of its opposition to UN sanctions against Sudan, that it will oppose the imposition of multilateral sanctions on an energy-producing state in which Chinese companies operate. In private conversations, senior Chinese diplomats and party officials describe Beijing's policy on the Iranian nuclear issue as seeking to balance a range of interests: a secure supply of oil, nonproliferation and regional stability, the defense of important international norms (including the peaceful resolution of disputes and the sovereign right of states to develop civil nuclear capabilities), securing China's northwest border (meaning Xinjiang province, where there is a significant Muslim population), the development of Chinese–Iranian relations, the development of U.S.–Chinese relations, and the positions of the European Union and Russia. It seems increasingly clear that, in their efforts to balance this set of interests, Chinese officials will remain deeply resistant to the imposition of sanctions on Iran. And as long as Russian opposition provides China with political cover, Chinese officials seem to calculate that they will not have to choose between relations with Iran and relations with the United States.

China's willingness to protect Iran from international pressure would also complicate Western efforts to impose meaningful sanctions on Iran through a "coalition of the willing." Without Chinese participation, a voluntary ban on investment in Iran's energy sector by Western powers would, at this point, be little more than a symbolic gesture, as U.S. companies are already barred from doing business in Iran by U.S. law, and most European IOCs have put potential projects on hold because of the political uncertainties. In recent years, though, Chinese NOCs have committed themselves, at least in principle, to substantial investments in Iran's energy sector, thereby mitigating the impact of restrictions on Western investment.

With the Bush Administration having ruled out direct and broad-based strategic discussions with Iran aimed at a "grand bargain" that would include a resolution of the nuclear issue, the United States and its European partners are headed down an ultimately futile path in the Security Council. The Security Council's failure to deal effectively with the Iranian nuclear issue will confront the United States, during the last two years or so of the Bush Administration's tenure, with the choice of doing nothing as Iran continues to develop its nuclear capabilities or taking unilateral military action in the hope of slowing down that development. Each of these choices is likely to damage American leadership in the world: Doing nothing will highlight U.S. fecklessness, while unilateral action without international legitimacy will further strain America's international standing (and probably not meaningfully impede Iran's nuclear development).

Beyond speculating whether Iran might cut off oil exports in response to sanctions or military action, commentators tend to overlook the implications of the current controversy's outcome for the geopolitics of global energy. How the nuclear issue plays out will largely determine Iran's future as an oil and gas supplier. Iranian oil production relies heavily on a small number of old, "super-giant" fields, where output has plateaued and could soon start to decline. These old fields need massive infusions of investment and technology to increase their recovery rates. Iran is not Saudi Arabia and cannot make the investments itself. Since reopening its upstream oil sector in 1994, Iran has actually taken in only around $10 billion of foreign investment in oil exploration and production, due to a lack of political consensus on the country's oil policy, a difficult and opaque negotiating process, and unattractive contractual terms. Similarly, Iran needs large-scale investment and technology transfers to develop its gas-exporting potential. If the nuclear controversy leads to Iran's further isolation from Western IOCs, there would be a powerful incentive for Tehran to turn to Chinese and other Asian NOCs, supplement their investment capital with expertise from more technologically advanced Russian companies, and rely on government-to-government marketing deals. This would significantly reinforce the economic and political logic behind the axis of oil.

Possible Policies

One step Washington needs to take is to facilitate broader and deeper cooperation between the International Energy Agency (IEA) and China and India. Because these states are not members of the OECD, they are not formally eligible for membership in the IEA, and they have not yet built up the minimum levels of stockpiled oil and petroleum products defined by the IEA for its members. Notwithstanding these barriers, it is clearly in the interests of the United States and its Western partners to establish much closer coordination between emerging Asian economies and the IEA, especially to persuade these states to rely more on international markets and less on exclusive supply deals to meet their energy needs.

At the same time, the United States needs to change its approach to promoting expansion of global energy supplies. It will take more than exhortations about market logic to change elite attitudes and government policies regarding upstream resource development in key energy-producing states. These elites have, by and large, determined that values other than pure market efficiency have priority in their calculations about resource development. Traditional American advocacy of liberalization and internationalization of upstream oil and gas sectors needs to shift decisively toward encouraging NOCs in key producing states to increase investment in productive capacity.

The larger reality is that U.S. foreign policy is ill suited to cope with the challenges to American leadership flowing from the new petropolitics. Current policy does not take energy security seriously as a foreign policy issue or prioritize energy security in relation to other foreign policy goals.

The United States cannot change the course of Moscow's energy policy or foreign policy, but American diplomacy can mitigate Russian policymakers' threat perceptions in exchange for more cooperative Russian behavior. This would require the United States to reach a set of strategic understandings with Moscow encouraging mutual respect for each side's critical interests—and also to make clear privately that Washington and its Western partners will not recognize Russia as a provider of energy security as long as it plays geopolitically on the energy security of others. Vice President Cheney's recent public denunciation of Moscow, coupled with the Bush Administration's refusal to reconsider its strategic approach to Russia, is hardly likely to achieve positive results.

To deal more effectively with China, Washington must recognize that, despite some acknowledgement in Beijing that the "going out" strategy may prove a poor energy security policy, there is still a widely held perception within the Chinese establishment that the international oil market is a foreign (primarily American) construction, operated by Western IOCs in accordance with their interests, and that China cannot bet its energy security on that construction. U.S. policy should encourage Chinese and other Asian NOCs to move along their own paths of internationalization. In this regard, the U.S. Congress's resistance to CNOOC's potential acquisition of Unocal last year sent precisely the wrong message to China.

More broadly, U.S. policymakers need to remember that, even for a global hegemon, to govern is to choose. Washington cannot continue to disregard the impact of its foreign policy choices on the interests of key energy-producing states like Russia if it expects these states not to use their market power in ways that run counter to U.S. preferences. And, similarly, Washington cannot ignore the energy security interests and perceptions of rising consumer countries like China and avoid consequences reflected in these countries' foreign policy choices.

Notes

1. The term "axis of oil" is not new and has been used by various commentators to describe a number of oil-focused relationships, such as the U.S.–Saudi strategic partnership or a possible coordination between India and China in their quest to secure external energy resources. We use the term, in a manner similar to Irwin Stelzer, to describe a shifting coalition of both energy exporting and energy importing states centered in ongoing Sino–Russian collaboration.

2. The authors are grateful to their colleague Fiona Hill for this point.

FLYNT LEVERETT is senior fellow at the Brookings Institution's Saban Center for Middle East Policy and has been appointed visiting professor of political science at the Massachusetts Institute of Technology. **PIERRE NOËL** is research fellow at the French Institute of International Relations (IFRI) in Paris. He will join the Electricity Policy Research Group at Cambridge University's Judge Business School in September.

The Coming Financial Pandemic

The U.S. financial crisis cannot be contained. Indeed, it has already begun to infect other countries, and it will travel further before it's done. From sluggish trade to credit crunches, from housing busts to volatile stock markets, this is how the contagion will spread.

Nouriel Roubini

For months, economists have debated whether the United States is headed toward a recession. Today, there is no doubt. President George W. Bush can tout his $150 billion economic stimulus package, and the Federal Reserve can continue to cut short-term interest rates in an effort to goose consumer spending. But those moves are unlikely to stop the economy's slide. The severe liquidity and credit crunch from the subprime mortgage bust is now spreading to broader credit markets, $100 barrels of oil are squeezing consumers, and unemployment continues to climb. And with the housing market melting down, empty-pocketed Americans can no longer use their homes as ATMs to fund their shopping sprees. It's time to face the truth—the U.S. economy is no longer merely battling a touch of the flu; it's now in the early stages of a painful and persistent bout of pneumonia.

Meanwhile, other countries are watching anxiously, hoping they don't get sick, too. In recent years, the global economy has been unbalanced, with Americans spending more than they earn and the country running massive external deficits. When the subprime mortgage crisis first hit headlines last year, observers hoped that the rest of the world had enough growth momentum and domestic demand to gird itself from the U.S. slowdown. But making up for slowing U.S. demand will be difficult, if not impossible. American consumers spend about $9 trillion a year. Compare that to Chinese consumers, who spend roughly $1 trillion a year, or Indian consumers, who spend only about $600 billion. Even in wealthy European and Japanese households, low income growth and insecurities about the global economy have caused consumers to save rather than spend. Meanwhile, countries such as China rely on exports to sustain their high economic growth. So there's little reason to believe that global buyers will pick up the slack of today's faltering American consumer, whose spending has already begun to drop.

Because the United States is such a huge part of the global economy—it accounts for about 25 percent of the world's GDP, and an even larger percentage of international financial

transactions—there's real reason to worry that an American financial virus could mark the beginning of a global economic contagion. It may not devolve into a worldwide recession, but at the very least, other nations should expect sharp economic downturns, too. Here's how it will happen:

Trade will drop. The most obvious way that a U.S. recession could spill over elsewhere in the world is through trade. If output and demand in the United States fall—something that by definition would happen in a recession—the resulting decline in private consumption, capital spending by companies, and production would lead to a drop in imports of consumer goods, capital goods, commodities, and other raw materials from abroad. U.S. imports are other countries' exports, as well as an important part of their overall demand. So such a scenario would spell a drop in their economic growth rates, too. Several significant economies—including Canada, China, Japan, Mexico, South Korea, and much of Southeast Asia—are heavily dependent on exports to the United States. China, in particular, is at risk because so much of its double-digit annual growth has relied on the uptick of exports to the United States. Americans are the world's biggest consumers, and China is one of the world's largest exporters. But with Americans reluctant to buy, where would Chinese goods go?

China is also a good example of how indirect trade links would suffer in an American recession. It once was the case that Asian manufacturing hubs such as South Korea and Taiwan produced finished goods, like consumer electronics, that were exported directly to American retailers. But with the rise of Chinese competitiveness in manufacturing, the pattern of trade in Asia has changed: Asian countries increasingly produce components, such as computer chips, for export to China. China then takes these component parts and assembles them into finished goods—say, a personal computer—and exports them to American consumers. Therefore, if U.S. imports fall, then Chinese exports to the United States would fall. If Chinese exports fall, then Chinese demand for component parts from the rest of Asia would fall, spreading the economic headache further.

A weak dollar will make matters worse. Already, the economic slowdown in the United States and the Fed's interest rate cuts have caused the value of the dollar to drop relative to many floating currencies such as the euro, the yen, and the won. This weaker dollar may stimulate U.S. export competitiveness, because those countries will be able to buy more for less. But, once again, it is bad news for other countries, such as Germany, Japan, and South Korea, who rely heavily on their own exports to the United States. That's because the strengthening of their currencies will increase the price of their goods in American stores, making their exports less competitive.

Housing bubbles will burst worldwide. The United States isn't the only country that experienced a housing boom in recent years. Easy money and low, long-term interest rates were plentiful in other countries, too, particularly in Europe. The United States also isn't the only country that has experienced a housing bust: Britain, Ireland, and Spain lag only slightly behind the United States as the value of their flats and villas trends downward. Countries with smaller but still substantial real estate bubbles include France, Greece, Hungary, Italy, Portugal, Turkey, and the Baltic nations. In Asia, countries including Australia, China, New Zealand, and Singapore have also experienced modest housing bubbles. There's even been a housing boom in parts of India. Inevitably, such bubbles will burst, as a credit crunch and higher interest rates poke holes in them, leading to a domestic economic slowdown for some and outright recession for others.

Commodity prices will fall. One need only look at the skyrocketing price of oil to see that worldwide demand for commodities has surged in recent years. But those high prices won't last for long. That's because a slowdown of the U.S. and Chinese economies—the two locomotives of global growth—will cause a sharp drop in the demand for commodities such as oil, energy, food, and minerals. The ensuing fall in die prices of those commodities will hurt the exports and growth rate of commodity exporters in Asia, Latin America, and Africa. Take Chile, for example, the world's biggest producer of copper, which is widely used for computer chips and electrical wiring. As demand from the United States and China falls, the price of copper, and therefore Chile's exports of it, will also start to slide.

Financial confidence will falter. The fallout from the U.S. subprime meltdown has already festered into a broader and more severe liquidity and credit crunch on Wall Street. That, in turn, has spilled over to financial markets in other parts of the world. This financial contagion is impossible to contain. A huge portion of the risky, radioactive U.S. securities that have now collapsed—such as the now disgraced residential mortgage-backed securities and collateralized debt obligations—were sold to foreign investors. That's why financial losses from defaulting mortgages in American cities such as Cleveland, Las Vegas, and

Phoenix are now showing up in Australia and Europe, even in small villages in Norway.

Today, central banks' ability to stimulate their economies and dampen the effect of a global slowdown is far more limited than in the past.

Consumer confidence outside the United States—especially in Europe and Japan—was never strong; it can only become weaker as an onslaught of lousy economic news in the United States dampens the spirits of consumers worldwide. And as losses on their U.S. operations hit their books, large multinational firms may decide to cut back new spending on factories and machines not just in the United States but everywhere. European corporations will be hit especially hard, as they depend on bank lending more than American firms do. The emerging global credit crunch will limit their ability to produce, hire, and invest.

The best way to see how this financial flu spreads is by watching global stock markets. Investors become more risk averse when their economies appear to be slowing down. So whenever there's bad economic news in the United States—say, reports of higher unemployment or negative GDP growth—there are worries that other economies will suffer, too. Investors sell off their stocks in New York and the Dow Jones plunges. You can expect a similarly sharp fall when the Nikkei opens in Tokyo a few hours later, and the ripple effect then continues in Europe when opening bells ring in Frankfurt, London, and Paris. It's a vicious circle; the market volatility culminates in a kind of panicky groupthink, causing investors to dump risky assets from their portfolios en masse. Such financial contagion was on prime display when global equity markets plummeted in January.

Money for Nothing

Optimists may believe that central banks can save the world from the painful side effects of an American recession. They may point to the world's recovery from the 2001 recession as a reason for hope. Back then, the U.S. Federal Reserve slashed interest rates from 6.5 percent to 1 percent, the European Central Bank dropped its rate from 4 percent to 2 percent, and the Bank of Japan cut its rate down to zero. But today, the ability of central banks to use monetary tools to stimulate their economies and dampen the effect of a global slowdown is far more limited than in the past. Central banks don't have as free a hand; they are constrained by higher levels of inflation. The Fed is cutting interest rates once again, but it must worry how the disorderly fall of the dollar could cause foreign investors to pull back on their financing of massive U.S. debts. A weaker dollar is a zero-sum game in the global economy; it may benefit the United States, but it hurts the competitiveness and growth of America's trading partners.

Monetary policy will also be less effective this time around because there is an oversupply of housing, automobiles, and other consumer goods. Demand for these goods is less sensitive to changes in interest rates, because it takes years to work out such gluts. A simple tax rebate can hardly be expected to change this fact, especially when credit card debt is mounting and mortgages and auto loans are coming due.

The United States is facing a financial crisis that goes far beyond the subprime problem into areas of economic life that the Fed simply can't reach. The problems the U.S. economy faces are no longer just about not having enough cash on hand; they're about insolvency, and monetary policy is ill equipped to deal with such problems. Millions of households are on the verge of defaulting on their mortgages. Not only have more than 100 subprime lenders gone bankrupt, there are riding delinquencies on more run-of-the-mill mortgages, too. Financial distress has even spread to the kinds of loans that finance excessively risky leveraged buyouts and commercial real estate. When the economy falls further, corporate default rates will sharply rise, leading to greater losses. There is also a "shadow banking system," made up of non-bank financial institutions that borrow cash or liquid investments in the near term, but lend or invest in the long term in nonliquid forms. Take money market funds, for example, which can be withdrawn overnight, or hedge funds, some of which can be redeemed with just one month's notice. Many of these funds are invested and locked into risky, long-term securities. This shadow banking system is therefore subject to greater risk because, unlike banks, they don't have access to the Fed's support as the lender of last resort, cutting them off from the help monetary policy can provide.

Beyond Wall Street, there is also much less room today for fiscal policy stimulus, because the United States, Europe, and Japan all have structural deficits. During the last recession, the United States underwent a nearly 6 percent change in fiscal policy, from a very large surplus of about 2.5 percent of GDP in 2000 to a large deficit of about 3.2 percent of GDP in 2004. But this time, the United States is already running a large structural deficit, and the room for fiscal stimulus is only 1 percent of GDP, as recently agreed upon in President Bush's stimulus package. The situation is similar for Europe and Japan.

President Bush's fiscal stimulus package is too small to make a major difference today, and what the Fed is doing now is too little, too late. It will take years to resolve the problems that led to this crisis. Poor regulation of mortgages, a lack of transparency about complex financial products, misguided incentive schemes in the compensation of bankers, wrongheaded credit ratings, poor risk management by financial institutions—the list goes on and on.

Ultimately, in today's flat world, interdependence boosts growth across countries in good times. Unfortunately, these trade and financial links also mean that an economic slowdown in one place can drag down everyone else. Not every country will follow the United States into an outright recession, but no one can claim to be immune.

NOURIEL ROUBINI is chairman of RGE Monitor and professor of economics at New York University's Stern School of Business.

UNIT 7

U.S. Military Strategy

Unit Selections

Key Points to Consider

- Is military power an effective instrument of foreign policy today? What problems is it best and least capable of solving?

- Does arms control have a future? Can it make the United States more secure, or does it weaken U.S. security?

- How should we think about nuclear weapons today? What is their purpose? Who should they be targeted against? What dangers must we guard against?

- How great is the terrorist threat to the United States? What steps should the United States take to protect itself from terrorist attacks?

- Develop a list of "dos and don'ts" to guide American troops when they are called upon to act as occupation forces.

- Under what conditions should the United States engage in peace-keeping activities?

- Can nuclear proliferation be stopped? What strategy would you recommend?

Student Web Site

www.mhcls.com/online

Internet References

Arms Control and Disarmament Agency (ACDA)
   http://dosfan.lib.uic.edu/acda/
Counterterrorism Page
   http://counterterrorism.com
DefenseLINK
   http://www.defenselink.mil/news/
Federation of American Scientists (FAS)
   http://www.fas.org
Human Rights Web
   http://www.hrweb.org

During the peak of the Cold War, American defense planners often thought in terms of needing a two-and-a-half war capacity: the simultaneous ability to fight major wars in Europe and Asia plus a smaller conflict elsewhere. The principal protagonists in this drama were well known: the Soviet Union and China. The stakes were also clear. Communism represented a global threat to American political democracy and economic prosperity. It was a conflict in which both sides publicly proclaimed that there could be but one winner. The means for deterring and fighting such challenges included strategic, tactical, and battlefield nuclear weapons; large numbers of conventional forces; alliance systems; arms transfers; and the development of a guerrilla war capability.

Until September 11, 2001, the political-military landscape of the post-Cold War world lacked any comparable enemy or military threat. Instead, the principal challenges to American foreign policy-makers were those of deciding what humanitarian interventions to undertake and how deeply to become involved. Kosovo, East Timor, Somalia, Bosnia, Rwanda, and Haiti each produced its own answer, which presented American policy-makers with a new type of military challenge in the form of humanitarian interventions. The challenge of formulating an effective military policy to deal with situations where domestic order has unraveled due to ethnic conflict and bottled-up political pressures for reform still remains unmet. However, they are no longer viewed as first-order security problems in the post-Cold War era.

With the terrorist attacks on the World Trade Center and the Pentagon, a more clearly defined enemy has emerged. Formulating a military strategy to defeat this enemy promises to be no easy task. President George W. Bush acknowledged as much in defining his war against terrorism as a new type of warfare and one that would not end quickly. To date, the war against terrorism has led to two wars, one that brought down the Taliban government in Afghanistan and one that brought down Saddam Hussein in Iraq. It also brought forward a new national security strategy centered on preemption in place of deterrence. And, most unexpectedly, from the point of view of the Bush administration, it has placed the American military squarely in the business of nation building and face-to-face with the problem of fighting counterinsurgencies.

The first essay in this unit is by Andrew Bacevich. In "Requiem for the Bush Doctrine" he argues that the Iraq War demonstrated that the United States cannot implement a policy of preventive war. Bacevich outlines the requirements for such a strategy to work and finds that the U.S. military is not up to the task. The second essay, "Outsourcing War," looks at the reasons why the United States has begun to rely on private military firms such as Blackwater to carry out tasks that once were performed by professional military units and the problems this causes for U.S. security interests. The third essay looks at the history of preemptive military strikes. In "Preemption Paradox" Bennett Ramberg finds that such attacks only buy time and that they hold profound risks for the attackers. Steve Metz looks at the problem of

understanding 21st century insurgencies in "New Challenges and Old Concepts." He argues that today's insurgencies are different from those of the 20th century that strategists turn to for lessons. Instead of viewing them in a war context, Metz argues they should be looked at as violent competitive markets. The goal now should be to deter insurgencies and end them quickly rather than try to fight and win in the long struggle. The final essay in this section, "A Nuclear Posture for Today" raises the question of what type of nuclear strategy should the United States pursue. John Deutch, a former head of the CIA, argues against abolishing the nuclear force and calls for one that is capable of preventing a nuclear attack on the United States and responding to lesser contingencies.

Changes in the nature of the military threats that confront the United States have led to changes in the arms control agenda. The old arms control agenda was dominated by a concern for reducing the size of U.S. and Soviet nuclear inventories. A much broader agenda exists today and it is one with many more players. Its core is the problem of dealing with weapons of mass destruction, and the question of whether a national ballistic missile system is an important part of the solution to the problem. In the first essay, David Albright takes up the question of "When Could Iran Get the Bomb?" The present scenarios suggest that it will take at least three years and he calls for renewed international efforts to slow or stop movement in this direction. Jack Mendelsohn argues that the United States is suffering from nuclear amnesia and have forgotten how destructive nuclear weapons really are. In "The New Threats" he calls for delegitimizing nuclear weapons and relegating them to the status of weapons of last resort. In the final essay, "Ban the Bomb. Really.," long time nuclear commentator Michael Krepon calls for abolishing nuclear weapons. He argues we have entered into a fourth wave of nuclear abolitionist thinking that differs from the three that preceded it in terms of its underlying dynamics. Krepon argues that it may be difficult to reach this goal, but it is the United States that has more steering capacity than any other country, to move the world in this direction.

Requiem for the Bush Doctrine

"The Iraq War has revealed that the armed forces possess nothing like the depth required to implement a policy of preventive war on a sustained basis."

ANDREW J. BACEVICH

The claim that 9-11 "changed everything" is demonstrably false. What did change as a consequence of that awful day was basic US policy regarding the use of force. Having now been tested and found wanting, that new policy—known as the Bush Doctrine—may already be on its way to the ash heap of history.

Before September 11, 2001, American presidents routinely insisted that when the United States went to war it did so only defensively and as a last resort. Although not always supported by the facts related to the nation's rise to the status of sole superpower, this sentiment accorded nicely with America's self-image as a peaceful nation.

According to President George W. Bush, the events of 9-11 rendered those views obsolete, if not dangerous. In the face of violent Islamic radicals for whom no act, however barbarous, was beyond the pale, the administration concluded that cold war-style deterrence could no longer be counted on to work. Convinced that the prospect of these radicals gaining possession of weapons of mass destruction was not only real but becoming more acute by the day, Bush and his lieutenants determined that the United States could not afford to let the other side fire the first shot. Waging war against the unprecedented menace posed by global terror now obliged the United States to go permanently on the offensive.

Henceforth, the United States needed to shoot first even if that meant acting on fragmentary evidence. In a post–9-11 world, the Bush administration insisted, the risks of delay outweighed the risks of precipitate action. As then-national security adviser Condoleezza Rice famously remarked with regard to Iraq, "We don't want the smoking gun to be a mushroom cloud." The new imperative was to eliminate threats before they could mature.

President Bush unveiled this new doctrine in a speech to graduating cadets at West Point delivered on June 1, 2002. "The gravest danger to freedom," he declared, was to be found at "the perilous crossroads of radicalism and technology." Old conceptions of deterrence meant "nothing against shadowy terrorist networks with no nation or citizens to defend." Rather than passively allowing this enemy to seize the initiative, Bush told the cadets that "we must take the battle to the enemy, disrupt his plans, and confront the worst threats before they emerge. In the world we have entered, the only path to safety is the path of action. And this nation will act."

The president went on to explain that the United States would "be ready for preemptive action when necessary." But the substance of his remarks indicated clearly that he was referring not to preemption,

but to preventive war. The distinction is crucial. Preemption implies launching a war when facing the clear prospect of imminent attack—as, for example, the state of Israel did in June 1967. Preventive war implies initiating hostilities to eliminate the possibility that an adversary might pose a future threat, again as Israel did in its 1981 attack on the partially assembled Iraqi nuclear reactor at Osirak. Effective June 2002, the United States embraced the concept of preventive war. This is the essence of the Bush Doctrine.

Assuming Power

Formidable moral and legal objections have been raised against the doctrine of preventive war. Critics have charged that the Bush Doctrine violates the Charter of the United Nations, and that it opens a Pandora's box, inviting any number of other nations to cite the US precedent as a pretext for their own preventive wars. According to the doctrine's logic, Israel could easily find justification for attacking Iran—and Iran could justifiably attack Israel.

But even leaving such objections aside, a doctrine of preventive war makes sense only if it works—that is, if its implementation yields enhanced security at a reasonable cost. In the American case, the Bush administration's belief in the efficacy of preventive war stemmed from its confidence in American military power. In his introduction to the *National Security Strategy* that the White House issued in September 2002, President Bush wrote that "today the United States enjoys a position of unparalleled military strength." The assumption underlying the Bush Doctrine, never made explicit, was that the unparalleled quality and capabilities of America's armed services made preventive war plausible.

In March 2003, the president implemented the Bush Doctrine, ordering the invasion of Iraq. In doing so, he also put to the test his administration's assumptions about American military power. That test has now continued long enough for us to draw some preliminary conclusions.

The most important of these conclusions is the following: as measured by the effectiveness and capacity of American arms, the quality of American generalship, and the adherence of American soldiers to professional norms, this administration has badly misread what the US military can and cannot do. The sword of American military power is neither sharp enough nor hard enough to meet the demands of preventive war.

At the very top, US military leadership has been at best mediocre if not altogether unsatisfactory.

Stalemate in Iraq

The Bush Doctrine requires military forces able, in the words of the *National Security Strategy,* to "conduct rapid and precise operations to achieve decisive results." Preventive war demands a quick kill. Victory gained swiftly and economically is not only a value in itself. It also conveys an exemplary message to others: resistance is pointless. Such a victory can serve to overawe other would-be adversaries, thereby limiting the occasions requiring the actual use of force.

In Iraq, decisive results have proved elusive. Although the initial march on Baghdad provided ample opportunity for US forces to demonstrate speed and impressive precision, successfully toppling the regime of Saddam Hussein produced not an end to war, but a wider conflict. As is so often the case in war, the enemy has refused to follow our script.

Whether this wider war resulted from carefully laid enemy plans or emerged spontaneously out of the chaos created by Hussein's overthrow hardly matters. The fact is that over two and a half years after launching Operation Iraqi Freedom with high hopes and great fanfare, the United States finds itself mired in a conflict that in a strictly military sense may be unwinnable. The armed forces that innumerable commentators have proclaimed the most advanced and most sophisticated that the world has ever seen have been stymied by 10,000 to 20,000 insurgents equipped with an arsenal of weapons dating from the 1940s and 1950s.

The enterprise launched with expectations of pocketing a quick military success has now evolved into a project that even administration officials concede may drag on for a decade or more. Although President Bush continues to insist that his aim in Iraq is "victory," senior military officers have been signaling just as clearly that extricating the United States from Iraq will require a political solution, which implies something less than vanquishing the enemy. "This insurgency is not going to be settled . . . through military options or military operations," Brigadier General Donald Alston, the chief US military spokesman in Baghdad, acknowledged this summer. "It's going to be settled in the political process."

In Iraq, the American way of war devised in the 1980s and refined during the 1990s has come up short. In the heady aftermath of Operation Desert Storm, the Pentagon had grandly announced that this novel approach to warfare, with its emphasis on advanced technology and air power, was providing US forces with what it called "full spectrum dominance." According to its proponents, the new model of waging war promised to banish "fog" and "friction," the terms coined by Karl von Clausewitz to describe the qualities that had throughout history made combat such an arduous, perplexing, and chancy proposition. But in Iraq fog blankets the battlefield: after more than two years of fighting, the enemy remains a cipher. And friction, which according to Clausewitz "makes even the simplest thing difficult" on the battlefield, has been omnipresent.

The significance of this military failure—and by the standards of preventive war, the Iraq War cannot be otherwise categorized—extends beyond the conflict immediately at hand. As the astute commentator Owen Harries has noted, the conflict in Iraq has shattered the "mystique" of US forces. All the world now knows that an army once thought to be unstoppable can be fought to a standstill. Thirty years after its defeat in Vietnam, it turns out that the United States still does not know how to counter a determined guerrilla force. Far from overawing other would-be opponents, the Iraq War has provided them with a template for how to fight the world's most powerful military to a stalemate—a lesson that other potential adversaries from Pyongyang to Tehran have no doubt taken to heart.

According to an ancient principle of statecraft, the reputation of power is itself power. By deflating the reputation of US forces, the Iraq War has considerably diminished the power of the United States and by extension has called into question the continued utility of the Bush Doctrine.

Empty Boots

The Bush Doctrine assumed not only that the United States had devised methods that endowed coercion with unprecedented effectiveness, but also that US forces possessed the wherewithal to employ these methods anywhere in the world. America's global leadership rests, in this view, on a capacity for global power projection. Yet the Iraq War has revealed that the armed forces possess nothing like the depth required to implement a policy of preventive war on a sustained basis. Our actual staying power has turned out to be far more limited than expected.

In *Imperial Grunts,* his just published tribute to militarized global empire, the author Robert Kaplan writes that "by the turn of the twenty-first century, the United States military had already appropriated the entire earth, and was ready to flood the most obscure areas of it with troops at a moment's notice." While an effective policy of preventive war may well require an ability to flood obscure areas with troops, recent events have demonstrated conclusively that the United States does not possess that ability. A commitment of approximately 140,000 troops to Iraq along with a far smaller contingent in Afghanistan has just about exhausted the resources of the US Army and Marine Corps.

Some of those most critical of the Bush administration's handling of the Iraq War argue that the key to breaking the stalemate in Iraq is to send more American troops. In fact, the soldiers needed to do so do not exist.

In September 2001, when President Bush committed the United States to an open-ended global war against terror, he chose not to increase the size of America's military establishment. It was the first time in its history that the United States embarked on a major conflict without expanding its armed services, the president and his advisers tacitly assuming that the existing active duty force of 1.4 million backed up by reserves would suffice for whatever tasks lay ahead. Rather than summoning his fellow citizens to the colors, President Bush famously urged them to go on vacation to rescue the ailing airline industry.

The president's belief that the existing military was large enough turned out to be deeply flawed. Four years after 9-11, the reserves are close to breaking—both recruiting and reenlistment are in free-fall. As for active duty forces, in fiscal year 2005 the heavily burdened US Army experienced its worst recruiting year in over a quarter-century. Whether or not sufficient numbers of volunteers can be found to maintain even the existing force has emerged as a pressing question, despite the fact that at present only 0.5 percent of the American population is in uniform.

The Strange Triumph of Unilateralism

G. John Ikenberry

Over the past few years almost all of the world's global and regional governance institutions have weakened. Indeed, it is possible to observe a systematic erosion of the authority and capacities of international institutions and regimes in the security, economic, and political realms. In the 1970s, Samuel Huntington, Michel Crozier, and Joji Watanuki wrote about the "crisis of governability" in the advanced democratic world, in which governments were losing the ability and public confidence to confront fundamental problems of managing domestic economies and addressing crime and welfare. Today, it appears as if the governance crisis has gone global.

- *The United Nations.* At a September summit, member states failed to agree on "grand bargain" reforms of the Security Council. The UN is still vital in peacekeeping and supervising elections, but efforts to make it a central vehicle for global security cooperation and collective decision-making on the use of force have failed. UN management is under a cloud, and efforts to implement reforms have been frustrated.
- *The European Union.* Voters this spring rejected the EU constitution, and Europeans are in the midst of a continent-wide rethinking about what comes next. This is a setback for those who would like Europe to play a more active global role in providing leadership and public goods. The federal vision of Europe is dead. In its place is European political drift.
- *NATO.* The Atlantic alliance still exists, but it has declined as a vehicle for serious strategic cooperation between the United States and Europe. Washington is drawing down its troop deployments in Germany, and the idea of an Atlantic security community increasingly has a ring of nostalgia about it.
- *The G-8 Summit.* Aside from the Bonn summit of 1978, the Group of Eight has always been a disappointment as a mechanism for summoning collective action.
- *World Trade Organization.* The WTO is perhaps the strongest link in the global system of rule-based cooperation. But efforts to reach agreement on agriculture subsidies and other tough issues so far have failed. In the meantime, narrow bilateral or regional trade agreements are proliferating. Some argue that the age of big, multilateral trade agreements is over.
- *The nuclear nonproliferation regime.* Most people outside of Washington think the nuclear Non-Proliferation Treaty is in crisis. The bargains have broken down. Washington has ignored NPT obligations; the Bush administration did not even send the secretary of state to this year's five-year review meeting. Overall, treaty-based arms control is going nowhere, and the United States has pulled back from or resisted a wide range of global security treaties.
- *The American provision of governance.* It is often remarked that the United States itself is a "private" provider of governance through enlightened—if self-interested—rule making and institution building. This "liberal hegemonic" logic of international order, which informed American foreign policy in the past, has been partially replaced by a conservative nationalist logic that questions the whole idea of global governance and rule-based order.

More Demand, Less Supply

It is not unfair to ask: where are the vibrant and growing global and regional institutions to help us collectively tackle the great problems of our age? If the United States is not providing "private" global governance, and if the postwar institutions and functional regimes run by the United States and the other "stake holders" of the international system are in decline or disrepair, where is this taking us? Are we in an era when the demand for cooperative mechanisms and institutionalized collective action is growing but the supply is dwindling? It sure looks like it.

There are several possible explanations for this observed crisis of governance. First, it is possible that the basic observation is wrong—governance is not in decline. Realists would say: certainly there is a crisis in global governance, but it is a 500-year crisis, if not longer. The underprovision of cooperation is inherent in world politics. Things are neither worse nor better than at earlier moments. We should be thankful for the long pause in great-power war and the failure of other major states to balance against the United States.

Second, much of the crisis may have to do with shifts in US policy. This is the hegemonic stability argument—namely, that the supply of rules and institutions ultimately hinges on the logic of behavior that informs the most powerful state in the system. Today, the United States does not have an inclination to sponsor, support, fund, and enforce global rules and institutions.

Third, the crisis may be driven by an inability to infuse international regimes and institutions with democratic accountability and legitimacy. The failure of the European constitution may be the most direct casualty of this sort of constraint. But it may be a more general problem of building and pooling authority above the level of states.

Fourth, more cooperation may be taking place, but just not in the old-style global treaty-based institutional way. Princeton's Anne-Marie Slaughter argues that an entire world of intergovernmental networks is flourishing below the political radar screen. They tend to be informal, practical, and executive-based. They escape the problem of democratic accountability largely because they operate unnoticed. The implication of this view is that there is really not a crisis of governance, merely a shift in the forms of governance.

Finally, there is a view that the crisis is real but is driven by deep shifts in the nature of the challenges that states face. In the economic realm, for example, multilateral trade rules and cooperation were possible during the long postwar era when tariff barriers were the most important impediments to open trade. Tariff reduction lent itself to multilateral exercises. Today, the blockages are built into domestic legislation—blockages that are more difficult to negotiate in global multilateral settings. Likewise, some observers argue that the new security threats—weapons of mass destruction in the hands of illegitimate, unstable, or untrustworthy states—cannot be handled by treaty-based arms control regimes that emerged in the decades of US-Soviet bipolar nuclear summitry. The crisis of governance in this view is driven by a mismatch between the nature of the problems confronting states and the traditional ways in which collective action has been organized.

Made in Washington

So which is it? As descriptions of the current landscape, these are not all competing or mutually exclusive. New forms of informal cooperation are evident. Still, it is clear something is very wrong with the current system of governance. Looking into the future—with the growing complexities and dangers associated with continued globalization of economies, societies, and cultures and the privatization of technologies of violence—it is obvious that the world will need more, not less, institutionalized cooperation. If we are in an age of declining institutionalized cooperation, well, ergo—we do have a growing problem or, yes, crisis.

In my view, the crisis is generated primarily from choices made by the United States. Washington does not appear to be doing as much today as in the past to sponsor and operate within a system of consensual rule-based governance. Why America is less willing to do so is actually a complex issue. Some of it is very specifically about the Bush administration, and thus about biases and viewpoints that eventually will pass from the scene as President Bush and his team leave office.

But there are also deeper structural shifts in the United States and the global system that make Washington less interested in rule and governance provision. American unipolarity seems to have created problems in how the United States thinks about the provision of international rules, institutions, and public goods. In the past, America provided globbal "services"—such as security protection and support for open markets—that made other states willing to work with rather than resist US preeminence. The public goods provision tended to make it worthwhile for these states to endure the day-to-day irritations of American foreign policy. But the trade-off seems to be shifting. Today, the United States appears to be providing fewer global public goods while at the same time the irritations associated with US dominance seem to be growing.

It might be useful to think of the dynamic this way: the United States is unique in that it is simultaneously both a provider of global governance and a great power that pursues its own national interest. When America acts as a "liberal hegemon,"championing the WTO, for example, or reaffirming its commitment to cooperative security in Asia and Europe, it is seeking to lead or manage the global system of rules and institutions. When it is acting as a nationalist great power, by protecting its steel and textile industries, for example, it is seeking to respond to domestic interests and its relative power position among nations. And today, these two roles—liberal hegemon and traditional great power—increasingly are in conflict.

G. John Ikenberry, a *Current History* contributing editor, is a professor of politics and international affairs at Princeton University. A version of this commentary originally appeared in "America Abroad" at TPMCafe.com.

Without question, the Pentagon's arsenal contains a sufficient number of bombers, missiles, and attack aircraft carriers to launch strikes against Syria or Iran or North Korea, as some supporters of the Bush Doctrine might advocate. But if the requirement goes beyond inflicting punishment—if it includes putting "boots on the ground"—then the men and women to fill those boots are in increasingly scarce supply.

The Bush Doctrine has brought into sharp relief a mismatch between the administration's declared ambitions and the military resources available to pursue those ambitions. Yet, having decided after 9-11 not to mobilize the country, President Bush cannot now ask Americans to cancel their vacations and instead report to their local recruiter.

Habits of the Highly Ineffective

A doctrine of preventive war also assumes the availability of military leaders who can effectively translate into action the directives of their political masters. It is one thing to order a preventive war; it is another thing to win it.

Ever since the armed services recovered from the debacle of Vietnam, quality leadership has been a hallmark of the American military establishment. Members of the officer corps take their profession seriously. Nothing in the tactical performance of US forces in Iraq or Afghanistan ought to raise second thoughts on that score. The lieutenants, captains, and colonels know their business. They are smart, seasoned, and tough. Whether military leaders at the topmost echelon of command understand the operational and strategic imperatives of preventive war may be another matter, however.

In all of the controversy that the Iraq War has generated, the performance of the most senior US officers—the three- and four-star commanders— has attracted surprisingly little attention. Yet a strong argument can be made that at the very top, US military leadership has been at best mediocre if not altogether unsatisfactory. Two examples will suffice to make the point: General Tommy Franks and Lieutenant General Ricardo Sanchez.

As commanding general of US Central Command, Franks planned and directed the invasions of Afghanistan and Iraq. In Afghanistan, the forces commanded by Franks handily toppled the Taliban regime and scattered, but did not destroy, the Al Qaeda cadres that had used Afghanistan as a safe haven. Osama bin Laden, Al Qaeda's supreme leader and the chief architect of the 9-11 attacks, eluded capture and remains at large. Although ousted from power, the Taliban refused to submit to the new American-installed political order. The effort to pacify Afghanistan continues, a low-level war that may become virtually perpetual. The decision gained by Franks in Afghanistan qualifies at best as partial and incomplete.

By comparison with Iraq, however, Afghanistan looks like a triumph. When it came to planning Operation Iraqi Freedom, General Franks counted on "shock and awe" to paralyze the Iraqi army and facilitate a lightning advance on the Iraqi capital, seen as the centerpiece of Baathist legitimacy. For Franks, Baghdad in 2003 became like Berlin in 1945: capturing it, he believed, meant endgame.

The sword of American military power is neither sharp enough nor hard enough to meet the demands of preventive war.

Even before the war began, dissenting voices warned otherwise. Studies undertaken by the State Department and the US Army War College forecast major challenges *after* Hussein and his henchmen had been removed. Most famously, General Eric Shinseki, then the army chief of staff, suggested that the occupation of Iraq was likely to require "several hundred thousand" soldiers.

These warnings turned out to be prescient. Franks failed to appreciate the political forces that Hussein's removal from power would unleash. His planning for "Phase IV"—the occupation of Iraq—verged on the non-existent. As a consequence, the disorder produced by the overthrow of Hussein caught Franks and his subordinates flat-footed. Out of that disorder there emerged an intense struggle to determine the future of Iraq, a struggle that soon became an insurgency that aimed to oust the "occupying" Americans.

Hardly had the outlines of that insurgency begun to emerge than Franks departed the scene, retiring to write his best-selling memoirs (in which he dismisses Shinseki as an ill-informed meddler). The man inheriting the mess that Franks left in his wake was General Sanchez, who served as senior US ground commander in Iraq for the insurgency's first full year. His mission was clear: snuff out the insurgency. Instead, Sanchez fueled it.

Historians of the Iraq War will likely remember Sanchez as this conflict's William C. Westmoreland—the senior commander who, in failing to grasp the political-military nature of the problem he faced, set US forces on an erroneous course from which recovery became all but impossible.

General Westmoreland, of course, was the senior US commander in South Vietnam from 1964 to 1968. Working within the very narrow constraints imposed on him by the Johnson administration, he concluded that the best way to defend South Vietnam was to capitalize on superior US firepower and mobility to crush the North Vietnamese communists. Westmoreland committed the United States to a protracted war of attrition, confident that his forces could inflict casualties at a rate that the enemy could not sustain. He miscalculated and the ultimate result was American defeat.

Similarly, Sanchez in 2003 judged the correlation of forces in Iraq to be in his favor and decided that a tough, aggressive strategy would disarm the insurgency before it could gain momentum. He too miscalculated, as badly as Westmoreland had. Rather than intimidating the insurgents, his kick-down-the-door tactics emboldened them and alienated ordinary Iraqis who came to see the Americans not as liberators but as an alien occupying force. Over the course of Sanchez's tenure in Baghdad, the insurgency grew in scope and sophistication. His successors have been struggling ever since to regain the upper hand. Today, the conflict drags on, eroding American popular support for the war and sapping the strength of the forces engaged. A doctrine of preventive war requires that the forces engaged accomplish their mission swiftly, economically, and without leaving loose ends. The generals employed to implement the Bush Doctrine have not demonstrated an ability to deliver those results.

The Tarnished Military

Especially in a democracy, a doctrine of preventive war also requires soldiers who manifest a consistently high level of professionalism. To maintain public support for what is, stripped to its essentials, a policy of aggression, the military forces committed to the enterprise must acquit themselves with honor, thereby making it easier to suppress questions about the war's moral justification. As long as US soldiers in Iraq behave like liberators, for example, it becomes easier for President Bush to maintain the position that America's true purpose is to spread the blessings of freedom and democracy.

Sadly, in the dirty war that Iraq has become, a number of American soldiers have behaved in ways that have undermined the administration's liberation narrative. This is a story in which the facts are as yet only partially known. But this much we can say for sure: after the revelations from Abu Ghraib prison and the credible allegations lodged recently by Captain Ian Fishback regarding widespread detainee abuse in the 82d Airborne Division, and with other accounts of misconduct steadily accumulating from week to week, it is no longer possible to pass off soldierly misbehavior as the late-night shenanigans of a few low-ranking sadists lacking adequate supervision. Unprofessional behavior in the ranks of the American military may not have reached epidemic proportions, but it is far from rare.

More sadly still, the chain of command seems determined to turn a blind eye to this growing problem. The courageous Fishback labored for 18 months to interest his superiors in the problem that he had witnessed in Iraq. Only when he brought his concerns to the attention of Human Rights Watch and the US Congress did anyone take notice. A year and a half after the Abu Ghraib scandal broke, the only senior officer to have been held accountable is a female reservist, Brigadier General Janis Karpinski, who was demoted and forced to retire. Karpinski's complaint of an old boy's club using her as a convenient scapegoat is self-serving, but it may well contain an element of truth. The American officer corps once professed to hold sacrosanct the principle of command responsibility. No more. At the very least it no longer applies to those occupying the executive suites in Baghdad and Washington.

The US military may well be teetering on the brink of a profound moral crisis. Another conflict like Iraq could easily prove the tipping point. That prospect alone ought to temper the Bush administration's enthusiasm for any further experiments with preventive war. At its conception, the Bush Doctrine represented a radical departure from the best traditions of American statecraft. Efforts to implement the doctrine have cost the nation and especially its military dearly without appreciably enhancing American security. It is too much to expect that this administration, committed to the proposition that it must never acknowledge error, will officially abrogate the Bush Doctrine. But the administration ignores reality at its peril. As it contemplates the wreckage caused by its preventive war in Iraq, the White House may well come to see the wisdom of allowing the Bush Doctrine to die a quiet and unlamented death.

ANDREW J. BACEVICH is a professor of international relations at Boston University. His most recent book is *The New American Militarism: How Americans Are Seduced by War* (Oxford University Press, 2005).

Outsourcing War

P. W. SINGER

Understanding the Private Military Industry

The tales of war, profit, honor, and greed that emerge from the private military industry often read like something out of a Hollywood screenplay. They range from action-packed stories of guns-for-hire fighting off swarms of insurgents in Iraq to the sad account of a private military air crew languishing in captivity in Colombia, abandoned by their corporate bosses in the United States. A recent African "rent-a-coup" scandal involved the son of a former British prime minister, and accusations of war profiteering have reached into the halls of the White House itself.

Incredible as these stories often sound, the private military industry is no fiction. Private companies are becoming significant players in conflicts around the world, supplying not merely the goods but also the services of war. Although recent well-publicized incidents from Abu Ghraib to Zimbabwe have shone unaccustomed light onto this new force in warfare, private military firms (PMFs) remain a poorly understood—and often unacknowledged—phenomenon. Mystery, myth, and conspiracy theory surround them, leaving policymakers and the public in positions of dangerous ignorance. Many key questions remain unanswered, including, What is this industry and where did it come from? What is its role in the United States' largest current overseas venture, Iraq? What are the broader implications of that role? And how should policymakers respond? Only by developing a better understanding of this burgeoning industry can governments hope to get a proper hold on this newly powerful force in foreign policy. If they fail, the consequences for policy and democracy could be deeply destructive.

Private Sector and Public Interest

PMFs are businesses that provide governments with professional services intricately linked to warfare; they represent, in other words, the corporate evolution of the age-old profession of mercenaries. Unlike the individual dogs of war of the past, however, PMFs are corporate bodies that offer a wide range of services, from tactical combat operations and strategic planning to logistical support and technical assistance.

The modern private military industry emerged at the start of the 1990s, driven by three dynamics: the end of the Cold War, transformations in the nature of warfare that blurred the lines between soldiers and civilians, and a general trend toward privatization and outsourcing of government functions around the world. These three forces fed into each other. When the face-off between the United States and the Soviet Union ended, professional armies around the world were downsized. At the same time, increasing global instability created a demand for more troops. Warfare in the developing world also became messier—more chaotic and less professional—involving forces ranging from warlords to child soldiers, while Western powers became more reluctant to intervene. Meanwhile, advanced militaries grew increasingly reliant on off-the-shelf commercial technology, often maintained and operated by private firms. And finally, many governments succumbed to an ideological trend toward the privatization of many of their functions; a whole raft of former state responsibilities—including education, policing, and the operation of prisons—were turned over to the marketplace.

The PMFs that arose as a result are not all alike, nor do they all offer the exact same services. The industry is divided into three basic sectors: military provider firms (also known as "private security firms"), which offer tactical military assistance, including actual combat services, to clients; military consulting firms, which employ retired officers to provide strategic advice and military training; and military support firms, which provide logistics, intelligence, and maintenance services to armed forces, allowing the latter's soldiers to concentrate on combat and reducing their government's need to recruit more troops or call up more reserves.

Although the world's most dominant military has become increasingly reliant on PMFs (the Pentagon has entered into more than 3,000 such contracts over the last decade), the industry and its clientele are not just American. Private military companies have operated in more than 50 nations, on every continent but Antarctica. For example, European militaries, which lack the means to transport and support their forces overseas, are now greatly dependent on PMFs for such functions. To get to Afghanistan, European troops relied on a Ukrainian firm that, under a contract worth more than $100 million, ferried them there in former Soviet jets. And the British military, following in the Pentagon's footsteps, has begun to contract out its logistics to Halliburton.

Nowhere has the role of PMFs been more integral—and more controversial—than in Iraq. Not only is Iraq now the site of the single largest U.S. military commitment in more than a decade; it is also the marketplace for the largest deployment of PMFs and personnel ever. More than 60 firms currently employ more than 20,000 private personnel there to carry out military functions (these figures do not include the thousands more that provide nonmilitary reconstruction and oil services)—roughly the same number as are provided by all of the United States' coalition partners combined. President George W. Bush's "coalition of the willing" might thus be more aptly described as the "coalition of the billing."

These large numbers have incurred large risks. Private military contractors have suffered an estimated 175 deaths and 900 wounded so far in Iraq (precise numbers are unavailable because the Pentagon does not track nonmilitary casualties)—more than any single U.S. Army division and more than the rest of the coalition combined.

More important than the raw numbers is the wide scope of critical jobs that contractors are now carrying out, far more extensive in Iraq than in past wars. In addition to war-gaming and field training U.S. troops before the invasion, private military personnel handled logistics and support during the war's buildup. The massive U.S. complex at Camp Doha in Kuwait, which served as the launch pad for the invasion, was not only built by a PMF but also operated and guarded by one. During the invasion, contractors maintained and loaded many of the most sophisticated U.S. weapons systems, such as B-2 stealth bombers and Apache helicopters. They even helped operate combat systems such as the Army's Patriot missile batteries and the Navy's Aegis missile-defense system.

PMFs—ranging from well-established companies such as Vinnell and mpri to startups such as the South African firm Erinys International—have played an even greater role in the postinvasion occupation and counterinsurgency effort. Halliburton's Kellogg, Brown & Root division, the largest corporate PMF in Iraq, currently provides supplies for troops and maintenance for equipment under a contract thought to be worth as much as $13 billion. (This figure, in current dollars, is roughly two and a half times what the United States paid to fight the entire 1991 Persian Gulf War, and roughly the same as what it spent to fight the American Revolution, the War of 1812, the Mexican-American War, and the Spanish-American War combined.) Other PMFs are helping to train local forces, including the new Iraqi army and national police, and are playing a range of tactical military roles.

An estimated 6,000 non-Iraqi private contractors currently carry out armed tactical functions in the country. These individuals are sometimes described as "security guards," but they are a far cry from the rent-a-cops who troll the food courts of U.S. shopping malls. In Iraq, their jobs include protecting important installations, such as corporate enclaves, U.S. facilities, and the Green Zone in Baghdad; guarding key individuals (Ambassador Paul Bremer, the head of the Coalition Provisional Authority, was protected by a Blackwater team that even had its own armed helicopters); and escorting convoys, a particularly dangerous task thanks to the frequency of roadside ambushes and bombings by the insurgents.

PMFs, in other words, have been essential to the U.S. effort in Iraq, helping Washington make up for its troop shortage and doing jobs that U.S. forces would prefer not to. But they have also been involved in some of the most controversial aspects of the war, including alleged corporate profiteering and abuse of Iraqi prisoners.

Five Obstructions

The mixed record of PMFs in Iraq points to some of the underlying problems and questions related to the industry's increasing role in U.S. policy. Five broad policy dilemmas are raised by the increasing privatization of the military.

The first involves the question of profit in a military context. To put it bluntly, the incentives of a private company do not always align with its clients' interests—or the public good. In an ideal world, this problem could be kept in check through proper management and oversight; in reality, such scrutiny is often absent. As a result, war-profiteering allegations have been thrown at several firms. For example, Halliburton—Vice President Dick Cheney's previous employer—has been accused of a number of abuses in Iraq, ranging from overcharging for gasoline to billing for services not rendered; the disputed charges now total $1.8 billion. And Custer Battles, a startup military provider firm that was featured on the front page of the Wall Street Journal in August 2004 has since been accused of running a fraudulent scheme of subsidiaries and false charges.

Still more worrisome from a policy standpoint is the question of lost control. Even when contractors do military jobs, they remain private businesses and thus fall outside the military chain of command and justice systems. Unlike military units, PMFs retain a choice over which contracts they will take and can abandon or suspend operations for any reason, including if they become too dangerous or unprofitable; their employees, unlike soldiers, can always choose to walk off the job. Such freedom can leave the military in the lurch, as has occurred several times already in Iraq: during periods of intense violence, numerous private firms delayed, suspended, or ended their operations, placing great stress on U.S. troops. On other occasions, PMF employees endured even greater risks and dangers than their military equivalents. But military operations do not have room for such mixed results.

The second general challenge with PMFs stems from the unregulated nature of what has become a global industry. There are insufficient controls over who can work for these firms and for whom these firms can work. The recruiting, screening, and hiring of individuals for public military roles is left in private hands. In Iraq, this problem was magnified by the gold-rush effect: many firms entering the market were either entirely new to the business or had rapidly expanded. To be fair, many PMF employees are extremely well qualified. A great number of retired U.S. special forces operatives have served with PMFs in Iraq, as have former members of the United Kingdom's elite sas (Special Air Service). But the rush for profits has led some corporations to cut corners in their screening procedures. For example, U.S. Army investigators of the Abu Ghraib prisoner-abuse scandal found that "approximately 35 percent of the contract interrogators [hired by the firm caci] lacked formal military training as interrogators." In other cases, investigations of contractors serving in Iraq revealed the hiring of a former British Army soldier who had been jailed for working with Irish terrorists and a former South African soldier who had admitted to firebombing the houses of more than 60 political activists during the apartheid era.

Similar problems can occur with PMFs' clientele. Although military contractors have worked for democratic governments, the UN, and even humanitarian and environmental organizations, they have also been employed by dictatorships, rebel groups, drug cartels, and, prior to September 11, 2001, at least two al Qaeda-linked jihadi groups. A recent episode in Equatorial Guinea illustrates the problems that PMFs can run into in the absence of external guidance or rules. In March 2004, Logo Logistics, a British-South African PMF, was accused of plotting to overthrow the government in Malabo; a planeload of employees was arrested in Zimbabwe, and several alleged funders in the British aristocracy (including Sir Mark Thatcher, the son of Margaret Thatcher) were soon implicated in the scandal. The plotters have been accused of trying to topple Equatorial Guinea's government for profit motives. But their would-be victim, President Teodoro Obiang Nguema Mbasogo, is a corrupt dictator who took power by killing his uncle and runs one of the most despicable regimes on the continent—hardly a sympathetic victim.

The third concern raised by PMFs is, ironically, precisely the feature that makes them so popular with governments today: they can accomplish public ends through private means. In other words, they allow governments to carry out actions that would not otherwise be possible, such as those that would not gain legislative or public approval. Sometimes, such freedom is beneficial: it can allow countries to fill unrecognized or unpopular strategic needs. But it also disconnects the public from its foreign policy, removing certain activities from popular oversight.

The increased use of private contractors by the U.S. government in Colombia is one illustration of this trend: by hiring PMFs, the Bush administration has circumvented congressional limits on the size and scope of the U.S. military's involvement in Colombia's civil war. The use of PMFs in Iraq is another example: by privatizing parts of the U.S. mission, the Bush administration has dramatically lowered the political price for its Iraq policies. Were it not for the more than 20,000 contractors currently operating in the country, the U.S. government would have to either deploy more of its own troops there (which would mean either expanding the regular force or calling up more National Guard members and reservists) or persuade other countries to increase their commitments—either of which would require painful political compromises. By outsourcing parts of the job instead, the Bush administration has avoided such unappealing alternatives and has also been able to shield the full costs from scrutiny: contractor casualties and kidnappings are not listed on public rolls and are rarely mentioned by the media. PMF contracts are also not subject to Freedom of Information Act requests. This reduction in transparency raises deep concerns about the long-term health of American democracy. As the legal scholar Arthur S. Miller once wrote, "democratic government is responsible government—which means accountable government—and the essential problem in contracting out is that responsibility and accountability are greatly diminished."

PMFs also create legal dilemmas, the fourth sort of policy challenge they raise. On both the personal and the corporate level, there is a striking absence of regulation, oversight, and enforcement. Although private military firms and their employees are now integral parts of many military operations, they tend to fall through the cracks of current legal codes, which sharply distinguish civilians from soldiers. Contractors are not quite civilians, given that they often carry and use weapons, interrogate prisoners, load bombs, and fulfill other critical military roles. Yet they are not quite soldiers, either. One military law analyst noted, "Legally speaking, [military contractors] fall into the same grey area as the unlawful combatants detained at Guantánamo Bay."

This lack of clarity means that when contractors are captured, their adversaries get to define their status. The results of this uncertainty can be dire—as they have been for three American employees of California Microwave Systems whose plane crashed in rebel-held territory in Colombia in 2003. The three have been held prisoner ever since, afforded none of the protections of the Geneva Conventions. Meanwhile, their corporate bosses and U.S. government clients seem to have washed their hands of the matter.

Such difficulties also play out when contractors commit misdeeds. It is often unclear how, when, where, and which authorities are responsible for investigating, prosecuting, and punishing such crimes. Unlike soldiers, who are accountable under their nation's military code of justice wherever they are located, contractors have a murky legal status, undefined by international law (they do not fit the formal definition of mercenaries). Normally, a civilian's crimes fall under the jurisdiction of the country where they are committed. But PMFs typically operate in failed states; indeed, the absence of local authority usually explains their presence in the first place. Prosecuting their crimes locally can thus be difficult.

Iraq, for example, still has no well-established courts, and during the formal U.S. occupation, regulations explicitly exempted contractors from local jurisdiction. Yet it is often just as difficult to prosecute contractors in their home country, since few legal systems cover crimes committed outside their territory. Some states do assert extraterritorial jurisdiction over their nationals, but they do so only for certain crimes and often lack the means to enforce their laws abroad. As a result of these gaps, not one private military contractor has been prosecuted or punished for a crime in Iraq (unlike the dozens of U.S. soldiers who have), despite the fact that more than 20,000 contractors have now spent almost two years there. Either every one of them happens to be a model citizen, or there are serious shortcomings in the legal system that governs them.

The failure to properly control the behavior of PMFs took on great consequence in the Abu Ghraib prisoner-abuse case. According to reports, all of the translators and up to half of the interrogators involved were private contractors working for two firms, Titan and caci. The U.S. Army found that contractors were involved in 36 percent of the proven incidents and identified 6 employees as individually culpable. More than a year after the incidents, however, not one of these individuals has been indicted, prosecuted, or punished, even though the U.S. Army has found the time to try the enlisted soldiers involved. Nor has there been any attempt to assess corporate responsibility for the misdeeds. Indeed, the only formal inquiry into PMF wrongdoing on the corporate level was conducted by caci itself. Caci investigated caci and, unsurprisingly, found that caci had done no wrong.

In the absence of legislation, some parties have already turned to litigation to address problems with PMFs—hardly the best forum for resolving issues related to human rights and the military. For example, some former Abu Ghraib prisoners have already tried to sue in U.S. courts the private firms involved with the prison. And the families of the four Blackwater employees murdered by insurgents in Fallujah have sued the company in a North Carolina court, claiming that the deceased had been sent into danger with a smaller unit than mandated in their contracts and with weapons, vehicles, and preparation that were not up to the standards promised.

The final dilemma raised by the extensive use of private contractors involves the future of the military itself. The armed services have long seen themselves as engaged in a unique profession, set apart from the rest of civilian society, which they are entrusted with securing. The introduction of PMFs, and their recruiting from within the military itself, challenges that uniqueness; the military's professional identity and monopoly on certain activities is being encroached on by the regular civilian marketplace.

Most soldiers thus have a deeply ambivalent attitude toward PMFs. On the one hand, they are grateful to have someone help them bear their burden, which, thanks to military overstretch in Iraq, feels particularly onerous at the moment. Even though the job of the U.S. armed services has grown, the force has shrunk by 35 percent since its Cold War high; the British military, meanwhile, is at its smallest since the Napoleonic wars. PMFs help fill the gap as well as offer retired soldiers the potential for a second career in a field they know and love.

Some in the military worry, on the other hand, that the PMF boom could endanger the health of their profession and resent the way these firms exploit skills learned at public expense for private profit. They also fear that the expanding PMF marketplace will hurt the military's ability to retain talented soldiers. Contractors in the PMF industry can make anywhere from two to ten times what they make in the regular military; in Iraq, former special forces troops can earn as much as $1,000 a day.

Certain service members, such as pilots, have always had the option of seeking work in the civilian marketplace. But the PMF industry marks a significant change, since it keeps its employees within the military, and thus the public, sphere. More important, PMFs compete directly with the government. Not only do they draw their employees from the military, they do so to play military roles, thus shrinking the military's purview. PMFs use public funds to offer soldiers higher pay, and then charge the government at an even higher rate, all for services provided by the human capital that the military itself originally helped build. The overall process may be brilliant from a business standpoint, but it is self-defeating from the military's perspective.

This issue has become especially pointed for special forces units, which have the most skills and are thus the most marketable. Elite force commanders in Australia, New Zealand, the United Kingdom, and the United States have all expressed deep concern over the poaching of their numbers by PMFs. One U.S. special forces officer described the issue of retention among his most experienced troops as being "at a tipping point." So far, the U.S. government has failed to respond adequately to this challenge. Some militaries now allow their soldiers to take a year's leave of absence, in the hope that they will make their money quickly and then return, rather than be lost to the service forever. But Washington has failed to take even this step; it has only created a special working group to explore the issue.

Caveat Emptor and—and Renter

As all of these problems suggest, governments that use PMFs must learn to recognize their responsibilities as regulators—and as smart clients. Their failure to do so thus far has distorted the free market and caused a major shift in the military-industrial complex. Without change, the status quo will result in bad policy and bad business.

To improve matters, it is first essential to lift the veil of secrecy that surrounds the private military industry. There must be far more openness about and public oversight of the basic numbers involved. Too little is known about the actual dollars spent on PMFs; the Pentagon does not even track the number of contractors working for it in Iraq, much less their casualties.

To start changing matters, clients—namely, governments that hire PMFs—must exercise their rights and undertake a comprehensive survey to discern the full scope of what they have outsourced and what have been the results. Washington should also require that, like most other government documents, all current and future contracts involving nonclassified activities be made available to the public on request. Each contract should also include "contractor visibility" measures that list the number of employees involved and what they are to be paid, thus limiting the possibility of financial abuse.

The U.S. military must also take a step back and reconsider, from a national security perspective, just what roles and functions should be kept in government hands. Outsourcing can be greatly beneficial, but only to the point where it begins to challenge core functions. According to the old military doctrine on contracting, if a function was "mission-critical" or "emergency-essential"—that is, if it could affect the very success or failure of an operation—it was kept within the military itself. The rule also held that civilians were to be armed only under extraordinary circumstances and then only for self-protection. The United States should either return to these standards or create new ones; the present ad-hoc process is yielding poor results.

A third lesson is self-evident but has often been ignored: privatize something only if it will save money or raise quality. If it will not, then do not. Unfortunately, the Pentagon's current, supposedly business-minded leadership seems to have forgotten Economics 101. All too often, it outsources first and never bothers to ask questions later. That something is done privately does not necessarily make it better, quicker, or cheaper. Rather, it is through leveraging free-market mechanisms that one potentially gets better private results. Success is likely only if a contract is competed for on the open market, if the winning firm can specialize on the job and build in redundancies, if the client is able to provide oversight and management to guard its own interests, and if the contractor is properly motivated by the fear of being fired. Forget these simple rules, as the U.S. government often does, and the result is not the best of privatization but the worst of monopolization.

Tapping simple business expertise would help the government become a better client. A staggering 40 percent of Defense Department contracts are currently awarded on a noncompetitive basis, adding up to $300 billion in contracts over the last five years. In the case of caci, the firm linked to abuses at Abu Ghraib, Army investigators subsequently reported not only that a caci employee may have helped write the work order, but also that the Abu Ghraib interrogators had been hired by simply amending an existing contract from 1998—for computer services overseen by the Department of the Interior.

When hiring contractors, the Defense Department must learn to better guard its own and the public's interest. Doing so will require having sufficient eyes and ears to oversee and manage contracts. So far, the military woefully lacks this capacity. The U.S. government has only twice as many personnel overseeing contractors in Iraq, for example, as it had during the 1990s for its Balkans contracts—even though there are now 15 times more contracts and the context is much more challenging.

The government should also change the nature of the contracts it signs. Too often, the "cost plus" arrangement has become the default form for all contracts. But this setup, in effect, gives companies more profit if they spend more. When combined with inadequate oversight, it creates a system ripe for inefficiency and abuse. In addition to insisting on more stringent terms, the government should start to use the power of market sanctions to shape more positive results. These days, the opposite seems to happen far more often: Halliburton and caci were both granted massive contract extensions for work in Iraq, despite being in the midst of government investigations.

Finally, more must be done to ensure legal accountability. To pay contractors more than soldiers is one thing; to also give them a legal free pass (as happened with Abu Ghraib) is unconscionable. Loopholes must be filled and new laws developed to address the legal and jurisdictional dilemmas PMFs raise. Laws should be written to establish who can work for these companies, who the firms can work for, and who will investigate, prosecute, and punish any wrongdoing by contractors. Because this is a transnational industry, the solution will require international involvement. Proposals to update the international antimercenary laws and to create a UN body to sanction and regulate PMFs have already been made. But any such international effort will take years. In the meantime, every state that has any involvement with the private military industry, as a client or a home base, should update its laws. One hopes that countries will coordinate their efforts and involve regional bodies to maximize coverage. The United Kingdom, for example, could coordinate its present efforts with the rest of the European Union, and the United States should do the same with its allies.

The forces that drove the growth of the private military industry seem set in place. Much like the Internet boom, the PMF bubble may burst if the current spate of work in Iraq ever ends, but the industry itself is unlikely to disappear anytime soon. Governments must therefore act to meet this reality. Using private solutions for public military ends is not necessarily a bad thing. But the stakes in warfare are far higher than in the corporate realm: in this most essential public sphere, national security and people's lives are constantly put at risk. War, as the old proverb has it, is certainly far too important to be left to the generals. The same holds true for the CEOs.

Preemption Paradox

Using military force to destroy an adversary's nuclear program is a compelling option, so how come most nations have decided against it?

BENNETT RAMBERG

Twenty-five years ago, on a late spring afternoon, eight Israeli bombers streaked across the desert sky on a top-secret mission to destroy Osirak, Iraq's emerging nuclear reactor complex. A dramatic military action to prevent nuclear weapons proliferation, the June 7, 1981 strike left a legacy that echoes today in the "all options are on the table" drumbeat emanating from Washington and Jerusalem. The seemingly straightforward message to Iran and other would-be proliferators: Abrogate nonproliferation pledges in this post-9/11 era and risk being "Osiraked."

These aggressive declarations, however, butt against historical reality. Save for two major exceptions—the Allied effort to scuttle Nazi Germany's nuclear program, and attempts by Iran, Israel, and the United States to wipe out Saddam Hussein's nuclear ambitions—countries with incentives to use force to halt nuclear proliferation have spent more time conducting tabletop exercises than taking action. The result: nations such as the Soviet Union, China, and Pakistan produced the Bomb despite the interest and capacity of adversaries to stop them.

A Desperate Race

At the beginning of the nuclear age, there was no nonproliferation norm, no concept of nuclear deterrence, and no taboos against nuclear war. All that existed was an apparent race for the Bomb in the midst of history's bloodiest conflict.

Adolf Hitler's Third Reich lacked the resources, organization, scientific understanding, and even commitment to be in the pursuit.[1] But the United States did not know this early in the war. "At best, I do not see how we can catch up with the Germans unless they have overlooked some possibilities we recognize, or unless our military action should delay them," warned physicist Arthur Compton in a 1942 communiqué to Gen. Leslie R. Groves.[2]

In response, the Allies applied a two-pronged strategy: They would try to cross the nuclear finish line first, and simultaneously, they would destroy the Nazi effort. Planners targeted German-occupied Norway's Norsk Hydro hydrogen-electrolysis plant—marking the first instance of nuclear preemption.[3] With so much at stake, the hesitation that would characterize post-World War II coercive nonproliferation had no place in this decision.

The Allies targeted the Norsk Hydro plant because it was the world's only commercial processor of heavy water (deuterium oxide), which can be used in some reactors to turn natural uranium into weapons-usable plutonium. From late 1942 to February 1944, the Allies spared no effort to destroy the plant and its contents.[4]

In the first attempt, two gliders ferried 34 British commandos to their sabotage mission. But one glider crashed at sea, the other onto Norway's rocky terrain. The next Allied effort parachuted a team of Norwegian commandos into their native country; the nine saboteurs, scaling a steep, icy canyon wall, conducted a dramatic winter evening assault. The attack effectively destroyed eight weeks' worth of heavy water production, but the Germans rebuilt the installation in six weeks. The undertaking offered a cautionary note that would reverberate in post-war planning: Force can fall short; adversaries can absorb a blow and then recoup.

Desperate to finish the mission, Washington ordered hundreds of bombers to take out the plant in a single air raid. Only 12 of the 1,000 dropped bombs struck the target, but the attack was a success; Germany decided not to rebuild. A final act of sabotage sunk a transport ferry that was to carry remaining stocks of heavy water to Germany.

Though intelligence demonstrated that Germany's nuclear program had sputtered, Washington still worried. In its view, only the Reich's defeat combined with occupation, dismantlement, and destruction of nuclear facilities, and the incarceration of senior Nazi scientists would put an end to Hitler's nuclear ambitions. Preemptive military strikes alone were not enough.

The Reluctant Superpower

At war's end, the United States stood atop the nuclear pinnacle. But it could sense the Soviet Union striving to reach the same heights. In 1946, the Kremlin rejected the U.S.-proposed Baruch Plan that would have placed the most worrisome elements of the nuclear fuel cycle under the auspices of an International Atomic Development Authority. Coupled with tensions over occupation rights in Germany and the Soviet Union's consolidation of its hold on Eastern Europe, some public figures and members of the nuclear scientific establishment—including

Winston Churchill, Bertrand Russell, Leo Szilard, and John von Neumann—called for military action to stop the Kremlin before it got the Bomb.[5]

General Groves, the head of the Manhattan Project, reflected: "If we were ruthlessly realistic, we would not permit any foreign power with which we are not firmly allied . . . to make or possess atomic bombs. If such a country started to make atomic weapons, we would destroy its capacity to make them before it had progressed far enough to threaten us."[6] But President Harry S. Truman seemed resigned to the inevitability of proliferation. In a September 18, 1945 conversation with White House confidant Joseph E. Davis, Truman said, "Are we going to give up these [atomic] locks and bolts which are necessary to protect our house? . . . Clearly we are not. Nor are the Soviets. Nor is any country if it can help itself."[7]

The idea of preemption also found resistance in the military. "It might be desirable to strike the first blow, [but] it is not politically feasible under our system to do so or to state that we will do so," Pentagon planner George Lincoln acknowledged in 1945.[8] As Cold War historian John Lewis Gaddis has observed, U.S. reluctance was partly rooted in self-image: "America did not start wars."[9]

The practical question of whether the United States could actually "win" a preemptive war against the Soviet Union also loomed large. In a statement that presaged the dilemma currently confronting U.S. advocates of preemption, Truman's defense secretary, James Forrestal, observed, "Conquering the Russians is one thing, and finding what to do with them afterward is an entirely different problem."[10]

Truman's successor also contemplated the merits of preemption. President Dwight D. Eisenhower endorsed a December 1954 National Security Policy paper that concluded, "The United States and its allies must reject the concept of preventive war or acts intended to provoke it."[11] But the principle would never be as immutable as the policy document suggested. The Eisenhower administration generated a plethora of conflicting statements about the use of preemptive force against a coiled Soviet Union, suggesting a policy of ambiguity that neither embraced nor rejected the option.[12]

By 1962, the United States had learned to live with a nuclear-armed Kremlin for 13 years. But "geographic proliferation" on Washington's doorstep—the placement of Soviet nuclear missiles in Cuba—would be another matter.[13] While there would be no repetition of the Norsk Hydro attacks, during the Cuban Missile Crisis President John F. Kennedy forced Soviet leader Nikita Khrushchev to back down by crystallizing Washington's preemptive intentions. Given the balance of interests and military power favoring Washington—coupled to a side agreement to remove U.S. missiles from Turkey—the Soviets decided that they would not risk Moscow for Havana.

The idea of preemption found resistance in the military. U.S. reluctance was partly rooted in self-image: "America did not start wars."

No Good Options

China began its nuclear weapons research in the 1950s. By December 1960, U.S. satellite imagery and U-2 intelligence pieced together the fragmentary basis for a National Intelligence Estimate that forecast a Chinese nuclear weapon test by as early as 1963.[14]

That China might get the Bomb generated tremors among U.S. policy makers.[15] In June 1961, the Joint Chiefs of Staff warned that Beijing's "attainment of a nuclear capability will have a marked impact on the security posture of the United States and the free world."[16] In their subsequent review of diplomatic, economic, and military options—which included sabotaging nuclear facilities, an invasion by Chinese nationalists, a maritime blockade, renewing the Korean War, and U.S. conventional or tactical nuclear weapon strikes on the nuclear plants—the Joint Chiefs made no specific recommendation. Yet their aversion to preemption was evident. "Many of the [military] actions . . . above are obviously acts of war, [and] should be initiated only after all other means have been exhausted, and then only after full and careful consideration of the implications at the time," they argued in a 1963 memorandum.[17]

The State Department arrived at a similar cautionary conclusion. Robert Johnson, the department's leading analyst on the issue, sought to dampen the sense of mounting panic within the U.S. bureaucracy, arguing that the "great asymmetry in Chinese Communist and U.S. nuclear capabilities and vulnerabilities" made it unlikely that Beijing would ever contemplate nuclear first-use, except in the event of an attack that "threatened the existence of the regime."[18] And even if U.S. military strikes were successful—an uncertain outcome given incomplete intelligence on China's nuclear facilities—preemption would, at best, "buy some time."[19] If anything, such an attack could strengthen Beijing's resolve to obtain a nuclear deterrent, and a hardened successor program could be constructed in as few as four or five years.

Military action entailed other risks: It could prompt Chinese retaliation against Taiwan or U.S. allies in East Asia, entangle the Soviets (who were unwilling to join in such an attack), degrade Washington's international prestige and alliances, and reduce the prospects for arms control initiatives to constrain China. Johnson concluded, "Action with no justification other than a general argument that the U.S. was seeking to preserve the peace of the world through depriving a potential aggressor of nuclear weapons" could not be defended.[20]

The arguments resonated. On September 15, 1964, the secretaries of State and Defense and the national security adviser met with President Lyndon B. Johnson in the Cabinet Room to present their recommendation: "We are not in favor of unprovoked unilateral U.S. military action against Chinese nuclear installations at this time. We would prefer to have a Chinese test take place than to initiate such action now. If for other reasons we should find ourselves in military hostilities at any level with the Chinese Communists, we would expect to give very close attention to the possibility of an appropriate military action against Chinese nuclear facilities."[21] Johnson, running on a peace platform in the upcoming election, concurred. On October 16, 1964, China conducted its first nuclear test and became the world's fourth nuclear weapon state.

Israel's Gamble

In the 1960s, the United States was willing to adopt a "wait and see" approach with China. Decades later, Israel would not give Iraq the same benefit. On September 8, 1975, Iraqi Vice President Saddam Hussein declared publicly that Baghdad's purchase from France of a 70-megawatt test reactor called Osiris and a small Isis reactor— collectively called Osirak—would be "the first actual step in the production of an Arab nuclear weapon."[22]

Jerusalem's 1981 attack against Osirak marked the culmination of a failed multiyear campaign to halt the construction of Iraq's reactor by means other than military action. The government of Prime Minister Menachem Begin first lobbied Paris and Washington. Rebuffed, Israel tried assassination, but the deaths of three scientists affiliated with the nuclear program barely hindered Iraq's efforts. Israel attempted sabotage next, but the demolition of Osirak's core as it awaited shipment and the firebombing of an Italian firm contracted to provide reprocessing technology delayed Osirak only marginally.[23]

The decision to use military force was not made easily; Israel debated the option intensely. In cabinet discussions, Israel's deputy prime minister, defense minister, health minister, chief of military intelligence, and head of Mossad all preferred the "wait and see" approach.[24] They feared that an unprovoked attack could spark war, stimulate region-wide nuclear proliferation, and make Israel a global pariah. Furthermore, some doubted that Iraq even had the scientific ability to build the Bomb.

The preemption option itself posed serious logistical problems.[25] A commando raid in which agents were inserted into and extracted from hostile territory was too daunting. But an air strike was also risky, as demonstrated by a botched Iranian aircraft strike on the plant in September 1980, shortly after the start of the Iran-Iraq War. Some Israeli officials questioned whether Israel's Phantom or F-15 aircraft could travel 600 miles over hostile territory to do the job.

As it turned out, these aircraft did not have to take on the task. In the aftermath of the 1979 Iranian Revolution, Shah Reza Pahlevi's order of U.S. F-16s did not go through. Superior to Israel's Phantoms and F-15s, Jerusalem scooped up the F-16s after Washington put them on the block. Still, it was not the acquisition of the aircraft that tipped Israel's scales in favor of a preemptive strike; it was the determination of Prime Minister Begin.

Eight F-16s each carrying two 2,000-pound gravity bombs flew toward Osirak; a phalanx of F-15s hovered nearby to jam Iraqi radar, intercept Iraq's air force, and provide a communication link to Israel. Search and rescue helicopters were at the ready. The attack took place before Osirak went critical to avoid the release of the plant's radioactive contents. All but two bombs hit the plant, leaving the reactor in ruins.

Israel's assault sent shock waves through the world, garnering condemnation and grudging admiration. But despite the destruction the preemptive strike wrought, it did not extinguish Iraq's ambitions. Baghdad, which had committed 400 scientists and $400 million to the nuclear program before the attack, enlarged its nuclear staff to 7,000 and upped its budget to $10 billion.[26]

South Asian Standoff

One country that took particular note of Israel's raid on Osirak was India. Throughout the 1970s and 1980s, India had watched apprehensively as Pakistan, its perennial adversary, followed a nuclear weapons path similar to its own. In addition to the acquisition of a "peaceful" heavy water reactor from Canada, the other telltale signs included an expanding number of reprocessing and enrichment installations. Given the diminutive size of Pakistan's nuclear power program, the fuel-cycle plants likely served only one purpose: nuclear weapons.

Adding to these concerns would be the program's principal political promoter. In 1971, in the aftermath of Pakistan's loss of Bangladesh to India's armed forces, Zulfikar Ali Bhutto became prime minister. Bhutto had been a patron of the atom as far back as 1960 when he became minister of minerals and natural resources. As foreign minister, in 1965, he laid the foundation for later nuclear weapons assistance from the Chinese. In the same year, he made his ambitions clear: "If India builds the bomb, we will eat grass or leaves, even go hungry, but we will get one of our own."[27] True to his word, as Pakistan's leader, he was determined to move forward. On January 24, 1972, he gathered the country's top scientists for a meeting in Multan, Punjab, to set the program in motion.

Although Bhutto would never see his ambition come to fruition—in 1977 the military overthrew and later executed him— his successors continued his efforts. India watched Pakistan's development at first with disdain—it couldn't possibly build the Bomb—but, in time, with mounting anxiety.[28] By the early 1980s, Indian analysts concluded that Pakistan had enriched sufficient uranium for one or two bombs.

Israel's bombing of Osirak provided inspiration for a military solution. The Indian Air Force—energized by the procurement of new British Jaguar strike aircraft—studied the application of Israel's example to Pakistan's Kahuta enrichment plant. Military planners concluded that the attack could succeed, but at a cost of half the bomber force. Such losses would not be the gravest risk. "What will happen next?" the chief of operations asked. "The international community would condemn us for doing something in peacetime, which the Israelis could get away with but India would not be able to get away with. In the end, it will result in a war."[29]

The specter of war prompted another concern. Pakistan's retaliatory response could include striking Indian nuclear reactors and reprocessing sites situated near urban settings— effectively mounting a devastating radiological attack upon India.[30] A high-ranking official commented, "We knew we would have to live with Pakistan's nuclear capability, and there was no way around it."[31]

But living together required some insurance; overcoming the temptation for nuclear preemption was in the interest of both parties. The two countries negotiated a 1985 accord (which was fully implemented in 1993) not to attack one another's nuclear facilities. However, as years passed, events would call into question whether the agreement would stand. The countries' tit-for-tat 1998 nuclear weapons detonations, coupled with the unresolved Kashmir dispute, periodically raised the preemption specter anew.

Targeting North Korea

As South Asia wrestled with its nuclear conundrum, another would-be nuclear power emerged in the Far East. North Korea's ambitions to obtain nuclear weapons lay rooted in U.S. threats to use the Bomb during the Korean War and the North's unease over the Soviet Union's retreat during the Cuban Missile Crisis. With assistance from Moscow, Pyongyang steadily expanded its indigenous nuclear program over the next couple of decades. However, in 1985, Moscow made it clear that further support was contingent upon North Korea joining the Nuclear Non-Proliferation Treaty (NPT).

From the beginning, signs were not good for international control. Seven years would pass before Pyongyang signed the International Atomic Energy Agency's (IAEA) Safeguards Agreement. And afterward, the North persistently denied IAEA inspectors access to sites of concern. In spring 1994, matters came to a head when North Korea began removing spent fuel from its five-megawatt reactor in Yongbyon.

Diplomacy was at the heart of the Clinton administration's effort to curb North Korea, but the president's advisers could not ignore the military option. The administration's senior national security staff evaluated the prospects in June 1994, against the backdrop of Pyongyang's announced intention to withdraw from the NPT and expel inspectors.[32] But armed force posed too many risks.[33] A commando or cruise missile attack might stop the future extraction of weapon-grade material, but it would not guarantee the destruction of material the North may have removed in advance. Attacking the reactor would substantially set back Pyongyang's program (albeit risking a radiological release), but doing so could prompt international opprobrium. Also, a strike against the North could spark a full-scale war. In the view of Gen. Gary Luck, commander of U.S. forces in South Korea, "If we pull an Osirak, they will be coming south." This could result in as many as 750,000 U.S. and South Korean military casualties alone.[34]

U.S. officials decided, at least for the time being, that sanctions offered a far more attractive option than preemption. Air Force Chief of Staff Gen. Merrill McPeak commented, "We can't find nuclear weapons now except by going on a house-to-house search," suggesting that, when it came to military options, he felt that only the occupation of North Korea, rather than limited preemptive strikes, would succeed.[35]

The matter became moot when former President Jimmy Carter visited Pyongyang in June 1994. Laying the foundation for what would become the Agreed Framework, the United States consented to lead an international consortium to provide the communist state with a light water reactor and heavy oil to meet its immediate energy needs.

In January 2003, confronted with U.S. intelligence that it had violated its nonproliferation vows by pursuing a secret enrichment program, President Kim Jong Il bolted from the NPT. On February 10, 2005, Pyongyang officially claimed that it had manufactured nuclear weapons.

Cautionary Tales

This recounting has summarized the "big" events in the history of nuclear preemption, save one: Washington's 2003 attack on Iraq.[36] Built on the false premise that Saddam had an active nuclear program, America's invasion was an exercise in preemptive overkill. Baghdad's nuclear program was already dead—not because of Saddam's aversion to the Bomb, but due to an earlier war that marked nuclear preemption by serendipity.[37] But for Iraq's defeat in 1991—or had Saddam delayed his invasion of Kuwait by a year or more—Baghdad might have joined the nuclear club.

While this and other cases are different from one another, viewed comparatively they suggest some tentative findings to answer a nonproliferation conundrum: Why has history not witnessed more consistent application of the Osirak template?

First, nuclear preemption in peacetime poses profound political risks. In confronting the prospects of a nuclear-armed Soviet Union and China, the United States was reluctant to be seen as the aggressor. India had similar reservations. Even Israel's security establishment—well aware of Iraq's declared ambition to obtain nuclear weapons—was mindful of the potential political costs of instigating an unprovoked attack.

A second lesson is that nuclear states appear reluctant to preempt emerging nuclear powers if the latter have a significant capacity to strike back. The geographic proximity of adversaries has long accentuated this dilemma. India feared ruinous reprisals from neighboring Pakistan. U.S. military planners worried that China would lash out across the Taiwan Straits and that North Korea would head south against Seoul. In today's world, strike-back could also include spectacular surrogate terrorist acts or military counterattacks against vital economic lifelines, such as petroleum production or distribution.

Radiological risks add novel concerns. India was not alone in its apprehension about retaliation against its nuclear sites. Japan, for example, feared that U.S. preemption of North Korea could result in attacks on its nuclear power plants.[38] Even without this prospect, successful destruction of Pyongyang's plants risked radioactive releases.[39] (By contrast, anxiety over nuclear contamination actually accelerated Israel's decision to bomb Osirak. Prime Minister Begin pressed for the strike before the reactor became "hot.")

The use of an atomic weapon by a preemptor would have even greater consequences. Even the lowest-yield nuclear "bunker buster" promises significant local damage and contamination.[40] The National Academy of Sciences estimates that high-yield nuclear attacks on hardened sites could result in hundreds of thousands of casualties depending on the depth of the burst, weather patterns, and the proximity of populations.

The resulting fallout—which would be even greater if the target were a nuclear facility—could reach beyond the borders of the country that was attacked to include a neighboring initiator or its allies.[41]

Facilities that have been destroyed can be rebuilt. As former U.N. weapons inspector David Kay once pointedly asked, "How do you roll back knowledge?"

In Israel's raid on Osirak, geography played a different role. The distance separating the adversaries made Jerusalem's decision easier, since Baghdad could not easily retaliate. However, in the 2003 Iraq War, geography was less important for another reason: the proximity of Washington's regional allies to Baghdad did not deter preemption because American planners believed that U.S. military superiority and destructiveness would more than compensate.

Another lesson from history is that preemptive military strikes are a logistical nightmare. Absent complete intelligence, a nation cannot be certain that a military attack will sufficiently devastate a rival country's nuclear program. In that respect, Osirak was an anomaly, in that the key elements of Iraq's nuclear infrastructure were clustered within one site. Other would-be nuclear proliferators have learned that lesson well, and today an adversary's nuclear program is likely to be scattered across several hardened facilities. As General McPeak acknowledged regarding North Korea in the early 1990s, nothing less than a "house-to-house search" would suffice. The effectiveness of international inspectors in Iraq after the 1991 war demonstrated that point.

But, even then, another dilemma remains: What has been destroyed can be rebuilt, a fact first evidenced in the initial "successful" sabotage of Norsk Hydro. As former U.N. weapons inspector David Kay once pointedly asked, "How do you roll back knowledge?"[42] During the Cold War, U.S. analysts recognized that China could reconstitute a nuclear program within a few years. Israeli bombers were able to destroy Osirak, but they could not destroy Iraq's technical and scientific infrastructure. Consequently, Iraq was able to reconstitute its nuclear program by the beginning of the 1990s.[43]

If nations are unable to deny adversaries the means and know-how to develop nuclear weapons, then the preemptive option with the best chance of long-term success is the World War II template of regime change. Yet, as the current U.S. occupation of Iraq reveals, this is not an option to be considered lightly. The costs of foreign rule and nation building—in terms of lives and economic resources—can be daunting.

The final lesson from the history of preemption is that surgical military strikes can only buy time. That said, buying time should not be as readily dismissed as some argue.[44] Israel's 1981 attack clearly set back Iraq's program. Indeed, time bought by military or other means allows international incentives, disincentives, and/or domestic political changes to curtail nuclear

ambitions. Libya's 2003 nuclear surrender proves that, given sufficient time, a country can decide to relinquish its nuclear ambitions.[45] But as North Korea and Iraq in 1981 demonstrated, time purchased, either through diplomacy or coercion, is no sure path to stem nuclear ambitions.

Ultimately, the legacy of Osirak lies in the fact that it effectively legitimized military means as a way to halt proliferation if other measures fail. But as history reveals, preemption is no easy solution. It is just one of many competing tactics in dealing with a predicament that has proven time and again to have few good options.[46]

Notes

1. Thomas Powers, *Heisenberg's War: The Secret History of the German Bomb* (New York: Knopf, 1993).

2. Quoted in Dan Kurzman, *Blood and Water: Sabotaging Hitler's Bomb* (New York: Henry Holt & Co., 1997), p. 17.

3. I use the term "preemptive" rather than "preventive" throughout to reflect the temporal opportunity to eliminate an adversary's nuclear program. See Alan Dershowitz, *Preemption* (New York: W. W. Norton, 2006), p. 96.

4. Ibid., pp. 195–202, 211–213; and Kurzman, *Blood and Water*.

5. George H. Quester, *Nuclear Monopoly* (New Brunswick: Transaction Publishers, 2000), pp. 37–56.

6. Ibid., quoted on p. 42.

7. Quoted in John Lewis Gaddis, *The United States and the Origins of the Cold War, 1941–1947* (New York: Columbia University Press, 1972), p. 273.

8. Quoted in John Lewis Gaddis et al., eds., *Cold War Statesmen Confront the Bomb* (New York: Oxford University Press, 1999), p. 88.

9. John Lewis Gaddis, *We Now Know* (New York: Oxford University Press, 1997), p. 88.

10. Ibid., quoted on p. 89.

11. David Alan Rosenberg, "The Origins of Overkill: Nuclear Weapons and American Strategy, 1945–1960," *International Security,* Spring 1983, p. 34.

12. Ibid.; Marc Trachtenberg, *A Constructed Peace: The Making of the European Settlement, 1945–1963* (Princeton: Princeton University Press, 1999), chap. 5; Marc Trachtenberg, "A Wasting Asset: American Strategy and the Shifting Nuclear Balance, 1949–1954," *International Security,* Winter 1988/89, p. 34, fn. 121; private communication from David Alan Rosenberg, March 2006.

13. White House tapes on the Cuban Missile Crisis reveal different views on the significance of Moscow's geographic proliferation. Robert McNamara reported that the Joint Chiefs believed the presence of Soviet nuclear weapons in Cuba would "substantially" change the strategic balance. McNamara's opinion: "Not at all." The first view dominated decision making. Marc Trachtenberg, "The Influence of Nuclear Weapons in the Cuban Missile Crisis," and "White House Tapes and Minutes of the Cuban Missile Crisis," *International Security,* Summer 1985, pp. 137–203.

14. William Burr and Jeffrey T. Richelson, "Whether to Strangle the Baby in the Cradle: The United States and the Chinese

Nuclear Program, 1960–64," *International Security,* Winter 2000/01, p. 59.

15. Ibid., pp. 54–99.

16. Ibid., p. 61.

17. Joint Chiefs of Staff, "Memorandum for the Secretary of Defense: Study of Chinese Communist Vulnerability," JCSM-343-63, April 29, 1963, p. 3.

18. Robert H. Johnson, "A Chinese Communist Nuclear Detonation and Nuclear Capability: Major Conclusions and Key Decisions," State Department, October 15, 1963, p. 1.

19. Burr and Richelson, "Whether to Strangle the Baby in the Cradle," p. 80.

20. Robert H. Johnson, "The Chinese Communist Nuclear Capability and Some Unorthodox Approaches to the Problem of Nuclear Proliferation," June 1, 1964; Burr and Richelson, "Whether to Strangle the Baby in the Cradle," pp. 78–80.

21. McGeorge Bundy, "Memorandum for the Record," White House, September 15, 1964.

22. Dan Reiter, "Preventive Attacks Against Nuclear Programs and the Success at Osirak," *Nonproliferation Review,* July 2005, p. 357.

23. Rodger W. Claire, *Raid on the Sun* (New York: Broadway Books, 2004), pp. 40– 41, 47–50, 61–65, 81, 97.

24. Ibid., p. xvii.

25. Claire's book provides the best insider account of the attack; see chap. 4–7.

26. Reiter, "Preventive Attacks," p. 263.

27. Quoted in Carey Sublette, "Pakistan's Nuclear Weapons Program," Nuclear Weapon Archive, January 2, 2002 (nuclearweaponarchive.org/Pakistan/PakOrigin.html).

28. George Perkovich, *India's Nuclear Bomb* (Berkeley: University of California Press, 1999), pp. 275–276.

29. Ibid., quoted on p. 240.

30. Ibid., p. 241.

31. Ibid.

32. Joel Wit et al., *Going Critical: The First North Korean Nuclear Crisis* (Washington: Brookings Institution, 2004), p. 210.

33. Ibid., pp. 210–211, 244–245, 410. See also Don Oberdorfer, *The Two Koreas* (New York: Basic Books, 1997), pp. 306–326 for a more pessimistic view of the odds of war.

34. Wit, *Going Critical,* p. 102.

35. Ibid., p. 104.

36. There are a number of lesser-known cases involving contemplation of preemption. For instance, in 1969, Sino-Soviet border clashes prompted Moscow to contemplate a preemptive strike against China. See Lyle J. Goldstein, "Do Nascent WMD Arsenals Deter? The Sino-Soviet Crisis of 1969," *Political Science Quarterly,* vol. 118, no. 1, 2003, pp. 53–79. In 1976, the Soviet Union approached the United States to consider cooperating in a joint effort to preempt South Africa's nuclear weapons program. See David Albright, "South Africa and the Affordable Bomb," *Bulletin of the Atomic Scientists,* July/August 1994.

37. While the United States did not use Iraq's nuclear program to justify the 1991 Gulf War, some in Congress did seek to rationalize the war on these grounds. See Michael J. Mazarr et al., *Desert Storm: The Gulf War and What We Learned* (Boulder: Westview, 1993), p. 85.

38. Wit, *Going Critical,* p. 178.

39. Ibid., p. 211.

40. Robert W. Nelson, "Low-Yield Earth Penetrating Nuclear Weapons," *Science and Global Security,* vol. 10, no. 1, 2002, pp. 1–20.

41. Committee on the Effects of Nuclear Earth-Penetrator and Other Weapons, "Effects of Nuclear Earth-Penetrator and Other Weapons" (Washington, D.C.: National Research Council, 2005), pp. 2, 6. For a depiction of the radioactive plume generated by a 300-kiloton earth-penetrator on North Korea, see Christopher Paine et al., "The Bush Administration's Quest for Earth-Penetrating and Low-Yield Nuclear Weapons" (Washington: Natural Resources Defense Council, 2003), p. 8. In Bennett Ramberg, *Nuclear Power Plants as Weapons for the Enemy: An Unrecognized Military Peril* (Berkeley: University of California Press, 1984), pp. 51, 54–56, the author illustrates the consequences of nuclear strikes against civil reactors.

42. David Kay, "With More at Stake, Less Will Be Verified," *Washington Post,* November 17, 2002.

43. Jeremy Bernstein, "Atomic Secrets," *New York Review of Books,* May 25, 2006, p. 43.

44. See, for example, Richard Betts, "The Osirak Fallacy," *The National Interest,* Spring 2006, p. 22.

45. Bruce W. Jentleson and Christopher A. Whytock, "Who 'Won' Libya? Force-Diplomacy Debate and Its Implications for Theory and Policy," *International Security,* Winter 2005/06, pp. 47–86; Judith Miller "How Gadhafi Lost His Groove," *Wall Street Journal,* May 16, 2006, p. A14; and Judith Miller, "Gadhafi's Leap of Faith," *Wall Street Journal,* May 17, 2006, p. A18.

46. The author wishes to thank Michael Intriligator, Kent Harrington, George H. Quester, and Robert Pendley for their helpful comments.

BENNETT RAMBERG, author of *Nuclear Power Plants as Weapons for the Enemy* (1984), served in the State Department's Bureau of Politico-Military Affairs in the first Bush administration. He can be reached at bennettramberg@aol.com.

New Challenges and Old Concepts

Understanding 21st Century Insurgency

STEVEN METZ

From the 1960s to the 1980s stopping Communist-backed insurgents was an important part of American strategy, so counterinsurgency was an important mission for the US military, particularly the Army. Even when most of the Army turned its attention to large-scale warfighting and the operational art following Vietnam, special operation forces preserved some degree of capability. In the 1980s American involvement in El Salvador and a spate of insurgencies around the world linked to the Soviets and Chinese sparked renewed interest in counterinsurgency operations (as a component of low-intensity conflict). By 1990 what could be called the El Salvador model of counterinsurgency, based on a limited US military footprint in conjunction with the strengthening of local security forces, became codified in strategy and doctrine.[1]

Interest then faded. Policymakers, military leaders, and defense experts assumed that insurgency was a relic of the Cold War, posing little challenge in the "new world order." With the demise of the Soviet Union and the mellowing of China, insurgency—even though it persisted in the far corners of the world—was not viewed as a strategic challenge to the world's sole superpower. With American involvement in Somalia, Bosnia, Kosovo, and Haiti, multinational peacekeeping—a previously unimportant role for the military—moved to the fore. In a burst of energy, the military revamped its peacekeeping doctrine and concepts. Professional military education and training shifted to accommodate these missions. Wargames, conferences, and seminars proliferated. Counterinsurgency was forgotten by all but a tiny handful of scholars.

Then, one clear September morning, the world turned. Al Qaeda and its affiliates adopted a strategy relying heavily on the methods of insurgency—both national insurgency and a transnational one.[2] Insurgency was again viewed as a strategic threat and the fear grew that insurgent success would create regimes willing to support and protect organizations like al Qaeda. The global campaign against violent Islamic extremists forced the United States military to undertake counterinsurgency missions in Iraq and Afghanistan. Once again, the Department of Defense was required to respond to a major strategic shift. The military services scrambled to develop new concepts and doctrine.[3] Counterinsurgency reentered the curriculum of the professional military educational system in a big way. It became a centerpiece for Army and Marine Corps training. Classic assessments

of the conflicts in Vietnam and Algeria became required reading for military leaders. Like the mythical phoenix, counterinsurgency had emerged from the ashes of its earlier death to become not just a concern of the US military but the central focus.

This is all to the good. Augmenting capabilities to respond to new strategic threats is exactly what the Department of Defense is supposed to do. There is a problem, however: As the American military relearned counterinsurgency strategy and doctrine, it may not have gotten them right. During the 1970s America's national security strategy was shaped by what became known as the "Vietnam syndrome"—a reluctance to intervene in internal conflicts based on the assumption that some disaster would ensue. Ironically, while the United States eventually overcame the Vietnam syndrome, a new one emerged. Vietnam has been treated as a universal model, the Viet Cong as the archetypical foe. Defense experts even concluded that insurgents who did not use the Vietnamese approach (derived from the teaching of Mao Zedong) stood little chance of success.[4]

This tendency to look back to the classic insurgencies of the twentieth century was pervasive. For instance, as the Army sought to understand the conflict in Iraq, the books most recommended for its officers were John Nagl's *Learning to Eat Soup with a Knife* (which dealt with the British involvement in Malaya and the American experience in Vietnam) and David Galula's *Counterinsurgency Warfare* (drawn from the French campaigns in Indochina and Algeria).[5] Both were excellent choices. But both deal with wars of imperial maintenance or nationalistic transition, not with complex communal conflicts where armed militias and organized crime play a key role.

In a sense, the United States has once again derived new strategies from old conflicts, while again preparing to fight the last war. Rather than rigorously examining twenty-first century insurgencies, America simply assumed that their logic, grammar, organization, and dynamics were the same as the classic insurgencies of the twentieth century. Such assumptions may be dangerously misguided. In many ways contemporary insurgencies are more like their immediate forebears—the complex internal conflicts of the 1990s—rather than twentieth century insurgencies. Somalia, Bosnia, Sierra Leone, Congo, Colombia, and Kosovo are possibly better models than Vietnam or Algeria. If that is true, the military and the defense analytical community need to rethink the insurgency challenge once again, this time seeking to distinguish its persisting elements from its evolving ones.

The Dynamics of Contemporary Insurgencies

Normally a twentieth century insurgency was the only game in town (or at least the most important one). Nations facing serious insurgencies such as South Vietnam or, later, El Salvador, certainly had other security problems, but they paled in comparison to the insurgent threat. Insurgencies were organizationally simple. They involved the insurgents, the regime, and, sometimes, outside supporters of one side or the other. When the United States finally engaged in counterinsurgency operations, many government agencies played a supporting role, but it was primarily a military effort. After all, Americans now viewed counterinsurgency as a variant of war. In war, the military dominates and the objective is the decisive defeat of the enemy. Why should counterinsurgency operations be any different?

This perception was always problematic, leading the United States to pursue military solutions to threats that could only be solved politically. This disconnect is even more dangerous today, largely because twenty-first century insurgencies have diverged significantly from their forebears. Rather than being discrete conflicts between insurgents and an established regime, they are nested in complex, multidimensional clashes having political, social, cultural, and economic components. In an even broader sense, contemporary insurgencies flow from systemic failures in the political, economic, and social realms. They arise not only from the failure or weakness of the state, but from more general flaws in cultural, social, and economic systems. Such complex conflicts involve a wide range of participants, all struggling to fill the voids created by failed or weak states and systemic collapse. In addition to what might be labeled "first forces" (the insurgent and the regime) and "second forces" (outside sponsors of the insurgents or the regime), there are "third forces" (armed groups such as militias, criminal gangs, or private military corporations) and "fourth forces" (the international media and nongovernmental organizations) all with the capability to impact the outcome.[6] The implications are stark; in the face of systemic failure, simply crushing insurgents and augmenting local security forces may not be enough to stem instability.

Contemporary insurgencies are less like traditional war where the combatants seek strategic victory, they are more like a violent, fluid, and competitive market. This circumstance is the result of globalization, the decline of overt state sponsorship of insurgency, the continuing importance of informal outside sponsorship, and the nesting of insurgency within complex conflicts associated with state weakness or failure. In economic markets, participants might dream of strategic victory—outright control of the market such as that exercised by Standard Oil prior to 1911—but seldom attained it. The best most can hope for is market domination. Even these trends tend to be transitory. Most businesses have more limited objectives—survival and some degree of profitability. This phenomenon of limited objectives also describes many insurgencies, particularly those of the twenty-first century. Competition and the absence of state sponsors mitigate against outright conquest of states in the mode

of Fidel Castro or Ho Chi Minh. It is nearly impossible for a single entity, whether the state or a nonstate player, to monopolize power. Market domination and share are constantly shifting.

In contemporary complex conflicts, profitability often is literal rather than metaphorical. There is an extensive body of analytical literature that chronicles the evolution of violent movements such as insurgencies from "grievance" to "greed."[7] The idea is that political grievances may instigate an insurgency but, as a conflict progresses, economic motives may begin to play a greater role. While combatants "have continued to mobilize around political, communal, and security objectives," as Karen Ballentine and Jake Sherman write, "increasingly these objectives have become obscured and sometimes contradicted by their more businesslike activities."[8] Conflict gives insurgents access to money and resources out of proportion to what they would have in peacetime. As Paul Collier, one of the pioneers of this idea, explains:

> Conflicts are far more likely to be caused by economic opportunities than by grievance. If economic agendas are driving conflict, then it is likely that some groups are benefiting from the conflict and these groups, therefore, have some interest in initiating and sustaining it.[9]

The counterinsurgents—the regime or its supporters—also develop vested political and economic interests in sustaining a controllable conflict. A regime facing an armed insurgency is normally under somewhat less outside pressure for economic and political reform. It can justifiably demand more of its citizens and, conversely, postpone meeting their demands. Insurgency often brings outside financial support and provides opportunities for corrupt members of the regime to tap into black markets. Even though internal conflict may diminish economic activity overall, it may increase profit margins by constraining competition. This too can work to the advantage of elites, including those in the government or security services. Collier continues:

> Various identifiable groups will "do well out of the war." They are opportunistic businessmen, criminals, traders, and the rebel organizations themselves. The rebels will do well through predation on primary commodity exports, traders will do well through the widened margins on the goods they sell to consumers, criminals will do well through theft, and opportunistic businessmen will do well at the expense of those businesses that are constrained to honest conduct.[10]

Internal wars "frequently involve the emergence of another alternative system of profit, power, and protection in which conflict serves the political and economic interests of a variety of groups."[11] Hence the insurgents, criminals, militias, or even the regime have a greater interest in sustaining a controlled conflict than in attaining victory.

The merging of armed violence and economics amplifies the degree to which complex conflicts emulate the characteristics and dynamics of volatile, hypercompetitive markets. For instance, like all markets, complex conflicts operate according to rules (albeit informal, unwritten ones). In the most basic sense, these rules dictate what is and is not acceptable as participants compete for market domination or share. Participants may violate the rules, but doing so entails risk and cost. The more risk averse a participant the less likely it is to challenge the rules—and governments are normally more risk averse than nongovernment participants, and participants satisfied with their market position and with a positive expectation about the future are more risk averse than those who are unsatisfied and pessimistic. These rules are conflict- and time-specific; they periodically evolve and shift. This year's rule or "road map" might not be next year's.

As in commercial markets, participants in a complex conflict may enter as small, personalistic companies. Some may resemble family businesses built on kinship or ethnicity. As in a commercial market, the more successful participants evolve into more complex, variegated corporate structures. Insurgencies then undertake a number of the same practices as corporations:

- Acquisitions and mergers (insurgent factions may join in partnerships, or a powerful one may integrate a less powerful one).
- Shedding or closing unproductive divisions (insurgencies may pull out of geographic regions or jettison a faction of the movement).
- Forming strategic partnerships (insurgencies may arrange relationships with internal or external groups—political, criminal, etc.—which share their objectives).
- Reorganizing for greater effectiveness and efficiency.
- Developing, refining, and at times abandoning products or product lines (insurgencies develop political, psychological, economic, and military techniques, operational methods, or themes. They refine these over time, sometimes dropping those which prove ineffective or too costly).
- Advertising and creating brand identity (insurgent psychological activities are akin to advertising. Their "brands" include political and psychological themes, and particular methods and techniques).
- Accumulating and expending capital (insurgents accumulate both financial and political capital, using it as required).
- Subcontracting or contracting out functions (contemporary insurgents may contract out tasks they are ineffective at or which they wish to dis-associate themselves from).
- Bringing in outside consultants (this can be done by physical presence of outside advisers or, in the contemporary environment, by "virtual" consultation).
- Entering and leaving market niches.
- Creating new markets and market niches.
- Creating and altering organizational culture.
- Professional development and establishing patterns of career progression.

As in commercial markets, a conflict market is affected by what happens in other markets. Just as the automobile market is affected by the petroleum market, or the American national market by the European market, the Iraq conflict market is affected by the Afghan conflict market or by the market of political ideas in the United States and other parts of the Arab world.

That contemporary insurgents emulate corporations in a hyper, competitive (violent) market shapes their operational methods. Specifically, insurgents gravitate toward operational methods which maximize desired effects while minimizing cost and risk. This, in conjunction with a profusion of information, the absence of state sponsors providing conventional military material, and the transparency of the operating environment, increases the value that terrorism provides the insurgent. Insurgents have always used terrorism. But one of the characteristics of this quintessentially psychological method of violence is that its effect is limited to those who know of or are impacted by the act. When, for instance, the Viet Cong killed a local political leader, it may have had the desired psychological effect on people in the region, but the act itself did little to shape the beliefs, perceptions, or morale of those living far away. Today, information technology amplifies the psychological effects of a terrorist incident by publicizing it to a much wider audience. This technology includes satellite, 24-hour media coverage, and, more importantly, the Internet which, Gordon McCormick and Frank Giordano believe, "has made symbolic violence a more powerful instrument of insurgent mobilization than at any time in the past."[12]

So terrorism is effective. It is easier and cheaper to undertake than conventional military operations. It is less costly and risky to the insurgent organization as a whole (since terrorist operations require only a very small number of personnel and a limited investment in training and material). It is efficient when psychological effects are compared to the resource investment. It allows insurgents to conjure an illusion of strength even when they are weak. Terrorism is less likely to lead to outright victory, but for an insurgency which does not seek victory, but only domination or survival, terrorism is the tool of choice.

As the second decade of the twenty-first century approaches, there are still a few old-fashioned insurgencies trying to militarily defeat established governments, triumphantly enter the capital city, and form their own regime. The more common pattern, though, is insurgencies satisfied with domination of all or part of the power market in their particular environment. The insurgents in Iraq, Colombia, India, Sri Lanka, Uganda, and even Afghanistan have little hope of or even interest in becoming an established regime—whether for their entire country or some breakaway segment. To continue conceptualizing contemporary insurgency as a variant of traditional, Clausewitzean warfare, where two antagonists each seek to impose their will and vanquish the opponent in pursuit of political objectives, does not capture the reality of today's geostrategic environment. Clausewitz may have been correct that war is always fought for political purposes, but not all armed conflict is war.

Rethinking Counterinsurgency

In today's world it is less the chance of an insurgent victory which creates a friendly environment for transnational terrorism than persistent internal conflict shattering any semblance of control and restraint in the state. During an insurgency, both the insurgents and the government focus on each other, often leaving parts of the country with minimal security and control.

Transnational terrorists exploit this phenomenon. Protracted insurgency tends to create a general disregard for law and order. Organized crime and corruption often blossom. A significant portion of the population also tends to lose its natural aversion to violence. A society brutalized and wounded by a protracted insurgency is more likely to spawn a variety of evils, dispersing violent individuals around the world long after a particular conflict ends.

Such actions suggest that the US military and broader defense community need a very different way of thinking about and undertaking counterinsurgency strategies and operations. At the strategic level, the risk to the United States is not that insurgents will "win" in the traditional sense, gain control of their country, or change it from an American ally to an enemy. The greater likelihood is that complex internal conflicts, especially ones involving an insurgency, will generate other adverse effects: the destabilization of regions; reduced access to resources and markets; the blossoming of transnational crime; humanitarian disasters; and transnational terrorism. Given these possibilities, the US goal should not automatically be the direct defeat of the insurgents by the established regime (which often is impossible, particularly when a partner regime is only half-heartedly committed), but, rather, the rapid resolution of the conflict. A quick and sustainable outcome which integrates most of the insurgents into the national power structure is less damaging to US national interests than a protracted conflict that may lead to the total destruction of the insurgent base. Protracted conflict, not insurgent victory, is the threat.

Because Americans consider insurgency a form of warfare, US strategy and doctrine are based on the same beliefs that are associated with a general approach to warfare: War is a pathological action which evil people impose on an otherwise peace-loving society. It is a disease which sometimes infects an otherwise healthy body politic. This metaphor is a useful one. Today, Americans consider a body without parasites and pathogens "normal." When parasites or pathogens invade, medical treatment is required to eradicate them and restore the body to its "normal" condition. Throughout human history, persistent parasites and pathogens were, in fact, normal. Societies and their members simply tolerated them. Today, this analogy characterizes conflict in many parts of the world. Rather than an abnormal and episodic condition which should be eradicated, it is viewed as normal and tolerated.

Because Americans see insurgency as a form of war and, following Clausewitz, view war as quintessentially political, they focus on the political causes and dimensions of insurgency. Certainly insurgency does have an important political component. But that is only part of the picture. Insurgency also fulfills the economic and psychological needs of the insurgent. It provides a source of income out of proportion to what the insurgent could otherwise earn, particularly for the lower ranks. It provides a source of identity and empowerment for those members with few sources for such things. Without a gun, most insurgent soldiers are simply poor, uneducated, disempowered people with no prospects and little hope. Insurgency changes all that. It makes the insurgent important and powerful and provides a livelihood. Again, the economic metaphor is useful; so

long as demand exists, supply and a market to link supply and demand will appear. So long as there are unmet human needs that can be addressed by violence, markets of violence will be created.

The tendency of insurgencies to evolve into criminal organizations suggests that counterinsurgency strategy itself needs to undergo a significant shift during the course of any conflict. If an insurgency has reached the point that it is motivated more by greed than grievance, addressing the political causes of the conflict will not prove effective. The counterinsurgency campaign needs to assume the characteristics of a program to defeat organized crime or gangs. Law enforcement should replace the military as the primary manager of a mature counterinsurgency campaign. This evolving cycle of insurgency also implies that there may be a window of opportunity early in the insurgency before its psychological, political, and economic dynamics are set. For the outsiders undertaking counterinsurgency operations, a rapid, large-scale security, political, law enforcement, intelligence, or economic effort in the nascent stages of an insurgency has the potential for providing greater results than any incremental increase in assistance following the commencement of conflict. Timing does matter.

Because Americans view insurgency as political, American counterinsurgency strategy and doctrine stress the need for political reform in those societies threatened by the insurgency. This is in fact necessary but not always sufficient. A comprehensive counterinsurgency strategy requires the simultaneous raising of the economic and psychological costs and risks for those participating in the insurgency (or other forms of conflict) while providing alternatives. David Keen explains:

> In order to move toward more lasting solution to the problem of mass violence, we need to understand and acknowledge that for significant groups this violence represents not a problem but a solution. We need to think of modifying the structure of incentives that are encouraging people to orchestrate, fund, or perpetuate acts of violence.[13]

Economic assistance and job training are as important to counter-insurgency as political reform. Businesses started and jobs created are as much "indicators of success" as insurgents killed or intelligence provided. Because the margins for economic activity tend to widen during conflict, counterinsurgency should attempt to make markets as competitive as possible.[14] Because economies dependent on exports of a single commodity or a few commodities are particularly vulnerable to protracted conflict, counter-insurgency operations need to include a plan for economic diversification.[15] A comprehensive counterinsurgency strategy should offer alternative sources of identity and empowerment for the bored, disillusioned, and disempowered. Simply providing low-paying, low-status jobs or the opportunity to attend school is not enough. Counterinsurgents—including the United States when it provides counterinsurgency support—need to recognize that becoming an insurgent gives the disenfranchised a sense of belonging, identity, and importance. Counterinsurgency cannot succeed unless it finds alternative sources of power and worth. It is in this environment where the military and other government agencies involved with counterinsurgency support need to look beyond their normal sources of inspiration and motivation. For starters, counterinsurgent planners should consult law enforcement personnel associated with antigang units, inner-city community leaders, social psychologists, and cultural anthropologists.

"Counterinsurgency cannot succeed unless it finds alternative sources of power and worth."

Women's empowerment—a brake on the aggression of disillusioned young males—should also be a central component of a successful counterinsurgency strategy. This illustrates one of the enduring problems and paradoxes of any counterinsurgency: What are foreign or external counterinsurgency supporters to do when some element of a nation's culture directly supports the conflict? Evidence suggests that cultures based on the repression of women, a warrior ethos, or some other social structure or factor are more prone to violence. Should counterinsurgency operations try to alter the culture or simply accept the fact that even once the insurgency is quelled, it may reappear?

The core dilemma, then, is that truly resolving an insurgency requires extensive social reengineering. Yet this may prove to be extremely difficult and expensive. This problem has many manifestations. In some cases, it may be impossible to provide forms of employment and sources of identity that are more lucrative than those offered by the insurgency. Regimes and national elites—the very partners the United States seeks to empower in counterinsurgency operations—often view actions necessary to stem the insurgency as a threat to their own power. They may view the conflict itself as a lesser evil. For many regimes, the insurgents pose less of a threat than a unified and effective security force. It is a basic fact that more regimes have been overthrown by coups than by insurgencies. Hence threatened governments will deliberately keep their security forces weak and divided. Alas, those with the greatest personal interest in resolving the conflict—the people—have the least ability to create peace.[16] Yet American strategy and doctrine are based on the assumption that our partners seek the same objective we do: the quickest possible resolution of the conflict. The United States assumes its partners will wholeheartedly pursue political reform and security force improvement. We are then often perplexed when insurgencies like the ongoing one in Colombia fester for decades; we are unable to grasp the dissonance between our objectives and those of our allies.

The implications of this are profound. If, in fact, insurgency is not simply a variant of war, if the real threat is the deleterious effects of sustained conflict, and if such actions are part of a systemic failure and pathology where key elites and organizations develop a vested interest in the sustainment of the conflict, the objective of counterinsurgency support should be systemic reengineering rather than simply strengthening the government so that it can impose its will more effectively on the insurgents. The most effective posture for outsiders is not to be viewed as

an ally of the government and thus a sustainer of the flawed sociopolitical-economic system, but rather to be seen as a neutral mediator and peacekeeper, even when the outsiders may have a greater ideological affinity for the existing regime than the insurgent.[17] If this is true, the United States should only undertake support of counterinsurgency operations in the most pressing instances.

When considering such support, we cannot assume that the regime of a particular nation views the conflict as we do. We need to remember that our allies often consider the reforms which the United States defines as key to long-term success as more of a threat than the insurgency itself. Elites in states faced with an insurgency do not want a pyrrhic victory in which they defeat the insurgents only to lose their own grip on power. The cure may be worse than the disease. America has to understand that many of its friends and allies view their own security forces with as much apprehension as they do the insurgents. So while the United States may press for strengthening of local security forces political leaders may resist. Ultimately, this dissonance may be irresolvable. Where the United States, viewing insurgency as a variant of war, seeks "victory" over the enemy, our allies often find that a contained insurgency which does not threaten the existence of a particular nation or regime is perfectly acceptable.

Conclusion

What, then, does all this mean? Outside of America's historic geographic area of concern (the Caribbean basin), the United States should only consider undertaking counterinsurgency operations as part of an equitable, legitimate, and broad-based multinational coalition. Unless the world community is willing to form a neo-trusteeship such as those in Bosnia, Eastern Slavonia, Kosovo, or East Timor in order to reestablish a legitimate administration, security system, or stable society, the best that can be done is ameliorating the human suffering associated with the violence.[18] In most cases, American strategic resources are better spent in the prevention of the insurgency or its containment. Clearly, systemic reengineering is not a task for the United States acting unilaterally. Nor is it a task for the US military. When America is part of a coalition, the primary role for the US military should be the protection of noncombatants until other security forces, preferably local ones, can assume that mission.

Rather than a "one size fits all" American strategy for counterinsurgencies, the United States should recognize three distinct insurgency environments, each demanding a different response:

- A functioning and responsible government with some degree of legitimacy in a nation with significant US national interests or traditional ties can be rescued by foreign internal defense (El Salvador model).
- There is no functioning or legitimate government but there is a broad international and regional consensus favoring the creation of a neo-trusteeship until systemic reengineering is complete. In such instances, the United States should provide military, economic, and political

support as part of a multinational force operating under the auspices of the United Nations.

- There is no functioning and legitimate government and no international or regional consensus for the formation of a neo-trusteeship. In such cases, the United States should pursue containment of the conflict through the support of regional states and, in cooperation with friendly states and allies, creating humanitarian "safe zones" within the region of the conflict.

In the long term, counterinsurgency operations may or may not remain a mission for the US military. It is possible that Iraq and Afghanistan were unique events caused by a combination of political factors not likely to be repeated. It is possible that future political leaders will decide that the control of ungoverned spaces or support to fragile regimes will not constitute a central pillar in American foreign policy or military strategy.

Counterinsurgency may, in fact, remain a key mission. If it does, continued analysis of insurgencies by the US military and—perhaps even more importantly, other agencies of the government—is essential. We cannot assume that twenty-first century insurgency is so like its twentieth century predecessor and that old solutions can simply be dusted off and applied. Perhaps we need to transcend the idea that insurgency is simply a variant of conventional war and amenable to the same strategic concepts. Such a conceptual and strategic readjustment will not come easily. It will be hard to simply contain an insurgency and possibly witness the ensuing humanitarian costs when no salvageable government or multinational consensus exists that is capable of reengineering the failed social, political, or economic system. It will be particularly difficult to conform to the notion of serving as mediators or honest-brokers rather than as active allies or supporters of a regime. But to not do so—to confront new security problems with old ideas and strategies—is a recipe for disaster.

Notes

1. Field Manual 100-20/Air Force Pamphlet 3-2, *Military Operations in Low Intensity Conflict* (Washington: Headquarters, Department of the Army and Department of the Air Force, 1990).

2. The most important treatment of this is David Kilcullen, "Countering Global Insurgency," *Journal of Strategic Studies,* 28 (August 2005), 597–617.

3. Field Manual 3-24/Marine Corps Warfighting Publication 3-33.5, *Counterinsurgency* (Washington: Headquarters, Department of the Army and Headquarters, United States Marine Corps, December 2006). Joint counterinsurgency doctrine is under development.

4. For instance, see Gary Anderson, "The Baathists' Blundering Guerrilla War," *The Washington Post,* 26 June 2003, A29.

5. John A. Nagl, *Learning to Eat Soup with a Knife: Counterinsurgency Lessons from Malaya and Vietnam*

(Westport, Conn.: Praeger, 2002), reprinted in paperback by the Univ. of Chicago Press, 2005; and David Galula, *Counterinsurgency Warfare: Theory and Practice* (Westport, Conn.: Praeger, 1964), reprinted 2006. Also popular is Galula's *Pacification in Algeria 1956–1958* (Santa Monica, Calif.: RAND, 1963), reprinted 2006. Nagl is a US Army officer who served multiple tours in Iraq after writing the book (which was derived from his Ph.D. dissertation). Galula was a French Army officer who based his analysis on his experience in Indochina and Algeria.

6. I explain this idea of "third" and "fourth" forces in *Rethinking Insurgency* (Carlisle, Pa.: US Army War College, Strategic Studies Institute, June 2007), 15–42.

7. Paul Collier and Anke Hoeffler, "Greed and Grievance in Civil War," *Policy Research Working Paper* No. 2355 (Washington: The World Bank, 2000).

8. Karen Ballentine and Jake Sherman, "Introduction," in Karen Ballentine and Jake Sherman, eds., *The Political Economy of Armed Conflict: Beyond Greed and Grievance* (Boulder, Colo.: Lynne Rienner, 2003), 3.

9. Paul Collier, "Doing Well Out of War: An Economic Perspective," in Mats Berdal and David M. Malone, eds., *Greed and Grievance: Economic Agendas in Civil Wars* (Boulder, Colo.: Lynne Rienner, 2000), 91.

10. Ibid., 103–104.

11. Mats Berdal and David Keen, "Violence and Economic Agendas in Civil Wars: Some Policy Implications," *Millennium,* 26 (No. 3, 1997), 797.

12. Gordon H. McCormick and Frank Giordano, "Things Come Together: Symbolic Violence and Guerrilla Mobilisation," *Third World Quarterly,* 28 (No. 2, 2007), 312.

13. David Keen, "Incentives and Disincentives for Violence," in Berdal and Malone, 25.

14. Collier, 107.

15. Ballentine and Sherman, 3.

16. Collier, 105.

17. James Fearon described and advocated such an approach in "Iraq's Civil War," *Foreign Affairs,* 86 (March/April 2007), 2–15.

18. On "neo-trusteeships," see James D. Fearon and David D. Laitin, "Neotrusteeship and the Problem of Weak States," *International Security,* 28 (Spring 2004), 4–43; and Richard Caplan, "From Collapsing States to Neo-Trusteeships: The Limits of Solving the Problem of 'Precarious Statehood' in the 21st Century," *Third World Quarterly,* 28 (No. 2, 2007), 231–44.

Dr. Steven Metz is Research Professor and Chairman of the Regional Strategy and Planning Department at the US Army War College Strategic Studies Institute. This article is based on his monograph *Rethinking Insurgency* (Carlisle, Pa.: US Army War College, Strategic Studies Institute, June 2007).

A Nuclear Posture for Today

JOHN DEUTCH

A Threat Transformed

The collapse of the Soviet Union was a dramatic geopolitical shift that should have led to major changes in the nuclear posture of the United States. The policy reviews undertaken by the Clinton administration in 1994 and the Bush administration in 2002, however, led to only minor alterations. As a result, the United States lacks a convincing rationale for its current nuclear force structure and for the policies that guide the management of its nuclear weapons enterprise.

The end of the Cold War did not mean that the United States could eliminate nuclear weapons altogether. Their existence is a reality, and the knowledge required to make them is widespread. But over the last decade, the nature of the nuclear threat has fundamentally changed, from large-scale attack to the use of one or a few devices by a rogue nation or subnational group against the United States or one of its allies. Countering the proliferation of nuclear weapons—by slowing the spread of nuclear capabilities among states, assuring that nuclear devices do not get into the hands of terrorist groups, and protecting existing stockpiles—has thus become as high a priority as deterring major nuclear attacks.

Unfortunately, the current U.S. nuclear posture does not reflect this shift. Washington still maintains a large nuclear arsenal designed for the Cold War, and it fails to take into account the current impact of its nuclear policies on those of other governments. In fact, with its overwhelming conventional military advantage, the United States does not need nuclear weapons for either war fighting or for deterring conventional war. It should therefore scale back its nuclear activity significantly. Policymakers should sharply decrease the number of warheads deployed with active military forces and make U.S. stockpile activities (of active and retired warheads and nuclear material) more transparent, setting a security standard for other nations. The United States should not, however, abandon effective nuclear forces, and it should even leave open the possibility of certain limited kinds of nuclear tests. A new U.S. nuclear posture, in short, should encourage international nonproliferation efforts without sacrificing the United States' ability to maintain a nuclear posture that deters attack.

Dual Purpose

In the past, U.S. policymakers have considered many potential roles for nuclear weapons: massive retaliation, damage limitation in nuclear exchanges, or controlling escalation in more limited scenarios. Still, they have always understood that the purpose of nuclear weapons is to deter war, not to fight it. For deterrence to work, however, the threat of preemptive or retaliatory use must be credible. It follows that, regardless of the number or the mix of weapons in the nuclear arsenal, they must be maintained ready for use, not kept as "wooden cannon."

During the Cold War, a range of nuclear scenarios defined strategic deterrence of the Soviet Union. The number of weapons in the Single Integrated Operation Plan (SIOP), the nuclear-attack strategy drawn up by the military and approved by the president, depended on the number of attack options, the number of targets (military as well as urban and industrial), and the desired "expected damage" to each target. "Expected damage" depended on the "hardness" of the target, the probability of a weapon's reaching it, and the explosive yield and accuracy of the programmed weapon. It does not require much imagination to appreciate that such a calculation could justify acquiring several thousand strategic weapons, as was indeed the case. In the 1970s and 1980s, the United States and the Soviet Union also accumulated several thousand tactical nuclear weapons, smaller devices intended for regional or battlefield use.

Although the nature of today's threats calls into question the usefulness of the United States' large nuclear arsenal, nuclear weapons continue to play a key role in U.S. security. After all, there is no guarantee that geopolitical circumstances will not change dramatically, and the emergence of a more militant China or Russia's return to totalitarianism might compel the United States to place greater reliance on its nuclear forces. Moreover, Washington's commanding nuclear posture still works to limit the nuclear ambitions of other countries. U.S. allies, most notably Germany and Japan, have forsworn establishing their own nuclear programs in exchange for protection under the U.S. security umbrella. Were the United States to give up its arsenal, other countries might be tempted to develop their own.

The possession of weapons by current nuclear powers does not directly influence the ambitions of states or terrorist groups that already want their own. They believe, rightly or wrongly, that acquiring a nuclear weapon will improve their security situation. A change in the U.S. nuclear posture would certainly not have dissuaded any of the newest members of the nuclear club—Israel, India, and Pakistan from seeking the bomb. North Korea and Iran, meanwhile, are vastly more concerned by the United States' conventional power than they are by its nuclear forces. They would probably seek nuclear weapons even if the United States had none, perhaps even with greater determination.

At the same time, the United States relies on the cooperation of many nations to achieve its nonproliferation objectives, and in this regard the U.S. nuclear posture has important consequences. An effective nonproliferation effort requires restricting the transfer of nuclear materials and technology, encouraging effective inspection by the International Atomic Energy Agency, and strengthening standards for the protection of nuclear materials and facilities. Cooperation is also essential for establishing an international norm that forbids the nuclear ambitions of non-nuclear states. (This goal, in fact, raises a basic hypocrisy on the part of nuclear powers: they retain their own arsenals while denying others the same right. This contradiction prompted Washington unwisely to commit under Article 6 of the Nonproliferation Treaty [NPT] "to pursue good-faith negotiations" toward complete disarmament, a goal it has no intention of pursuing.)

Ultimately, Washington must strike a balance between conflicting goals: maintaining a modern nuclear weapons posture, on the one hand, and curbing the spread of nuclear weapons, on the other. The Bush administration has not struck this balance well. Some officials have made unfortunate policy statements about preemption, implying that the U.S. government might even consider a first nuclear strike. The administration's 2002 nuclear posture review unwisely treats non-nuclear and nuclear strike capabilities as part of a single retaliatory continuum. Policymakers have invoked technical and geopolitical uncertainty as an argument for modernizing the weapons complex and maintaining robust testing and production capabilities. Most unfortunately, the Bush administration has proposed work on a new warhead—a low-yield "robust nuclear earth-penetrator." Although it could have argued that some conceptual work on generic warheads is needed to preserve the competence of weapons designers, the administration has instead justified this weapon on the basis of its military utility, hinting at the possibility of development and production in the future. The tone of this proposal ignores the indirect effect that new U.S. warhead research programs have on international attitudes toward nonproliferation.

How Low Can You Go?

Today, the U.S. nuclear arsenal should be managed with two purposes in mind: to deter a nuclear attack against the United States or its allies by retaining an overwhelming nuclear force with high "survivability," and to respond flexibly and precisely to a broad range of contingencies, including chemical or biological attack. The goal is to force any nation or subnational group that contemplates use of a weapon of mass destruction for an act of catastrophic terrorism to consider the possibility of U.S. nuclear retaliation and the complete destruction of its interests or sanctuary.

These purposes are not so different from those of the past, but the new nature of the threat means that many fewer weapons are needed to achieve them. In May 2001, President George W. Bush said at the National Defense University, "I am committed to achieving a credible deterrent with the lowest-possible number of nuclear weapons consistent with our national security needs, including our obligations to our allies." But just what is the "lowest possible number"?

The answer cannot be calculated using the classic SIOP method: there are no suitable target lists analogous to those drawn during the Cold War. But even a crude estimate of numerical requirements gives a sense of how much smaller the U.S. nuclear arsenal could be.

A fleet of nine Trident ballistic-missile-equipped nuclear submarines—half the size of the current fleet of 18 boats, which is capable of carrying about 3,000 warheads—would constitute a retaliatory force with sufficient survivability. Three partially loaded submarines would be on continuous station, each carrying 16 D-5 missiles with 8 nuclear warheads (a combination of the w76 and the w88), for a total of 384 warheads on alert. Another three would be in transit (carrying an additional 384 warheads in strategic reserve), and still another three would be in overhaul (and thus unarmed) at any given time. (Because each Trident can carry 24 missiles, such a deployment would add up to 1,728 accountable warheads under the counting rules of the Strategic Arms Reduction Treaty, suggesting that these rules may no longer be relevant to either the United States or Russia.) Another 200 operational nuclear warheads would complement the fleet, providing for flexible response. These would be placed on other delivery systems, such as land-based intercontinental ballistic missiles and cruise missiles on sea and air platforms that permit easier command and control.

Such a deployment—less than 1,000 warheads in total—would be smaller than the reduced target proposed by Bush as part of the Strategic Offensive Reductions Treaty: between 1,700 and 2,200 deployed strategic warheads by 2012. But for the sake of deterrence and response, this smaller nuclear force would be enough. China, the nation most likely to try to match the U.S. nuclear capability, is thought to have a total inventory of 400 nuclear weapons, including a small but growing ballistic missile force capable of reaching the United States.

In the past, all nuclear force reductions took place within U.S.-Russian arms control agreements. Given today's geopolitical realities, it is not necessary to wait for formal agreements before moving toward lower numbers. To be sure, the pace of reduction should consider Russian force levels as well as political developments there. But Washington's concern with Moscow's nuclear stockpile has as much, if not more, to do with security and the threat of "loose nukes" than with the threat of Russian attack.

Alarm over the security of nuclear stockpiles also points to the need to change the way nuclear warheads are counted. In the past, Washington counted only operational military warheads and delivery vehicles, the weapons that posed the most immediate threat. Now, however, preventing proliferation requires focusing not only on a country's deployed nuclear capability, but also on the security of its nuclear material and the intentions of those who control it. Accordingly, all nuclear weapons and material—including deployed warheads, warheads undergoing maintenance or modification, decommissioned warheads, and all weapons-grade highly enriched uranium and separated plutonium—should be counted as part of a nation's nuclear inventory.

This revised accounting scheme would do away with the anachronistic distinction between long-range strategic and short-range tactical weapons; today, all nuclear weapons are of equal concern. It would also drive home the importance of securing a country's entire nuclear inventory, including decommissioned warheads and nuclear-related materials (such as spent fuel and low-enriched uranium). Removing a warhead from the active force would shift it to a different accounting category, not drop it from the inventory altogether, because the device and its nuclear material would still require secure supervision.

Meanwhile, the United States should make its own total nuclear inventory known to the public, reporting the number of warheads and the amount of material in each category as an example to other governments. During the Cold War, there was good reason to keep this information secret. Now, however, greater transparency, consistent with proliferation concerns, would enhance U.S. security by giving allies comfort and prospective proliferators pause. Nations resisting disclosure would be inviting increased international scrutiny of their capabilities and intentions.

Low-Profile Management

Responsibility for managing the United States' nuclear weapons complex falls to the National Nuclear Security Administration (NNSA) of the Department of Energy (DOE). The NNSA's budget request for fiscal year 2005 was $6.6 billion, and this is expected to grow to $7.5 billion by 2009. The agency, which has some 35,000 employees, faces significant obstacles, including assuring the competence of its staff. The generation of scientists and engineers that developed, built, and tested nuclear weapons has long since retired. The current work force at the three main weapons laboratories—at Los Alamos, New Mexico; Livermore, California; and Sandia, New Mexico—has little direct experience designing or testing weapons. And the DOE's stringent response to recent unfortunate security lapses has hurt morale and clouded the atmosphere in the laboratories.

In 1992, the Exon-Hatfield-Mitchell amendment barred nuclear tests except those motivated by concern about the safety and reliability of weapons already in the stockpile. Since then there has been general agreement that there is no such need (affirmed by annual Defense Department reviews of nuclear safety and reliability), and the United States has observed a testing moratorium.

In the absence of a test program, the DOE has established a "stockpile stewardship program" designed to preserve the knowledge and technology required to extend the life of existing warheads. Advanced computing technology—bolstered by the DOE's impressive Accelerated Strategic Computing Initiative—has allowed modeling and simulations that can partially substitute for instrumented laboratory tests. The program also includes nuclear-weapons-related subcritical laboratory experimentation, conducted, for example, in the x-ray radiographic test facility at Los Alamos and the laser ignition facility at Livermore.

The premise behind the stockpile stewardship program is that computer simulation of the nuclear explosion sequence (beginning with chemical explosive detonation in the primary and ending with fission and thermonuclear burn in the secondary), confirmed with data from experimental facilities, can give technicians confidence in new or modified weapons. Scientists disagree, however, about whether this premise is correct. Some argue that the current program is enough to confirm the safety and reliability of existing weapons. The only way to prove the effectiveness of the strategy, however, is to demonstrate that computer codes can in fact predict the results of a nuclear explosion, as the program assumes. This suggests the need for a "scientific confirmation test," meant not to ensure stockpile security or to develop new weapons but to prove that the practical physics underpinning the nuclear program still holds. Accordingly, scientific confirmation should be added as an acceptable rationale for testing, in addition to the verification of the correction of a safety or reliability problem that cannot be verified by other means. Indeed, in the past, confidence in the stockpile came largely from development tests, rather than from tests specifically designed to confirm weapons reliability.

The NNSA program also includes several large and costly facilities intended to modernize the production infrastructure. These include a new tritium extraction facility at Los Alamos, a pit disassembly and conversion facility at the Savannah River Laboratory in South Carolina, and plans for a modern pit facility. Each individual project may be justified, but the quantity, size, and timing of such developments contribute to an impression that the U.S. weapons complex is growing and that the United States is not, in fact, reducing the role of nuclear weapons.

A more realistic U.S. nuclear posture would require a smaller but still high-quality weapons research and engineering program and a consolidated production complex. The existing stockpile stewardship program's approach is reasonable, but confirmation that physics knowledge remains adequate may require (and, from a technical point of view, ideally would require) occasional "scientific confirmation tests." Careful timing and management of such tests could mitigate the adverse international reaction they would inevitably cause. Meanwhile, conceptual work on the design of new warheads should not be precluded per se, but if it is proposed and performed there must be no ambiguity about future development. Greater transparency with regard to the activities of the NNSA would also help convince domestic and international audiences that Washington is striking the right balance in managing its nuclear weapons.

Rethinking Arms Control

A new U.S. nuclear posture should include consideration of several current and prospective arms control measures. The most controversial is the Comprehensive Test Ban Treaty (CTBT), which would permanently ban all future nuclear tests, with no provision for withdrawal. The United States has not ratified the CTBT (nor have India, Iran, Israel, North Korea, and Pakistan), but 109 nations (including the United Kingdom, France, Russia, and China) have.

Proponents of the CTBT see its potential for strengthening international norms against nuclear weapons as vital to nonproliferation efforts. They argue that it is especially worthwhile because, with the stockpile stewardship program in place, the United States does not need testing to confirm stockpile safety or reliability. Opponents respond that the CTBT has verification problems, that testing has no direct effect on either the pace or the likelihood of success by determined proliferators such as North Korea and Iran, and that, given the uncertainty of future requirements for new weapons, forgoing forever the possibility of new tests is a mistake.

Both sides in this debate have strengths and weaknesses. Opponents of the CTBT are correct that testing should be allowed if the assurance of stockpile safety or reliability requires it. However, they exaggerate the treaty's verification problems: only very low-yield tests (or tests that insulate the explosion from the surrounding earth) have much of a chance of escaping detection. CTBT advocates, meanwhile, are correct that the treaty would bolster international nonproliferation norms, even if their assertion that no test will ever again be necessary to assure stockpile safety is dubious. (In fact, some CTBT advocates may oppose testing precisely because they believe that confidence in the reliability of nuclear weapons will erode without it—to the point that nuclear weapons will lose their deterrent value and become irrelevant.) Those who attempt to sidestep the issue by claiming that a future president could invoke the supreme national interest to renounce the treaty are implying that it is better to accept a treaty despite major reservations than to work to craft one that resolves difficult issues.

There is, fortunately, a sensible middle ground in this dispute: a CTBT of limited term. Former national security officials Brent Scowcroft and Arnold Kanter have proposed entering into the CTBT for a five-year term (since all agree that U.S. nuclear tests will not be necessary anytime soon), with possible five-year extensions, after ratification by the Senate. Such a compromise would have the advantage of strengthening nonproliferation efforts and thus be preferable to having no CTBT—while leaving open the possibility of not extending the treaty if geopolitical circumstances or stockpile considerations change. A similar approach worked with the NPT, which was ratified in 1969 for a 25-year period, with review conferences every five years, and then made permanent in 1995. Opponents argue that it would be difficult or impossible at this stage to change the terms of the internationally negotiated CTBT. But the CTBT does not enter into force until 44 countries, including the United States, have ratified it, so the choice is whether the United States prefers a renewable five-year CTBT to no CTBT at all.

The U.S. nuclear posture must change to meet a transformed nuclear threat.

A second still-unratified arms control treaty is the fissile material production cutoff treaty, originally proposed by President Bill Clinton at the United Nations in 1993; it would prohibit new production of separated plutonium or highly enriched uranium. This is an attractive measure, because the United States and other nuclear states have ample amounts of weapons-usable material. The ban would prohibit any state from undertaking new production, thus serving basic nonproliferation objectives, and would limit the total amount of material that must be kept secure.

The UN Conference on Disarmament has been deliberating the cutoff treaty for several years. On August 4, 2004, the U.S. ambassador to the UN, John Danforth, announced that the Bush administration, although supportive of the ban, does not believe that effective verification is feasible. This and earlier statements by the Bush administration imply that alleged verification shortcomings will be a barrier to an agreement. But with a new nuclear posture, opposition to this treaty would be inexplicable. No arms control treaty is perfectly verifiable; there is always a risk that a violation will go undetected. Verification could be enhanced if signatory countries agreed to inspections. Traditionally, the United States and other nuclear weapons states have not accepted such inspections, but there is now little reason for the United States to resist them. Here again, transparency is in the interest of the United States. A signatory violating the treaty would be stigmatized as a proliferator before the international community. And a state that refused to sign the treaty would be signaling its interest in acquiring material suitable for making a bomb.

Arms control advocates have proposed two other major changes to U.S. nuclear policy: pledging "no first use" and de-alerting

nuclear forces. Even with a changed nuclear posture, however, the arguments for such reforms are not convincing.

Since 1978, Washington has committed to not using nuclear weapons against non-nuclear states that are signatories to the NPT, unless they attack the United States with the backing of a nuclear state. Successive U.S. administrations, however, have also maintained a policy of "strategic ambiguity," refusing to rule out a nuclear response to a biological or chemical attack. Supporters of a stronger no-first-use policy argue that strategic ambiguity sends the wrong signal to other governments: even the United States, with its overwhelming conventional military advantage, sees value in leaving open the possibility of first use. And this impression, they argue, undermines nonproliferation. They underestimate, however, just how much strategic ambiguity aids deterrence by keeping potential adversaries uncertain about a U.S. response.

De-alerting nuclear forces would mean increasing the amount of time between the decision to launch a nuclear weapon and its actual launch, in order to prevent accidental or unauthorized attacks, avoid misunderstanding, and add time to negotiate in a crisis. During the Cold War, a prompt launch capability was necessary to assure the survivability of land-based forces. Those who support de-alerting U.S. nuclear forces correctly argue that such a concern is no longer relevant. But they underestimate the practical obstacles to de-alerting submarine-launched warheads. If warheads were removed from the submarines, maintaining a continuous sea-based deployment would not be possible; the ships would need to be kept close to port, near the warheads, where they would be more vulnerable. Alternatively, communications to submarines on station could be managed to lengthen the time to launch, but it is hard to see how this could serve as a verifiable confidence-building measure. Such a step would be easily reversible anyway, making its usefulness quite limited.

Finally, the United States should make clear that any reduction is not a first step toward the abolition of the U.S. nuclear force. The U.S. nuclear posture should be consistent with foreseeable U.S. security interests. In the distant future, depending on the state of the world, a move to even lower—or potentially back to higher—levels might make sense.

Even with the Cold War over, nuclear weapons remain far more than empty symbols; they cannot simply be eliminated, despite the hopes of some arms-control advocates and the stated goals of the NPT. Nonetheless, the U.S. nuclear posture must change to meet a transformed nuclear threat. The U.S. nuclear force must be strong enough to deter and to survive attack even as it serves, as much as possible, to advance Washington's nonproliferation goals. Instead of treating nonproliferation and the maintenance of a nuclear deterrent as mutually exclusive, the United States must shape and manage its nuclear force in a way that does both.

JOHN DEUTCH is Institute Professor at the Massachusetts Institute of Technology. He served as Deputy Secretary of Defense, Chairman of the Nuclear Weapons Council, and Director of Central Intelligence during the Clinton administration and as Undersecretary of Energy during the Carter administration.

When Could Iran Get the Bomb?

What We Know and What We Don't Know about Iran's Nuclear Program

DAVID ALBRIGHT

Though hardly transparent, Director of National Intelligence John Negroponte's testimony on Iran before the Senate Intelligence Committee on February 2 was clearly cautious. The U.S. intelligence community judges that Iran probably has neither a nuclear weapon nor the necessary fissile material for a weapon, he stated. If Iran continues on its current path, it "will likely have the capability to produce a nuclear weapon within the next decade," he added. The basis for this estimate remains classified, although Iran's lack of knowledge and experience in building and running large numbers of centrifuges for uranium enrichment was reportedly an important consideration. When pressed, U.S. officials have said that they interpret Negroponte's remark to mean that Iran will need roughly 5–10 years before it possesses nuclear weapons.

Despite this caution, a handful of U.S. officials have since attempted to overstate Iran's nuclear progress, contradicting even this latest estimate. It appears that in the ongoing crisis between Iran and the United States, the crucial struggle for public perception of the Iranian nuclear threat is well under way.

Following an International Atomic Energy Agency (IAEA) briefing of U.N. Security Council permanent members and Germany in mid-March about a group of 164 centrifuges at Iran's Natanz uranium enrichment site, U.S. officials began to distort what the IAEA had said. Under the cloak of anonymity, these officials told journalists that Iran's actions represented a significant acceleration of its enrichment program. The IAEA was "shocked," "astonished," and "blown away" by Iran's progress on gas centrifuges, according to these U.S. officials, leading the United States to revise its own timeline for when Iran will get the bomb. In reality, IAEA officials said they were not surprised by Iran's actions. These U.S. statements, a senior IAEA official told the Associated Press, came "from people who are seeking a crisis, not a solution."[1]

Some outside experts and officials, including Defense Secretary Donald Rumsfeld, may be trying to undermine U.S. intelligence assessments on Iran's timeline to the bomb by highlighting the intelligence community's failure to correctly assess Iraq's weapons of mass destruction efforts.[2] Although the intelligence community deserves strong criticism for its analysis of Iraq's weapons programs, the more recent Iranian analysis has been subject to more thorough review and is more consensual than the Iraqi assessments. For example, centrifuge experts at Oak Ridge National Laboratory, who challenged faulty CIA conclusions that Iraqi aluminum tubes were for a reconstituted nuclear weapons program long before the war, have been central in assessing Iran's gas centrifuge program for the intelligence community, according to a U.S. intelligence official.

Iran is indeed on the verge of mastering a critical step in building and operating a gas centrifuge plant that would be able to produce enriched uranium for either peaceful or military purposes. However, it can be expected to face serious technical hurdles before it can reliably produce large quantities of enriched uranium.

Many details about Iran's technical nuclear capabilities and plans are unknown, and the IAEA has neither been able to verify that Iran has declared its nuclear activities in full nor to establish conclusively that Iran does not have hidden nuclear enrichment sites. Western governments view with skepticism Iranian denials of intentions to produce highly enriched uranium (HEU) or to build nuclear weapons. Yet there is no evidence of an Iranian decision to build a nuclear arsenal, let alone any knowledge of an official Iranian schedule for acquiring nuclear weapons.

During the past three years of IAEA inspections, the international community has learned a great deal of information about the Iranian program that can be used to estimate the minimum amount of time Iran would need to produce enough HEU for a nuclear bomb. According to several possible scenarios, Iran appears to need at least three years before it could have enough HEU to make a nuclear weapon. Given the technical difficulty of the task, it could take Iran much longer.

With political rhetoric likely to intensify during the coming months, it is essential to have as clear an evaluation as possible of Iranian nuclear capabilities. It is also essential to avoid repeating the mistakes that were made prior to the Iraq War, when senior Bush administration officials and their allies outside government hyped the Iraqi nuclear threat to gain support in confronting Iraq.

Out of the Gate

Iran's recent actions appear aimed at rapidly installing and running gas centrifuges, which can be used to separate uranium 235 from uranium 238—the process known as enrichment. In early January 2006, Iran removed 52 IAEA seals that verified the suspension of Iran's P-1 centrifuge uranium enrichment program that had been in effect since October 2003. (The P-1 centrifuge is a design that Iran developed from plans acquired through the nuclear smuggling network of Pakistani scientist A. Q. Khan.) The seals were located at the Natanz, Pars Trash, and Farayand Technique sites, Iran's main centrifuge facilities. On February 11, Iran started to enrich uranium in a small number of centrifuges at Natanz.

After removing the seals, Iran also started to substantially renovate key portions of its main centrifuge research and development facility, the Pilot Fuel Enrichment Plant at Natanz. Iran secretly began construction on the pilot plant in 2001, and it installed about 200 centrifuges in 2002 and 2003. The pilot plant is designed to hold six 164-machine cascades, groups of centrifuges connected by pipes that work together to enrich greater amounts of uranium to higher enrichment levels than a group of individual centrifuges. The plant has space for additional, smaller test cascades, for a total of about 1,000 centrifuges.

At Natanz and Farayand Technique, Iran quickly restarted testing and checking centrifuge components to determine if they were manufactured precisely enough to use in a centrifuge. By early March, Iran had restarted enriching uranium at the pilot plant in 10- and 20-centrifuge cascades.

Iran also moved processing tanks and an autoclave—used to heat centrifuge feed material known as uranium hexafluoride into a gas prior to insertion into a centrifuge cascade—into its main production facility, the underground Fuel Enrichment Plant (FEP) at Natanz. This plant is designed to eventually hold 50,000–60,000 centrifuges. Iran told the IAEA that it intends to start installing the first 3,000 P-1 centrifuges at the FEP in the fourth quarter of 2006. A key outstanding question is whether Iran has procured from abroad or domestically manufactured all the equipment and materials it needs to finish the first module of 3,000 centrifuges.

Iran's Uranium Conversion Facility at Isfahan, which converts natural uranium into uranium hexafluoride, has continued to operate since restarting in August 2005, following the beginning of the breakdown in the suspension. By May 2006, Iran had produced 110 metric tons of uranium hexafluoride.[3] Assuming that roughly 5 metric tons of uranium hexafluoride are needed to make enough HEU for a nuclear weapon, this stock represents enough natural uranium hexafluoride for more than 20 nuclear weapons. Although this uranium hexafluoride contains impurities that can interfere with the operation of centrifuges and reduce their output or cause them to fail, most IAEA experts believe that Iran can overcome this problem and that the issue of hexafluoride impurity has been overblown in the media. Iran is known to be working to improve the purity of its uranium hexafluoride. If necessary, Iran could use its existing stock of impure material, either further purifying this uranium hexafluoride or settling for reduced output and a higher centrifuge failure rate.

Centrifuge Know-How

A key part of the development of Iran's gas centrifuge program is the operation of the 164-machine test cascades at the Natanz pilot plant, which will be the workhorses of any future centrifuge plant. Iran finished installing its first test cascade in the fall of 2003, but the cascade never operated with uranium hexafluoride prior to the October 2003 suspension. On April 13, 2006, Iran announced that it had produced low-enriched uranium (LEU) in its 164-machine cascade. Soon afterward, it announced that it had enriched uranium up to a level of almost 5 percent.

Restarting the cascade took several months because Iran had to repair damaged centrifuges. According to IAEA reports, many centrifuges crashed or broke when the cascade was shut down at the start of the suspension in 2003. Before introducing uranium hexafluoride, Iran had to reconnect all the pipes, establish a vacuum inside the cascade, and prepare the cascade for operation with uranium hexafluoride.

Beyond the technical unknowns, answering the question of how soon Iran could produce enough HEU for a nuclear weapon is complicated and fraught with uncertainty.

The initial performance of the P-1 centrifuges in this cascade has been lower than expected. Based on the April 12 statements of Gholam Reza Aghazadeh, head of the Atomic Energy Organization of Iran, the average annualized output of the centrifuges in this cascade is relatively low.[4] In the same interview, Aghazadeh implied that he expects the average output of each P-1 centrifuge to almost double in the main plant.

In addition, Iran has not yet run this cascade continuously to produce enriched uranium. According to a Vienna diplomat, the cascade operated with uranium hexafluoride only about half of its first month of operation, although it continued to operate under vacuum the rest of the time. During this period, according to a May 19 Agence France Presse report, the cascade produced only "dozens of grams" of enriched uranium, far below the more than 2,000 grams Aghazadeh predicted the cascade would produce running continuously for that length of time. The Iranian centrifuge operators do not yet have sufficient understanding of cascade operation and must conduct a series of longer tests to develop a deeper understanding.

The IAEA reported in April that Iran is building the second and third cascades at the pilot plant. A senior diplomat in Vienna said in a late-April interview that the second and third cascades could start by early summer. This schedule would allow Iran to test multiple cascades running in parallel, a necessary step before building a centrifuge plant composed of such cascades. The diplomat speculated that Iran could continue with this pattern, installing the fourth and fifth in July and August, respectively. The space for the sixth cascade is currently occupied by the 10- and 20-machine cascades, he said.

Iran would likely want to run its cascades individually and in parallel for several months to ensure that no significant problems develop and to gain confidence that it can reliably enrich uranium in the cascades. Problems could include excessive vibration of the centrifuges, motor or power failures, pressure and temperature instabilities, or breakdown of the vacuum. Iran may also want to test any emergency systems designed to shut down the cascade without losing many centrifuges in the event of a major failure. Absent major problems, Iran is expected to need until the fall or later to demonstrate successful operation of its cascades and their associated emergency and control systems.

Once Iran overcomes the technical hurdle of operating its demonstration cascades, it can duplicate them and even create larger cascades. Iran would then be ready to build a centrifuge plant able to produce significant amounts of enriched uranium either for peaceful purposes or for nuclear weapons.

The Underground Path

Answering the question of how soon Iran could produce enough HEU for a nuclear weapon is complicated and fraught with uncertainty. Beyond the technical uncertainties, several other important factors are unknown. Will Iran develop an enrichment capability but produce only LEU for use in nuclear power reactors and not any HEU for use in a nuclear weapon? Will Iran withdraw from the Nuclear Non-Proliferation Treaty (NPT), expel IAEA inspectors, and concentrate on building secret nuclear facilities? How does the Iranian regime perceive the political risks of a particular action, such as trying to make HEU in the pilot plant? What resources will Iran apply to finishing its uranium enrichment facilities? Will there be preemptive military strikes against Iranian nuclear sites?

For the purposes of these estimates, a crude fission nuclear weapon is estimated to require 15–20 kilograms of weapon-grade uranium (HEU containing more than 90 percent uranium 235).[5] Iran's most direct path to obtaining HEU for nuclear weapons is to build a relatively small gas centrifuge plant that can make weapon-grade uranium directly.[6] If Iran built such a plant openly, it would be an acknowledgement that it seeks nuclear weapons and would invite a harsh response from the West and the IAEA.

As a result, Iran would likely pursue such a path in utmost secrecy, without declaring to the IAEA the facility and any associated uranium hexafluoride production facilities. Because Iran announced earlier this year that it was ending its implementation of the Additional Protocol—an advanced safeguards agreement created in the 1990s to fix traditional safeguards' inability to provide adequate assurance that a country does not have undeclared nuclear facilities or materials—the IAEA would face a difficult challenge discovering such a clandestine facility. The IAEA has already reported that it can no longer effectively monitor centrifuge components, unless they are at Natanz and within areas subject to IAEA containment and surveillance.

A centrifuge plant containing about 1,500–1,800 P-1 centrifuges is sufficient to make more than enough HEU for one nuclear weapon per year. (Each P-1 centrifuge is assumed to have an output of about 2.5–3 separative work units [swu] per year.[7] With a capacity of 4,500 swu per year, this facility could produce as much as 28 kilograms of weapon-grade uranium a year.[8])

Worst-Case Scenarios

If Iran decides to obtain highly enriched uranium (HEU) for use in a nuclear weapon, its two most likely paths would be to develop a clandestine or a "breakout" centrifuge enrichment capability. In either worst-case estimate, the earliest Iran would have enough HEU for a nuclear weapon would be in 2009.

Beginning of 2006–End of 2007
If the construction of a secret plant with 1,500–1,800 centrifuges had begun in early 2006, its completion would not be likely before the end of 2007.

Beginning of 2008–End of 2008
It would take approximately one year for this plant to produce enough HEU for a nuclear weapon.

Beginning of 2009–Months later
Converting the HEU into weapon components would take a few months, meaning the earliest Iran could have a nuclear weapon would be sometime in 2009.

Late 2006–2009 or 2010
Iran has said it will begin installing 3,000 centrifuges in its production-scale plant in late 2006. If there are no major delays, this module could be complete in 2009 or 2010.

Months later
Centrifuges in the production-scale plant could be reconfigured relatively easily to make HEU and could produce enough material for a weapon in as little as a few months. Converting the HEU into weapon components would take an additional few months.

Iran has enough components to build up to 5,000 centrifuges, according to some senior diplomats in Vienna. Other senior diplomats, however, have said that Iran may not have 5,000 of all components, and that many components are not expected to pass quality control. In total, Iran is estimated to have in hand enough decent components for at least 1,000 to 2,000 centrifuges, in addition to the roughly 800 centrifuges already slated for the pilot plant. Iran could also build new centrifuge components, and, in fact, may have already started to do so.

If Iran had started to build a clandestine plant with 1,500–1,800 centrifuges in early 2006, it could assemble enough additional usable machines in about 15–18 months, or by about mid-2007. It would need to assemble centrifuges at the upper limit of its past rate, about 70–100 centrifuges per month, to accomplish this goal. In the meantime, Iran would need to identify a new facility where it could install the centrifuge cascades, since it is unlikely to choose Natanz as the location of a secret plant. It would also need to install control and emergency equipment, feed and withdrawal systems, and other peripheral equipment. It would then need to integrate all of these systems, test them, and commission the plant. Iran could start immediately to accomplish these steps, even before the final testing of the 164-machine cascades at Natanz, but final completion of a clandestine plant would be highly unlikely before the end of 2007.

Given another year to make enough HEU for a nuclear weapon, and a few more months to convert the uranium into weapon components, Iran could have its first nuclear weapon in 2009. By this time, Iran could have had sufficient time to prepare the other components of a nuclear weapon, although the weapon may not be small enough to be deliverable by a ballistic missile.

This result reflects a worst-case assessment for arms control. Iran can be expected to take longer, as it is likely to encounter technical difficulties that would delay bringing a centrifuge plant into operation. Factors causing delay could include difficulty assembling and installing so many centrifuges in such a short time period, inability to achieve the relatively high separative work output used in these estimates, difficulty acquiring sufficient dual-use equipment overseas, taking longer than expected to overcome difficulties in operating the cascades as a single production unit, or a holdup in commissioning the secret centrifuge plant.

Iranian officials have recently announced that they are also working on developing the more advanced P-2 centrifuge, the designs for which were also obtained from the Khan network. Iran's progress on this centrifuge appears to lag behind that of the P-1 centrifuge, as evidenced by a lack of procurement records for P-2 parts. The IAEA has been unable to determine the exact status of the P-2 program, but what is known appears to exclude the existence of undeclared P-2 facilities sufficiently advanced to significantly shift projections of the amount of time Iran would need to produce nuclear weapons.

Readying a "Breakout"

Another way that Iran could produce HEU for nuclear weapons would be to use its Natanz production facility, even though the centrifuge module is being designed to produce LEU for use in nuclear reactors. Iran has said it intends to start installing its first module of 3,000 centrifuges in the production facility's underground halls in late 2006, though it doesn't presently have enough centrifuge parts to complete the module. Since the pilot plant would likely have already produced a relatively large amount of LEU, the time to produce enough HEU for a nuclear weapon in this facility could be dramatically shortened.

At the above rates of centrifuge assembly, and assuming that it has, can produce, or acquire abroad enough P-1 centrifuges and associated equipment, Iran could finish assembling the module's 3,000 centrifuges sometime in 2008. Although Iran would likely build and operate some cascades before all the centrifuges are assembled, it will probably need at least another year to finish this module, placing the completion date in 2009

or 2010. Unexpected complications could delay the commissioning date. Alternatively, Iran could accelerate the pace by manufacturing, assembling, and installing centrifuges more quickly. Given all the difficult tasks that must be accomplished, however, Iran is unlikely to commission this module much before the start of 2009.

If Iran decided to make HEU in this module, it would have several alternatives. Because of the small throughput and great operational flexibility of centrifuges, HEU for nuclear weapons could be produced by reconfiguring the cascades in the module or by batch recycling, which entails feeding the cascade product back into the same cascade for subsequent cycles of enrichment.

Reconfiguration could be as straightforward as connecting separate cascades in series and carefully selecting the places where new pipes interconnect the cascades. Iran's 3,000-centrifuge module is slated to be composed of almost 20 164-centrifuge cascades, operating together under one common control system. With such a setup, reconfiguration would not require the disassembly of the individual cascades and could be accomplished within days. Such a setup could lessen by 10 percent the enrichment output, and the HEU's final enrichment level may reach only 80 percent, which is still sufficient for use in an existing implosion design, albeit with a lower explosive yield.

With a reconfigured plant, and starting with natural uranium, 20 kilograms of HEU could be produced within four to six months. If Iran waited until it had produced a stock of LEU before reconfiguring and then used this stock as the initial feedstock in the reconfigured plant, it could produce 20 kilograms of HEU in about one to two months.

Batch recycling would entail putting the cascade product back through the cascade several times, without changing the cascade's basic setup. Starting with natural uranium, cascades of the type expected at Natanz could produce weapon-grade uranium after four to five recycles. Twenty kilograms of weapon-grade uranium could be produced in about six to twelve months. If the batch operation started with an existing stock of LEU, the time to produce 20 kilograms of weapon-grade uranium would drop to about one to two months.

Whether using batch recycling or reconfiguration, Iran would likely operate the module to make LEU so that any production of HEU would be expected to happen quickly. Still, using either of these breakout approaches, Iran is not likely to have enough HEU for a nuclear weapon until 2009, and technical obstacles may further delay the operation of the module in the production facility.

Looking at a timeline of at least three years before Iran could have a nuclear weapons capability means that there is still time to pursue aggressive diplomatic options and time for measures such as sanctions to have an effect, if they become necessary.

In the short term, it is imperative for the international community to intensify its efforts to disrupt or slow Iran's ongoing overseas acquisition of dual-use items for its centrifuge program. Iran has encountered greater difficulty acquiring these items because of the increased scrutiny by key supplier states and companies, forcing Iranian smugglers to look elsewhere. As Iran applies more devious methods or seeks these items in other countries, greater efforts will be required to thwart it from succeeding.

It is vital to continue to understand what Iran has accomplished, what it still has to learn, and when it will reach a point when a plan to pursue nuclear weapons covertly or openly could succeed more quickly than the international community can react. Although these estimates include significant uncertainties, they reinforce the view that Iran must foreswear any deployed enrichment capability and accept adequate inspections. Otherwise, we risk a seismic shift in the balance of power in the region.

Notes

1. George Jahn, "U.N. to Inspect Iran Enrichment Program," Associated Press, March 25, 2006.

2. In an April 18, 2006 interview on the *Laura Ingraham Show,* Rumsfeld said he was "not confident" that the U.S. intelligence community's estimate of Iran's nuclear timeline was accurate (transcript available at www.defenselink.mil/transcripts/2006/tr20060418-12862.html). At a May 9, 2006 press conference, he said that the "wrong" intelligence used to justify the U.S. invasion of Iraq should "give one pause" when evaluating the credibility of intelligence regarding Iran ("Rumsfeld: Iraq Errors Affect Assessment of Iran," CNN, May 9, 2006).

3. This quantity refers to the amount of uranium mass in the uranium hexafluoride.

4. The annualized average output of each centrifuge was about 1.4 separative work units (swu) per machine per year, based on Aghazadeh's statement of a maximum feed rate of 70 grams per hour and the production of 7 grams per hour of 3.5 percent enriched uranium. The feed and product rates imply a tails assay (the fraction of fissionable uranium 235 in the waste stream) of 0.4 percent. This relatively low output could mean that the aluminum centrifuge rotors are spinning at a lower speed than possible. For the main plant, Aghazadeh said that 48,000 centrifuges would produce 30 metric tons of low-enriched uranium per year. Assuming a tails assay of 0.4 percent and a product of 3.5 percent enriched uranium, the estimated average output of each machine would be about 2.3 swu/year. With an assumed tails assay of 0.3 percent, the estimated output rises to 2.7 swu/year, high for a Pakistani P-1 design but possible if the centrifuge is further optimized.

5. Iran could be expected to initially build a crude, implosion-type fission weapon similar to known designs. In 1990, Iraq initially planned to use 15 kilograms of weapon-grade uranium in its implosion design. An unclassified design using almost 20 kilograms was calculated in a study by the author and Theodore Taylor in about 1990. A larger quantity of HEU is needed than the exact amount placed into the weapon because of inevitable losses during processing, but such losses can be kept to less than 20 percent with care.

6. Alternatively, Iran could secretly build a "topping plant" of about 500 centrifuges and use a stock of low-enriched uranium produced in the pilot plant as feed to produce HEU. However, the estimated timeline for this alternative route is not significantly different from the one outlined in this scenario.

7. These values for separative work are at the high end of the possible output of Iran's P-1 centrifuge. Actual values may be less.

8. This calculation assumes a relatively high tails assay of 0.5 percent. As a centrifuge program matures and grows, it typically reduces the tails assay to conserve uranium supplies.

DAVID ALBRIGHT is president of the Institute for Science and International Security and a member of the *Bulletin's* Editorial Advisory Board.

The New Threats: Nuclear Amnesia, Nuclear Legitimacy

"It will be up to the next U.S. administration to remove nuclear arms from the quiver of threat responses and war-fighting scenarios and begin the process of delegitimizing nuclear weapons."

JACK MENDELSOHN

The most urgent national security issue facing the United States is the possibility that a nuclear weapon might be used against the nation as an instrument of war or terror. If Americans are to avoid such a catastrophe and its unprecedented environmental, economic, and social effects, this threat must be addressed vigorously and soon.

Facing up to the threat will require tracking down terrorists and warning rogue states that they will be held accountable for their actions. But it also will require delegitimizing nuclear weapons as usable instruments of warfare and relegating them to a deterrent role or, in certain cases, to weapons of last resort. This policy change will be difficult to adopt because America's leaders as well as the general public have lost sight of the devastating power of nuclear weapons and tend to dismiss the political and moral taboos surrounding their use.

Memory Loss

A nuclear weapon has not been detonated in war since 1945. The 1962 Cuban missile crisis is ancient history for anyone under 50. There have been less than a handful of nuclear tests during the past decade. And the vast majority of nuclear tests between 1963 (when the Limited Test Ban Treaty came into effect) and 1996 (when the Comprehensive Test Ban Treaty was signed) were conducted underground, literally and figuratively burying the "shock and awe" effects of a nuclear explosion. In the meantime, presidents and politicians have come to view nuclear weapons as a seamless extension of the nation's military capabilities and the threat of their potential use as an acceptable part of its political rhetoric.

This nuclear amnesia is critically dangerous for several reasons. First, nuclear weapons are enormously more destructive than conventional explosives. During 10 months of air raids on Britain in 1940 and 1941, the German Luftwaffe dropped

bombs with the equivalent of 18.8 kilotons and killed more than 43,000 people. At Hiroshima, one bomb with an estimated yield of 15 kilotons killed 70,000 in one day, with the toll reaching 140,000 by the end of 1945 because of subsequent deaths from injuries and radiation exposure.

Second, despite efforts by the Clinton and Bush administrations to equate the dangers of chemical, biological, and nuclear weapons by lumping them together as weapons of mass destruction, nuclear weapons are the only ones that could devastate the United States, irreparably altering the lives of its citizens. Chemical weapons (CWS) tend to be localized in their effects and difficult to deliver over large areas. Sensors can detect them and protective measures can mitigate their effects. Biological weapons (BWS) are a more serious threat, but they can be tricky to produce, difficult to disseminate, and unpredictable in their effects. Against unprepared civilians, BWS could be devastating, but vaccinations, masks, antidotes, protective clothing, quarantines, and small-scale evacuations could attenuate the severity of an attack.

The effects of nuclear weapons in relation to CWS and BWS are indicated in a comparative lethality risk model developed by the now-defunct congressional Office of Technology Assessment. The release of 300 kilograms of sarin nerve gas would create a .22-square-kilometer lethal area and cause 60 to 200 deaths. The release of 30 kilograms of anthrax spores would create a 10-square-kilometer lethal area and cause 30,000 to 100,000 deaths. The explosion of a hydrogen bomb with a 1-megaton yield would create a 190-square-kilometer lethal area and cause 570,000 to 1,900,000 deaths.

Third, unlike CWS and BWS, there are no effective defenses against a nuclear weapon delivered by long-range missile or clandestinely placed in a target country. Although command authorities of the nuclear weapon states have a high level of confidence in the reliability of offensive warheads going off over the target if launched by missiles, there is no comparable confidence in the reliability of defenses that are deployed or being developed against ballistic or cruise missile attack. Strategic missile defenses currently under development are unproven against a determined small-scale attack, unworkable against a large-scale attack, and irrelevant to the threat from rogue states or terrorists, whose delivery systems are unknown but not likely to be long-range ballistic missiles.

Fourth, the public is generally unaware of the large numbers of nuclear weapons around the world. About 27,000 are believed to exist in nine countries, including North Korea, which apparently exploded a nuclear device in October. Most of these weapons (26,000) are in U.S. or Russian arsenals. Weapons that are deployed and ready to be used on short notice generally are secure from theft or diversion. But security problems, particularly in Russia, continue to exist with weapons that are kept in storage or reserve.

The 2002 U.S.-Russian Strategic Offensive Reduction Treaty (SORT, also referred to as the Moscow Treaty) will reduce the long-range strategic nuclear weapons of the two countries to between 1,700 and 2,200 deployed warheads each by 2012. The treaty, however, does not apply to strategic nuclear weapons in storage or reserve, or to any tactical nuclear weapons, which together constitute the overwhelming majority of warheads in the arsenals. Nor does the treaty affect the 2,500 to 3,000 warheads that the United States and Russia each still maintain ready to be launched on short notice. (The other nuclear powers generally keep their systems in a lower state of readiness, often without the war-heads mated to missiles or aircraft.)

Holes in the Treaty

Nuclear amnesia is also dangerous because, even though CWS and BWS are banned by international treaty, nuclear weapons are not. International agreements outlaw the possession, use, and transfer of CWS and BWS. Notwithstanding the fact that some countries have acquired and used these weapons, the international community has established an explicit norm against their use, and the relevant CW and BW agreements call for an international response to violations of this norm, orchestrated through the UN Security Council.

Most states seem to recognize implicit political and moral constraints against the use of nuclear weapons. (These would, of course, not restrain nonstate actors.) Also, some large areas of the world have declared nuclear weapons off limits. These so-called nuclear-weapon-free zones include Latin America, Africa, the South Pacific, Southeast Asia, and Antarctica.

Nevertheless, the major international agreement regarding nuclear weapons, the nuclear Non-Proliferation Treaty (NPT), bans only the proliferation, not the use, of nuclear weapons beyond the United States, United Kingdom, France, China, and Russia—which also happen to be the five permanent members (P-5) of the UN Security Council. The NPT, moreover, grants non-nuclear-weapon states the right to "peaceful" use of nuclear technology. This essentially permits any state to develop the capability to produce the enriched uranium fuel used in a nuclear power plant. Unfortunately, this fuel can also be used to build nuclear weapons. This is the basis for the current concern about the Iranian program to enrich uranium.

A U.S. first-use policy reinforces the value and prestige attributed to nuclear weapons and undermines efforts to persuade other nations to refrain from developing their own nuclear arsenals.

To counterbalance the continued possession of nuclear weapons by the P-5 nations, the NPT calls for these states to work toward ending the arms race and for all NPT members to seek general and complete disarmament. This nuclear disarmament goal is explicit, and the non-nuclear-weapon states frequently cite it as an "unequivocal obligation" that the nuclear powers have yet to fulfill. But no timetable and no political or security criteria for disarmament were established. Not surprisingly, no nuclear nation has committed to a date for its own denuclearization (although the debate has some resonance in the United Kingdom).

In addition, there is no explicit ban on the further development or modernization of nuclear weapons by the nuclear weapon states. The U.S. Senate in 1999 rejected the Comprehensive Nuclear Test Ban Treaty (CTBT), which would have essentially halted the development of more sophisticated weapons. The treaty's entry into force any time soon, if ever, looks improbable.

Right of First Use

A final source of danger in nuclear amnesia results from the desire of every nuclear weapon state except China to continue to maintain the right of first use of nuclear weapons against any kind of attack, as well as the right of preventive or preemptive attack. As President Jacques Chirac of France stated in January 2006, "The leaders of states who would use terrorist means against us, as well as those who would consider using in one way or another weapons of mass destruction, must understand that they would lay themselves open to a firm and adapted response on our part. This response could be a conventional one. It could also be of a different kind."

All nuclear first-use policies stand in sharp conflict with the findings of the International Court of Justice (ICJ). In 1996, the ICJ concluded that "the threat or use of nuclear weapons would generally be contrary to the rules of international law applicable in armed conflict, and in particular the principles and rules of humanitarian law." The ICJ, however, could not agree on whether nuclear weapons could be used "in an extreme circumstance of self-defense, in which the very survival of a State would be at stake." First-use policies also contravene the so-called negative security assurances, a solemn political commitment by the P-5 not to carry out a nuclear attack against non-nuclear-weapon states that are NPT members.

Yet Bush administration strategic statements and development plans clearly envision first-use scenarios. The administration argued in its 2001 Nuclear Posture Review that "new capabilities must be developed to defeat emerging threats such as hard and deeply buried targets, to find and attack mobile and relocatable targets, to defeat chemical or biological agents, and to improve accuracy and limit collateral damage."

Concern about current nuclear weapon use policies has evoked a strong reaction from some members of Congress. In a December 2005 letter to the president, 16 lawmakers objected to a March 15, 2005, draft of the Pentagon's Doctrine for Nuclear Operations that would allow combat commanders to request presidential approval for the preemptive use of nuclear weapons under various conditions. "We believe this effort to broaden the range of scenarios in which nuclear weapons might be contemplated is unwise and provocative," the letter said.

By supporting a variety of justifications for nuclear use, the administration is sending a clear message that nuclear weapons are indispensable, legitimate war-fighting weapons required by the world's most powerful country to ensure its security. The administration's policies also indicate that the United States does not intend to eliminate these weapons from its own arsenal. On the contrary, it plans to modernize and retain the arsenal indefinitely.

Delegitimizing Nukes

There are no indications that the Bush administration in its remaining years in office will reexamine its ill-considered and self-endangering policy of threatening to use nuclear weapons in a proliferating variety of contingencies. Nor will it abandon the push to develop new specialized nuclear weapons to support this first-use policy. If America is to avoid the unmitigated disaster surrounding any nuclear weapons use, it will be up to the next U.S. administration to remove nuclear arms from the quiver of threat responses and war-fighting scenarios and begin the process of delegitimizing nuclear weapons.

To this end, several actions can be taken. The next administration should renounce the current U.S. nuclear use policy, extend a moratorium on nuclear weapons tests while slowing the development of tactical nuclear weapons, propose an international ban on the first use of nuclear weapons, and encourage the spread of nuclear-weapon-free zones.

The first step is to declare that the United States does not consider nuclear arms a weapon of war and will not use them unless an adversary uses them. Issuing this statement would not require congressional approval or presage costly military acquisitions. It might also be coordinated with the other nuclear powers. As Linton Brooks, the head of the Department of Energy's National Nuclear Security Administration, noted recently, "We can change our declaratory policy in a day."

The current U.S. nuclear use policy is unwise in that it lacks any strategic rationale. The threat during the cold war to use nuclear weapons in response to non-nuclear aggression, however contradictory such a policy might have been, was considered helpful in reassuring the Western alliance that some military response was available to counter the quantitative, conventional military advantages of the Warsaw Pact. Today, the United States enjoys the greatest conventional superiority

in history over any potential enemy or combination of enemies and, with the exception of nuclear weapons, cannot be put at risk by any adversary.

In 1993, three respected members of the U.S. national security establishment, McGeorge Bundy, William J. Crowe, and Sidney Drell, wrote: "There is no vital interest of the U.S., except the deterrence of nuclear attack, that cannot be met by prudent conventional readiness. There is no visible case where the U.S. could be forced to choose between defeat and the first use of nuclear weapons." Nothing has occurred since this statement was written to make nuclear weapons more critical to maintaining stability and security.

To the contrary, for the United States to insist that it needs the threat of the use of nuclear weapons to deter potential state and nonstate adversaries raises the question of why other, much weaker nations, confronted by hostile neighbors, do not need them as well (or even more). Moreover, a U.S. first-use policy reinforces the value and prestige attributed to nuclear weapons and undermines efforts to persuade other nations to refrain from developing their own nuclear arsenals.

"Calculated Ambiguity"

Current U.S. nuclear use policy is also unwise in that it lacks any political rationale. As its series of post–cold war interventions has demonstrated, the United States is prepared to undertake military missions for a number of reasons: to promote democracy (Haiti), resolve civil conflicts (Somalia), protect allies (Kuwait), initiate regime change (Iraq), pursue terrorists (Afghanistan), and protect human rights (Kosovo). At the same time, the United States has made it clear that it seeks to perform these mainly humanitarian missions with a minimum amount of harm to innocent civilians and the target country.

In none of these interventions would nuclear weapons have been an appropriate or necessary means to a political end. Yet, as long as the United States refuses to rule out the potential use of nuclear weapons in virtually any contingency, it is difficult to avoid creating the impression that the spread of democratic values is being backed by a nuclear threat. To many countries, this policy seems both deceitful and dangerous and suggests that the only way to meet the U.S. challenge is to possess nuclear weapons of their own.

Some proponents of the current nuclear use policy argue that the United States will probably never employ nuclear weapons except in retaliation for an actual nuclear attack or to prevent an imminent one. Certainly, memoirs by senior policy makers during the first Gulf War make it clear that whatever was implied, the United States never had, under any circumstances, the intention of using nuclear weapons during the war. Nonetheless, proponents claim that the uncertainty or "calculated ambiguity" of the U.S. response to a high-profile security challenge still serves to deter a potential aggressor from initiating a CW or BW attack.

Yet, if the United States continues to maintain that all options are on the table but does not actually intend to use nuclear weapons in the situations envisaged by the Pentagon's draft Doctrine for Nuclear Operations, then "calculated ambiguity" as a policy loses its credibility—and the United States is saddled with a doctrine that provokes hostility rather than promoting security.

America's leaders have lost sight of the devastating power of nuclear weapons and tend to dismiss the political and moral taboos surrounding their use.

Toward a Test Ban

The next administration could also make it clear that the United States does not intend to resume nuclear testing in order to develop new nuclear weapons. There will be a new Congress in 2009 that, if the new administration is so committed, might be persuaded to reconsider the Senate's 1999 rejection of the CTBT. If China joined with the United States and the three other members of the P-5 that have already ratified the treaty, it would make it considerably more difficult (though not impossible) for the major nuclear powers to begin nuclear testing again.

Ratifying the CTBT would not immediately solve the challenges involving India, Pakistan, North Korea, or Israel, which currently do not seem to have the political incentive to sign and ratify the agreement. It would, however, delegitimize nuclear testing, curb substantial arsenal modernization by the P-5, and reinforce U.S. credibility in efforts to convince other nations of the need to stem proliferation.

If the next administration cannot muster enough senatorial support to see the CTBT through to ratification, it should publicly recommit to the self-imposed testing moratorium—as the current administration has done after a fashion—that has been in place for all of the P-5 since 1996. (Russia has not tested a nuclear weapon since 1990; the United States and the United Kingdom have not tested one since 1992.)

The continued testing moratorium should be combined with a disavowal of efforts to develop new warheads to carry out nuclear use policies. The Bush administration has been seeking funds to explore three new nuclear weapons: a "bunker-buster" (an earth-penetrating bomb intended to destroy underground facilities); a "mini-nuke" (purportedly to reduce collateral damage); and a "reliable replacement warhead" (RRW) to increase the longevity, reliability, and safety of the nuclear stockpile.

One or another of these devices might be developed without testing. The bunker-buster, for example, is more a question of enhancing the casing than changing the physics package, and there are existing low-yield warhead designs available for a mini-nuke. Yet those who champion these new weapons are likely to use the uncertain performance of these new systems, most egregiously the RRW, as a compelling reason to abandon the testing moratorium and resume nuclear tests.

Nuclear "Newspeak"

The new nuclear weapons that the administration is seeking are not ideal or even necessary for carrying out their designated missions. Finding hard and deeply buried targets of high value is a strenuous and uncertain intelligence task. If such sites are correctly identified—a big "if"—many of them could be destroyed or disabled or access to them denied by precision-guided conventional munitions. On the other hand, if they are misidentified and a nuclear weapon destroys a nonmilitary industrial site and the neighborhood surrounding it, the United States would be subject to international outrage of the sort that has shrouded the invasion of Iraq.

In addition, any potential adversary would seek to put its important command and control or other military assets deeply enough underground or within mountains or inside tunnels to make them safe from such attack. In that case, the hardened targets would either be unreachable or would require weapons with such high yields that they would unfailingly inflict significant collateral damage (a mission already within the capabilities of weapons in the existing arsenal).

Alternatively, adversaries might embed their high-value targets in civilian neighborhoods, inviting the United States to face widespread condemnation if these targets were attacked with nuclear weapons. The same paradox surrounds attacks against BW or CW agents. The deeper the bunker and the larger the yield required to destroy it, the greater the collateral damage. Moreover, if the attack fails to neutralize the chemical and biological agents by thermal effects or radiation, then the agents themselves may be dispersed and compound the lethality of the attack.

The administration argues that the current U.S. nuclear arsenal is self-deterring because a rogue state leader could doubt that the United States would employ large-yield warheads against an adversary. Low-yield mini-nukes, the administration claims, would be a much more credible deterrent or response.

But there are serious drawbacks to this argument. One is that making nuclear weapons more usable, particularly when they are not militarily required, ultimately endangers U.S. security by breaking down the barriers to the use of any nuclear device. Second, the idea that a mini-nuke will reduce collateral damage is truly nuclear "newspeak," given the destructive power of even a small-yield weapon. (A 12.5-kiloton weapon could cause 20,000 to 80,000 deaths. The severe blast damage radius of a 5-kiloton weapon would extend more than 0.6 kilometers.) Finally, the call for usable mini-nukes implies that the current force of 6,000 deployed nuclear warheads, including some weapons with very small yields, is neither a valid deterrent nor a credible retaliatory threat.

Weapons of Last Resort

Rather than preserving and heralding the right of first use, the next U.S. administration should urge the international community to ban the use of nuclear weapons except in retaliation for nuclear use by others or—particularly in the case of small states such as Israel—as a last resort if the nation's survival is at risk. This, too, would help efforts to begin reversing the increased legitimization of nuclear weapons. (Eliminating the possession of nuclear weapons, the ultimate ideal outcome, will be obtained incrementally, if at all, after transparency and confidence are gradually established and specific regional security concerns are removed.)

The NATO alliance came close to this no-first-use formulation in its London Communiqué of 1990, when it sought to reassure Russia by deeming nuclear forces "truly weapons of last resort" and again in its 1999 Strategic Concept, when it noted that "the circumstances in which any use of nuclear weapons might have to be contemplated . . . are therefore extremely remote."

The European allies of the United States can be helpful in this regard. They need to abandon their attachment to European-based U.S. tactical nuclear weapons: the 200 to 400 bombs deployed in Belgium, Germany, Italy, the Netherlands, Turkey, and the United Kingdom, which constitute the last remnants of the cold war "flexible response" policy. In the early years of the Clinton administration, the Pentagon concluded that there was no longer any military requirement for these weapons in Europe. The allies, however, were loath to cut the nuclear umbilical cord at that time, and the weapons remain as a symbol in the European mind of American commitment to continental security.

If the Europeans can wean themselves of this perverse sign of solidarity, which might have been made easier by erratic and bellicose U.S. behavior in this decade, a half-dozen NATO allies might finally be cleared of nuclear weaponry. In turn, this move might encourage Russia to reciprocate by constraining its tactical nuclear weapons stockpile.

A declaration of nonuse would be difficult, but perhaps not impossible, to negotiate. The nuclear weapon states have already committed not to attack non-nuclear states with nuclear weapons except in defense against attacks on their own nations or their allies. According to a 2004 poll conducted by the University of Maryland's Center on Policy Attitudes, 57 percent of Americans believe that the United States should "reconfirm" this commitment "so as to discourage countries from trying to acquire or build nuclear weapons."

The existing "negative security assurances" could easily be rewritten to make nuclear weapons use justified only in response to nuclear attack. Of course, drafting such a statement is much easier than marshalling the political forces to endorse it. But if the United States took the lead in seeking to delegitimize the use of nuclear weapons under any but the most extenuating circumstances, it might be possible to rally the other P-5 members to the declaration.

Finally, the next U.S. administration should encourage the creation of more nuclear-weapon-free zones (NWFZs), the goal of which would be to make increasing areas of the globe off limits to nuclear arms. Although the NPT is a nearly universal agreement, it is also an agreement with 187 very diverse members stretched over vast geographical and cultural distances and whose ultimate arbiter is the United Nations. Regional NWFZs are smaller units and, in theory at least, deal with the national security concerns of a "neighborhood" of member states. The treaty-based NWFZs that already exist could provide model frameworks for the negotiation of new ones. (Nonsovereign territories such as Antarctica, outer space, and the seabed are already off limits to nuclear weapons.)

Thus far, Washington has resisted going along fully with new zones being created. The United States signed the protocol to the African NWFZ Treaty, but with a reservation allowing the use of nuclear weapons against states in the NWFZ that use CWs or BWs. The United States, along with other nuclear weapon states, also has not signed the relevant protocol to the Southeast Asia NWFZ Treaty, claiming that it conflicts with the right of passage—that is, with the transport of nuclear cargoes through international waters and airspace.

Because the United States no longer has nuclear weapons on surface ships, this objection could be reconsidered. And, rather than taking exception to these zones, Washington should welcome them as reinforcing its own security goals. It should seek to strengthen efforts elsewhere in the world to rule out the presence of nuclear weapons.

The Amnesia Cure

Nuclear weapons are a clear and present danger, especially to the United States. Because Washington is at present unwilling to negotiate treaties or enter into binding agreements, the burden of securing the nation's future while advancing global security will fall on the next president. If his (or her) administration hopes to enhance U.S. security against the most serious threats, it will have to do more than pursue terrorists or enforce nonproliferation. It will also have to reduce the attractiveness of nuclear weapons to the United States and to the rest of the world. This entails adopting policies that delegitimize nuclear weapons by reducing the incentives to acquire them and by relegating them to a deterrent or retaliatory role or to weapons of last resort.

If Americans fail to wean themselves from the idea that the threat or use of nuclear weapons can ensure their security, they are likely to find that the cure for nuclear amnesia involves a nasty shock and an acrid smell.

JACK MENDELSOHN, an adjunct professor at George Washington University and American University, was a member of the U.S. SALT I and START II delegations. This essay is adapted from an article that appeared in *Issues in Science and Technology*.

Ban the Bomb. Really.

MICHAEL KREPON

The idea of abolishing nuclear weapons comes and goes in cycles, usually when external events either evoke uncommon fear or present great opportunities. So far, there have been three abolitionist waves. The first and most powerful came immediately after the use of atomic weapons to end World War II. This wave was short lived, driven by the profound fears evoked by weapons ideally suited for devastating surprise attacks, as well as by hopes that the newly created United Nations might somehow prevent the Bomb from becoming a fixture in international politics. The second wave rolled in during the first Reagan Administration. It was accompanied by a sharp downturn in superpower relations and fears of a "nuclear winter" in the aftermath of massive nuclear exchanges. The third wave, which quickly rose and fell in the mid-1990s, was driven by hopes that the end of the Soviet Union and the Cold War might prompt a wholesale devaluation of nuclear weapons. Each wave has been weaker and more ineffectual than the one before.

A fourth abolitionist wave is now building. This wave is unusual because it is moving from the center outward. Its leading advocates—statesmen like George Shultz, Sam Nunn, Henry Kissinger, William Perry and Max Kampelman—have long resumes of distinguished public service. Because of their leadership, the fourth wave has more potential than its predecessors. When foreign policy realists who have served in positions of great responsibility in the Nixon, Ford, Carter and Reagan Administrations join with a Democratic presidential candidate like Barack Obama in calling for nuclear abolition, clearly something noteworthy is unfolding.

The fourth abolitionist wave is also different because it is powered by subtle, slow-motion events rather than sharp external shocks. All abolitionist waves are driven by anticipatory dread of one kind or another. The sense of dread this time around derives from the erosion of global structures built to prevent proliferation, and the possibility of a horrific act of nuclear terrorism. This wave is also different because it comes at a time when *all* major powers face two common enemies: nuclear terrorism and the demise of the global nonproliferation system. The fourth wave seeks to leverage these common concerns, and the best way to do that, in the view of Shultz & Co., is to reaffirm and take seriously nuclear abolition as the declaratory policy of the U.S. government.

They are correct. It makes particularly good sense for the United States to champion the elimination of nuclear weapons. After six decades without being used on the battlefield, the Bomb's military utility has never been lower. In addition, its political utility for the United States has never been lower, thanks to America's conventional military superiority. Today, only nuclear weapons pose an existential threat to the United States.

The political stars may also be well aligned for a new look at abolition. Significant discontinuities in foreign and national security policy from one administration to the next are rare in post-nuclear American history. One such discontinuity occurred more than 25 years ago, when Ronald Reagan replaced Jimmy Carter in the White House, and another occurred when George W. Bush succeeded Bill Clinton. Yet another shift of similar magnitude is possible in January 2009, when George W. Bush leaves office. Whoever replaces him will have both sufficient motive and leeway to alter the status quo in significant ways. An opportunity beckons.

The Abolitionist Legacy

The first abolitionist wave in 1946–47 was the strongest of all because it was generated by the biggest tremor: the nuclear devastation of Hiroshima and Nagasaki. At that time, the A-bomb constituted the most powerful threat known to humankind. An attack could come suddenly, and there was no defense against it. Military historian Bernard Brodie labeled the A-bomb "the absolute weapon", but in less than five years, far more powerful nuclear weapons, hydrogen bombs, appeared. By then, abolition seemed to be an impossible dream, given the intractability of the U.S.-Soviet divide.

In contrast, the A-bomb appeared at an optimistic time. The Cold War had not fully emerged; Nazi Germany and Imperial Japan were defeated; and great hopes were placed in the United Nations. No less a luminary than Albert Einstein warned that unless humanity found a way to put an end to war, war would put an end to humanity. The Acheson-Lilienthal plan, which called for international control of the means of producing bomb-making material, arose during this brief springtime, but an early winter, in the forms of Josef Stalin and the Iron Curtain, put an end to those hopes. The Acheson-Lilienthal plan wasn't shy about describing the risks involved in its implementation, one of which was "the probable acceleration of the rate at which our present monopoly will disappear." For those who assumed that the United States could compete effectively against the Soviet Union and that Stalin couldn't be trusted, this risk seemed unacceptable.

The second wave of nuclear abolition crested on the Reagan Administration, whose plans for a nuclear arms build-up, tough talk about prevailing in a nuclear war and early disinterest in negotiations stoked public anxieties. Scientific studies about nuclear winter underpinned the second abolitionist movement. Its most influential wave-runner and voice was Jonathan Schell, who wrote two powerful and widely read books, *The Fate of the Earth* and *The Abolition,* during this period.

The abolitionist wave of the 1980s was less powerful than the first for several reasons. Superpower nuclear arsenals had grown so large and animosities so great that abolition seemed a bridge much too far. Besides, the Kremlin walked out of nuclear talks in 1983 to protest NATO missile deployments in Europe, so there was no negotiating vehicle for deep cuts, let alone abolition. Organized public opposition to the Reagan Administration's initiatives in the United States and Western Europe focused instead on freezing new nuclear force deployments in general and blocking new NATO missile deployments in particular.

The Reagan Administration trumped the nuclear freeze movement, first, by championing deep cuts in nuclear forces and, then, by actually achieving them. Reagan's play of trump, however, was no game: No one believed more fervently in abolition than Reagan himself. He consistently disparaged the logic and morality of mutual assured destruction, and he believed sincerely in missile defenses to diminish the relevance of nuclear weapons and eventually make the Bomb "impotent and obsolete."

Reagan was a shock not only to the Kremlin, but also to the U.S. nuclear establishment. Before Reagan, it was exceedingly hard to find anyone who was both staunchly anti-Communist and anti-nuclear. Reagan and Mikhail Gorbachev were a mesmerizing odd couple: two supremely confident risk-takers with little use for convention. At the unscripted Reykjavik summit in October 1986, Reagan and Gorbachev engaged in what then-Secretary of State Shultz called "the highest-stakes poker game ever played", entertaining deep cuts before embracing the bare outlines of a plan for nuclear abolition. At the 11th hour, Gorbachev demanded the sacrifice of Reagan's heartfelt Strategic Defense Initiative, abruptly ending the most astonishing negotiations of the nuclear age.

These talks nonetheless laid the groundwork for path-breaking nuclear arms reduction treaties and the abolition of several categories of ballistic missiles. Reagan and Gorbachev broke the back of the nuclear arms race. The second abolitionist wave, which had begun with deep public anxieties over renewed superpower rivalry, ended with treaties that shifted the competition into reverse gear.

The third and weakest wave of interest in abolition occurred after the Soviet Union dissolved. In the early 1990s, as in 1945, the world seemed reborn, and radical possibilities arose in sober and sensible minds. The paramount nuclear security threats to American primacy now related to Russian weakness, not Soviet strength. All the more reason to reconsider abolition, said supporters. So in January 1994, the Henry L. Stimson Center

enlisted General Andrew Goodpaster and a distinguished panel of national security experts including Paul Nitze to take a fresh look at the role of nuclear weapons in the post-Cold War world. General Goodpaster had worked as a key staff aide to General Dwight D. Eisenhower in Europe and later in the White House. He also served as NATO commander and deputy commander of American forces in Vietnam. Nitze was present at all key junctures of the nuclear competition. He was the principal author of NSC-68, the seminal policy blueprint of Cold War deterrence and containment, the most powerful voice of the Committee on the Present Danger, which opposed the Strategic Arms Limitation Talks during the Carter Administration, and the key arms control adviser to Secretary of State Shultz during the Reagan Administration. No one could gainsay Goodpaster's and Nitze's credentials as defense-minded patriots.

What emerged from the Goodpaster-Nitze reports was an argument for a phased approach to abolition on national security grounds, identifying the security conditions required to move from one stage to the next. The study concluded: "Without a more radical approach to non-proliferation, the challenges posed to the non-proliferation regime can only mount over time, and the United States, eventually, is sure to face new nuclear threats." Other panels of experts convened by the Australian and Japanese governments around this time also made the case for abolition. The Canberra Commission and the Tokyo Forum reports stressed global security and moral considerations.

These reports had little public effect. The best way to explain their lack of impact is the abolition paradox. The abolition paradox holds that when abolition is most needed, it is also most difficult to achieve, and that when opportunities to champion abolition are most evident, its pursuit appears to be least needed. The most dangerous stages of any arms competition are accompanied by intense political fears and dysfunctions that make abolition appear impractical. Conversely, when political conditions appear favorable, hugely ambitious undertakings seem less warranted, and near-term concerns crowd out visionary pursuits.

The Goodpaster-Nitze, Canberra Commission and Tokyo Forum initiatives occurred after the Soviet Union dissolved and free nations raised their own flags around Russia's periphery. Deep cuts in nuclear forces were being implemented, the security environment appeared to be much improved, and the Clinton Administration had more pressing matters to attend to. The pursuit of abolition wasn't a priority.

The New Wave

The fourth abolitionist wave is building at a time when nuclear concerns are rising but opportunities for breakthroughs appear limited. In this sense, the current state of play has most in common with the second abolitionist wave. U.S.-Russian relations have deteriorated markedly and await top-down impulses to change course. Missile defenses have again become a source of contention—not because the Bush Administration aspires to an astrodome defense, but because it seeks to deploy modest defenses in Russia's backyard to defend against future Middle Eastern threats. The Kremlin's paranoia, which ran so deep during the worst phases of the Cold War nuclear competition, has readily revived during the current period of U.S. military dominance.

The fourth abolitionist wave also comes at a time when the global structures built over many decades to prevent proliferation are deteriorating. The Nonproliferation Treaty, the foundation upon which subsequent construction has been built, was not designed to deal with nuclear terrorism or underground proliferation networks like that of A. Q. Khan. These structures were, in effect, period pieces reflecting the architectural collaboration of Washington and Moscow. Despite all of their competitive pursuits, the United States and the Soviet Union could and did work well together to prevent proliferation.

Constructing a global nonproliferation system atop the divides created by nuclear weapons and the Cold War could only have occurred if states possessing the Bomb pledged abolition and states without pledged continued abstinence. Norms of nuclear disarmament and nonproliferation needed to apply to everyone; otherwise construction could never have begun. A selective approach of helping friends and penalizing bad actors was impossible because the two master builders—the United States and the Soviet Union—could never have agreed about who the good guys were. The load-bearing walls of these structures were treaties ending atmospheric nuclear testing and reducing superpower arsenals. These structures became stronger over time, with tougher export controls and intrusive verification procedures.

The "unipolar moment" tilted this construction site, as the world's sole superpower embraced military dominance as a means of preventing and combating proliferation threats. The Bush Administration's preventive war against Saddam Hussein, based on false assumptions and faulty intelligence, tilted the playing field further. North Korea and Iran accelerated their nuclear programs, and other countries began to hedge their nuclear bets, especially in the Middle East. Moreover, the Bush Administration held in low regard what previous administrations considered to be the most important parts of the edifice: treaties banning nuclear testing and downsizing nuclear forces. Constraints on U.S. freedom of action were systematically denigrated or thrown overboard, especially protections for monitoring satellites and provisions mandating intrusive monitoring.

The Bush Administration also adopted a "good guy/bad guy" approach to proliferation. Nuclear programs in friendly states, like India, weren't the problem: The character of the government, not the essence of the Bomb, mattered most. Inspections and treaties have been deemed essential for bad guys, not good guys. The goal of abolition has been treated dismissively as have multilateral treaty negotiations. For two years, as Pakistan edged closer to a meltdown, the Bush Administration made its highest regional priority a civil nuclear cooperation agreement with India, in which lax rules would be allowed for a friend, while seeking to tighten rules on Iran, a foe. In effect, the Bush Administration attempted to construct a second story atop the Nonproliferation Treaty using a very different building code. What previous contractors considered to be load-bearing walls, the Bush Administration considered to be a nuisance, or worse.

With global nonproliferation norms becoming shaky, and with the promise of a new administration on the horizon, the timing of Shultz, Nunn, Kissinger, Perry and Kampelman couldn't have been better. But the first part of the abolition paradox still applies: The need for abolition is great precisely because dangers and obstacles appear to be growing.

Getting to zero will not be easy. It requires, first of all, reaffirming the end state of abolition as desirable, and even that has proved difficult in recent decades. It also means the absence of nuclear nightmares, including: any use of a nuclear weapon in warfare between states; the destabilization of Pakistan; failure to stop and reverse the Iranian and North Korean nuclear weapon programs; failure to stop the spread of enrichment and reprocessing plants to new nations that can be a "screwdriver's turn" away from producing the Bomb; failure to lock down and properly safeguard existing weapons and nuclear materials; acts of nuclear terrorism directed against states; the demise of the international inspections regime and other nuclear monitoring arrangements; a resumption and cascade of nuclear-weapons testing; and continued production of highly enriched uranium and plutonium for nuclear weapons. Getting to zero requires not just the absence of negatives, however. Many key positives are also required, beginning with significant cooperation among the major powers.

The absence of damaging negatives and the profusion of positives needed to reach zero seems fanciful. And yet a succession of very hard-headed thinkers about the nuclear dilemma have concluded, at the end of many years of public service and reflection, that zero is exactly the right destination. Henry L. Stimson arrived at this conclusion before leaving the War Department in 1945—not out of remorse about authorizing the use of the atomic bomb, but from a hard-headed sense of realism. Stimson's analysis still holds:

> The riven atom, uncontrolled, can be only a growing menace to us all, and there can be no final safety short of full control throughout the world. Nor can we hope to realize the vast potential wealth of atomic energy until it is disarmed and rendered harmless. Upon us, as the people who first harnessed and made use of this force, there rests a grave and continuing responsibility for leadership in turning it toward life, not death.[1]

Paul Nitze ultimately came to the same conclusion. Like Stimson, Nitze held no romantic notions about abolition. Instead, the starting point for his recommendation was the revolutionary advance of U.S. conventional warfare:

> The technology of our conventional weapons is such that we can achieve accuracies of less than three feet from the expected point of impact. The modern equivalent of a stick of dynamite exploded within three feet of an object on or near the earth's surface is more than enough to destroy the target. In view of the fact that we can achieve our objectives with conventional weapons, there is no purpose to be gained through the use of our nuclear arsenal. To use it would merely guarantee the annihilation of hundreds of thousands of people, none of whom would have been responsible for the decision invoked in bringing about the weapons' use, not to mention incalculable damage to our natural environment.[2]

In addition to pragmatic reasons for setting the goal of zero nuclear weapons, the fourth abolitionist wave is values-based. Many serious thinkers, religious leaders and former practitioners of the art of the possible have reached a similar conclusion. The Reverend Billy Graham came to this same conviction as a "teaching of the Bible." Nunn, Shultz, Kissinger and Perry wrote, "Reassertion of the vision of a world free of nuclear weapons and practical measures toward achieving that goal would be, and would be perceived as, a bold initiative consistent with America's moral heritage." These authors can by no means be considered naive waifs.

The leaders of the fourth abolitionist wave are not arguing for the elimination of U.S. nuclear weapons without reciprocal, verifiable and permanent elimination by all other states. No one is arguing that the rogue state Bomb-in-the-basement problem isn't real. It clearly must be solved before reaching this end state. No one denies the dilemma posed by the fact that U.S. conventional military superiority, which we rightly wish to preserve, can be a goad to proliferation. Nor can the nuclear umbrella provided by the United States to friends and allies in troubled regions be withdrawn without substituting suitable assurances by non-nuclear means.

Even with these obstacles acknowledged, the goal of nuclear disarmament tends to invite reactions of depression or derision. This end-state seems as implausible as, say, hoping in 1948–49 that the United States and the Soviet Union could somehow manage to avoid incinerating each other for the duration of the Cold War. This implausible goal was achieved; others can be, as well. Paul Nitze's advice in this regard, given during a particularly virulent period of U.S.-Soviet competition, is worth recalling: "Try to reduce the dangers of nuclear war within the relevant future time period as best you can; you just get depressed if you worry about the long-term future."[3] Working the problem of nuclear disarmament requires the same focus: day by day, month by month, and year by year.

What other end state makes more sense than abolition? "Managed" proliferation and arms control do not provide compelling answers; nuclear anarchy is the worst of all possible outcomes; and attempts to assert U.S. nuclear dominance would accelerate the demise of global non-proliferation and disarmament norms. Abolition as an agreed aim provides the best framework for national leaders to progressively reduce new nuclear dangers. Nuclear disarmament is a process, not an on/off switch—a journey as well as a destination. The destination will not be reached unless public safety and national security are enhanced every step along the way. If security and political conditions cannot support this journey, it will grind to a halt.

How, then, shall we proceed? Pragmatic steps can lead to ideal objectives, and ideal objectives can open the aperture for pragmatic steps. Washington may not be able to reach the safe harbor of nuclear abolition, but it has more steering capacity than any other capital. As the panel led by General Goodpaster wisely noted, "By contemplating the unthinkable, the boundaries of the feasible might well be stretched."[4] That was right a dozen years ago, and it is still right today. Our safe harbor remains a long way off, but an impressive list of people is determined to undertake the journey.

Notes

1. Stimson, "The Challenge to Americans", *Foreign Affairs* (October 1947).

2. Nitze, "A Threat Mostly to Ourselves", *New York Times,* October 28, 1999; and Nitze, "Is It Time To Junk Our Nukes? The New World Disorder Makes Them Obsolete", *Washington Post,* January 16, 1994.

3. Quoted in Strobe Talbott, *The Master of the Game: Paul Nitze and the Nuclear Peace* (Alfred A. Knopf, 1988).

4. "An Evolving U.S. Nuclear Posture", The Henry L. Stimson Center, Second Report of the Steering Committee, Project on Eliminating Weapons of Mass Destruction, Report no. 19 (December 1995).

Michael Krepon is the co-founder of the Henry L. Stimson Center and a Diplomat Scholar at the University of Virginia. He is the author of *Better Safe than Sorry: The Ironies of Living with the Bomb* (forthcoming).

UNIT 8

The Iraq War and Beyond

Unit Selections

Key Points to Consider

- How important are allies and the United Nations in the reconstruction of Iraq?

- How important is Iraq to the security interests of the United States?

- Make a list of dimensions along which you would measure the success or failure of the U.S. foreign policy toward Iraq? How would you rate the present situation along these dimensions?

- How quickly should the United States undertake another "Iraq War?" What words of advice would you give policy makers about to embark on such a war?

- When and under what conditions should the United States leave Iraq?

- How would you rate the terrorist threat to the United States today compared to September 10, 2001? What about five years from now?

Student Web Site

www.mhcls.com/online

Internet References

White House: Renewal In Iraq
http://www.whitehouse.gov/infocus/iraq/

The Iraq War, right from its planning and conduct, to post-war occupation and reconstruction, has been the single defining feature of the George W. Bush administration's foreign policy. The Iraq War has come to sharply divide the American public. To its supporters, the Iraq War is the second campaign of the first war of the 21st century, the war against terrorism. For its detractors, the Iraq War has served to detract the United States from more critical threats that are emanating from terrorist groups such as al-Qaeda, and has isolated the United States from its traditional allies. Conflicts of opinion extend beyond the war to questions about the handling of intelligence and decision-making procedures prior to the terrorist attacks of September 11, 2001. Because it is so central to American foreign policy, we have organized a separate section around evaluations of the Iraq War and it implications for American foreign policy.

In order to better understand the chain of events that led the authors of these essays to take the positions that they did, we present a timeline of the Iraq War, beginning with President Bush's 2002 State of the Union address. While rumors that the Bush administration was determined to go to war with Iraq after the defeat of the Taliban in Afghanistan were widespread in Washington, they took on a new intensity following this speech.

- **January 29, 2002:** In his State of the Union address, Bush identifies Iraq, North Korea, and Iran as an "axis of evil" and promises that the United States would not allow "the world's most dangerous regimes to threaten us with the world's most destructive weapons."

- **September 12, 2002:** Bush addresses the opening session of the United Nations and challenges it to confront the "grave and gathering danger" of Iraq or become irrelevant.

- **September 17, 2002:** The Bush administration releases its national security strategy that replaces deterrence with preemption.

- **October 10, 2002:** Congress authorizes the use of force against Iraq.

- **November 27, 2002:** Weapons inspections resume in Iraq, following a unanimous November 8 Security Council resolution that called for tougher arms inspections in Iraq.

- **December 21, 2002:** Bush approves deployment of U.S. forces to the Persian Gulf.

- **February 14, 2003:** UN Weapons Inspector, Hans Blix, asserts that progress has been made in Iraq.

- **February 24, 2003:** The United States, Great Britain and Spain introduce a resolution at the Security Council, authorizing the use of military force against Iraq. France, Germany and Russia oppose the resolution.

U.S. Air Force photo by Staff Sgt. Manuel J. Martinez

- **March 17, 2003:** Bush presents Saddam Hussein with a 48 hour ultimatum to leave Iraq.

- **March 19, 2003:** Operation 'Iraq Freedom' begins with a decapitation strike, aimed at Iraqi leadership targets in Baghdad.

- **March 21, 2003:** Major fighting in Iraq begins.

- **April 9, 2003:** Baghdad falls.

- **May 1, 2003:** President Bush declares an end to major combat operations.

- **May 19, 2003:** Thousands in Baghdad peacefully protest U.S. presence.

- **May 23, 2003:** UN Security Council lifts sanctions and gives U.S. and Great Britain authority to control Iraq until an elected government is in place.

- **July 9, 2003:** Secretary of Defense, Donald Rumsfeld, admits that the cost of the war was underestimated by one-half. He now places it at $3.9 billion/month and acknowledges that far more troops than anticipated will be needed for the occupation.

- **July 17, 2003:** U.S. combat deaths in Iraq reach the level of the Persian Gulf War.

- **December 13, 2003:** Saddam Hussein is captured.

- **April 29, 2004:** Photos of torture and mistreatment of Iraqi prisoners by U.S. personnel at the Abu Ghraib prison.

- **June 8, 2004:** UN Security Council passes resolution ending formal occupation and outlining a role for the UN in post-transition Iraq.

- **June 28, 2004:** The United States transfers power to the new Iraqi government.

- **September 8, 2004:** U.S. casualties reach 1,000 dead. One month later a report estimates Iraqi war-related casualties to be as high as 10,000.

- **October 6, 2004:** U.S. top weapons inspector issues a report concluding that Iraq destroyed its illegal weapons months after the 1991 Persian Gulf War.

- **December 1, 2004:** The United States announces that it plans to expand its military presence in Iraq to 150,000 troops.

- **January 30, 2005:** Iraq holds first multiparty election in 50 years.

- **April 28, 2005:** Prime Minister Ibrahim al-Jaafari and his cabinet are approved by the National Assembly.

- **June 16, 2005:** Agreement reached on increasing Sunni participation in drafting a new constitution.

- **October 15, 2005:** Iraqi's vote on new constitution.

- **October 25, 2005:** Number of deaths of U.S. soldiers in Iraq reaches 2,000.

- **December 15, 2005:** Iraq holds parliamentary elections.

- **March 15, 2006:** Saddam Hussein testifies for the first time at his trial.

- **April 22, 2006:** Nuri al-Maliki of the Shiite Dawa Party is approved as Prime Minister, breaking a long political deadlock.

- **June 8, 2006:** Abu Musab al-Zarqari, head of al Qaeda in Iraq, is killed in a U.S. air strike.

- **June 22, 2006:** Republican controlled Senate rejects a Democrat proposal to start a withdrawal of troops from Iraq.

- **December 6, 2006:** The Iraq Study Group Report [Baker-Hamilton Report] calling for disengagement from Iraq is released.

- **December 30, 2006:** Saddam Hussein is executed.

- **January 2007:** President Bush announces a surge of U.S. forces into Iraq to stem the violence and create conditions for peace.

- **March 19, 2008:** Fifth anniversary of the start of the Iraq War.

- **March 24, 2008:** 4,000th U.S. combat death in Iraq War.

The first reading in this section, "Lifting the Veil," provides findings from recent public opinion polls from the Middle East. The author concludes that defeating terrorism will require defeating the rage that fuels it. The next set of essays present contrasting view points on how to evaluate the Iraq War experience. The second essay, "The Right Way" presents a strategy for victory, but holds doubts about the American public's willingness to give it time to succeed. The next article is by William Odom, who sees the Iraq War as having been a flawed policy from the outset. John McCain presents the opposing view in his essay, "Stay to Win" in which he argues that the United States incurred a moral responsibility to protect the Iraqi people when it removed Saddam Hussein from power. The last of the interpretative essays is by John Judis. He argues that the Iraq War is not simply another example of unilateralism in American foreign policy as many suggest, but represents an embrace of a traditional great-power imperialism and a rejection of Wilsonian thinking. The final essay looks beyond the Iraq War and to the future. Marc Sageman, in "The Next Generation of Terror," asserts that the generation of terrorists that carried out the 9/11 attacks have been replaced by a new more dangerous generation. Not under the control of al-Qaeda Central, they present the United States with a major security threat that must be addressed and the author outlines how this might be done.

Lifting the Veil
Understanding the Roots of Islamic Militancy

Henry Munson

In the wake of the attacks of September 11, 2001, many intellectuals have argued that Muslim extremists like Osama bin Laden despise the United States primarily because of its foreign policy. Conversely, US President George Bush's administration and its supporters have insisted that extremists loathe the United States simply because they are religious fanatics who "hate our freedoms." These conflicting views of the roots of militant Islamic hostility toward the United States lead to very different policy prescriptions. If US policies have caused much of this hostility, it would make sense to change those policies, if possible, to dilute the rage that fuels Islamic militancy. If, on the other hand, the hostility is the result of religious fanaticism, then the use of brute force to suppress fanaticism would appear to be a sensible course of action.

Groundings for Animosity

Public opinion polls taken in the Islamic world in recent years provide considerable insight into the roots of Muslim hostility toward the United States, indicating that for the most part, this hostility has less to do with cultural or religious differences than with US policies in the Arab world. In February and March 2003, Zogby International conducted a survey on behalf of Professor Shibley Telhami of the University of Maryland involving 2,620 men and women in Egypt, Jordan, Lebanon, Morocco, and Saudi Arabia. Most of those surveyed had "unfavorable attitudes" toward the United States and said that their hostility to the United States was based primarily on US policy rather than on their values. This was true of 67 percent of the Saudis surveyed. In Egypt, however, only 46 percent said their hostility resulted from US policy, while 43 percent attributed their attitudes to their values as Arabs. This is surprising given that the prevailing religious values in Saudi Arabia are more conservative than in Egypt. Be that as it may, a plurality of people in all the countries surveyed said that their hostility toward the United States was primarily based on their opposition to US policy.

The issue that arouses the most hostility in the Middle East toward the United States is the Israeli-Palestinian conflict and what Muslims perceive as US responsibility for the suffering of the Palestinians. A similar Zogby International survey from the summer of 2001 found that more than 80 percent of the respondents in Egypt, Kuwait, Lebanon, and Saudi Arabia ranked the Palestinian issue as one of the three issues of greatest importance to them. A survey of Muslim "opinion leaders" released by the Pew Research Center for the People and the Press in December 2001 also found that the US position on the Israeli-Palestinian conflict was the main source of hostility toward the United States.

It is true that Muslim hostility toward Israel is often expressed in terms of anti-Semitic stereotypes and conspiracy theories—think, for example, of the belief widely-held in the Islamic world that Jews were responsible for the terrorists attacks of September 11, 2001. Muslim governments and educators need to further eliminate anti-Semitic bias in the Islamic world. However, it would be a serious mistake to dismiss Muslim and Arab hostility toward Israel as simply a matter of anti-Semitism. In the context of Jewish history, Israel represents liberation. In the context of Palestinian history, it represents subjugation. There will always be a gap between how the West and how the Muslim societies perceive Israel. There will also always be some Muslims (like Osama bin Laden) who will refuse to accept any solution to the Israeli-Palestinian conflict other than the destruction of the state of Israel. That said, if the United States is serious about winning the so-called "war on terror," then resolution of the Israeli-Palestinian conflict should be among its top priorities in the Middle East.

Eradicating, or at least curbing, Palestinian terrorism entails reducing the humiliation, despair, and rage that drive many Palestinians to support militant Islamic groups like Hamas and Islamic Jihad. When soldiers at an Israeli checkpoint prevented Ahmad Qurei (Abu al Ala), one of the principal negotiators of the Oslo accords and president of the Palestinian Authority's parliament, from traveling from Gaza to his home on the West Bank, he declared, "Soon, I too will join Hamas." Qurei's words reflected his outrage at the subjugation of his people and the humiliation that Palestinians experience every day at the checkpoints that surround their homes. Defeating groups like Hamas requires diluting the rage that fuels them. Relying on force alone tends to increase rather than weaken their appeal. This is demonstrated by some of the unintended consequences of the US-led invasion and occupation of Iraq in the spring of 2003.

On June 3, 2003, the Pew Research Center for the People and the Press released a report entitled *Views of a Changing World June 2003*. This study was primarily based on a survey of nearly 16,000 people in 21 countries (including the Palestinian Authority) from April 28 to May 15, 2003, shortly after the fall of Saddam Hussein's regime. The survey results were supplemented by data from earlier polls, especially a survey of 38,000 people in 44 countries in 2002. The study found a marked increase in Muslim hostility toward the United States from 2002 to 2003. In the summer of 2002, 61 percent of Indonesians held a favorable view of the United States. By May of 2003, only 15 percent did. During the same period of time, the decline in Turkey was from 30 percent to 15 percent, and in Jordan it was from 25 percent to one percent.

Indeed, the Bush administration's war on terror has been a major reason for the increased hostility toward the United States. The Pew Center's 2003 survey found that few Muslims support this war. Only 23 percent of Indonesians did so in May of 2003, down from 31 percent in the summer of 2002. In Turkey, support dropped from 30 percent to 22 percent. In Pakistan, support dropped from 30 percent to 16 percent, and in Jordan from 13 percent to two percent. These decreases reflect overwhelming Muslim opposition to the war in Iraq, which most Muslims saw as yet another act of imperial subjugation of Muslims by the West.

The 2003 Zogby International poll found that most Arabs believe that the United States attacked Iraq to gain control of Iraqi oil and to help Israel. Over three-fourths of all those surveyed felt that oil was a major reason for the war. More than three-fourths of the Saudis and Jordanians said that helping Israel was a major reason, as did 72 percent of the Moroccans and over 50 percent of the Egyptians and Lebanese. Most Arabs clearly do not believe that the United States overthrew Saddam Hussein out of humanitarian motives. Even in Iraq itself, where there was considerable support for the war, most people attribute the war to the US desire to gain control of Iraqi oil and help Israel.

Not only has the Bush administration failed to win much Muslim support for its war on terrorism, its conduct of the war has generated a dangerous backlash. Most Muslims see the US fight against terror as a war against the Islamic world. The 2003 Pew survey found that over 70 percent of Indonesians, Pakistanis, and Turks were either somewhat or very worried about a potential US threat to their countries, as were over half of Jordanians and Kuwaitis.

This sense of a US threat is linked to the 2003 Pew report's finding of widespread support for Osama bin Laden. The survey of April and May 2003 found that over half those surveyed in Indonesia, Jordan, and the Palestinian Authority, and almost half those surveyed in Morocco and Pakistan, listed bin Laden as one of the three world figures in whom they had the most confidence "to do the right thing." For most US citizens, this admiration for the man responsible for the attacks of September 11, 2001, is incomprehensible. But no matter how outrageous this widespread belief may be, it is vitally important to understand its origins. If one does not understand why people think the way they do, one cannot induce them to think differently.

Similarly, if one does not understand why people act as they do, one cannot hope to induce them to act differently.

The Appeal of Osama bin Laden

Osama bin Laden first engaged in violence because of the occupation of a Muslim country by an "infidel" superpower. He did not fight the Russians in Afghanistan because he hated their values or their freedoms, but because they had occupied a Muslim land. He participated in and supported the Afghan resistance to the Soviet occupation from 1979 to 1989, which ended with the withdrawal of the Russians. Bin Laden saw this war as legitimate resistance to foreign occupation. At the same time, he saw it as a *jihad,* or holy war, on behalf of Muslims oppressed by infidels.

When Saddam Hussein invaded Kuwait in August 1990, bin Laden offered to lead an army to defend Saudi Arabia. The Saudis rejected this offer and instead allowed the United States to establish bases in their kingdom, leading to bin Laden's active opposition to the United States. One can only speculate what bin Laden would have done for the rest of his life if the United States had not stationed hundreds of thousands of US troops in Saudi Arabia in 1990. Conceivably, bin Laden's hostility toward the United States might have remained passive and verbal instead of active and violent. All we can say with certainty is that the presence of US troops in Saudi Arabia did trigger bin Laden's holy war against the United States. It was no accident that the bombing of two US embassies in Africa on August 7, 1998, marked the eighth anniversary of the introduction of US forces into Saudi Arabia as part of Operation Desert Storm.

Part of bin Laden's opposition to the presence of US military presence in Saudi Arabia resulted from the fact that US troops were infidels on or near holy Islamic ground. Non-Muslims are not allowed to enter Mecca and Medina, the two holiest places in Islam, and they are allowed to live in Saudi Arabia only as temporary residents. Bin Laden is a reactionary Wahhabi Muslim who undoubtedly does hate all non-Muslims. But that hatred was not in itself enough to trigger his *jihad* against the United States.

Indeed, bin Laden's opposition to the presence of US troops in Saudi Arabia had a nationalistic and anti-imperialist tone. In 1996, he declared that Saudi Arabia had become an American colony. There is nothing specifically religious or fundamentalist about this assertion. In his book *Chronique d'une Guerre d'Orient,* Gilles Kepel describes a wealthy whiskey-drinking Saudi who left part of his fortune to bin Laden because he alone "was defending the honor of the country, reduced in his eyes to a simple American protectorate."

In 1996, bin Laden issued his first major manifesto, entitled a "Declaration of Jihad against the Americans Occupying the Land of the Two Holy Places." The very title focuses on the presence of US troops in Saudi Arabia, which bin Laden calls an "occupation." But this manifesto also refers to other examples of what bin Laden sees as the oppression of Muslims by infidels. "It is no secret that the people of Islam have suffered from the oppression, injustice, and aggression of the alliance of Jews and Christians and their collaborators to the point that the blood of the Muslims became the cheapest and their wealth was loot in the hands of the enemies," he writes. "Their blood was spilled in Palestine and Iraq."

Bin Laden has referred to the suffering of the Palestinians and the Iraqis (especially with respect to the deaths caused by sanctions) in all of his public statements since at least the mid-1990s. His 1996 "Declaration of Jihad" is no exception. Nonetheless, it primarily focuses on the idea that the Saudi regime has "lost all legitimacy" because it "has permitted the enemies of the Islamic community, the Crusader American forces, to occupy our land for many years." In this 1996 text, bin Laden even contends that the members of the Saudi royal family are apostates because they helped infidels fight the Muslim Iraqis in the Persian Gulf War of 1991.

A number of neo-conservatives have advocated the overthrow of the Saudi regime because of its support for terrorism. It is true that the Saudis have funded militant Islamic movements. It is also true that Saudi textbooks and teachers often encourage hatred of infidels and allow the extremist views of bin Laden to thrive. It is also probably true that members of the Saudi royal family have financially supported terrorist groups. The fact remains, however, that bin Laden and his followers in Al Qaeda have themselves repeatedly called for the overthrow of the Saudi regime, saying that it has turned Saudi Arabia into "an American colony."

If the United States were to send troops to Saudi Arabia once again, this time to overthrow the Saudi regime itself, the main beneficiaries would be bin Laden and those who think like him. On January 27, 2002, a *New York Times* article referenced a Saudi intelligence survey conducted in October 2001 that showed that 95 percent of educated Saudis between the ages of 25 and 41 supported bin Laden. If the United States were to overthrow the Saudi regime, such people would lead a guerrilla war that US forces would inevitably find themselves fighting. This war would attract recruits from all over the Islamic world outraged by the desecration of "the land of the two holy places." Given that US forces are already fighting protracted guerrilla wars in Iraq and Afghanistan, starting a third one in Saudi Arabia would not be the most effective way of eradicating terror in the Middle East.

Those who would advocate the overthrow of the Saudi regime by US troops seem to forget why bin Laden began his holy war against the United States in the first place. They also seem to forget that no one is more committed to the overthrow of the Saudi regime than bin Laden himself. Saudi Arabia is in dire need of reform, but yet another US occupation of a Muslim country is not the way to make it happen.

In December 1998, Palestinian journalist Jamal Abd al Latif Isma'il asked bin Laden, "Who is Osama bin Laden, and what does he want?" After providing a brief history of his life, bin Laden responded to the second part of the question, "We demand that our land be liberated from the enemies, that our land be liberated from the Americans. God almighty, may He be praised, gave all living beings a natural desire to reject external intruders. Take chickens, for example. If an armed soldier enters a chicken's home wanting to attack it, it fights him even though it is just a chicken." For bin Laden and millions of other Muslims, the Afghans, the Chechens, the Iraqis, the Kashmiris, and the Palestinians are all just "chickens" defending their homes against the attacks of foreign soldiers.

In his videotaped message of October 7, 2001, after the attacks of September 11, 2001, bin Laden declared, "What America is tasting now is nothing compared to what we have been tasting for decades. For over 80 years our *umma* has been tasting this humiliation and this degradation. Its sons are killed, its blood is shed, its holy places are violated, and it is ruled by other than that which God has revealed. Yet no one hears. No one responds."

Bin Laden's defiance of the United States and his criticism of Muslim governments who ignore what most Muslims see as the oppression of the Palestinians, Iraqis, Chechens, and others, have made him a hero of Muslims who do not agree with his goal of a strictly Islamic state and society. Even young Arab girls in tight jeans praise bin Laden as an anti-imperialist hero. A young Iraqi woman and her Palestinian friends told Gilles Kepel in the fall of 2001, "He stood up to defend us. He is the only one."

Looking Ahead

Feelings of impotence, humiliation, and rage currently pervade the Islamic world, especially the Muslim Middle East. The invasion and occupation of Iraq has exacerbated Muslim concerns about the United States. In this context, bin Laden is seen as a heroic Osama Maccabeus descending from his mountain cave to fight the infidel oppressors to whom the worldly rulers of the Islamic world bow and scrape.

The violent actions of Osama bin Laden and those who share his views are not simply caused by "hatred of Western freedoms." They result, in part at least, from US policies that have enraged the Muslim world. Certainly, Islamic zealots like bin Laden do despise many aspects of Western culture. They do hate "infidels" in general, and Jews in particular. Muslims do need to seriously examine the existence and perpetuation of such hatred in their societies and cultures. But invading and occupying their countries simply exacerbates the sense of impotence, humiliation, and rage that induce them to support people like bin Laden. Defeating terror entails diluting the rage that fuels it.

HENRY MUNSON is Chair of the Department of Anthropology at the University of Maine.

The Right Way

Seven Steps Toward a Last Chance in Iraq

KENNETH M. POLLACK

I raq hangs in the balance. December's elections once again demonstrated the desire of Iraqis for a prosperous, pluralist, and pacific country. There should be little doubt that the vast majority of the Iraqi people want to see reconstruction succeed. This is the most powerful of the positive factors that could enable a new Iraqi state to overcome sectarian differences and serve as a force for stability in the larger Middle East.

But both the Iraqi people and the American people are growing increasingly frustrated with the persistent failings of reconstruction. They worry that the United States and the new Iraqi government do not have a strategy that can succeed. For this reason, 2006 will likely prove decisive for the future of Iraq: reconstruction efforts must finally begin to show tangible results, or else people in both Iraq and America will lose faith that positive outcomes are even possible. And the brutal reality is that time is running out. A six- to twelve-month window of opportunity may be all that remains before the spiral toward possible chaos and civil war is beyond control.

Iraq is beset by a host of deep-seated problems. In some cases these are masked by superficial aspects of progress. For instance, security has increased somewhat in many parts of Iraq because sectarian militias have taken control there and because looters and petty criminals have been consolidated into organized crime rings. This is not a meaningful improvement, because it carries within it the seeds of its own destruction. While Iraq may seem "safer" for the moment, it is, in fact, less secure for the longer term.

The most damaging reality of all is that the United States created a security vacuum in April of 2003 that it has never properly filled. This has given rise to two related and interlinked phenomena: a full-blown insurgency, largely based in the Sunni tribal community of western Iraq; and a failed state, in which the governmental architecture has essentially collapsed. Thus, Iraq not only faces problems similar to those that the United States confronted in Vietnam—and the British in Northern Ireland, the French in Algeria, and the Russians in Afghanistan—but also many that plagued Lebanon in the 1970s and 1980s, and Yugoslavia in the 1990s. Confronting the problems of Iraq means crafting a strategy that will not only defeat the insurgency but will simultaneously deal with the myriad problems stemming from Iraq as a failed state, one that is at this point held together almost entirely by the American military presence.

The clock may be ticking, but all is not lost; it is possible to imagine a different strategic approach. Over the past several months the Saban Center for Middle East Policy at the Brookings Institution brought together a group of experts on Iraq, military affairs, reconstruction, and democratization to undertake a thorough review of U.S. policy on Iraq. This group, the Iraq Policy Working Group, reflected a wide range of beliefs and politics. It included military and civilian personnel who have served in various governments. Most of them have also had significant on-the-ground experience in Iraq. The group met to try to answer this question: If America can't leave Iraq precipitately, what should we be doing differently to give ourselves the greatest prospect of success? The result is a 70,000-word report on all aspects of Iraq policy, from security to economics to politics.

What follows is a summary of some key points about shifting American strategy to make it more likely that reconstruction will succeed. Solutions to the many problems that the United States faces in Iraq do exist. Indeed, there was not a single problem that the Iraq Working Group addressed—from stamping out the insurgency to reconciling Iraq's warring factions to eradicating the corruption plaguing Iraq's new ministries—for which an effective response cannot be envisaged. The real question facing the United States is not whether there are workable ideas but whether the administration is willing to change its strategy, quickly and decisively—and whether the American people are willing to give these workable ideas the time they need to show results.

1. Make Protecting the Iraqi People and Civilian Infrastructure Our Highest Priority

There is a large, coherent body of literature on the practice and history of counterinsurgent warfare, and what is most remarkable about it is that it all draws on the same lessons. So does the literature on stability operations—operations that address the problems of failed states. The principal one is that the most important mission of counterinsurgency forces is to provide basic safety for the population against attack, extortion, threat, and simple fear. If the people are afraid to leave their homes—or worse still, if they are afraid even while in their homes—the guerrillas and other forces of chaos have effectively won. The people will not support the government; they will be susceptible to insurgents and extremist militias; they will not go about their normal business; and the economy will suffer, as will the political system. This is precisely what any insurgent seeks to accomplish, and what the Iraqi insurgents largely have done. Consequently, American forces must fundamentally reorient their priorities to make what is called "area security"—protecting Iraqi towns and neighborhoods—their highest concern.

The United States and the Iraqi security forces must focus on making the Iraqi people feel safe in their homes, their streets, and their places of business. This does not mean simply deploying soldiers in defensive positions around Iraqi population centers (although in some cases that can be helpful). It means establishing a constant presence throughout those areas to reassure the population and deter (or defeat) insurgents or militias. Constant patrols (principally on foot); checkpoints; and security personnel deployed at major gathering points—markets, entertainment, religious or political events, and even main intersections or thoroughfares—create that sense of constant presence. Security personnel should conduct searches routinely for any person entering a large facility—a business or apartment complex, a *suq* or shopping mall, a sports arena, etc. Fixed defensive positions, checkpoints, or ambushes can be employed against known routes of attack or infiltration by the insurgents. Key infrastructure must be guarded—with personnel for a single facility; and with sensors, patrols, and quick-reaction teams for pipelines, roads, communications lines, or water/sewage lines.

2. Shift the Strategic Emphasis from Offensive to Defensive Military Operations

President Bush stated last summer that "the principal task of our military is to find and defeat the terrorists, and that is why we are on the offense." While this is an accurate description of the American military approach, it is, unfortunately, wrong in terms of what is needed. The right formulation would be that "the principal task of our military is to protect the Iraqi people, and that is why we are mainly on the defense." Instead, the approach we are employing in Iraq—concentrating our forces in Iraq's western provinces where the insurgents are thickest and support for reconstruction weakest—means committing the cardinal military sin of reinforcing failure. Such an approach has resulted in failures against guerrilla warfare throughout history. Moreover, it has meant ceding control over much of the populace to the forces of chaos (the militias), which is the cardinal sin of stability operations (the name for operations designed to deal with failed states). Our efforts to "take the fight to the enemy" and mount offensive sweep operations designed to kill insurgents and eliminate their strongholds have failed to work, and likely will continue to do so, as was the case in Vietnam and other lost guerrilla wars.

Large-scale offensive military operations cannot succeed, and can be counterproductive, against a full-blown insurgency. The guerrilla does not need to stand and fight, but can run or melt back into the population and so avoid crippling losses. If the counterinsurgency forces do not remain and pacify the area for the long term, the guerrillas will be back within weeks, months, or maybe years, but they will be back nonetheless. Meanwhile, the concentration of forces on these sweep operations means a major diversion of effort away from securing the population.

This is precisely what is happening in Iraq. While there needs to be an offensive component to any strategy no matter how defensive in orientation, the offensive component in counterinsurgency campaigns should mostly consist of limited attacks on unequivocally clear and important insurgent strongholds, or immediate counterattacks

against guerrilla forces when they are vulnerable after an attack of their own. One of the hardest things for highly effective conventional militaries like ours to understand is that in unconventional warfare, like counterinsurgency and stability operations, the path to victory is to remain on the strategic defensive in the military arena while going on the offensive in the political and economic arenas.

Our efforts to "take the fight to the enemy" have failed to work. Large-scale offensive military operations cannot succeed against a full-blown insurgency. We should concentrate on defense.

The administration's recently adopted "clear, hold, and build" strategy is a step in the right direction, but still falls short of the mark. Of greatest importance, it is being implemented in the wrong part of Iraq (the Sunni Triangle) and so is continuing to draw off forces from where they are most needed, in southern and central Iraq, where the public favors reconstruction but is souring on it because of the persistent state of insecurity. However, even within the Sunni Triangle, the United States is not employing enough troops to meaningfully "hold" areas or enough resources to really "build" there. For instance, during Operation Iron Hammer last September, the U.S. 3rd Armored Cavalry Regiment, boasting nearly 5,000 troops, cleared Tal Afar, but was replaced just a few weeks later by a battalion roughly one-tenth its size. That is simply not enough troops to "hold" Tal Afar. Similarly, after the Marine reduction of Fallujah, the United States left only a brigade-sized formation there, which has been large enough to prevent the town from reverting back to the control of the insurgents and Sunni militias but not enough to actually preserve security and stability there or make it possible for meaningful economic and political reconstruction to begin.

3. Emphasize Population Security in the South and Center of Iraq

In a pattern reminiscent of our disastrous early experiences in Vietnam, the American (and Iraqi) military forces have concentrated on trying to capture or kill insurgents and clear out their strongholds in western Iraq, where both the population and support for American reconstruction is thinnest. As noted above, not only is this unlikely to succeed but, in so doing, we have denuded central and southern Iraq of the forces so desperately needed to maintain order, enable the economy to revive, and prevent the militias from taking over. By leaving these areas without adequate protection, the Coalition has left the people there prey not only to insurgent attacks but to crime and lawlessness more generally, which has crippled economic and political revival. It has also left the vast bulk of Iraq's population vulnerable to the militias, which take over wherever there is not a significant Coalition military presence and provide the people the protection, food, and other basic necessities that the Americans and the Iraqi central government have not supplied. In this way, through intimidation or accommodation, the sectarian militias have taken over much of central and southern Iraq, where most of Iraq's population resides.

215

The security vacuum the United States created after the fall of Saddam Hussein is what made it possible for the militias—which are probably a greater threat than the insurgents—to establish themselves. The only way to reverse this phenomenon is to fill that vacuum.

Not only do the militias distort reconstruction but, along with the Sunni insurgents, they are the force most likely to bring civil war to Iraq. In fact, the militias are probably a greater threat to the future of Iraq than is the insurgency. As President Bush rightly pointed out, the insurgency is itself composed of at least three different primary groups: the Salafi Jihadists like Abu Musab al-Zarqawi's al-Qaeda in Mesopotamia; the last of Saddam Hussein's leading henchmen, who know that the new Iraq has nothing to offer them except the hangman's noose; and a large group of Sunni tribes and others who are much more like the Shiite (and Sunni) militias that now dominate central and southern Iraq than they are like the other two groups. Like the other militias, these groups are fighting because they seek power and control over swaths of Iraq, they fear what the new Iraqi government will mean for them, and they fear the violence of the Shiite militias just as the Shia fear them. Incidents of ethnic cleansing, assassination, and other violence by Shiite militias and Sunni militias/insurgents against one another and against Iraqi civilians are becoming more and more common in Iraq and will provoke a civil war if they are not brought under control.

The security vacuum the United States created after the fall of Saddam Hussein is what made it possible for the militias to establish themselves; the only way to reverse this phenomenon is to fill that vacuum. Very few of the Shiite militias have ever tried to resist Coalition forces when they moved into an area in strength, because they understood that doing so was essentially suicidal. Once the Coalition has concentrated sufficient forces to move back into a population center in central or southern Iraq, it should be able to do so. Then, Iraqi and American forces must remain in strength over time, and in so doing obviate the rationale that drove the locals to support the militia. This is critical, not only to create a basis for defeating the insurgency but to prevent the failed-state aspects from causing the country to spiral out of control.

Once these enclaves are secured, and as additional Iraqi security forces are trained, they should be slowly expanded to include additional communities. This approach, which has been put forward most notably by the military analyst Andrew Krepinevich, is typically referred to either as a "spreading ink spot" or as a "spreading oil stain" because the counterinsurgency forces slowly spread their control over the country, depriving the guerrillas of support piece by piece. The administration has embraced this idea rhetorically, but not operationally.

If implemented properly, a true counterinsurgency approach can succeed in winning back the entire country. However, it means ceding control over some parts at first and taking some time before all of Iraq will be seen as a stable, unified, pluralist state. Nevertheless, it is worth considering that the United States and the Iraqi government currently do not control much of the country, because it is in the hands of insurgent groups or militias. Thus, the strategy is really about *acknowledging* that we can control only part of the country

with the forces currently available—and using them to exert our control over the most important parts rather than squandering them playing Whac-A-Mole with insurgents in parts that we cannot control.

The key to this approach is that it "solves" the problem of inadequate force levels, which was one of the original mistakes of the war. The problem here was that we did not have an adequate concentration of forces to secure the country against either the insurgents or the problems of Iraq as a failed state (like organized crime and the militias). The guiding principle of a spreading-oil-stain approach is that it allows the counterinsurgent force to concentrate in part of the country and then slowly pacify the rest, using time to substitute for numbers.

Numbers in warfare are always slippery, but it is impossible to avoid them for planning purposes. For both counterinsurgency operations and stability operations, the canonical figure is that there need to be twenty security personnel (military and police) per 1,000 of the population. The population of Iraq today is roughly 26 million, which would suggest the need for 520,000 security personnel. However, the 4 million or so Kurds who live inside Iraqi Kurdistan enjoy considerable safety because they are protected by approximately 70,000 peshmerga fighters. To secure the remaining 22 million people, then, would require about 440,000 security personnel. This number is the baseline figure for what will be required ultimately to stabilize Iraq. Unfortunately, we are far from that number. At present, the United States has 135,000 to 160,000 troops in Iraq at any given time. They are joined by roughly 10,000 British and Australian troops, along with a grab bag of other detachments that may withdraw in 2006 and so should not be considered for planning purposes. There are probably some 40,000 to 60,000 Iraqi security personnel in the army, national guard, police force, and other units that are capable of participating in security operations in a meaningful way. This yields a total of 185,000 to 230,000 Coalition security personnel, a force that should be capable of securing a population of 9 million to 11.5 million, or about half of Iraq's population outside Kurdistan.

If the United States and the Iraqi government were to begin with only this baseline of troops and were to employ a traditional counterinsurgency strategy, withdrawing most of their forces from those areas of Iraq most opposed to reconstruction and instead concentrating the troops and resources on areas of high importance and high support for reconstruction, its starting oil stain could encompass Baghdad, all of central Iraq, and a significant portion of southern Iraq, with a smaller "economy of force" presence in northwest Iraq to prevent the situation there from deteriorating. Different strategists might draw the oil stain differently, but that is a very big area to start with and would allow the further pacification of the rest of Iraq within a number of years.

4. Train Iraqi Forces Properly. A Showy "Acceleration" Is Worse than Useless

The single greatest problem with all American efforts to train a new Iraqi military has been (and to some extent, continues to be) political pressure to quickly produce more trained Iraqi units in order to "show progress" in Iraq. This has been disastrous. The first training program instituted by Major General Paul Eaton's team was a perfectly reasonable one, and could have achieved its objectives had the Bush administration not demanded that Eaton both speed up the training course and increase the numbers of Iraqis trained. Even today, both the administration and its critics continue to press for *accelerated* training—meaning getting people through the training pipeline in shorter amounts of time—and a more rapid deployment of Iraqi forces to take over for American soldiers.

This is the worst approach we could take. The quality of Iraqi forces is far more important than their quantity if our goal is for the Iraqis to shoulder a greater and greater share of the burden of securing their country. The only way to produce troops sufficiently capable of doing so is to give them the time, in both formal and informal training, to develop such quality.

Like all new military units, Iraqi formations, even after their formal training is completed, need time to further jell. Unit cohesion starts to be formed in training, but it is inevitably tested by the first operations that a formation undertakes and can really emerge only in an operational environment—and only if the unit survives its early experiences. So, too, with the confidence of Iraqi recruits, and with the leadership skills of their officers. What's more, the process of vetting—weeding out those unsuited for the tasks at hand or those working for the enemy—is a lengthy one, and it is not unusual for soldiers and officers to do well in training but fail once placed in actual combat situations. Therefore, Iraqi troops not only need longer periods of formal training; they desperately need longer periods of informal training in the kind of permissive conditions that will enable them to learn and bond without being thrown into high-intensity combat.

The United States believed, at least twice since the fall of Baghdad, that it had adequately trained and prepared Iraqi security forces only to have them collapse in combat. In April of 2004, roughly half of the security forces in southern and central Iraq melted away when confronted by the revolt of Muqtada al-Sadr's Mahdi Army. Similarly, in November of 2004, coalition personnel believed that the Iraqi security forces around Mosul were doing fine: they had gone through the existing training programs, were deployed in and around the city, and seemed to be doing an excellent job maintaining law and order. However, that month, Sunni insurgents mounted a series of major attacks, and all but one battalion of these Iraqi security forces evaporated.

The nagging question plaguing Iraq's security forces is, how can we be sure that this latest force, which also seems to be fully capable and participating in combat operations, does not fall apart like its predecessors in southern and central Iraq in April of 2004 and around Mosul in November of 2004? The only answer to that question is time. The more time we give Iraqi formations to train, conduct exercises, and operate first in conditions that favor success, the more likely they will be to survive the test of real combat.

5. Create a Unified Command Structure

This is another well-known lesson that the United States continues to ignore. First, there needs to be a single "campaign chief" heading the entire effort. That person should have complete control over both the civilian and military sides of the American effort. There are arguments as to why that person should be from the military, but equally good ones as to why he or she should be a civilian. The historical evidence is equally mixed, but what it suggests is that the personality and skills of the individual are far more important than where he or she comes from. This campaign chief should have the authority and purview of something like a Roman proconsul, and be capable of making executive decisions on all matters to achieve the goal.

If America does not begin to get things right—and this means making sweeping changes to our approach—within the next few months, we face the prospect of a vicious cycle propelling Iraq toward full-blown civil war.

Beneath that campaign chief and his or her deputy there must be a fully integrated chain of command. Every division, brigade, and battalion must be part of it, as should the personnel of every civilian agency in country. Ideally the United States would create reconstruction committees at every level of the chain of command, and these committees would bring together, at a minimum, the relevant military commander, the relevant State Department officer, a USAID official, and an intelligence officer, and their Iraqi counterparts. At present, American military personnel are often the only Americans in any given town or neighborhood in Iraq. They have neither the skills, the resources, nor the time to spend on aid contracts, political negotiations, engineering projects, and the like. These are jobs that should be handled by civilian agencies, but because those personnel are not present outside the Green Zone, their jobs fall on the shoulders of the military. Military officers have risen admirably to that challenge, but it is one they should not have to bear.

The administration's nascent plan to deploy Provincial Reconstruction Teams to Iraq has some merit, but is by no means enough, because it will not erect an integrated hierarchy reaching from the bottom to the top of Iraqi society. The PRTs in Iraq rely too heavily on military personnel and so are better suited to helping with security-sector than civilian-sector reforms. More important, PRTs are teams that work with local Iraqi officials; they are not a hierarchy that integrates the reconstruction effort both horizontally and vertically, which is what Iraq desperately needs.

6. Decentralize Power and Oil Revenues

Iraq's central government is now fully constituted but essentially powerless. It lacks the resources and the institutions to tackle any of the challenges facing the country. Iraq's ministries are understaffed and eviscerated by endemic corruption of a kind that compares unfavorably even with Saddam Hussein's regime. Iraq's political leaders are consumed by discussions over power-sharing, and often care little about their constituents. The Iraqi capital is incapable of doing much for the Iraqi people, but quite capable of preventing the rest of the country from providing for itself. In the long run Washington must try to build the capacity of Iraq's central government. But in the short term it is critical to shift authority and outside resources away from Baghdad and toward local governments that might be able to start delivering the basic necessities Iraqis crave. The United States can help with this process by expanding its efforts to provide funds directly to local governments to be spent at their discretion, and by pressing the new Iraqi government to transfer control over the country's various police forces from the Ministry of the Interior to local authorities. Without control over financial or security power, local governments will be irrelevant. Washington also needs to help reduce the role of Iraqi ministries by shifting implementation, contracting, and some elements of regulation to local governments.

Iraq's oil revenues must be used both to build central-government capacity and to decentralize power and authority. That oil can be a blessing or a curse. At present it is mostly a curse, fueling the vicious infighting among political elites looking for a bigger (illegal) cut of Iraq's oil revenue. This revenue must be used instead to create incentives for Iraqi politicians to start caring about their constituents, to promote the decentralization of power beyond Baghdad, and to foster the process of national reconciliation by removing oil as an issue to be fought over.

The only way this will be possible is if Iraq switches to a relatively fixed system of distribution that provides funds to several "baskets." Some money would still have to go to the central government to pay for national defense, government salaries, and other indivisible functions, but this will cost a lot less if decentralization is pursued. Other money should be provided directly to local governments, preferably in two forms: one portion divided up on a fixed basis by population in each province and municipality, and another in which varying amounts would be apportioned to different communities based on the deliberations of the Iraq National Assembly. The purpose of this latter pool would be to force Iraq's parliamentarians—who currently pay little attention to the needs of their constituents—to fight for their communities or risk losing their jobs. Finally, yet another basket should provide some money directly to the people in the form of regular deposits into individual bank accounts, which would help capitalize Iraq's withered banking system. Giving the Iraqi people a direct stake in oil revenues would also galvanize them to oppose both organized crime and the insurgents who steal the oil and its revenues. Finally, putting money into the hands of the people and giving them a choice over how to spend it would allow market forces to help lead Iraq's economic recovery.

7. Bring in the International Community

Although the topic has largely faded from the op-ed pages, there are important roles to be played by the United Nations and the international community. Now that the December elections have ushered in what is to be Iraq's permanent and fully sovereign new government, it is a fitting moment for the United States to begin handing over some of the burden of guiding Iraq's reconstruction to an international body. This would be helpful because the United States is increasingly wearing out its welcome; shifting to a more international approach would allow us to prolong the process of reconstruction longer than would a go-it-alone approach.

Moreover, it remains the case that the United Nations, through its various agencies, can call upon a vast network of personnel and resources vital to nation-building. One of the greatest problems the United States has faced is that we simply do not have enough people who know how to do all of the things necessary to rebuild the political and economic system of a shattered nation. We have not tried to do such a thing since at least Vietnam—if not since South Korea, Germany, and Japan. The UN has worked with thousands of people with the relevant skills in Cambodia, Bosnia, Kosovo, East Timor, Afghanistan, and elsewhere. The ability to tap into a much bigger network is, in and of itself, a crucial virtue of the United Nations.

Is UN participation possible? Very much so, if the United States is willing to address two key problems: security and political cover. The violence plaguing Iraq has driven out most UN and nongovernmental organization, or NGO, personnel, and they are unlikely to return until the security situation improves. Here the answer, once again, is to implement a spreading-oil-stain approach in accord with traditional counterinsurgency doctrine. It is one of the many reasons why this strategy, and no other, succeeds in situations like the one the United States faces in Iraq. If Washington (and Baghdad) can demonstrate to UN agencies and NGOs that there are parts of Iraq that are largely safe—and that their personnel will remain in those safe zones—there is every reason to believe they would be willing to send more help.

The politics might be a bit more tricky. The problem here is that many UN member states cannot or will not participate in a post-conflict occupation that is not under UN auspices. Likewise, many NGOs do not want to be part of something that they see as an act of American imperialism. Their politics notwithstanding, the obvious solution would be for the United States to accept a UN-authorized high commissioner, as we did in Bosnia—a move that senior American military officers in fact favor, precisely because it would help bring in more international personnel and would reduce some of the need for the United States to prevent the newly empowered Iraqi government from doing anything rash. Instead, that thankless task would largely fall to the high commissioner.

The United States must approach 2006 as a watershed year in Iraq. Either America—and it really is America, because the Iraqis simply do not have the military, political, or economic capacity to solve their own problems yet—really begins to get things right or we face the prospect of a vicious cycle propelling Iraq toward a full-blown civil war. For this reason, the gradual, evolutionary changes that the United States has made to its military, political, and economic approaches to Iraq since April of 2003 will no longer suffice. Within the next year—that is all the time they have—Washington and Baghdad must make sweeping changes to prove that they understand the problems and are putting in place new policies that can solve them.

KENNETH M. POLLACK is the director of research at the Saban Center for Middle East Policy at the Brookings Institution. His most recent book is *The Persian Puzzle* (2004).

Withdraw Now

"The invasion of Iraq may well turn out to be the greatest strategic disaster in U.S. history. And the longer America stays, the worse it will be."

WILLIAM ODOM

U ntil Congressman John Murtha's call this fall for a pullout from Iraq, there was little serious public debate in the United States about whether it makes sense to continue a struggle that had been launched unwisely. Belatedly, that seems to be changing.

The Bush administration responded quickly to the Pennsylvania Democrat's challenge with a speech by the president at the U.S. Naval Academy at the end of November, and with the release of a document entitled *A National Strategy for Victory in Iraq.* Neither the speech nor the strategy document indicated a significant change of course. Both appeared to suggest that President George W. Bush will continue to dig deeper into the hole he has created. The arguments trotted out for "staying the course" are the same ones we have long heard from the White House and the Defense Department.

A subtle reading of the administration's response might lead one to see it as the beginning of the end—a cover for a failed strategy by progressively redefining "victory" in Iraq to such a low standard that withdrawal seems acceptable. At this point, however, the former reading, suggesting intent to dig even deeper, seems the more plausible.

It never made sense to invade Iraq, and the longer U.S. forces stay there, the greater the damage to America's interests. The war was and remains in the interest of Al Qaeda and Iran, both longtime enemies of Saddam Hussein. It has detracted from America's pursuit of Al Qaeda, and it has nearly destroyed the Atlantic alliance. From enjoying incredibly strong worldwide support in the fall of 2001 the United States has sunk to a new low in its standing in the world.

Darkness at the Tunnel's End

Supporters of the current policy offer a long list of justifications, most of which consist of dire predictions about what would transpire if the United States withdraws from Iraq. Yet most of these warnings—of civil conflict, lost U.S. credibility, bolstered terrorists, hampered democracy, inadequate security, regional instability, and the like—already have come true. And others may come to pass no matter how long American forces remain in Iraq. I believe a much stronger case can be made that an early

withdrawal will not make the situation all that much worse, and in some regards will improve it.

Consider the danger of leaving a civil war in the aftermath of an American withdrawal. The Iraqis, in fact, are already fighting Iraqis. Insurgents have killed far more Iraqis than Americans. This is civil war. The United States created a civil war when it invaded; it cannot prevent a civil war by staying. As for American credibility: What will happen to it if the course the administration is pursuing proves a major strategic disaster? Would it not be better for America's long-term standing to withdraw earlier than later in this event?

Proponents of staying the course argue that withdrawal will embolden the insurgency and cripple the move toward democracy. There is no question the insurgents or other anti-American parties will take over the government once the United States leaves. But that will happen no matter how long the United States stays in Iraq. Any government capable of holding power there will be anti-American, because the Iraqi people are increasingly becoming anti-American.

The United States will not leave behind a liberal, constitutional democracy in Iraq no matter how long it stays. Holding elections is easy. It is impossible to make a constitutional democracy in a hurry. President Bush's statements about progress in Iraq are increasingly resembling President Lyndon Johnson's assurances during the Vietnam War. Johnson's comments about the 1968 election are very similar to what Bush said in February 2005 after the election of a provisional parliament. Why should we expect an outcome in Iraq different from what occurred in Vietnam?

Leaving a pro-American liberal regime in place in Iraq is impossible. Postwar Germany and Japan are not models for Iraq. Each had mature—at least one generation old—constitutional orders by the end of the nineteenth century. Their states had both endured as constitutional orders until the 1930s. Thus General Lucius Clay in Germany and General Douglas MacArthur in Japan were merely reversing a decade and a half of totalitarianism—returning to nearly a century of liberal political change in Japan and a much longer period in Germany.

To impose a liberal constitutional order in Iraq would be to accomplish something that has never been done before. Of all the world's political cultures, an Arab-Muslim one may be the most resistant of any to such a change. The administration's supporters cite Turkey as an example of a constitutional order in an Islamic society. But Turkey (which has been known to backslide occasionally) has a decidedly anti-Arab culture.

A Terrorist Training Ground

It is also said that Iraq will become a haven for terrorists without a U.S. military presence. But Iraq is already a training ground for terrorists—having become one since the United States invaded. The CIA has pointed out to the administration and Congress that Iraq is spawning so many terrorists that they are returning home to many other countries to further practice their skills there. The quicker a new dictator wins political power in Iraq and imposes order, the sooner the country will stop producing well-experienced terrorists.

Another argument made is that American training and support are essential to the creation of a viable Iraqi military. As President Bush puts it, "We will stand down as the Iraqis stand up." Yet the insurgents are fighting very effectively without U.S. or European military advisers to train them. Why do the soldiers and police in the service of the present Iraqi government not do their duty as well? Because they are uncertain about committing their lives to this regime. They are being asked to take a political stand, just as the insurgents are. Political consolidation, not military—technical consolidation, is the challenge.

The issue, in other words, is not military training; it is institutional loyalty. The United States trained the Vietnamese military effectively. Its generals took power and proved to be lousy politicians and poor fighters in the final showdown. In many battles over a decade or more, South Vietnamese military units fought very well, defeating Vietcong and North Vietnamese Army units. But South Vietnam's political leaders lost the war.

Even if Washington were able to successfully train an Iraqi military and police force, the likely result, after all that, would be another military dictatorship. Experience around the world teaches us that military dictatorships arise when the military's institutional modernization gets ahead of political consolidation.

The Region at Risk

For those who worry about destabilizing the region, the sensible policy is not to stay the course in Iraq. It is rapid withdrawal, with Washington reestablishing strong relations with its allies in Europe, showing confidence in the UN Security Council, and trying to knit together a large coalition—including Europe's major states, Japan, South Korea, China, and India—to back a strategy for stabilizing the area from the eastern Mediterranean to Afghanistan and Pakistan. Until the United States withdraws from Iraq and admits its strategic error, no such coalition can be formed. Those who fear leaving a mess are actually helping make things worse while preventing a new strategic approach with some promise of success.

Iranian leaders see U.S. policy in Iraq as being so much in Tehran's interests that they have been advising Iraqi Shiite leaders to do exactly what the Americans ask them to do. The December parliamentary elections have allowed the Shiites to take power legally. Once firmly in charge, they can settle scores with the Baathists and Sunnis. If U.S. policy in Iraq begins to undercut Iran's interests, then Tehran can use its growing influence among Iraqi Shiites to stir up trouble, possibly committing Shiite militias to an insurgency against U.S. forces.

The American invasion has vastly increased Iran's influence in Iraq, not sealed it out, and it is unlikely to shrink as the Shiite majority grasps the reins of government. Would it not be better to pull out now rather than continue America's present course of weakening the Sunnis and Baathists, opening the way for a Shiite dictatorship?

The civil conflict America leaves behind may well draw in Syria, Turkey, and Iran. But today each of those states is already deeply involved in support for or opposition to factions in the ongoing Iraqi Civil war. The very act of invading Iraq almost ensured that violence would involve the larger region. And so it has and will continue, with or without U.S. forces in Iraq.

Yet this does not mean the United States would leave the area. I believe that stabilizing the region from the eastern Mediterranean to Afghanistan is very much an American interest, one it shares with all its allies as well as with several other countries, especially China, Russia, and India.

The Global Balkans

Former national security adviser Zbigniew Brzezinski has called this region the "global Balkans," a name that recalls the role of the European Balkans during the two or three decades leading up to the outbreak of World War I. By themselves the Balkan countries were not that important. Yet several great powers, especially Russia and Austria, were jockeying for strategic advantage there as they anticipated the collapse of the Ottoman Empire and competition for control of the straits leading from the Black Sea into the Mediterranean. Britain and France wanted neither Russia nor Austria to dominate; Germany, although uninterested in the Balkans, was allied to Austria.

From a strategic viewpoint, the assassination of Archduke Ferdinand in Sarajevo in 1914 was unimportant, but it set in motion actions that soon brought all of the major powers in Europe to war. Four empires collapsed, and the doors were opened to the Communists in Russia and the Nazis in Germany as a result.

Many U.S. officers in Iraq know that while they are winning every tactical battle, they are losing strategically.

Brzezinski's point is that the Middle East and Southwest Asia have precisely that kind of potential for catalyzing wars among the major powers of the world today, although nothing in the region objectively merits such wars. (Middle East oil as a "strategic" factor is largely a red herring. Oil producers have always been willing to sell their oil, even to bitter enemies. The

Soviet Union sold oil to the "imperialist" West during the height of the cold war.)

Brzezinski calls for the United States to lead the states of Europe plus Russia, Japan, and China in a cooperative approach to stabilizing this region so that it cannot spark conflicts among them. As he rightly argues, the task of stabilization is beyond the power of the United States alone. With allies, however; it can manage the challenge.

After Al Qaeda's attacks in the United States in September 2001, the European members of NATO invoked Article Five of the North Atlantic Treaty, meaning that they considered the attack on America as an attack on them all Article Five had never been invoked before. Moreover, more than 90 countries worldwide joined one or more of five separate coalitions to support the U.S. war against Al Qaeda. Seldom has the United States had so much international support. It was a most propitious time, therefore, for dealing with "the global Balkans" in precisely the way Brzezinski suggested.

Over the next year and a half, however, in the run-up to the invasion of Iraq, many neoconservatives, both inside and outside the administration, disparaged NATO and other U.S. allies as unnecessary for "transforming the Middle East." Because the United States is a superpower, they insisted, it could handle this task alone. Accordingly, we witnessed Secretary of Defense Donald Rumsfeld's team and some officials in the State Department and the White House (especially in the vice president's office) gratuitously and repeatedly insult the Europeans, dismissing them as irrelevant. The climax of this sustained campaign to discard America's allies came in the UN Security Council struggle for a resolution to legitimize the invasion of Iraq in February–March 2003.

From that time on, we have seen most U.S. allies stand aside and engage in schadenfreude over America's painful bog-down in Iraq. Winston Churchill's glib observation that "the only thing worse than having allies is having none" was once again vindicated.

The Wrong Strategy

Two areas of inquiry follow naturally from this background. First, how could the United States induce its allies to join its efforts in Iraq now? Why should they put troops in Iraq and suffer the pain with Americans? Could Washington seriously expect them to do so? Second, is remaining in Iraq the best strategy for a coalition of major states to stabilize the region? Would a large NATO coalition of force plus some from India, Japan, and China enjoy more success?

On the first point, there is no chance that America's allies will join it in Iraq. How could the leaders of Germany; France, and other states in Europe convince their publics to support such a course of action? They could not, and their publics would not be wise to agree if their leaders pleaded for them to do so.

On the second point, Iraq is the worst place to fight a battle for regional stability. Whose interests were best served by the U.S. invasion of Iraq in the first place? It turns out that Iran and Al Qaeda benefited the most, and that continues to be true every day U.S. forces remain there. A serious review of America's

regional interests is required. Until that is accomplished and new and compelling aims for managing the region are clarified, continuing the campaign in Iraq makes no sense.

Once these two realities are recognized, it becomes clear that U.S. withdrawal from Iraq is the precondition to America's winning the support of allies and a few others for a joint approach to the region. Until that has been completed, they will not join such a coalition. And until that has happened, America's leaders cannot even think dearly about what constitutes U.S. interests there, much less gain agreement about common interests for a coalition.

By contrast, any argument for "staying the course," or seeking more stability before the United States withdraws—or pointing out tragic consequences that withdrawal would cause—is bound to be wrong, or at least unpersuasive. Putting it bluntly, those who insist on staying in Iraq longer make the consequences of withdrawal more terrible and also make it harder to find an alternative strategy for achieving regional stability.

Once the invasion began in March 2003, all of the ensuing unhappy results became inevitable. The invasion of Iraq may well turn out to be the greatest strategic disaster in U.S. history. And the longer America stays, the worse it will be. Until that is understood, the United States will make no progress with its allies or in devising a promising alternative strategy.

"Staying the course" may make a good sound bite, but it can be disastrous for strategy. Several of Hitler's generals told him that "staying the course" at Stalingrad in 1942 was a strategic mistake, that he should allow the Sixth Army to be withdrawn, saving it to fight defensive actions on reduced frontage against the growing Red Army. He refused, lost the Sixth Army entirely, and left his commanders with fewer forces to defend a wider front. Thus he made the subsequent Soviet offensives westward easier.

To argue, as some do, that the United States cannot leave Iraq because "we broke it and therefore we own it" is to reason precisely the way Hitler did with his commanders. Of course America broke it! But the Middle East is not a pottery store. It is the site of major military conflict with several different forces that the United States is galvanizing into an alliance against America. To hang on to an untenable position is the height of irresponsibility. Beware of anyone, including the president, who insists that this is the "responsible" or "patriotic" thing to do.

The Refuge of Scoundrels

Many U.S. officers in Iraq, especially at company and field grade levels, know that while they are winning every tactical battle, they are losing strategically. And they are beginning to voice complaints about Americans at home bearing none of the pains of the war. One can only guess about the enlisted ranks, but those on a second tour—perhaps the majority today—are probably anxious for an early pullout. It is also noteworthy that U.S. generals in Iraq are not bubbling over with optimistic reports the way they were during the first few years of the Vietnam War.

Their careful statements and caution probably reflect serious doubts that they do not, and should not, express publicly. The more important question is whether repressive and vindictive behavior by the secretary of defense and his deputy against the senior military—especially the Army leadership, which is the critical component in the war—has made it impossible for field commanders to make the political leaders see the facts.

Most officers and probably most troops do not believe that it is unpatriotic and a failure to support the troops to question the strategic wisdom of the war. They are angry at the deficiencies in material support they get from the Department of Defense, and especially about the irresponsibly long deployments they must now endure because Rumsfeld and his staff have refused to enlarge the ground forces to provide shorter tours. In the meantime, they know that the defense budget lavishes funds on the maritime forces and programs like the Strategic Defense Initiative while the Pentagon refuses to increase dramatically the size of the Army.

One could justly anticipate that in conditions such as these, the opposition party—the Democrats today—would be advocating a pullout. Yet none were until Congressman Murtha surprised both the White House and his own party by putting things as plainly as I have. Although he has infuriated the administration and terrified some of his fellow Democrats, he seems to have catalyzed a political debate that is long overdue.

Why was it so late in coming? And why are so many Democrats still dodging and weaving on an issue of such dramatic important for the country? Why such an egregious evasion of political responsibility? I can only speculate. The biggest reason is because Democrats were not willing to oppose the war during the 2004 presidential campaign. Former Vermont Governor Howard Dean alone took a clear and consistent stand on Iraq, and the rest of the Democratic Party trashed him for it. Most

Democratic leaders in Congress voted for the war and let that vote shackle them later on. Now they are scared to death that the White House will smear them with lack of patriotism if they suggest pulling out.

Aid and Comfort

No one will be able to sustain a strong case for withdrawal in the short run without going back to the fundamental misjudgment of invading Iraq in the first place. Once the enormity of that error is grasped, the case for pulling out becomes easy to see.

The U.S. invasion of Iraq mainly served the interests of three groups. It benefited Osama bin Laden's Al Qaeda, by making Iraq safe for Al Qaeda, by positioning U.S. military personnel in places where jihadist operatives could kill them, by helping to radicalize youth throughout the Arab and Muslim world, by alienating America's most important and strongest allies—the Europeans—and by squandering U.S. military resources that otherwise might be used to finish off Al Qaeda in Pakistan.

The invasion also benefited the Iranians, who had been invaded by Hussein's army and suffered massive casualties in an eight-year war with Iraq. And it benefited extremists in both Palesllnian and Israeli political circles, who do not really want a peace settlement and who probably believe that bogging the United States down in a war in Iraq will give them the time and cover to wipe out the other side. The Iraq War was never in America's interest. It has not become so since the war began.

General **WILLIAM ODOM,** a senior fellow at the Hudson Institute, served as director of the National Security Agency under President Ronald Reagan from 1985 to 1988.

From *Current History,* January 2006, pp. 3–7. Copyright © 2006 by Current History, Inc. Reprinted by permission.

Stay to Win

JOHN MCCAIN

The news from Iraq is filled with numbers. The number of Iraqis streaming to the polls to determine their future democratically. A new constitution, enshrining fundamental rights, approved by a 4-to-1 margin, with two Sunni-dominated provinces dissenting. More than 2,000 Americans killed in action since the war began.

It is all being counted: the number of safe areas, the daily attacks, the Iraqi troop units trained, the billions spent per month. And yet, as has been so often the case in Iraq, these numbers cannot indicate where that country is heading, because the figures themselves point in different directions. There is, at the same time, both great difficulty and great hope. And just as Americans would be unwise to focus solely on the hopeful signs, so too would they be foolish merely to dwell on the difficulties.

I mention this not because I seek to whitewash the situation in Iraq. On the contrary, not all is well there. But as we look on events there, let us not forget that the Iraqi people are in the midst of something unprecedented in their history.

The world has witnessed Iraqis of all stripes exercising those very democratic habits that critics predicted could never take root in a country with little democratic tradition. On December 15, 2005, Iraqis braved death threats to elect their first free and independent parliament. Before that, they voted in January for an interim government. They put Saddam Hussein on trial and dictators throughout the world on notice. They produced a landmark constitution that, while not perfect, nevertheless upholds critical rights that go far beyond standards elsewhere in the region. And they adopted that constitution by free vote—the first time in history for an Arab country. Try as they might, the terrorists and the insurgents have proved unable to muster a veto against Iraqi democracy.

Despite the daily bombings and attacks, the terrorists have not achieved their goals. They have failed to incite a civil war, because Kurds and Shiites still have faith in the future and in American and Iraqi security efforts. The insurgents have not prevented Iraqis from joining the military and police, in spite of horrific attacks at recruiting centers. Oil exports continue, despite concerted efforts at sabotage. And the insurgents have not stopped the political process, even while they assassinate government officials and attack polling places.

Amid the debate about Iraq, the stakes for the United States, and current American policy, it is important not to forget just how far the Iraqi people have come. With US help, the dictator who ruled their lives is gone from power and the Iraqi people are establishing a true democracy. The Middle East will be forever changed by the choices American policy makers have made, and by the choices they will continue to make over the next months. They must get Iraq right.

Transcendent Stakes

The United States must get Iraq right because America's stake in that conflict is enormous. All Americans, whether or not they supported the US action to topple Hussein, must understand the profound implications of their country's presence there. Success or failure in Iraq is the transcendent issue for US foreign policy and national security, for now and years to come. And the stakes are higher than in the Vietnam War.

There is an understandable desire, nearly three years after the invasion, to seek a quick and easy end to the intervention in Iraq. We see this in the protests of antiwar activist Cindy Sheehan; we saw it recently in Senator John Kerry's call to withdraw troops whether or not the country is secured. But should America follow these calls, it would face consequences of the most serious nature. Because Iraqi forces are not yet capable of carrying out most security operations on their own, great bloodshed would occur if the main enforcer of government authority—coalition troops—drew down prematurely. If the United States were to leave, the most likely result would be full-scale civil war.

When America toppled Saddam Hussein, it incurred a moral duty not to abandon the Iraqi people to terrorists and killers. If the United States withdraws prematurely, risking all-out civil war, it will have done precisely that. I can hardly imagine that any US senator or any other American leader would want his nation to suffer that moral stain.

And yet the implications of premature withdrawal from Iraq are not moral alone; they directly involve America's national security. Instability in Iraq would invite further Syrian and Iranian interference, bolstering the influence of two terror-sponsoring states firmly opposed to US policy in the region. Iraq's neighbors—from Saudi Arabia to Israel to Turkey—would feel their own security eroding, and might be induced to act. This uncertain swirl of events would have a damaging impact on America's ability to promote positive change in the Middle East, to say the least.

Withdrawing before there is a stable and legitimate Iraqi authority would turn Iraq into a failed state in the heart of the Middle East. We have seen a failed state emerge after US disengagement before, and it cost Americans terribly. Before Al Qaeda's attacks on the United States on September 11, 2001, terrorists found sanctuary in Afghanistan to train and plan operations with impunity. We know that there are today in Iraq terrorists who are planning attacks against Americans. The United States cannot make this fatal mistake twice.

If America leaves Iraq prematurely, the jihadists will interpret the withdrawal as their great victory against a great power. Osama bin Laden and his followers believe that America is weak, unwilling to suffer casualties in battle. They drew that lesson from Lebanon in the 1980s and Somalia in the 1990s, when US troops hastily withdrew after being attacked. Today they have their sights set squarely on Iraq.

Zawahiri's Plan

A recently released letter from Ayman al-Zawahiri, bin Laden's lieutenant, to Abu Musab al-Zarqawi, the leading terrorist in Iraq, draws out the implications. The Zawahiri letter is predicated on the assumption that the United States will quit Iraq, and that Al Qaeda's real game begins as soon as the United States abandons the country. In his missive, Zawahiri lays out a four-stage plan—including the establishment of a caliphate in Iraq, the extension of a "jihad wave" to the secular countries neighboring Iraq, and renewed confrontation with Israel—none of which shall commence until the completion of stage one: *expel the Americans from Iraq.* Zawahiri observes that the collapse of American power in Vietnam—"and how they ran and left their agents"—suggests that "we must be ready starting now."

The United States cannot let them start, now or ever. America must stay in Iraq until the government there has a fully functioning security apparatus that can keep Zarqawi and his terrorists at bay, and ultimately defeat them. Some argue that it is America's very presence in Iraq that has created the insurgency; if America ends the occupation, it ends the insurgency. In fact, by ending military operations, the United States would likely empower the insurgency. Zarqawi and others fight not just against foreign forces but also against the Shiite Muslims, whom they believe to be infidels, and against all elements of the government. Sunni Muslim insurgents attack Kurds, Turkmens, Christians, and other Iraqis not simply to end the US occupation, but to recapture lost Sunni power. As the military analyst Frederick Kagan has written, these Sunnis are not yet persuaded that violence is counterproductive; on the contrary, they believe the insurgency might lead to an improvement in their political situation. There is no reason to think that an American drawdown would extinguish these motivations to fight.

Because it cannot pull out and simply hope for the best, because it cannot withdraw and manage things from afar, because morality and national security compel it, the United

States has to see this mission through to completion. Calls for premature withdrawal of American forces represent, I believe, a major step on the road to disaster. Drawdowns must be based on conditions in Iraq, not arbitrary deadlines rooted in domestic American politics.

President Bush and his advisers understand this, and I praise their resolve. They know that the consequences of failure are unacceptable and that the benefits of success in Iraq remain profound. And yet at the same time there is an undeniable sense that things are slipping—more violence on the ground, declining domestic support for the war, growing incantations among Americans that there is no end in sight. To build on what has been accomplished, and to win the war in Iraq, the United States needs to make several significant policy changes.

A Counterinsurgency Strategy

The first is to adopt an effective military counterinsurgency strategy. For most of the occupation, US military strategy has been built around trying to secure the entirety of Iraq at the same time. With the Americans' current force structure and the power vacuum that persists in many areas of Iraq, that is not possible today. In their attempt to secure all of Iraq, coalition forces engage in search and destroy operations to root out insurgent strongholds, with the aim of killing as many insurgents as possible. But coalition forces cannot hold the ground indefinitely, and when they move on to fight other battles, the insurgent ranks replenish and the strongholds fill again. US troops must then reenter the same area and refight the same battle.

The example of Tal Afar, a city in northwestern Iraq not far from the Syrian border, is instructive. Coalition forces first fought in Tal Afar in September 2003, when the 101st Airborne Division took the city, then withdrew. Over the next year insurgents streamed back into the area. In September 2004 Stryker brigades and Iraqi security forces returned to Tal Afar, chasing out insurgents. They then left again, moving on to fight insurgents in other locations. Then in September 2005, the Third Armored Calvary Regiment swept into Tal Afar, killing rebels while others retreated into the countryside. Most US troops have already redeployed, and they may well be back again. The battles of Tal Afar, like those in other areas of Iraq, have become seasonal offensives, where success is measured most often by the number of insurgents captured and killed. But that is not success. And "sweeping and leaving" is not working.

Instead, coalition forces need to clear and stay. They can do this with a modified version of traditional counterinsurgency strategy. Andrew Krepinevich, Tom Donnelly, Gary Schmitt, and others have written about this idea. Whether called the "ink blot," "oil spot," or "safe haven" strategy, it draws on successful counterinsurgency efforts in the past. Rather than focusing on killing and capturing insurgents, this strategy emphasizes protecting the local population and creating secure areas where insurgents find it difficult to operate. US forces with Iraqi assistance would begin by clearing areas, with heavy force if necessary, to establish a zone as free of insurgents as possible. Security forces can then cordon off the zone and establish constant patrols, by American and Iraqi military and police, to protect the population from insurgents and common crime, and to arrest remaining insurgents as they are found.

In this newly secure environment, many of the tasks critical to winning in Iraq can take place—tasks that are not being carried out today. Massive reconstruction can go forward without fear of attack and sabotage. Political meetings and campaigning can take place in the open. Civil society can emerge. Intelligence improves, as it becomes increasingly safe for citizens to provide tips to the security forces, knowing that they can do so without being threatened. The coalition must then act on this intelligence, increasing the speed at which it is transmitted to operational teams. Past practice has shown that "actionable intelligence" has a short shelf life, and the lag involved in communicating it to security forces costs vital opportunities.

As these elements positively reinforce each other, the security forces then expand the territory under their control. Coalition and Iraqi forces have done this successfully in Falluja. They cleared the area of insurgents and held the city. Today Iraqi police and soldiers patrol the streets, with support from two US battalions. And when the Iraqi forces are at a level sufficient to take over the patrolling responsibilities on their own, American troops can hand over the duties. Falluja today is not perfect, but the aim is not perfection—it is an improvement over the insecurity that plagues Iraq today.

The Costs of Success

This kind of a counterinsurgency strategy has some costs. Securing ever increasing parts of Iraq and preventing the emergence of new terrorist safe havens will require more troops and money. It will take time, probably years, and mean more American casualties. Those are terrible prices to pay. But with the stakes so high, I believe Americans must choose the strategy with the best chance of success. The Pentagon seems to be coming around on this, and top commanders profess to employ a version already. If the United States is on its way to adopting a true counterinsurgency strategy, that is wonderful, but it has not been the case thus far. Soon after the recent operations in Tal Afar, most US troops were redeployed, leaving behind Iraqi units with Americans embedded. I hope this will be sufficient to establish security there, but it is also clear that there has been no spike in reconstruction activity in that city.

To enhance chances of success with this strategy, and enable coalition forces to hold as much territory as possible, America needs more troops in Iraq. For this reason, I believe that current ideas to effect a partial drawdown during 2006 are exactly wrong. While the United States and its partners are training Iraqi security forces at a furious pace, these Iraqis should supplement, not substitute for, the coalition forces on the ground. Instead of drawing down, the United States should be ramping up, with more civil-military soldiers, translators, and counterinsurgency operations teams. Decisions about troop levels should be tied to the success or failure of the mission in Iraq, not to the number of Iraqi troops trained and equipped. And while American policy makers seek higher troop levels for Iraq, they should at last face facts and increase the standing size of the US Army. It takes time to build a larger army, but had the United States

done so even after its invasion of Iraq, its military would have more soldiers available for deployment now.

Knowing the enemy is the essential precondition to defeating him, and I believe US counterinsurgency strategy can do more to exploit divisions in the strands of the insurgency. Foreign jihadists, Baathist revanchists, and Sunni discontents do not necessarily share tactics or goals. Recent Sunni participation in the constitutional process—and especially the decision by Sunni parties to contest the December parliamentary elections—present opportunities to split Sunnis from those whose only goal is death, destruction, and chaos.

Building Support for Victory

Besides changing military strategy, US policy makers need to take several other steps to assure success in the war. To begin with, they need to start keeping senior officers in place. The Pentagon has adopted a policy of rotating generals in and out of Iraq almost as frequently as it rotates the troops. General David Petraeus, a fine officer who was the military's foremost expert in the training of Iraqi security forces, now uses his hard-earned experience and expertise at Fort Leavenworth. Others, including Generals James Conway, Ray Odierno, and Peter Chiarelli, have been transferred to Washington or elsewhere. This is deeply unwise. If these were the best men for the task, they should still be on the job. These generals and other senior officers build, in their time in Iraq, the on-the-ground and institutional knowledge necessary to approach this conflict with wisdom. They know, for example, the difference between a battle in Falluja and one in Tal Afar, or what kind of patrols are most effective in Shiite areas of Baghdad. These commanders—and their hard-won experience—need to stay in place.

Second, policy makers need to integrate counterinsurgency efforts at senior levels. While it is critical to focus American military efforts on insurgents, particularly against Sunni fighters using violence to improve their political position, the nonmilitary component is also essential. All Iraqis need to see a tangible improvement in their daily lives or support for the new government will slip. Sunnis need to feel that, should they abandon violence once and for all, there will be some role in the political process for them. The Iraqi people must feel invested in a newly free, newly powerful and prosperous country at peace.

There is a role for each element of the US government in this, whether it implies aid, trade, wells, schools, training, or anything else. US Ambassador Zalmay Khalilzad has done a fine job coordinating these efforts with the military campaign and the political process, but it needs to be done in Washington too. This should be the highest priority of President Bush's team, and must be managed by the most senior levels at the State Department, the Pentagon, the National Security Council, the US Agency for International Development, and any other agency that can contribute to the effort. To consign Iraq to the Pentagon to win or lose will simply not suffice.

In this regard, I am encouraged by Secretary of State Condoleezza Rice's recent testimony before the Senate Foreign Relations Committee, which laid out a more comprehensive, integrated political-military-economic strategy for Iraq. Implementing it is essential and will require a more formal interagency structure than we have seen to date.

Third, the United States needs to build loyalty in Iraq's armed forces. In building the armed forces at a rapid pace, US and Iraqi authorities have invited former militia members to join. In the short run, it is most practical to do what has been done thus far: swallow former militia units whole. In the long run, the focus must be on building diversified individual military units.

The lesson of Afghanistan is instructive. There, the United States insisted—over initial objections from the Afghan Ministry of Defense—that each new military unit be carefully calibrated to include Pashtuns, Tajiks, Uzbeks, and others. This diversification within units serves several important functions. Over time, it helps build loyalty to the central government. It makes it more difficult for militias to reconstitute, should any decide to oppose the government. And, more broadly, it helps build support for a unified nation. The multiethnic Afghan National Army has provided a powerful psychological boost in a deeply divided country. Simply seeing Pashtuns and Tajiks and Uzbeks, in uniform and working together, has had a great impact on Afghan public opinion and the way Afghans imagine their country.

In Iraq the policy has been to recruit former militia members as individuals, rather than as units, but the reality has fallen short. Building units in this way is more difficult and will require more time than accepting homogeneous Kurdish, Shiite, or Sunni units, for reasons of language, culture, and expediency. But that is precisely why it is so important to do. Standing up the Iraqi army is about more than generating manpower so that American troops can withdraw. The composition and character of the force that Americans leave behind will have social and political ramifications far beyond the military balance of power.

Fourth, policy makers should increase pressure on Syria. For too long, Syria has refused to crack down on Iraqi insurgents and foreign terrorists operating from its territory. President Bashar Assad said recently that his government distinguishes between those insurgents who attack Iraqis and those who attack American and British troops, suggesting they are "something different." This is the same mindset that has led Syria to defy the United Nations over the assassination of former Lebanese Prime Minister Rafik Hariri, give sanctuary to Palestinian terrorist organizations, and attempt to maintain some hold on Lebanon.

With the UN Security Council now engaged, the international community has an opportunity to apply real pressure on Syria to change its behavior on all these fronts. While multilateral sanctions keyed to Syrian cooperation with the Hariri investigation may be the starting point, that should not be the end. Any country that wishes to see the Iraqi people live in peace and freedom should join in pressuring Syria to stop Iraqi and foreign terrorists from using its soil.

The Other Battlefront

Finally, the United States needs to assure success in Iraq by winning the war on the home front. Even as the political-military strategy is being improved, the latest polls and protests suggest that the American public's support increasingly is at risk. If it disappears, the country will have lost this war as soundly as if its forces were defeated on the battlefield. A renewed effort at home starts with explaining precisely what is at stake in this war—not to alarm Americans, but so that they see the nature of this struggle for what it is. The president cannot do this alone. The media, so efficient in portraying the difficulties in Iraq, need to convey the consequences of success or failure there. Critics in the Democratic Party should outline precisely what they believe to be the stakes in this battle, if they are willing to suffer the consequences of withdrawal.

Another part of the effort includes avoiding rosy aspirations for near-term improvements in Iraq's politics or security situation, and more accurately portraying events on the ground, even if they are negative. The American people have heard many times that the violence in Iraq will subside soon—when there is a transitional government in place, when Hussein is captured, when there are elections, when there is a constitution, when there is an elected parliament. It would be better to describe the situation as it is—difficult right now, but not without progress and hope, and with a long, hard road ahead—and to announce that things have improved only when they in fact have.

Above all, winning the home front means reiterating the nation's commitment to victory and laying out a realistic game plan that will take America there. I believe that the vast majority of Americans, even those who did not support the initial invasion, wish to see their country prevail. They are prepared to pay the human and financial costs of this war if—but only if—they believe their government is on a measurable path to victory. That their government must give them. In this war as in all others, there are two fronts, the battlefield and the home front, and leaders must tend to both.

The Number That Counts

Despite bombs, daily attacks, and untold threats against the democratic process, Iraq has held free elections, with open campaigns and a truly free press. Iraq has ratified the most progressive constitution in the Arab world and instilled justice in a country that for so long lacked it. Iraq has put Hussein on trial and held his henchmen accountable for their murderous rule. In doing all these things and more, the Iraqi people have issued to their more peaceful, prosperous neighbors a profound challenge.

We have seen responses already in Lebanon's Cedar Revolution, Egypt's recent elections, and a proliferation of calls for democracy in the Arab world. As Iraq consolidates its democratic process, the challenge to its neighbors—and their necessary responses—will be starker still. The Iraqi people have shown their impulse toward democracy; they need security to hash out the many remaining differences that still divide them. They can get there, but they need America's support.

This much should be obvious: America, Iraq, and the world are better off with Hussein in prison rather than in power. Does anyone believe the stirrings of freedom in the region would exist if he still ruled with an iron fist? Does anyone believe the region would be better off if he were in power, using oil revenue to purchase political support? Does anyone believe meaningful sanctions would remain or that there would be any serious checks on his ambitions? The costs of this war have been high, especially for the more than 2,000 Americans, and their families, who have paid the ultimate price. But liberating Iraq was in America's strategic and moral interests, and Americans must honor their sacrifice by seeing this mission through to victory.

Victory will not come overnight. On the contrary, it will take more time, more commitment, and more support—and more brave Americans will lose their lives in the service of this great cause. And despite US cajoling, nagging, and pleading, few other countries around the world will share much of the burden. Iraq is for Americans to do, for them to win or lose, for them to suffer the consequences or share in the benefits. Progress in Iraq can be charted with all sorts of numbers. But in the end, there is only one United States of America, and it is to that nation that history will look for courage and commitment.

Bush's Neo-Imperialist War

Our Iraqi occupation not only rejects American foreign policy since Wilson, it's a throwback to the great power imperialism that led to World War I.

JOHN B. JUDIS

In 1882 the British occupied Egypt. Although they claimed they would withdraw their troops, the British remained, they said, at the request of the khedive, the ruler they had installed. The *U.S. Army Area Handbook* aptly describes the British decision to stay:

> At the outset of the occupation, the British government declared its intention to withdraw its troops as soon as possible. This could not be done, however, until the authority of the khedive was restored. Eventually, the British realized that these two aims were incompatible because the military intervention, which Khedive Tawfiq supported and which prevented his overthrow, had undermined the authority of the ruler. Without the British presence, the khedival government would probably have collapsed.

The British would remain in Egypt for 70 years until Gamel Abdel Nasser's nationalist revolt tossed them out. They would grant Egypt nominal independence in 1922, but in order to maintain their hold over the Suez Canal, the gateway to British India and Asia, they would retain control over Egypt's finances and foreign policy.

On Sept. 13, 2007, George W. Bush issued his report to the nation on the progress of "the surge" in Iraq. Echoing the British in Egypt, he promised "a reduced American presence" in Iraq, but he added ominously that "Iraqi leaders from all communities . . . understand that their success will require U.S. political, economic, and security engagement that extends beyond my presidency. These Iraqi leaders have asked for an *enduring relationship* with America. And we are ready to begin building that relationship—in a way that protects our interests in the region and requires many fewer American troops." (Emphasis mine.) In other words, Iraqi leaders who owe their positions to the U.S. occupation want the Americans to stay indefinitely, and Bush is ready to oblige them, albeit with a smaller force.

British Prime Minister William Gladstone insisted in 1882 that the British would not make Egypt a colony. He wanted, his private secretary recorded, "to give scope to Egypt for the Egyptians were this feasible and attainable without risk." But that appeared too risky, and Egypt quickly became part of the British Empire. Bush,

too, has insisted that the United States is not engaged in imperialism. America is not "an imperial power," but a "liberating power," he has declared. But Bush's denial rings as hollow as Gladstone's. What Bush has done in Iraq, rather than what he says he has done, is to revive an imperialist foreign policy, reminiscent of the British and French in the Middle East, and of the kind that the United States practiced briefly under William McKinley and Theodore Roosevelt.

Bush's foreign policy has been variously described as unilateralist, militarist, and hyper-nationalist. But the term that fits it best is imperialist. That's not because it is the most incendiary term, but because it is the most historically accurate. Bush's foreign policy was framed as an alternative to the liberal internationalist policies that Woodrow Wilson espoused and that presidents from Franklin D. Roosevelt to Bill Clinton tried to put into effect as an alternative to the imperialist strategies that helped cause two world wars and even the Cold War. Bush's foreign policy represents a return not to the simple unilateralism of 19th-century American foreign policy, but to the imperial strategy that the great powers of Europe—and, for a brief period, America, too—followed and that resulted in utter disaster.

There have been empires since the dawn of history, but the term "imperialism," and its modern practice, originated in the late 19th century. During that time, Britain and the major European powers struggled to carve up the less developed world into colonies, protectorates, and spheres of influence. The new empires spawned during this period didn't consist of "settler colonies" like the original American colonies or Australia, but indigenous possessions like British India or French Indochina. The United States got into the great game in 1898 when, after successfully ousting Spain from Cuba and the Pacific, the McKinley administration, prodded by Theodore Roosevelt and Henry Cabot Lodge, decided to annex the Philippines.

There were two kinds of imperial rule: direct, where the colonial power assigned an administrator—a viceroy or proconsul—who ran the country directly; and indirect, where the colonial power used its financial and military power to prop up a native administration that did its bidding and to prevent the rise of governments that did not. The latter kind of imperial rule was developed by the

United States in Cuba in 1901 after Roosevelt's Secretary of War Elihu Root realized that direct rule could bring war and rebellion, as it had done, to the McKinley administration's surprise, in the Philippines. The British later adopted this kind of imperial rule in Egypt and Iraq.

The impetus for the growth of empires in the 19th century was economic. Britain and the imperial powers sought secure access to raw materials, including rubber, cotton, and foodstuffs—oil would come later—and to outlets for capital investment in railroads and other major projects. As their colonial investments grew, they tried to erect an international system of islands and port facilities and canals that could protect their trade routes. (The U.S. originally saw the Philippines as a stepping stone to the lucrative Chinese market.) But the impetus wasn't only economic. By the early 20th century, as the countries strove to divide up the globe, the acquisition of colonies became a source of national power and prestige, and acquired its own elaborate and malignant ideological justification. It gained a life of its own.

This growth of imperialism eventually created the conditions for its undoing. By encouraging not merely trade rivalry, but growing competition for national power—epitomized in the pre–World War I naval arms race between Britain and Germany—imperialism helped spawn wars among the great powers themselves. The rivalry between top dog England and challenger Germany, and between Germany and Austria, on the one hand, and France and Russia, on the other, contributed to the outbreak of World War I. The Second World War also represented, among other things, an attempt by the Axis powers, a subordinate group of capitalist nations, to redivide the world at the expense of the U.S., Great Britain, France, and the USSR. And the Cold War stemmed from the attempt by the Soviet Union, one of the most vocal critics of Western imperialism, to fulfill the imperial dreams of Czarist Russia by expanding westward and to the south.

In addition, the system of imperialism spawned nationalist and anti-imperialist movements in the colonies themselves. Some of these movements, particularly in the Middle East, had a religious coloration. Others took their ideology from Soviet or Chinese communism or from the Wilsonian vision of national self-determination. These movements made it difficult, and finally impossible, for the imperial powers to maintain their control.

In the United States, Woodrow Wilson came to realize the pitfalls of imperialism not only from the six-year war with the Filipino rebels and Wilson's own unsuccessful intervention in Mexico in 1914, but also from the outbreak of World War I, which Wilson privately blamed on imperial rivalry. After World War I, Wilson set out to create new international arrangements to replace those of imperialism. Wilson sought an agreement among the great powers through the League of Nations to prevent new conquests and wars over conquests. He wanted to phase out the existing imperialism through "mandates" that would put countries, and groups of countries, that had no vested interest in acquiring colonies in charge of assisting colonies in making the transition to self-government. And Wilson favored economic agreements to ease conflicts over access to markets and raw materials.

Wilson didn't think the United States should abandon the leadership role it acquired at the end of World War I. But he wanted the United States to exercise it through international institutions that could ensure a peaceful world in which the United States would not have to prepare perpetually for war and in which America's vaunted economic superiority could come to the fore. Wilson failed to win over his European counterparts and the Republicans at home. But during and after World War II, Franklin Roosevelt and Harry Truman attempted to put Wilson's liberal internationalism into practice. It was embodied not only in the U.N., but in the IMF, World Bank, and GATT agreements, and in America's multilateral approach to the Cold War.

Roosevelt had planned to force Britain and France to divest themselves of their empires—the new U.N. had a "trusteeship" system for that purpose—but American resolve was blunted by the onset of the Cold War. Faced with Soviet support for anti-imperialist movements in Africa, Asia, and the Middle East, the United States sided with the former colonial powers. That policy came to a disastrous culmination in the Vietnam war, which was an outgrowth of American support for French colonialism. The American defeat in Vietnam dealt a fatal blow to U.S. attempts to prop up the Western imperialism. Subsequently, Portugal's colonies in Africa gained their independence. That left only the Soviet empire. When it collapsed in the early 1990s, the age of empire was over.

There were still colonies and quasi-colonies like Chechnya or Tibet, but they were contested extensions of the larger power itself. Some political scientists in the United States and Europe claimed that America remained an imperial power because of its worldwide system of military bases and its clout in international financial institutions, but while America was capable of influencing governments, it could no longer exercise a veto over critical regimes coming to power. The invasion of Panama in 1989 appeared to be the last gasp of America's indirect imperialism.

Indeed, the 1990s became a high water mark of liberal internationalism. George H.W. Bush's administration built a coalition through the U.N. to drive Iraq out of Kuwait. Acting through NATO, the Clinton administration built a coalition to end the wars in Bosnia and Kosovo and to oversee the transition to a peaceful breakup of former Yugoslavia. The United States also took leadership in the formation of the World Trade Organization—which, whatever its imperfections, was designed to prevent the kind of rival trade blocs that could eventually lead to war. At Maastricht, Western Europe, once the center of imperial rivalry, became a model of post-imperial integration. And the world's nations seemed on the verge of agreeing to a new set of accords, including the Kyoto Protocol, that would address problems Wilson never dreamed of—problems that could not be addressed except through international agreements.

When George W. Bush took office in January 2001, however, his foreign policy echoed not only that of neo-isolationist Republicans like former Majority Leader Dick Armey, but also that of America's foreign policy before we decided in 1898 that we had to get involved in the struggle for empire. That was an America that not only scorned empire but was oblivious to much of the outside world. Bush disdained international organizations. He withdrew the United States from the Kyoto climate treaty and whatever other international agreements had yet to be ratified. He was a unilateralist, but he was reluctant to use America's singular power to affect the governments of other countries. His highest defense priority was the erection of an anti-missile system, the purpose of which was not only to make the United States impregnable from foreign attack, but also to reduce the reliance of the U.S. on other countries for its security.

All that changed after September 11. Bush retained his unilateralism, but he now wedded it to an aggressive strategy for dealing with America's enemies.

In developing a response to September 11, Bush fell under the influence of neo-conservatives in his administration and in Washington policy circles. These neo-conservatives believed that the United States should use its superior military power to intimidate and overthrow the regimes of "rogue states" like Iraq that challenged American hegemony. (One typical slogan was "rogue state rollback.") The neocons didn't favor colonialism, but believed that by exerting its power the United States could produce regimes that did its bidding. After September 11, they spoke openly of creating a new American empire. "People are now coming out of the closet on the word 'empire,' " *Washington Post* columnist Charles Krauthammer exulted.

The neo-conservatives found common cause with Bush officials, including Vice President Dick Cheney and Secretary of Defense Donald Rumsfeld, who were concerned about protecting American access to foreign oil in a period of rising demand and stagnating supply. That made them particularly interested in ousting Saddam Hussein, whose government sat atop the third largest oil reserve in the world, and in installing a regime more friendly to the United States.

In the buildup to the war, and during the invasion and occupation, Bush officials, who were eager to advertise Iraq's nuclear threat, were reluctant to talk about oil, but in off-the-record interviews I conducted in December 2002, neo-conservatives waxed poetic about using Iraq's oil wealth to undermine OPEC. After he left office, former Treasury Secretary Paul O'Neill recounted National Security Council discussions about Iraqi oil. And in his recently published memoir, Alan Greenspan wrote, "I'm saddened that it is politically inconvenient to acknowledge what everyone knows—the Iraq war is largely about oil."

Bush and other administration officials denied that the United States was trying to create a new empire. But they were less guarded in their private communications. When the White House offered former Sen. Bob Kerrey the job of head of the Provisional Authority in Iraq—the job that eventually went to Paul Bremer—officials asked him if he were interested in being "viceroy." Kerrey, taken aback, turned down the job.

The administration's actions also belied its denials. In March 2004, the *Chicago Tribune* reported that the U.S. Army was constructing what it called 14 "enduring bases" in Iraq. These would provide a continuing American military presence in Iraq. And the administration continues work on these bases, including a new one perched on the Iranian border, even as it professes to be committed to turning Iraq over to its government and army.

If there is any lesson to be learned from the 130-year history of imperialism, it is that the natives eventually grow restless.

Though opposition to the American presence in Iraq has grown both there and in the U.S., Bush's televised address and Gen. David Petraeus' congressional testimony in September made clear that the administration has grown even more determined to remain there. As Spencer Ackerman points out, Bush's promise to stay in Iraq "as long as necessary, not one day longer" has given way to the promise of an "enduring relationship." And American projections of troop presence in Iraq now extend indefinitely into the future. If the administration's experience in Iraq does not parallel that of the British in Egypt, it won't be for lack of trying.

Indeed, this brand of imperialism, as practiced by the Bush administration, is remarkably similar to the older European variety. Its outward veneer is optimistic and even triumphalist, when articulated by a neo-conservative like Max Boot or William Kristol, and is usually accompanied by a vision of global moral-religious-social transformation. The British boasted of bringing Christianity and civilization to the heathens; America's neoconservatives trumpet the virtues of free-market capitalism and democracy. And like the older imperialism, Bush's policy toward Iraq and the Middle East has been driven by a fear of losing out on scarce natural resources. Ultimately, his policy is as much a product of the relative decline of American power brought about by the increasingly fierce international competition for resources and markets as it is of America's "unipolar moment."

Bush sought privileged access to Iraq's oil, sparking a new oil diplomacy in which nations use oil wealth as a political weapon.

Bush and Cheney were hardly unique in worrying about the dwindling supply of oil. Bush's father and Bill Clinton also worried about it. But George H.W. Bush and Clinton acted on the premise that petroleum and natural gas were international commodities to which any purchaser should have access. Oil companies, which pressed for the removal of sanctions on Iraq and Iran, shared this view. When the elder Bush and Clinton sought to prevent Iraq from monopolizing the region's oil—and using it as a political instrument—they did so through the United Nations.

But George W. Bush has differed from his predecessors in both his concerns and his methods. Bush, prodded by Cheney, sought to win privileged access to Iraq's oil—not necessarily for any particular company (although Cheney clearly wanted a role for Halliburton in building Iraq's oil infrastructure), but for American producers and consumers in general. That is similar to the strategy of the older imperial powers. And the method they employed was unilateral invasion—oh yes, with the support of Britain, the former great imperial power in the region.

Bush's imperial strategy is sparking a new phase in oil diplomacy, where oil consumers like China are trying to lock up long-term deals with countries in Africa, Asia, and Latin America, and where the producers—notably at this point Venezuela—are beginning to use their oil wealth as a political weapon. The eventual outcome—if this rivalry is not regulated through new international agreements—could be the kind of tension that gave rise to World War I.

As the war in Iraq has turned into a quagmire, neo-conservatives who had goaded the president into action have blamed the war's failure on the administration's flawed strategy. They have propounded a series of "if only's": If only the administration had sent more troops, if only it had not disbanded the Ba'ath army, if only it had handed the leadership of Iraq over immediately to con man Ahmed Chalabi. Of these, only the addition of more troops might have quelled the insurgency, and then only temporarily. If there is any lesson from the 130-year history of imperialism, it is that the natives eventually grow restless. Since World War II, the peoples of the Middle East, Asia, and Africa have been throwing off rather than welcoming foreign control.

The Middle East, where Muslims still blanch at the Crusades and later British and French attempts to divide and rule, is particularly sensitive to outside attempts at domination. Osama bin Laden and al-Qaeda didn't spring from Mecca but from the battlefield in Afghanistan, from resentment of American support for Israel and of American bases on Arab soil. Bush's policy in the region has reflected a profound ignorance of this history. Wrote former National Security Advisor Zbigniew Brzezinski in January 2007, "America is acting like a colonial power in Iraq. But the age of colonialism is over. Waging a colonial war in the post-colonial age is self-defeating."

What, then, should the United States be doing in Iraq and elsewhere to repair the damage wrought by Bush's exercise in neo-imperialism? On one level, this is an enormously complicated question that is beyond my capacity to answer. But on a simple, much less specific level, the answer is obvious: A new administration has to repudiate Bush's policy of imperialism and reaffirm America's commitment to liberal internationalism. That will entail at least these three kinds of initiatives:

- The new administration needs to repudiate Bush's strategy of preemptive regime change and reaffirm the United Nations charter, which allows nations to act unilaterally only in their own immediate self-defense. That would have an immediate effect on American policy toward Iran, whose regime the United States is now officially trying to overthrow.

- The new administration needs to reaffirm the idea behind internationally sanctioned and administered "mandates" and "trusteeship" for countries and peoples going through a difficult transition toward independence and statehood. If countries intervene to prevent war or genocide, they must do so in a manner that assures the peoples targeted that their right of self-determination will be respected. If the United States, for instance, had tried to intervene in the Balkans by itself, it might still be fighting an insurgency there.

- The new administration needs to reaffirm the importance of international action and agreements—through the U.N. and other bodies—to aid in the prevention of wars, pandemics, and environmental catastrophe, and to ease the struggle over scarce resources, including oil and water. That means at a minimum returning to the negotiations over global warming; and attempting to revive the Non-Proliferation Treaty, which the U.S. undermined in signing a nuclear deal with India.

But what about Iraq? Should the U.S. withdraw immediately? Should it leave a rump force in place to fight international terrorists? These questions—now at the forefront of the debate in Washington—are secondary to questions of diplomacy. A new administration should declare the invasion and occupation of Iraq a mistake and pledge to remove American troops from the country. It should not do so, however, with any hope of ending the civil war there, but rather of gaining international support for a "trusteeship" that would guide Iraq back toward genuine self-government and independence. The U.S. can contribute financially, but it will have to take a subordinate role in any international peace-keeping force that enters the country.

None of this will be easy. At this point, the Bush administration might have dug such a huge hole in the region that nothing the United States does will prevent more war and greater chaos. But it is certain that the Bush administration will not change course, and, equally, that a new administration will enjoy a honeymoon not only with American voters, but with the rest of the world in which it could advance a new foreign policy that breaks decisively with that of the Bush administration. If it doesn't do this—if it equivocates and seeks half-measures, or if it tries (as some Republican candidates threaten) to reinforce the American occupation—then its actions will not lead to an enduring relationship with the Iraqis and the peoples of the Middle East, but to an enduring nightmare.

JOHN B. JUDIS is a senior editor at *The New Republic* and a visiting scholar at the Carnegie Endowment for International Peace. He is author most recently of *The Folly of Empire*.

The Next Generation of Terror

The world's most dangerous jihadists no longer answer to al Qaeda. The terrorists we should fear most are self-recruited wannabes who find purpose in terror and comrades on the Web. This new generation is even more frightening and unpredictable than its predecessors, but its evolution just may reveal the key to its demise.

MARC SAGEMAN

When British police broke down Younis Tsouli's door in October 2005 in a leafy west London neighborhood, they suspected the 22-year-old college student, the son of a Moroccan diplomat, of little more than having traded e-mails with men planning a bombing in Bosnia. It was only after they began examining the hard drive on Tsouli's computer that they realized they had stumbled upon one of the most infamous—and unlikely—cyberjihadists in the world.

Tsouli's online username, as they discovered, was Irhabi007 ("Terrorist007" in Arabic). It was a moniker well known to international counterterrorism officials. Since 2004, this young man, with no history of radical activity, had become one of the world's most influential propagandists in jihadi chatrooms. It had been the online images of the war in Iraq that first radicalized him. He began spending his days creating and hacking dozens of Web sites in order to upload videos of beheadings and suicide bombings in Iraq and post links to the texts of bomb-making manuals. From his bedroom in London, he eventually became a crucial global organizer of online terrorist networks, guiding others to jihadist sites where they could learn their deadly craft. Ultimately, he attracted the attention of the late leader of al Qaeda in Iraq, Abu Musab al-Zarqawi. When British police discovered this young IT student in his London flat, he was serving as Zarqawi's public relations mouthpiece on the Web.

Tsouli's journey from computer geek to radical jihadist is representative of the wider evolution of Islamist terrorist networks today. Since Sept. 11, 2001, the threat confronting the West has changed dramatically, but most governments still imagine their foe in the mold of the old al Qaeda. The enemy today is not a product of poverty, ignorance, or religious brainwashing. The individuals we should fear most haven't been trained in terrorist camps, and they don't answer to Osama bin Laden or Ayman al-Zawahiri. They often do not even adhere to the most austere and dogmatic tenets of radical Islam. Instead, the new generation of terrorists consists of home-grown wannabes—self-recruited, without leadership, and globally connected through the Internet. They are young people seeking thrills and a sense of significance and belonging in their lives. And their lack of structure and organizing principles makes them even more terrifying and volatile than their terrorist forebears.

The New Face of Terror

The five years between Osama bin Laden's 1996 declaration of war against the United States from his safe haven in Afghanistan to the attacks of 9/11 were the "golden age" of what could be called al Qaeda Central. Those days are long over, but the social movement they inspired is as strong and dangerous as ever. The structure has simply evolved over time.

Today's new generation of terrorists constitutes the third wave of radicals stirred to battle by the ideology of global jihad. The first wave to join al-Qaeda was Afghan Arabs who came to Pakistan and Afghanistan to fight the Soviets in the 1980s. They were, contrary to popular belief, largely well educated and from solidly middle-class backgrounds. They were also mature, often about 30 years old when they took up arms. Their remnants still form the backbone of al Qaeda's leadership today, but there are at most a few dozen of them left, hiding in the frontier territories of northwest Pakistan.

The second wave that followed consisted mostly of elite expatriates from the Middle East who went to the West to attend universities. The separation from family, friends, and culture led many to feel homesick and marginalized, sentiments that hardened into the seeds of their radicalization. It was this generation of young men who traveled to al Qaeda's training camps in Afghanistan in the 1990s. They were incorporated into al Qaeda Central, and today there are at most about 100 of them left, also in hiding in northwest Pakistan.

The new, third wave is unlike its predecessors. It consists mostly of would-be terrorists, who, angered by the invasion of Iraq, aspire to join the movement and the men they hail as heroes. But it is nearly impossible for them to link up with al Qaeda Central, which was forced underground after 9/11. Instead, they form fluid, informal networks that are self-financed and self-trained. They have no physical headquarters or sanctuary, but the tolerant, virtual environment of the Internet offers them a semblance of unity and purpose. Theirs is a scattered, decentralized social structure—a leaderless jihad.

Take the case of Mohammed Bouyeri, perhaps the most infamous member of a network of aspiring jihadists that Dutch authorities dubbed the "Hofstad Netwerk," in 2004. Bouyeri, then a 26-year-old formerly secular social worker born to Moroccan immigrants in Amsterdam, could also trace his radicalization to outrage over the Iraq war. He became influential among a loosely connected group of about 100 young Dutch Muslims, most of whom were in their late teens and born in the Netherlands. The network informally coalesced around three or four active participants, some of whom had acquired a local reputation for trying (and failing) to fight the jihad abroad. Some of the initial meetings were at demonstrations for international Muslim causes, others at radical mosques, but mostly they met in Internet chatrooms. Other popular meeting spots included Internet cafes or the few apartments of the older members, as most of the network still lived with their parents. The group had no clear leader and no connection to established terrorist networks abroad.

On Nov. 2, 2004, Mohammed Bouyeri brutally murdered Dutch filmmaker Theo van Gogh on an Amsterdam street, nearly sawing off van Gogh's head and pinning a five-page note threatening the enemies of Islam to his victim's chest. Bouyeri had been enraged by van Gogh's short film, *Submission,* about Islam's treatment of women and domestic violence, and written by former Dutch parliamentarian Ayaan Hirsi Ali. After killing van Gogh, Bouyeri calmly waited for the police in the hope that he would die in the gunfight that he expected would follow. He was only wounded and, less than a year later, sentenced to life in prison. A series of raids against other members of the network uncovered evidence of plans to bomb the Dutch parliament, a nuclear power plant, and Amsterdam's airport, as well as assassination plots against prominent Dutch politicians.

The fluidity of the Hofstad Netwerk has created problems for Dutch prosecutors. The first few trials succeeded in convicting some members as belonging to a terrorist organization because they met regularly. But at later trials, when defendants faced more serious charges, the prosecutors' cases began to break down. Some guilty verdicts have even been subsequently overturned. In January, a Dutch appeals court threw out the convictions of seven men accused of belonging to the Hofstad Netwerk because "no structured cooperation [had] been established." It is difficult to convict suspects who rarely meet face to face and whose cause has no formal organization.

The perpetrators of the Madrid bombings in March 2004 are another example of the self-recruited leaderless jihad. They were an unlikely network of young immigrants who came together in haphazard ways. Some had been lifelong friends from their barrio in Tetouan, Morocco, and eventually came to run one of the most successful drug networks in Madrid, selling hashish and ecstasy. Their informal leader, Jamal Ahmidan, a 33-year-old high school dropout who liked to chase women, wavered between pointless criminality and redemptive religion. When he was released from a Moroccan jail in 2003 after serving three years for an alleged homicide, he became increasingly obsessed with the war in Iraq. He linked up with Tunisian-born Sarhane Ben Abdelmajid Fakhet, who had moved to Madrid to get his doctorate in economics. They were part of a loose network of foreign Muslims in Spain who spent time together after soccer games and mosque prayers. They later masterminded the Madrid bombings, the deadliest Islamist terror attack on European soil. As Spanish authorities closed in on their hideout several weeks after the bombings, Fakhet, Ahmidan, and several accomplices blew themselves up as the police moved in.

The tolerant, virtual environment of the Web offers these wannabes a semblance of unity and purpose.

Try as they may, Spanish authorities have never found any direct connection between the Madrid bombers and international al Qaeda networks. The 2007 trials of collaborators concluded that the bombings were inspired by al Qaeda, but not directed by it.

Evidence of hopeful young jihadists is not limited to Western Europe. In June 2006, Canadian security forces conducted a series of raids against two clusters of young people in and around Toronto. The youths they apprehended were mostly second-generation Canadians in their late teens or early 20s and from secular, middle-class households. They were accused of planning large-scale terrorist attacks in Toronto and Ottawa, and when they were arrested, they had already purchased vast quantities of bomb-making materials. The core members of the group were close friends from their early high school years, when they had formed a "Religious Awareness Club," which met during lunch hours at school. They also created an online forum where they could share their views on life, religion, and politics. Eventually, a number of the young men and women intermarried while still in their teens.

The group expanded their network when they moved to other parts of the greater Toronto area, attending radical mosques and meeting like-minded young people. They also reached out in international chatrooms, eventually linking up with Irhabi007 prior to his arrest. Through his forum, they were directed to Web sites providing them with information on how to build bombs. Other militants in Bosnia, Britain, Denmark, Sweden, and even Atlanta, Georgia, also virtually connected through this forum and actively planned attacks. Again, there is no evidence that any of the core Toronto plotters were ever in contact with al Qaeda; the plot was completely homegrown.

What makes these examples of the next generation of terrorists so frightening is the ease with which marginalized youths are able to translate their frustrations into acts of terrorism, often on the back of professed solidarity with terrorists halfway around the world whom they have never met. They seek to belong to a movement larger than themselves, and their violent actions and plans are hatched locally, with advice from others on the Web. Their mode of communication also suggests that they will increasingly evade detection. Without links to known terrorists, this new generation is more difficult to discover through traditional intelligence gathering. Of course, their lack of training and experience could limit their effectiveness. But that's cold comfort for their victims.

Why They Fight

Any strategy to fight these terrorists must be based on an understanding of why they believe what they believe. In other words, what transforms ordinary people into fanatics who use violence for political ends? What leads them to consider themselves special, part of a small vanguard trying to build their version of an Islamist utopia?

The explanation for their behavior is found not in how they think, but rather in how they feel. One of the most common refrains among Islamist radicals is their sense of moral outrage. Before 2003, the most significant source of these feelings were the killings of Muslims in Afghanistan in the 1980s. In the 1990s, it was the fighting in Bosnia, Chechnya, and Kashmir. Then came the second Palestinian intifada beginning in 2000. And since 2003, it has been all about the war in Iraq, which has become the focal point of global moral outrage for Muslims all over the world. Along with the humiliations of Abu Ghraib and Guantánamo, Iraq is monopolizing today's conversations about Islam and the West. On a more local level, governments that appear overly pro-American cause radicals to feel they are the victims of a larger anti-Muslim conspiracy, bridging the perceived local and global attacks against them.

In order for this moral outrage to translate into extremism, the frustrations must be interpreted in a particular way: The violations are deemed part of a unified Western strategy, namely a "war against Islam." That deliberately vague worldview, however, is just a sound bite. The new terrorists are not Islamic scholars. Jihadists volunteering for Iraq are interested not in theological debates but in living out their heroic fantasies.

How various individuals interpret this vision of a "war against Islam" differs from country to country, and it is a major reason why homegrown terrorism within the United States is far less likely than it is in Europe. To a degree, the belief that the United States is a melting pot protects the country from homegrown attacks. Whether or not the United States is a land of opportunity, the important point is that people believe it to be. A recent poll found that 71 percent of Muslim Americans believe in the "American Dream," more than the American public as a whole (64 percent). This is not the case in Europe, where national myths are based on degrees of "Britishness," "Frenchness," or "Germanness." This excludes non-European Muslim immigrants from truly feeling as if they belong.

Feeling marginalized is, of course, no simple springboard to violence. Many people feel they don't belong but don't aspire to wage violent jihad. What transforms a very small number to become terrorists is mobilization by networks. Until a few years ago, these networks were face-to-face groups. They included local gangs of young immigrants, members of student associations, and study groups at radical mosques. These cliques of friends became radicalized together. The group acted as an echo chamber, amplifying grievances, intensifying bonds to each other, and breeding values that rejected those of their host societies. These natural group dynamics resulted in a spiral of mutual encouragement and escalation, transforming a few young Muslims into dedicated terrorists willing to follow the model of their heroes and sacrifice themselves for comrades and cause. Their turn to violence was a collective decision, rather than an individual one.

During the past two or three years, however, face-to-face radicalization has been replaced by online radicalization. The same support and validation that young people used to derive from their offline peer groups are now found in online forums, which promote the image of the terrorist hero, link users to the online social movement, give them guidance, and instruct them in tactics. These forums, virtual marketplaces for extremist ideas, have become the "invisible hand" that organizes terrorist activities worldwide. The true leader of this violent social movement is the collective discourse on half a dozen influential forums. They are transforming the terrorist movement, attracting ever younger members and now women, who can participate in the discussions.

At present, al Qaeda Central cannot impose discipline on these third-wave wannabes, mostly because it does not know who they are. Without this command and control, each disconnected network acts according to its own understanding and capability, but their collective actions do not amount to any unified long-term goal or strategy. These separate groups cannot coalesce into a physical movement, leaving them condemned to remain leaderless, an online aspiration. Such traits make them particularly volatile and difficult to detect, but they also offer a tantalizing strategy for those who wish to defeat these dangerous individuals: The very seeds of the movement's demise are within the movement itself.

Islamist terrorism will likely disappear for internal reasons—if America has the sense to allow it.

The Beginning of the End?

There has been talk of an al Qaeda resurgence, but the truth is that most of the hard-core members of the first and second waves have been killed or captured. The survival of the social movement they inspired relies on the continued inflow of new members. But this movement is vulnerable to whatever may diminish its appeal among the young. Its allure thrives only at the abstract fantasy level. The few times its aspirations have been translated into reality—the Taliban in Afghanistan, parts of Algeria during its civil war, and more recently in Iraq's Anbar Province—were particularly repulsive to most Muslims.

What's more, a leaderless social movement is permanently at the mercy of its participants. As each generation attempts to define itself in contrast to its predecessor, what appeals to the present generation of young would-be radicals may not appeal to the next. A major source of the present appeal is the anger and moral outrage provoked by the invasion of Iraq. As the Western footprint there fades, so will the appeal of fighting it. And new hotheads in the movement will always push the envelope to make a name for themselves and cause ever escalating atrocities. The magnitude of these horrors will, in turn, likely alienate potential recruits.

The U.S. strategy to counter this terrorist threat continues to be frozen by the horrors of 9/11. It relies more on wishful thinking than on a deep understanding of the enemy. The pursuit of "high-value targets" who were directly involved in the 9/11 operation more than six years ago was an appropriate first step to bring the perpetrators to justice. And the United States has been largely successful in degrading the capability of al Qaeda Central.

But this strategy is not only useless against the leaderless jihad; it is precisely what will help the movement flourish. Radical Islamist terrorism will never disappear because the West defeats it. Instead, it will most likely disappear for internal reasons—if the United States has the sense to allow it to continue on its course and fade away. The main threat to radical Islamist terrorism is the fact that its appeal is self-limiting. The key is to accelerate this process of internal decay. This need not be a long war, unless American policy makes it so.

Terrorist acts must be stripped of glory and reduced to common criminality. Most aspiring terrorists want nothing more than to be elevated to the status of an FBI Most Wanted poster. "[I am] one of the most wanted terrorists on the Internet," Younis Tsouli boasted online a few months before his arrest in 2005. "I have the Feds and the CIA, both would love to catch me. I have MI6 on my back." His ego fed off the respect such bragging brought him in the eyes of other chatroom participants.

Any policy or recognition that puts such people on a pedestal only makes them heroes in each other's eyes—and encourages others to follow their example. These young men aspire to nothing more glorious than to fight uniformed soldiers of the sole remaining superpower. That is why the struggle against these terrorists must be demilitarized and turned over to collaborative law enforcement. The military role should be limited to denying terrorists a sanctuary.

It is equally crucial not to place terrorists who are arrested or killed in the limelight. The temptation to hold press conferences to publicize another "major victory" in the war on terror must be resisted, for it only transforms terrorist criminals into jihadist heroes. The United States underestimates the value of prosecutions, which often can be enormously demoralizing to radical groups. There is no glory in being taken to prison in handcuffs. No jihadi Web site publishes such pictures. Arrested terrorists fade into oblivion; martyrs live on in popular memory.

This is very much a battle for young Muslims' hearts and minds. Any appearance of persecution for short-term tactical gains will be a strategic defeat on this battlefield. The point is to regain the international moral high ground, which served the United States and its allies so well during the Cold War. With the advent of the Internet, there has been a gradual shift to online networks, where young Muslims share their hopes, dreams, and grievances. That offers an opportunity to encourage voices that reject violence.

It is necessary to reframe the entire debate, from imagined glory to very real horror. Young people must learn that terrorism is about death and destruction, not fame. The voices of the victims must be heard over the bragging and posturing that go on in the online jihadist forums. Only then will the leaderless jihad expire, poisoned by its own toxic message.

Marc Sageman, a forensic psychiatrist and former CIA case officer, is author of *Leaderless Jihad: Terror Networks in the Twenty-First Century* (Philadelphia: University of Pennsylvania Press, 2008).

Test-Your-Knowledge Form

We encourage you to photocopy and use this page as a tool to assess how the articles in *Annual Editions* expand on the information in your textbook. By reflecting on the articles you will gain enhanced text information. You can also access this useful form on a product's book support Web site at *http://www.mhcls.com/online/*.

NAME: DATE:

_____

TITLE AND NUMBER OF ARTICLE:

_____

BRIEFLY STATE THE MAIN IDEA OF THIS ARTICLE:

_____

LIST THREE IMPORTANT FACTS THAT THE AUTHOR USES TO SUPPORT THE MAIN IDEA:

_____

WHAT INFORMATION OR IDEAS DISCUSSED IN THIS ARTICLE ARE ALSO DISCUSSED IN YOUR TEXTBOOK OR OTHER READINGS THAT YOU HAVE DONE? LIST THE TEXTBOOK CHAPTERS AND PAGE NUMBERS:

_____

LIST ANY EXAMPLES OF BIAS OR FAULTY REASONING THAT YOU FOUND IN THE ARTICLE:

_____

LIST ANY NEW TERMS/CONCEPTS THAT WERE DISCUSSED IN THE ARTICLE, AND WRITE A SHORT DEFINITION: